# 16th International PEAT Congress (IPC 2021)



Oral Presentations

Tallinn, Estonia
3-6 May 2021

ISBN: 978-1-7138-3868-5

**Printed from e-media with permission by:**

Curran Associates, Inc.
57 Morehouse Lane
Red Hook, NY 12571

**Some format issues inherent in the e-media version may also appear in this print version.**



Printed by Curran Associates, Inc. (2021)

For permission requests, please contact International Peatland Society (IPS) at the address below.

International Peatland Society (IPS)
Vapaudenkatu 12
40100 Jyvaskyla Finland

Phone: 358 14 3385 440
Fax: 358 14 3385 410

ips@peatlands.org

**Additional copies of this publication are available from:**

Curran Associates, Inc.
57 Morehouse Lane
Red Hook, NY 12571 USA
Phone: 845-758-0400
Fax: 845-758-2633
Email: curran@proceedings.com
Web: www.proceedings.com

International Peatland Society

IPC 2021

# 16th INTERNATIONAL PEATLAND CONGRESS

## 3-6 May 2021 • Tallinn, Estonia

## Oral presentations

Argo Argel • Suru bog, Estonia

# THANK YOU TO
# ALL SPONSORS AND EXHIBITORS

## Gold sponsor

## Silver Sponsor

## Bronze sponsor

## PEAT Talks Sponsor

## Exhibitors

**Proceedings of the 16th International Peatland Congress**

**Publisher: Publicon PCO, Kastani 42, Tartu, Estonia**
**Published: June 2021**

# FOREWORD

When in April 2019 we invited the international peatlands community to join the next big event – the 16th IPS International Peatland Congress (IPC2020) in Tallinn, Estonia – we had no idea about the global challenges ahead. Due to the COVID-19 pandemic, various international events, including the IPC2020, had to change their traditional ways of planning and management completely.

As a result, the first fully virtual IPC in history – the 16th IPC2021 – was launched in Tallinn in May 2021.

The main theme of the Congress, PEATLANDS AND PEAT – SOURCE OF ECOSYSTEM SERVICES, proposed by the Organising Committee of the Congress already in 2012, remained the same. In collaboration with executive Board of the IPS the Programme was structured into 27 sub-topics of seven key topics.

Initially, 429 abstracts were accepted by the Scientific Committee of the Congress, out of which 220 presentations (including 58 poster presentations) were made in the virtual environment. During the four Congress working days, it was possible to enjoy excellent presentations by eight international keynote speakers, six Peat Talks, 12 intriguing talks from the Industry Summit programme and six from the Peatwise Session. In total, the 16th IPC2021 had presentations from 31 countries and participants from 34 countries.

The Congress left a clear impression that there is a consensus among wide range of stakeholders about the uniqueness of peatland ecosystems and their services.

The *Carbon sequestration and climate regulation* sessions attracted the largest number of presentations, clearly influenced by the global carbon neutrality policy. Significant changes in land-use in tropical peatlands have led scientists and stakeholders to adopting innovative techniques and research methods to raise awareness about these unique ecosystems in the world.

Several presentations emphasised that the use of peat as an energy source is rapidly declining. At the same time, the demand for peat-based growing media and the high value of peat-based products is increasing. In addition, the COVID-19 crisis has shown that the importance of locally produced food cannot be underestimated. Therefore, we are still in a situation where the challenges in developing high-quality and cost-effective growing substrates have remained, while companies are actively turning their attention to the climate policy and society needs.

In recent decades, great developments have taken place in the collection of experiences and scientific know-how in the field of restoration and reclamation of peatland ecosystems. In Europe, such activities have been financially supported by continuous contributions from different base and applied science funds. However, there are still several tasks which need to be tackled in relation to changes in climate, freshwater resources, GHG emissions, aquatic and terrestrial biodiversity, and anthropogenic pressure. Furthermore, it seems that it is time look toward such integrated research areas such as socio-ecology or socio-hydrology, aiming to involve social scientists more deeply into the research and management policy of ecosystem services of peatlands or peat, for example.

With this publication, we aim to maintain the ideas and experiences shared in the 16th IPC2021 for future use and to contribute closer communication development between scientists, peat industry professionals, conservationists, officials and other stakeholders of peatlands and peat.

We thank all participants of the Congress and the Secretariat for realising our ideas in a 100% online environment.

May 15, 2021

**Elve Lode**
Chair of the Scientific Committee

**Martin Küttim**
Deputy Chair of the Scientific Committee

**Erki Niitlaan** Chairman

**Jaanus Paal** Congress General

# ORGANISING COMMITTEE

**Erki Niitlaan** Chair of the Congress, Estonian Peat Association
**Jaanus Paal** Scientific Congress General, University of Tartu
**Elve Lode** Chair of the Scientific Committee, Tallinn University
**Martin Küttim** Vice-Chair of the Scientific Committee, Tallinn University
**Edgar Karofeld** University of Tartu
**Marko Kohv** Estonian Wetlands Society
**Gilbert Ludwig** International Peatland Society
**Susann Warnecke** International Peatland Society

# SCIENTIFIC COMMITTEE

**Rachel Carmenta** University of Cambridge, England
**Gerald Jurasinski** The University of Rostock, Germany
**Marko Kohv** University of Tartu, Estonian Fund for Nature, Estonia
**Randall Kolka** USDA Forest Service Northern Research Station, USA
**Aino Korrensalo** University of Eastern Finland, Finland
**Marika Kose** Estonian University of Life Sciences, Estonia
**Ingrida Krigere** Latvian Peat Association, Latvia
**Ain Kull** University of Tartu, Estonia
**Liisa Küttim** Tallinn University, Estonia
**Martin Küttim** Tallinn University, Estonia
**Anna Laine** University of Eastern Finland, Finland
**Elve Lode** Tallinn University, Estonia
**Aleksei Lotman** Estonian Fund for Nature, Estonia
**Lars Lundin** Swedish University of Agricultural Sciences, Sweden
**Shailendra Mishra** Asian School of the Environment, Singapore
**Katri Ots** Estonian University of Life Sciences, Estonia
**Jaanus Paal** University of Tartu, Estonia
**Jan Peters** Michael Succow Foundation, Germany
**Piret Pungas-Kohv** University of Tartu, Estonian Fund for Nature, Estonia
**Mart Reimann** Tallinn University, Estonia
**Jack Rieley** The University of Nottingham and UK Peatland Society, United Kingdom
**Line Rochefort** Laval University, Canada
**Jüri-Ott Salm** Estonian Fund for Nature, Estonia
**Hannu Salo** Bioenergia ry, Finland
**Budi Indra Setiawan** Bogor Agricultural University, Indonesia
**Dace Silina** Latvia University of Life Sciences and Technologies, Latvia
**Pete Whittington** Brandon University, Canada
**Meng Xianmin** Northeast Normal University, China Humic Acid Industry Association, China

I PROVISING SERVICES



II SUPPORTING SERVICES



III REGULATING SERVICES

## *VI PROTECTION AND RECLMATION OF PEATLANDS*

# I PROVISING SERVICES

IPC 2021

ID 61475

# BALNEOLOGICAL PEAT IN ESTONIA – RESOURCES AND PROPERTIES

*Mall Orru[1], Hans Orru[2,3]

[1]Institute of Geology, Tallinn University of Technology, Estonia
[2]Institute of Family Medicine and Public Health, University of Tartu, Estonia
[3]Loodusmark OÜ, Estonia

*mall.orru@taltech.ee*

Peat and various peat preparations have been worldwide successfully used in balneology. When considering the biological properties of balneological peat, humic substances have been found to be of particular importance. Current analysis aimed to describe the resources, properties and current use of balneological peat in Estonia.

The balneological peat has been searched based on mapping of Estonian peatlands, followed by chemical analysis in seven selected peat deposits. Altogether 0.9 million tons of suitable peat resources with the 0.85–1.00 m deep peat layer, have been found in Estonia. Chemical analyses have revealed that content of humic substances (HS) in studied peat layers in Estonia can be relatively high, up to 60%. All three useful humic subtsnaces: humic, hymatomelanic and fulvic acids can be found with highest concentration in well humified lignum–cottongrass peat. As the peat used in balneological practise has to be ecologically clean from heavy metals, the deposites with the content lover than Estonian peat's average, had been selected.

Balneological peat has physical effect through temperature and biochemical effect through bioactive substances. In clinical studies patients with Heberden-Bouchard disease (Osteoarthrosis) in lingers experienced improvement in their condition when threated with balneological peat. According to the International Classification of Functioning Disability and Health scale we could be observe pain reduction in 95% of the cases, improved mobility of finger joints with 74% of the patient, improved mobility of the middle finger 35% of patients (tested with moving the finger towards the palm) and ability of picking objects improved in 42% of the cases.

Currently, in Estonia peat and various peat products are successfully used in balneological practice in rehabilitation as well as in spa, and sauna treatments, face masks, peat shampoos, peat soaps and in hair salons.

ID 72825

# HYDROPHOBICITY EVALUATION OF OMBROGEN PEAT SOIL USING FTIR SPECTROSCOPY WITH WATER LEVEL SIMULATION TREATMENT

*Wahida Annisa[1], Hendri Sosiawan[2], Muhammad Saleh[1], Mawardi[1], Nurkwakhid[1]

[1]Indonesian Swampland Agricultural Research Institute (ISARI), South Kalimantan, Indonesia
[2]Indonesian Agroclimatology and Hydrology Research Institute (IAHRI) Bogor, Indonesia

*annisa_balittra@yahoo.com*

Irreversible dryness or not being able to reabsorb water is an obstacle problem of peat soils that were used for food crops cultivation. The peat characteristic was changed from hydrophilic to hydrophobic. Peat hydrophobicity occurs due to the association and interaction of polar functional groups which causes the orientation of the non-polar groups on the surface of the organic colloid. Fourier Transform Infrared (FTIR) data spectroscopy is a quantitative indicator of soil organic matter composition that potentially can be used for peat hydrophobicity evaluation because it can characterize the functional groups of organic matter.

The research was conducted in a greenhouse at Indonesian Swampland Research Institute, Banjarbaru, Indonesia using a factorial randomized block design with 3 factors and 3 replications. The first factor was peat type which consists of hydrophilic peat with a bulk density (BV) of (1) 0.1 g/cm3 and (2) 0.2 g/cm3. The second factor was water level, namely (1) -100 cm, (2) -70 cm, and (3) -40 cm.

After 2 months of soil incubation, the results showed that the highest capillary potential was peat type with a BV of 0.2 g/cm3 and water level of -40 cm, indicated by the value of groundwater content attain to 205%. The lowest capillary potential was peat type with a BV of 0.1 g/cm3 and water level of -100 cm (the water content value was only 82%). The hydrophobic functional groups of the peat type with a BV of 0.2 g/cm3 and water level of -100 cm were increased and decreased, respectively, from 18.2 to 18.8% and 48.6 to 39.1% of the absorption area.

*Keywords: Irreversible dryness, functional group, bulk density, capillary potential*

ID 61311

# REGENERATION OF *SPHAGNUM* MOSS BIOMASS HARVESTING SITES IN FINLAND

Niko Silvan[1]*, Liisa Särkkä[2], Juha Näkkilä[2], Risto Tahvonen[2]

1*. Natural Resources Institute Finland, Production systems, Biomass characterization and properties; Parkano Unit, Finland.

2. Natural Resources Institute Finland, Natural resources, Plant production; Turku Unit, Finland

*niko.silvan@luke.fi*

## SUMMARY

Horticultural peat is a microbiologically active and physically favourable growing medium, which risks of plant diseases are also markedly smaller than when using synthetic growing media. Unfortunately, horticultural peat is a very slowly renewable biomass and good quality horticultural peat is not so common even in peatland-rich countries. Thus, good-quality and simultaneously renewable growing media alternatives are needed. According to our results from several shallow (to depth of ca. 30 cm) *Sphagnum* moss biomass harvesting sites in Central Finland, sites will regenerate swiftly after harvesting. Vegetation colonization started immediately after harvesting, and in the fourth year after harvesting already over a half of the surface was covered with *Sphagnum* and other mire vegetation. The mire vegetation of the oldest harvesting sites (ten and thirteen years after harvesting) was already almost completely regrown. However, some species composition alterations were observed due to the harvesting compared to the situation before it, for instance *Sphagnum* species growing on lawns and hollows became more abundant due to the harvesting. Additionally, especially the abundance of *Eriophorum vaginatum* was much higher compared to the situation before harvesting, although it seems that the phase of abundant *Eriophorum vaginatum* will probably remain rather short, only couple of years. Renewability of the *Sphagnum* is based both remained living auxiliary buds and also dropped *Sphagnum* material during harvesting. According to our results, *Sphagnum* moss material is partly living biomass at least to a depth of 30 cm, i.e. the harvesting depth used in Finland. The observed height growth of *Sphagnum* mosses on the harvesting sites was on average 1−2 cm $y^{-1}$, thus adequate to compensate the removed *Sphagnum* moss biomass during ca. three decades. According to our results, responsibly harvested *Sphagnum* moss biomass can be regarded as a renewable biomass, and also as a good, ecologically acceptable alternative for growing medium constituent.

***Keywords**: Sphagnum moss biomass, vegetation regeneration, growing media*

## INTRODUCTION

*Sphagnum* in top soil (i.e. peat moss) has been used for centuries as a litter for cattle (Roderfeld et al. 1996), insulation in different buildings and absorbing material in open wound care, for instance. However, other more easily available materials have nearly fully replaced the use of *Sphagnum* moss in these traditional ways. For decades, non-professional orchid growers have also used *Sphagnum* moss on a smaller scale as a growing medium constituent. As a result, *Sphagnum* moss based growing media have gained small global markets (Whinam & Buxton 1997, Whinam et al. 2003). The recent broader commercial interest in *Sphagnum* mosses has resulted from the high suitability of *Sphagnum* moss biomass for use as other growing media to replace white horticultural peat (Gaudig & Joosten 2002, Näkkilä et al. 2013, Tahvonen et al. 2012, Silvan et al. 2017). *Sphagnum* farming, or "paludiculture", has prompted growing interest in the more sustainable use of peatlands. In paludiculture, plant-based biomass is produced by maintaining a high water level on peatlands to make their water management and carbon sequestering qualities close to peatlands in a pristine state (Wichtmann et al. 2016). In Central Europe, *Sphagnum* farming on re-wetted peat fields and former peat production areas has increased, while retaining experimental operations on a smaller scale (Gaudig et al. 2013, Vos 2016). In Finland, small-scale *Sphagnum* moss harvesting started on low-productive drained peatlands from the middle of the last decade, and there are significant expectations that it will produce growing media ecologically and sustainably in the future.

*Sphagnum* moss biomass comprises the living undecomposed surface layer, dominated by *Sphagnum* moss, and more than half of its projected coverage and volume should consist of living *Sphagnum* moss cell tissue (Näkkilä et al. 2015). As a natural material, it may also contain some other moss species, sedgelike plants and shoots, and their roots (Näkkilä et al. 2015). This biomass constitutes the topmost layer on a peatland, being mainly living, usually less than 50 years old (Clymo 1984) and extending to a depth of 20–30 cm (Clymo & Duckett 1986). Below this layer, Sphagnum moss largely comprises dead moss material mainly accumulated in oxygen-free conditions, i.e. peat. However, the line between moss biomass and peat is often difficult to distinguish and observe. Auxiliary buds of *Sphagnum* moss may extend to a depth of at least 30 cm, even if they appear dead to the naked eye (Clymo & Duckett 1986).

In addition to peatlands in their natural state, Sphagnum moss grows on many drained peatland areas. The more nutrient-poor the drained area and the deteriorated the drainage state, the more *Sphagnum* mosses there usually exist. Especially on poorly drained low-productive peatland forests, the surface layer formed after drainage is normally dominated by *Sphagnum* mosses (Saarinen 2002). Instead, drained peatlands that have a highly advanced drainage succession and more trees, the amount of *Sphagnum* mosses is smaller, and the surface layer contains more dwarf shrubs and upland forest moss species (e.g. Laine et al. 1995).

In Finland, mechanical harvesting systems have been developed for harvesting *Sphagnum* moss biomass. So far, at most 100 000 $m^3 a^{-1}$ of biomass have been harvested during the last three years using a single prototype (patented, Ecomoss Oy) installed on a forest machine base. *Sphagnum* moss biomass can be harvested during winter also, but recently only during summer. During summer, harvesting is more challenging due to the low load-bearing capacity of the soil, while, however, it is easier to select the harvested material and dewater it during harvesting. This possibility to dewater *Sphagnum* moss material makes the summer the most feasible harvesting period in Finland.

Although *Sphagnum* moss biomass has thus far been harvested on a fairly small scale in Finland, the potential is large. If demand is sufficient, and the price of the material enables financially feasible and ecologically sustainable harvesting, *Sphagnum* moss will have highly promising uses. Finland, with its large peatlands suitable for harvesting, will have an excellent opportunity to become a significant *Sphagnum* moss producer.

Furthermore, no negative loads on watercourses, at least in the short term, have been identified in the only study conducted thus far (Silvan 2019). This is possible because in Sphagnum moss biomass harvesting, the area is not drained, and no water is discharged away from the area (e.g. by pumping). On the other hand, clear cuttings in low-productive forestry-drained peatlands has been found to increase loads on watercourses, the leaching of soluble phosphorus, especially due to reduction reactions in peat caused by the wetting of the previously dry surface layer (Kaila et al. 2014, Koskinen et al. 2017). It is therefore highly possible that larger-volume Sphagnum moss biomass harvesting may cause some harmful effects on watercourses too; especially the leaching of humus (DOC) and phosphorus. On the other hand, the nutrient leaching volume may in some cases even decrease when the nutrient-containing surface layer, which has otherwise been the primary source of loads, is removed. Such results have been found, for example, in the remediation of peat fields, from where the surface layer has been removed (Zak et al. 2018). However, runoff from peatlands and runoff peaks may increase after harvesting, at least temporarily, when the storage capacity of the surface layer and evaporation from it decrease. Water chemistry monitoring on several larger harvesting areas with longer-term period (10–20 years) will be necessary to identify the possible harmful effects of moss biomass harvesting on watercourses.

According to observations made in Central Europe, the removal of the 20–30 cm surface layer may improve the restoration of the area into peatlands (Zak et al. 2018). This probably accelerates restoration, especially compared with a situation in which no activities are carried out, because water content in the peatland surface increases when the relatively dry surface layer is removed, evaporation decreases and the peatland level lowers. In a situation where no re-harvesting is carried out, this could increase biodiversity and help to regenerate peat. However, no studies support this assumption.

## CONCLUSION

In Finland, Sphagnum moss biomass has thus far been harvested on a fairly small scale. Currently, the harvesting area totals slightly more than 100 hectares. This has mainly been caused by the relatively high price of Sphagnum moss material compared with white peat, although its price can be a little higher, because it is a renewable natural product. Ultimately, the future of Sphagnum moss depends on how strictly the production of horticultural peat is regulated, how many other replacement products are launched, and whether Sphagnum moss can be produced in a truly sustainable and environmentally friendly manner. Access to large international markets would require certified production and products, which in turn would require more comprehensive information about the environmental impact of moss production. If demand is sufficient, and the price of the material enables financially feasible and ecologically sustainable harvesting, Sphagnum moss will have highly promising uses. Finland, with its large peatlands suitable for harvesting, will have an excellent opportunity to become a significant Sphagnum moss producer.

## REGENERATION OF SPHAGNUM MOSSES AFTER HARVESTING

Currently, methods where harvesting does not extend below the lower level of the living surface layer, i.e. no deeper than 30 cm, are considered to be sustainable options for harvesting Sphagnum moss. This ensures the regeneration of Sphagnum moss and minimises the spread of other mire vegetation (mainly sedges) to the harvested area (Reinikainen et al. 2012, Silvan et al. 2012, Silvan et al. 2017). In other words, the aim is to peel a thin layer of the existing living surface so that living Sphagnum moss, able to regrow, remains below the harvested layer. As a result of this type of harvesting, Sphagnum moss can regenerate naturally on the basis of local auxiliary buds, without any re-introduction (Silvan et al. 2017).

Some studies have been conducted in Finland regarding the impact of the intensity of Sphagnum moss biomass harvesting on regeneration, on which the aforementioned recommendations of the harvesting depth are largely based. Two alternative harvesting depths in the surface layer were tested in pilot harvesting trials of Vapo Oy and the former Finnish Forest Research Institute: "normal" (surface layer removed up to a depth of roughly 30 cm) and "deep" (surface layer removed up to a depth of roughly 60 cm) (Reinikainen et al. 2012, Silvan et al. 2012). S. balticum colonized the most quickly harvested surfaces. The majority (approx. 80%) of regeneration was achieved by S. balticum during the first three years after harvesting (Näkkilä et al. 2015). According to later observations, however, variation between areas can be high, depending on the nutrient level and hydrology of the harvesting area, for example.

When post-harvest succession advanced, S. fuscum and S. medium (former magellanicum) also started to regenerate within a few years after harvesting (Näkkilä et al. 2015). In parts of the normal area, the regeneration of Sphagnum moss already had a coverage of nearly 100% during the third year after harvesting (Näkkilä et al. 2015). According to preliminary observations made in the oldest areas being monitored, the Sphagnum moss surface seems to have almost completely taken the original harvested surface over ten years after harvesting. However, as only two areas of this age can be monitored, these observations are highly preliminary. A surface originally dominated by Sphagnum moss is often replaced first by lawn species similar to S. balticum, at least during the first years after harvesting (Näkkilä et al. 2015). In comparison, hummock Sphagnum moss species also grow in areas from which peat moss has been harvested a few decades after harvesting.

In deep harvesting, regeneration after harvesting has been much slower than after normal harvesting (Reinikainen et al. 2012, Silvan et al. 2012). In deep harvesting areas, regeneration mainly consisted of S. balticum and of S. cuspidatum and S. majus in places, because water-filled deep hollows are formed in deep harvesting. New Sphagnum moss has formed much more slowly in deep harvesting areas than on average in normal harvesting areas. Significantly more sedgelike plants (particularly Eriophorum vaginatum) have spread onto deep harvesting areas than to normal harvesting areas. The increase in sedgelike plants may have a negative impact on the quality of the next Sphagnum moss harvest in the same area. Furthermore, sedgelike plants, Eriophorum vaginatum in particular, may significantly increase methane emissions from harvested areas (Tuittila et al. 2000).

According to our preliminary (Reinikainen et al. 2012, Silvan et al. 2012, Silvan et al. 2017), previous (Lainevesi 1990) and ongoing unpublished estimates, the average growth rate of the Sphagnum moss surface could be approx. 1 cm $a^{-1}$ in Finland, considering variation in the growth rate in different eco-hydrological conditions on harvesting areas. If the thickness of the harvested Sphagnum moss layer is assumed to be at most 30 cm, Sphagnum moss biomass can be harvested in the planned cycle of roughly 30 years (Reinikainen et al. 2012, Silvan et al. 2012, Silvan et al. 2017).

Based on previous studies, the average volume harvested at any one time on a certain peatland has been approximately 1,000 $m^3$ $ha^{-1}$ (Ecomoss Oy). If the harvesting target was ca. 200 000 $m^3$ $a^{-1}$, i.e. an amount equalling Finland's domestic annual horticultural peat consumption volume in greenhouse cultivation, some 300 hectares of new harvesting area for Sphagnum moss biomass would be needed every year. With a cycle of 30 years, slightly under 10 000 hectares of new production area would be needed. For a comparison, this passes clearly underneath the area of current peat production areas (horticultural and energy peat areas included) in Finland. Based on the experiences of the last years, these calculations have proved realistically feasible in the harvesting of Sphagnum moss biomass from forestry-drained peatlands in low-productive forest land (Ecomoss Oy).

## ENVIRONMENTAL IMPACTS OF SPHAGNUM MOSS BIOMASS HARVESTING

Because Sphagnum moss biomass has only been harvested on a commercial scale for a few years in Finland, and because operations have so far remained on a smaller scale, it is impossible to say anything certain of the long-term environmental impact of these operations. Vegetation has been monitored on a smaller scale in seven areas, but the monitoring information is partly unpublished. The impact on the carbon balance and watercourses has only been assessed in one separate test area for a few years after harvesting. Studies conducted during the first years after harvesting suggest that at least the short-term environmental impact of operations is minor. In peatlands, vegetation regenerates in a few years. However, there are distinct changes in species at early stages of succession after harvesting. For example, the relative proportion of Sphagnum moss in the lawn layer and Eriophorum vaginatum has increased compared with the situation before harvesting (Silvan et al. 2017). The harvested area may already return to a carbon-sequestering ecosystem in less than five years after harvesting (Silvan et al. 2017).

## ACKNOWLEDGEMENTS

The Finnish Ministry of Agriculture and Forestry, the Natural Resources Institute Finland and Vapo Ltd. have gratefully acknowledged for making the Sphagnum moss biomass studies possible.

## REFERENCES


Clymo R S (1984) The limits to peat bog growth. *Philosophical Transactions of the Royal* ***Society of London B*; 303: 605–654.**

Clymo RS and Duckett JG (1986) Regeneration of Sphagnum. *New Phytologist*; 102: 589-614. https://doi.org/10.1111/j.1469-8137.1986.tb00834.x

Gaudig G and Joosten H (2002) Peat moss (*Sphagnum*) as a renewable resource - an alternative to *Sphagnum* peat in horticulture. In G. Schmilewski and L. Rochefort (eds.), *Peat in horticulture*. Quality and environmental challenges. International Peat Society, Jyväskylä, pp. 117-125.

Gaudig G, Fengler F, Krebs M, Prager A, Schulz J, Wichmann S, Joosten H (2013) Sphagnum farming in Germany - a review of progress. *Mires and Peat*; 13: Article 8.

Kaila A, Sarkkola S, Laurén A, Ukonmaanaho L, Koivusalo H, Xiao L, O'Driscoll C, Asam Z-u-Z, Tervahauta A, Nieminen M (2014) Phosphorus export from drained Scots pine mires after clear-felling and bioenergy harvesting. *Forest Ecology and Management* ; 325: 99-107. doi:10.1016/j.foreco.2014.03.025

Koskinen M, Tahvanainen T, Sarkkola S, Menberu M W, Laurén A, Sallantaus T, Marttila H, Ronkanen A-K, Tolvanen A, Parviainen M, Koivusalo H, Nieminen M (2017) Restoration of fertile peatlands poses a risk for high exports of dissolved organic carbon, nitrogen, and phosphorus. *The Science of the Total Environment*; 586: 858–869. doi:10.1016/j.scitotenv.2017.02.065.

Laine J, Vasander H, Laiho R (1995) Long-term effects of water level drawdown on the vegetation of drained pine mires in southern Finland. *Journal of Applied Ecology*; 32: 785–802.

Lainevesi S (1990) Korjuunjälkeinen turpeen kasvu ja suokasvillisuuden palautuminen Kihniön Aitonevan palaturvesoilla. Pro gradu-tutkielma, Oulun yliopisto.

Näkkilä J, Jokinen K, Särkkä L, Tahvonen R, Silvan K, Silvan N (2013) Rahkasammalessa vihannestaimi kasvaa hyvin. *Puutarha & Kauppa*; 2013(3): 20-21.

Näkkilä J, Silvan N, Jokinen K, Särkkä L, Tahvonen R (2015) Rahkasammalen tuotanto ja käyttö kasvihuonekasvien kasvualustana. MMM-Makera-loppuraportti. 16 pp.

Reinikainen O, Korpi J, Tahvonen R, Näkkilä J, Silvan N (2012) Harvesting of Sphagnum biomass and its use as a growing medium constituent. In: Proceedings of the 14th International Peat Congress, session Peat for Horticulture, extended abstract number 137.

Roderfeld H, Vasander H, Tuittila E-S (1996) A cut-over bog in the stage of regeneration in southern Finland. *Telma*; 26: 223–235.

Saarinen M (2002) Kasvillisuuden ja maanmuokkauksen vaikutus männyn ja koivun taimettumiseen varpu- ja puolukkaturvekankailla. (Summary: Effect of vegetation and site preparation on the restocking of Scots pine and birch in dwarf-schrub and Vaccinium vitis-idaea type peatland forests). *Suo - Mires and Peat*; 53(2): 41-60.

Silvan N, Silvan K, Näkkilä J, Tahvonen R, Reinikainen O (2012) Renewability, use and properties of Sphagnum biomass for growing media purposes. In: Proceedings of the 14th International Peat Congress, session Sphagnum Farming, extended abstract number 55.

Silvan N, Jokinen K, Näkkilä J, Tahvonen R. (2017) Swift recovery of *Sphagnum* carpet and carbon sequestration after shallow *Sphagnum* biomass harvesting. *Mires and Peat*; 20(01): 1–11.

Silvan N (2019) Short-term effects of shallow *Sphagnum* moss biomass harvesting on the runoff water quality. *International Journal of Environmental Monitoring and Analysis*; 7(1): 34-39.

Tahvonen R, Näkkilä J, Silvan N, Reinikainen O, Väre I (2012) Rahkasammalista kasvualustaa. *Puutarha & Kauppa*; 2012(3): 12-13.

Tuittila E-S, Vasander H, Laine J (2000) Impact of rewetting on vegetation of a cut-away peatland. *Applied Vegetation Science*; 3: 205–212.

Vos R (ed.) (2016) Cultivation of Sphagnum in Northeast Friesland. Ideas, Methods, and Experiences for Spgahnum Farming. Raportti, Wageningen University, Hollanti. 28 s. (http://kenniswerkplaatsnoordoostfryslan.nl/uploads/files/ACT-1636-Case-Business-Peat-moss-final-report-april-2016.pdf)

Whinam J and Buxton R (1997) *Sphagnum* peatlands of Australasia: an assessment of harvesting sustainability. *Biological Conservation*; 82: 21–29. https://doi.org/10.1016/S0006-3207(97)00015-3.

Whinam J, Hope G S, Clarkson B R, Buxton R P, Alspach P A, Adam P (2003) *Sphagnum* in peatlands of Australasia: Their distribution, utilisation and management. *Wetlands Ecology and Management*; 11: 37–49.

Wichtmann W, Schröder C, Joosten H, (ed.) (2016) Paludiculture - productive use of wet peatlands. Climate protection - biodiversity - regional economic benefits. Schweizerbart Science Publishers, 272 p. ISBN 978-3-510-65283-9

Zak D, Goldhammer T, Cabezas A, Gelbrecht J, Gurke R, Wagner C, Reuter H, Augustin J, Klimkowska A, McInnes R J (2018) Top soil removal reduces water pollution from phosphorus and dissolved organic matter and lowers methane emissions from rewetted peatlands. *Journal of Applied Ecology*; 55: 311-20.

ID 62497

# GREENHOUSE GAS BALANCE OF A YOUNG, MICROPROPAGATED SPHAGNUM FARMING CROP ON A CUT-OVER LOWLAND PEATLAND IN NORTHERN ENGLAND

*Simon Caporn[1], Anna Keightley[1], Chris Field[1], Richard Lindsay[2], Jack Clough[2], Catharine Dawson[3], Paul Thomas[4], Neal Wright[5]

[1]Manchester Metropolitan University, UK
[2]University of East London, UK
[3]Melcourt Industries Ltd, UK
[4]Natural England, UK
[5]Micropropagation Services Ltd, UK

*s.j.m.caporn@mmu.ac.uk*

Peat is the preferred growing media in horticulture but is also a vital global carbon store. In many world regions, the supply is limited, and peat use in the UK is being phased out. There are, therefore, growing pressures to find alternatives in horticulture. Farmed, fresh Sphagnum is one peat substitute, and, in this project, we trialled a new method of growing a Sphagnum crop (patent pending). We aimed to grow a young crop and explore the consequences of crop management methods for $CO_2$ and CH4 exchange with the air. Sphagnum was grown from micropropagated plants and planted as either Sphagnum plugs or liquid gel (BeadaHumok™ and BeadaGel™ respectively) onto a cut-over peatland in Autumn 2018. Irrigation, when required, using water from adjacent peatland reservoirs was supplied by either spray or by drip. The water table was not controlled and varied from -2 cm to -38 cm. Different ways of protecting early-stage Sphagnum plant growth were compared: either straw, plastic mesh, plastic sheet (rain permeable) or a no-cover control. Each month, Sphagnum growth (% cover) was measured along with real-time fluxes of carbon greenhouse gases ($CO_2$ and CH4) using a Los Gatos Ultraportable analyser and a clear flux chamber. During the trial, the Sphagnum % cover on plug-planted plots increased from less than 4% at planting and reached almost complete cover (100%) by August (i.e. around 10 months). The cover material protected the developing Sphagnum crop and growth was faster than in the unprotected controls. Methane flux was negligible throughout the trial. The carbon dioxide exchange of the soil and crop switched from a net source to a sink at the stage when Sphagnum cover reached 100%. This approach to Sphagnum farming appears promising for both biomass production and climate change benefits by reducing carbon losses from cut-over peatlands.

# ID 62465

# SELECTING HIGHLY PRODUCTIVE SPHAGNUM PROVENANCES AND ITS MASS-PROPAGATION – FIRST RESULTS OF THE JOINT SPHAGNUM FARMING RESEARCH PROJECT,MOOSZUCHT'

*Anja Prager[1], Eva Decker[2], Greta Gaudig[1], Melanie Heck[2], Hans Joosten[1], Mira Kohl[1], Matthias Krebs[1], Paul Lamkowski[1], Volker Lüth[2], Ingrida Melkova[3], Clemens Posten[3], Ralf Reski[2], Christian Schade[4], Mira Schaefer[4], Martin Schnittler[1]

[1]Institute of Botany and Landscape Ecology, University of Greifswald, Germany
[2]Albert-Ludwigs-University of Freiburg, Faculty of Biology, Department Plant Biotechnology, Germany
[3]Karlsruhe Institute of Technology – KIT, Department Bioprocess Engineering, Germany
[4]Enterprise Niedersächsische Rasenkulturen NIRA GmbH & Co. KG – NIRA, Germany

*anja.prager@uni-greifswald.de*

To reach the zero $CO_2$ emission goal 2050 of the 'Paris Agreement' both, the drainage-based use of peatlands and the use of peat in growing media is no longer appropriate. Sphagnum (peatmoss) offers a climate-friendly alternative for both, when it is cultivated as a renewable crop on degraded rewetted peatlands (Sphagnum farming) and the produced biomass is used in growing media substituting peat. Field trails on rewetted former bog grassland and cut-over bogs showed the feasibility of Sphagnum farming, but so far only wild parent material was used as donor material. The 'Mooszucht' project addresses the potential of increasing Sphagnum productivity by selecting highly productive wild provenances and the large-scale mass propagation of selected provenances as founder material for implementing Sphagnum farming or for restoration purpose (www.mooszucht.paludiculture.com).

So far, 474 moss samples of 12 Sphagnum species have been collected from 31 mires (10 European countries). The most productive mosses were selected in a common-garden and a climate chamber experiment (comparing increment of lawn height, cover of capitula, and increase in dry weight). First results showed 40 % higher biomass productivity for Sphagnum papillosum (Georgian provenance) and 12 % for S. palustre (Czech provenance) compared to currently cultivated mosses in our pilot field. To explore the relationship between and distribution of Sphagnum genotypes most productive wild provenances were genetically characterized by SSR marker assays.

A protocol for both axenic in-vitro cultures, generated from spore and vegetative moss material was developed. The optimization of culture conditions in a stirred tank-reactor allowed e.g. a 40-fold biomass increase within 23 days for a S. palustre clone. To further scale up the photo-bioreactor approach, a trickle bed-reactor was developed. In this reactor a productivity of 300 g/m2/d was reached for a Sphagnum palustre clone. Additionally, non-axenic Sphagnum mass propagation was successful tested on irrigated fleeces.

ID 62795

# PALUDICULTURE ON FORMER BOG GRASSLAND: SUSTAINABLE BIOMASS PRODUCTION AND ADDITIONAL BENEFITS OF SPHAGNUM FARMING IN NW GERMANY

Greta Gaudig, Anja Prager, Matthias Krebs, *Sabine Wichmann

Institute of Botany and Landscape Ecology, University of Greifswald, Germany

*wichmann@uni-greifswald.de*

Sphagnum farming is paludiculture on bogs. *Sphagnum* mosses are cultivated as permanent culture and the biomass is harvested e.g. as a raw material for horticultural growing media. Field trails on rewetted former bog grassland and cut-over bogs in Northwest Germany showed the feasibility of Sphagnum farming, both on peat and on floating mats. Here we present the results we achieved on our 14-ha study site in the peatland Hankhauser Moor (Lower Saxony, Germany) on formerly drained bog grassland.

• *Sphagnum* growth: A mainly closed *Sphagnum* lawn was established within 18 months and had accumulated 39 t dry mass per hectare eight years after installation. *Sphagnum* biomass was mechanically harvested after five years on part of the area. The regeneration after harvest was slow.

• Water demand: In a drained landscape, irrigation with 160 mm of water is needed to compensate the water deficit during summer.

• Water quality: *Sphagnum* mosses grow well due to low bicarbonate concentrations and pH values in the peat pore water. The *Sphagnum* production fields act as an active nutrient sink as the *Sphagnum* mosses achieved high nutrient sequestration rates.

• Greenhouse gas emissions: Our Sphagnum farming site represented a slight GHG source of 2.5 t $ha^{-1}$ $a^{-1}$ $CO_{2e}$ during the establishment phase, representing a significant reduction compared to previous use.

• Biodiversity: The study site provides a substitute habitat for bog species, but also for other partly rare flora and fauna species (spiders, dragonflies).

• Economics: Sphagnum farming is economically feasible when harvested biomass is traded as founder material or as raw material for higher prised cultures. The profitability as an alternative to peat can be achieved e.g. by reducing currently high production costs and slightly higher prices for peat-free produced plants.

For the large-scale implementation of Sphagnum farming more research is needed to reach technological maturity and to reduce costs.

# II SUPPORTING SERVICES

IPC2021

ID 62580

# CYCLING OF NUTRIENTS IN DIFFERENT INTENSITY REGENERATION FELLINGS: MINERAL SOIL VS. PEAT SOIL

*Ivars Klavins[1,2], Zane Kalvīte[1,2], Arta Bārdule[1], Zane Lībiete[1],

[1]Latvian State Forest Research Institute 'Silava'
[2]University of Latvia, Latvia

*ivars.klavins@silava.lv*

With the growing importance of climate goals and related increase of renewable energy use, forestry intensification is ongoing and expected to continue in Latvia, therefore, its risks and opportunities must be better understood. Whole-tree harvesting (WTH) with removal of entire above-ground biomass in regeneration fellings is becoming a common practice. The impacts on the natural ecosystem and connected waterbodies varies according to different forest site types, nutrient pools and soil.

To evaluate the impacts of WTH on the cycling of nutrients, study objects in locally typical forest site types *Hylocomiosa*(mineral soil) and *Oxalidosa. turf. mel.* (drained peat soil) were established. Soil water, groundwater, rainwater, surface water in nearby streams/ditches, soil, foliage of the young stands and litter were sampled in each site in three subplots: control (C; not harvested); conventional harvest (CH); WTH. In addition, height growth of the young stands is measured yearly. Continuous and still ongoing observations date back to 2012 – with one year retrospection before the fellings were carried out.

The most direct responses after fellings were observed in parameters of soil water. Nitrate nitrogen (N-$NO_3^-$) and total nitrogen (TN) concentrations notably increased in *Hylocomiosa* site in both WTH and CH subplots with peaks 2-4 years after felling; the concentrations remained stable in CH subplot of *Oxalidosa. turf. mel.* site while in WTH subplot increased with peaks 1-3 years after felling. N-$NH_4^+$ concentrations in *Hylocomiosa* site increased in all three subplots 1-3 years after felling while elevated concentrations in *Oxalidosa. turf. mel.* site were observed only in WTH subplot. Height growth of the young stand in WTH subplot of *Oxalidosa. turf. mel.* site was slightly higher than that in CH subplot during all study years while no significant differences were observed between subplots of the *Hylocomiosa* site.

ID 61729

# GEOLOGICAL SURVEY OF FINLAND'S LABORATORY ANALYSES DATABASE – DETAILED INFORMATION ON THE BACKGROUND LEVELS OF ELEMENTS IN FINNISH PEATLANDS

Teuvo Herranen[1], Anna Laine-Petäjäkangas[1], Jukka Turunen[1], Tuija Vähäkuopus[1]

[1]Geological Survey of Finland

*teuvo.herranen@gtk.fi*

## SUMMARY

The Geological Survey of Finland (GTK) has thus far studied 2.3 million ha of the total geological peatland area of Finland (5.1 million ha). Samples have been taken over 19 000 sampling points for detailed laboratory analyses, which include over 1 800 elemental analyses points. The data covers almost 10 000 individual peatlands throughout Finland and provides information on the background levels of elements in peat.
The majority of the peat sample series covers the peat column from the surface to the bottom of the peat layer, with the samples taken at continuous 20-cm intervals. The majority of the elemental analyses include the top and bottom sections of the peat columns, with analyses also conducted on several middles sections. Most elements have been analysed in over 7 000 samples; however, sulphur content has been analysed in over 66 000 samples.

The concentrations of most elements in the peat samples are lower or significantly lower than in mineral soil and are often at the same level as in the humus layer. Sulphur clearly appears to be enriched in the peat and humus layer. Exceptionally high element concentrations in peat often indicate the presence of black schist zones nearby, and high element concentrations can also be useful in ore prospecting.

The highest elemental concentrations are usually in the middle and bottom part of the peat stratum. In contrast to other elements, lead is clearly enriched in the peat surface. This derives from the immobility of lead in peat and from the fact that much of the lead has come from fall-out. Often the highest element concentrations are found in the samples with high ash content. Lead is an exception. The samples with high lead content have low ash content.

***Keywords***: analyses, elements, peat, black schist, Finland

## INTRODUCTION

The Geological Survey of Finland (GTK) has studied Finnish peatlands since the second world war and more effectively after the energy crisis in the seventies. The big increase in research capacity occurred in the year 1981. So GTK has thus far studied 2.3 million ha of Finnish peatland. The peat data generated in peat mapping has been saved in a peat database maintained by GTK. The database contains data on nearly 18 000 peatlands, totalling more than 1.75 million study and depth points. Samples have been taken for more detailed laboratory analyses from nearly 9 900 peatlands. There are in all over 19 000 sampling points, which include over 1 800 elemental analyses points. Elemental assays have been carried out since the 1970s. Most elements have been analysed in over 7 000 samples; however, sulphur content has been analysed in over 66 000 samples.

The Hakku service lets you search for and start using a range of spatial data products. The service includes Finnish spatial data, documents and metadata from the 19th century to the present day. The service is continuously expanded with new products (https://hakku.gtk.fi/en). There you can also find nearly 470 municipal peat reports and the report Turpeen alkuainemääritykset GTK:ssa Summary: The element assays of peat in the GTK (http://tupa.gtk.fi/raportti/arkisto/73_2018.pdf).

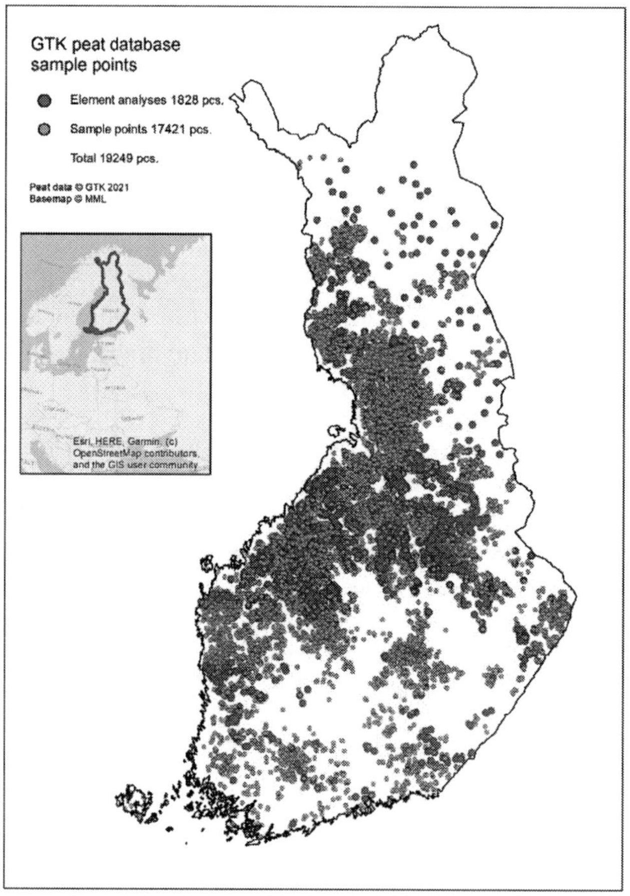


Fig. 1. The peat sample points and element analysis points of the peatlands investigated by GTK. Blue peat sample points in the database of the Geological Survey of Finland are presented on the map, representing the situation in February 2021. The peat sample points for element analysis are marked with a red colour. There are altogether 9 965 peatlands with samples, 19 249 peat sample points and 1 828 element sample points. (Base map © National Land Survey of Finland).

## MATERIALS AND METHODS

In addition to recording the peat type and humification, the peat samples have also nearly always been assayed for their ash and water content. Nearly 220 000 ash content and over 218 000 water content assays have been conducted. For those samples that have been precisely volume weighted (nearly 183 000), the dry bulk density has been assayed. Over 175 000 pH value and over 125 000 calorific value determinations have been performed. The majority of the peat sample series taken in connection with peat studies have extended from the surface to near the bottom of the peat layer, with the samples being a continuum of 20 cm sub-samples. Most of the elemental assays in connection with peat mapping have been carried out so that in addition to samples taken from surface and bottom parts, assays have also been conducted on several samples between them.

Elemental assays were formerly carried out in the chemistry laboratory of GTK, but following its incorporation in 2006, they have been carried out by Eurofins Labtium. The assay method used is that involving nitric acid dissolution of dried and comminuted peat (0.5 g) in a microwave oven (US EPA 3051A), and the element concentrations are determined by ICP-OES and ICP-MS. ICP-MS (method 503M of Labtium) can detect elements at very low concentrations.

The element studies of peat does not quite cover the whole Finland, because formerly less element determinations of peat were assayed. During the last few years the regional scope has become better, and elements of peat have been systematically assayed. So the quantity of analyses has grown outstandingly. At the same time lower determination limits for As and Cd have been used.

Formerly the samples were taken with the volume exact piston drill developed by Dr Martti Korpijaakko, the diameter of which is 10 cm. Nowadays we take surface peat samples 0–100 cm with box sampler. With that we get volume exact samples even from slightly humified surface peat. Samples from bottom peat layer are taken with Russian peat borer, the diameter of which is 5 cm.

## RESULTS

The peat sulphur content has been assayed for nearly 66 000 samples. In addition, the carbon and nitrogen content has been determined for over 8 800 samples. Most elements have over 7 000 determinations (table 1).

Table 1. The summarize results of the element assays of peat. All assays (ash content max. 25 %). The state on the fourth of October 2019.

| | mg/kg | | | | | | | | | | | | | |
|---|---|---|---|---|---|---|---|---|---|---|---|---|---|---|
| | Al | As | B | Ba | Be | Ca | Cd | Co | Cr | Cu | Fe | K | La | Li |
| N | 7195 | 7133 | 7171 | 7171 | 7145 | 7195 | 7273 | 7272 | 7202 | 7272 | 7272 | 7195 | 822 | 2301 |
| Min | 26 | 0 | 0 | 1.96 | 0 | 148 | 0 | 0.05 | 0.1 | 0.2 | 74.1 | 5 | 0* | 0* |
| Max | 25300 | 4220 | 67 | 1090 | 18 | 33000 | 6.5 | 1550 | 220 | 389 | 142000 | 7390 | 348 | 14 |
| Mean | 2679 | 3.80 | 2.68 | 57.9 | 0.23 | 3998 | 0.26 | 1.63 | 5.67 | 11.26 | 6529 | 166.4 | 9.69 | 0.45 |
| Median | 1860 | 2.50 | 2.50 | 45 | 0.1 | 2870 | 0.25 | 0.5 | 3 | 5.4 | 4420 | 50 | 4 | 0.1 |
| St. deviation | 2753 | 51.6 | 1.52 | 56.5 | 0.58 | 3456 | 0.16 | 18.9 | 9.34 | 18.1 | 11006 | 350.8 | 21.8 | 1.06 |

| | mg/kg | | | | | | | | | | | | | |
|---|---|---|---|---|---|---|---|---|---|---|---|---|---|---|
| | Mg | Mn | Mo | Na | Ni | P | Pb | S | Sb | Sc | Si | Sr | Th | Ti |
| N | 7195 | 7272 | 4648 | 7171 | 7272 | 7196 | 7271 | 7173 | 7171 | 770 | 819 | 7171 | 39 | 7170 |
| Min | 23 | 0.5 | 0 | 2.5 | 0.1 | 52 | 0.025 | 64.5 | 0* | 0* | 4.2 | 0.5 | 0.02 | 0.25 |
| Max | 4260 | 3590 | 75 | 1010 | 4270 | 7430 | 3840 | 147000 | 51 | 10.3 | 1030 | 355 | 3 | 928 |
| Mean | 659 | 78.7 | 0.73 | 47.1 | 6.38 | 550 | 4.5 | 2853 | 2.99 | 1.17 | 143 | 27.5 | 0.72 | 70.9 |
| Median | 523 | 36.3 | 0.5 | 25 | 3.0 | 471 | 2.5 | 1770 | 0.01 | 0.60 | 132 | 23.3 | 0.21 | 38 |
| St. deviation | 494 | 129.8 | 2.76 | 58.2 | 59.8 | 1135 | 45.5 | 5743 | 3.71 | 1.55 | 88.2 | 19.44 | 0.93 | 105.6 |

| | mg/kg | | | | | % | | | | |
|---|---|---|---|---|---|---|---|---|---|---|
| | U | V | Y | Zn | Zr | C | H | N | S | |
| N zero values | 60 | 7170 | 770 | 7271 | 2022 | 8515 | 233 | 852358482 | | * = notably |
| Min | 0.018 | 0.05 | 0* | 0.5 | 0* | 27.0 | 5.3 | 0.06 | 0 | |
| Max | 80.8 | 786 | 115 | 6750 | 46.2 | 62.7 | 7.91 | 4.52 | 14.6 | |
| Mean | 4.19 | 12.32 | 5.28 | 13.88 | 2.18 | 51.67 | 6.69 | 1.80 | 0.25 | |
| Median | 0.64 | 5.44 | 2.5 | 3.9 | 1 | 52.1 | 6.93 | 1.84 | 0.18 | |
| St. deviation | 12.9 | 29.95 | 8.96 | 140 | 3.84 | 3.73 | 0.65 | 0.58 | 0.37 | |

The contents of most elements in peat are lower or clearly lower than in mineral soil and are often at the same level as in the humus layer (fig. 2). The cadmium content of peat in the analysis results used in calculation is on average clearly higher than in mineral soil and on average lower than in humus. In reality, the difference is not so clear, because the element contents of many elements in peat samples analysed have been under the assay limit. The sulphur content of peat is nearly one-fifth higher than the corresponding value of humus. Compared with mineral soil, the sulphur content of peat is approximately 8–39 times higher. Sulphur therefore clearly appears to be enriched in the peat and humus layer, which mostly results from the presence of black schist zones nearby (Herranen 2009, Herranen & Toivonen 2018).

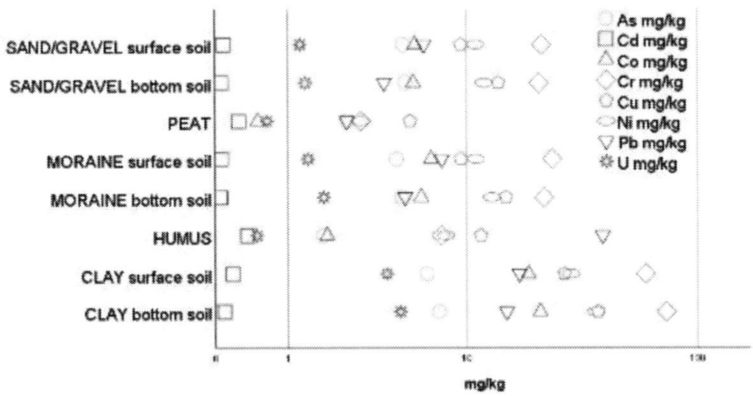


Fig. 2. The median contents of arsenic, cadmium, cobalt, chromium, copper, nickel, lead and uranium in peat, humus and various soil types.

The median content of noxious element in peat is generally clearly below the threshold value, but the maximum values are generally clearly above the threshold values. The maximum content of arsenic in peat is over eight hundred-fold, the maximum content of nickel and cobalt about eighty-fold compared with the threshold values.

## DISCUSSION

High element contents of peat often indicate the presence of black schist zones nearby, but high element contents can additionally be useful in ore prospecting, because the surrounding bedrock is also otherwise reflected in the element content of peat (Salmi 1955). Black schists are rock types, which contain carbon as graphite, and they form thin belts in schist series. They are easily weathered (Virtanen & Lerssi 2006, 2008).

In black schist areas (fig. 3) the average aluminium, arsenic, barium, cadmium, cobalt, chromium, copper, iron, manganese, nickel, lead, sulphur, titanium, uranium, vanadium, zinc and ash contents of peat are often higher than normal. Taking note of black schist zones and having a denser spacing of analysis points in the neighbourhood of these zones might be reasonable, if a peatland is found to be either a potential peat harvesting area or suitable for other use.

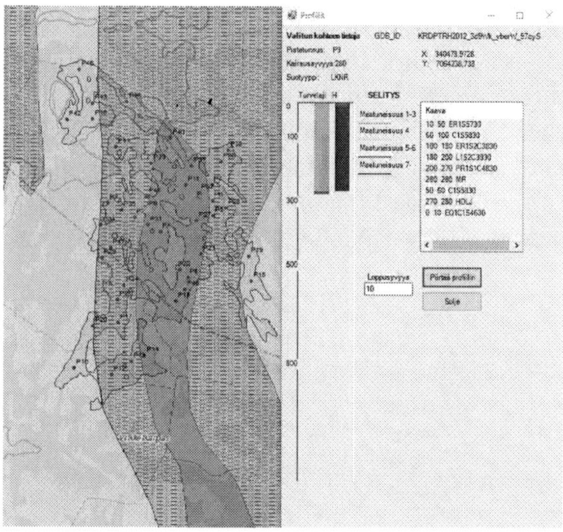


Fig. 3. The peatland on the black schist zone and the boring profile. Kairaussyvyys = boring depth, suotyyppi = peatland type, LKNR = low-sedge pine fen, turvelaji = peat type, Maatuneisuus = humification.
Base map © National Land Survey of Finland.

Many elements in peat have quite large scattering, and on the other hand many elements in peat have quite even distribution (fig. 4).

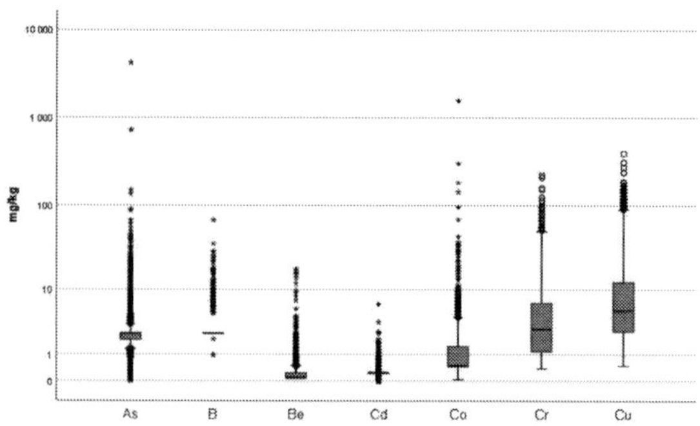


Fig. 4. The distribution of arsenic, boron, beryllium, cadmium, cobalt, chromium and copper in peat presented as a box plot (N = 6 920).

## CONCLUSION

The results of the element assays of peat can be utilized regionally in the planning of land use and after-use of peat harvesting areas, for instance. In addition it is possible to gain a more exact understanding of regional geochemistry and the risk areas of heavy metals. The data have a very important role in developing new ways and possibilities to use peat and peatlands.


## ACKNOWLEDGEMENTS

We thank Arto Laiho for technical support for getting the analysis data summary from the peat database of GTK.


## REFERENCES


**Herranen, T. 2009.** Turpeen rikkipitoisuus Suomessa. Abstract: The sulfur concentration of peat in Finland. Geological Survey of Finland,
Report of Peat Investigation 398, 55 pages, 19 figures and 27 tables. Available at: http://tupa.gtk.fi/raportti/turve/ttr_398.pdf

**Herranen, T. & Toivonen, T. 2018** Turpeen alkuainemääritykset GTK:ssa. Summary: The element assays of peat in the GTK. Geological Survey of Finland, Open File Research Report
73/2018, 45 pages, 37 figures and 3 tables. Available at: http://tupa.gtk.fi/raportti/arkisto/73_2018.pdf

**Salmi, M. 1955**. Prospecting for bog-covered ore by means of peat investigations. Bull. Comm.Geol. Finlande 169. 34 p. Available at:
http://tupa.gtk.fi/julkaisu/bulletin/bt_169.pdf

**Virtanen, K. & Lerssi, J. 2006** Mustaliuskekivilajin vaikutus turpeen alkuainepitoisuuksiin. Influence of black schists to element content of peat. Geological Survey of Finland. 33 p, 2 appendixes and 30 figures. Available at: http://tupa.gtk.fi/raportti/arkisto/s42_0000_2006_1.pdf

**Virtanen, K. & Lerssi, J. 2008**. The influence of metal bearing black schist bedrock on metal and sulphur contents of peat deposits. Farrell, C. & Feehan, J. (eds) After Wise Use – The Future of Peatlands. Proceedings of the 13th International Peat Congress, Tullamore, Ireland 8–13 June 2008. Volume 2, Poster presentations. International Peat Society, 55–59.

ID 62280

# THE INTERATION OF NITROGEN AND PHOSPHORUS ON THE EXTRACELLULAR ENZYMES IN A MINEROTROPHIC PEATLAND

*Meng Wang[1], Tong Li[1,2], Yan Chen[1], Zhaojun Bu[1], Changhui Peng[3],

[1]Northeast Normal University, China
[2]Northwest A&F University, China
[3]University of Quebec at Montreal, Canada

*wangm581@nenu.edu.cn*

Extracellular enzymes play critical roles in regulating the biogeochemical cycles and carbon (C) sequestration in northern peatlands. The substantial increase in the reactive nitrogen (N) deposition has remarkably compromised the C storage of northern peatlands via the impact on the activities of the key extracellular enzymes and their interactions. However, there is still a dearth of knowledge regarding the interactions of N and P on the enzymatic activities and hence the organic matter decomposition. Here we conducted two sets of field experiments to assess the effect of different loadings and duration of N and P addition on the key extracellular enzymes in a minerotrophic fen in northeast China.

We found that the long-term (10 years) N addition had significantly reduced the growth of *Sphagnum* mosses and dwarf shrubs, whereas P addition increased the growth of both. Long-term P addition led to the shift in vegetation composition from being *Sphagnum*-dominated to shrub-dominated, resulting in the increased input of lignin and phenolics from shrub litters. The indirect effect of long-term P addition through the shift to shrub-dominated plant community generally regulated the activities of β-glucosidase, N-acetyl-β-D-glycosaminidase and phosphatase. However, the long-tern N addition was of great importance in regulating the stoichiometry of the enzymatic activities. In contrast, the short-term (2 years) N and P addition only posed significant effects on the phenol oxidase activity. Over the course of fertilization, the interaction of N and P predominated once the significant shift in vegetation composition occurred. In summary, the traditional 'enzymatic latch' mechanism failed to regulate the decomposition of organic matter as the cumulative external N and P input shifted the chemistry of the litter and peat. Therefore, the interactions between N and P is likely of primary significance in regulating the biogeochemical cycling of peatlands.

72818

# THE ORGANIC SULFUR DYNAMICS ASSOCIATED WITH MERCURY METHYLATION IN A BOREAL PEATLAND

*Caroline Pierce[1], Olha Furman[2], Sarah Nicholas[3], Jill Coleman-Wasik[4], Steven Sebestyen[5], Randall Kolka[5], Carl Mitchell[6], Natalie Griffiths[7], Edward Nater[1], Brandy Toner[1]

[1]University of Minnesota, USA
[2]Department of the Environment and Energy, Australia
[3]Brookhaven National Laboratory - National Synchrotron Light Source II, USA
[4]University of Wisconsin, USA
[5]USDA Forest Service, Northern Research Station, USA
[6]University of Toronto, Canada
[7]Oak Ridge National Lab, USA

*pierc521@umn.edu*

Peatlands hold large quantities of atmospherically deposited mercury (Hg) and can be significant sources of neurotoxic methylmercury (MeHg) to the surrounding surface waters. Because peatlands are anaerobic, they provide ideal conditions for Hg methylation, so much so that the percentage of wetlands in a watershed is positively correlated with MeHg concentrations in fish. It is known that sulfur is important to the methylation of mercury but the sulfur species in organic soils, such as peatlands, remains vague in terms of reactants, products, and effect on bioavailability of mercury. This study aims to characterize the interaction of sulfur and mercury within a boreal peatland. We examined the size, composition, and spatial correlation of sulfur and mercury pools in peat depth profiles. A significant positive correlation ($p < 0.05$) between MeHg and organic disulfide (R-S-S-R') concentrations with depth was observed and is consistent with these chemical species being products of dissimilatory sulfate reduction processes. Peaks of MeHg and organic disulfide were co-located in the zone of water table fluctuation. Conversely, a significant negative correlation between organic monosulfides (R-S-H , R-S-R') with MeHg concentrations was observed and is consistent with the reduction of Hg(II) bioavailability via complexation reactions between Hg(II) and organic monosulfides in peat. Finally, a significant positive correlation between ester sulfate concentrations and potential methylation constants was observed and is consistent with ester sulfate being the substrate that drives mercury methylation via dissimilatory sulfate reduction. The relationships between sulfur species and mercury were assessed by measuring sulfur speciation using sulfur 1s X-ray absorption near-edge structure (XANES) spectroscopy, measuring total mercury (THg) and MeHg concentrations by cold vapor atomic fluorescence spectrometry (CVAFS) and measuring instantaneous potential methylation and demethylation constants.

ID 61445

# IMPACT OF RESTORATION OF BOG MARGIN AREAS ON MOOR FROG (RANA ARVALIS) IN ESTONIA

*Liina Remm, Riinu Rannap

University of Tartu, Estonia

*liina.remm@ut.ee*

Moor frog (Rana arvalis) is threatened species in several European countries. In Estonia, its status has deteriorated over the last decades, being today near threatened. In natural hemiboreal Europe the wetland-originating biomass of this species contributes greatly to various food chains. A main threat factor for that amphibian is loss of breeding habitats. Moor frogs spawn in shallow floods and tolerate more acid waters than other Estonian amphibians. Flooded fen and lagg areas have been reduced as a result of drainage for forestry and agriculture as well as due to peat mining. Such habitats have served as massive breeding sites for moor frogs. Studies about the impact of large-scale hydrological restoration on amphibians are scarce. We explored, how large-scale mire restoration (implemented in frame of the project LIFE Mires of Estonia in six bog complexes) could improve the breeding conditions of moor frog. At first we conducted a pre-restoration inventory and searched for existing breeding sites in 57 km of ditches and 24 ha of flooded sites. The spawn of moor frog was abundant in flooded fens and transitional mires as well in ditches impounded by beavers, but scarce in forest drainage ditches. Possible restoration dilemmas appeared in ditches where beaver impoundments had to be removed to enable machinery access for restoration works. After restoration works spawn numbers greatly increased in places where ditches were blocked not only within bog massive but also in fen and lagg areas. This result emphasises that it is important to incorporate whole mire complexes, not only bog massives, to protected areas in order to enable restoration of the species rich fen and lagg habitats.

ID 62691

# LONG-TERM RESPONSE OF VEGETATION ON THE WATER LEVEL DROP-DOWN ON A LARGE CALCAREOUS FEN (NW ESTONIA)

*Laimdota Truus[1], Mati Ilomets[1], Raimo Pajula[1], Kairi Sepp[1]

[1]Institute of Ecology, Tallinn University, Tallinn, Estonia

*laimi@tlu.ee*

**SUMMARY**

Mires are usually drained for economic use – for peat extraction, tree plantation or agricultural production. Sedge fen with area over 3 000 ha on the border of Suursoo-Leidissoo mire complex (over 20 000 ha) was drained at theend of the 19$^{th}$ Century for hay cutting. In reality, the hay was cut there in short period and locally, so the area hasbeen subject only to weak but long-term drainage over 100 years. Hence the vegetation succession has been spontaneous with only human-induced influence – constant drainage.
Peat composition shows that pre-drainage vegetation consisted of low-growth sedges (Carex sp., Schoenus ferrugineus) and brown mosses. Similar vegetation is still there in a small area but for the most part it has changeddramatically because of decline of a mineral-rich mire water table level.
As a result, different trends are observed in vegetation composition.
First, water table (WT) deepened but still available mineral-rich water supports transition from previous low- sedge vegetation to tall-growing grasses and sedges (Molinia caerulea, Trichophorum caespitosum) that make high tussocks. Dense litter covers spaces between tussocks and brown mosses have mostly disappeared.
The second trend is afforestation. We have recognised different successional stages from open fen to treed fen and to thick mixed forest of birches, pines and spruces. The latter is accompanied by the lowest WT and the mostdecomposed topmost peat in the soil.
The third and the most common trend of the succession is similar to the natural succession – development from mineral-rich fen to bog-like vegetation, but that succession goes hundred times faster than it happens in natural way. Previous low-growing sedge vegetation is overgrowing by Sphagnum-dominant vegetation, both treed and open sites.
The last trend is often seen nowadays in fens in Estonia, whether the WT of the mire is lowered by land use, landuplift or by drainage through the trees evapotranspiration.

**Keywords**: Calcareous fen, drainage, groundwater level, peat mineralization, vegetation succession

## INTRODUCTION

State and quality of calcareous fen ecosystems is controlled by relatively constant groundwater exfiltration that assures constant close to surface water level (WL), high ionic concentration and low plant nutrients supply (Hayeket al., 2006). When WL drops down because of drainage the proportion of rainwater in mire water balance increases and pore water pH decreases provoking lose the basic feeding type (Johansen et al., 2011). Higher proportion of rainwater in formation of the mire water lowers water pH. Decline in water level leads to decomposition of peat that increases nutrients supply for plants (Devito and Dillon, 1997; Haraguchi et al., 2003). Drainage causes multidirectional disturbances in quality and quantity of peatland feeding system and modifies the structure of vegetation composition. The fall down of WL fosters the increase of vascular plant cover (such as dwarf shrubs) with corresponding reduction in the moss cover (Goud et al., 2018). Changes from one type to another may proceed with short successional time-frame. Thus, changes caused by drainage are complex but always resulting with impoverishment of typical fen vegetation.

Fens were widely distributed in Estonia, making up to ca 50% (420 000 ha) of the Estonian mire area. Calcareousfens as typical vegetation type, especially in the western Estonia have been drained, mostly for hay mowing and for pasturing because fen soils are very suitable for agriculture (Laasimer, 1965). Management of fens largely ended in the 1960s-1970s. By the estimations (Ilomets, 2017) only up to 10-15% of calcareous fens are left in near-natural state today. But, once dug ditches still drain and the area of fens in natural state is constantly decreasing.

Restoration of fen ecosystems sets complex tasks for restoration measures application and results are hard to predict because of complex hydrological system and heterogeneity of vegetation units.

We set up a comprehensive and integrated monitoring system in the Suursoo-Leidissoo calcareous fen site undertaken for restoration. We aimed to understand the share of different abiotic drivers affecting state development of plant cover during over 100 years lasting weak drainage what may give valuable information for predictions about changes following restoration measures.

Our hypothesis was that there are other abiotic drivers besides the water level drop down responded into the formation of patterned vegetation.

STUDY SITE

A B

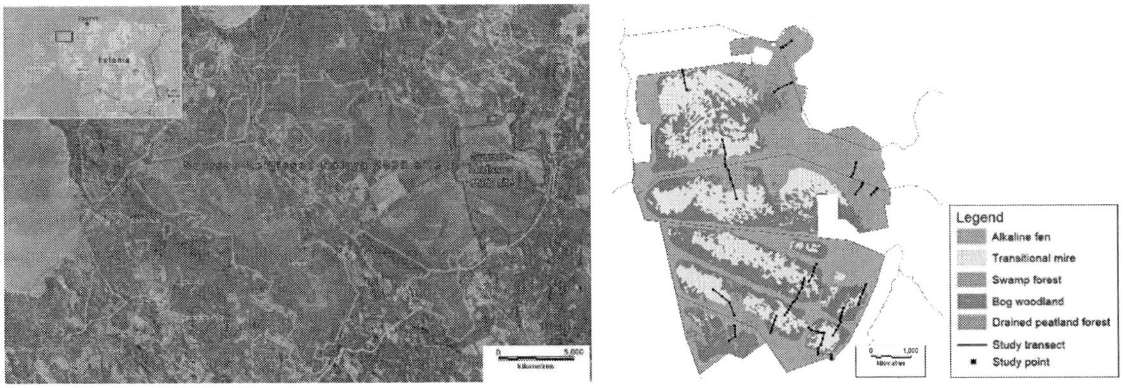


Figure 1. A – Location of the Suursoo-Leidissoo study site (also LIFE Peat Restore project site; with red border) Läänemaa Suursoo mire complex in NW Estonia; B – drainage-induced vegetation pattern with study transects and study points.

Suursoo-Leidissoo study site (ca 3 400 ha) as part of the Suursoo-Leidissoo Natura 2000 site (EE0040202) is an eastern part of Läänemaa Suursoo mire complex (over 20 000 ha) and is project LIFE Peat Restore peatland restoration site. Originally the site was an extensive wet fen (dominantly ass. *Drepanoclado-Schoenetum*). At theend of the 19$^{th}$ century the sparse hand-dug drainage system was made with total length of narrow ditches of ca 45km, with ca 1 km distance between each other. The ill-fated amelioration resulted in the development of peatlandwith patterned plant cover from still open fen to different Sphagnum dominated transitional mire and drained forested peatland communities.

## METHODS

For the vegetation survey we analysed plant species (vascular plants and mosses) coverage on 95 sample plots (10x10 m) on transects cross ditches over the site (Figure 1B). In the nested-plot design 3 subplots by 2x2 m (divided into four 1x1 m squares) were nested into 10x10 m plot for vascular plant analyses and 36 subplots of 0.25x0.25 m in every 2x2 m plot for moss layer analyses where coverage (%) of every species estimated. Trees and shrubs estimated on 10x10 m plots (Figure 2).

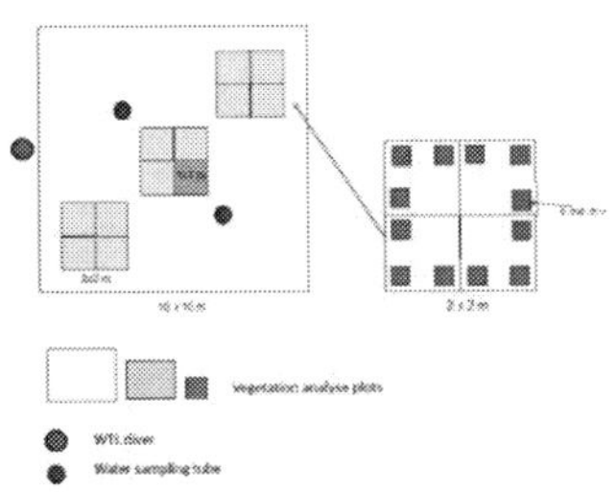

Figure 2. Analyse design for vegetation and water sampling.

Water level monitored from PVC tubes inserted to every vegetation analyse plot since 2017 and with automatic divers (record the water level every 2 hours) close to 60 vegetation analyse plots in 2018-2020.

Water chemistry samples collected every summer and autumn from perforated PVC tubes inserted on all analyseplots. Electrical conductivity, pH, inorganic carbon (IC), SO $^{2-}$, $Ca^{2+}$ etc. content analysed. Means of water and peat parameters calculated and statistical differences found between parameters (Table 1).

Peat samples (from 0-10 cm and 10-20 cm depth) were taken for their later bulk density and ash content analysesclose to vegetation plots.

On the base of Lidar data, satellite maps and UAV-photos, the distribution map of vegetation types compiled at start in 2017. PCA ordination of vegetation data in relation to water and peat parameters provided.

## RESULTS

Five vegetation types were distinguished (Figure 1B) which all lie on quite uniform weakly to medium decomposed (2-4 after van Post) Carex-brown moss peat. It means that all types have been evolved from one – the calcareus fen type.

The main parameters of water and peat distinguishing vegetation types are given in Table 1. Subdivisions of calcareus fen and transitional mire types indicate about different successional stages of these types. Calcareous fen type differs from others by significantly higher electrical conductivity (EC) of pore water and by peat bulk density and ash content of the upper 0-10 cm peat. Peat density and ash content of drained peatland forest were also higher than in other successional vegetation units. WL measured in summer and in autumn 2017 did not showstatistical differences. WL was always high in 2017 because of extreme weather – long and cold spring and rainy August and September. These parameters differentiated significantly between vegetation types in two following years, 2018 and 2019 with dryer weather (data of the Estonian Weather Service).

Table 1. General water and peat properties in the vegetation types of Suursoo-Leidissoo study site. Data taken inJuly 2017, just WL_aut taken in September; EC – Electrical conductivity, µS/cm; WL – water table level; BD_1 – bulk density of upper 0-10 cm peat, g dm$^3$; BD_2 – bulk density of 10-20 cm peat depth, g dm$^3$; Ash _1 – ash content (%) of 0-10 peat depth; Ash _2 – ash content (%) of 10-20 peat depth. Indexes a and b show statistical differences.

| | | Calcareous fen | | Transitional mire | | | |
|---|---|---|---|---|---|---|---|
| | **Parameter** | Small sedges | Molinia | Tall sedges | Sphagnum-Menyanthes | **Transitional mire forest** | **Drained peatland forest** |
| **Water** | EC_sum17 | 322a | 328a | 82b | 85b | 85b | 116b |
| | WL_sum17 | -3b | 0b | -6b | -14b | -8b | -31b |
| | WL_aut17 | +15b | +11b | +4b | +2b | +2b | +2b |
| | BD_1 | 106a | 105a | 79b | 84b | 85b | 113a |
| | Ash_1 | 14a | 12a | 6b | 7 b | 6b | 10 a |
| **Peat** | BD_2 | 91b | 90b | 72b | 80b | 74b | 115a |
| | Ash_2 | 9b | 9b | 4b | 6b | 6b | 18a |

Based on plant cover data from 95 plots we made PCA ordination biplot of vascular plant assemblages distributionin relation to WL and water chemistry (sampled in May 2019) and on relation to minimal, maximum water levelsand to WL amplitude (Figure 3). We found that distribution of plant assemblages (sedges and other fen species, bog species and species typical for minerotrophic forests) are related on peat water mineral content and on water level fluctuation differently.

Assemblage 1 (with light green circle on Figure 3) on sites with high EC, high mineral content and high water level represents the best preserved fen site (Myrica+Carex+fen mosses group). It is related to higher carbon (carbonates) content in mire water and on constantly high WL during the vegetation period.

If water and peat indicator values of typical fen are declining, a continuous transition to Sphagnum-dominated transition mire associations (assemblages 3, 4 and 5) starts. Treed fen (assemblage 2) locates close to the transitionmire assemblages 4 and 5. There is no sharp line between them but rather a continuous transition. Assemblages 3, 4 and 5 (with purple circle) represent plots with mixture of certain fen species in complex with Sphagnum and Calluna vulgaris – classified here as transitional mire with different stages of afforestation. It is characterised withlow content of $Ca^{2+}$, SO $^{2-}$ and inorganic carbon and with deep WL during summer period.

Distribution of plant assemblages 6 (swamp forest) and 7 (drained peatland forest) on the ordination biplot is characterised by high WL amplitude indicating about considerable WL fluctuations during the vegetation period.The deep and fluctuating WL results in high total organic content indicating about increased surface peat decay processes.

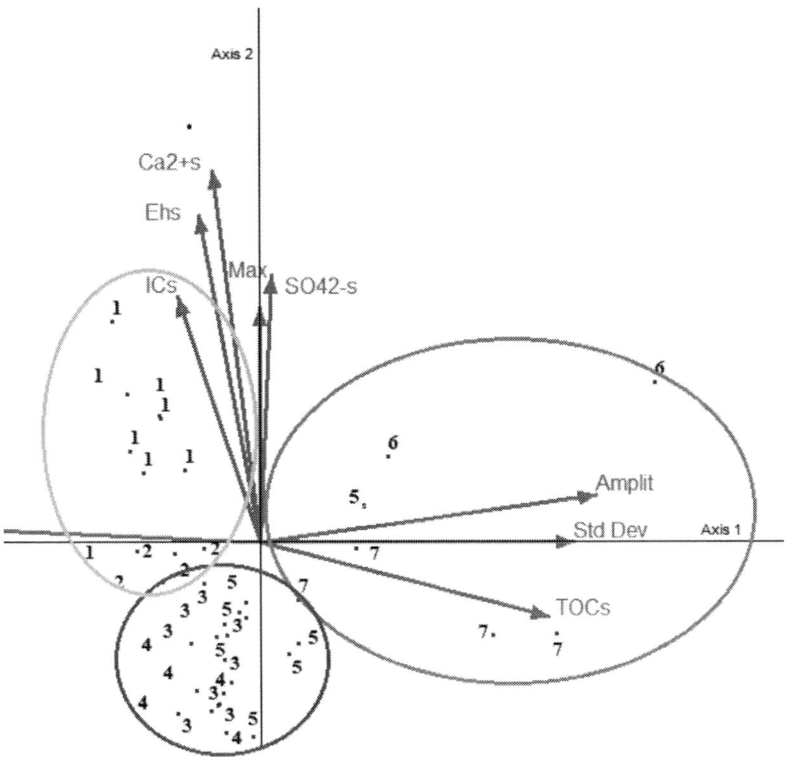


Figure 3. PCA ordination biplot of vascular plant distribution in relation to water level and certain water chemistry parameters (sampled in May 2019). Plant assemblages: 1-open fen, 2-treed fen, 3-open transitional mire, 4-treedtransitional mire, 5-transitional mire forest, 6-swamp forest, 7-

drained peatland forest. Symbols on figure are: Ca2+s –$Ca^{2+}$, SO42s – $SO_4^{2-}$, ICs – inorganic carbon, Ehs – electrical conductivity (EC), TOCs – total organic carbon contents. Ampl – water level (WL) amplitude, Max – WL maximum depth of water level, Min – WL minimum, Std Dev – WL standard deviation, s- sampling in spring.

## DISCUSSION

Changes in varying magnitudes occurred due to changed moisture conditions due to ditching. Groups 1 and 2 onFigure 3 represent fen vegetation, 3-5 transitional mire and transitional mire forest, group 6 swamp forest and group 7 is formed from drained peatland forest analyses. Group 1 is still in almost natural state but changes as conditions become drier. The trends occurring on the study site due to long-lasting but weak drainage are presentedon Figure 4.

PCA ordination biplot indicates about two general trends of succession: from sedge-dominated fen to Sphagnum-dominated transitional mire, and from open vegetation to closed (treed) vegetation. WL drop down can led to acidification (Van Heasebroek et al., 1997) and peat drying to nutrient release due to peat decomposition (Devitoand Dillon, 1997; Haraguchi et al., 2003). Changed pH promote growth of Sphagnum (Hájek et al., 2006). As strong dominants, Sphagnum species become shaping the environment and contribute to vegetation change.

In the vegetation of near-natural part of the calcareous fen (group 1 on Figure 3) the depth to water level and porewater pH are the main abiotic drives. In the parts of the site with dropped down of water level the species composition in the field layer responds to pore water pH and EC, topsoil ash content and the coverage of the tree layer.

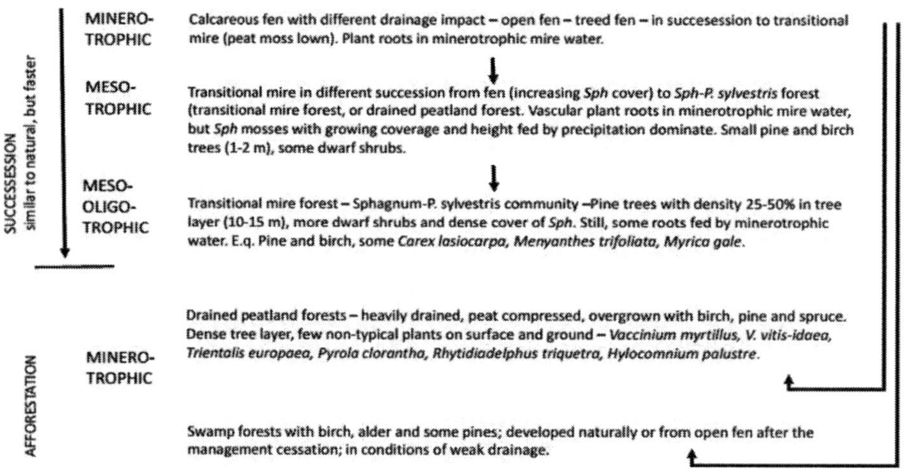


Figure 4. Pathways of drainage induced successions of the Suursoo-Leidissoo calcareous fen.

## CONCLUSION

The drainage systems ever built in fens operate even though the economic need has ceased and the role of groundwater in ecosystem succession is decreasing. The changes in plant communities often occur in the same direction as the natural peatland ecosystem transition from minerotrophic to ombrotrophic peatland, but the rate of this process is importantly accelerated.

## ACKNOWLEDGEMENTS

We thank Elve Lode for hydrology data modeling, Galina Kapanen for laboratory water and peat sampling and Matrin Küttim and Anna-Helena Purre for field assistance.

The study was funded by LIFE Climate Change project Life Peat Restore 2016-2021 (LIFE15 CCM/DE/000138).

## REFERENCES

- Devito K.J., Dillon P.J. (1997) The influence of hydrologic conditions and peat oxia on the phosphorusand nitrogen dynamics of a conifer swamp. Water Resources Research; 29: 2675–2685.
- Goud E.M., Watt C., Moore T.R. (2018) Plant community composition along a peatland margin followsalternate successional pathways after hydrologic disturbance. *Acta Oecologica*; 91: 65–72.
- Hájek M., Horsák M., Hájková P., Dite D. (2006) Habitat diversity of central European fens in relation environmental gradients and an effort to standardize fen terminology in ecological studies. *Perspectivesin Plant Ecology, Evolution and Systematics*; 8: 97–114.
- Haraguchi A., Hasegawa C., Hirayama A., Kojima H. (2003) Decomposition activity of peat soils ingeogenous mires in Sasakami, central Japan. *European Journal of Soil Biology*; 39: 191–196.
- Ilomets M. (2017) Estonia. In: *Mires and peatlands of Europe* (H. Joosten, F. Tanneberger and A.Moen, eds), Schweizerbart Science Publishers, Stuttgart, pp. 360–371.
- Johansen O.M., Petersen M.L., Jensen J.B. (2011) Effect of groundwater abstraction on fen ecosystems.Journal of Ecology; 402: 357–366.
- Lode, E. (2021). Groundwater dynamics in Life Peat Restore project area located on the Läänemaa–Suursoo Mire Complex. The Third Report for the EU Life+ project LIFE15 CCM/DE/000138.
- Van Haesebroek V., Boeye D., Verhagen B., Verheyen R.F. (1997) Experimental investigation ofdrought induced acification in a rich fen soil. *Biogeochemistry*; 37: 15–32.

ID 62729

# EFFECTS OF PERSISTENT WATER-TABLE LEVEL DRAWDOWN ON FINE ROOT BIOMASS AND PRODUCTION IN BOREAL FORESTED PEATLANDS

*Maija Lampela[1], Kari Minkkinen[1], Petra Straková[2], Wei He[2], Päivi Mäkiranta[2], Paavo Ojanen[1], Timo Penttilä[2], Raija Laiho[2]

[1]University of Helsinki, Finland
[2]Natural Resources Institute Finland

*maija.lampela@gmail.com*

Peat accumulation is one of the large-scale processes that sequester carbon from the atmosphere to stable deposits. Yet, the information on one of the main components that contribute to these deposits, roots of vascular plants, is very little studied. The aim of this study was to increase the knowledge on fine root biomass (FRB) and production (FRP) in different forested peatland site types and their drained counterparts. We studied the effect of environmental variables and species and species group contribution to FRB and FRP and their depth distribution.

The study was conducted in a partly drained Lakkasuo mire area (61°48' N, 24°19' E) in the southern Finland. We chose four pairs of forested undrained and drained sites with differing nutrient characteristics. FRB (root diameter < 0.5 mm) was studied with 50 cm deep peat cores divided into 10 cm compartments by depth. FRP was studied with ingrowth core method with 2 years incubation period. Environmental variables such as ground water table level, soil temperature, soil properties and above-ground vegetation were monitored in sites. Fine roots were identified to species or species group level with two methods: in FRB by visual identification and in FRP with infrared spectroscopy.

Overall variation in both FRB and FRP was great within and between sites. Drainage decreased FRB in the nutrient-poor pine-dominated sites whereas in the more nutrient-rich spruce dominant sites drainage increased FRB. Results in FRP were less clear with mostly non-significant differences between the drained and undrained sites. Depth distribution was generally shallower in FRB than in FRP, but differences between sites were great. FRB and FRP in species and species groups had clear differences between undrained and drained sites. Based on these results we can conclude that drainage has diverse effects on FRB and FRP depending on the mire site type.

ID 61963

# IMPACT OF DRAINAGE ON VEGETATION STRUCTURE IN ESTONIAN RAISED BOGS

Jaanus Paal, *Ain Kull

Institute of Ecology and Earth Sciences, University of Tartu, Estonia

*ain.kull@ut.ee*

We studied the extent of drainage impact on vegetation structure in 15 raised bogs along a hydrosequence. Sampling was performed along a straight line transects aligned perpendicular to the drainage ditch. The drawdown effect of the drainage ditches on the minimum water depends on drainage type but can extend more than 690 m. Correlation coefficients between the distance from the drainage ditch and sum of trees height (-0.71), sum of their girth (-0.70), canopy closure (-0.69), tree layer height by LIDAR (-0.71), canopy closure by LIDAR (-0.66) and trees annual increment (-0.67) are all highly significant. For vascular plant species the minimum water level of -50 cm appears to be critical: by that level even Scots pines almost disappear and the number of bog-specific species stabilizes. Sum of trees girth decreases with moving farther away from the cutoff ditch up to 190 m; the tree layer height and canopy closure are decreasing at least up to 690 m, but here it is not possible to separate the direct drainage impact from the natural state of bogs. The number of shrub stems and their height starts to increase at the distance of 16 m and continues to grow up to 400 m from the cutoff ditch. The percentage of bog-specific species begins to increase remarkably at a distance of about 200 m from the cutoff ditch. Total cover of Sphagnum mosses stabilizes at 90-440 m from the drainage diches depending on the drainage type.

ID 77540

# RESTORATION IN ACTION – HOW THE LIFE WELSH RAISED BOGS PROJECT IS RESTORING SEVEN OF THE MOST IMPORTANT RAISED PEAT BOGS IN WALES

Patrick Green

Natural Resources Wales, European Union LIFE+ Nature and Biodiversity Programme (LIFE16 NAT/UK/000646), Welsh Government, Snowdonia National Park Authority

*patrick.green@cyfoethnaturiolcymru.gov.uk*

The Natural Resources Wales (NRW) LIFE Welsh Raised Bogs project aims to restore seven of the most important raised peat bogs in Wales.
All seven of the bogs in the project are designated as Special Areas of Conservation (SAC).

**Why is this project important?**

All active (H7110*) and degraded (H7120) raised bog SAC features in Wales are in unfavourable condition. Active raised bog is a threatened element of the EU peatland resource. It has suffered more habitat loss than any other peatland type and remains under acute pressure.
The aim of this project is to improve the conservation status of 694 hectares of Active raised bogs, 275.6 hectares of Degraded raised bog, and associated H7150 and H7140, within the seven raised bog SACs wholly in Wales by implementing favourable management.

**What will restoration look like?**

To restore hydrological regimes the project will create 64km of low-level banks of peat (also known as bunds). These will improve natural water levels on the peatland.
Invasive vegetation such as molinia grass, scrub (small trees) and rhododendron have encroached and now dominate part of the bogs. Several innovative methods are being used by the project to remove this vegetation.
Monitoring is a key part of the project and it is working with UKCEH, UEL and BGS to monitor Greenhouse Gas Emissions, hydrology, and vegetation on all seven sites in the project with the aim of measuring the impact of the project's restoration work.

# ID 62565

# DEVELOPMENT HISTORY OF ORGANIC SOILS AND RECENT CHANGES IN CARBON ACCUMULATION IN SVALBARD, NORWAY

*Teemu Juselius[1], Sanna Piilo[1], Mitro Mûller[2], Minna Väliranta[1], Virve Ravolainen[3]

[1]Environmental Change Research Unit, University of Helsinki, Finland
[2]University of Helsinki, Finland
[3]Norwegian Polar Institute

*teemu.juselius@helsinki.fi*

The Arctic area has warmed more than twice as fast as the rest of the Northern hemisphere since 1970's. During 20th century, increasing trend in both temperature and precipitation has been recorded in Svalbard. These improved growth conditions increase vegetation productivity and carbon accumulation to organic soils, if sufficient moisture regime is maintained. In addition, other factors such as fertilization and grazing by reindeer and birds can affect both development and carbon accumulation of organic soils.

Aim of this research is to study the development history of organic soils in Svalbard and recent changes in carbon accumulation by palaeoecological and remote sensing methods.

14 organic soil cores were collected from 4 different sites, Alkehornet, Björndalen, Bolterdalen and Colesdalen, in Svalbard during 2018. Laboratory measurements (LOI%, BD, C/N) were conducted in 2019. Basal age of the cores were dated by radiocarbon ($^{14}C$) accelerator mass spectrometry analysis method. In addition, 8 of the cores were also dated using lead ($^{210}Pb$) dating method to acquire ages from more recent organic soil layers.

Changes in NDVI between 1970 and 2018 will be calculated from Landsat satellite imagery series.

The oldest study site (Alkehornet) was dated to be at least 5600 years old. The other sites were markedly younger with basal dates being 135, 59 and 55 years old. All sites had also younger basal dates varying from 1808 AD (Alkehornet) to 1989 AD (Bolterdalen). Mean carbon accumulation rates between 1970-2018 varied both within and between sites. Both highest (118 g C $m^2$ $a^{-1}$) and lowest (2 g C $m^2$ $a^{-1}$) accumulation rates were found in the oldest site. Younger sites had mean carbon accumulation rates of 72.5, 60.5 and 53 g C m2 a-1.

We expect to finalize our data analysis within next 2 months to be ready for manuscript and for IPC2020 long abstract.

ID 63352

# THE IMPORTANCE OF MONITORING RESEARCH IN ASSESSING IMPACTS OF ANTHROPOGENIC ACTIVITIES ON TROPICAL PEATLAND BIODIVERSITY: EXAMPLES FROM CENTRAL KALIMANTAN, INDONESIA

Mark E. Harrison[1,2], Darmae Nasir[3], William Healy[1], Ici P. Kulu[3], Simon J. Husson[4], Santiano[3,5], Ari Purwanto[3,5], Iwan[3,5], Susan E. Page[2], Frank van Veen[1], Muhammad Ali Imron[6]

[1]Centre for Ecology and Conservation, College of Life and Environmental Sciences, University of Exeter, Penryn, UK
[2]School of Geography, Geology and the Environment, University of Leicester, Leicester, UK
[3]Centre for the International Cooperation in Sustainable Management of Tropical Peatlands, University of Palangka Raya, Palangka Raya, Central Kalimantan, Indonesia
[4]Borneo Nature Foundation International, Penryn, Cornwall, UK
[5]Yayasan Borneo Nature Indonesia, Palangka Raya, Central Kalimantan, Indonesia
[6]Faculty of Forestry, University Gadjah Mada, Yogyakarta, Indonesia

*m.e.harrison@exeter.ac.uk*

## SUMMARY

Tropical peatlands worldwide are subject to a variety of anthropogenic disturbances, leading to a variety of documented climate, social-economic and ecological impacts. In response, various protection and restoration strategies are being implemented to reduce and ideally reverse the impacts of these disturbances. Understanding the nature of the ecosystem's responses to these anthropogenic activities is thus critical to informing effective adaptive management strategies, yet the impacts of anthropogenic activities on tropical peatland biodiversity remain poorly understood. Here, we illustrate how both temporal and spatial datasets can be used to assess the impacts of two anthropogenic threats on biodiversity (illegal logging and fire), and subsequent recovery following management interventions on three different taxa in Sebangau National Park, Central Kalimantan: trees, fruit-feeding butterflies and orangutans. These data demonstrate negative impacts of illegal logging and fire, as expected, but also show an ability for all three taxa to recover post-disturbance in the presence of active conservation interventions, though ~7 and 12 years, respectively, were needed for mean tree size and orangutan population density to recover to pre-logging disturbance levels in our dataset, and far longer will be needed to recover from fire. This illustrates both the harmful and beneficial impact that anthropogenic activities can have on tropical peatland biodiversity, but in particular highlights the critical need to protect relatively undisturbed ecosystems, to avoid the need for difficult, costly and lengthy biodiversity recovery efforts.

***Keywords***: *Borneo, conservation, fire, logging, peat-swamp forest*

## INTRODUCTION

The value of tropical peat-swamp forests for biodiversity and the threats these ecosystems face are becoming increasingly recognised (Yule 2010, Posa *et al.* 2011, Dargie *et al.* 2019, Harrison *et al.* 2020). This is particularly so in Kalimantan (Indonesian Borneo), with for example our teams' past studies in Sebangau National Park, Central Kalimantan revealing a high diversity of flora and fauna (Husson *et al.* 2018), which includes the world's largest population of the critically endangered Bornean orangutan (*Pongo pygmaeus*: Morrogh-Bernard *et al.* 2003), and important populations of the Bornean white-bearded gibbon (*Hylobates albinarbis*: Cheyne *et al.* 2008), plus threatened Borneo wild cats (Cheyne and MacDonald 2011) and birds, such as the Storm's stork (*Ciconia stormi*: Cheyne *et al.* 2014). Despite this, Kalimantan's peat-swamp forests have experienced extensive loss and degradation over the last several decades, resulting primarily from agricultural conversion, peat drainage and subsequent fire (Miettinen *et al.* 2016, Harrison *et al.* 2020).

Research to assess the impacts of this disturbance on peatland biodiversity in Kalimantan has, however, been relatively scant, though see for example Yeager *et al.* (2003), Thornton *et al.* (2018) and Harrison *et al.* (2016) for impacts of fire, and Husson *et al.* (2015) for impacts of logging. Here, we combine datasets collected in the Sebangau peat-swamp forest, with the aim to conduct a preliminary assessment of the impacts of both fire and logging disturbance on forest structure, an invertebrate ecological disturbance indicator species (fruit-feeding butterflies) and a flagship conservation species (orangutans). We do this through both spatial comparisons of data collected in burned, relatively heavily logged and relatively undisturbed forest areas; and through temporal comparisons of trends in long-term datasets spanning periods of past illegal logging and major fire events.

## MATERIALS AND METHODS

All data were collected in the 500 $km^2$ Natural Laboratory of Peat-swamp Forest (NLPSF; 2°19' S, 113°54' E), in Sebangau National Park (5,421 $km^2$), Central Kalimantan, Indonesia. This is an ombrogenous peat-swamp forest exhibiting a transition in main habitat sub-types, from tall-interior forest (TIF) in the centre, to low-pole forest (LPF) and finally mixed-swamp forest (MSF), with the riverine forest around the edge now almost completely deforested (see Page *et al.* 1999 for detailed description). The study area has experienced a number of disturbances over the last several decades, most notably including concession logging up to 1997, immediately followed by illegal logging until 2004. Logging is considered to have been most intense between the two old logging railways running south-east from the research camp, which thus represents the "logging" condition in this study. The adjacent forest to the west of these logging railways is considered to have been less intensively logged and is used as the relatively "undisturbed" condition in our study. The study area has also experienced several major fire events, including burning of a large area of mostly TIF in 1997-98 and a large area of MSF close to the research camp in 2015 (Husson *et al.* 2015, Harrison *et al.* 2016), the latter of which is used as the "new burn" site in this study. The former riverine forest areas are now deforested sedge swamp that experiences regular fires that often set back the natural regeneration that is slowly occurring, including an area burned close to the research camp in 2006, which we use as an "old burn" site in this study.

Spatial differences in trees ≥ 10 cm diameter at breast height (DBH) were assessed through 15 plots of 10 x 10 m in each of the four disturbance conditions described above (new burn, old burn, logged and undisturbed), in which the DBH of all trees was measured and used to calculate total cross-sectional area per plot, as a proxy of above-ground biomass. Within these tree plots, nested sub-plots were used to assess abundance of tree sapling (DBH < 10 cm and height ≥ 1 m; in 5 x 5 m sub-plot) and seedings (height < 1 m; in 2 x 2 m sub-plot). Temporal trends in total basal area of trees ≥ 7 cm DBH were monitored in separate MSF plots from 2003 to present, in addition to previous pre-illegal logging plot data from 1993 presented by Shepherd *et al.* (1997) and Page *et al.* (1999). Although in the same habitat sub-type and locale, our plots are not in the exact same locations as those established by Shepherd *et al.* (1997) and Page *et al.* (1999), and consequently our temporal comparisons may be confounded to some extent by potential spatial variations between these plot locations.

Fruit-feeding butterflies were sampled monthly from August 2018-July 2019, following methods in Marchant *et al.* (2015). Specifically, ten fruit-baited canopy traps (five each at 1-2 m and ~15 m height) along three transects in each of three disturbance conditions (burnt in 2015, relatively intensively logged up to 15 years previously and relatively undisturbed; termed "new burn", "logged" and "undisturbed" hereafter). Orangutan population density was assessed through counting of nests (sleeping platforms) along line transects using standardised methods (Husson *et al.* 2015). Surveys were conducted every 40 days along six transects totaling 11.5 km in length in the mixed-swamp forest, and at 1-2-year intervals in the low-pole (4 transects; 7.5 km) and tall-interior forest (4 transects; 4 km).

## RESULTS

Differences in tree abundance and cross-sectional area, plus total butterfly abundance and orangutan population density, between the different disturbance conditions are shown in Table 1. Significant differences were found for all forest structure variables among disturbance conditions, with post-hoc tests indicating lower seedling and sapling abundance in new burn plots, and lower tree and cross-sectional area in both new and unburned plots, compared to logged and undisturbed plots. Orangutan surveys indicate a density of 920 nests km$^{-2}$ in 2020. Formal surveys have not been conducted in the burned or logged areas, but while conducting other research our team has seen neither orangutans nor their nests in burned areas, indicating that they are most likely absent from these. Orangutans and their nests are commonly seen in the logged area, however, with these informal observations suggesting a similar population density to the undisturbed area.

**Table 1.** Tree and fruit-feeding butterfly indices in different disturbance conditions in Sebangau. Values are means ± SD. K-W = Kruskal-Wallis $X^2$ value; *** = $p < 0.001$. Different super-script letters indicate significant differences among each variable in post-hoc tests.

| Variable | Disturbance condition | | | | K-W |
|---|---|---|---|---|---|
| | New burn | Old burn | Logged | Undisturbed | |
| No. seedlings / plot | 4.1 ± 4.5 [a] | 12.1 ± 10.2 [a,b] | 20.3 ± 12.3 [b] | 20.2 ± 10.2 [b] | 25.1 *** |
| No. saplings / plot | 9.9 ± 3.4 [a] | 19.5 ± 14.8 [b] | 22.0 ± 15.7 [b] | 25.1 ± 9.0 [b] | 26.4 *** |
| No. trees ≥ 10 cm DBH / plot | 0.1 ± 0.3 [a] | 1.1 ± 1.4 [a] | 10.5 ± 2.8 [b] | 12.6 ± 4.8 [b] | 48.0 *** |
| Perc. plots with no trees ≥ 10 cm DBH | 93% | 47% | 0% | 0% | - |
| Total X-section area trees ≥ 10 cm DBH / plot ($cm^2$) | 6 ± 24 [a] | 115 ± 141 [a] | 3,201 ± 1,938 [b] | 4,240 ± 1,904 [b] | 48.3 *** |
| Total no. butterflies / transect / mo | 0.3 ± 0.6 [a] | N/A | 18.8 ± 15.0 [b] | 19.7 ± 11.6 [b] | 72.6*** |

Trends in tree basal area and orangutan nest density in the mixed-swamp forest are shown in Figure 1. These trends follow a similar pattern, with values for both decreasing during the concession and illegal logging periods, followed by an overall gradually increasing trend (which, for orangutans at least, started during the latter half of the illegal logging period). By 2011, tree basal area values had reached comparable levels to the pre-illegal logging 1993 baseline, after which this remains relatively constant. For orangutans, the lowest nest density occurred in 2001 and 1995 baseline levels were reached in 2016, after which nest density has continued to increase. The major 2015 fires are not associated with any marked change in tree basal area, but do coincide with a relatively large annual increase in orangutan nest density.

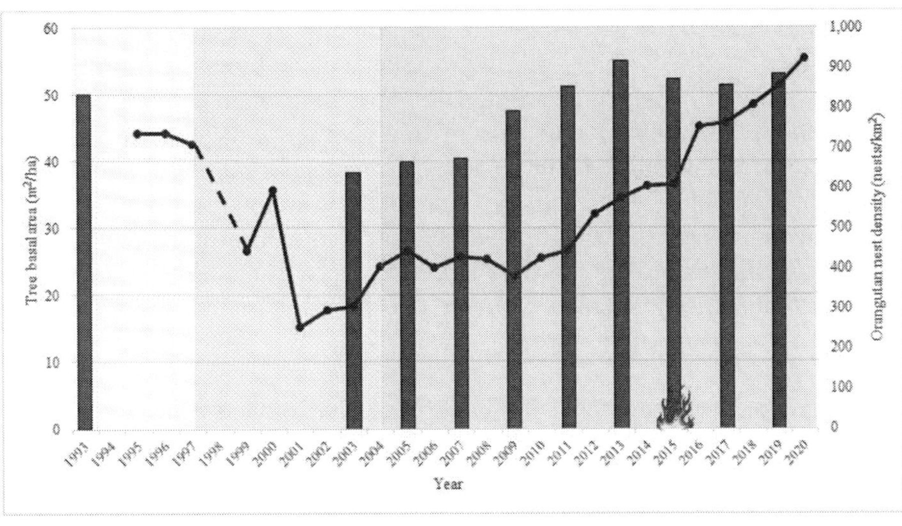


**Figure 1.** Long-term trends in total basal area of trees ≥ 7 cm DBH (bars) and orangutan nest density (line) in Sebangau mixed-swamp forest from 1993-2017. Values are means across all plots/transects. No bar and dashed line indicate no survey in that year. Shading indicates periods of concession logging (light orange), illegal logging disturbance (darker orange) and protection (green).

## DISCUSSION

Our data indicate that both logging and particularly fire disturbance have negative impacts on forest condition (structure) and fauna (fruit-feeding butterflies, orangutans), but also suggest that recovery from these disturbances appears possible under conditions of forest protection and the absence of fire. This is evidenced by the decrease in total tree basal area and orangutan population density following illegal logging disturbance, and their subsequent increases following protection in the absence of fire; together with dramatically lower tree abundance, cross-sectional area and fruit-feeding butterfly abundance in burned areas, and no significant differences in these variables between forest that was relatively heavily logged up to ~15 years previously vs. relatively lightly logged (undisturbed) forest. Although post-hoc tests in tree numbers and basal area were not significant between new and old burn, and logged and undisturbed areas, the observed trends are also in line with this. We also observed that seedling abundance was significantly lower in new burned compared to all other plots (with the exception of old burn), yet not significantly different between old burn, logged and undisturbed plots; whereas sapling abundance was significantly lower only in new burn plots. This also aligns with the above interpretation; i.e., that fire would have killed almost all original forest trees (Harrison *et al.* 2016), with early signs of recovery evidenced through the seedling, sapling and tree data, but with insufficient time having passed for recovery of larger trees (≥ 10 cm DBH) to the undisturbed forest baseline in even old burn plots (burnt 13 years previously). Given that trees larger than 10 cm and particularly 20 cm DBH produce more fruit, and that the mean DBH of trees fed on by orangutans in Sebangau has been reported as 27.7 cm (Morrogh-Bernard 2009), this suggests that it may be many more years before orangutans are able to habitually use these burned areas again.

Conversely, total tree basal area and orangutan nest density, respectively, returned to pre-illegal logging levels within 7 and 12 years, following the onset of effective forest protection (illegal logging and fire prevention). While again encouraging, this observation comes with at least two important caveats. Firstly, TPSF tree size is relatively stunted owing to low levels of nutrient availability in the flooded peat ecosystem (Page *et al.* 1999). The onset of illegal logging in the study area was associated with construction of canals for extracting timber (Morrogh-Bernard *et al.* 2003) which, despite extensive canal blocking efforts over the last decade, may have artificially helped encourage tree growth through creating drier conditions and thus increasing availability of nutrients to tree root systems via peat mineralisation. Second, the major 2015 fires burned a large area of forest adjacent to our study area and the sharp increase in orangutan nest density immediately following this likely therefore represents an influx of orangutans from this burned forest into our study area, which probably accounts for most of the immediate increase in density seen at this time and lower-yet-still-artificially-elevated densities thereafter, as some but not all orangutans disperse away from our study area into other parts of the forest.

These findings build on earlier evidence indicating negative impacts of fire on peatland trees, fish, orangutans and other species (Yeager *et al.* 2003, Page *et al.* 2009, Harrison *et al.* 2016, Thornton *et al.* 2018), and of logging on peatland orangutans (Husson *et al.* 2015). While this is concerning in light of the ongoing nature of fire and logging disturbance in Kalimantan and tropical peatlands more widely, the indications from our data that forest condition (as indicated through forest structure and an invertebrate ecological disturbance indicator group) and flagship species (orangutan) populations are likely able to recover from these disturbances over time also provides reason for optimism. Our observation that tree density and cross-sectional area did not differ significantly between new and old burned areas represents a potential caveat to this. Although the time period from the last fire event to our data collection was still relatively short (~12 years), the trend in these data is in the expected direction and previous research suggests that peatland tree flora can regenerate following fire, provided that repeat fires and a resultant switch to retrogressive succession do not occur (Page *et al.* 2009).

## CONCLUSION

1. Fire and logging disturbance in tropical peat-swamp forest have negative impacts on forest structure, fruit-feeding butterflies (ecological disturbance indicator) and orangutans (flagship species).
2. Evidence suggests that recovery of these is likely possible following forest protection and in the absence of future fires, though particularly in the case of fire, many years or even decades may be required until tree biomass and orangutan populations are able to recover to pre-disturbance levels.

## ACKNOWLEDGEMENTS

We thank RISTEK-BRIN and LIPI for research permissions; Sebangau National Park for support; all researchers and staff who contributed to data collection; and Suwido Limin, Yusurum Jagau, Susan Cheyne, Helen Morrogh-Bernard, Jack Rieley and Matthew Struebig for discussion and support. We are grateful all of our funders over the years, in particular the Arcus Foundation, US Fish and Wildlife Great Apes Conservation Fund, The Orangutan Project, Save the Orangutan, the Orangutan Land Trust, Ocean Parks Conservation Foundation Hong Kong, Orangutan Outreach and Darwin Initiative, plus NERC-GCRF (grant no.: NE/T010401/1) for analysis and writing.

## REFERENCES

Cheyne S. M., Husson S. J., Dragiewicz M. L., Thompson L. J., Adul, Jeffers K. A., Limin S. H., Ehlers Smith D. A. (2014). Kalimantan's tropical peat-swamp forests are important for Storm's stork (*Ciconia stormi*) conservation. *Journal of Indonesian Natural History* 2(1): 45-50.

Cheyne S. M., MacDonald D. W. (2011). Wild felid diversity and activity patterns in Sabangau peat-swamp forest, Indonesian Borneo. *Oryx* 45(1): 119-124.

Cheyne S. M., Thompson C. J. H., Phillips A. C., Hill R. M. C., Limin S. H. (2008). Density and population estimate of gibbons (*Hylobates albibarbis*) in the Sabangau catchment, Central Kalimantan, Indonesia. *Primates* 49: 50-56.

Dargie G. C., Lawson I. T., Rayden T. J., Miles L., Mitchard E. T. A., Page S. E., Bocko Y. E., Ifo S. A., Lewis S. L. (2019). Congo Basin peatlands: threats and conservation priorities. *Mitigation and Adaptation Strategies for Global Change* 24(4): 669-686.

Harrison M. E., Ottay J. B., D'Arcy L. J., Cheyne S. M., Anggodo, Belcher C., Cole L., Dohong A., Ermiasi Y., Feldpausch T., Gallego-Sala A., Gunawan A., Höing A., Husson S. J., Kulu I. P., Soebagio S. M., Mang S., Mercado L., Morrogh-Bernard H. C., Page S. E., Priyanto R., Ripoll Capilla B., Rowland L., Santos E., Schreer V., Sudyana I. N., Bin Bakeri Taman S., Thornton S. A., Upton C., Wich S. A., van Veen F. (2020). Tropical forest and peatland conservation in Indonesia: Challenges and directions. *People and Nature* 2: 4-28.

Harrison M. E., Ripoll Capilla B., Thornton S. A., Cattau M. E., Page S. E. (2016). Impacts of the 2015 fire season on peat-swamp forest biodiversity in Indonesian Borneo. In. *Peatlands in Harmony - Agriculture, Industry & Nature. Proceedings of the 15th International Peat Congress: Oral Presentations. 15-19 August 2016, Sarawak, Malaysia.* International Peat Society. pp: 713-717.

Husson S. J., Limin S. H., Adul, Boyd N. S., Brousseau J. J., Collier S., Cheyne S. M., D'Arcy L. J., Dow R. A., Dowds N. W., Dragiewicz M. L., Smith D. A. E., Iwan, Harsanto F. A., Hendri, Houlihan P. R., Jeffers K. A., Jarrett B. J. M., Kulu I. P., Morrogh-Bernard H. C., Page S. E., Perlett E. D., Purwanto A.,

Capilla B. R., Salahuddin, Santiano, Schreven S. J. J., Struebig M. J., Thornton S. A., Tremlett C., Yeen Z., Harrison M. E. (2018). Biodiversity of the Sabangau tropical peat-swamp forest, Indonesian Borneo. *Mires and Peat* 22(05): 1-50.

Husson S. J., Morrogh-Bernard H., Santiano, Purwanto A., Harsanto F. A., McLardy C., D'Arcy L. J. (2015). Bornean orangutans in the Sabangau peat-swamp forest. In: Lanjouw A., Rainer H., White A. (eds) *State of the Apes: Industrial Agriculture and Ape Conservation.* The Arcus Foundation, New York.pp: 200-207.

Marchant N. C., Purwanto A., Harsanto F. A., Boyd N. S., Harrison M. E., Houlihan P. R. (2015). 'Random-flight' dispersal in tropical fruit-feeding butterflies? High mobility, long lifespans and no home ranges. *Ecological Entomology* 40(6): 696-706.

Miettinen J., Shi C., Liew S. C. (2016). Land cover distribution in the peatlands of Peninsular Malaysia, Sumatra and Borneo in 2015 with changes since 1990. *Global Ecology and Conservation* 6: 67–78.

Morrogh-Bernard H. (2009). Orang-utan Behavioural Ecology in the Sabangau Peat-Swamp Forest, Borneo PhD thesis, University of Cambridge.

Morrogh-Bernard H., Husson S., Page S. E., Rieley J. O. (2003). Population status of the Bornean orang-utan (*Pongo pygmaeus*) in the Sebangau peat swamp forest, Central Kalimantan, Indonesia. *Biological Conservation* 110: 141-152.

Page S., Hoscilo A., Wösten H., Jauhiainen J., Silvius M., Rieley J., Ritzema H., Tansey K., Graham L., Vasander H., Limin S. (2009). Restoration ecology of lowland tropical peatlands in Southeast Asia: current knowledge and future research directions. *Ecosystems* 12(6): 888-905.

Page S. E., Rieley J. O., Shotyk W., Weiss D. (1999). Interdependence of peat and vegetation in a tropical peat swamp forest. *Philosophical Transactions of the Royal Society of London B* 354: 1885-1897.

Posa M. R. C., Wijedasa L. S., Corlett R. T. (2011). Biodiversity and conservation of tropical peat swamp forests. *BioScience* 61(1): 49-57.

Shepherd P. A., Rieley J. O., Page S. E. (1997). The relationship between forest structure and peat characteristics in the upper catchment of the Sungai Sebangau, Central Kalimantan. In: Rieley J. O., Page S. E (eds). *Biodiversity and Sustainability of Tropical Peatlands.* Samara Publishing, Cardigan, UK.pp: 191-210.

Thornton S. A., Dudin, Page S. E., Upton C., Harrison M. E. (2018). Peatland fish of Sebangau, Borneo: Diversity, monitoring and conservation. *Mires and Peat* 22(04): 1-25.

Yeager C. P., Marshall A. J., Stickler C. M., Chapman C. A. (2003). Effects of fires on peat swamp and lowland dipterocarp forests in Kalimantan, Indonesia. *Tropical Biodiversity* 8(1): 121-138.

Yule C. M. (2010). Loss of biodiversity and ecosystem functioning in Indo-Malayan peat swamp forests. *Biodiversity and Conservation* 19: 393-409.

ID 62957

# CARBON STORAGE IN AMAZONIAN PEATLANDS: DISTRIBUTION AND DYNAMICS

*Adam Hastie[1], Ed Mitchard[1], Charlotte Wheeler[1], José Reyna[2], Julio Irarica[2], Julio Sanchez[2], Jhon del Aguila Pasque[1,2], Euridice Honorio Coronado[2], Greta Dargie[3], Stephen Frolking[4], Claire Treat[4], Christine Åkesson[5], Lydia Cole[5], Katy Roucoux[5], Ian Lawson[5]

[1] University of Edinburgh, United Kingdom
[2] Instituto de Investigaciones de la Amazonía Peruana, Peru
[3] University of Leeds, United Kingdom
[4] University of New Hampshire, USA
[5] University of St Andrews, United Kingdom

*adam.hastie@ed.ac.uk*

The Pastaza-Marañon foreland basin (PMFB) in Peru is among the largest area of intact peatlands in the tropics. However, the uncertainties on current estimates of carbon storage in the basin, particularly the below ground component, remain unacceptably large. This is due to a limited understanding of the spatial distribution of peatland ecosystems and peat depth across the basin, and of what drives their variation. Moreover, we are only just beginning to understand the drivers of temporal variation in peat accumulation in the PMFB and, in turn, the vulnerability of these ecosystems to climate change.

Here we present data from new field sites in the PMFB and beyond, and explain how these data are being used to improve our understanding of the spatial and temporal variation of peat-forming ecosystems in the Amazon. Water table, litter fall and decomposition data from monitoring sites are being used to parametrise the HPMTrop model to assess the hydrological and productivity limits to peat accumulation. In addition, peat depth and vegetation survey data are being used in combination with remote sensing data to narrow the uncertainty on current carbon storage estimates.

ID 72717

# CARBON FOOTPRINT OF BLACK PEAT FROM DEGRADED PEATLAND PREVIOUSLY USED FOR AGRICULTURE IN GERMANY

Heinz Stichnothe[1]

[1]Thünen Institute of Agricultural Technology, Braunschweig, Germany

*heinz.stichnothe@thuenen.de*

## SUMMARY

On a worldwide scale, drained peatlands contribute substantially to anthropogenic greenhouse gas (GHG) emissions. Reducing GHG from drained peatland is the most space- and cost-effective climate change mitigation option within the land use and agricultural sectors. Peat, particularly black peat, is currently a major compound in substrates for horticulture, where it cannot be immediately replaced. One option is to extract black peat from degraded peatland, which cannot be rewetted.
In order to calculate the carbon footprint (CF) a life cycle approach is applied and three scenarios are defined. The carbon footprint varies widely for nutrient-rich peat in the best-case 70, default 107 and worst-case 161 kg $CO_{2eq}$ per $m^3$ stored black peat. For nutrient-poor peat the carbon footprint is significantly lower best case 49, default 64 and worst case 70 kg $CO_{2eq}$ per $m^3$ stored black peat. If German national EFs are used, the CF values are even lower, 28, 45 and 70 kg $CO_{2eq}$ per $m^3$ stored black peat. The difference between nutrient-rich and nutrient-poor peat is caused by the respective carbon density provided in the IPCC guidelines.

Despite substantial differences in diesel consumption and extraction rate, the carbon footprint of black peat extracted from degraded peatlands is dominated by two factors, the GHG emissions during black peat storage and the period assumed for land restoration. Surprisingly little is known or reported in the literature concerning these factors. In order to get more precise results, the existing knowledge gaps, particularly methane emissions during black peat storage, have to be examined.
In order to calculate the carbon footprint of black peat from degraded peatland in a transparent and reproducible manner, a conceptional model and a decision tree for selecting area-based EFs is presented.

***Keywords**: LCA approach, emission factor, rewetting, climate impact, conceptual model*

## INTRODUCTION

Land provides the principal basis for human livelihoods and well-being including the supply of food, freshwater and multiple other ecosystem services (Shukla 2019). Peatland ecosystems contain disproportionally more organic carbon than other terrestrial ecosystems. Peatlands cover only 3% of the world's land area and contain 550 Gigatons (Gt) of carbon. This is equivalent to 30% of all soil carbon and twice the carbon stock of all forest biomass of the world. This makes peatlands one of the most important long-term carbon storage options in the terrestrial biosphere (Parish 2008). Sustainable (peat)land management can

contribute to reducing GHG-emissions. Carbon sequestration in soil or vegetation, such as afforestation, reforestation, or carbon storage in harvested wood products, do not continue to sequester carbon indefinitely. Peatlands, however, can continue to sequester carbon for centuries (Shukla 2019).
Carbon sequestration in peatland depends on the delicate balance between production and decay of organic material. On seasonal and inter-annual time scales natural peatlands shift between being carbon sinks and sources. The carbon accumulation rate varied substantially during the Holocene. However, the long-term natural balance is positive (Parish 2008). On a worldwide scale, drained peatlands contribute substantially to anthropogenic greenhouse gas (GHG) emissions (Barthelmes 2018). Long-term GHG monitoring in boreal sites has demonstrated that rewetting and restoration noticeably reduce emissions compared to degraded drained sites and can restore the carbon sink function when vegetation is re-established although, restored ecosystems may not yet be as resilient as their undisturbed counterparts (Wilson 2016). Several studies have demonstrated the co-benefits of rewetting specific degraded peatlands for biodiversity, carbon sequestration (Renou-Wilson, Moser et al. 2019). Reducing GHG-emissions from drained peatland is the most space- and cost effective climate change mitigation option within the land use and agricultural sectors (Barthelmes 2018).

Peat has excellent properties for use in the horticultural sector, but is also used for energy generation. While it is easier to substitute peat as fuel, it is much harder to replace peat, particularly (frozen) black peat, in substrates for horticulture. Frozen black peat is mainly used for potting soil for raising vegetable plants and bedding plants (Bos 2011). There is no single material that is able to replace peat, Thus, various materials have to be mixed in order to replace peat in substrates, which increases complexity and requires various management adaptations for plant growers. Therefore, the horticultural sector is reluctant to replace peat. Simultaneously reducing GHG-emissions is a requirement and several nations, including Germany, have signed the Paris agreement and defined GHG reduction targets for all economy sectors, including agriculture. That includes the reduction of peat. However, it is important to understand to consequences of peat reduction with respect to GHG-emissions. While for national GHG reporting a harmonised approach exist, various approached are used to calculate GHG-emissions from peat extraction (Peano 2012, Höglund 2013, Eymann 2015, Murphy, Devlin et al. 2015).

In this paper, a conceptual model is presented for calculating the carbon footprint of black peat, which is on one hand in line with the internationally agreed GHG-reporting guidelines and on the other land uses a transparent and reproducible life cycle approach that can be extended for business-to-business and business-to-consumer communication.

Black peat from degraded peatland is used as examples, because frozen black peat is the component most difficult to be replaced in substrates in horticulture. Moreover, critical values and knowledge/data gaps are identified for calculating the carbon footprint of black peat.

## MATERIALS AND METHODS

In order to calculate the greenhouse gas (GHG) intensity of black peat and its carbon footprint respectively, a life cycle approach is used. For this model a cut-off approach is used, i.e. emissions from dewatering peatland are allocated to the former economic activity, agricultural use in this case. The system boundary included land use from land transformation to land rehabilitation, black peat extraction by milling and the peat storage. One ha is used as functional unit but results are expressed for nutrient rich and nutrient poor peat per m³ black peat stockpiled.

All activities from preparing the area for peat extraction and the restoration of the area are included. GHG-emissions from area preparation are calculated using area-based emissions from peat extraction multiplied by the ratio of transformation_period/extraction_period and for restoration the emission factor for rewetting multiplied by the ratio of restoration_period/ extraction_period, respectively. Area-based GHG emission factors (EF) are taken from the latest IPCC Guidelines for National GHG Inventories from Wetlands (Hiraishi 2014). Fuel consumption data are collected from peat producers in Germany. The conceptual model is displayed in Fig.1. Peat processing and transport after stockpiling are not included in this analysis but can easily be added when the required data becomes available.

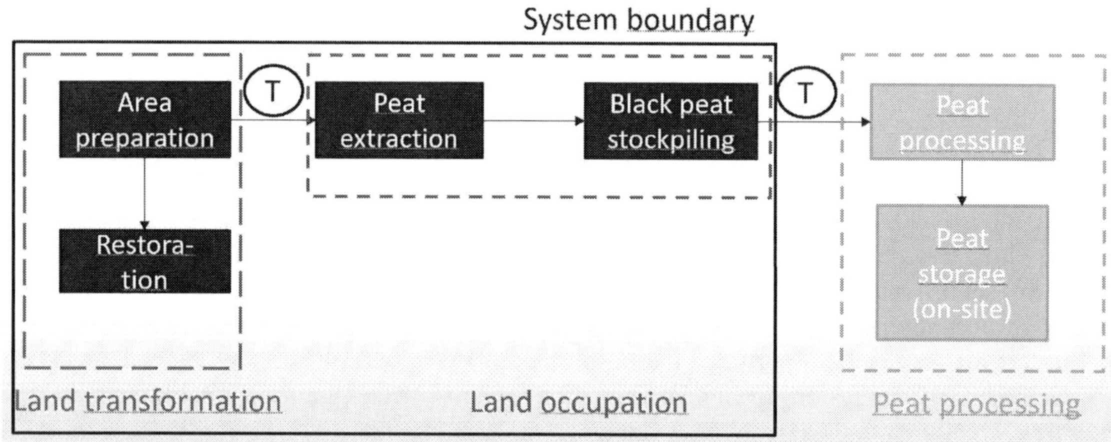


Fig. 1: Conceptual model for calculating the Carbon Footprint of black peat extraction

According to IPCC "Boreal countries that do not have information on areas of nutrient-rich and nutrient-poor peatlands should use the emission factor for nutrient-poor peatlands. Temperate countries that do not have such data should use the emission factor for nutrient-rich peatlands" (Blain 2006). Although just nutrient-poor peat is usually used for horticulture for sake of consistency the carbon footprint for both is calculated.

An important question is, which area-based EFs should be used for peat extraction and rewetting? Fig. 2 shows a decision tree for selecting appropriate emission factors; this approach is in agreement with IPCC guidelines for national GHG emission reporting.

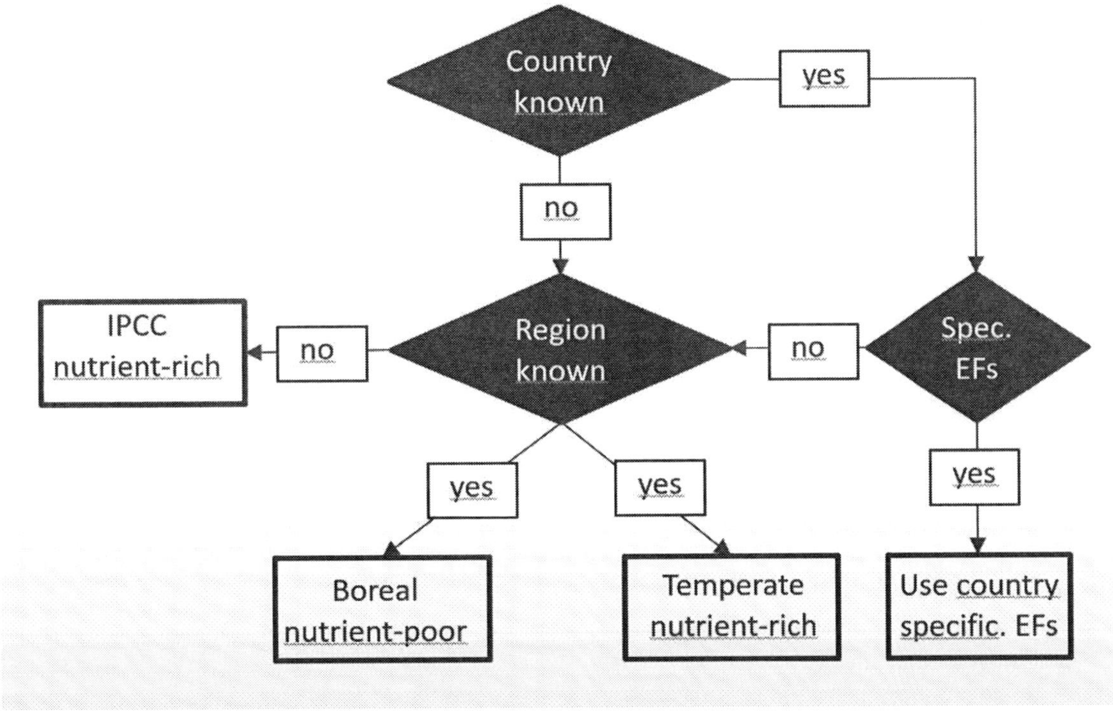


Fig. 2: Decision tree for selecting area-based EFs for peat extraction and land restoration

## RESULTS

There is an inherent variability of GHG-emissions due to local and seasonal variations, that is also accompanied with a variability of emission factors for peat extraction and rewetting (Alm 2007, Wilson 2016, Tiemeyer, Freibauer et al. 2020). The diesel consumption ranges from approximately 300 to 800 l per ha and the peat extraction rate from 750 to more than 1.000 $m^3$ per ha. Therefore, a scenario analysis is conducted by defining best case, default and worst case changing the most important parameters governing the carbon footprint. The restoration period is assumed to be between 10 to 45 years, the peat, respectively carbon, degradation rate during storage between 4 to 6% per year and methane emissions between 1 to 10% of the degraded carbon. All modelling parameters for each scenario are shown in Table 1. The only difference between nutrient-poor and nutrient-rich peat, considered here, is the carbon content per $m^3$ air-dried peat.

Table 1: Modelling parameters for the defined scenario

| Modelling parameter | Best case | Default | Worst case | Reference |
|---|---|---|---|---|
| Transformation period [yr] | 1 | 1 | 1 | assumed |
| EF peat extraction | | | | (Hiraishi 2014) or (Tiemeyer, Freibauer et al. 2020) |
| Extraction period [yr] | 20 | 20 | 20 | (Byrne 2004) |
| EF rewetting | | | | (Hiraishi 2014) or (Tiemeyer, Freibauer et al. 2020) |
| Restoration period [yr] | 10 | 20 | 45 | (Alm 2007) |
| Diesel for land preparation [$l*ha^{-1}$] | 10 | 20 | 20 | KTBL[1] |
| Diesel for peat extraction [$l*ha^{-1}$] | 600 | 600 | 600 | Anonymous |
| Carbon content of peat [kg C *$m^3$ air dried] | 70 (nutrient poor) - 240 (nutrient rich) | | | (Blain 2006) |
| Yield [$m^3*ha^{-1}$] | 890 | 890 | 890 | anonymous |
| C-degradation during stockpiling [%-C*$yr^{-1}$] | 4 | 5 | 6 | (Peano 2012) |
| $CH_4$ from stockpiling [% of degraded C] | 1 | 5 | 10 | Estimate from green-waste composting |
| Stockpiling period [yr] | 1.1 | 1.1 | 1.1 | Assumed |

Calculation results for each scenario are shown in Tab. 2.

Table 2: Carbon footprint of stockpiled black peat

| | **Nutrient-rich peat** | | | **Nutrient-poor peat** | | | **Germany** | | |
|---|---|---|---|---|---|---|---|---|---|
| | Best case | Default | Worst case | Best case | Default | Worst case | Best case | Default | Worst case |
| | kg $CO_{2eq}$ *$m^{-3}$ | | | | | | | | |
| CF | 70 | 107 | 161 | 49 | 64 | 70 | 28 | 45 | 77 |

## DISCUSSION

The carbon footprint varies widely for nutrient-rich peat in the best-case 70, default 107 and worst-case 161 kg $CO_{2eq}$ per $m^3$ stored black peat. For nutrient-poor peat the carbon footprint is significantly lower best case 49, default 64 and worst case 70 kg $CO_{2eq}$ per $m^3$ stored black peat. The CF values are lower, 28, 45 and 70 kg $CO_{2eq}$ per $m^3$ stored black peat, if German national EFs are used. The difference between nutrient-rich and nutrient-poor peat is caused by the carbon density provided in the IPCC guidelines. The contribution of $CO_2$ and $CH_4$ changes within each scenario group, while in the best-case scenario $CO_2$ contributes the most, in the worst case scenario $CH_4$ is the dominant contributor. In the default scenario both gases contribute almost equally to the carbon footprint. The trend is the same for nutrient-rich and nutrient-poor black peat, although the overall figure differs. The EFs for peat extraction in

[1] https://daten.ktbl.de/feldarbeit/entry.html

Germany are lower than IPCC Tier1 EF, e.g. $EF_{CH4}$ 4.2 compared to 6.1 kg $*ha^{-1}$ and $EF_{CO2}$ 1300 compared to 2800 kg $*ha^{-1}$ (Tiemeyer, Freibauer et al. 2020). Despite substantial differences in diesel consumption and extraction rate, the carbon footprint of black peat extracted from degraded peatlands is dominated by two factors, the GHG emissions during black peat storage and the period assumed for land restoration. Surprisingly little is known or reported in the literature concerning these factors. In order to get more precise results, the existing knowledge gaps, particularly methane emissions during black peat storage, have to be examined.

## CONCLUSION

In order to calculate the carbon footprint of black peat from degraded peatland in a transparent and reproducible manner, a conceptional model and a decision tree for selecting area-based EFs is presented. The conceptional model is built in a modular way and it is in line with IPCC GHG reporting guidelines. Moreover, the model can be easily modified to calculate the CF of white peat; because the land-based emissions and per ha diesel consumption is basically the same as for black peat and stockpiling is not required for white peat. The model can be extended by a peat processing module as shown in Fig.1. Transparency is key for a credible method that can be used for policy makers but also for informing consumers.

## ACKNOWLEDGEMENTS

We are thankful to several peat producers in Germany that provided crucial data and valuable input to this paper.

## REFERENCES

Alm, J., Shurpali, N. J., Minkkinen, K., Aro, L., Hytönen, J., Laurila, T., Lohila, A., Maljanen, M., Martikainen, P. J., Mäkiranta, P., Penttilä, T., Saarnio, S., Silvan, N., Tuittila, E.-S. & Laine, J. (2007). "Emission factors and their uncertainty for the exchange of CO2, CH4 and N2O in Finnish managed peatlands." BOREAL ENVIRONMENT RESEARCH **12**: 191-209.

Barthelmes, A. (eds). (2018). Reporting greenhouse gas emissions from organic soils in the European Union: challenges and opportunities. Greifswald, Greifswald Mire Centre**:** 17.

Blain, D. C. R., C; Alm, J; Byrne, K; and Parish, F (2006). IPCC Guidelines for National Greenhouse Gas Inventories (Chapter 7: Wetlands). IPCC. Geneva, IPCC. **Volume 4: Agriculture, Forestry and Other Land Use:** 24.

Bos, M. G. D., W.H. and Verhagen, A. (eds.) (2011). Sustainable Peat Supply Chain. Alterra report 2167. Alterra. Wageningen, Alterra**:** 134.

Byrne, K. A. C., B.; Christensen, T.R.; Drösler, M.; Friborg, T.; Frolking, S.; Lindroth, A. Mailhammer, J.; Malmer, N.; Selin, P.; Turunen, J. Valentini, R. Zetterberg, L. (2004). EU Peatlands: Current Carbon Stocks and Trace Gas Fluxes. Brussels**:** 58.

Eymann, L. M., A.; Stucki, M.; Amrein, S. (2015). Torf und Torfersatzprodukte im Vergleich; Eigenschaften, Verfügbarkeit, ökologische Nachhaltigkeit und soziale Auswirkungen. Wädenwill, Zürcher Hochschule für Angewandte Wissenschaften ZHAW**:** 130.

Hiraishi, T. K., T; Tanabe, K; Srivastava, N; Jamsranjav, B; Fukuda, M and Tiffany Troxler, T (eds) (2014). 2013 Supplement to the 2006 IPCC Guidelines for National Greenhouse Gas Inventories: Wetlands. Switzerland, IPCC**:** 354.

Höglund, J. a. M., F. (2013). Comparative review of variations in LCA results and peatland emissions from energy peat utilisation. Stockholm, Swedish Environmental Reserach Instittue.

Murphy, F., G. Devlin and K. McDonnell (2015). "Benchmarking Environmental Impacts of Peat Use for Electricity Generation in Ireland—A Life Cycle Assessment." Sustainability **2015**: 6376-6393.

Parish, F., Sirin, A., Charman, D., Joosten, H., Minayeva, T., Silvius, M. and Stringer, L. (Eds.) (2008). Assessment on Peatlands, Biodiversity and Climate Change: Main Report. Malaysia, Global Environment Centre, Kuala Lumpur and Wetlands International, Wageningen.**:** 206.

Peano, L. a. L., Y. (2012). Comparative life cycle assessment of horticultural growing media based on peat and other prowing media constituents. Bruessels, QUANTIS**:** 156.

Renou-Wilson, F., G. Moser, D. Fallon, C. A. Farrell, C. Müller and D. Wilson (2019). "Rewetting degraded peatlands for climate and biodiversity benefits: Results from two raised bogs." Ecological Engineering **127**: 547-560.

Shukla, P. R. S., J.; Calvo Buendia, E.; Masson-Delmotte, V.; Pörtner, H.-O.; Roberts, D.C.; Zhai, P.; Slade, R.; Connors, S.; van Diemen, R.; Ferrat, M.; Haughey, E.; Luz, S.; Neogi, S.; Pathak, M.; Petzold, J.; Portugal Pereira, J.; Vyas, P.; Huntley, P.; Kissick, K.; Belkacemi, M.; Malley, J. (eds.) (2019). Climate Change and Land: An IPCC special report on climate change, desertification, land degradation, sustainable land management, food security, and greenhouse gas fluxes in terrestrial ecosystems. Switzerland, IPCC**:** 906.

Tiemeyer, B., A. Freibauer, E. A. Borraz, J. Augustin, M. Bechtold, S. Beetz, C. Beyer, M. Ebli, T. Eickenscheidt, S. Fiedler, C. Förster, A. Gensior, M. Giebels, S. Glatzel, J. Heinichen, M. Hoffmann, H. Höper, G. Jurasinski, A. Laggner, K. Leiber-Sauheitl, M. Peichl-Brak and M. Drösler (2020). "A new methodology for organic soils in national greenhouse gas inventories: Data synthesis, derivation and application." Ecological Indicators **109**: 105838.

Wilson, D. B., D.; Couwenberg, C.; Evans, C.D.; Murdiyarso, D.; Page, S.E.; Renou-Wilson, F.; Rieley, J.O.; Sirin, A.; Strack, M. and TuittilaE.-S. (2016). "Greenhouse gas emission factors associated with rewetting of organic soils." Mires and Peat **17**(Article 4): 1-28.

ID 62440

# EFFECTS OF PEAT FIRES ON SOIL CHEMICAL AND PHYSICAL PROPERTIES: A CASE STUDY IN SOUTH SUMATRA

*Dede Sulaeman[1], Eli Nur Nirmala Sari[1], Thomas Westhoff[2]

[1]World Resources Institute, Indonesia
[2]Wageningen University, The Netherlands

*dede.sulaeman@wri.org*

Peat fires have been an annual environmental crisis in Indonesia. In 2015, the country suffered one of its worst burning seasons in years, impacting the health, education, and livelihoods of millions of Indonesians living in the affected areas. Peat fires still occur in Indonesia from 2016 to 2019, and the fires of 2019 are the worst since 2015. These fires are a significant cause of land surface changes with impacts on the climate system, vegetation composition, and the chemical composition of the atmosphere. Communities, who are living on peat, have practiced the burning of peatland for a long time because they are convinced that this process will improve the peat soil fertility. However, this assumption is not entirely justified. This research expects to determine the impact of fires on soil chemical and physical properties of tropical peat. This study examined the effect of a peat fire in 2019 in South Sumatra by comparing samples taken on an affected and unaffected smallholder palm oil plantation. These samples are analyzed for a broad set of properties. Results show that peat fires produce ashes which increased drastically by 57%. The fires improved the soil pH, which was 6% higher than in the unburned area. However, the severe peat fires also caused negative impacts on soil fertility by reducing the amount of potassium (18%), nitrogen (6%), and cation exchange capacity (8%). Besides, this study also shows that peat fires decreased water retention capacity by 1 and 12 % for pF 2.54 and pF 4.2, respectively. Contrary to popular belief among local farmers, this study shows the negative consequences of slash and burn activities on the fertility of peat and hopes to contribute to a change in the use of this land clearing method.

# III REGULATING SERVICES

IPC2021

ID 61434

# EXPERIMENTAL EVIDENCE FOR RETENTION OF SULPHUR AND IRON IN REWETTED FEN PEAT

Lydia Roesel

Humboldt-Universität zu Berlin, Berlin, Germany
Research Institute of Post-Mining Landscapes (FIB), Finsterwalde, Germany

*lydia.k.roesel@googlemail.com*

**SUMMARY**

Long-time lignite mining activities and agriculture in East Germany went along with large-scale drawdown of the water table which also destroyed peatlands. Both the mine dumps and peatlands contain pyrite, an iron disulphide. When the mineral encounters with oxygen and water, it wears and release sulphuric acid and iron. The groundwater and the surface water are already acidic and polluted with sulphate and iron. Many measures went in for clean up the water. While iron in the form of iron-hydroxide can be removed very easy, sulphate remains in the water. Sulphate in the water makes concrete porous and removing in the water treatment plant is very expensive. So, there is a need for action. It is necessary to bring both components of the mineral, iron and sulphur, together again, so sulphate can also be eliminated from the water. The mineral forming process needs anaerobic conditions, organic matter and sufficient amounts of iron and sulphate. I conduct an experiment and use rewetted peat as a filter to rebuild pyrite, and thus reduce iron and sulphate in the water. For this purpose, I filled columns with peat and flooded them with groundwater rich in iron and sulphate. I use different timesteps between 3 and 7 months, controlling for percolation speed. Preliminary results show a significant increase of pH values from 4.5 to 6.4 and a decrease in electrical conductivity of 58.5 %. The ferrous iron concentration decreases by 87.1 % and sulphate concentration decreases by 87.4 %. The results indicate a significant reduction of iron and sulphate in the water while percolating through a peat column implication that pyrite was formed in peat.

***Keywords**: iron, sulphate, peat, rewetting, post-mining, pyrite*

## INTRODUCTION

Mining is responsible for acidification and salinisation of the environment all over the world (Kefeni et al. 2017). This causes server problems for groundwater and surface water ecosystems (Luís et al. 2009). Released soluble iron and sulphate in very high concentrations as acid mine drainage (AMD) is a result of pyrite weathering. Pyrite bearing material is relocated to mine dumps where the mineral encounters oxygen and precipitation. Seepage water carry the dissolved ions into the groundwater (Blodau 2006; Graupner et al. 2012). Polluted groundwater and surface water transport and distribute iron and sulphate in the landscape. While iron oxidises in the surface water and precipitates as an ochre-colored sediment (RoyChowdhury et al. 2015), sulphate remains in the water, aggravate drinking water conditioning (Fernando et al. 2018) and attacking concrete buildings such as bridges and weirs (Ekolu et al. 2016; Wisotzky 2015). Re-joining iron and sulphur may solve both problems simultaneously. However, specific conditions are required for this process. Where point treatment of acid mine drainage is feasible, artificial wetlands, modeled as a kind of peatland, are the chosen measure for water (Parviainen et al. 2014). The aim here is to initiate anaerobic conditions in an environment with high content of organic matter and suitable plants. Under such conditions, microorganism reduce iron and sulphate, form insoluble sulphides like pyrite (Sobolewski 1999) and produce alkalinity (McCullough and Lund 2011). However, in case of a diffuse distribution of iron and sulphate, constructed wetlands are not capable of counteracting groundwater pollution. Therefore, alternative ways of groundwater remediation have to be investigated.

The Lusatia region in East Germany is an ideal natural laboratory to study pyrite formation in peat because numerous peatland relicts exists in the landscape. Peatlands were drained because of long time mining (Leclair et al. 2015) and agricultural activities (Gosling and Baker 1980). These human interventions caused also pyrite weathering in the peat. Nowadays, after mine closure, the groundwater table rises again. Thus, and sulphate-laden water may infiltrate these peatland relicts.

Little is known about reductive processes of iron and sulphate distributed in a post-mining landscape (Blodau 2006), which include degraded peatlands as well. In case of rising groundwater table, it is not clear how degraded peat saturated with groundwater rich in iron and sulphate can provide conditions to form pyrite and thus alter groundwater chemistry to a significant degree. Examinations with different organic matter (wood-dust, litter, compost, detritus) as well as peat in constructed wetlands and sediments receiving AMD were done. All the studies show strong evidence between organic matter and a high activity of sulphate reducing bacteria. These microbes use organic matter as a carbon and energy source for sulphate reduction. (Tuttle et al. 1969; Vile and Wieder 1993; Gazea et al. 1996; Batty and Younger 2007; Peiffer 2016; Pat-Espadas et al. 2018). As an interstage product of pyrite formation, hydrogen sulphate forms from sulphate reduction. However, comparable research on degraded peatlands is still scarce. Here I present first results of an experiment with degraded peat and mining affected groundwater. I investigate the quantitative reduction of ferrous iron and sulphate across different time periods and setups, the latter focusing on the importance of water percolation rate through the peat core.

## MATERIALS AND METHODS

My experiment comprises three variants with five columns each. The columns contain degraded peat and mining affected groundwater. The columns have a height of 50 cm and a diameter of 10 cm. A tool on the bottom with a fleece inside the columns holds a tap. On the top of the column there is a short tube and a cap. Every column is fixed on a wooden rack. Peat samples were taken from a degraded fen which is extensively used as a grassland and for cattle grazing. The sedge peat is middle to strongly degraded. For every column, I took five peat cores next to each other with a metallic cylinder in the depth of 30 cm, i.e. the depth of the groundwater table during sampling time. I stacked the peat cores in the columns and saturated them with groundwater, rich in iron and sulphate. The groundwater originates from a mining affected aquifer in Lusatia, Germany. I took the peat cores in June 2019 (V3 and V7) and October 2019 (variant V5). For the time of the experiment, all columns sat in a climate chamber at 24°C (Figure 1).

Figure 1: Peat columns in the climate chamber

Table 1 shows the operation time, the number of samples and the exchanged water volume of every sampling of the three variants. Every second week, a specific water volume was taken for water analysis and the same water volume of fresh stored groundwater was added on the top of the column. To avoid too much gas exchange, I piled up water to 7 cm above the peat core top. Finally, circa 3800 ml groundwater in total percolated through every column during the whole specific operation time. Therefore, longer operation time comes with smaller quantities of exchanged water volume. My routine of the water monitoring and analysis comprised concentration measurement of dissolved ferrous iron, sulphate, sulphur and total iron as well as pH value and electrical conductivity.

Table 1: Scheme of the experimental variants

| Variant label | V3 | V5 | V7 |
|---|---|---|---|
| Operation time [weeks] | 12 | 20 | 28 |
| Percolation speed [ml/d] | 42.2 | 25.3 | 18.1 |
| Number of samples | 6 | 10 | 14 |
| Exchanged water volume [ml] | 620 | 380 | 270 |
| Number of columns | 5 | 5 | 5* |

* One of the five columns have to be excluded from the data evaluation

## RESULTS

Figure 2 shows the trends of ferrous iron and sulphate concentration. For every variant, ferrous iron and sulphate concentration decrease over the operation time. For V3 and V5 the presented data are the average over five data series, for V7 is the average over four data series. Based on the input water conditions, ferrous iron concentrations decreased from 251 mg/l to 56.1 mg/l, from 275 mg/l to 54.4 mg/l and from 251 mg/l to 32.4 mg/l during 3, 5 and 7 months equalling a reduction of 77.7 % (V3), 80.2 % (V5) and 87.1 % (V7), respectively. The ferrous iron concentration of V3 and V7 pronouncedly decreased at the beginning and flatted after circa 6 weeks. During the same time, the ferrous iron concentration of V5 increase and also starts from a different level compared to the other variants. Sulphate concentrations decrease from 773 mg/l to 393.9 mg/l, from 766 mg/l to 136.1 mg/l and from 773 mg/l to 97.2 mg/l during 3, 5 and 7 months, which equals a reduction of 49 % (V3), 82.2 % (V5) and 87.4 % (V7), respectively. At the beginning of variant V3, the concentration decreases more intensive then V5 and V7. In contrast to V3, V5 and V7 may still not have converge to the final level of sulphate concentration.

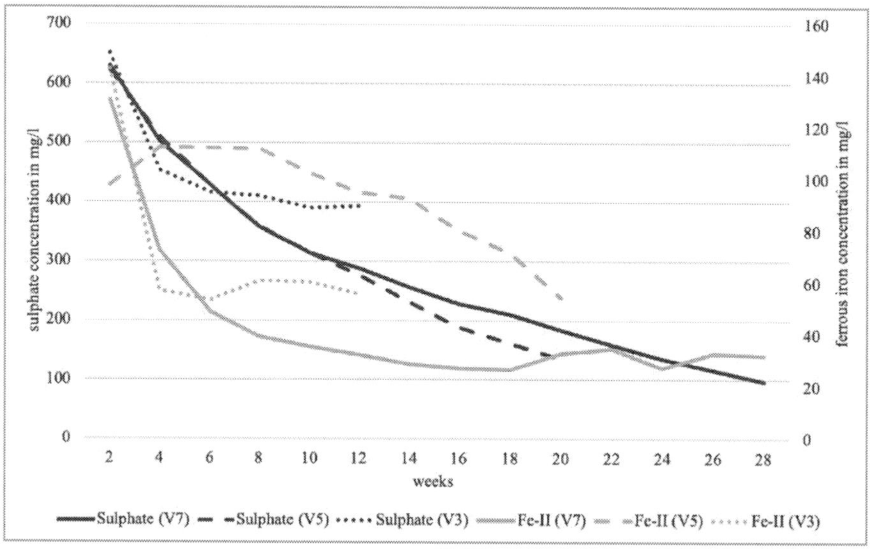


Figure 2: Measured sulphate and ferrous iron concentrations at an operation time of 3 (V3), 5 (V5) and 7 (V7) months.

Figure 3 shows the electrical conductivity and the pH value measured during the operation time of the three variants every second week. The chart presents the average over all five columns of V3 and V5 and the average over four columns of V7. Based on the input water conditions, electrical conductivity decreases from 1418 µS/cm to 965 µS/cm, from 1297 µS/cm to 636.4 µS/cm and from 1418 µS/cm to 588.8 µS/cm during 3, 5 and 7 months, equalling a reduction of 31.9 % (V3), 50.9 % (V5) and 58.5 % (V7). The pH value increase from 4.9 to 6.9 from 4.4 to 6.1 and from 4.5 to 6.3 during 3, 5 and 7 months. After 14 weeks, the pH values of V5 and V7 converge to pH 6.1 and 6.3 until the end of operation time. The electrical conductivity steadily decreases during the operation time.

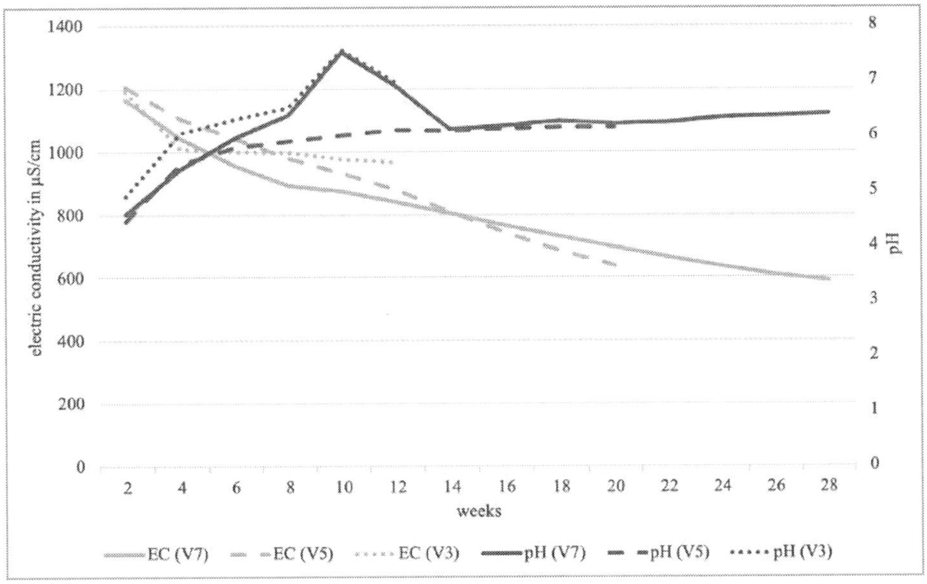


Figure 3: Measured electrical conductivity and pH value at an operation time of 3 (V3), 5 (V5) and 7 (V7) months.

## DISCUSSION

Water ion concentrations as well as the electrical conductivity decreased, and the pH value increased in every variant of my experiment. Despite the same place of soil sampling, the peat sampled in October (V5) was much drier than June samples (V3, V7). Probably the groundwater table dipped below under the ground surface during the hot summer of 2019, causing the layer where I took the peat cores to partially dry. Iron hydroxide in the peat cores of V5, I observed during the sampling, indicate that the peat was not continuously saturated and under anaerobic conditions. The trend of the pH value also shows the difference between V7 and V3 comparted to V5. However, the pH value of V5 and V7 converge at about 6.2 after 14 weeks in both cases. An operation time of three months is maybe not long enough to approach a constant pH level. The trend of the ferrous iron concentration of V5 is different from the other two variants. The already mentioned iron hydroxide in the peat cores of V5 probably reduced under anaerobic conditions in the column during my experiment and release iron as ferrous iron. As a result, the ferrous iron concentration increase. This process was already observed in a previous experiment (Rösel et al. 2019).

All observations strongly indicate that pyrite was formed. A steady decreased electrical conductivity is attended by the decreased sulphate concentration and also for reducing acidity. A slightly acidic pH value was reached during the operation time, implying considerable activity of sulphate reducing bacteria (Herlihy and Mills 1985; Koschorreck and Wendt-Potthoff 2012). As shown in Figure 3, the first measurement of every variant offers pH < 5 but sulphate concentration already decreased. Sulphate reducing bacteria usually operate at pH > 5. The high organic content of the peat is a more important driver of the sulphate reduction. However, wetlands host specific sulphate-reducing bacteria which are also active at low pH (Koschorreck 2008). Those microorganisms are important for the process of pyrite forming. I observed gas release during sampling which I interpret as dissolved carbon dioxide in the water. $CO_2$ is formed as a product of sulphate and ferric reduction under anaerobic conditions. This is an intermediate of pyrite formation (Blodau 2006).

Further research will be done to determine the pyrite amount in the peat cores. To fill the remaining data gaps, further variants with operation times of 4 and 6 months are now in progress.

## CONCLUSION

Mining affected groundwater is rich in ferrous iron and sulphate. If the acidic groundwater enters the surface water, iron oxidise and precipitate as iron hydroxide whereas dissolved sulphate remains in the water and becomes a serious environmental problem. Constructed wetlands provide an anaerobic milieu and a high content of organic matter, altering acid mine drainage by reducing iron and sulphate, and forming pyrite. I conducted a column experiment involving degraded peat and mining affected groundwater. The results show a decrease of electrical conductivity between 31.9 % and 58.5 % whereas the pH increased until a slightly acidic value. The ferrous iron and sulphate concentrations decreased between 77.7 % and 87.1 % as well as 49 % and 87.4 %. The results indicate pyrite forming in different intensities. My findings indicate that the slower a specific water volume percolates through the peat core, the more iron and sulphur can retain in the peat. Because of the high content of organic carbon of degraded peat, specific microorganism may reduce sulphate also at low pH. Translated to natural large-scale conditions, the results of my research give reasons to hypothesis the rewetting peatlands can help to decontaminate mining affected groundwater in the Lusatian post-mining landscape to a significant degree.

## ACKNOWLEDGEMENTS

I acknowledge the support of lab and technician department' stuff of Research Institute of Post-Mining Landscapes. I thank Jutta Zeitz and Frank Riesbeck (HU Berlin) for all the helpful discussions and sharing their field and experimental experiences. My research is founded by the Friedrich-Naumann-Stiftung für die Freiheit.

## REFERENCES


1. Batty, L.C.; Younger, P.L. (2007) The effect of pH on plant litter decomposition and metal cycling in wetland mesocosms supplied with mine drainage. *Chemosphere*; 66: 158–164
2. Blodau, C. (2006) A review of acidity generation and consumption in acidic coal mine lakes and their watersheds. *Science of the Total Environment*; 369: 307–332
3. Ekolu, S.O.; Diop, S.; Azene, F.; Mkhize, N. (2016) Disintegration of concrete construction induced by acid mine drainage attack. *Journal of the South African institution of civil engineering*; 58(1): 34–42
4. Fernando, W.A.M.; Ilankoon, I.M.S.K.; Syed, T.H.; Yellishetty, M. (2018) Challenges and opportunities in the removal of sulphate ions in contaminated mine water: A review. *Minerals Engineering*; 117: 74–90
5. Gazea, K.A.; Kontopoulos, A. (1996) A review of passive systems for the treatment of acid mine drainage. *Minerals Engineering*; 9(1): 23–42
6. Gosling, L.M.; Baker, S.J. (1980) Acidity fluctuations at a broadland site in Norfolk. *Journal of Applied Ecology*; 17: 479–490
7. Graupner, B.J.; Koch, C.; Prommer, H.; Werner, F. (2012) Process oriented quantification of mine dump pollutant inventories on the large scale – The case of the lignite mining district Lusatia, Germany. *Journal of Geochemical Exploration*; 112: 161–173
8. Herlihy, A.T. and Mills, A.L. (1985) Sulfate Reduction in Freshwater Sediments Receiving Acid Mine Drainage. *Applied and Environmental Microbiology*; 49(1): 179–186
9. Kefeni, K.K.; Msagati, T.A.M.; Mamba, B.B. (2017) Acid mine drainage: Prevention, treatment options, and resource recovery: A review. *Journal of Cleaner Production*; 151: 475–493
10. Koschorreck, M. (2008) Microbial sulphate reduction at a low pH. *FEMS Microbiological Ecology*; 64: 329–342
11. Koschorreck, M.; Wendt-Potthoff (2012) A sediment exchange experiment to assess the limiting factors of microbial sulfate reduction in acid mine pit lakes. *Journal of Soils Sediments*; 12: 1615–1622
12. Leclair, M.; Whittington, P.; Price, J. (2015) Hydrological functions of a mine-impacted and natural peatland-dominated watershed, James Bay Lowland. *Journal of Hydrology: Regional Studies*; 4: 732–747
13. Luís, A.T.; Teixeira, P.; Almeida, S.F.P; Ector, L.; Matos, J.X.; Ferreira da Silva, E.A. (2009) Impact of Acid Mine Drainage (AMD). *Water, Air, and Soil Pollution*; 200: 147–167
14. McCullough, C.D.; Lund, M.A. (2011) Bioremediation of Acidic and Metalliferous Drainage (AMD) through organic carbon amendment by municipal sewage and green waste. *Journal of Environmental Management*; 92: 2419–2426
15. Parviainen, A.; Mäkilä, M; Loukola-Ruskeeniemi, K. (2014) Pre-mining acid rock drainage in the Talvivaara Ni-Cu-Zn-Co deposit (Finland): Natural peat layer as a natural analog to constructed wetlands. *Journal of Geochemical Exploration*; 143: 84–95
16. Pat-Espadas, A.M.; Loredo-Portales, R.; Amabilis-Sosa, L.E.; Gómez, G.; Vidal, G. (2018) Review of Constructed Wetlands of Acid Mine Drainage Treatment. *Water*; 10(11)
17. Peiffer, S. (2016) Reaction time scales for sulphate reduction in sediments of acidic pit lakes and its relation to in-lake acidity neutralisation. *Applied Geochemistry*; 73: 8–12
18. Rösel, L.; Hildmann, C.; Reissmann, R.; Zingelmann, M. (2019) Mineralogische und bodenkundliche Charakterisierung von Eisenhydroxidsedimenten (mineralogical and pedological properties of iron hydroxide sediments) in German. Jahrestagung der DBG/BGS 2019: Erd-Reich und Boden-Landschaften, 24.–29.08.2019, Bern
19. RoyChowdhury, A.; Sarkar, D.; Datta, R. (2015) Remediation of Acid Mine Drainage-Impacted Water. *Current Pollution Reports*; 1: 131–141
20. Sobolewski, A. (1999) A Review of Processes Responsible for Metal Removal in Wetlands Treating Contaminated Mine Drainage. *International Journal of Phytoremediation*. 1(1): 19–51
21. Tuttle, J.H.; Dugan, P.R.; Randles, C.I. (1969) Microbial Sulfate Reduction and Its Potential Utility as an Acid Mine Water Pollution Abatement Precedure. *Applied Microbiology*; 17(2): 297–302
22. Vile, M.A.; Wieder, R.K. (1993) Alkalinity generation by Fe(III) reduction versus sulfate reduction in wetlands constructed for acid mine drainage treatment. *Water, Air, and Soil Pollution*; 69: 425–441
23. Wisotzky, F. (2015) Bedeutung von Pyritmineralen für die Grundwasserchemie (Importance of pyrite minerals for groundwater chemistry) in German. *Grundwasser – Zeitschrift der Fachsektion Hydrogeologie*; 20: 107–115

ID 62768

# THE IMPACT OF SOIL FERTILIZATION EXPERIMENT ON SOIL WATER CHEMISTRY IN FOREST STANDS ON DRAINED ORGANIC SOIL, IN LATVIA

Ilze Karklina[1, 2], Arta Bardule[1], Ieva Licite[1, 3]

[1] Latvian State Forest Research Institute 'Silava', Salaspils, Latvia
[2] University of Latvia, Riga, Latvia
[3] Latvia University of Life Sciences and Technologies, Jelgava, Latvia

*ilze.karklina@silava.lv*

## SUMMARY

Enhanced forest growth may respond to demand of woody resources and contribute to the climate change mitigation. The forest soil treatment with fertilizers along with drainage and thinning is acknowledged as a measure of enhanced forest growth. Potassium and phosphorus are usually the tree growth limiting nutrients in forest stands on drained organic soil. The deficit of these elements can be compensated with wood ash. The study was conducted in three forests stands on drained organic soil, located in eastern part of Latvia. Forest soil was enriched with wood ash fertilizer or combined wood ash and ammonium nitrate fertilizer. The soil water samples were collected during the period 2017–2019. The aim of this study is to investigate the impact on forest soil fertilization on soil water chemistry. There was a statistically significant increase in total nitrogen concentrations in soil water samples from wood ash and combined fertilizer treated plots. However, the elevated concentrations decreased within three months after fertilization. We detected also significant increase in concentrations of phosphate and calcium in soil water from some stands. In addition to soil water monitoring, a canopy throughfall water samples were collected in all plots. In order to evaluate the impact of throughfall water on soil water chemistry, a Spearman correlation analysis was conducted between variables of soil and throughfall water chemistry. There were only few significant correlations detected, mostly for pH. The strongest relationship was found for potassium in the control plot of Norway spruce stand ($r = 0.70$; $p<0.05$). The results suggest that most pronounced effect on soil water chemistry ($N_{TOT}$, Ca, Mg, $PO_4^{3-}$) was caused by the forest soil enrichment with ammonium nitrate rather by wood ash spreading or the impact of throughfall water.

***Keywords**: wood ash, ammonium nitrate, nutrient leaching, throughfall water*

## INTRODUCTION

Nutrient inputs into forest ecosystem are usually considered to be stable. The major sources of N (nitrogen) are atmospheric deposition and biotic/abiotic fixation, but Ca (calcium), Mg (magnesium), K (potassium) and P (phosphorus) come generally from mineral weathering. However, nutrient, particularly P and N, losses increase, when logging residues are removed from forest ecosystem, especially softwood stands, in comparison to stem-only harvesting. In contrast to acid mineral soil, organic soil layers are able to preserve released base cations more effectively (Paré, Thiffault, 2016).

Wood ash can be used with the efficiency of commercial P and K containing fertilizers, especially in forest on organic soil (Pitman, 2006). Wood ash properties depend on biomass, combustion process, fraction of wood ash and additional treatment. More nutrients, also trace metals are found in untreated fly ash. Although relatively higher pH of untreated fly ash induce element availability for trees in acid, nutrient poor sites, rapid change in alkalinity may impact an ecology of forest ecosystem. Therefore, wood ash should be granulated or at self-hardened (Pitman, 2006). Wood ash in combination with N containing fertilizer may also be used in soil improvement of N limited forest stand. However, it is suggested to reduce usage of wood ash in forests that are heavily enriched with atmospheric input of N that would enhance N leaching into groundwater or surface water.

Experiments of forest soil fertilization exhibit the importance of N in forest growth, particularly in boreal and temperate regions (Aber et al., 1989; Paré, Thiffault, 2016). Atmospheric input of N may compensate the removal of harvested wood products to some extent, but there is a gradient of N deposition across the North America and Nordic countries, indicating that in some regions atmospheric input would not be enough to compensated N losses by harvesting (Paré, Thiffault, 2016). The inputs of base cations and P through deposition, on the contrary, are relatively small in comparison to the removal of these nutrients with harvested wood products (Paré, Thiffault, 2016). The atmospheric deposition of N has an impact on N cycling in a forest ecosystem. The threshold value of atmospheric input of N is considered to be 10 kg $ha^{-1}$ $yr^{-1}$ and may induce N leaching (Dise, Wright, 1995; Kristensen et al. , 2004). Therefore, it is thus of interest, how nutrient input with throughfall water affects the chemical properties of soil water in trial like this in order to better estimate the nutrient fluxes. Furthermore, there are determined threshold values of N content in coniferous foliage. For instance, N content in needles above 17 mg $g^{-1}$ indicates enhanced $NO_3^-$ leaching in soil water (Kristensen et al., 2004). The purpose of this paper is to estimate impact of organic forest soil fertilization on chemical properties of soil water.

## MATERIALS AND METHODS

Three experimental sites were established in coniferous stands on drained organic soil, in Latvia (**Error! Reference source not found.**). The dominant tree species is the Norway s pruce (*Picea abies* (L.) H.Karst.). Established experimental objects are located in eastern part of the state, in Kalsnava and Viesite parishes. Each of the experimental sites had one control plot and one trial plot. The control plots were left without any treatment, while the trial plots were fertilized. Hardened bottom ash was spread in all forest stands. In this experiment N was given in a form of ammonium nitrate. Forest soil was improved with both fertilizers in the object No. 3. Fertilizer was spread manually in 500 $m^2$ circle-type trial plots, in experimental sites No. 1 and No. 2, and mechanically with forest machinery moving through technological corridors, crossing margins of a 500 $m^2$ circle-type trial plot No. 3.

Table 2. The characteristics and fertilization of forest stands

| No. | Forest type | Tree species | Stand age | Fertilizer[1] | Dose of WA: t $ha^{-1}$/ $NH_4NO_3$: kg $ha^{-1}$ | Spreading of fertilizer | Date of treatment |
|---|---|---|---|---|---|---|---|
| 1 | OTM | Norway spruce | 49 | WA | 2 | manually | 11.2014 |
| 2 | OTM | Norway spruce | 54 | WA | 2 | manually | 11.2014 |
| 3 | OTM | Norway spruce | 54 | WA/ $NH_4NO_3$ | 3/ 150 | mechanically | 10.2016/ 07.2017 |

[1] WA – wood ash; $NH_4NO_3$ – ammonium nitrate
OTM – *Oxalidosa turf. mel*

Each of the plot had three pairs of vacuum lysimeters installed at the depths of 30 cm and 60 cm and three throughfall water collectors installed below the canopies of trees, hence ensuring three replicates for each of the plot. The water samples were collected once per month, in period from April/May to September/October, depending on the meteorological conditions in during 2017–2019. K (mg $L^{-1}$), Ca (mg $L^{-1}$), Mg (mg $L^{-1}$), $PO_4^{3-}$ (mg $L^{-1}$), $N_{TOT}$ (mg $L^{-1}$) and pH were determined in the collected water samples using ISO standard methodology.
First, statistical significance was tested between parameters of soil water collected from 30 cm and 60 cm depth at the individual plot and research object level, using Wilcoxon signed-rank test with continuity correction. If there was no significant difference, the two data sets of one chemical parameter were combined. Next, the differences were tested between the control plot and the fertilized plot at the individual research object level, using Wilcoxon rank sum test with continuity correction. In addition, to estimate the impact of throughfall water on chemical parameters of soil water, a Spearman correlation analysis was used. The statistical tests were conducted in RStudio (R Core Team, 2018).

## RESULTS

The results of chemical parameters of three-year soil water monitoring are summarized in **Error! Reference source not found.**. Soil water pH was lower in all treated plots, whether t he soil was improved with wood ash or with both fertilizers. However, the wood ash had significant effect on soil water alkalinity only in trial plots fertilized with wood ash 3 years before the monitoring. The results show that the tendency of relatively higher nutrient concentrations occur in trial plot treated with wood ash and ammonium nitrate. The total N is important chemical parameter of soil leachate in terms of ammonium nitrate impact and release of nutrients as a result of wood ash induced mineralization. The N concentration was higher in fertilizer treated plots and most of the observed increased concentrations were statistically significant. Ca and K concentrations were mostly elevated in soil water samples, collected from the trial plots. On the contrary, Mg and $PO_4^{3-}$ concentrations were mostly decreased.

Table 3. The average concentrations of chemical parameters of soil water collected from control and treated plots in the 3-year monitoring, commenced in the 3rd year (WA) and 1st year (WAN) after the treatment

| **Chemical parameters/ depth** | | **WA experiment** | | | | **WAN experiment** | |
|---|---|---|---|---|---|---|---|
| | | Norway spruce stand (49 years) | | Norway spruce stand (54 years) | | Norway spruce stand (54 years) | |
| | | C | WA | C | WA | C | WAN |
| pH | 30 cm | *7.21 ±0.05 | *7.03↓ ±0.05 | 7.20 ±0.06 | 7.13↓ ±0.09 | 6.58 ±0.08 | 6.39↓ ±0.07 |
| | 60 cm | **7.41 ±0.06 | **7.12↓ ±0.06 | **7.25 ±0.07 | **6.85↓ ±0.07 | 6.61 ±0.07 | 6.61 ±0.07 |
| $N_{TOT}$ | 30 cm | *10 ±1 | *12↑ ±1 | 5.3 ±0.5 | 6.7↑ ±0.6 | **4.4 ±0.4 | **15↑ ±6 |
| | 60 cm | **6.8 ±0.9 | **11↑ ±1 | **3.2 ±0.4 | **4.4↑ ±0.2 | **3.6 ±0.2 | **7↑ ±2 |
| Ca | 30 cm | *37 ±2 | *44↑ ±2 | 31 ±2 | 35↑ ±2 | 22 ±2 | 27↑ ±4 |
| | 60 cm | 47 ±1 | 49↑ ±1 | *42 ±2 | *36↓ ±2 | 26 ±1 | 26 ±2 |
| Mg | 30 cm | 10.4 ±0.7 | 10.2↓ ±0.8 | 7.3 ±0.5 | 6.7↓ ±0.6 | 4.2 ±0.3 | 5↑ ±1 |
| | 60 cm | **16.1 ±0.5 | **12.0↓ ±0.3 | **11.0 ±0.7 | **8.0↓ ±0.3 | 5.0 ±0.3 | 4.9↓ ±0.4 |
| K | 30 cm | 0.32 ±0.03 | 0.31↓ ±0.06 | 0.39 ±0.04 | 0.42↑ ±0.09 | 0.5 ±0.2 | 0.9↑ ±0.4 |
| | 60 cm | | | | | 0.4 ±0.1 | 0.4 ±0.1 |
| $PO_4^{3-}$ | 30 cm | **0.016 ±0.001 | **0.030↑ ±0.004 | 0.04 ±0.01 | 0.018↓ ±0.002 | 0.030 ±0.004 | 0.032↑ ±0.004 |
| | 60 cm | | | | | 0.03 ±0.02 | 0.028↓ ±0.004 |

C – control plot; WA – wood ash treated plot; WAN – wood ash and ammonium nitrate treated plot; * significant difference between the control and the treated plot ($p<0.05$); ** significant difference between the control and the treated plot ($p<0.01$); ↑ – a higher value compared to a control plot; ↓ – a lower value compared to a control plot

If the average concentrations are compared on the 3-years' time scale (data not shown), the acidity shows similar variations in both plots at the individual object level. As expected, a comparatively higher total N concentration detected in the first year of the monitoring in the trial plot of the forest stand received the combined treatment, because ammonium nitrate is very soluble in water. Likewise, Ca and Mg concentrations were higher in the trial plot of combined fertilizers in the first year of the monitoring. In comparison to the control, elevated leaching of K observed in the wood ash treated 54-year old stand and combined fertilizer stand in the first year of the monitoring – in the third and first year after the treatment, respectively. The 5-month sums (from May to September) of atmospheric input of analyzed elements range in diapasons: $N_{TOT}$ 1.10 – 2.78 kg $ha^{-1}$, K 1.43 – 7.18 kg $ha^{-1}$, Ca 2.40 – 5.95 kg $ha^{-1}$, Mg 0.70 – 1.66 kg $ha^{-1}$ and $PO_4^{3-}$ 0.04 – 1.28 kg $ha^{-1}$ (data not shown).

Table 4 summarizes only statistically significant correlations that are found between throughfall and soil water properties. Most of the detected correlations were positive, except for K at the control plot of combined fertilizer experimental site. It was noted that on average soil water's pH was lower in trial plots (**Error! Reference source not found.**). The c orrelation analysis showed a throughfall water's pH impact on soil water's acidity in the treated plots.

Table 4. The Spearman rank correlation ($p<0.05$) between chemical parameters of soil water and throughfall water

| Chemical parameters/ depth | | WA experiment | | WAN experiment | |
|---|---|---|---|---|---|
| | | Norway spruce stand (49 years) | Norway spruce stand (54 years) | Norway spruce stand (54 years) | |
| | | C | WA | C | W-AN |
| pH | 30 cm | | 0.57 | | 0.63 |
| | 60 cm | | 0.58 | | 0.53 |
| Mg | 30 cm | 0.56 | | | |
| K | 30 cm | | | 0.56 | |
| $PO_4^{3-}$ | 30 cm | 0.70 | | | |

C – control plot; WA – wood ash treated plot; WAN – wood ash and ammonium nitrate treated plot

## DISCUSSION

Wood ash is an alkaline material, and contrary to our results, elevated soil water's pH is usually detected in wood ash treatment experiments in forests on mineral soil, thought (Pitman, 2006). Wood ash increased pH may mobilize Fe, Al and induce a leaching of these elements. It is essential, since low concentrations of Fe and Al in peat enhance P loss from fertilized peatland (Renou-Wilson, Farrell, 2007). Ca and Mg leaching is reported to be a long-term effect of wood ash fertilization, whereas the soluble form of P is released gradually from wood ash (Piirainen et al., 2013; Pitman, 2006). We observed a similar tendency of significantly elevated Ca and $PO_4^{3-}$ concentrations in 49-year-old forest stand, treated with wood ash. It is also reported on K leaching into surface water immediately in the first year after the afforested peatland treatment with wood ash, which can be explained with the comparatively higher leachability of the element. Thus wood ash spreading in winter on snow facilitates K leaching during the snow melt (Piirainen et al., 2013). We observed a comparatively higher K concentration in combined treatment trial plot in the first year of monitoring (the first year after the soil fertilization). While wood ash treatment experiment in forest on mineral soil indicate significant increase of K concentration in soil solution of mor layer, in mineral podzol layer and Ca increase in soil solution from mineral layer in the first year after fertilization (Norström et al., 2012).

Higher N concentration, which was observed in trial plots fertilized with wood ash, is an indirect by-effect of wood ash application as a result of elevated pH, N mineralization and increased soil microbial biomass (Pitman, 2006). And on the contrary, it is also reported on decreased N concentrations in drainage water of fertilized afforested peatland (Piirainen et al., 2013). Similarly, N leachates in form of $NO_3^-$ from limed soil (Pitman, 2006). It must be noted that released N is taken up by trees (Piirainen et al., 2013). Soil matrix and microbial activity have also an essential impact of N and P leaching. For instance, $NO_3^-$ and $PO_4^{3-}$ were added in restored cutaway peatland. As a result, 0,5 % $NO_3^-$ and 7 % $PO_4^{3-}$ drained through peatland buffer within three years of monitoring, besides 70 % of added $NO_3^-$ were bound in microbial biomass and 43 % of $PO_4^{3-}$ – in peat matrix (Silvan et al., 2005).

It is observed that atmospheric deposition of N to forest land ranges from less than 5 kg N $ha^{-1}$ $yr^{-1}$ in Northern Europe (Sponseller et al., 2016) to greater than 60 kg N $ha^{-1}$ $yr^{-1}$ in Central and Western Europe (Butterbach-Bahl et al., 2011; Dise, Wright, 1995). Rates of atmospheric deposition, particularly of N, have declined since 1980's in Europe (Ruoho-

Airola et al., 2012), still it is important to take into account the threshold values of atmospheric input of N. Considering that atmospheric input of N was calculated for five months of each monitoring year, still the estimated input of N is relatively lower than on average in Europe and does not exceed the threshold values of 12 kg N $ha^{-1}$ $yr^{-1}$ (Pitman, 2006) or even 10 kg N $ha^{-1}$ $yr^{-1}$ (Dise, Wright, 1995; Kristensen et al., 2004). The threshold values indicate elevated $NO_3^-$ leaching that may suggest limiting fertilization of forest soil. Although atmospheric input of N may have an impact on $NO_3^-$ leaching, there was no significant correlation between total N concentration in soil solution and throughfall water (Kristensen et al., 2004). Atmospheric input of N may also explain the acidity of soil (Dise, Wright, 1995); however, no significant correlation was found between N concentration in throughfall water and pH of soil water.

## CONCLUSION

Forest soil improvement with wood ash or combined wood ash and N containing mineral fertilizer resulted in significantly elevated total N concentrations and decreased pH in the soil water samples from treated plots. The forest soil enrichment with combined fertilizer had more distinct effect on the chemistry of soil water rather than wood ash spreading or the impact of throughfall water. However, the results may be explained with the larger dosage of fertilizers and initiated monitoring in the same year of ammonium nitrate treatment, while wood ash was spread few months earlier. Contrary to expectations, we did not observe a tendency of elevated pH of soil water in wood ash treated plots. There were significant increase in concentrations of Ca and $PO_4^{3-}$ 3 – 5 years after the soil improvement with wood ash. There were significant correlations between pH of canopy throughfall water and soil water in some treated plots. However, the most distinct effect on soil water chemistry was due to the forest soil fertilization, in particular with combined fertilizer, rather than due to the impact of canopy throughfall water.

## ACKNOWLEDGEMENTS

The study is implemented within the scope of the memorandum between the Joint Stock Company ‘Latvia’s State Forests’ and LSFRI ‘Silava’ on ‘Collaboration in scientific research’ from October 11, 2011. The research was conducted within the scope of the Joint Stock Company ‘Latvia’s State Forests’ research project ‘Research program on forest fertilization’ (2016-2021).

## REFERENCES


1. Aber, J.D., Nadelhoffer, K.J., Steudler, P., Melillo J.M. (1989) Nitrogen Saturation in Northern Forest Ecosystems. *BioScience*; 39: 378–286.
2. Butterbach-Bahl, K., Gundersen, P., Ambus, P., Augustin, J., Beier, C., Boeckx, P., ... Zechmeister-Boltenstern, S. (2011) Nitrogen processes in terrestrial ecosystems. No M. A. Sutton, C. M. Howard, J. W. Erisman, G. Billen, A. Bleeker, P. Grennfelt, ... B. Grizzetti (Red.), *The European Nitrogen Assessment*. Cambridge: Cambridge University Press: 99–125.
3. Dise, N. B., Wright, R. F. (1995) Nitrogen leaching from European forests in relation to nitrogen deposition. *Forest Ecology and Management*; 71: 153–161.
4. Kristensen, H. L., Gundersen, P., Callesen, I., Reinds, G. J. (2004) Throughfall Nitrogen Deposition Has Different Impacts on Soil Solution Nitrate Concentration in European Coniferous and Deciduous Forests. *Ecosystems*; 7: 180-192.
5. Norström, S. H., Bylund, D., Vestin, J. L. K., Lundström, U. S. (2012) Initial effects of wood ash application to soil and soil solution chemistry in a small, boreal catchment. *Geoderma*; 187–188: 85–93.
6. Paré, D., Thiffault, E. (2016) Nutrient Budgets in Forests Under Increased Biomass Harvesting Scenarios. *Current Forestry Reports*; 2: 81–91.
7. Piirainen, S., Domisch, T., Moilanen, M., Nieminen, M. (2013) Long-term effects of ash fertilization on runoff water quality from drained peatland forests. *Forest Ecology and Management*; 287: 53–66.
8. Pitman, R. M. (2006) Wood ash use in forestry - a review of the environmental impacts. *Forestry*; 79: 563–588.
9. R Core Team. (2018) *R: A language and environment for statistical computing*. Vienna, Austria: R Foundation for Statistical Computing.
10. Renou-Wilson, F., Farrell, E. (2007) The use of foliage and soil information for managing the nutrition of Sitka and Norway spruce on cutaway peatlands. *Silva Fennica*; 41: 409-424.
11. Ruoho-Airola, T., Eilola, K., Savchuk, O. P., Parviainen, M., Tarvainen, V. (2012) Atmospheric Nutrient Input to the Baltic Sea from 1850 to 2006: A Reconstruction from Modeling Results and Historical Data. *Ambio*; 41: 549–55.
12. Silvan, N., Sallantaus, T., Vasander, H., Laine, J. (2005) Hydraulic nutrient transport in a restored peatland buffer. *Boreal Environment Research*; 10: 203–210.
13. Sponseller, R. A., Gundale, M. J., Futter, M., Ring, E., Nordin, A., Näsholm, T., Laudon, H. (2016) Nitrogen dynamics in managed boreal forests: Recent advances and future research directions. *Ambio*; 45: 175–187.

ID 72807

# ASSESSING THE WATER BALANCE AS BASIS FOR WATER MANAGEMENTAND HYDROLOGICAL RESTORATION IN TROPICAL PEATLAND

*Sigit Sutikno[1,5,6], Andy Hendri[1], Besri Nasrul[2,5], Budi Triadi[3], Haris Gunawan[4]

[1]Civil Engineering Department, University of Riau, Indonesia
[2]Department of soil Science, University of Riau, Indonesia
[3]Ministry of Public Work and Housing, Indonesia
[4]Peatland and Mangrove Restoration Agency, Republic of Indonesia
[5]Center for Disaster Studies, University of Riau, Indonesia
[6]Center of Excellence in Peat Research, University of Riau, Indonesia

*sigit.sutikno@lecturer.unri.ac.id*

## SUMMARY

A key factor in tropical peatland restoration is a hydrological restoration that keeps the peat always wet and restores its hydrological function. Therefore, water management is an important aspect for the hydrological restoration of the degraded tropical peatland due to the uneven distribution of water during the dry and rainy seasons. Good water management should be designed with considering the water balance that explains the time and the amount of water surplus and the deficit along years in the study area. However, analysis of the water balance in tropical peatlands is not simple due to the difficulty of estimating the outflow from many canals in themost of degraded peatlands. This study applied the Thornthwaite water balance (TMWB) model in Pulau Tebing Tinggi peatland hydrological unit (PHU), Riau Province, Indonesia to analyze the water balance and the impact of water management on degraded peatlands. The data required for analysis were monthly rainfall and temperature, land use, degree of peat decomposition, and the latitude of the location. The model was calibrated by comparing the calculated discharge and the measured outflow discharge from canals. This study found that thecalculated discharge corresponds closely to the measured values with the correlation value and the root mean square error of about 0.87 and 0.91 respectively. These results indicate that the TMWB model can be satisfactorilyapplied to estimate the average monthly outflow discharge and to analyze the water balance in tropical peatlands with numerous canals outflow. The model also can be used to understand the impact of water management interventions using canal blocking on the water balance. It was found that the water balance in Pulau Tebing Tinggi PHU will not be deficit if it is implemented at least 50% of the ideal number of canal blocking plan.

***Keywords**: water balance, tropical peatland, water management, peatland restoration*

## INTRODUCTION

The degraded peatlands because of over drained and land conversion for certain purposes will continuously causesubsidence, carbon emissions, and peat fires (Holden et al., 2006). The disturbance of the peat ecosystem is generally triggered by logging, land-use conversion to other uses such as plantation, agriculture, and transmigration that is accompanied by excessive development of drainage canal networks (Bonn et al., 2016). Peatlands that have been degraded from their natural conditions will also decrease their function as carbon storageand climate regulation, habitat for biodiversity, and for water regulation (Simil et al., n.d.). Due to the important role of the peatlands in preserving the environment, it is urgent to restore them immediately.

A key factor in tropical peatland restoration is a hydrological restoration that keeps the peat always wet andrestores its hydrological function (Giesen & Nirmala, 2018), (S. Sutikno et al., 2020). Therefore, water management is an important aspect for the hydrological restoration of the degraded tropical peatland due to the uneven distribution of water during the dry and rainy seasons. Good water management should be designed with considering the water balance that explains the time and the amount of water surplus and the deficit along years inthe study area. However, analysis of the water balance in tropical peatlands is not simple due to the difficulty of estimating the outflow from many canals in the most of degraded peatlands. This study applied the Thornthwaite water balance (TMWB) model in Pulau Tebing Tinggi peatland hydrological unit (PHU), Riau Province, Indonesiato analyze the water balance and the impact of water management on degraded peatlands.

## MATERIALS AND METHODS

This research focused in the Pulau Tebing Tinggi PHU, Kepulauan Meranti Regency, Riau Province, Indonesia, as presented in Fig-1. The peatland area is the most priority for restoration by Peatland Restoration Agency, The Republic of Indonesian due to its degradation status (Dohong et al., 2017). The PHU and many peatland areas in Riau suffered big peat fires in 2013-2015, which caused a haze disaster that lasted nearly two months and affectednot just Indonesia but neighboring countries as well (Sigit Sutikno et al., 2020).

For more detailed water balance analysis, this study divided the PHU into five sub-PHUs, such as sub- PHU-1, sub-PHU-2, sub-PHU-3, sub-PHU-4, and sub-PHU-5. Sub-PHU-1 was picked up for hydrologic modeling, because of the fewest canal outlet identified. The data required for analysis were monthly rainfall and temperature, land use, degree of peat decomposition, and the latitude of the location. We installed five discharge monitoring equipment at canal outlets to estimate the direct runoff (DRO) from the Sub-PHU-1. These data wereused for model calibration. This research used TMWB model for water balance analysis in the tropical peatland that originally was developed by Thornthwaite (Fish, 2011), (Suryatmojo et al., 2013), (Nugroho et al., 2019). Themodel uses the concept of soil moisture capacity to explain the water balance in the peatland as shown in Fig-2.

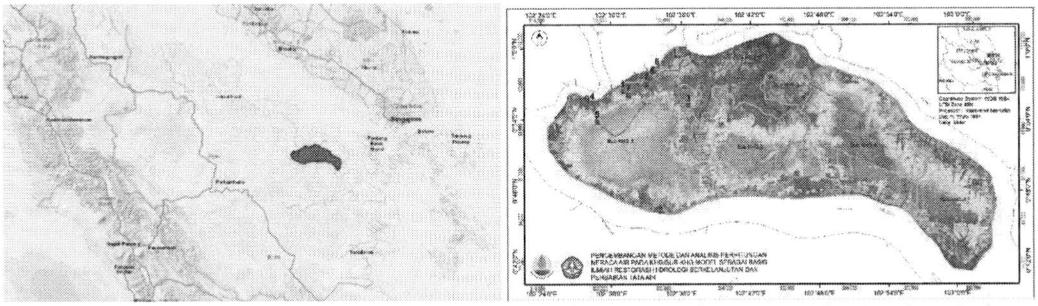

Fig-1. The study area at Pulau Tebing Tinggi PHU, Kepulauan Meranti Regency, Riau Province, Indonesia andthe division of Sub-PHU

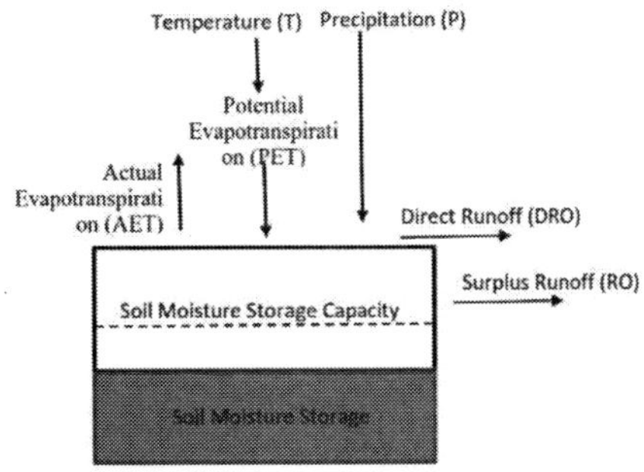


Fig-2. Thornthwaite-Matter water balance model diagram (Source: McCabe, modified)

## RESULTS AND DISCUSSION

The calculation process of the water balance analysis is presented in Table-1. Thornthwaite and Mather suggest that there is only 50 percent of the surplus water in the large watersheds which will become runoff in any month. The remaining 50% is assumed to be detained and will become runoff during the next month (Nugroho et al., 2019). In this research, that percentage is described in *k* value which can be calibrated by comparing the calculateddischarge and the measured outflow discharge from canals. Ideally, the measured discharge for the calibration should be at least one year, but this research started to measure the outflow discharge from August 2020. The calibration process using five months data is presented in Fig-3. This study found that the calculated discharge corresponds closely to the measured values with the correlation value and the root mean square error of about 0.99and 0.91 respectively. These results indicate that the TMWB model can be satisfactorily applied to estimate the average monthly outflow discharge and to analyze the water balance in tropical peatlands with numerous canals outflow. This research found that the Thornthwaite and Mather suggestion still can be applied in the tropical peatland condition.

The calibrated model was used to analyze and to simulate the water balance for several water managementscenarios. Fig-4 shows the ideal design of the canal blockings for water management. They were designed to blockthe water flow in all of the canals in a distance of each 0.5 m elevation interval to reduce the direct runoff. For thisdesigned criteria, Pulau Tebing Tinggi PHU needs about 186 canal blocks. Due to the limited budget that the government usually faces, this research justified making several scenarios of implementing the number of canal blocking and simulated their impact on the water balance, such as 100%, 75%, 50%, and 25% of the ideal designof canal blocking (Table-2). Fig-4 (right) shows the impact of implementing those scenarios on reducing the direct runoff, and Fig-5 shows the impact of implementing 50%-scenario on water balance in comparison with no canalblocking. The annual water balance for each canal blocking scenario is presented in Table-2. It was found that thewater balance in Pulau Tebing Tinggi PHU will not be deficit if it is implemented at least 50% of the ideal numberof canal blocking plan.

Table-1 The calculation process of the water balance analysis

| Parameters | Symbol | Unit | Jan | Feb | Mar | Apr | Mei | Jun | Jul | Agust | Sep | Okt | Nop |
|---|---|---|---|---|---|---|---|---|---|---|---|---|---|
| Temperature | T | °C | 24.73 | 24.79 | 25.17 | 25.33 | 25.23 | 24.58 | 23.96 | 24.05 | 24.75 | | |
| Presipitasi | P | mm | 127.99 | 76.22 | 160.61 | 175.62 | 154.16 | 105.69 | 106.70 | 136.91 | | | |
| Potential Evapotranspiration | PE | mm | 112.85 | 102.78 | 119.35 | 118.26 | 120.26 | 107.49 | 102 | | | | |
| Accumulated Potensial Water Loss | APWL | mm | 15.15 | 41.71 | 0.00 | 0.00 | 0.00 | | | | | | |
| Available Water Capacity | AWC | % | 288.87 | 288.87 | 288.87 | 288.87 | | | | | | | |
| Soil Moisture Storage | ST | mm | 277.32 | 258.16 | 288.8 | | | | | | | | |
| Monthly Soil Moisture Storage Differenc | ΔST | mm | -11.55 | -1 | | | | | | | | | |
| Actual Evapotranspiration | AE | m | | | | | | | | | | | |
| Surplus | Surp | m | | | | | | | | | | | |
| Deficit | | | | | | | | | | | | | |
| Direct Run of Surplus | | | | | | | | | | | | | |

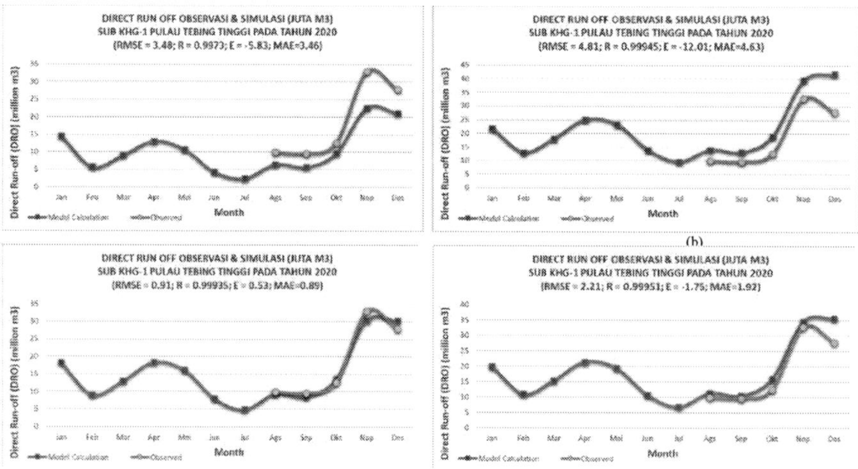


(a) (b) (c) (d)

Fig-3. The calibration process using measured discharge from August-December 2020 with *k* value of 0.4 (a),0.6 (b), 0.5 (c), and 0.55 (d)

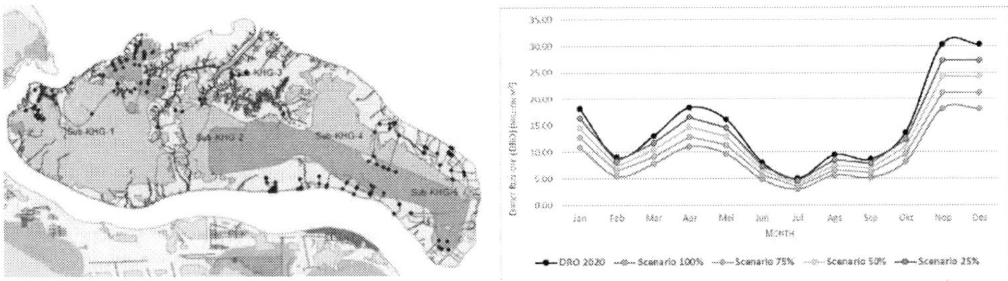


Fig-4. The ideal canal blocking design (left) and their impact scenarios on reducing direct runoff (right)

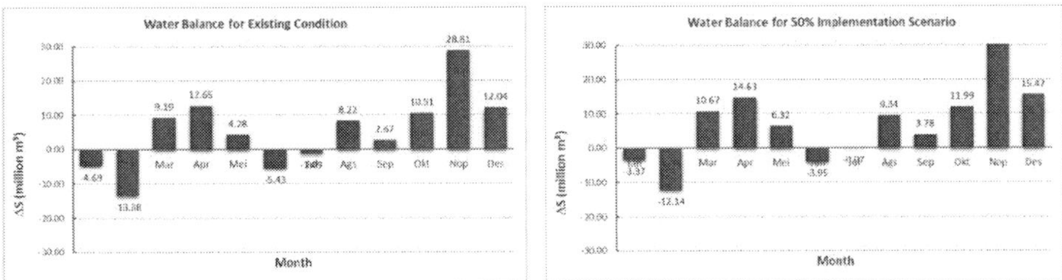


Fig-5. The water balance of the existing condition and with the implementation 50% of the ideal canal blockingdesign

Table-2 The effect of the implementation of canal blocking scenarios on the annual water balance of each sub-PHU in Pulau Tebing Tinggi PHU

| Scenario for the canal blocking implementation | The number of canal blocking implementation | The reducing DRO assumed | Best $k$ value | Annual deficit/surplus (million $m^3$) | | | | | |
|---|---|---|---|---|---|---|---|---|---|
| | | | | Sub PHU-1 | Sub PHU-2 | Sub PHU-3 | Sub PHU-4 | Sub PHU-5 | PHU |
| 100% | 186 | 40% | 0.35 | 63.79 | 33.74 | 5.04 | 40.42 | 38.08 | 181.07 |
| 75% | 140 | 30% | 0.40 | 45.74 | 24.19 | 3.34 | 26.69 | 28.31 | 128.27 |
| 50% | 93 | 20% | 0.44 | 27.69 | 14.65 | 1.64 | 12.96 | 18.54 | 75.48 |
| 25% | 47 | 10% | 0.47 | 9.64 | 5.10 | -0.07 | -0.78 | 8.78 | 22.67 |
| Existing | | | 0.50 | -8.41 | -4.45 | -1.78 | -14.50 | -0.98 | -30.12 |

## CONCLUSION

This study applied the Thornthwaite water balance (TMWB) model in Pulau Tebing Tinggi peatland hydrologicalunit (PHU), Riau Province, Indonesia to analyze the water balance and the impact of water management on degraded peatlands. This study found that the TMWB model can be satisfactorily applied to estimate the average monthly outflow discharge and to analyze the water balance in tropical peatlands with numerous canals outflow. The model also can be used to understand the impact of water management interventions using canal blocking onthe water balance. It was found that the water balance in Pulau Tebing Tinggi PHU will not be deficit if it is implemented at least 50% of the ideal number of canal blocking plan.

## ACKNOWLEDGEMENTS

The authors would like to thank the Mangrove and Peatland Restoration Agency (BRG), The Republic ofIndonesia for supporting the research funds.

## REFERENCES

Bonn, A., Allott, T., Evans, M., Joosten, H., & Stoneman, R. (2016). Peatland restoration and ecosystem services:Nature-based solutions for societal goals. *Peatland Restoration and Ecosystem Services: Science, Policy and Practice, July 2018*, 402–417. https://doi.org/10.1017/CBO9781139177788.021

Dohong, A., Cassiophea, L., Sutikno, S., Triadi, B. L., Wirada, F., Rengganis, P., & Lubendik Sigalingging. (2017). *Modul pelatihan Pembangunan Infrastruktur Pembasahan Gambut Sekat Kanal Berbasis Masyarakat* (Issue April). Kedeputian Bidang Konstruksi, Operasi dan Pemeliharaan Badan Restorasi Gambut (BRG), Republik Indonesia.

Fish, R. E. (2011). *Using Water Balance Models To Approximate the Effects of Climate Change on Spring Catchment Discharge : Mt . Hanang , Tanzania.*

Giesen, W., & Nirmala, E. (2018). *Tropical Peatland Restoration Report: the Indonesian case* (Issue March). https://doi.org/10.13140/RG.2.2.30049.40808

Holden, J., Evans, M. G., Burt, T. P., & Horton, M. (2006). Impact of Land Drainage on Peatland Hydrology. *Journal of Environment Quality*. https://doi.org/10.2134/jeq2005.0477

Nugroho, A. R., Tamagawa, I., Riandraswari, A., & Febrianti, T. (2019). Thornthwaite-Mather water balance analysis in Tambakbayan watershed, Yogyakarta, Indonesia. *MATEC Web of Conferences*, *280*(May), 05007. https://doi.org/10.1051/matecconf/201928005007

Simil, M., Aapala, K., & Penttinen, J. (n.d.). *Ecological restoration in drained peatlands* (M. Similä, K. Aapala,& J. Penttinen (eds.)). Metsähallitus – Natural Heritage Services.

Suryatmojo, H., Fujimoto, M., Yamakawa, Y., Kosugi, K., & Mizuyama, T. (2013). Water balance changes in thetropical rainforest with intensive forest management system. *International Journal of Sustainable Future for Human Security*, *1*(2), 56–62. https://doi.org/10.24910/jsustain/1.2/5662

Sutikno, S., Rinaldi, R., Saputra, E., Kusairi, M., Saharjo, B. H., & Putra, E. I. (2020). Water management for hydrological restoration and fire prevention in tropical peatland. *IOP Conference Series: Materials Science and Engineering*. https://doi.org/10.1088/1757-899X/933/1/012053

Sutikno, Sigit, Afdeni, S., Rinaldi, & Handayani, Y. L. (2020). Analysis of tropical peatland fire risk using drought standardized precipitation index method and TRMM rainfall data. *AIP Conference Proceedings*. https://doi.org/10.1063/5.0013880

ID 60783

# AFFORESTATION AS A MEANS OF OFFSETTING $CO_2$ EMISSIONS ON CUTAWAY PEATLANDS

Lasse Aro[1], Jyrki Hytönen[2], Paula Jylhä[2]

[1] Natural Resources Institute Finland, Turku, Finland

[2] Natural Resources Institute Finland, Kokkola, Finland

*lasse.aro@luke.fi*

## SUMMARY

On cutaway peatlands the non-vegetated residual peat decomposes aerobically and emits $CO_2$. Afforestation of cutaway peatlands could offset soil $CO_2$ emissions due to an increase in the sequestration of atmospheric carbon ($CO_2$-C) into the growing tree biomass. In the afforestation, the two main options are growing of dense energy forests with short-rotation principles or traditional forestry aiming at timber production. We studied the biomass production and carbon sequestration in the above- and below-ground biomass in 25 dense 10–30-year old downy birch (*Betula pubescens* Ehrh.) stands and in two 31–32-year old Scots pine (*Pinus sylvestris* L.) experiments comparing stand establishment by planting and sowing in peat cutaway areas in Finland. We measured the tree stands, calculated their leafless above-ground, stump and root biomass and carbon content of the components. We also measured the organic matter and C accumulated in the O-layer on the top of the residual peat. The O-layer contributed significantly to the C sink. Finally, we compared annual C sink to decomposition measurements of the residual peat in afforested, fertilised cutaway peatland. Growing dense downy birch stands converted most of the sites into C sinks and growing of Scots pine would offset considerably the peat emissions.

***Keywords***: *carbon sink, cutaway peatland, downy birch, Scots pine, tree biomass*

## INTRODUCTION

Cutaway peatlands, i.e. former peat production sites, can be used in agriculture and forestry, or mires can be restored or flooded to form bird sanctuaries, game reserves or fishing lakes (Hytönen at al. 2018). Forestry is considered to be the major reuse option for cutaway peatlands in Finland (Selin 1999; Laasasenaho et al. 2017). Peat cutaway areas are characterized by variation in peat thickness, low pH levels, high nitrogen concentration, and low phosphorus and potassium concentrations (Aro et al. 1997). Afforestation of cutaway peatlands may encounter nutritional problems and consequently success in afforestation in many cases depends on fertilisation (e.g. Hytönen et al. 1995, Aro et al. 1997, Aro & Kaunisto 2003).

On cutaway peatlands the non-vegetated residual peat decomposes aerobically and emits $CO_2$ (Tuittila and Komulainen 1995; Sundh et al. 2000; Waddington et al. 2002). Afforestation of cutaway peatlands could offset soil $CO_2$ emissions due to an increase in the sequestration of atmospheric carbon ($CO_2$-C) into the growing tree biomass. However, the annual $CO_2$ emissions from the peat even on afforested cutaway peatlands can be high (Mäkiranta et al.

2007; Silvan and Hytönen 2016). Following the establishment of tree stands a new organic layer starts gradually to develop on top of the residual peat layer, originating mainly from tree litterfall. In the afforestation, the two main options are growing of dense energy forests with short-rotation principles or traditional forestry aiming at timber production.

The aim of this study was to compare the biomass production and carbon sequestration in the above- and below-ground biomass in 10–33-year old downy birch (short-rotation production) and Scots pine stands (traditional forestry) to the $CO_2$ emissions from the residual peat.

## MATERIALS AND METHODS

We studied the biomass production and carbon sequestration in the above- and below-ground biomass in 25 dense 10–30-year old downy birch (Betula pubescens Ehrh.) stands (Hytönen et al. 2018) and in two 31-32-year old Scots pine (Pinus sylvestris L.) experiments comparing planting and sowing in peat cutaway areas in Finland. The stand density of the birch stands varied from 122,000 trees $ha^{-1}$ (stand age of 10 years) to 10,000 trees $ha^{-1}$ (25–30 years), and in the Scots pine stands 856–4,583 trees $ha^{-1}$ (31–32 years). We measured the tree stands, calculated their leafless above-ground, stump and root biomass and carbon (C) content of the components. For birch stands the estimation of annual fine root C flux into the soil was based on the study of Uri et al. (2017). For Scots pine fine roots, the corresponding C amount was assumed to account 25% of the total C bound into the tree stand biomass. We also measured the organic matter and C accumulated in the new O-layer on the top of the residual peat. C concentration was assumed to be 50% in all tree stand compartments and in the organic soil layer.

Published values for the $CO_2$ emissions from the residual peat of the afforested cutaway peatlands were used. The annual soil $CO_2$-C emissions due to the decomposition of the remaining peat layer on recently ash fertilised cutaway peatland was on the average 284 g C $m^{-2}$ $a^{-1}$ (Silvan and Hytönen 2016) and 381 g C $m^{-2}$ $a^{-1}$ 15–43 years after PK fertilisation, on average (Mäkiranta et al. 2007).

## RESULTS

The O-layer contributed significantly to the C sink. Growing dense downy birch stands converted most of the sites into C sinks and growing of Scots pine would offset considerably the peat emissions (Figure 1).

## DISCUSSION

Dense birch stands can be established on cutaway peatlands in a cost-efficient manner applying natural afforestation or direct seeding and grown with relatively short rotations. In short-rotation production of downy birch biomass, extending rotations up to 20 years is recommended from the perspectives of biomass production (Hytönen et al. 2018) and profitability (Jylhä et al. 2015). Afforestation of cutaway peatlands with downy birch would also turn most of the sites to C sinks and compensate for the high $CO_2$ emissions from cutaway peat. In line with our study, young and middle-aged downy birch stands (12–30-years-old) growing on drained peatlands have also acted as C sink in Estonia (Uri et al. 2017).

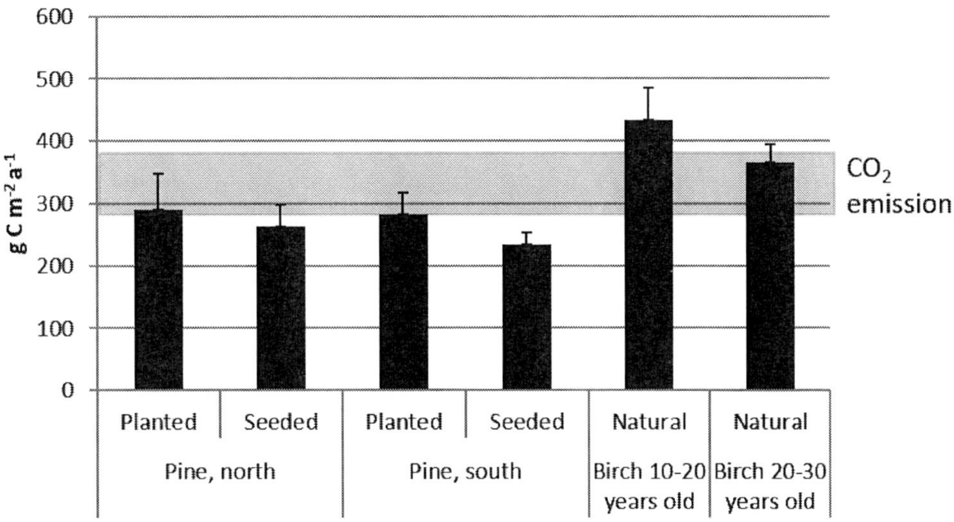


Figure 1. Annual carbon sequestration in above- and below-ground biomass of trees and in the O-layer. The horizontal grey area represents the range of means for decomposition measurements of peat in afforested, fertilised cutaway peatlands according to Mäkiranta et al. (2007) and Silvan and Hytönen (2016). Standard deviation is marked on top of the bars.

Scots pine stand establishment on cutaway peatlands generally requires seeding or planting. Thus, the growing density is much lower compared to short-rotation birch stands. Lower growing density and slower initial growth of Scots pine results smaller short-term carbon sequestration compared to birch. However, our study was confined to the first 30 years of Scots pine stand development.

The new organic layer formed on the top of the residual peat accumulates also C into the ecosystem and forms considerable C sink. Afforestation of cutaway peatlands is climatically beneficial and would turn the sites in carbon sinks or compensate considerably the C emissions from the peat. Therefore, forest owners should be encouraged to afforest their peat cutaway areas.

## ACKNOWLEDGEMENTS

Seppo Vihanta is acknowledged for measurements and assistance in the analysis.

## REFERENCES


1. Aro L., Kaunisto S. (2003) Jatkolannoituksen ja kasvatustiheyden vaikutus nuorten mäntymetsiköiden ravinnetilaan sekä puuston ja juuriston kehitykseen paksuturpeisella suonpohjalla. Summary: Effect of refertilisation and growing density on the nutrition, growth and root development of young Scots pine stands in a peat cutaway area with deep peat layers. *Suo*; 54(2): 49–68.
2. Aro L., Kaunisto S., Saarinen M. (1997) Summary: Afforestation of peat cutaway areas. Project report in 1986-1995. *Finnish Forest Research Institute, Research papers*; 634, 51 p.
3. Hytönen J., Aro L., Jylhä P. (2018) Biomass production and carbon sequestration of dense downy birch stands on cutaway peatlands. *Scandinavian Journal of Forest Research*; 33(8): 764–771.
4. Hytönen J., Saarsalmi A., Rossi P. (1995) Biomass production and nutrient uptake of short-rotation plantations. *Silva Fennica*; 29(2): 117-139.
5. Jylhä P, Hytönen J, Ahtikoski, A. (2015) Profitability of short-rotation biomass production on downy birch stands on cut-away peatlands in northern Finland. *Biomass & Bioenergy*; 75: 272—281.
6. Laasasenaho K., Lensu A., Rintala J., Lauhanen R. (2017) Landowners' willingness to promote bioenergy production on wasteland – future impact on land use of cutaway peatlands. *Land Use Policy*; 69: 167–175.
7. Mäkiranta P, Hytönen J, Aro L, Maljanen M, Pihlatie M, Potila H, Shurpali N, Laine J, Lohila A-L, Martikainen PJ, Minkkinen K. (2007) Soil greenhouse gas emissions from afforested organic soil croplands and cutaway peatlands. *Boreal Environment Research*; 12: 159–175.
8. Selin P. (1999) Turvevarojen teollinen käyttö ja suopohjien hyödyntäminen Suomessa. *University of Jyväskylä. Jyväskylä studies in biological and environmental sciences*; 79, 239 p.
9. Silvan N, Hytönen J. (2016) Impact of ash-fertilization and soil preparation on soil respiration and vegetation colonization on cutaway peatlands. *American Journal of Climate Change*; 5: 178–192.
10. Sundh I, Nilsson M, Mikkelä C, Granberg G, Svensson BH. (2000) Fluxes of methane and carbon dioxide on peat-mining areas in Sweden. *Ambio*; 29(8): 499–503.
11. Tuittila E.-S, Komulainen V.-M. (1995) Vegetation and $CO_2$ balance in an abandoned harvested peatland in Aitoneva, southern Finland. *Suo*; 46(3): 69–80.
12. Uri V, Kukumägi M, Aosaar J, Varik M, Becker H, Morozov G, Karoles, K. (2017) Ecosystems carbon budgets of differently aged downy birch stands growing on well-drained peatlands. *Forest Ecology and Management*; 399: 82–93.
13. Waddington J. M., Warner K. D., Kennedy G. W. (2002) Cutover peatlands: A persistent source of atmospheric $CO_2$. *Global Biogeochemical Cycles*; 16(1): 2-1–2-7.

ID 61325

# PEAT USE, CLIMATE IMPACTS AND MITIGATION POLICIES IN EUROPE

Olivier Hirschler[1], Bernhard Osterburg[1]

[1]Thünen Institute, Braunschweig, Germany

*olivier.hirschler@thuenen.de*

## SUMMARY

Peat is a carbon-rich material used as a component of horticultural growing media and as fuel. The extraction and the use of peat is a source of greenhouse gases, mostly through the metabolism and combustion of peat itself. Greenhouse gas emissions from peat extraction and use are reported by UNFCCC[2] Parties in their National Inventory Reports in the categories 4.D "LULUCF - Wetlands" for extraction sites and extracted non-energy peat, and 1. "Energy" for peat fuel consumption. In the European Union, they amounted to a total of 20.4 million tons CO2-eq per year for the period 2013-2017. In a context of climate debates, the issue of peat emissions triggers political questions. In some countries, goals have been set to reduce the extraction and use of peat in both horticultural and energy sectors. In the European Union, peat extraction will be included in mitigation targets defined in the LULUCF regulation (EU) 2018/841 as part of the category Wetlands from 2026 onwards. Some countries decided to include this category already from 2021 onwards. Policies and measures regarding peat in the European countries will then become relevant for internationally binding mitigation targets. Ireland and Finland have recently set goals to reduce peat use for energy purpose. The UK, Switzerland and more recently Germany are developing strategies to reduce the use of horticultural peat. The goal to phase out peat use is also part of the protocol on soil conservation of the Alpine Convention ratified by the EU in 2006. Based on the policy analysis and the calculation of emissions from peat extraction and use, the absolute climate potential in the case of an achievement of national goals is evaluated. Because of possible strong displacement or leakage effects in the case of national strategies, the emissions of horticultural peat should also be addressed at a European scale.

Keywords: Peat, Horticulture, Energy, GHG emissions, Mitigation policy

---

[2] United Nations Framework Convention on Climate Change

## INTRODUCTION

Peat is a material extracted from drained peatland soils, used as constituent for horticultural growing media in Europe (Schmilewski, 2017) and as fuel for the production of electricity and heat (EPE, 2018). Because of its high carbon content, peat releases $CO_2$ in the atmosphere through its combustion or its aerobic decomposition. Drained peatlands for extraction are also a source of greenhouse gases (GHG). In the context of growing climate concerns (UNFCCC, 2015), emissions from peat trigger political debates. In the European Union, GHG emissions from peat for fuel in the emission category 1. Energy have been taken into account in the Emissions Trading System (ETS) since 2005 and in the EU targets since 2009 (EC, 2020). Emissions from peat for horticulture (off-site) and from extracting sites (on-site) are reported in the land use, land use change and forestry sector (LULUCF), in the sub-category 4.D Wetlands, in which they contribute to around 80% (calculation based on UNFCCC, 2021 for the period 2013-2017 for the EU). As set by the regulation (EU) 2018/841, emissions from wetlands will also become relevant for the legally binding

mitigation targets of the EU member states from 2026 onwards. As a result, emissions from peat extraction are expected to gain relevance in the climate policy in the near future. The regulation offered the possibility to voluntary include this category from 2021 onwards, which was applied in Ireland (Irish government, 2021), and in Germany (Umweltbundesamt, personal communication, 2021). The total of the emissions from fuel and horticultural peat reported to the UNFCCC by the European Union amounts to 20.4 million tons $CO_2$-eq per year on average (calculation based on UNFCCC, 2021 for the period 2013-2017). In order to address these emissions, some countries have set goals to reduce the extraction and/or the use of peat. This paper aims to provide a description of the policies on peat reduction in Europe, quantify the emissions to be reduced and discuss the potential policy impacts.

## MATERIALS AND METHODS

The analysis was conducted for each country of the European Union, the United Kingdom and Switzerland. The policies of each country were analysed based on official documents, articles and presentations, derived from systematic online research. The strategies presented are only explicit political goals to reduce either the production or the use of peat. Other policies leading to limiting land availability or mining concessions with no explicit purpose to reduce peat extraction are not included in the study.

The mitigation potential is calculated for policies aiming to reduce peat extraction and use in the energy sector, and only peat use in the horticultural sector. Policies to reduce peat extraction for horticulture (only in Germany) are not considered based on the assumption that the reduction of extraction is compensated by imports. Any other displacement effects in both sectors are not considered in the calculations. Since the reference year for these policies is rarely clearly defined and in order to compare and sum up the amounts calculated, the data used refer to an average for the years 2013-2017.

The types of emissions considered are the emissions associated with peat extraction and use included in the IPCC[3] Guidelines for National Greenhouse Gas Inventories, concerning peat extraction sites (on-site) and peat use for energy and non-energy use (off-site) (Eggleston et al., 2006; Hiraishi et al., 2014). These emissions concern the following GHG: $CO_2$, $CH_4$ and $N_2O$. Emissions from the extraction machinery and the transport of peat are not included. The emissions reported to the UNFCCC are not suited to evaluate the impacts of political

[3] Intergovernmental Panel on Climate Change

measures regarding peat for the following reasons. 1) The on-site emissions from both energy and non-energy peat and the off-site emissions of non-energy peat are not differentiated in the reporting system of the UNFCCC. 2) The emissions from energy peat are reported on a consumption-based basis, whereas the emissions from extraction sites and non-energy peat are reported on a production-based basis. 3) The systematic analysis of the National Inventory Report (NIR) of all countries reporting emissions from peat shows a large variation of emissions factors for off-site emissions of non-energy peat. 4) Moreover, for some countries, the activity data and the factors used could not be found in the NIR or other sources were found to be more reliable.
Therefore, the potential reduction of GHG emissions of these policies are evaluated based on our own calculations. For this analysis, existing data on production and trade are combined to provide a balanced model and calculate consumption of peat. An overview of the methodology is a publication of the ISHS (Hirschler and Osterburg, 2021). The results might differ because it was enhanced with newer data and by considering the presence of alternative materials in traded growing media. Emission factors from on-site emissions and off-site emissions from energy peat were taken from the literature, mostly from countries' national inventory reports, or from the default values from the IPCC Guidelines. Emission factors from off-site non-energy peat were calculated for each country by differentiating the following three types of peat in the production and consumption: white bog peat (low decomposition rate H1-H5), black bog peat (high decomposition rate H6-H10) and fen peat. For each type of peat, a standard dry matter and C-content was found in the literature.

## RESULTS: PEAT REDUCTION POLICIES IN EUROPE

In Ireland, the half-public peat extracting company Bord na Móna and the Ministry for Energy announced in 2015 their intention to phase-out the harvesting of peat for the production of electricity and heat by 2030 (Bord na Móna, 2015). The situation of the extracting industry facing a sudden shutdown since 2020 is the result of a legal procedure and not a governmental decision (GMI, 2021).
In Finland, the reduction of peat use for energy was first set in the National Energy and Climate Strategy in 2013 with a reduction goal of a third by 2025 (Finnish Government, 2013). In 2019, in the scope of the Finland's carbon neutrality target, the government set a new goal of 50 % by 2030 (Finnish Government, 2019). This strategy is implemented by increasing the energy tax on peat set by the government, which was almost doubled in 2019 (Statistics Finland, 2021). A statement of the Ministry of the Environment in 2020 implies that peat should be phased-out on the long term, although no official target year was defined (Finnish Government, 2020).
The United Kingdom was the first country to address the use of horticultural peat with a target of 40 % alternative constituents in soil improvers and growing media by 2005 set in Minerals Planning Guidance 13 in 1995, extended to 90% by 2010 in the Lowland raised bog Habitat Action Plan in 1999 (HM Government, 1995; UK Biodiversity Group, 1999). In 2011, the natural environment white paper set a new goal to phase-out peat in the UK with a target by 2015 in the public sector, 2020 for amateur gardening and 2030 for professional growers (HM Government, 2011). In January 2018, the goal and the timeframe to end peat use were reaffirmed in the 25-Years Environment Plan, with a possibility to introduce further measures in case the target for 2020 was not reached (HM Government, 2018). In addition, an England Peat Strategy was announced, which is expected for 2021. The government supports research projects and works with the growing media and horticultural industry, without economically restrictive measures.

Switzerland banned peat extraction in 1987 by law. In 2012, in coherence with its goal to reduce overall impacts of peat extraction, the government decided to address imports and to ban peat use, without timeframe and restrictive measures (BAFU, 2020). Following the political discussions, the horticultural sector for ornamental plants committed itself to reduce peat rate in growing media to 50% by 2025 and to 5% by 2030, and the hobby sector committed itself to 5% by 2020. Additionally, the Swiss government supports research projects and farm counselling services and leads a working group to adapt the guidelines on fertilization to peat-free products.

In Germany, peat extraction is addressed in the Climate Action Plan 2050 (BMU, 2016) and is planned to be "progressively reduced with a view to shutting it down one day". Because peat extraction rights are delivered by local authorities under state's law, no measures are taken on federal level. The reduction of the use of peat in horticulture was also set in the Climate Action Plan 2050, the Agreement between the governing parties (Koalitionsvertrag, 2018) and the Climate Action Programme 2030 (BMU, 2019). Following these decisions, the Ministry of Agriculture set a goal to phase-out peat in the hobby sector by 2026 and to significantly reduce the peat rate in the professional sector by 2030 (BMEL, 2019). The government also supports research and demonstration projects for the development of peat-reduced production systems in the horticultural sector. Following round table discussions, the industry committed itself to increase the rate of alternative constituents by 50% in 2025 and 70% in 2030 for the hobby sector and by 20% in 2025 and 30% in 2030 for the professional sector (BHB et al., 2020; IVG, 2020).

The complete end of peat use on the medium term is also part of the protocol on soil conservation (SCP) of the Alpine Convention, signed and ratified by Austria (SCP in force since 2002), Germany (2002), France (2005), Italy (2013), Lichtenstein (2002), Macedonia (2003), Slovenia (2004) and the European Union (2006).

The climate potential of the national strategies on peat is presented in the table 1.

Table 1: Potential GHG mitigation through the achievement of political goals on peat extraction for energy and use for horticulture in European countries (EU, United Kingdom and Switzerland). Average data per year for the period 2013-2017. Source: own calculations.

| **Country** | **Category** | **Sector** | **Reduction goal** | **Decision year** | **Goal year** | **Quantity of peat Mt** | **Emissions avoided Mt CO2-eq** |
|---|---|---|---|---|---|---|---|
| Ireland | Extraction | Energy | 100% | 2015 | 2030 | 4.56 | 4.83 |
| Finland | Extraction | Energy | 50% | 2019 | 2030 | 2.33 | 3.35 |
| | | Total amounts extracted for energy to be reduced in Europe | | | | 6.90 | 8.18 |
| | | Total amounts extracted for energy in Europe (2013-2017) | | | | 11.18 | 14.95 |
| | | | | *Share to be reduced* | | 62% | 55% |
| UK | Use | Horticulture | 100% | 2011 | 2030 | 0.67 | 0.66 |
| Switzerland | Use | Horticulture | 100% | 2012 | ? | 0.07 | 0.07 |
| Germany | Use | Horticulture | 90%* | 2016 | 2030 | 1.41 | 1.45 |
| | | Total amounts used for horticulture to be reduced in Europe | | | | 2.15 | 2.18 |
| | | Total amounts used for horticulture in Europe (2013-2017) | | | | 6.97 | 7.20 |
| | | | | *Share to be reduced* | | 31% | 30% |
| | Total amounts for energy and for horticulture to be reduced in Europe | | | | | 9.05 | 10.35 |
| | Total amounts used for energy and for horticulture in Europe (2013-2017) | | | | | 18.26 | 22.30 |
| | | | | *Share to be reduced* | | 50% | 46% |

*Interpretation of Germany's goal (hobby sector: phase-out, professional sector: significant reduction)

83% of the peat used for energy is produced in Finland and Ireland and 66% of the total emissions from peat comes from its energy use. Therefore, the contribution of the policies in Finland and Ireland is very significant for the overall peat emission mitigation. Germany plays an important role as producer and as consumer of horticultural peat in Europe, and therefore can contribute significantly to the mitigation of the emissions from horticultural peat use. Overall, around half of the GHG emissions from peat are addressed through national peat reduction policies.

## DISCUSSION

In both Ireland and Finland, the use of peat for energy purposes is politically maintained for energy dependency and employment-related reasons. However, the climate impacts of energy peat, the financial costs through subsidies and the possibility to use renewable energy sources make the energy use of peat controversial (Kettunen, 2016; The Irish Times, 2018). Peat for energy purposes is consumed where it is produced and is hardly traded. Therefore, a limitation of the reduction of the production or use of peat for energy at a national level can be expected not to lead to displacement of the peat extraction in other countries. Thus, national strategies seem to be adapted to reduce the emissions from energy peat. However, the overall climate impact of these policies must consider the alternatives and displacement effect towards other fuels. Further, reduced use of peat for energy purposes could increase the supply of peat for horticulture.

On the other hand, because horticultural peat is intensively traded within Europe, the reduction of the extraction of horticultural peat in a country can easily lead to a displacement through import of peat, indirectly increasing the production in other countries, which limits the effect on peat use globally. Such displacement triggered by a political strategy is called climate leakage (Marcu et al., 2013). Peat is the major component of horticultural substrates in Europe (Schmilewski, 2017) and many actors of the growing media sector claim to have no immediate solution for a massive replacement of peat due to limitation in the quality and quantity of available alternative materials (IVG; Growing Media Europe, 2016). Thus, a reduction of peat in growing media could affect the competitiveness of the growing media and the horticultural industry. Since around half of the horticultural plants and flowers production is traded within the EU (calculation in value, based on Eurostat data for 2013-2017), a one-sided limitation of peat use in one country could lead to a distortion of competition and carbon leakage through imports of growing media and horticultural products. In order to avoid leakage effects between countries, the emissions of horticultural peat should be addressed both on national and European level. Although Germany is the leader of the growing media production in Europe, it is now, after Brexit, the only country in the EU aiming to reduce peat extraction and use for horticulture. The development of a European strategy on peat would imply involving other key countries in the growing media sector in Europe, in particular the Baltic States which produce most of the horticultural peat and the Netherlands who owns the second biggest growing media industry.

## CONCLUSION

European countries report emissions of 20.4 Mt $CO_2$-eq per year for peat extraction and use. In the case of peat used for energy purposes, the major producers Finland and Ireland intend to respectively halve and end the use by 2030. Due to limited trade of energy peat, these policies on the national level are expected not to create displacement effects. In the case of horticultural peat, the goal to phase-out or strongly reduce its use has been set by the UK,

Switzerland and Germany, and is also part of the Alpine Convention engaging the countries of the Alpine region and the EU. With the implementation of the LULUCF Regulation on Wetlands in 2026, emissions from horticultural peat are expected to gain relevance in the climate policy. Current national policies to reduce peat extraction or use for the horticultural sector address around half of the total emissions. However, they could induce displacement effects and carbon leakage through imports of peat, growing media and horticultural products. Therefore, the reduction of peat use in the horticultural sector should be addressed both on national and on a European level.

## AKNOWLEDGMENTS

The authors would like to thank Hannu Salo (IPS), Susanna Hönle (Thünen Institute) and Joseph Rocchio for their help.

## REFERENCES

1. BAFU (2020). Torfausstieg. Marktteilnehmer setzen gemeinsam Reduktion des Torfverbrauches um. https://www.bafu.admin.ch/torfausstieg. 16.3.2020.
2. BHB, BdB, VDG, and ZVG (2020). Branchenempfehlung zum Torfeinsatz.
3. BMEL (2019). Gartenbau - Torfverwendung reduzieren - Klima schützen. https://www.bmel.de/DE/themen/landwirtschaft/pflanzenbau/gartenbau/torf.html;jsessionid=2B5DFF02C09CB3A0DC935F470C45079A.intranet921. 29.03.2021.
4. BMU (2016). Klimaschutzplan 2050. Klimapolitische Grundsätze und Ziele der Bundesregierung (BMUB Berlin).
5. BMU (2019). Klimaschutzprogramm 2030 der Bundesregierung zur Umsetzung des Klimaschutzplans 2050. https://www.bundesregierung.de/resource/blob/975226/1679914/e01d6bd855f09bf05cf7498e06d0a3ff/2019-10-09-klima-massnahmen-data.pdf?download=1. 15.11.2019.
6. Bord na Móna (2015). Bord na Móna announces biggest change of land use in modern Irish history. https://www.bordnamona.ie/company/news/articles/bord-na-mona-announces-biggest-change-of-land-use-in-modern-irish-history/. 16.3.2020.
7. EC (2020). 2030 climate & energy framework - Climate Action. https://ec.europa.eu/clima/policies/strategies/2030_en. 16.3.2020.
8. Eggleston, S., Buendia, L., Miwa, K., Ngara, T., and Tanabe, K. (2006). 2006 IPCC guidelines for national greenhouse gas inventories (Hayama, Japan: Institute for Global Environmental Strategies).
9. EPE (2018). Energy Peat in Europe | Energy Peat Europe. https://www.energypeat.eu/single-post/2018/02/21/Energy-Peat-in-Europe. 03.06.2019.
10. (2018). Regulation (EU) 2018/841 of the European Parliament and of the Council of 30 May 2018 on the inclusion of greenhouse gas emissions and removals from land use, land use change and forestry in the 2030 climate and energy framework, and amending Regulation (EU) No 525/2013 and Decision No 529/2013/EU. European Union.
11. Finnish Government (2013). National Energy and Climate Strategy.
12. Finnish Government (2019). "Finland has an excellent opportunity to rebuild itself in line with the principles of sustainable development". 3.1 Carbon neutral Finland that protects biodiversity. https://valtioneuvosto.fi/en/article/-/asset_publisher/3-1-hiilineutraali-ja-luonnon-monimuotoisuuden-turvaava-suomi. 17.3.2020.
13. Finnish Government (2020). Minister of the Environment and Climate Change Krista Mikkonen: Budget brings welcome boost to climate work - Ympäristöministeriö. https://ym.fi/en/-/minister-of-the-environment-and-climate-change-krista-mikkonen-budget-brings-welcome-boost-to-climate-work. 19.03.2021.
14. GMI (2021). Irish Horticultural Peat Industry 2021. Opening Statement.
15. Growing Media Europe (2016). About Growing Media. https://www.growing-media.eu/single-post/2019/09/13/peat-between-now-and-2050-peat-is-part-of-the-answer. 19.03.2021.
16. Hiraishi, T., Krug, T., Tanabe, K., Srivastava, N., Baasansuren, J., Fukuda, M., and Troxler, T.G. (2014). 2013 supplement to the 2006 IPCC guidelines for national greenhouse gas inventories: Wetlands. IPCC, Switzerland.

17. Hirschler, O., and Osterburg, B. (2021). Peat market in Europe: evolution and climate relevance. Acta Hortic., 357-364. https://doi.org/10.17660/ActaHortic.2021.1305.47.
18. HM Government (1995). Minerals Planning Guidance 13: Guidelines for peat provision in England.
19. HM Government (2011). The natural choice. Securing the value of nature (London: TSO).
20. HM Government (2018). A Green Future: Our 25 Year Plan to Improve the Environment.
21. Irish government (2021). Ireland will now report greenhouse gas emissions and removals from managed wetlands (and including bogs) as part of progress towards EU greenhouse gas targets. https://www.gov.ie/en/press-release/005d3-ireland-will-now-report-greenhouse-gas-emissions-and-removals-from-managed-wetlands-and-including-bogs-as-part-of-progress-towards-eu-greenhouse-gas-targets/. 18.03.2021.
22. IVG. 10 Fragen zum Thema Torf. Beiträge zur aktuellen politischen Diskussion. https://www.ivg.org/fileadmin/downloads/Flyer/flyer-10fragentorf.pdf. 19.03.2021.
23. IVG (2020). Selbstverpflichtung der Substratindustrie zur Torfminderung (Düsseldorf).
24. Kettunen, M. (2016). Tax on the use of peat for energy in Finland.
25. Koalitionsvertrag (2018). Ein neuer Aufbruch für Europa. Eine neue Dynamik für Deutschland. Ein neuer Zusammenhalt für unser Land. Koalitionsvertrag zwischen CDU, CSU und SPD.
26. Marcu, A., Egenhofer, C., Roth, S., and Stoefs, W. (2013). Carbon leakage. An overview (Brussels: Centre for European Policy Studies).
27. Schmilewski, G. (2017). Growing media constituents used in the EU in 2013. Acta Horticulturae, 85-92. https://doi.org/10.17660/ActaHortic.2017.1168.12.
28. Statistics Finland (2021). Appendix table 1. Energy taxes, precautionary stock fees and oil pollution fees. http://www.stat.fi/til/ehi/2020/04/ehi_2020_04_2021-03-11_tau_001_en.html. 23.03.2021.
29. The Irish Times (2018). Government still providing millions in subsidises for fossil fuels – CSO. €115m was provided for peat extraction in 2016 while just €88m went to retrofitting. https://www.irishtimes.com/business/economy/government-still-providing-millions-in-subsidises-for-fossil-fuels-cso-1.3462554. 16.3.2020.
30. UK Biodiversity Group (1999). Lowland raised bog Habitat Action Plan. In Tranche 2 Action Plans. Terrestrial and Freshwater Species and Habitats.
31. UNFCCC (2021). Greenhouse Gas Inventory Data - Flexible queries Annex I countries. https://di.unfccc.int/flex_annex1. 18.03.2021.
32. UNFCCC, V. (2015). Adoption of the Paris agreement. I: Proposal by the President (Draft Decision), United Nations Office, Geneva (Switzerland).

ID 61667

# DOES NITROGEN DEPOSITION LEAD TO A WEAKER OR STRONGER CARBON SINK IN NUTRIENT-POOR PEATLANDS?

Tuula Larmola[1], Jani Antila[2], Liisa Maanavilja[1], Sari Juutinen[3], Jill L. Bubier[4], Elyn Humphreys[5], Heikki Kiheri[1, 6], Tim R. Moore[7], Mats Nilsson[8], Matthias Peichl[8]

[1] Natural Resources Institute Finland, Helsinki, Finland
[2] Department of Forest Sciences, University of Helsinki, Helsinki, Finland
[3] Faculty of Environmental and Biosciences, University of Helsinki, Helsinki, Finland
[4] Environmental Studies Department, Mount Holyoke College, South Hadley, MA, USA
[5] Department of Geography, Carleton University, Ottawa, ON, Canada
[6] University of Helsinki, Helsinki, Finland
[7] Department of Geography, McGill University, Montreal, QC, Canada
[8] Department of Forest Ecology and Management, Swedish University of Agricultural Sciences, Umeå, Sweden

*tuula.larmola@luke.fi*

## SUMMARY

We examined vegetation feedbacks of Nitrogen (N) deposition at two of the longest-running nutrient addition experiments on peatlands at Mer Bleue Bog, Canada, and Degerö Stormyr Fen, Sweden. The contrasting carbon (C) sink responses to long term N load may be explained by the type of vegetation and the water table depth Counterbalancing effects between nutrient load and increasing wetness may partly explain a larger bog C sink potential at intermediate N levels, whereas long term treatments did not alter wetness at fen but led to a weaker C sink.

***Keywords***: *bog, carbon dioxide, fen, photosynthesis, Sphagnum*

## INTRODUCTION

Atmospheric nitrogen (N) deposition is increasing owing to fossil fuel burning and agriculture. In nutrient limited peatland ecosystems, atmospheric nitrogen (N) deposition has been found to increase vascular plant growth, decrease Sphagnum growth, and alter decomposability of plant litter. These changes may affect net imbalance of production and decomposition and thus, carbon (C) accumulation in peatlands. We studied whether the vegetation feedbacks of N deposition lead to stronger or weaker C sink in nutrient-poor peatlands.

## MATERIALS AND METHODS

We investigated vegetation and ecosystem carbon dioxide ($CO_2$) exchange at two of the longest-running nutrient addition experiments on peatlands, Mer Bleue Bog, Ottawa, Canada (45°N, 75.5°W) and Degerö Stormyr poor fen, Vindeln, Sweden (64°11N, 19°13E) that have been fertilized with $NH_4NO_3$ (2-15 times ambient annual wet deposition) for 12-23 years. At Mer Bleue Bog, nutrients have been applied in soluble form on triplicate 3 x 3 m plots every three weeks from May to August (e.g., Larmola et al. 2013). At Degerö Stormyr fen, one third of seasonal $NH_4NO_3$ dose is applied on duplicate plots after snow melt in May, and the rest in four equal doses from June to September (e.g. Granberg et al. 2001). In these nutrient poor peatlands, the vegetation is dominated by ericaceous shrubs, Chamaedaphne calyculata, Rhododendron groenlandicum at Mer Bleue, Andromeda polifolia, Vaccinium oxycoccos at Degerö, Sphagnum mosses and sedge Eriophorum vaginatum. Gross photosynthesis, ecosystem respiration and net $CO_2$ exchange were measured weekly during June-August using chambers. To examine vegetation changes with increasing N influx, we determined the peak growing season aboveground biomass and coverage of vascular plants using the point intercept method.

## RESULTS

After 12-23 years of nutrient addition, the two sites revealed contrasting patterns: At Mer Bleue the highest nutrient additions were associated with up to 3-fold net $CO_2$ uptake potential than in the control, whereas N addition treatments at Degerö Stormyr with only 0.3 fold net $CO_2$ uptake potential, compared to the control. The stronger C sink potential at Mer Bleue was mainly due to up to 50% increase in the gross photosynthesis and a diminished C sink potential at Degerö Stormyr due to down to 40 % lower gross photosynthesis. Ecosystem respiration was unaltered or increased to a lesser extent under N load at both peatlands. Most of the N addition treatments showed an increase of up to 60% in total vascular aboveground plant abundance and a concomitant loss of Sphagnum (Fig. 1). At Mer Bleue along with the decrease in Sphagnum cover, the plots under highest N additions had become wetter, counterbalancing the impact of dry summer conditions in the study year whereas at Degerö Stormyr long term treatments did not alter wetness of the site.

## DISCUSSION AND CONCLUSION

The contrasting C sink responses to long term N load may be explained by the type of vegetation and the water table depth. Shrubs were strong competitors at the dry Mer Bleue Bog while sedges had gained in abundance under N load at the wetter Degerö Stormyr. Our study emphasizes the value of the long-term experiments in examining the ecosystem response of peatlands to N deposition, possible nonlinear responses, whether low dose manipulations follow those of high-dose, and whether the key feedback mechanisms to ecosystem C sink potential differ in two main types of peatlands.


## ACKNOWLEDGEMENTS

We acknowledge Mike Dalva, Kristiina Myller, Reija Heinonen, Julia Palorinne, Leszek Bledzki and Mike Treberg for their help in the field and laboratory. The study was funded by the Academy of Finland (projects 286731, 293365, 319262 to TL).


## REFERENCES


Granberg G, Sundh I, Svensson B H, Nilsson M. (2001) Effects of temperature, and nitrogen and sulfur deposition, on methane emission from a boreal mire *Ecology*, 82: 1982–1998.

Larmola T, Bubier JL, Kobyljanec C, Basiliko N, Juutinen S, Humphreys E, Preston M, Moore, T. (2013) Vegetation feedbacks of atmospheric nitrogen deposition lead to a weaker carbon sink in an ombrotrophic bog. *Global Change Biology*, 19: 3729-3739.

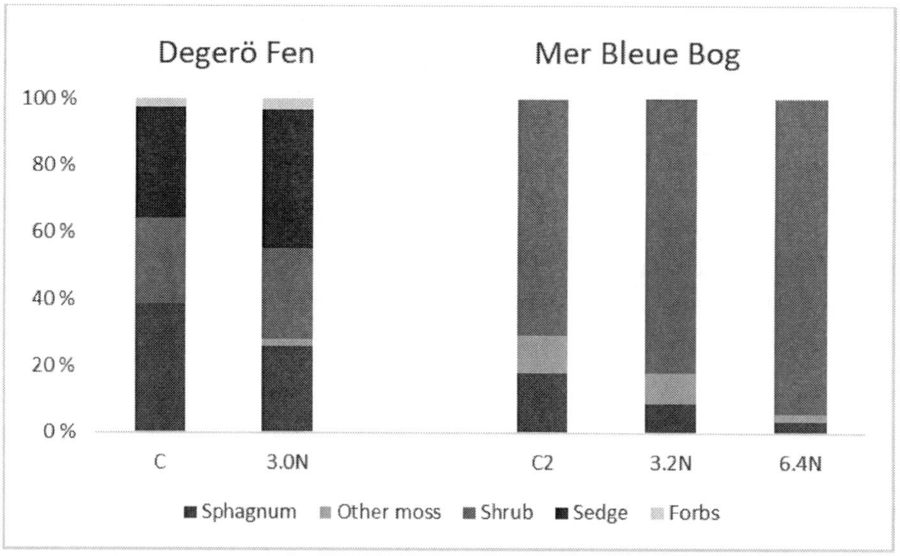


Figure 1. Vegetation structure after 12-23 years of experimental nitrogen addition at Degerö Stormyr and Mer Bleue peatlands. Values are proportions of point intercept hits to different plant groups under selected treatments (Degerö: C unfertilized control, 3.0N addition of 3.0 g N $m^{-2}$ $y^{-1}$, Mer Bleue C2 control, 3.2N and 6.4N additions of 3.2 and 6.4 g N $m^{-2}$ $y^{-1}$, respectively, number of observation per treatment =2-3).

ID 62038

# LONG-TERM WATER LEVEL DRAW-DOWN AFFECTS FUNCTIONAL PLANT TRAIT COMPOSITION OF NORTHERN PEATLANDS

*Anna M. Laine[1], Aino Korrensalo[2], Nicola Kokkonen[2], Eeva-Stiina Tuittila[2]

[1]Geological Survey of Finland, Finland and School of Forest Sciences, University of Eastern Finland, Finland
[2]School of Forest Sciences, University of Eastern Finland, Finland

*anna.laine-petajakangas@gtk.fi*

Understanding how plant communities respond to climate change is critical for forecasting the future peatland functions. Water level has been shown to have a stronger impact on peatland functioning than warming itself. Functional plant traits provide a link between species communities and ecosystem functions and therefore constitute a highly useful concept for forecasting changes in ecosystem functions.

In here we apply long term experiment in Lakkasuo, Finland to study how water level drawdown (WLD) impacts functional traits of vascular plants and mosses at different peatland types. WLD was initiated at year 2001 and vegetation change in a rich fen, poor fen and bog was followed until 2016. During year 2016 we measured several functional plant traits from the most common vascular plant and moss species. We analysed the level of intraspecific trait variability, community weighted mean (CWM) trait differences between sites and changes over the study period. We used structural equation modeling (SEM) to address how photosynthesis related traits were directly or indirectly via other traits affected by WLD.

We found equally high interspecific traits variation for Sphagnum mosses and vascular plants, while the intraspecific variation was higher in mosses. CWM traits varied between sites; WLD most affected and strengthened traits typical of dominating plant group. In rich fen WLD led to taller plants with higher specific leaf area. In bog, WLD further enhanced moss stands' ability to retain moist under drier conditions. SEM models showed that in fens WLD increased photosynthetic capacity, while in the bog the impact was opposite. Overall, the traits of vascular plant and Sphagnum communities formed a more densely connected network in the bog than in the fens.

It seems evident that fens and bogs adapt differently to WLD and this should be considered when predicting the effects of climate change on peatland carbon cycling.

ID 62243

# OLDEST KNOWN EXTANT PEATLANDS COMPRISE A LONG-TERM CARBON SINK FROM THE LAST GLACIAL TO THE HOLOCENE

*Monika Ruwaimana[1,2], Daniel G. Gavin[1], Gusti Z. Anshari[3]

[1] University of Oregon, USA
[2] Universitas Atma Jaya Yogyakarta, Indonesia
[3] Faculty of Forestry, Universitas Tanjungpura (UNTAN), West Kalimantan Province, Indonesia

*mruwaima@uoregon.edu*

Tropical peat soils are widespread in coastal and inland areas of Kalimantan (Indonesia). While coastal peats are attributed to sea level stabilization in the middle Holocene, a few studies have from inland areas indicate the earliest ages close to 40 ka. Our basal radiocarbon dates from a peat dome near Putussibau, Upper Kapuas Basin, dated to 45 to >50 ka; the oldest dates were from deepest depths cored (15 m) but were not basal. At 4 other locations in West Kalimantan, basal peat dates dated to approximately 4 ka at coastal sites and over 9 ka at inland sites. This indicates that the upper-Kapuas contains exceptionally old and deep peat accumulations that are currently under threat by land development. It also indicates that the glacial-maximum climate was not sufficiently dry to preclude peat formation and that these areas likely functioned as an important carbon sink during the last glacial period.

Our preliminary estimation suggest that the inland peat dome contains on average 4390 Mg C/ha, and a simple extrapolation shows the inland peat of the Upper Kapuas Basin contains 1.214 Gt C within an area of 2,461.32 km2. Further, the estimate of 1.214 Gt C suggests a share of 2.2% of the total estimate carbon stored in tropical peats in Indonesia, despite the area only covers 1.1% peat in Indonesia, suggest that this area contains double the amount of carbon stock compared to the typical tropical peat in Indonesia. Thus, not only have these deep inland peats provided a carbon sink that has persisted from the glacial to interglacial climates, they are one of the most carbon-dense ecosystems in the world.

ID 62329

# THE IMPACTS OF LONGTERM DRAINAGE AND AGRICULTURE ON THE CARBON DYNAMICS OF SHALLOW AND DEEP PEATS IN THE FENLAND REGION OF EAST ANGLIA, UK

Thomas Newman, Jörg Kaduk, Susan Page

Geography, Geology and the Environment, University of Leicester, Leicester, UK

*trn2@leicester.ac.uk*

**SUMMARY**

In the UK, many lowland fen peatlands have a long history of drainage and agricultural use resulting in peat subsidence through initial consolidation followed by long term oxidation. Today, 1922 $km^2$ (13.5%) of UK peatlands are classified as 'wasted' - i.e. the peatland has lost its peat-forming vegetation cover along with a significant depth of peat. As a result, these depleted peat soils are increasingly dominated by the underlying mineral layer.

The East Anglian Fens have a long history of drainage for agriculture, and today comprise some of the most productive arable farmland within the UK. Due to historical losses of up to 3.9 m of the original peat layer, large swathes of this remaining peatland are classified as wasted. Studies on C emissions from non-wasted agricultural peatlands within the Fens suggest emission factors of 5.2 to 8.3 t $CO_2$-C $ha^{-1}$ $yr^{-1}$, indicating their significance as a component of the UK's national greenhouse gas inventory. However, to date there has been no representative study on emissions from agriculturally managed wasted peats.

Using Eddy Covariance, the $CO_2$ emissions of two fen peatlands co-located in the East Anglian Fens and under intensive agricultural use were quantified. One site (EF-DA) was situated on deep peat (>1 m organic layer), whilst the other (EN-SP3) was on severely depleted peat (< 40 cm organic layer). An initial analysis of emissions from EN-SP3 over two cropping periods (Maize; May - Dec 2018, Celery; May 2019 - May 2020) indicated a net C balance of 438 and 540 g C $m^{-2}$ respectively.

We present a comparison of initial data from EN-SP3 with data collected from EF-DA over the last ~6 years. We highlight key differences between sites, enabling us to draw early insights into how C dynamics may differ between shallow and deep lowland agricultural peat soils.

***Keywords***: *wasted peat, agriculture,* $CO_2$, *fens, Eddy Covariance.*

## INTRODUCTION

Peatlands are found on every continent, storing ~30% of the Earth's terrestrial soil carbon (C) in just 3% of its land area (Gorham, 1991). In England there are 6799 $km^2$ of peatland (5% of land area) of which 958 $km^2$ are classed as fen peatlands that are fed by groundwater as opposed to precipitation alone (Natural England, 2010).

Over the last few centuries, nearly all of the UK's fen peatlands have been drained for agriculture. This has causes loss of peat depth, both through consolidation as the peat dries out and through oxidation (loss of peat as $CO_2$ via decomposition). Consequently large areas of once deep and shallow peats (depth > 0.4 m) are now being classified as 'wasted' (defined as a peatland which has lost its peat forming vegetation, undergone a significant loss of peat depth (typically to < 0.4 m), and has an increasing mineral content from the underlying mineral layer, (JNCC, 2011)). Today, the UK's wasted peatlands occupy 1922 $km^2$ (Natural England, 2010).

The East Anglian Fens are no exception to this trend, having been drained since the mid-19$^{th}$ century (Hutchinson, 1980). Once thought of as almost uninhabitable, today the Fens support some of the most productive arable farmland in the UK, producing large quantities of salad (such as lettuce) and vegetable crops. However, long term drainage has resulted in the loss of over 4.8 m of the original peat layer (Hutchinson, 1980) with a continued annual loss of 1-2 cm (Holman, 2009), primarily through oxidation. This has led to continued high emissions of C (as $CO_2$) to the atmosphere and lowering of the peat surface which is now close to or below sea level across the Fenland region. C flux measurements from non-wasted agricultural peatlands in the Fens suggest emissions of between 5.2 to 8.3 t $CO_2$-C $ha^{-1}$ $yr^{-1}$ (Evans et al., 2017) indicating their significance as a component of the UK's national greenhouse gas inventory. To date, there has been no representative study on emissions from agriculturally-managed wasted fen peats.

We present a first initial estimate of C emissions from a wasted peat under horticulture (EN-SP3) over the three years (2018/20) of measurements and compare with emissions from a co-located deep peat site (EF-DA) under similar management, and with other studies conducted in the East Anglian fen region. We highlight key differences between the years, allowing initial insights into how agricultural management practices impact C emissions. We compare emissions data across sites and studies, enabling us to draw early insights into how C dynamics may differ between wasted and deep agricultural peatlands. We aim to produce a more accurate estimate of C emissions from agriculturally managed fen peatlands in the UK and to provide insights into mitigation strategies to help reduce C emissions and preserve the peatland resource.

## MATERIALS AND METHODS

Using Eddy Covariance (EC) the $CO_2$ emissions of a wasted peatland (EN-SP3) under intensive agricultural use were quantified. EN-SP3 is situated on a wasted peatland (< 0.4 m organic layer atop fen clay) to the east of Ely, UK on a 67.7 ha field with homogeneous terrain. The field has been under intensive agriculture for the last few decades under the management of the G's Fresh group (G's Fresh, 2019) and is used to grow a mixture of arable and horticultural crops, primarily lettuce and celery, but also maize and wheat in recent years.

EC instrumentation consisted of a CSAT3, 3-D sonic anemometer (Campbell Scientific Ltd.,

Logan, UK USA) and LI-COR Biosciences $H_2O/CO_2$ IRGA (LI-7500A) (LI-COR inc., Lincoln, Nebraska, USA) with supporting biometeorological system. All raw 20Hz flux data were processed using Eddy Pro version 6.2.2 (LI-COR inc., Lincoln, Nebraska, USA) into 30-minute flux averaging periods. Post processing (QA and gap filling) was performed using Tovi version 2.7.2 (LI-COR inc., Lincoln, Nebraska, USA). Finally, processed data were exported into R version 3.3.1 (R Core Team, 2013) and Microsoft Excel version 2002 (Microsoft inc, Redmond, Washington, USA) for graphical representation.

$CO_2$ flux data were collected from EN-SP3 between May 2018 and June 2020. Measurements encompass two cropping periods; Maize (2018) and Celery (2019), with the first full year of data collected at a wasted peat site between 17th May 2019 – 17th May 2020. Flux data were compared to historical data from multiple years collected from the co-located EF-DA site under multiple crops (Cumming, 2018) and from other studies within the Fenland region (Evans et al., 2017; Taft, Cross, Edwards-Jones, Moorhouse, & Jones, 2017) and reported Emission Factors (EF) (IPCC, 2014) for temperate peatlands.

## RESULTS

EN-SP3 had a net C balance of 540 g C $m^{-2}$ $yr^{-1}$ between 17th May 2019 – 17th May 2020 that included a celery crop and 438 g C $m^{-2}$ over the 208 day measurement period (17th May 2018 – 11th Dec 2018) that included the maize crop once C gained and lost through field inputs and crop removals was accounted for (Fig. 1). Despite measurements from the field being for 157 days less, cumulative emission from the 208 day period were just 102 g C $m^{-2}$ less than the full year value. When comparative 208 day periods are compared for both 2018 and 2019 (17th May – 11th Dec), a cumulative flux of 261 g C $m^{-2}$ was seen on the field in 2019, 177 g C $m^{-2}$ less than 2018 indicating that the 2018 period had a much higher level of emission. This is attributed to the higher C uptake caused by the maize's higher sequestration rate being negated by the removal of biomass from the field at harvest in 2018 (Fig. 1) and the effect of a cover crop in 2019. In the period after harvesting, the maize crop showed a higer rate of emission compared to the celery crop.

The celery planting caused a large C input as celery seedlings are firstly grown indoors within peat plugs which are then transferred into the field. In preparation for celery planting, between the 16th of May and the 1st June, a Lacy Phacelia (*Phacelia tanacetifolia*) and Buckwheat (*Fagopyrum esculentum*) cover crop was grown. The field therefore briefly became a net C sink until the field was prepared for celery planting and the cover crop was disked into the field (except for a 48m strip in front of the flux tower) (Fig. 1).

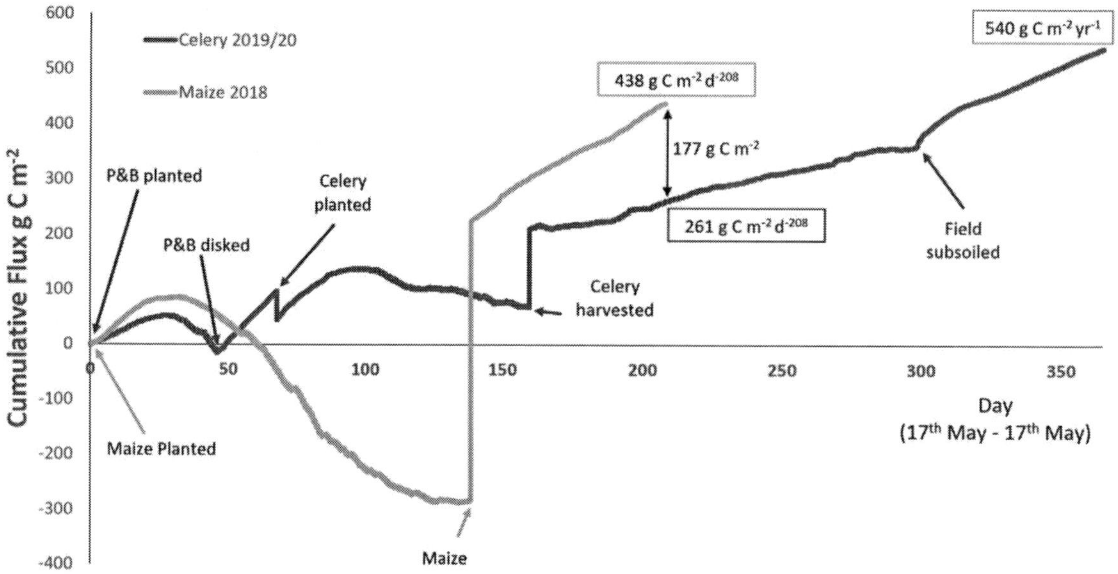


**Figure 1.** Cumulative C flux for EN-SP3 from data collected in 2018, 2019 & 2020 within two distinct periods: During the first period (17th May to 11th December 2018) a maize crop was grown. During the second period (17th May 19 to 17th May 2020) a phacelia and buckwheat cover crop was grown prior to a celery crop.

Daily C emissions were then compared to data recorded from 4 crops grown on EF-DA over 4 different years (Fig. 2) with 3 of those years (2a, 2b and 2c) having full yearly emissions budgets. The celery crop from EN-SP3 indicated lower C emissions than 3 of the 4 crops grown on deep peat at EF-DA with the exception being a lettuce crop that did not have a completed annual budget. The partial year data set which included the maize crop indicated a similar rate of emission. When compared to EF's derived from aggregate values of emissions from studies conducted on non-wasted peatlands, yearly emissions from EN-SP3 are at the lower end of estimated values (Fig 3, study 3a) whilst the partial year maize crop was found to have a comparable emission.

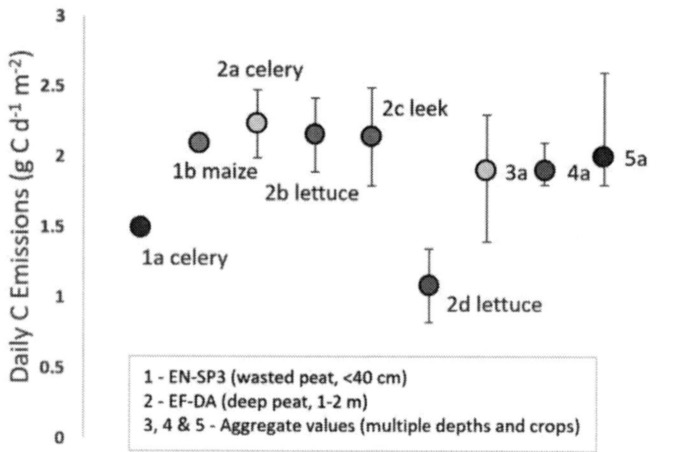


**Figure 2.** Daily field C emissions from multiple studies conducted on the East Anglian Fens. 1. EN-SP3, 2. EF-DA Cumming, 2018, 3. Taft et al., 2017, 4. Evans et al., 2017, and the current IPCC EF for agricultural peatlands 2017, 5. IPCC, 2013. Where possible, individual crops are indicated. Error bars indicate the error reported in each study for the values (2) or the minimum and maximum value reported (3, 4, 5).

## DISCUSSION

There were clear differences in the way that the crops grew, the amount of C sequestered over the growing period and the final cumulative values (Fig. 1), in contrast to other studies (Cumming, 2018; Norberg et al., 2016) which suggested that crop does not have an overall large impact on C emissions. The maize results show that a crop with the potential to sequester large amounts of C does not necessary lead to an overall reduction in net emissions from the field, especially when most of the biomass is removed. This is shown by the higher cumulative emissions from the maize cropping period despite much higher C sequestration.

There are several possible explanations for the differences observed in the cumulative C flux between the maize and celery crops: In part it can be explained by the additional C input from the peat plugs from celery planting, which added 52.1 g C $m^{-2}$. The cover crop planted before the celery crop likely also contributed, with the fastest rates of C sequestration observed over this period and the cover crop being ploughed into the soil rather than harvested, keeping the C on the field. In addition, the 48m strip of cover crop in front of the flux tower that was not ploughed in until March 3rd 2020 had an observable C drawdown effect that offset emissions from the rest of the flux tower footprint. It has been suggested that this can lead to a fertilization or 'priming' effect, with C not being 'stored' in already aerated soils, but instead becoming labile and leading to a period of increased emissions (Wen et al., 2019), however this effect is not well understood. In our study there was no observable long lasting increase in C emissions, other than immediately after the cover crop was ploughed on March 3rd 2020, suggesting a limited priming effect. Additionally, in part this increase can likely be attributed to the short term aeration of the organic layer after ploughing (Morrison et al., 2013).

Some of the difference in the final cumulative C flux can be explained by a difference in the rate of C emission in the short periods after harvesting, with the maize crop resulting in a greater C emission during this time period than the celery crop (Fig. 1). It is possible that this was due to the difference in the post-harvest conditions of the field; once the maize was harvested, the entire field was left bare (excluding maize stubble). In contrast, after the celery harvest, small patches of crop remained on the field and a dense cover of celery waste (~5cm deep) was left covering large parts of the field in addition to the 48m strip of cover crop. Both the cover crop strip and the remnants of the celery crop continued to grow until March 3rd 2020 when the field was ploughed, thereby offsetting some of the C emission from peat soil mineralization during this time.

Inter-annual variations in weather conditions between the corresponding 2018 and 2019 periods could also have affected crop emissions. 2018 was characterized by summer drought, particularly during June and July. This had an observable negative impact on the growth of the maize crop (pers. Comm. Rob Parker, farm manager), leaving it stunted. During this period soil conditions indicated substantial drying of the organic horizon. Despite the drought, the maize crop was not surface irrigated. In contrast, the celery crop was grown in a year with more average weather conditions and had consistent surface irrigation throughout the growing period. It has been shown that $CO_2$ emissions from peatlands are higher under lower water tables (Evans et al., 2017), with greater aeration of the peat layer leading to greater oxidative losses. The drier field conditions during summer 2018 could have led to a greater C emission than 2019. This suggests that field management practices may have a big impact, with consistent irrigation reducing heterotrophic emissions by maintaining a high peat moisture content.

Currently our results are not conclusive. While the full year budget indicates that there were lower emissions from the wasted peat (EN-SP3) site compared to full year budgets from the deep peat (EF-DA) site and studies of other deeper peat sites (Fig. 2), the 2018 partial year budget indicates similar emissions from the two sites. This variability in emissions is also reflected in the literature, with some studies suggesting lower oxidative losses from wasted peat owing to lower C availability (e.g. Norberg et al., 2016; Taft et al., 2017), while other studies have reported similar (Tiemeyer et al., 2016) or increasing emissions with decreasing peat depth or C content (Säurich et al., 2019). Further data collection over multiple years at EN-SP3 is required before we can draw precise conclusions on the scale of emissions from UK wasted lowland peatlands.

## CONCLUSION

Initial analyses of C emissions from the UK's first study on wasted fen peatland under intensive agriculture indicate that these peatlands are a significant C source. There was an observable difference between both the cumulative and daily C emissions over two crop cycles, with potentially higher net emissions from a maize crop compared to a celery crop. We identify several possible reasons for this, relating to inter-annual climatic variations and agricultural management practices such as cover cropping, irrigation and post-harvest field condition.

Future work includes the continued monitoring of emissions from the wasted peatland site to allow calculation of multiple yearly budgets. With this information we hope to develop improved emission factors for better accounting of C emissions from fen peatlands in the UK. We plan to analyze the differences between years and sites with different peat depths to better understand the drivers of C emissions form these systems, and to allow policy makers and farmers to make informed, future land management decisions to help preserve peatland C stocks into the near future.

## ACKNOWLEDGEMENTS

We would like to thank the University of Leicester for funding the PhD programme of Thomas Newman, G's Fresh Ltd for allowing access to their farms and Robert Parker, Martin Hammond and Emma Garfield for providing cropping, field and farm management information. Part of this work was funded by Defra (Department for Environment, Food and Rural Affairs) as part of project SP1218: *Managing agricultural systems on lowland peat for decreased greenhouse gas emission whilst maintaining agricultural productivity.*

# REFERENCES


Cumming, A. (2018). *Multi-annual carbon flux at an intensively cultivated lowland peatland in East Anglia, UK.* (Doctor of Philosophy). University of Leicester, University of Leicester.

Evans, C., Morrison, R., Burden, A., Williamson, J., Baird, A., Brown, E., . . . Dean, H. (2017). Final report on project SP1210: Lowland peatland systems in England and Wales–evaluating greenhouse gas fluxes and carbon balances.

G's Fresh. (2019). Grower Profiles. Retrieved from https://www.gs-growers.com/gs-growers/growers-profiles/

Gorham, E. (1991). Northern Peatlands Role in the Carbon Cycle and Probable Responses to Climatic Warming, Ecological Applications Volume 1, Issue 2. *Ecological Applications, 1*(2), 182-195.

Holman, I. (2009). An estimate of peat reserves and loss in the East Anglian Fens Commissioned by the RSPB. *Department of Natural Resources Cranfield University, Cranfield, Bedfordshire.*

Hutchinson, J. N. (1980). The Record of Peat Wastage in the East Anglian Fenlands at Holme Post, 1848-1978 A.D. *Journal of Ecology, 68*(1), 229-249. doi:10.2307/2259253

IPCC. (2014). 2013 supplement to the 2006 IPCC guidelines for national greenhouse gas inventories: Wetlands. On *IPCC, Switzerland.*

JNCC. (2011) Towards an assessment of the state of UK Peatlands. In.

Morrison, R., Cumming, A. M. J., Taft, H. E., Kaduk, J., Page, S. E., Jones, D. L., ... & Balzter, H. (2013). Carbon dioxide fluxes at an intensively cultivated temperate lowland peatland in the East Anglian Fens, UK. *Biogeosciences Discussions, 10*(3), 4193-4223.

Natural England. (2010). England's peatlands: carbon storage and greenhouse gases.

Norberg, L., Berglund, Ö., & Berglund, K. (2016). Seasonal CO 2 emission under different cropping systems on Histosols in southern Sweden. *Geoderma Regional, 7*(3), 338-345.

R Core Team. (2013). R: A language and environment for statistical computing. In. R Foundation for Statistical Computing, Vienna, Australia. URL: http://www.R-project.org/.

Säurich, A., Tiemeyer, B., Dettmann, U., & Don, A. (2019). How do sand addition, soil moisture and nutrient status influence greenhouse gas fluxes from drained organic soils? *Soil Biology and Biochemistry, 135*, 71-84. doi:https://doi.org/10.1016/j.soilbio.2019.04.013

Taft, H. E., Cross, P. A., Edwards-Jones, G., Moorhouse, E. R., & Jones, D. L. (2017). Greenhouse gas emissions from intensively managed peat soils in an arable production system. *Agriculture, Ecosystems & Environment, 237*(Supplement C), 162-172. doi:https://doi.org/10.1016/j.agee.2016.11.015

Tiemeyer, B., Albiac Borraz, E., Augustin, J., Bechtold, M., Beetz, S., Beyer, C., . . . Fiedler, S. (2016). High emissions of greenhouse gases from grasslands on peat and other organic soils. *Global change biology, 22*(12), 4134-4149.

Wen, Y., Zang, H., Freeman, B., Ma, Q., Chadwick, D. R., & Jones, D. L. (2019). Rye cover crop incorporation and high watertable mitigate greenhouse gas emissions in cultivated peatland. *Land Degradation & Development, 30*(16), 1928-1938.

ID 62186

# PHYSIOLOGICAL STRESS IN CALCAREOUS FEN MOSSES FOLLOWING AN EXPERIMENTAL CHANGE IN WINTER CLIMATE

*Martin Küttim[1], Anna M. Laine[2], Liisa Küttim[1], Mati Ilomets[1], Bjorn J.M. Robroek[3]

[1]Tallinn University, Institute of Ecology, Estonia
[2]Finnish Geological Survey, Finland
[3]Radboud University, Institute for Water and Wetland Research, The Netherlands

*kyttim@tlu.ee*

Calcareous spring fens are known as one of the rarest and most threatened type of peatlands worldwide, where moss layer has an essential role. The majority of them are located at high latitudes, where the rate of climate change is above the global average. The changes are especially rapid in winter, and can be most visibly seen as decreased snow cover. This can have a negative effect on plant performance. To study the effect of declining snowpack on two moss species that dominate in calcareous spring fens – *Campylium stellatum* and *Scorpidium scorpioides* – we conducted a field experiment in Paraspõllu fen, N-Estonia. While snow was removed throughout the winter from some of the experimental plots, photosystem II efficiency (Fv/Fm) and chlorophyll content of these mosses was periodically measured to estimate their physiological stress. In both species, Fv/Fm was the lowest in spring, indicating physiological stress. Chlorophyll contents were the highest in the autumn. Snow removal increased physiological stress in both species – an effect that cascaded to the growing season. The effect of the treatment appeared to be stronger in case of *C. stellatum*. Therefore, the overall impact of winter climate change is negative on calcareous spring fens and their moss layer. The changes in climate are thus likely to result in alterations of the community structure and in the carbon economics of these ecosystems.

# ID 62333

# HOLOCENE DEVELOPMENT, RADIATIVE FORCING AND CHANGES IN CARBON ACCUMULATION AND VEGETATION IN A SUBARCTIC FEN IN FINLAND

*S. R. Piilo[1,2], L. Heiskanen[3], J-P. Tuovinen[3], M. Aurela[3], S. Juutinen[1,2], J. Turunen, H. Marttila[4], M. Saari[4], A. Korhola[1,2], M. M. Väliranta[1,2]

[1]ECRU, Ecosystems and Environment Research Programme, Department of Environmental Sciences, University of Helsinki, Finland
[2]Helsinki Institute of Sustainability Science (HELSUS), Finland
[3]Finnish Meteorological Institute, Finland
[4]University of Oulu, Water, energy and Environmental Engineering Research Unit, Finland

*sanna.piilo@helsinki.fi*

Northern peatlands, globally important carbon sinks, mainly formed during the Holocene (the last ca. 11 700 years). In different stages of peatland development and succession, the aggregate effect of carbon fluxes (carbon dioxide ($CO_2$) and methane ($CH_4$)) and thus radiative forcing (RF) often changes from climate warming to cooling. However, the timing of these shifts varies. We investigated the lateral expansion of a subarctic fen in Finland and modelled the RF over the Holocene by using plant macrofossil data and carbon flux measurements.

Our results show that the peatland initiated at ca. 9500 cal. Before Present (BP) and the lateral expansion was greatest from ca. 9000 to ca. 7000 cal. BP. However, peat accumulation rates greatly differ in different parts of the peatland. The current surface microtopography with flarks and strings formed only after ca. 1000 years ago.

We tested two RF scenarios, which both indicate that for the first millennium the fen had a minor effect on climate. Based on the first scenario, the fen had a climate warming impact from ca. 9000 to ca. 4000 cal. BP after which it changed to a cooling impact. The second scenario shows a consistent cooling impact with an exception of warming impact lasting for ca. 500 years at ca. 6000 cal. BP. Both scenarios suggest a total net cooling effect for the peatland development, mainly driven by carbon uptake, with the greatest cooling effect ca. 1000 years ago after which the surface microtopography started to form. Overall, the study suggests that the contribution of the fen to climate, in terms of RF, has followed a typical pathway of northern fen ecosystems and in this case, with $CO_2$ uptake controlling the long term RF over CH4 emissions.

# ID 62432

# SIMULATING CLIMATE CHANGE IN NORTHERN PEATLANDS: INITIAL RESULTS OF THE SPRUCE EXPERIMENT

*Randy Kolka[1], Paul Hanson[2]

[1]USDA Forest Service Northern Research Station, United States
[2]Oak Ridge National Laboratory, United States

*randall.k.kolka@usda.gov*

The Spruce and Peatland Responses Under Changing Environments experiment, or SPRUCE, is an ambitious ecosystem-level experiment that is testing the response of high-carbon northern peatland ecosystems to increased temperatures and elevated carbon dioxide. The experiment is being conducted in a black spruce peatland in northern Minnesota, USA, at the USDA Forest Service's Marcell Experimental Forest (MEF). SPRUCE is supported by the US Department of Energy and is a collaboration between Oak Ridge National Lab, the USDA Forest Service and numerous other scientists from across the globe. Northern peatlands are an ecosystem considered especially vulnerable to climate change, and anticipated to be near their tipping point with respect to their carbon balance, especially at the southern margin of their range at MEF. Responses to warming and interactions with increased atmospheric $CO_2$ concentration are anticipated to have important feedbacks on the atmosphere and climate. The manipulation is evaluating the response of the existing communities to a range of warming levels from ambient to +9°C, with and without elevated $CO_2$, provided via large, open-top chambers. Belowground heating began in 2014, aboveground heating in 2015, and elevated $CO_2$ treatments commenced in June 2016. We anticipate running the experiment for 10 years. I will give an overview of SPRUCE and some of the initial results including including early treatment effects on the carbon balance and plant responses.

# ID 62455

# GREENHOUSE GAS PRODUCTION AND EMISSIONS FROM THE CENTRAL CONGO BASIN PEATLAND COMPLEX

*Nicholas T. Girkin[1], Emmanuel Mampouya[2], Mackline Mbemba[2], Yannick E. Bocko[2], Dafydd Crabtree[3], Greta C. Dargie[3], Suspense A. Ifo[2], Christopher H. Vane[4], Sofie Sjögersten[5], Simon L. Lewis[3]

[1]Cranfield University, UK; University of Nottingham, United Kingdom
[2]Marien Ngoube University, Republic of Congo
[3]University of Leeds, UK
[4]British Geological Survey, United Kingdom
[5]University of Nottingham, United Kingdom

*nicholas.girkin@gmail.com*

The Cuvette Centrale peatland complex (145,500 $km^2$) spans the Republic of Congo and Democratic Republic of Congo, storing approximately 30.6 Gt C. However, despite significant carbon storage, its contribution to regional greenhouse gas (GHG) budgets remains uncertain. We conducted the first on-the-ground measurement campaign to assess peat surface and plant stem emissions of carbon dioxide ($CO_2$), methane ($CH_4$) and nitrous oxide ($N_2O$), and understand their relative contributions to ecosystem scale fluxes. During sampling, measured peat surface GHG fluxes were 615 – 755 mg $CO_2$ m-2 hr-1, -0.02 – 0.63 mg $CH_4$ $m^{-2}$ $hr^{-1}$, and 0.03 – 0.04 mg $N_2O$ $m^{-2}$ $hr^{-1}$, broadly comparable to other tropical peatland sites, although tree stem fluxes were lower. An ex situ incubation experiment across a range of depths (0 – 1.7 m) indicated that potential GHG production was low under both aerobic and anoxic conditions. We used Rock-Eval pyrolysis to characterise organic matter properties throughout the peat profile, with results indicating a highly decomposed peat substrate limiting potential GHG production. These results are supported by recent top-down estimates, which indicate that, despite its significant size, the peatland is not a major contributor to regional $CH_4$ budgets. Ongoing studies of temporal and spatial variation of GHG production and emissions will be key to clarifying the contribution of the peatland complex to regional budgets. Taken together, our results show that trees are an important pathway for GHG transport in the peatland, but that rates of subsurface GHG production are low and limit subsequent emissions, most likely due to highly recalcitrant peat carbon. Disturbance processes that alter the hydrology or species composition in the region, alongside the impacts of climate change, have the potential to significantly increase emissions, meaning that protection of the Cuvette Centrale peatlands remains a priority.

ID 62623

# REWETTING OFFERS FAST CLIMATE BENEFITS FOR TROPICAL AND AGRICULTURAL PEATLANDS BUT NOT FOR FORESTRY-DRAINED PEATLANDS

*Paavo Ojanen, Kari Minkkinen

University of Helsinki, Finland

*paavo.ojanen@helsinki.fi*

Peat soils drained for agriculture and forestry are big sources of carbon dioxide and nitrous oxide. Rewetting effectively reduces these emissions. But rewetting also causes emissions as it increases methane emissions from soil and, on forestry-drained peatlands, decreases carbon storage of trees.

To inspect the effect of peatland rewetting on climate, we built radiative forcing scenarios for tropical peat soils, temperate and boreal agricultural peat soils and temperate and boreal forestry-drained peat soils. Also, the effect of tree and wood product carbon storage at boreal forestry-drained peatlands was estimated as a case study for Finland.

Rewetting of tropical peat soils resulted in immediate cooling. In temperate and boreal agricultural peat soils, the warming effect of methane emission offset a major part of the cooling for the first decades after rewetting. In temperate and boreal forestry-drained peat soils, the effect of rewetting was mostly warming for the first decades. In addition, taking into account the effects on trees and wood products further delayed the onset of the cooling effect for decades.

Global rewetting resulted in increasing climate cooling, reaching −70 mW ($m^2$ Earth)$^{-1}$ in 100 years. Tropical peat soils (9.6 million ha) accounted for ca. two thirds and temperate and boreal agricultural peat soils (13.0 million ha) one third of the cooling. Forestry-drained peat soils (10.6 million ha) had a negligible effect.

We conclude that rewetting of peatlands is beneficial and important for mitigating climate change, but concerning forestry-drained peatlands, the best option could be to abandon the tree stands instead.

# ID 62710

# $CO_2$ EXCHANGE AND PLANT ABOVE-GROUND BIOMASS OF RESTORED FORESTRY DRAINED AND MILLED PEATLANDS, AND PRISTINE MIRES

*Anna-Helena Purre[1], Mati Ilomets[2]

[1] School of Natural Sciences and Health, Tallinn University, Tallinn, Estonia
[2] Institute of Ecology, Tallinn University, Tallinn, Estonia

*annahele@tlu.ee*

## SUMMARY

In Northern Hemisphere anthropogenic influences like drainage and peat milling are affecting $CO_2$ emissions from large peatland areas. To mitigate the negative climate impact of such activities, activities are carried out in increasing rate, which intend to restore biodiversity and carbon accumulation on such areas so that these sites again become similar to natural peatlands. We aimed at relating growing season $CO_2$ fluxes with plant functional type biomass on restored forestry-drained and milled peatlands and compare those with similar pristine peatlands.
$CO_2$ fluxes were measured using manual chambers in growing seasons of 2015 and/or 2016 from six pristine mires (mainly bogs), four restored milled peatlands, and four rewetted forestry-drained peatlands in Estonia and in Finland. Once during the measurement period, plant above-ground biomass was also measured from each of the sites.

Pristine mires were in average $CO_2$ sinks throughout the growing seasons of 2015 (dry) and 2016 (wet). Rewetted forestry-drained peatlands and restored milled peatlands were $CO_2$ emitters during the dry year, and restored milled peatlands were $CO_2$ binders during the wet growing season of 2016. $CO_2$ fluxes from rewetted forestry-drained peatlands were not measured in 2016. Plant composition develops similar to pristine mires with time since restoration. Relationships between $CO_2$ fluxes and plant functional types biomass varied between the management types (rewetted forestry-drained, restored milled peatland, pristine mire).

Restoration of forestry-drained and milled peatlands supports the development of peatland specific vegetation and reduces their $CO_2$ emissions. This is dependent of weather conditions during the growing season, and amount of plant biomass and its composition. $CO_2$ fluxes on pristine mires are less dependent on interannual differences in weather conditions.

***Keywords***: *peatland restoration, forestry-drained peatlands, milled peatlands, carbon dioxide, plant functional types*

## INTRODUCTION

Peatlands in pristine state play an important role in global carbon cycling. In Estonia total peatland area is about 915 000 ha (Paal and Leibak 2011) from which peatland ecosystems on large areas have been altered during the past centuries. In Estonia, 158 000 ha of peatlands have been drained for forestry (Pikk 1997) and about 30 000 ha of mires are directly affected by current or past peat extraction (Ilomets 2017). Such anthropogenic impacts alter the environmental conditions; therefore plant communities and $CO_2$ exchange on these areas. Drainage for forestry supports the growth of trees, shrubs and forest mosses while having negative impact on *Sphagnum*, while on peat excavation sites top spit and upper layers of peat have been removed in addition to heavy drainage. Self-recovery of these sites is limited, especially in case of abandoned milled peatlands.

In longer time-scale pristine peatlands are considered to be carbon sinks, while drainage generally turn those areas to carbon sources. To restore the carbon sink function on raising the water table near the surface is beneficial. This creates suitable conditions for succession of mire plant communities and therefore lays foundation for carbon sequestration as in pristine peatlands. We aimed at relating growing season $CO_2$ fluxes with plant functional type biomass on restored forestry-drained and milled peatlands and compare those with similar pristine peatlands.

## MATERIALS AND METHODS

Study was conducted on eight peatland sites restored after anthropogenic disturbances such as forestry drainage or peat milling and on locating nearby six pristine peatland sites (Table 1). All sites were located in Estonia and Finland in the northern boreal, boreo-nemoral and southern boreal zones. Forestry-drained sites were rewetted and trees were removed from some of the sites. Former milled peatlands were restored by moss-layer-transfer technique (Rochefort et al. 2003) or rewetting (Smolders et al. 2003). Rewetting was done by filling-in the ditches or closing them with dams.

**Table 1. Locations, restoration methods and years of the study sites. Abbreviations are following: MP- milled peatlands, FD- forestry-drained, MLTT- moss-layer-transfer technique (Rochefort et al. 2003), REW – rewetting, PRI- pristine state.**

| Sites | State | | Year of restoration | Measurement year | Coordinates |
|---|---|---|---|---|---|
| | Pristine | Restored | | | |
| Viru | - | MP (MLTT) | 2008 | 2015 and 2016 | 59° 28'N, 25°39'E |
| Seli | - | MP (MLTT) | 2005/2006 | 2015 and 2016 | 59° 19'N, 25°0'E |
| Hara | Raised bog | MP (REW) | 2012 | REW 2015 and 2016, PRI 2016 | 59° 33'N, 25°36'E |
| Kõrsa | Raised bog | MP (REW) | 1980 | 2016 | 58°24' N, 24°41' E |
| Viljandi | Raised bog | FD (REW) | 2013 | 2015 | 58° 28'N, 25°12'E |
| Tammela | Raised bog | FD (REW) | 2005 | 2015 | 60° 38'N, 23°58'E |
| Sipoo | Raised bog | FD (REW) | 2006 - 2012 | 2015 | 60° 19'N, 25°20'E |
| Sodankylä | Aapa mire | FD (REW) | 2006 | 2015 | REW 67° 25'N, 26°30'E/ PRI 67° 22'N, 26°39'E |

In each of the site and state combination four to twelve $CO_2$ measurement collars were inserted so that heterogeneity of vegetation composition was taken into account. NEE measurements were carried out during the growing seasons of 2015 and 2016 at least once a month.

For $CO_2$ exchange measurements, we used transparent chamber (60×60×30 cm) equipped with a cooling system, a ventilator, and an infrared gas analyzer (EGM-4, PP System (USA) or Li-6400, Li-Cor (USA)). NEE measurements were done in full light and using one to two shades to develop light-response curves. For measuring ecosystem respiration ($R_{eco}$) chamber was covered with the opaque hood. Several variables were monitored and recorded during the $CO_2$ flux measurements: PAR inside the chamber, temperature inside and outside the chamber, peat temperatures at 5 and 15 cm depths, water table depth and leaf area of vascular plants ($LAI_{vasc}$).

$CO_2$ flux rates were calculated based on a linear change in $CO_2$ concentration in time. Gross photosynthesis ($P_g$) was calculated by adding $R_{eco}$ to NEE. We use sign convention so $P_g$ and $R_{eco}$ are always positive and thus positive NEE values indicate $CO_2$ net uptake to the ecosystem from the atmosphere.

Separate $P_g$ and $R_{eco}$ models were parameterized for each measurement plot in order to reconstruct hourly $CO_2$ fluxes for the growing season (May–September 2015 and 2016). The gross photosynthesis ($P_g$; mg $CO_2$ $m^{-2}$ $h^{-1}$) model is a non-linear model that uses the saturating response to PAR, which also takes into account the $LAI_{vasc}$ during the growing season. The respiration model consists of an exponential response of ecosystem respiration ($R_{eco}$; mg CO2 $m^{-2}$ $h^{-1}$) to the temperature inside the chamber.

Statistical significances of variable average values between the management types was tested with Kruskal-Wallis test and Mann-Whitney pairwise comparison with Bonferroni corrections. For correlations, Spearman correlation coefficient was used. Average values in tables, figures and text are brought with standard errors.

**RESULTS**

Vegetation in restored forestry-drained peatlands was more similar to pristine peatlands than in milled peatlands. Vascular plant and moss biomass were similar in pristine and restored-forestry drained peatlands (from 6.0 ± 0.6 g $dm^{-2}$ up to 7.4 ± 0.7 g $dm^{-2}$), while being significantly ($Z \geq -2.39$; $p < 0.05$) lower in milled peatlands (bryophytes 5.1 ± 0.9 g $dm^{-2}$, vascular plants 2.5 ± 0.4 g $dm^{-2}$; Figure 1a). In restored forestry-drained sites hummock-hollow microtopography was present. Restored milled peatlands had larger between-site and spatial variations in vegetation, but hummocks and hollows had developed only in the Kõrsa, the oldest restored milled peatland site.

Reconstructed growing season $CO_2$ fluxes differed statistically significantly between pristine and restored milled peatlands. Restored forestry-drained peatlands had similar $P_g$ and $R_{eco}$ to pristine peatlands, although somewhat lower NEE (Figure 1b). Restored milled peatlands had large variations between the sites, measurement plots and also measurement years. $R_{eco}$ and $P_g$ were higher in hummocks than in hollows, although in all studied management types, those differences were statistically insignificant.

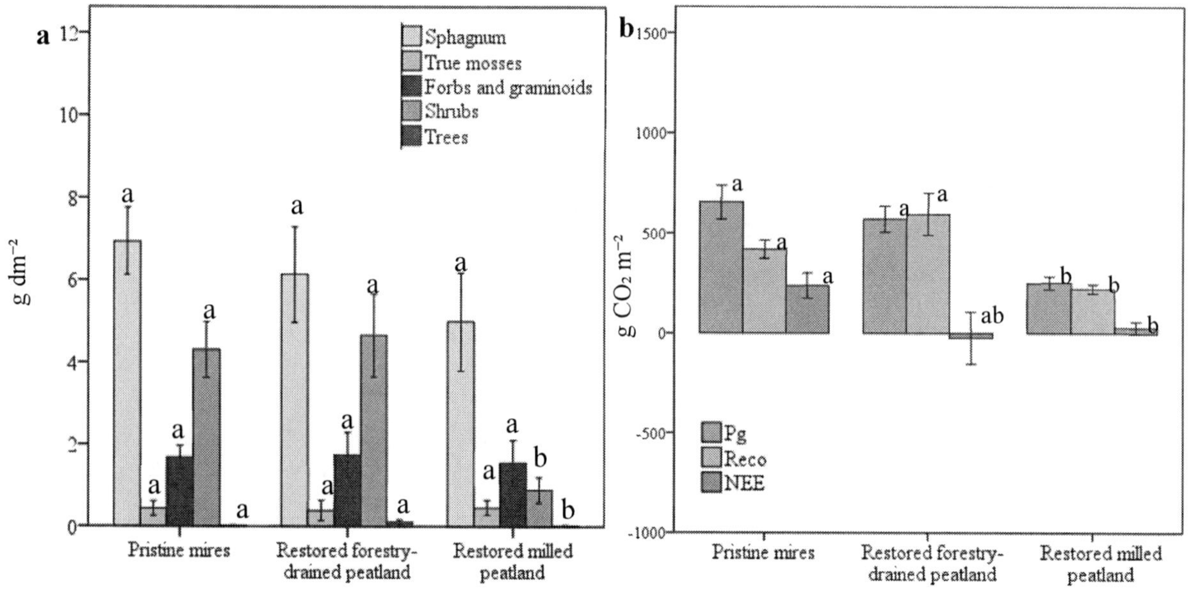


**Figure 1. Plant functional type (PFT) biomass (a) and growing season $CO_2$ flux components (b) in studied peatlands with different management. Average values are brought out with standard error. Different letters indicate the presence of statistically significant difference in $CO_2$ fluxes or PFT biomass between the management types.**

Variations in $CO_2$ fluxes were mainly explained by differences in *Sphagnum*, bryophyte, and forb and graminoid biomass, and number of PFTs present in the measurement collar. Correlations between growing season $CO_2$ fluxes and vegetation variables varied between management types (Figure 2). In pristine peatlands, measurement plots with higher bryophyte and *Sphagnum* biomass were lower $CO_2$ sinks during the growing season while NEE was positively connected with true moss, and forb and graminoid biomass. In restored milled peatlands, higher NEE was measured on plots with higher vascular plant, *Sphagnum*, and forb and graminoid biomass. In restored forestry-drained peatlands, NEE was only significantly and negatively related with tree biomass.

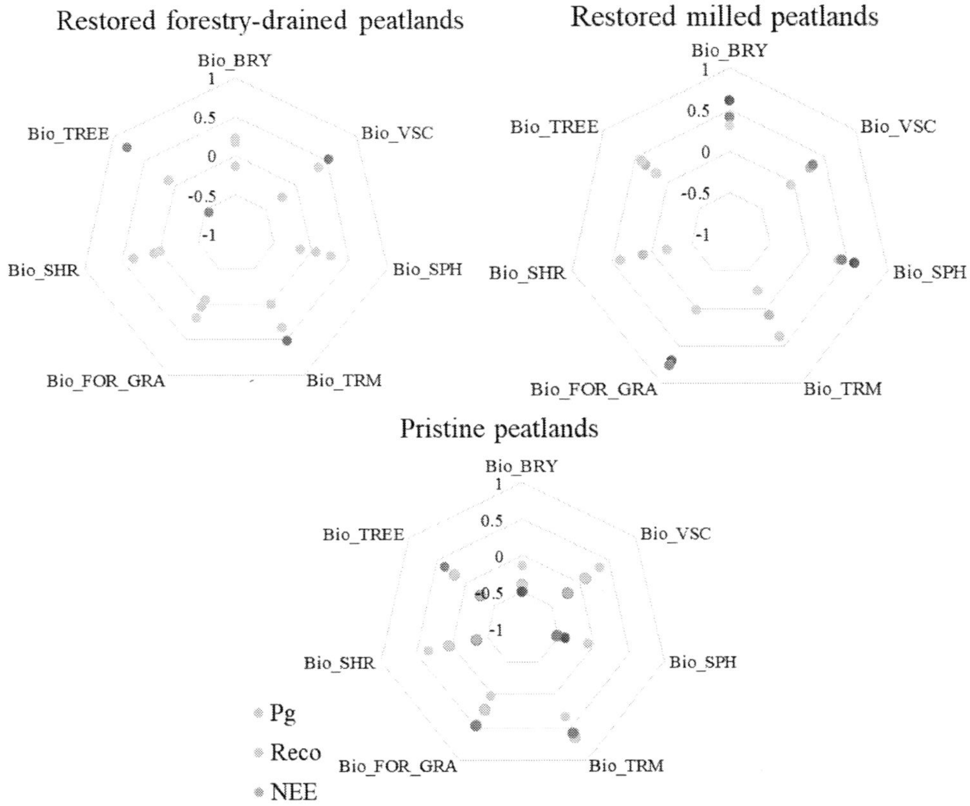


Figure 2. Correlations between plant functional type biomasses and $CO_2$ flux components in peatlands with different management. Stronger colors indicate statistically significant correlation between the variables. Bio-biomass, BRY- bryophytes, VSC-vascular plats, SPH- *Sphagnum*, TRM- true mosses, FOR_GRA- forbs and graminoids, SHR- shrubs, TREE-trees.

## DISCUSSION

Vegetation and $CO_2$ dynamics tends to develop faster in direction of pristine peatlands on restored forestry-drained sites than in restored milled peatlands. This is reported before on restored milled peatlands (Soini et al. 2010) and restored forestry-drained peatlands (Kareksela et al. 2015; Haapalehto et al. 2017). In restored milled peatlands vegetation development starts from bare peat surfaces whereas vegetation is present on forestry-drained peatlands. Restored milled peatlands had significantly lower biomass of shrubs trees than pristine and restored forestry-drained peatlands. Those plant functional types take more time to establish themselves on restored milled peatlands, especially if rewetting is done (Soini et al. 2010; González et al. 2013).

$CO_2$ dynamics in restored forestry-drained sites in current study did not differ statistically significantly from pristine reference sites, while having lower NEE due to higher respiration. Our results were strongly impacted by dry summer of 2015, which increased the respiration of the sites (Purre et al. 2019a), especially as restored forestry-drained peatlands were only measured in that year. It could be expected, that $CO_2$ sink function would be larger on those sites, if measurements would have been done in wetter conditions. Komulainen et al. (1999), Kareksela et al. (2015), and Laine et al. (2019) found that carbon accumulation on rewetted forestry-drained peatlands approach the pristine peatlands relatively fast within about five years, which is supported by part of this study (Purre et al. 2019b). Restored milled peatlands had significantly lower NEE, $P_g$ and $R_{eco}$ than pristine sites, mainly related with lower vegetation cover there. Restored milled peatlands in the study showed large differences in growing season $CO_2$ exchange between the measurement years (Purre et al. 2019b).

Correlations between the $CO_2$ fluxes and PFT biomass differed between the studied management types. Those correlations could be partly affected also by the fact, that in this study only growing season fluxes were measured. Korrensalo et al. (2017) reported that vascular plants are important in photosynthesis during the growing season, but bryophytes have active growth also outside that period (Küttim et al. 2020). Our results support that development of *Sphagnum* cover is important for $CO_2$ accumulation on restored milled peatlands, whereas restored forestry-drained sites already had similar high *Sphagnum* cover and therefore it was insignificant predictor.

## CONCLUSION

Our results provide into scarce dataset of peatland related $CO_2$ flux measurements in Baltic countries, especially as in Estonia transparent chamber measurements had not been done before in undisturbed raised bogs and restored forestry-drained sites. We found that restored forestry-drained peatlands move in the direction of pristine sites faster than restored milled peatlands. While pristine sites were $CO_2$ sinks during the growing seasons, restored sites were either small sinks or sources. The correlations between PFT abundances and $CO_2$ fluxes differed between the management types, even if the sites were structurally recovered as in restored forestry-drained sites in this paper, emphasizing the need to study peatlands with different management.

## ACKNOWLEDGEMENTS

We thank Timo Penttilä, Paavo Ojanen, Kari Minkkinen, Mika Aurela and Annalea Lohila for their help and support in measurements and analysis concerning rewetted forestry-drained peatlands and pristine sites in Finland, and Stephanie Gerin and Irene Zamblera for their important help in collecting data from the sites in Sodankylä. We also thank Aleksandra Krijer for help in biomass measurements in Estonian milled peatlands. Financial support has been provided by the Tallinn University Centre of Excellence of Natural Sciences and Sustainable Development, and Doctoral School of Earth Sciences and Ecology.

## REFERENCES


1. González E, Henstra S.W, Rochefort L, Bradfield G.E, Poulin M. (2013) Is rewetting enough to recover Sphagnum and associated peat-accumulating species in traditionally exploited bogs? *Wetlands Ecology and Management*; 22,: 49–62
2. Haapalehto T.O, Juutinen R, Kareksela S, Kuitunen M, Tahvanainen T, Vuori H, Kotiaho S.J. (2017) Recovery of plant communities after ecological restoration of forestry- drained peatlands. *Ecology and Evolution*; 7: 7848–7858
3. Ilomets M. (2017) Estonia. In: *Mires and peatlands of Europe: Status, distribution and conservation* (Joosten, H., Tanneberger, F., & Moen, A., (eds.)), pp. 360–371, E. Schweizerbart'sche Verlagsbuchhandlung, Stuttgart, Germany.
4. Karekesela S, Haapalehto T, Juutinen R, Matilainen R, Tahvanainen T, Kotiaho J.S. (2015) Fighting carbon loss of degraded peatlands by jump-starting ecosystem functioning with ecological restoration. *Science of the Total Environment*; 537: 268–276
5. Korrensalo A, Alekseychik P, Hájek T, Rinne J, Vesala T, Mehtätalo L, Mammarella I, Tuittila E-S. (2017) Species-specific temporal variation in photosynthesis as a moderator of peatland carbon sequestration. *Biogeosciences*; 14, 257–269
6. Küttim M, Küttim L, Ilomets M, Laine A.M. (2020) Controls of *Sphagnum* growth and the role of winter. *Ecological Research*; 35: 219–234
7. Laine A.M, Mehtätalo L, Tolvanen A, Frolking S, Tuittila E-S. (2019) Impacts of drainage, restoration and warming on boreal wetland greenhouse gas fluxes. *Science of the Total Environment*; 647:169–181
8. Paal J, Leibak E. (2011) *Estonian mires: Inventory of habitats.* Eestimaa Looduse Fond, Tartu.
9. Pikk J. (1997) Metsaparanduse tulemused turvasmuldadel. *Akadeemilise Metsaseltsi Toimetised*; 9: 12–16
10. Purre A-H, Pajula R, Ilomets M. (2019a) Carbon dioxide sink function in restored milled peatlands – the significance of weather and vegetation. *Geoderma*; 346: 30–42
11. Purre A-H, Penttilä T, Ojanen P, Minkkinen K, Aurela M, Lohila A, Ilomets M. (2019b) Carbon dioxide fluxes and phytomass structure on rewetted and pristine peatlands in Finland and Estonia. *Boreal Environment Research*; 24: 243–261
12. Rochefort L, Quinty F, Campeau S, Johnson K. Malterer T. (2003) North American approach to the restoration of Sphagnum dominated peatlands. *Wetlands Ecology and Management*; 11: 3–20
13. Smolders A.J.P, Tomassen H.B.M, Van Mullekom M, Lamers L.P.M, Roelofs J.G.M. (2003) Mechanisms involved in the re-establishment of Sphagnum-dominated vegetation in rewetted bog remnants. *Wetlands Ecology and Management*; 11: 403–418
14. Soini P, Riutta T, Yli-Petäys M, Vasander H. (2010) Comparison of vegetation and $CO_2$ dynamics between a restored cut-away peatland and a pristine fen: evaluation of the restoration success. *Restoration Ecology*; 18: 894–903

ID 62659

# SPATIO-TEMPORAL VARIABILITY OF GREENHOUSE GASES ALONG DRAINAGE GRADIENT IN 17 PEATLANDS ACROSS ESTONIA

Gert Veber[1], Ain Kull[1], Jaanus Paal[2]

[1] Department of Geography, Institute of Ecology and Earth Sciences, University of Tartu, Tartu, Estonia

[2] Department of Botany, Institute of Ecology and Earth Sciences, University of Tartu, Tartu, Estonia

*gert.veber@ut.ee*

## SUMMARY

Undisturbed peatlands are important sinks for carbon, whereas peatlands with strong anthropogenic disturbance, particularly drainage, are sources of carbon. To conduct our study, greenhouse gas (GHG) emission sampling points were established along transects following the water regime changes gradient in 17 peatlands in Estonia. Closed-chamber-based sampling lasted from July 2012 to August 2016 on a monthly basis. In total 7310 gas samples of $CO_2$, $N_2O$ and $CH_4$ were collected. During each sampling session groundwater table depth, temperature, $O_2$ content, pH, conductivity, redox potential, soil temperature were measured and water samples for determining carbon and nitrogen content collected. The flux of $CO_2$ had strong seasonal pattern, almost 90% was emitted during the growing season. Highest fluxes occurred near the drainage ditches, reaching average 139.1 mg $CO_2$-C $m^{-2}h^{-1}$ during the growing season while being 20.9 mg $CO_2$-C $m^{-2}h^{-1}$ in average during the winter. Methane emissions had remarkable seasonal and spatial variability, being lowest in the winter and near the drainage ditches, increasing up to 20310.3 µg $CH_4$-C $m^{-2}h^{-1}$ by August in the pristine parts of the raised bogs. Whereas the emission of $N_2O$ was insignificant in raised bogs, it reached 20.7 µg $N_2O$-N $m^{-2}h^{-1}$ in drained transitional bogs. The main drivers of $CH_4$ and $CO_2$ emissions were water table depth and soil temperature. Dissolved nitrogen content explained the differences in $N_2O$ emissions between raised and transitional bogs. Distance from the ditch and $O_2$ content were also relevant in explaining the emissions. The results of this study are applicable for wetland protection and restoration.

***Keywords***: *carbon dioxide; methane; nitrous oxide; raised bog; transitional bog*

## INTRODUCTION

Peatland ecosystems accumulate and store a disproportionately large amount of carbon in organic soils relative to their global areal coverage (Joosten and Clarke, 2002). However, changes in land use and associated drainage have transformed peatlands to significant sources of $CO_2$ and $N_2O$ (Maljanen et al., 2010). Approximately 70% of Estonian 1 009 100 ha of peatlands have been affected by drainage (Orru and Orru 2008; Salm et al., 2012). The wooded transitional mires are seriously affected by drainage for forestry and most Estonian bogs are affected by drainage at the margins (Ilomets, 2015). Natural wetlands are sources of $CH_4$ and sinks of $CO_2$, changes in the water level alter the ratio of $CH_4$ and $CO_2$ fluxes. Dryer conditions in peatlands reduce $CH_4$ emissions and increase $CO_2$ loss from the soil (Petrescu et al., 2015) converting efficient carbon sink ecosystems to a large $CO_2$ sources (Maljanen et al., 2010). Most commonly in previous studies, the water table position (Dise et al., 1993; Moore and Roulet, 1993; Waddington et al., 1996; Ojanen and Minkkinen, 2019) and soil temperature (Ballantyne et al., 2014; Le Mer and Roger, 2001; Levy and Gray, 2015; Nykanen et al., 1995; Pelletier et al., 2007; Salm et al., 2012) are considered the major control on GHG emissions from northern peatlands. While main factors controlling GHG fluxes in peatlands are known there is still high uncertainty how far the drainage effect reaches and especially, how it affects spatial and temporal GHG fluxes. The aim of this study was to quantify the drainage effect on spatial and temporal variation of GHG fluxes and their drivers along drainage gradient in transitional and raised bogs in Estonia.

## MATERIALS AND METHODS

Geographically representative selection of 17 peatlands based on stratified sampling method from all over Estonia was chosen. This selection contains 12 raised bogs and 5 transitional bogs. Transects perpendicular to the drainage ditch with sampling areas following water regime changes along gradient were established in each of these peatlands. Transect layout is described in detail by Paal et al., 2016.

Gas sampling was carried out throughout the year on a monthly basis from July 2012 to August 2016 in 17 peatlands at each transect minimum of four and maximum of six sampling areas (44 sampling areas in raised bogs, 23 in transitional bogs and 8 sampling areas in raised bogs with an old overgrown ditch). The closed static chamber method was used for the measurement of ecosystem respiration ($R_{eco}$) $CO_2$, $CH_4$ and $N_2O$ fluxes. $R_{eco}$ was used as $CO_2$ flux indicator of drainage effect because it combines both soil respiration and plant respiration, thus reflecting both faster C-turnover rate and also changes in mire species assemblage. Gas was sampled using pre-evacuated 100 mL glass vials every 20 minutes during an one-hour session (at 0, 20, 40 and 60 minutes from the enclosure of samplers). The gas concentration was determined using the gas chromatography system Shimadzu GC-2014, in the laboratory of the University of Tartu, Estonia. The emission rate was calculated assuming a linear change in the gas concentration of the gas in chamber, taking into account the volume of the chamber and the area covered by the chamber. Emission rate for one sampling area in the transect was calculated as the average of three chambers 2 meters apart of each other at the sampling area. A total of 7310 samples were collected and in statistical analysis, only samples with determination coefficient $R^2 \geq 0.90$ for goodness of fit to linear regression of gas concentration change and samples with near-zero fluxes below the gas-chromatographer accuracy (change of concentration < 20 ppb) with $R^2 < 0.90$ were used.

During each gas sampling session at every sampling area, the depth of the groundwater table

(cm) in the observation wells and soil temperature were measured at four depths (10, 20, 30, 40 cm). In observation wells water temperature, dissolved oxygen content $O_2$ (mg/l), dissolved $O_2$ saturation level (%), pH, conductivity (μS/cm2) and redox potential (ORP, mV) were measured. Concurrently water samples were collected for the analyses of total nitrogen (TN), dissolved nitrogen (DN), dissolved organic carbon (DOC), dissolved inorganic carbon (DIC), dissolved carbon (DC) determined with Vario TOC cube analyser in the laboratory of the University of Tartu.
Statistical analysis was carried out using the STATISTICA 7.1. The normality of the variable distributions was verified using the Kolmogorov–Smirnov and Lilliefors tests. Spearman's rank order correlation and Principal Component Analysis (PCA) were used to analyse the relationship between measured GHG emission and environmental parameters. In all cases, $p < 0.05$ was the standard by which statistical significance was accepted.

## RESULTS

Based on the results of our study the temporal variability of $R_{eco}$ based $CO_2$ flux and $CH_4$ emission in different sampling areas on transects in drained bogs, drained transitional bogs and bogs with an old overgrown ditch had strong correlations to water table position along with strong correlations to both water and soil temperature. The $N_2O$ flux in studied nitrogen-poor peatlands was low or insignificant and statistically significant correlations between the environmental variables and the emission of $N_2O$ were scarce. According to PCA the $N_2O$ emission was most often related to higher dissolved nitrogen and dissolved organic carbon concentration, particularly in drained transitional bogs in zone of strong drainage effect and large seasonal water level fluctuations.

Ecosystem respiration $CO_2$ flux

The $R_{eco}$ flux of $CO_2$ had strong seasonal pattern, almost 90% was emitted during the growing season (Figure 1A, B, C). In all studied peatlands, August was the month with the highest $CO_2$ flux (Figure 1A, B, C) having also the highest peat temperature at 20 cm depth and the lowest water table level (Figure 1D, E, F). Fluxes were higher closer to the drainage ditches and seasonal amplitude in $R_{eco}$ was decreasing towards mire in natural status (440 m from ditch) in all studied peatlands. In drained transitional bogs $R_{eco}$ was on average 139.1 mg $CO_2$-C $m^{-2}h^{-1}$ during the growing season while being only 20.9 mg $CO_2$-C $m^{-2}h^{-1}$ during the winter. The highest mean monthly flux was reached in natural background areas in July but in drainage affected zone in August. Drained transitional bogs had the highest $R_{eco}$ (202.8 mg $CO_2$-C $m^{-2}h^{-1}$) at the distance up to 15m from the ditch (Figure 1C) while in raised bogs it remained at 169 mg $CO_2$-C $m^{-2}h^{-1}$. Water table level had a large spatial and temporal fluctuations over the frost free season, both in drained raised bogs and transitional bogs. Only in raised bogs with overgrown ditches the water table depth was in average higher than -30 cm at 15m distance from the ditch all year round (Figure 1D). High $R_{eco}$ in drainage affected zone of transitional and raised bogs is related to faster C turnover indicated also by higher pore water dissolved $O_2$ content, DOC and DN concentration.

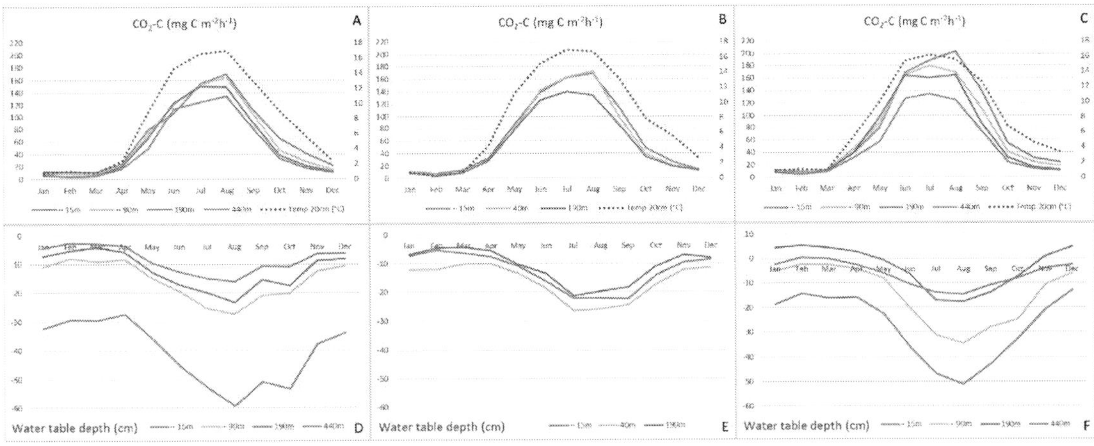


Figure 1. Seasonal dynamics of $CO_2$-C fluxes by distance from the drainage ditch, and mean soil temperature at 20 cm depth (right axis) in drained raised bogs (A), raised bogs with an old overgrown ditch (B) and drained transitional bogs (C). Seasonal dynamics of mean water table depth by distance from the ditch in drained raised bogs (D), raised bogs with an old overgrown ditch (E) and drained transitional bogs (F).

## $CH_4$ emissions

Methane emissions had remarkable seasonal and spatial variability, being lowest in the winter and near the drainage ditches, increasing up to 20310.3 μg $CH_4$-C $m^{-2}h^{-1}$ by August in the pristine parts of the raised bogs with ridge-hollow-pool subtype (Figure 2A, C). On the contrary to the raised bogs and transitional bogs the emission of methane in bogs with old overgrown ditches was higher close to the drainage (Figure 2B) though staying considerably lower than the emission in pristine parts of raised bogs and transitional bogs. The *Sphagnum* filled ditches kept optimal water table level for methane production during the summer month (Figure 1E) and avoided the major water table lowering present in other peatlands of the study (Figure 1D, F). However, *Sphagnum cuspidatum* filled old shallow ditches and partly blocked water movement had throughout the year sufficient dissolved oxygen level for oxidation of $CH_4$ produced in inundated zone.

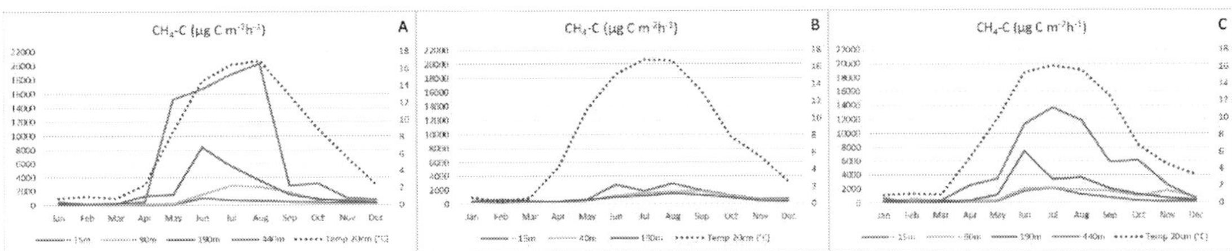


Figure 2. Seasonal dynamics of $CH_4$-C emission by distance from the drainage ditch (left axis) and mean soil temperature at 20 cm depth (right axis) in drained raised bogs (A), raised bogs with an old overgrown ditch (B) and drained transitional bogs (C).

## $N_2O$ emissions

Emission of $N_2O$ was insignificant and without any clear seasonal pattern staying below 3 μg $N_2O$-N $m^{-2}h^{-1}$ the whole year in nitrogen-poor raised bogs (Figure 3A, B). While the emission had slight tendency to increase in warm period since May next to the ditch in most drainage affected zone where peat decomposition is faster, dissolved nitrogen is more readily available and pore water content is highly fluctuating according to added rainwater. In areas less affected by drainage or in natural background sites $N_2O$ emission was slightly higher only in months of the lowest water table level and the sole determining factor was pore-water content fluctuating according to added rainwater. In drained transitional bogs soil nitrogen content was higher and emission reached 20.7 μg $N_2O$-N $m^{-2}h^{-1}$ at the distance up to 15 m from the ditch (Figure 3C). The $N_2O$ emission in strongly drainage affected zone up to 90 m in transitional bogs was higher all year round and had distinctive short-lasting peak in winter with freeze-thaw cycles when peat pores started to fill up with snow melt water and longer lasting peak in summer when water table level was low but fluctuant and DN was increased in pore water after rainfalls. Further from ditch in more intact parts of the transitional bogs the emission of $N_2O$ was similar to that in raised bogs (Figure 3C).

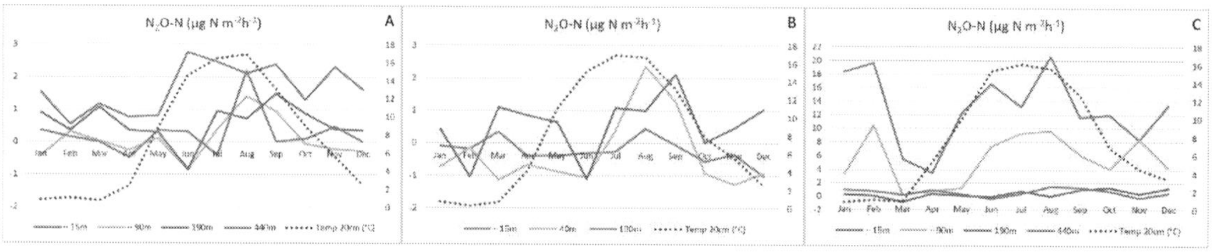


Figure 3. Seasonal dynamics of $N_2O$-N emission by distance from the drainage ditch (left axis) and mean soil temperature at 20 cm depth (right axis) in drained raised bogs (A), raised bogs with an old overgrown ditch (B) and drained transitional bogs (C).

## DISCUSSION

There is a clear seasonal and spatial pattern in the fluxes of $R_{eco}$ $CO_2$ and $CH_4$. During the winter months the fluxes are similarly low regardless drainage effect along the transects. In spring when soil starts to warm up the fluxes of GHG-s start to increase (Figure 1A, B, C). During the summer the differences in fluxes of GHG-s along the drainage gradient emerged and this is in good agreement with other studies (Metzger et al., 2019). Areas with lower water table level have higher fluxes of $CO_2$ rather than more natural parts of transects with higher water table (Figure 1). The relationship between the water table level and methane emission was the opposite, the lower the water level dropped the smaller the emission. Areas unaffected by drainage with natural water table showed increase in methane emission following the seasonal course of the surface temperature (Figure 2A, B, C and 1D, E, F). Although the emission of $CH_4$ in the natural parts of the peatlands are noticeable, the amount of carbon lost as $CH_4$-C is not comparable to the $CO_2$-C fluxes from the areas with lowered water table level. The $N_2O$ emission from peatlands is closely related to peat nitrogen content and thus raised bogs, transitional bogs and fens emissions vary highly after drainage. This is supported by previous studies by other authors (Martikainen et al., 1995) and furthermore, peat degradation in drainage affected zone is the main driver of $N_2O$ and DOC release (Liu et al., 2019). In general raised bogs are a very weak source of nitrous oxide while its share increases with anthropogenic disturbance (Frolking et al., 2011; Salm et al., 2012; Veber et al., 2018). Drained peatlands with high N stocks have increased $N_2O$ emissions (Liimatainen et al., 2018), approach applicable also in association with nutrient rich organic soils characteristic to drained transitional bogs.

## CONCLUSION

Strong seasonal and spatial pattern of GHG-s emission characteristic for northern peatlands is amplified in drainage affected zone. $R_{eco}$ and $N_2O$ emissions increased up to 190 m and 90 m respectively, from functioning drainage ditch in studied peatlands while raised bogs with shallow overgrown ditches had still increased $R_{eco}$ but reduced methane emission and $N_2O$ emission at the level typical of natural mires. The main drivers of $CH_4$ and $CO_2$ emissions were water table level and soil temperature. Dissolved nitrogen content explained the differences in $N_2O$ emissions between raised and transitional bogs, and between drainage affected zone and natural background area. Distance from the ditch and dissolved $O_2$ content were also relevant in explaining the emissions. The results of this study are applicable for wetland protection and restoration of peatlands.

## ACKNOWLEDGEMENTS

The study was financed by Environmental Investment Centre grants SLOOM12006 and SLOOM14103, and supported by the Estonian Research Council research grant PRG352 and Estonian State Forest Management Centre grant LLTOM17250.

## REFERENCES

1. Ballantyne, D.M., Hribljan, J.A., Pypker, T.G., Chimner, R.A. (2014) Long-term water table manipulations alter peatland gaseous carbon fluxes in Northern Michigan. *Wetlands Ecology and Management*, 22(1): 35–47, https://doi.org/10.1007/s11273-013-9320-8
2. Dise, N.B., Gorham, E., Verry, E.S. (1993) Environmental factors controlling methane emissions from peatlands in northern Minnesota. *Journal of Geophysical Research: Solid Earth*, 98(D6): 10583–10594.
3. Frolking, S., Talbot, J., Jones, M.C., Treat, C.C., Kauffman, J.B., Tuittila, E.-S., Roulet, N. (2011) Peatlands in the Earth's 21st century climate system. *Environmental Reviews*, 19: 371–396, https://doi.org/10.1139/a11-014
4. Ilomets, M. (2015) Estonia, in: Joosten, H., Tanneberger, F., Moen, A. (Eds.), *Mires and peatlands of Europe.* Schweizerbart Science Publishers, Stuttgart: 780 pp.
5. Joosten, H., Clarke, D. (2002) *Wise Use of Mires and Peatlands: Background and Principles Including a Framework for Decision-Making.* International Peat Society, Jyväskylä, Finland: 304 pp.
6. Le Mer, J., Roger, P. (2001) Production, oxidation, emission and consumption of methane by soils: A review. *European Journal of Soil Biology*, 37(1): 25–50, https://doi.org/10.1016/S1164-5563(01)01067-6
7. Levy, P.E., Gray, A. (2015) Greenhouse gas balance of a semi-natural peatbog in northern Scotland. *Environmental Research Letters*, 10(9): 094019, https://doi.org/10.1088/1748-9326/10/9/094019
8. Liimatainen, M., Voigt, C., Martikainen, P.J., Hytönen, J., Regina, K., Óskarsson, H., Maljanen, M. (2018) Factors controlling nitrous oxide emissions from managed northern peat soils with low carbon to nitrogen ratio. *Soil Biology and Biochemistry*, 122: 186–195, https://doi.org/10.1016/j.soilbio.2018.04.006
9. Liu, H., Zak, D., Rezanezhad, F., Lennartz, B. (2019) Soil degradation determines release of nitrous oxide and dissolved organic carbon from peatlands. *Environmental Research Letters*, 14(9): 094009, https://doi.org/10.1088/1748-9326/ab3947
10. Maljanen, M., Sigurdsson, B.D., Guðmundsson, J., Óskarsson, H., Huttunen, J.T., Martikainen, P.J. (2010) Greenhouse gas balances of managed peatlands in the Nordic countries – present knowledge and gaps. *Biogeosciences*, 7(9): 2711–2738, https://doi.org/10.5194/bg-7-2711-2010
11. Martikainen, P.J., Nykänen, H., Alm, J., Silvola, J. (1995) Change in fluxes of carbon dioxide, methane and nitrous oxide due to forest drainage of mire sites of different trophy. *Plant and Soil*, 168(1): 571–577, https://doi.org/10.1007/BF00029370
12. Metzger, C., Jansson, P.-E., Lohila, A., Aurela, M., Eickenscheidt, T., Belelli-Marchesini, L., Dinsmore, K. J., Drewer, J., van Huissteden, J., Drösler, M. (2019) $CO_2$ fluxes and ecosystem dynamics at five European treeless peatlands – merging data and process oriented modeling. *Biogeosciences*, 12, 125–146, https://doi.org/10.5194/bg-12-125-2015
13. Moore, T.R., Roulet, N.T. (1993) Methane flux: Water table relations in northern wetlands. *Geophysical Research Letters*, 20(7): 587–590, https://doi.org/10.1029/93GL00208
14. Nykanen, H., Alm, J., Lang, K., Silvola, J., Martikainen, P.J. (1995) Emissions of $CH_4$, $N_2O$ and $CO_2$ from

a virgin fen and a fen drained for grassland in Finland. *Journal of Biogeography*, 22(2/3): 351–357, https://doi.org/10.2307/2845930

15. Ojanen, P., Minkkinen, K. (2019) The dependence of net soil CO2 emissions on water table depth in boreal peatlands drained for forestry. *Mires and Peat*, 24(27): 1–8, https://doi.org/10.19189/MaP.2019.OMB.StA.1751
16. Orru, M., Orru, H. (2008) Sustainable use of Estonian peat reserves and environmental challenges. *Estonian Journal of Earth Sciences*, 57(2): 87–93, https://doi.org/10.3176/earth.2008.2.04
17. Paal, J.; Jürjendal, I., Suija, A., Kull, A. (2016). Impact of drainage on vegetation of transitional mires in Estonia. *Mires and Peat*, 18, 1−19, https://doi.org/10.19189/MaP.2015.OMB.183
18. Pelletier, L., Moore, T.R., Roulet, N.T., Garneau, M., Beaulieu-Audy, V. (2007) Methane fluxes from three peatlands in the La Grande Rivière watershed, James Bay lowland, Canada. *Journal of Geophysical Research: Biogeosciences*, 112(G1): G01018, https://doi.org/10.1029/2006JG000216
19. Petrescu, A.M.R., Lohila, A., Tuovinen, J.-P., Baldocchi, D.D., Desai, A.R., Roulet, N.T., Vesala, T., Dolman, A.J., Oechel, W.C., Marcolla, B., Friborg, T., Rinne, J., Matthes, J.H., Merbold, L., Meijide, A., Kiely, G., Sottocornola, M., Sachs, T., Zona, D., Varlagin, A., Lai, D.Y.F., Veenendaal, E., Parmentier, F.-J.W., Skiba, U., Lund, M., Hensen, A., Huissteden, J. van, Flanagan, L.B., Shurpali, N.J., Grünwald, T., Humphreys, E.R., Jackowicz-Korczyński, M., Aurela, M.A., Laurila, T., Grüning, C., Corradi, C.A.R., Schrier-Uijl, A.P., Christensen, T.R., Tamstorf, M.P., Mastepanov, M., Martikainen, P.J., Verma, S.B., Bernhofer, C., Cescatti, A. (2015) The uncertain climate footprint of wetlands under human pressure. *Proceedings of the National Academy of Sciences*, 112(15): 4594–4599, https://doi.org/10.1073/pnas.1416267112
20. Salm, J.-O., Maddison, M., Tammik, S., Soosaar, K., Truu, J., Mander, Ü. (2012) Emissions of CO2, CH4 and N2O from undisturbed, drained and mined peatlands in Estonia. *Hydrobiologia*, 692(1): 41–55, https://doi.org/10.1007/s10750-011-0934-7
21. Veber, G., Kull, A., Villa, J.A., Maddison, M., Paal, J., Oja, T., Iturraspe, R., Pärn, J., Teemusk, A., Mander, Ü. (2018) Greenhouse gas emissions in natural and managed peatlands of America: Case studies along a latitudinal gradient. *Ecological Engineering, Wetlands and Carbon Revisited*, 114: 34–45, https://doi.org/10.1016/j.ecoleng.2017.06.068
22. Waddington, J.M., Roulet, N.T., Swanson, R.V. (1996) Water table control of CH4 emission enhancement by vascular plants in boreal peatlands. *Journal of Geophysical Research: Atmospheres*, 101(D17): 22775–22785, https://doi.org/10.1029/96JD02014

ID 72837

# DO ANDIC SOIL PROPERTIES IMPACT CARBON DYNAMICS OF PEATLANDS IN VOLCANIC REGIONS?

*Susanne C. Möckel, Egill Erlendsson, Guðrún Gísladóttir

Institute of Life and Environmental Sciences, University of Iceland, Iceland

*scm2@hi.is*

Due to frequent volcanic activity and ongoing erosion of dryland soils induced by land use after the human settlement (c. 870 AD), peatlands in Iceland receive regular additions of mineral aeolian deposits (tephra and eroded material). Hence, their soils (histosols) may develop not only histic, but also andic (volcanic) characteristics. Yet, mineral aeolian deposition as an environmental determinant of peatland characteristics in Iceland is still poorly understood, not least with regard to the peatlands carbon stores. In this presentation, a concise outline is given on the state of knowledge on soil processes of peatlands within volcanically active regions. Then, we present findings of an ongoing project on the impact of tephra deposition on histosols, focusing on interactions between histic and andic soil properties and their impact on C storage. We evaluate datasets of the C structure of histosols derived by $^{13}C$ NMR spectroscopy and andic soil properties based on selective extractions of Al, Fe and Si with ammonium oxalate and sodium pyrophosphate. Soil organic matter of histosols with andic properties is less decomposed than of histosols without these properties. The interaction of andic and histic soil properties seems to impact the C structure of histosols by facilitating the formation of organo-mineral complexes, which particularly hamper the decomposition of chemically more labile C groups. Tephra layers appear to have the potential to serve as protective barriers. Hence, the interaction of andic and histic soil properties, accompanied by the protective role of major tephra deposits, may enable an unusual potential for long-term C stabilization in a natural peatland environment.

ID 72881

# THE USE OF SUBSIDENCE TO CALCULATE CARBON LOSS FROM DEFORESTED AND DRAINED TROPICAL PEATLAND

*Gusti Anshari[1,2], Evi Gusmayanti[1,3], Nisa Novita[4]

[1]Magister of Environmental Science, Universitas Tanjungpura, Indonesia
[2]Soil science department, Universitas Tanjungpura, Indonesia
[3]Agrotechnology department, Universitas Tanjungpura, Indonesia
[4]Yayasan Konservasi Alam Nusantara (TNC Indonesia), Indonesia

*gzanshari@live.untan.ac.id*

Carbon loss in drained tropical peat is enormous. The current carbon loss estimate is based on the groundwater table's single proxy, which is spatially and temporarily dynamic. The relation between the groundwater table and carbon emission is not linear. Peatland drainage or lowering the groundwater table provides plenty of oxygen into the upper layer of peat above the water table, where microbial activity becomes active. So, lowering the water table escalates subsidence and consequently emits carbon because of microbial oxidation. This paper reviews bulk density characteristics (BD), total organic carbon (TOC), and subsidence rate in the peat forest and drained peat. BD, TOC, and subsidence data are derived from published and unpublished sources. We used Pearson correlation, one-way Anova, and simple linear regression to analyze carbon loss from drained tropical peat. We found that BD is generally higher in the surface layer in both the peat forest and drained peat.

TOC values in the peat forest are less variable than TOC values in drained peat. The reduction of TOC values in the top surface suggests significant peat oxidation in the drained peat. We suggest that BD and TOC's default values in the peat forest and drained peats are 0.09 g cm-3 and 56%: and 0.14 g cm-3 and 50%, respectively. The estimated carbon emission from the drained peatland, assuming subsidence rate per year is 2 – 6 cm, range 30.9 to 92.7 t $CO_2$-eq ha-1 yr-1. In other words, subsidence 1 cm per year results in 15.46 t $CO_2$-eq ha-1 yr-1. This result is comparable to other studies. We are sure that subsidence rate is more practical to estimate carbon emission from drained tropical peat than the groundwater table.

**Keywords:** drained peat, subsidence, carbon loss, characteristics of peat forest and drained peat; changes of bulk density and TOC

ID 62746

# IMPROVING KNOWLEDGE IN THE PARAMETERS FOR ESTIMATING GHG EMISSIONS FROM PEAT SWAMP FORESTS FIRES IN INDONESIA

*Haruni Krisnawati[1], Liubov Volkova[2], Wahyu Catur Adinugroho[1], Rinaldi Imanuddin[1], Chris Weston[2]

[1]Forestry and Environment Research, Development and Innovation Agency, Indonesia
[2]University of Melbourne, Australia

*harunikrisnawati@gmail.com*

Tropical peatlands are the area of high carbon density and plays an important role in carbon-gas land-atmosphere interactions. Currently, this ecosystem is subject to rapid degradation due to strong economic and social pressures for timber and land for agriculture and plantations. Clearance and drainage of tropical peatlands over recent decades has resulted in an unprecedented increase in peat fires, with smoke and pollution affecting countries, not only Indonesia but also some other countries in South-eastern Asia. Emissions from peat fires is subject of a great uncertainty as only a few empirical based parameters of fuel loads and their combustion efficiency are currently reported in the literature. Lack of knowledge on how different fuels contribute to greenhouse gas emissions makes it difficult to develop well-targeted policy for emission reduction. At present, emissions from peat swamp forest fires are not currently reported in the greenhouse gas inventory due to high levels of uncertainty in the available data. Improving knowledge in the parameters for estimating GHG emissions from peat swamp forests fires is therefore needed, to support policy input for emission reduction.

ID 62640

# INVESTIGATION INTO PLANT-MEDIATED $CH_4$ TRANSPORT, PEAT INCUBATION AND MICROBIOME COMPOSITION REVEALS FIRE DEGRADED TROPICAL PEATLANDS AS A HOT SPOT OF $CH_4$

Hasan Akhtar[1,2,3*], Massimo Lupascu[1,2], Aditya Bandla[2,3], Omkar S. Kulkarni[3,7], Rahayu S. Sukri[4], Alexander R. Cobb[5], Thomas E. L. Smith[6], Sanjay Swarup[2,3,7]

[1] Department of Geography, National University of Singapore, Singapore;
[2] Integrated Tropical Peatland Research Program (INTPREP), NUS Environmental Research Institute, Singapore;
[3] Singapore Centre for Environmental Life Sciences Engineering, Singapore;
[4] Institute for Biodiversity and Environmental Research, Universiti Brunei Darussalam, Brunei Darussalam;
[5] Center for Environmental Sensing and Modelling, Singapore–MIT Alliance for Research and Technology, Singapore;
[6] Department of Geography and Environment, London School of Economics & Political Science, UK;
[7] Department of Biological Sciences, National University of Singapore, Singapore.

*hasanakhtar@u.nus.edu*

## SUMMARY

Tropical peatlands (TP) in Southeast (SE) Asia have been degraded for multiple land uses, mainly by employing drainage and fire. The extent of such areas, primarily covered with ferns and sedges, currently occupies one-tenth of the total peatland extent in SE Asia. Recent findings have confirmed these fire-degraded TPs as a hot spot of surface $CH_4$ emission; however, post-fire changes in microtopography, vegetation and underlying microbiome composition regulating carbon (C) dynamics basically remains unexplored. Therefore, within this context investigated the role of plant-mediated transport, water-saturation in peat due to microtopography, labile C, temperature, and microbiome composition in regulating the C dynamics of the fire-degraded TP in Brunei. Our study shows for the first time that sedges transported >70% of the total $CH_4$ emission at our site, with a significant spatio-temporal variation ($0.78 \pm 0.14$ to $4.86 \pm 0.66$ $mgCH_4m^{-2}hr^{-1}$) mainly attributed to water table position, and number of sedges. Further, using a controlled incubation experiment, we tried to disentangle the complex interplay of a) microtopography, creating an oxic and anoxic condition, b) labile C inputs from root exudates secretion from sedges and ferns, and c) diurnal temperature change in regulating C production. We found that the interaction of these factors significantly affected the rate of $CO_2$ and $CH_4$ production with mesic condition acting as a strong source of $CO_2$ and anoxic acted as a strong source of $CH_4$. Furthermore, using 16S rRNA gene-amplicon sequencing, we found significant differences in microbiome composition between non-burnt and burnt peat, where latter harboured higher abundance of methanogenic archaea *(Bathyarchaeia)* and lesser abundance of methane oxidizing bacteria *(Alphaproteobacteria, Gammaproteobacteria),* compared to non-burnt peat. These insights provide an important basis for future studies on $CH_4$ dynamics as the total emissions via these processes might increase in future with increase in the extent of degraded TPs due to more frequent fire episodes and flooding.
***Keywords:*** *Tropical peatlands, Fire, $CH_4$, Sedges, Microtopography, Root exudates, Microbiome*

## INTRODUCTION

Despite being one of the world's richest carbon (C) reserves, tropical peatlands in Southeast (SE) Asia have been heavily disturbed mainly by employing drainage and fire over past few decades (Hooijer et al., 2010; Miettinen, et al., 2016). Specifically, the extent of degraded tropical peatlands have increased to almost 10% (in 2015) of the total peatland area (approximately 1.42Mha) in SE Asia (Miettinen et al., 2016), with this land primarily occupied by ferns and sedges (van Eijk et al., 2009). However, under post-fire scenario the ecosystem's response in cycling C, which is likely affected due to change in vegetation composition, altered hydrology, microtopography, and microbiome composition, basically remains answered.

Fire-degraded tropical peatlands experiences frequent flooding, due to enhanced peat oxidative decomposition and subsidence, especially during wet season (Page et al., 2009). Subsequently, this area can expand up to five times and may experience shift in vegetation composition towards flood tolerant species such as sedges (Wösten et al., 2006). Sedges are well recognized as a significant source of $CH_4$ emission and their role in the production, oxidation, and transportation of $CH_4$ have been well studied in northern peatlands (Carmichael et al., 2014). Due to its distinct anatomy (presence of aerenchyma), the sedges can transport $CH_4$ directly to the atmosphere where rate of such bypass is in order of ~22% to >90% of total methane flux at ecosystem level (Bhullar et al., 2013; Carmichael et al., 2014). However, in tropics no study has investigated their role in $CH_4$ emissions. Along with the impact on vegetation structure, fire also affects porewater characteristics which can influence the recovery of these degraded areas to secondary peat swamp forest (Page et al., 2009).

Constant water logging, anoxia and high acidity are some of the key conditions which inhibit microbial activity and organic matter decomposition thereby supporting peat accumulation (Mezbahuddin et al., 2014; Yule & Gomez, 2009). Although microbes are one of the key drivers in regulating the biogeochemical cycling of C, there exists a scarcity of information regarding the microbiome composition for degraded tropical peatland areas, which currently occupies one-tenth of the total peatland extent in Southeast Asia (Miettinen et al., 2016). Recent studies have explored microbial diversity in tropical peatlands under different land-uses in SE Asia where *Proteobacteria* and *Acidobacteria* are reported as the most dominant phyla with varying results for methanogens (Jackson et al., 2009; Kanokratana et al., 2011; Mishra et al., 2014; Too et al., 2018). While recent studies have confirmed how fire-degraded tropical peatlands remain a source of $CH_4$ long after a fire event (Lupascu et al., 2020), the underlying microbiome composition regulating $CH_4$ dynamics remains unexplored.

The recurrent fires not only alters the vegetation composition but also degrade tropical peatland ecosystems by altering their hydrology, microtopography (hollows and hummocks), and associated changes in abiotic (pH, temperature, oxidation-reduction conditions, nutrients) and biotic (e.g. vegetation composition and hence labile C in the form of root exudates) factors (Lupascu et al., 2020). For intact tropical peatlands, studies have well reported the effects of these factors on the rate of greenhouse gases (GHGs; $CO_2$ and $CH_4$) emissions (Girkin et al., 2018; Hirano et al., 2009; Jauhiainen et al., 2005; Sjögersten et al., 2018). However, for fire-degraded tropical peatland areas, these effects remain unexplored.

Therefore, to address these important knowledge gaps, we adopted a three-way approach in this study, specifically looking at the role of 1) plant-mediated $CH_4$ transport, 2) underlying microbiome composition, and 3) physicochemical characteristics (microtopography, labile C, temperature) in regulating C dynamics in fire-degraded tropical peatlands in Brunei. A schematic of the processes integrating the three-way approach in this study is described in Figure 1 in form of 1) vegetation control, 2) physicochemical control, and 3) microbial control.

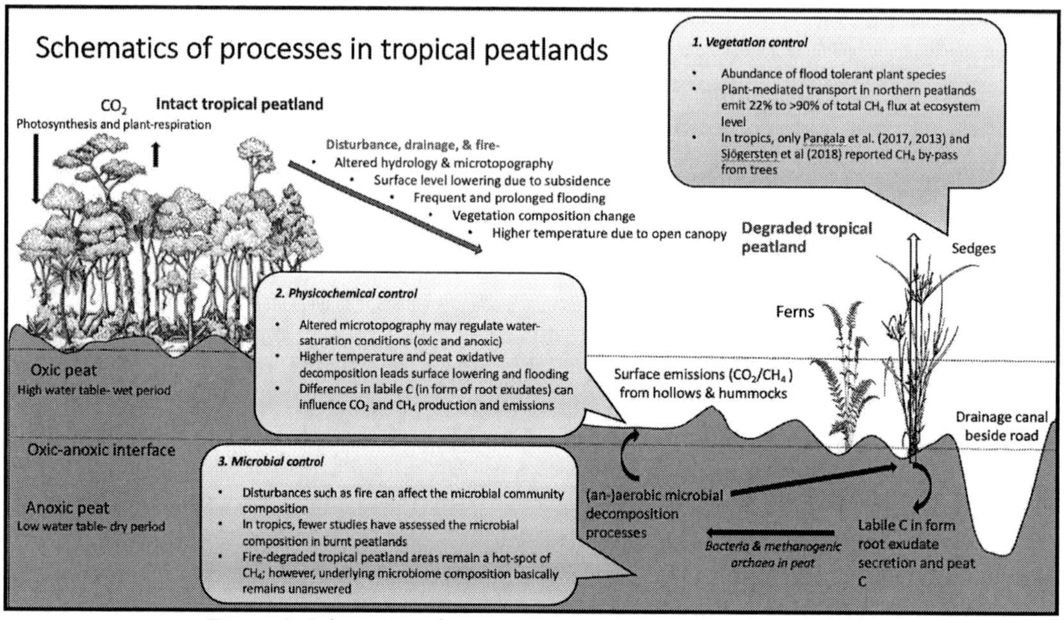


*Figure 1: Schematics of processes occurring in tropical peatlands*

## MATERIALS AND METHODS

The study area lies 20 km south of the coast in Belait District, Brunei Darussalam, with a fire-degraded or burnt site and a non-burnt site as a control (4°28'40" N, 114°18'19" E) (Figure 2a). The study area experiences wet period from October to January and May to June and dry period from February to March and June to August. Measurements and samples were collected from six plots (5m x 5m) at burnt sites (B0–5) and four plots at non-burnt or control site (C1–4), as described in Akhtar et al. 2021 and Lupascu et al. 2020 (Figure 2a).

1. ***Vegetation control:*** To estimate the sedge-mediated $CH_4$ transport, measurements with vegetation (n=3–8 sedges per collar) and without vegetation (bare peat surface) were recorded adjacent to each other in plots at burnt site (B0-5) using a GHG (GasScouter, Picarro Inc., CA, USA) connected to a transparent chamber (clear acrylic pipe, 11cm ID and up to 200 cm long with a total volume of 19.1 litre) (Figure 2b). Measurements were recorded between 09:00-17:00 hrs, to estimate net $CH_4$ contribution from sedges. The seasonal difference in $CH_4$ emissions was identified using Kruskal-Wallis test, while the correlation between $CH_4$ emissions and other parameters was determined using spearman correlation. The significance was accepted at $p \leq 0.05$ and tests were performed using Origin Pro (2019).

2. ***Microbial control:*** For microbiome composition, peat samples (in triplicate) were collected from plots at burnt site (B1–4) and non-burnt (C1–4) from different depths (0–5, 35–40, 95–100 cm below peat surface) in sterile tubes. Peat soil DNA was extracted using ZR Soil-Microbe DNA extraction kit (Zymo Research Corp., USA) following manufacturer's protocol, and stored at -80°C. PCR was performed in replicates (20 μL

reaction) using 5 nano gram of template DNA for amplification of 16S rRNA gene. Thereafter, an agarose gel electrophoresis was run to verify the amplified product size and concentration. Amplified products were cleaned using NucleoSpin® Extract II as per the protocol. Illumina library preparation and Illumina MiSeq sequencing was done at Singapore Centre for Environmental Life Sciences Engineering. Raw reads were processed using the DADA2 pipeline in order to infer sequence variants. Multivariate statistical analysis were performed to infer the diversity metrics.

3. ***Physicochemical control:*** To investigate the effects of water saturation (mesic, flooded oxic and anoxic) due to microtopography (hollows and hummocks), and labile C inputs in form of root exudates from sedges and ferns, burnt peat soil samples (13 gram dry-weight equivalent) were incubated under 26 °C and 30 °C in mason jars (1litre). For mesic treatments, peat with an initial field moisture content (75%) was used whereas flooded oxic treatment was filled with DI water and flooded anoxic treatment was further flushed with $N_2$ for 2 minutes to create oxygen-free conditions. Labile C were added in form of 1 ml of artificial root exudates solution (made of glucose, fructose, acetate, formate, succinate in DI water) in three concentration range R1–3 (0.1, 0.2 and 0.3 mgC/g of peat/day). Head gas concentration in each mason jar, fitted with two PVC bulkheads sealed with silicon-sealant and closed-loop nylon tubing, was recroded using a GHG analyser (Picarro Inc., USA) at 0, 6, 12, 24, 72 and 120 hours of labile C addition. ANOVA test was used for comparison of mean values with significance acceptance at $p \leq 0.05$.

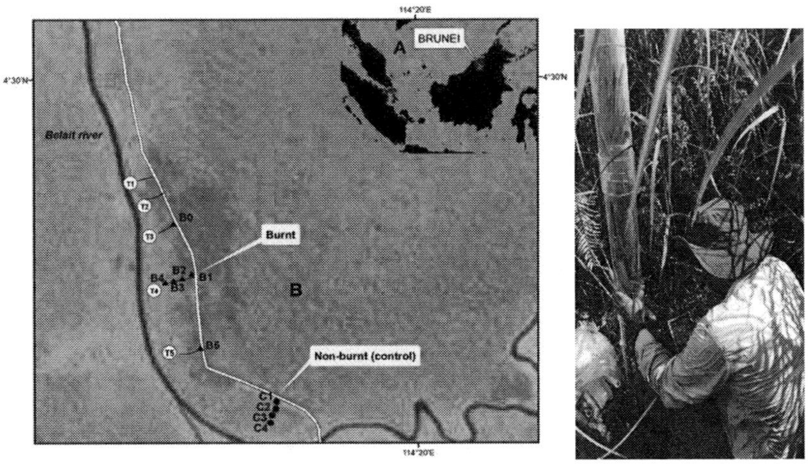


*Figure 2: a) Study sites location (left), and b) clear acrylic chamber (right) for sedge-mediated $CH_4$ measurement.*

## RESULTS

1. ***Vegetation control:*** We found sedge-mediated transported >70% of $CH_4$ directly into the atmosphere with significant ($p<0.001$; Kruskal-Wallis ANOVA, H=65.52) seasonal variation, following the water table levels (Figure 3). Lower values were recorded during the dry season (0.98–2.27 $mgCH_4m^{-2}hr^{-1}$ in August 2018 and July 2019). The peak in $CH_4$ emission was observed in wet period (4.53–7.49 $mgCH_4m^{-2}hr^{-1}$ in October 2018 and January 2019). We also observed significant ($p<0.001$; Kruskal-Wallis ANOVA, H=42.48) spatial variation in sedge-mediated $CH_4$ emission with higher values near

drainage canal (3.48–5.41 $mgCH_4m^{-2}hr^{-1}$) and lower values away from canal (0.63–1.75 $mgCH_4m^{-2}hr^{-1}$) (Figure 3). This spatial variation was was mainly attributed to the higher number of sedges ($r^2$=0.49; $p<0.001$) and higher water tables ($r^2$=0.78; $p<0.001$).

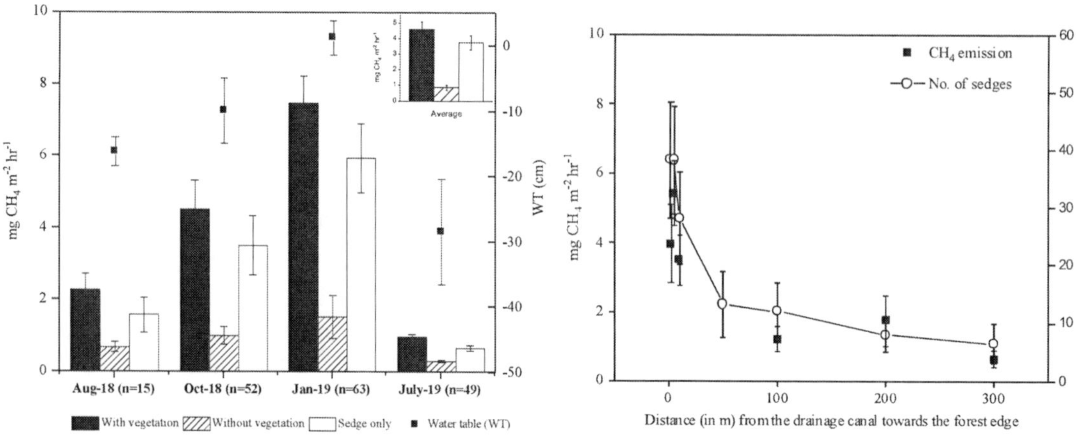


*Figure 3: Temporal (left) and spatial (right) variation in sedge-mediated $CH_4$ emissions over the sampling period; inset is the overall annual average of sedge-mediated $CH_4$ emissions.*

2. ***Microbial control:*** For microbiome composition, PERMANOVA analysis showed significant differences between burnt and non-burnt ($p<0.01$) as well as along the depths ($p<0.01$) (Figure 4). We also observed that burnt peat samples were enriched in *Bathyarchaeia,* a recently classified methane producing archaeal class, compared to non-burnt peat samples, particularly at depths of 35–40 cm (mid partially oxic layer, B_P_1–4) and 95–100 cm (deeper anoxic layer, B_B_1–4) (Figure 4). At the same time, burnt peat was depleted in *Alphaproteobacteria* and *Gammaproteobacteria,* known classes to encompass methane oxidizing bacteria, compared to non-burnt peat, further supporting the higher $CH_4$ emissions from burnt site (Figure 4).

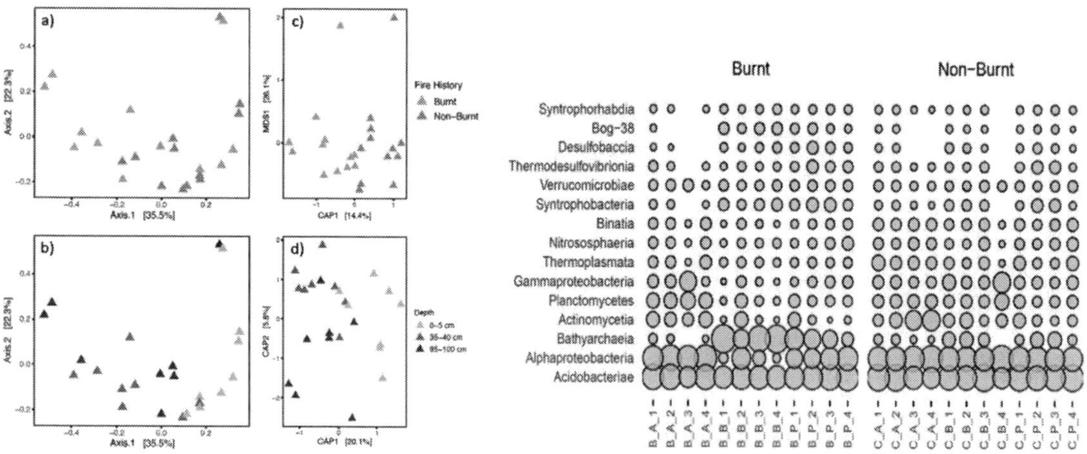


*Figure 4: Left side a-b shows unconstrained principal coordinates analysis (PCoA), and c-d shows constrained PCoA between burnt and non-burnt and three depths. Right side) shows relative abundance of top 15 bacterial and archaeal class between burnt and non-burnt along the three depths.*

3. ***Physicochemical control:*** Peat incubation results showed the effect of temperature increase on $CO_2$ production was most clear for mesic condition compared to flooded oxic and anoxic treatments with a rate of 232.90 ± 30.59 μg$CO_2$ $g^{-1}$ $hr^{-1}$ (at 26°C) to 337.98 ± 41.97 μg$CO_2$ $g^{-1}$ $hr^{-1}$ (at 30°C) (Figure 5). However, for $CH_4$ production, anoxic treatments clearly responded to temperature increase and acted as strong source (474.57 ± 69.10 at 26°C and 1097.06 ± 172.46 ng$CH_4$ $g^{-1}$ $hr^{-1}$ at 30°C) compared to other two treatments acting as a source of $CH_4$. Labile C addition, significantly ($p<0.001$) increased both $CO_2$ and $CH_4$ production rate across all the treatments (Figure 5). Overall, rates of $CO_2$ production increased with a corresponding increase in daily C addition (0.1<0.2<0.3 mgC $g^{-1}$) in mesic treatments whereas increased $CH_4$ production rate was observed in anoxic treatments only.

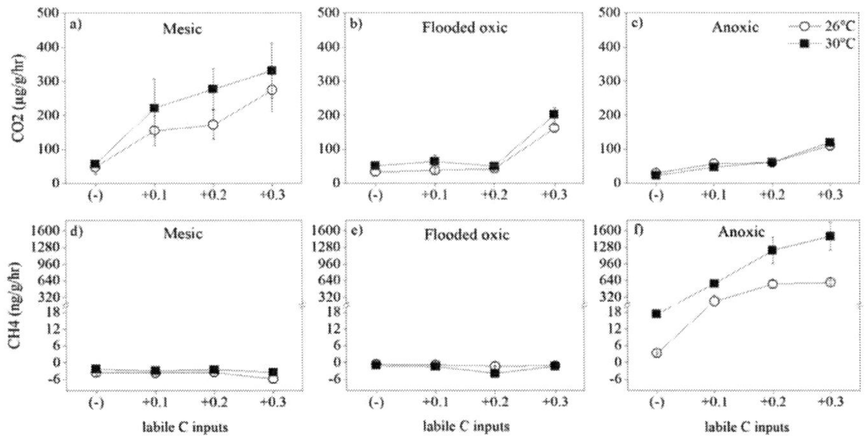


*Figure 5: Effects of water-saturation, due to microtopography, creating mesic, flooded oxic, and anoxic conditions, labile C inputs (+0.1, +0.2, +0.3 are daily carbon inputs rates in mgC$g^{-1}$ of peat soil; (-) is control), and diurnal temperature range (26°C for night-time and 30°C for day-time) on $CO_2$ (a–c) and $CH_4$ (d–f) production rates.*

## DISCUSSION

Our data shows for the first time that in fire-degraded tropical peatland sedge-mediated $CH_4$ transport to the atmosphere contributes >70% of total $CH_4$ emission at ecosystem level. This result is similar to plant-mediated $CH_4$ emissions in northern peatlands, which contributes ~22% to >90% of total $CH_4$ emission to the atmosphere at ecosystem level (Bhullar et al., 2013; Carmichael et al., 2014). Further, our microbiome composition analysis also revealed that burnt peat samples from deeper anoxic layer are enriched in *Bathyarchaeia*, a recently classified methane producing archaea. Concurrently, our results show that burnt peat samples are depleted in methanotrophs (*Alphaproteobacteria*, *Gammaproteobacteria*), compared to non-burnt peat samples. These results further explain higher $CH_4$ flux values from the burnt site. In fact, simulating the key-onsite conditions of water-saturation regulating oxic-anoxic interface, our incubation study also showed that fire-degraded tropical peat under mesic condition acted as a strong source of $CO_2$ whereas under anoxic conditions acted as a strong source of $CH_4$. However, with frequent fire episodes, the microtopography of such degraded areas tends to become relatively flat compared to intact tropical peatland areas, which may further result in prolonged flooding, creating anoxic and ORP conditions conducive to higher $CH_4$ production and emission. Furthermore, $CO_2$ and $CH_4$ production rates increased in response to the addition of plant root exudates, which shows how vegetation composition change can affect the quality and quantity of labile C in further regulating the GHG production and emissions. Taken together, the three-way approach adopted in this study i.e., effect of plant-mediated transport, changes in microbiome composition and oxic-anoxic interface in peat profile, highlights that fire-degraded tropical peatland areas may continue emitting significant amount of methane.

## CONCLUSION

We showed for the first time that sedges can be an important source of plant-mediated $CH_4$ emissions in a fire-degraded tropical peatland, similar to northern peatlands. These results are further confirmed by our microbiome composition data showing the enrichment of $CH_4$ producing archaea and depletion of $CH_4$ oxidizing bacteria in burnt tropical peat compared to non-burnt. Furthermore, our incubation study also confirmed that changes in oxic-anoxic interface can significantly affect the $CH_4$ production and emissions from fire-degraded tropical peat. Moreover, as the region is expected to encounter frequent fire episodes together with prolonged flooding in the subsiding degraded tropical peatland areas, these numbers are likely to shift towards higher in near future.

## ACKNOWLEDGEMENTS

This study was supported by grants received from Ministry of Education, Singapore (FY2015-SUG), Singapore Centre for Environmental Life Sciences Engineering (SCELSE Cluster 1: Plant Holobionts, WBS: R-711-500-008-271) and NUS Graduate Research Support Scheme for funding this research. We would also like to thank: the Brunei Forestry Department for entry and sampling permits (REF:[209]/JPH/UND/17 PT.1); the Biodiversity Research and Innovation Centre for export permits; the Biosecurity Division for phytosanitary certificates; the Universiti Brunei Darussalam for permission to conduct research, help with logistics, field support and various assistants for their help in the field.

# REFERENCES

Bhullar, G. S., Edwards, P. J., & Olde Venterink, H. (2013). Variation in the plant-mediated methane transport and its importance for methane emission from intact wetland peat mesocosms. Journal of Plant Ecology, 6(4), 298–304. https://doi.org/10.1093/jpe/rts045

Carmichael, M. J., Bernhardt, E. S., Bräuer, S. L., & Smith, W. K. (2014). The role of vegetation in methane flux to the atmosphere: Should vegetation be included as a distinct category in the global methane budget? Biogeochemistry, 119(1–3), 1–24. https://doi.org/10.1007/s10533-014-9974-1

Girkin, N. T., Turner, B. L., Ostle, N., Craigon, J., & Sjögersten, S. (2018). Root exudate analogues accelerate CO2 and CH4 production in tropical peat. Soil Biology and Biochemistry, 117, 48-55.

Hirano, T., Jauhiainen, J., Inoue, T., & Takahashi, H. (2009). Controls on the Carbon Balance of Tropical Peatlands. Ecosystems, 12(6), 873–887. https://doi.org/10.1007/s10021-008-9209-1

Hooijer, A., Page, S., Canadell, J. G., Silvius, M., Kwadijk, J., Woosten, H., & Jauhiainen, J. (2010). Current and future CO 2 emissions from drained peatlands in Southeast Asia. Biogeosciences, 7(5), 1505–1514. https://doi.org/10.5194/bg-7-1505-2010

Jackson, C. R., Liew, K. C., & Yule, C. M. (2009). Structural and functional changes with depth in microbial communities in a tropical Malaysian peat swamp forest. Microbial ecology, 57(3), 402-412.

Jauhiainen J, Takahashi H, Heikkinen JEP, Martikainen PJ, V. H. (2005). Carbon fluxes from a tropical peat swamp forest floor. Global Change Biology, 11, 1788–1797. https://doi.org/10.1111/j.1365-2486.2005.01031.x

Kanokratana, P., Uengwetwanit, T., Rattanachomsri, U., Bunterngsook, B., Nimchua, T., Tangphatsornruang, S., ... & Eurwilaichitr, L. (2011). Insights into the phylogeny and metabolic potential of a primary tropical peat swamp forest microbial community by metagenomic analysis. Microbial ecology, 61(3), 518-528.

Lupascu, M., Akhtar, H., Smith, T. E. L., & Sukri, R. S. (2019). Post-fire carbon dynamics in the tropical peat swamp forests of Brunei. Submitted to Global Change Biology.

Mezbahuddin, M., Grant, R. F., & Hirano, T. (2014). Modelling effects of seasonal variation in water table depth on net ecosystem CO 2 exchange of a tropical peatland. Biogeosciences, 11(3), 577-599.

Miettinen, J., Shi, C., & Liew, S. C. (2016). Land cover distribution in the peatlands of Peninsular Malaysia, Sumatra and Borneo in 2015 with changes since 1990. Global Ecology and Conservation, 6, 67–78. https://doi.org/10.1016/j.gecco.2016.02.004

Mishra, S., Lee, W. A., Hooijer, A., Reuben, S., Sudiana, I. M., Idris, A., & Swarup, S. (2014). Microbial and metabolic profiling reveal strong influence of water table and land-use patterns on classification of degraded tropical peatlands. Biogeosciences, 11(7), 1727-1741.

Page, S., Hosciło, A., Wösten, H., Jauhiainen, J., Silvius, M., Rieley, J., … Limin, S. (2009). Restoration ecology of lowland tropical peatlands in Southeast Asia: Current knowledge and future research directions. Ecosystems, 12(6), 888–905. https://doi.org/10.1007/s10021-008-9216-2

Sjögersten, S., Aplin, P., Gauci, V., Peacock, M., Siegenthaler, A., & Turner, B. L. (2018). Temperature response of ex-situ greenhouse gas emissions from tropical peatlands: Interactions between forest type and peat moisture conditions. Geoderma, 324, 47-55.

Too, C. C., Keller, A., Sickel, W., Lee, S. M., & Yule, C. M. (2018). Microbial community structure in a Malaysian tropical peat swamp forest: the influence of tree species and depth. Frontiers in microbiology, 9, 2859.

van Eijk, P., Leenman, P., Wibisono, I. T. C., & Giesen, W. (2009). Regeneration and restoration of degraded peat swamp forest in Berbak National Park, Jambi, Sumatra, Indonesia. Malayan Nature Journal, 61(November), 223–241.

Whalen, S. C. (2005). Biogeochemistry of methane exchange between natural wetlands and the atmosphere. Environmental Engineering Science, 22(1), 73-94.

Wösten, J. H. M., Van Den Berg, J., Van Eijk, P., Gevers, G. J. M., Giesen, W. B. J. T., Hooijer, A., … Wibisono, I. T. (2006). Interrelationships between hydrology and ecology in fire degraded tropical peat swamp forests. International Journal of Water Resources Development, 22(1), 157–174. https://doi.org/10.1080/07900620500405973

Yule, C. M., & Gomez, L. N. (2009). Leaf litter decomposition in a tropical peat swamp forest in Peninsular Malaysia. Wetlands Ecology and Management, 17(3), 231-241.

ID 62653

# REWETTING DEGRADED TROPICAL PEATLANDS TO SUBSTANTIALLY REDUCE CARBON EMISSIONS: A META-ANALYSIS AND EXPERIMENTAL STUDY

*Taryono Darusman[1], Daniel Murdiyarso[1,2], Impron[1], Iswandi Anas[3]

[1] Department of Geophysics and Meteorology, Bogor Agricultural University, Bogor 16680, Indonesia
[2] Center for International Forestry Research (CIFOR), Situgede, Bogor Sindang Barang 16115, Indonesia
[3] Departement of Soil Science and Land Resources, Bogor Agricultural University, Bogor 16680, Indonesia

*taryono.d@gmail.com*

## SUMMARY

The study on rewetting drained peatlands has been reported worldwide. To summarize the effect of rewetting on carbon emissions, we conducted a meta-analysis by which we could strategize in closing the gaps of information. Data was collected from 2,089 published articles, and 33 of these articles were then categorized as primary articles, eligible for further analysis, and represented temperate peat (24), boreal peat (8), and tropical peat (1). Subsequently, the meta-analysis was applied to generate overall random effects size (standardize effect size (d) between treatment and control). The overall random-effect size calculated from 22 effect sizes (cases) in high latitude peatlands showed rewetting had a reduction effect of $CO_2$ emissions of d = - 0.861 (95% CI -1.59 to -0.14), compared to the drained counterpart ecosystems. In addition, data from 24 cases showed rewetting high latitude peatlands increased $CH_4$ emissions of d = 1.11 (95% CI 0.43 to 1.78), compared to the drained counterpart ecosystems. Due to the limited availability of published data from tropical peatlands, carbon emissions of rewetted (treated site) and undrained (control site) peat swamp forest in Central Kalimantan, Indonesia, were compared. According to preliminary results, the averaged carbon emission from total respiration ($R_s$) in the rewetted sites was 6.05 ± 1.21 Mg-C ha$^{-1}$ y$^{-1}$, which is lower than undrained sites' counterpart of 7.27 ± 1.17 Mg-C ha$^{-1}$ y$^{-1}$. Meanwhile, the averaged carbon emission from heterotrophic respiration ($R_h$) of rewetted sites at 6.32 ± 1.06 Mg-C ha$^{-1}$ y$^{-1}$, was close with the counterpart of the undrained sites 6.21 ± 0.9 Mg-C ha$^{-1}$ y$^{-1}$. These suggest rewetting tropical peatlands has the potential to meet the restoration objective, as the $CO_2$ fluxes are similar to the undrained counterparts.

Keyoords: *Undrained, rewetted, heterotrophic respiration, and carbon fluxes.*

## INTRODUCTION

Degraded peatlands and deforested peat swamp forests are a source of carbon emissions. Furthermore, restoring these areas to the original states, and eventually, to the capacity to function as carbon sinks, is bound to take over 100 years, depending on the degradation severity. However, rewetting intervention on previously drained peatlands has been firmly believed to reduce carbon emission from the peat decomposition, at a relatively immediate timeline (Ojanen *et al.,* 2020). Rewetting is defined as the deliberate action of raising the water table in a previously drained peatland ecosystem. According to Wilson *et al.,* (2016), numerous individual findings related to the rewetting intervention's effect on carbon emission have been widely published, mostly from high latitude peatlands, however, the study on rewetted or, generally, on restored tropical counterparts is increasing but currently limited (Murdiyarso *et al.,* 2019). This study therefore aims to statistically summarize the individual effect of rewetting on previously drained peatland and estimate the in situ $CO_2$ as well $CH_4$ emissions, from rewetted tropical peat swamp forest.

## MATERIALS AND METHODS

### Systematic review and meta-analysis

For this research, peer-reviewed primary studies related to peatland rewetting and carbon flux measurement from 1990 to 2018 were collected. Subsequently, the primary studies were screened, based on inclusion criteria, for instance, measuring carbon fluxes ($CO_2$ and/or $CH_4$), experimental study (field study), and possessing a comparison site (rewetted and control site). The selected primary studies were then categorized as eligible for meta-analysis. Furthermore, the mean value, standard deviation (SD), and sample size data (N) were extracted from eligible studies, to calculate an effect size. In cases where the eligible studies reported only SE (standard error) value, this was converted into SD (standard deviation) using the formula SD = SE x $\sqrt{n}$ (Skinner *et al.*, 2014). Data was only extracted from the pair-site data, either before-after or using the comparison site approach, for instance, rewetted hummock measurement site with drained hummock measurement site, rewetted hollow site with drained hollow measurement site, or on the same site but applied before-after rewetting intervention. In addition, a random-effects meta-analysis was used to investigate the overall effect sizes of rewetting on carbon fluxes from peatland ecosystems (Borenstein *et al.*, 2009). The rewetting effect's magnitude and direction were evaluated using standardized mean difference (*d*) (SMD), without converting the primary studies' unit measurements into a single unit measurement. Meanwhile, the individual effect size (*d*) was calculated automatically from the mean, standard deviation, and sample size in Comprehensive Meta-Analysis Software (CMA™) from each study (Borenstein *et al.*, 2009). The results were then plotted using a forest plot graph.

### GHG fluxes in situ measurement

This study was conducted in Peatland Restoration and Conservation Project Area (Katingan Mentaya Project), Central Kalimantan, Indonesia. The rewetted site (treated plots) was located approximately 800 meters from the primary canal (Hantipan Canal), while the undrained site (control plots) was located nearly in the Katingan peat swamp forest area's center, about 3 km from the primary canal and 2.5 km from the rewetted site, in a northward direction. Furthermore, the plot's location was at -2° 55'25.93"; 113° 9'16.19" for the rewetted site and -2° 54'15.54"; 113° 9'14.92" for the undrained site. Carbon fluxes ($CO_2$ and $CH_4$) were measured using the static closed chamber method, at four circular plots in each site (rewetted and undrained), with 100 meters distance between plots. Each plot consists of 8 permanent chambers placed at each cardinal point, thus, a total of 64 (8 x 8) chambers, with 32 chambers in each site (undrained PSF and rewetted PSF), were obtained. Also, half of the chambers (16 in each site) were trenched to separate heterotrophic and autotrophic respiration. Data collection was commenced two months after trenching was established, and gas samples were collected to represent the dry (September 2019) and wet (February 2019) seasons, to cover seasonal variability. Gas sampling was performed from 08:00 am to 13:00 pm and collected at 0, 10, 20, and 30 minutes intervals using a 50 ml polypropylene syringe. Subsequently, the samples were analyzed with a gas chromatography equipped with an Electron Capture Detector (ECD) and with a Flame Ionization Detector (FID) for $CH_4$ and $CO_2$ analysis in CIFOR-Bogor. The fluxes rate was then calculated from the concentration change rate in the chamber headspace, determined by the slope of a linear regression of gas concentration and converted, using the ideal gas ideal (Pihlatie *et al.* 2013).

## RESULTS

### Systematic review and Meta-analysis

Initially, about 2,089 primary studies records were obtained, with 1,747 from website and online database searches, and 342 collected from previous article reviews. After conducting the screening process, only 33 records met our inclusion criteria, for instance, having a comparator site (comparing rewetted with drained or undrained sites). In regard to the comparator site, of the 33 studies, most used drained sites (20), while 5 used undrained sites, and 8 used both drained and undrained sites as comparators sites. In terms of climate zones, most of the primary studies were conducted in temperate regions (24), while 8 were conducted in boreal regions, and only one in the tropics.

Based on the meta-analysis performed, the rewetted peatlands showed lower $CO_2$ emissions, compared to drained peatlands, with a random overall effect size of d = - 0.861 (95% CI - 1.59 to – -0.14) (Table 1 and Figure 1). This was considered a large effect size, and differed significantly from 0 with Z-value = -2.328; p = 0.020. Conversely, the meta-analysis was performed on 24 individual effect sizes showed rewetting interventions had the overall effect of increasing $CH_4$ emissions, with d = 1.11 (95% CI 0.43 to 1.78), z-value of 3.223, and p = 0.001 (Table 1 and Figure 2).

**Table 1:** The overall random effect sizes, from peatland rewetting intervention on $CO_2$ and $CH_4$ fluxes. S = number of primary studies, EZ = total number of individual effect size extracted from the primary studies, d = standardized effect size, SE = standard error, Var. = variance. A negative d value indicates a reduction of carbon ($CO_2$) emission from rewetted peatland, while a positive d value indicates a rise in carbon ($CH_4$) emission from rewetted peatland

| | S | EZ | d | SE | Var. | Lower Limit | Upper Limit | Z | P |
|---|---|---|---|---|---|---|---|---|---|
| $CO_2$ | 11 | 22 | -0.86 | 0.37 | 0.14 | -1.59 | -0.14 | -2.33 | 0.020 |
| $CH_4$ | 13 | 24 | 1.11 | 0.34 | 0.12 | 0.43 | 1.78 | 3.22 | 0.001 |

| Study name | Std diff in means | Standard error | p-Value |
|---|---|---|---|
| Tuittila et al. (1999) (E. tussock-Rtu 3) | -0.003 | 0.428 | 0.994 |
| Tuittila et al. (1999) (Intertussock-Rin 2) | -1.202 | 0.475 | 0.011 |
| Waddington et al. (2010) (Bare peat) | -3.459 | 0.690 | 0.000 |
| Waddington et al. (2010) (Moss peat) | -4.097 | 0.768 | 0.000 |
| Waddington et al. (2010) (Eriphorum peat) | 4.420 | 0.810 | 0.000 |
| Urbanová et al. (2012) (Bog rewetted-high shrub) | -0.572 | 0.833 | 0.492 |
| Urbanová et al. (2012) (Bog rewetted-trich) | 0.703 | 0.841 | 0.403 |
| Strack & Zuback (2013) (Field) | -0.287 | 0.490 | 0.558 |
| Strack et al. (2014) (Wet) | 1.226 | 0.683 | 0.073 |
| Wilson et al. (2016) (Bare peat) | -2.072 | 1.012 | 0.041 |
| Wilson et al. (2016) (Juncuss efussus-Dominated) | -1.721 | 0.956 | 0.072 |
| Renou-Wilson et al. (2016) (Grazed) | -0.776 | 0.628 | 0.216 |
| Renou-Wilson et al. (2016) (Ungrazed) | -3.264 | 0.922 | 0.000 |
| Strack et al. (2016) | 0.484 | 0.223 | 0.030 |
| Luan et al. (2018) (Kobresia pussila) | -2.611 | 0.786 | 0.001 |
| Luan et al. (2018) (Carex enervis) | -2.963 | 0.836 | 0.000 |
| Luan et al. (2018) (Carex Muliensis) | -3.838 | 1.376 | 0.005 |
| Renou-Wilson et al. (2018) (Moyarwood) | -1.369 | 0.692 | 0.048 |
| Renou-Wilson et al. (2018) (Reeds- Blackwater) | 1.997 | 0.800 | 0.013 |
| Jauhiainen et al. (2008) (Drained forest, depression site) | 0.165 | 0.818 | 0.841 |
| Jauhiainen et al. (2008) (Drained-burnt peat, hummock site) | -0.679 | 0.650 | 0.296 |
| Jauhiainen et al. (2008) (Drained-burnt peat, depression site) | -0.621 | 0.724 | 0.391 |
| | -0.861 | 0.370 | 0.020 |

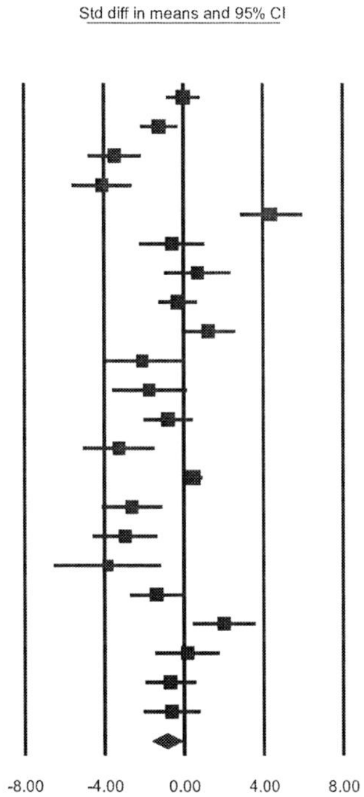


Figure 4. Forest-plot analysis of $CO_2$ fluxes. Std Diff is standardized difference and CI is confidence interval. The negative sign indicate $CO_2$ flux reduction and positive sign indicate $CO_2$ flux increase due to rewetting intervention. The overall effect size of rewetting (blue diamond) was -0.861±0.370 (p-value of 0.020).

| Study name | Std diff in means | Standard error | p-Value |
|---|---|---|---|
| Komulainen et al. (1998) (Fen site A) | 2.067 | 1.239 | 0.095 |
| Komulainen et al. (1998) (Fen site B) | 1.287 | 1.099 | 0.241 |
| Komulainen et al. (1998) (Bog site A) | 0.746 | 1.034 | 0.471 |
| Komulainen et al. (1998) (Bog site B) | 0.020 | 1.000 | 0.984 |
| Waddington and Day (2007) (2000 Bare peat) | 0.326 | 0.503 | 0.517 |
| Waddington and Day (2007) (2001 Bare peat) | 0.252 | 0.502 | 0.615 |
| Jauhiainen et al. (2008) (Drained forest - depression site) | -1.054 | 0.755 | 0.162 |
| Jauhiainen et al. (2008) (Drained-burnt peat - depression site) | 0.422 | 0.826 | 0.609 |
| Urbanová et al. (2012) (Bog rewetted-high shrub) | 1.055 | 0.972 | 0.278 |
| Strack et al. (2013) (Growing season-field) | 0.842 | 0.506 | 0.096 |
| Strack et al. (2013) (Non-growing season-field) | -0.669 | 0.499 | 0.180 |
| Strack et al. (2014) | 2.235 | 0.920 | 0.015 |
| Vanselow-Algan et al. (2015) (Purple moor grass) | 2.001 | 0.866 | 0.021 |
| Krause et al. (2015) (Meadow) | 1.374 | 0.556 | 0.013 |
| Renou-Wilson et al. (2016) | 0.989 | 0.641 | 0.123 |
| Strack et al. (2016) | 3.901 | 0.325 | 0.000 |
| Renou-Wilson et al. (2018) (Moyarwood) | 4.144 | 1.019 | 0.000 |
| Luan et al. (2018) (Kobresia pussila) | 0.424 | 0.584 | 0.468 |
| Luan et al. (2018) (Carex enervis) | 4.444 | 1.075 | 0.000 |
| Luan et al. (2018) (Carex muliensis) | 5.926 | 1.896 | 0.002 |
| Waddington and Day (2007) (2002 Bare peat) | 0.068 | 0.500 | 0.892 |
| Waddington and Day (2007) (2000 Moss peat) | 0.000 | 0.500 | 1.000 |
| Waddington and Day (2007) (2001 Moss peat) | 0.262 | 0.502 | 0.601 |
| Waddington and Day (2007) (2002 Moss peat) | -0.253 | 0.502 | 0.614 |
| | 1.107 | 0.343 | 0.001 |

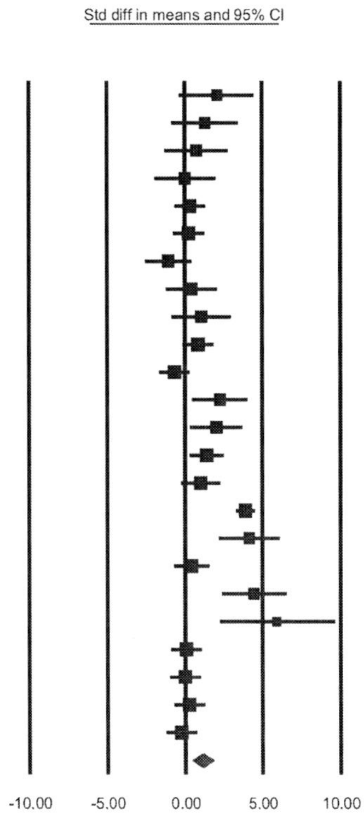


Figure 5. The forest-plot analysis of rewetting effect sizes on $CH_4$ emissions. Std Diff is standardized difference, while CI is confidence interval. Negative and positive values indicate the emission reduction and increase, due to rewetting intervention. The overall effect size (blue diamond) was 1.107 ± 3.223 (p-value of 0.001)

$CO_2$ and $CH_4$ fluxes

Carbon emissions ($CO_2$ and $CH_4$) were measured in February and September 2019, representing the wet and the dry season. The field observation showed $CO_2$ and $CH_4$ emissions fluctuated, according to ground water level (GWL) (Figure 3). Furthermore, the total soil respirations ($R_s$) and heterotrophic component of soil respirations ($R_h$) were lower in February 2019, compared to September 2019, in the two sites. The annual mean $R_h$ in February 2019 were at $86.37 \pm 18$ mg $m^{-2}$ $hr^{-1}$ and $76.38 \pm 21$ mg $m^{-2}$ $hr^{-1}$ in the rewetted and undrained sites, respectively, and increased to $493.22 \pm 74$ mg $m^{-2}$ $hr^{-1}$ and $443.25 \pm 33$ mg $m^{-2}$ $hr^{-1}$, respectively, in September. However, the $CH_4$ emissions showed an opposite pattern with the $CO_2$ emissions. The annual mean $CH_4$ emissions were $1.11 \pm 1.02$ mg $CH_4$ $m^{-2}$ $hr^{-1}$ in rewetted site and $2.66 \pm 1.32$ mg $CH_4$ $m^{-2}$ $hr^{-1}$ in undrained site, amounting to $54.93 \pm 50.45$ Kg $CH_4$ $ha^{-1}$ year-1 and $131.21 \pm 65.48$ Kg $CH_4$ $ha^{-1}year^{-1}$, respectively.

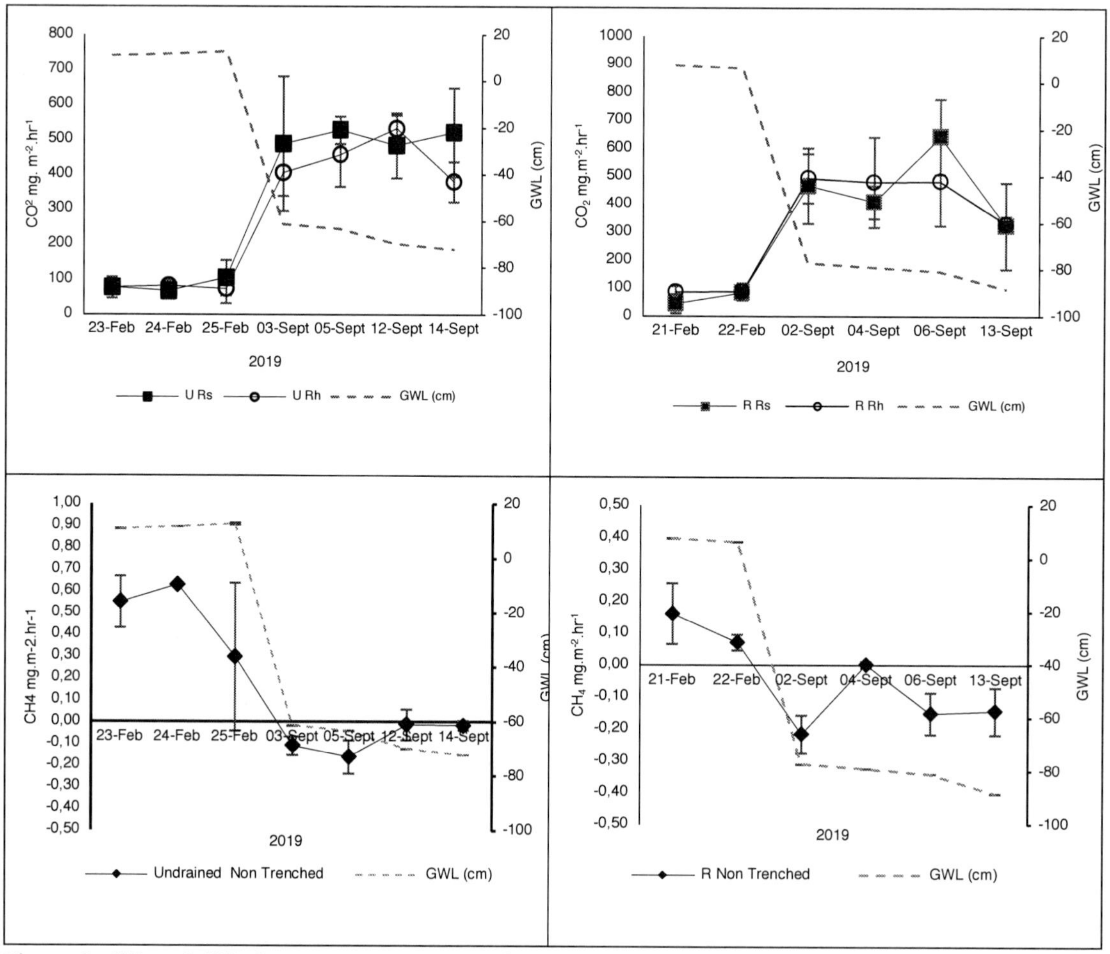


Figure 6: $CO_2$ and $CH_4$ fluxes response to groundwater level (blue-dash line) in rewetted and undrained sites. Symbols indicate mean fluxes and error bars in SE. R = rewetted, U= Undrained.

## DISCUSSION

Based on the meta-analysis study, rewetted peatland has lower $CO_2$ and higher $CH_4$ emission compared to drained peatland. The effect of rewetting intervention on $CO_2$ emission reduction was statistically significant, as indicated by confident interval (CI) value below the zero value and a p-value of 0.020. In contrast, the rewetting intervention significantly increased $CH_4$ emission with a p-value of 0.001. However, data from tropical peatlands related to the rewetting intervention is currently limited. A few recent studies have assessed the rewetting effect on carbon emission in tropical peatlands, but these findings were not incorporated in this paper. In addition to the meta-analysis study, the field observation showed the total soil respiration ($R_s$) from the rewetted site did not significantly differ from the undrained site, with values of 6.05 ± 1.21 Mg C $ha^{-1}year^{-1}$ and 7.27 ± 1.17 Mg C $ha^{-1}year^{-1}$, respectively. Interestingly, the $R_h$ from the rewetted site was 6.32 ± 1.06 Mg C $ha^{-1}year^{-1}$, leading to an $R_h/R_s$ ratio above 100%, while from the undrained site counterpart was at 6.21 ± 0.90 Mg C $ha^{-1}year^{-1}$, making the $R_h/R_s$ ratio 85%. High $R_h/R_s$ ratios were also reported by Ishikura *et al.*, (2019) and Hergoualc'h *et al.*, (2017) from pristine and undrained tropical peat swamp forests. During the measurement, litterfall was not removed from the trenched chambers. Litterfall possibly provides fresh and labile organic matters in the trenched chambers and eventually increases the $R_h$. In addition, the newly dead roots inside the trenching probably also contribute to the $R_h$, as gas sampling was conducted only two months after trenching establishment. The $R_h$ values in this study were slightly smaller compared to tropical PSFs, Tanjung Putting, Central Kalimantan (7.1 ± 0.4 Mg C $ha^{-1}$ $year^{-1}$) (Hergoualc'h *et al.,* 2017), undrained peat swamp forest, Sebangau, Central Kalimantan (8.9 ± 0.4 Mg C $ha^{-1}$ $year^{-1}$), and other values from the tropical PSFs reported by Itoh *et al.,* (2017). The relatively lower GWL probably influences the smaller $R_h$ fluxes in the study sites. The annual mean GWL in 2019 was -21 cm and -12 cm for the rewetted and undrained sites, respectively, and this is lower, compared to other studies' counterparts range from -20 cm to - 114 cm (Itoh *et al.* 2017). In contrast $CH_4$ emissions was increased in the rewetted sites; however, the $CH_4$ emissions from this preliminary study was not substantial. Carbon loss reduction from peat soil is a possible assumption for an incomplete success of the rewetting intervention because the ultimate goal is not to reduce carbon loss but also to restore the degraded peat swamp forests from carbon source to carbon sink. Therefore, the carbon loss from peat soil ($R_h$), is possibly coupled with the aboveground and belowground litter data (as a significant carbon input), to evaluate effect of rewetting on the carbon balance in tropical peat swamp forests.

## CONCLUSION

The meta-analysis study shows rewetting intervention on previously drained peatland has a significant effect on reducing $CO_2$ emission and increasing $CH_4$ emission. This finding was in line with the field study conducted in the rewetted tropical peat swamp forest, where rewetting intervention was able to reduce the carbon ($CO_2$) emission of previously drained tropical peat swamp forests, similar to the undrained peat swamp forest.

## ACKNOWLEDGEMENTS

The authors are grateful to the United States Agency for International Development (USAID), for providing a fellowship program through the Sustainable Wetlands Adaptation and Mitigation Program (SWAMP) of the Center for International Forestry Research (CIFOR). The authors also thanks Katingan Mentaya Project for additional support during the field work.

## REFERENCES


1. Borenstein M, Hedges LV, Higgins JPT and Rothstein HR. (2009) Introduction to meta-analysis. John Wiley & Sons Ltd, United Kingdom
2. Hergoualc'h K, Hendry DT, Murdiyarso D, Verchot LV. (2017) Total and heterotrophic soil respiration in a swamp forest and oil palm plantations on peat in Central Kalimantan, Indonesia. *Biogeochemistry* doi:10.1007/s10533-017-0363-4
3. Itoh M, Okimoto Y, Hirano T, Kusin K. (2017) Factors affecting oxidative peat decomposition due to land use in tropical peat swamp forests in Indonesia. *Sci Total Environ* 609:906–15.
4. Ojanen P, & Minkkinen K. (2020) Rewetting offers rapid climate benefits for tropical and agricultural peatlands but not for forestry drained peatlands. *Global Biogeochemical Cycles*, 34, e2019GB006503. https://doi.org/10.1029/2019GB006503. 2020
5. Pihlatie MK, Christiansen JR, Aaltonen H, Korhonen JFF, Nordbo A, Rasilo T, Benanti G, Giebels M, Helmy M, Sheehy J, Jones S, Juszczak R, Kefloth R, Lobo-do-Vale R, Rosa AP, Schreiber P, Serca D, Vicca S, Wolf B, and Pumpanen J. (2013) Comparison of static chambers to measure $CH_4$ emission from soils. Agricultur and Forest Meteorology. 171-172, 124-136. https://dx.doi.org/10.1016/j.agroformet.2012.11.008 .
6. Murdiyarso D, Saragi-Sasmito MF, Rustini A. (2019) Greenhouse gas emissions in restored secondary tropical peat swamp forests. *Mitig Adapt Strateg Glob Change* **24,** 507–520. https://doi.org/10.1007/s11027-017-9776-6
7. Wilson D, Blain D, Couwenberg J, Evans CD, Murdiyarso D, Page SE, Wilson R E, Rieley J, Sirin A, Strack M, Tuittila E. (2016) Greenhouse gas emissions factor associated with rewetting organic soils. *Mires and Peat,* **1**, 28.

ID 62724

# PEATLAND RESPONSE TO DRYING, COMPARING AND CONTRASTING PEATLANDS IN SWEDEN AND NEW ZEALAND

*Ratcliffe, JL[1], Campbel[1], DI2, Clarkson, BR[3], Nilsson, MB, Peichl, M[1]

[1] Department of Forest Ecology and Management, Swedish University of Agricultural Sciences, Sweden
[2] School of Science and Environmental Research Institute, University of Waikato, New Zealand
[3] Manaaki Whenua – Landcare Research, University of Waikato, New Zealand

*joss.ratcliffe@slu.se*

European peatlands are drying out, and are increasingly subject to droughts. There is much concern as to what may happen to carbon stored as peat. Peatlands, as a biome, are remarkably varied in terms of geographical distribution and vegetation composition. Restiad peats, endemic to the Southern Hemisphere, are one of the less-studied peat types and are formed from plants of the Restionaceae family. These plants are highly efficient peat-formers, in many ways analogous to Sphagnum, but contrast from Sphagnum in the sense they are vascular, with strong stomatal control, and a great many xeromorphic adaptations which allow them to survive desiccation. Restiad peat-formers can tolerate a wide range of water-table conditions and can maintain peatland carbon stocks even in light of exceptionally low water tables. Therefore, restiad peatlands can offer some unique insights into the resilience of peatlands to drying. Here we present Eddy Covariance data from Sphagnum and restiad dominated peatlands, comparing the response of the two peatland types to drying. We use plant functional traits as a lens through which to interpret the contrasting responses seen in the different peat types.

ID 62759

# GREENHOUSE GAS EMISSIONS FROM DEGRADED AND REWETTED PEATLANDS IN NORTHERN EUROPEAN LOWLAND

*Andreas Herrmann[1, 2], Anna-Helena Purre[3], Letícia Jurema[1], Tom Kirschey[1], Marc Kupetz[1], Andis Lazdiņš[4], Ainars Lupikis[4]

[1] NABU, International Peatland Conservation, Berlin, Germany
[2] Division of Soil and Site Science, Humboldt-Universität zu Berlin, Berlin, Germany
[3] School of Natural Sciences and Health, Tallinn University, Tallinn, Estonia
[4] Latvian State Forest Research – "Silava", Riga, Latvia

andreas.herrmann.1@agrar.hu-berlin.de

## SUMMARY

The north-eastern European countries as Estonia, Latvia and Lithuania have huge peatland areas, which partly reach several meters in depth. Due to peat excavating and the intensification of agriculture and forestry, peatlands were increasingly drained, leading to an accelerated peat mineralization and consequently to high greenhouse gas (GHG) emissions. At European level the Baltic States represent Hot Spots of GHG emissions, coming from drained peatlands as well as Germany and Poland. The EU aims to reduce greenhouse gas emissions currently by 50 to 55 percent until 2030 compared to 1990. Therefore the restoration of drained peatlands must be integrated in the climate policy.

The objective of the EU-LIFE Project "Peat Restore" is the rewetting of degraded peatlands in the partner countries Estonia, Latvia, Lithuania, Poland and Germany, covering a total area of 5.300 hectares. To assess the climate effect of the restoration measures and to obtain actual emission data, we monitored the greenhouse gas dynamic in ten different sites and ecosystems.

The measurements started in early summer 2018 in Estonia, Poland and Germany and 2019 in Latvia and Lithuania. We used a combination of different chambers (opaque and transparent ones) to quantify the Ecosystem Respiration ($R_{ECO}$) and the Net-Ecosystem-Exchange (NEE) by different Infrared Gas analyser (IRGA) systems. We also measured methane ($CH_4$) and nitrous oxide ($N_2O$) fluxes in-situ or in the laboratory by manual sampling in a 2-/4-weekly cycle.

Due to the dry summer we measured continuously high $R_{ECO}$-fluxes throughout the vegetation period in 2018, but depending on the vegetation composition and the water level with significant spatial differences. The calculated gross primary production (GPP) fluxes reflect a more typical seasonal course, with a pronounced interannual variation. The methane fluxes are low to moderate, but respond also with rates to beaver activities. The $N_2O$ fluxes are currently on a low level only.

***Keywords***: *restoration, carbon dioxide, methane, nitrous oxide, chamber method*

## INTRODUCTION

On the global scale peatlands store more than 600 gigatons carbon (C) (Leifeld & Menichetti 2018), which amounts to ca. 30 percent of the global soil carbon (Parish et al. 2008). Referred to a total area of ca. 4 to 5 million $km^2$, peatlands belong to the most space-effective terrestrial C-pools in the world. Contemporary peatlands affect also the global climate as important source and sink of greenhouse gases, like carbon dioxide ($CO_2$), methane ($CH_4$) and nitrous oxide ($N_2O$). Due to intensive drainage measures for agriculture and forestry, but also for peat mining activities most of the peatlands in Europe are degraded and emit huge amounts of $CO_2$ and $N_2O$.

More than 15 percent of the Baltic Countries (Estonia, Latvia, Lithuania) are covered by peatlands (Barthelmes et al. 2015), over 70 % of these areas are directly or indirectly affected by degradation. The estimated $CO_2$-emissions of the Baltic Countries extend to 29 megatons per year (Barthelmes et al. 2015). In Germany drained organic soils emit more than 55 million tons, accounting for ca. 6.6 % of the national GHG emissions in 2014 (Tiemeyer et al. 2020) and the emissions of drained organic soils in Poland amounts to ca. 580 kilotons per year (NIR_POL 2020). Therefore at European level drained peatlands in the Baltic States as well as in Poland and Germany constitute Hot Spots of GHG.

Within the Green Deal the EU signed on to reduce GHG emissions by 50 to 55 percent until 2030 compared to 1990. To achieve these ambitious goals, we have to focus on the restoration of drained peatlands in the climate policy. The objective of the EU-LIFE Project "Peat Restore" is the rewetting of degraded peatlands in the partner countries Estonia, Latvia, Lithuania, Poland and Germany, covering a total area of 5,300 hectares. To assess the climate effect of the restoration measures and to quantify the current emission, we observe the greenhouse gas dynamic on the project sites. Here we want to present the first GHG data of the last years in the Baltic Countries, as well as Poland and Germany.

## MATERIALS AND METHODS

In total we investigated the GHG dynamics in ten study sites: Suursoo-Leidissoo (SL) in Estonia, Augstroze Mire (AUG), Lake Engure Fen (ENG) and Baltezers Mire (BAL) in Latvia, Sachara (SAC), Puščia (PUS), Aukštumala (AUK) and Amalvas (AMA) in Lithuania, Slowinski National Park (SNP) in Poland and Biesenthaler Becken (BB) in Germany. A summary of some site characteristics is given in table 1

Table 1 Summary of site characteristics

| Site | Code | Habitat | WL* | Prec.** | Air Temp.** |
|---|---|---|---|---|---|
| | | | cm | mm | °C |
| Suursoo-Leidissoo | SL-1 | Calcareous Fen | -8 (+20 to -44) | 688 | 6.4 |
| | SL-2 | Transitional Mire | -15 (+4 to -43) | | |
| | SL-3 | Oligotrophic Forest | -15 (+3 to -52) | | |
| | SL-4 | Swamp Forest | -9 (+20 to -80) | | |
| | SL-5 | Drained Peatland Forest | -32 (+7 to -80) | | |
| Augstroze Mire | AUG | Degraded Raised Bog | -56.3 (-15.9 to -96.7) | 780 | 7.6 |
| Lake Engure Fen | ENG | Calcareous Fen | -67.4 (-10.5 to -116.0) | | |
| Baltezers Mire | BAL | Transitional Mire / Quaking Bogs | -72.0 (-24.3 to -116.4) | | |
| Sachara | SAC | Degraded Bog Woodland | -20.3 (+11.5 to -114.5) | 635 | 6.5 |
| Puščia | PUS | Former Peat cut-off area, Bare Peat | -18.0 (+22.1 to -44.8) | 630 | 6.1 |
| Aukštumala | AUK | Active and Former Peat cut-off area, Bare Peat | -56.4 (+8.4 to -118.6) | 775 | 7.2 |
| Amalvas | AMA | Degraded Bog Woodland | -84.1 (-35.1 to -146.2) | 630 | 6.6 |
| Slowinski National Park | SNP | Bog Heath | -37.1 (+4.7 to -94.4) | 661 | 8.1 |
| Biesenthaler Becken | BB | Swamp Forest | -12.8 (+8.0 to -61.7) | 520 | 8.6 |

*Average in cm beneath the surface with Minimum and Maximum values; ** Average values taken from the closest weather station

In general, we used the manual chamber technique for GHG-measurements with a combination of dark (for Ecosystem-Respiration ($R_{ECO}$), transparency level 0%) and light measurements (for net ecosystem exchange (NEE), different transparency levels). The study setup and the measurement equipment distinguished a bit between the different countries. In Estonian restoration site, four measurement points were positioned along a transect stretching from communities impacted by drainage close to the ditch up to the middle part of the restoration site, representing more "natural" communities with less drainage impact. Every point is represented by four measurement plots (collars), which allows the analysis of the spatial variance. In the other countries we installed three collars in Germany and Poland and five collars in Latvia and Lithuania in only one location per study site. NEE measurements were made by transparent chambers with volumes ranging from 65 up to 608 l in each country. For $R_{ECO}$-measurements an opaque hood on transparent chambers or opaque white plastic chambers were used. All chambers were equipped with fans for mixing the chamber air volume; a cooling systems to keep the temperature inside the chamber approximately close to the temperature outside the chamber; an air temperature and a PAR sensor to quantify these parameters inside the chamber.

To quantify the $CO_2$ concentration in the field we used in Estonia a Li-6400 Infrared gas analyzer (IRGA). In Latvia and Lithuania an EGM-4 IRGA and in Poland and Germany a Li-810. Methane and Nitrous Oxide was measured by a separate IRGA Gasmet DX-4030 directly in the field in Estonia. In all other countries we took manual samples by previously evacuated gas-tight syringes or bottles. Afterwards the samples were analyzed by a gas chromatograph (GC) equipped with an electron capture detector (ECD) and flame ionization detector (FID) within four to six weeks after the measurement campaign. Samples from Germany and Poland were analyzed by a GC-2010 Plus AF (Fa. Shimadzu) at the Humboldt-Universität zu Berlin and Samples from Latvia and Lithuania were analyzed by a GC-2014 and a Loftfield autosampler at the University of Tartu.

Furthermore we recorded additional environmental parameters like vegetation height and coverage, the leaf-area-index of vascular plants ($LAI_{vasc.}$), groundwater levels (GWL), photosynthetically active radiation (PAR), air and soil temperature in 5 or 10 cm as well as soil moisture for reconstructing spatial and temporal variability of greenhouse gas fluxes.

For the calculation of the GHG fluxes we used the ideal gas equation with a presumed simple linear change in concentration in time. Negative Fluxes stands for an uptake of GHG from the atmosphere, while positive values represent an emission of GHG to the atmosphere. To estimate the GHG balances for the studied periods, data sets were parameterized for each measurement plot in order to calculate hourly GHG fluxes. In case of $CO_2$ we have first calculated the ecosystem respiration with an Arrhenius approach, integrating the non-linear relationship between measured respiration rate and temperature. Then we used the calculated $R_{ECO}$ flux rates to calculate the gross primary production by simple subtraction from the measured net ecosystem exchange fluxes. In SL site, GHG fluxes were also modelled to whole growing season. $CO_2$ flux components were modelled similarly to Purre et al. (2019).

Methane and $N_2O$ fluxes were reconstructed by creating regression models with groundwater levels and air temperature respective. For other sites, the fluxes are presented here first as mean calculated values.

## RESULTS

Preliminary data of ecosystem respiration fluxes presented in Fig.1 show clear site-specific differences. The highest flux medians amount 1.33 and 0.96 g $CO_2$-C $m^{-2}$ $h^{-1}$ for AMA and SAC respective. Both sites are covered by highly degraded bog woodland. Measured singular $R_{ECO}$-Fluxes succeeded a seasonal course with higher fluxes in the summertime and lower fluxes in the early spring and late autumn. A clear "global" relationship with the water table could not be found, yet, but it seems that the water table fluctuations play a more important role.

Methane fluxes are presented in figure 2. The highest emissions were measured in all Latvian Sites, AUG, BAL and ENG with 630.5, 1952.3 and 870.63 µg $CH_4$-C $m^{-2}$ $h^{-1}$ respective. Interestingly we found also no clear dependence on water level. So there must be identify other site specific factors like nutrient conditions, pH-value or vegetation

composition (e.g. abundance of aerenchymus plant species), which could explain these differences. However, there could also be other factors like beaver activities, especially in the German project site, which strongly influence the hydrological regime.
$N_2O$ emissions were very low, only the in-alder swamp forest in Germany and in the active peat extraction area in Lithuania we observed slight higher $N_2O$ fluxes.

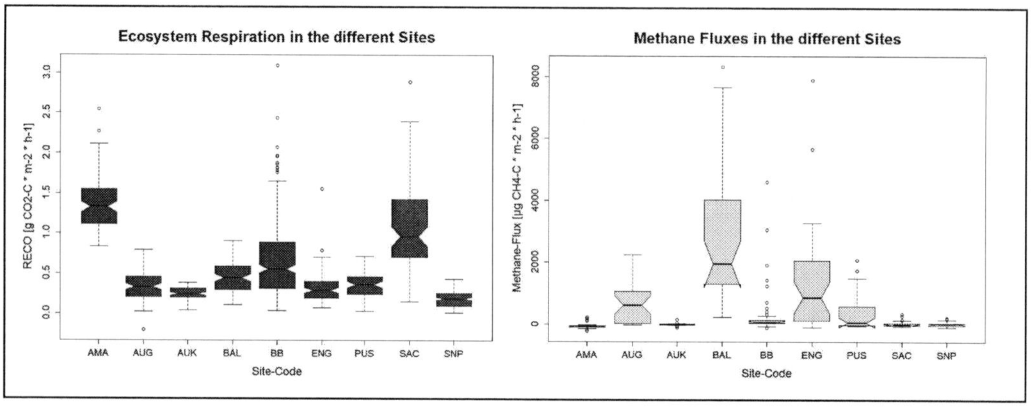


Figure 1 + 2: Mean calculated $R_{Eco}$ and Methane Fluxes in the different project sites in Latvia, Lithuania, Germany and Poland

Growing season GHG fluxes in Suursoo-Leidissoo were heavily affected by the drainage impact resulting in spatial variability of vegetation and groundwater levels. In both studied years, SL-2 and SL-5 were $CO_2$ sources to the atmosphere, while SL-1 and SL-3 were not so severely affected by the drought year of 2019. Methane emissions were larger on both studied years in less disturbed vegetation types (SL-1, SL-2, SL-3), or in SL-5 where measurement plots were close to the drainage ditch. Methane emissions were larger in 2019 (except in SL-1) than in 2018. This was most emphasized in SL-2 where large part of the $CH_4$ was emitted from the hollows, which had also open water during large part of the summer of 2019, but were completely dry in most of the summer period of 2018. $N_2O$ fluxes were very low in all of the studied vegetation types and years. It must be considered that the GHG fluxes related with trees were not covered with those measurements and reconstructions.

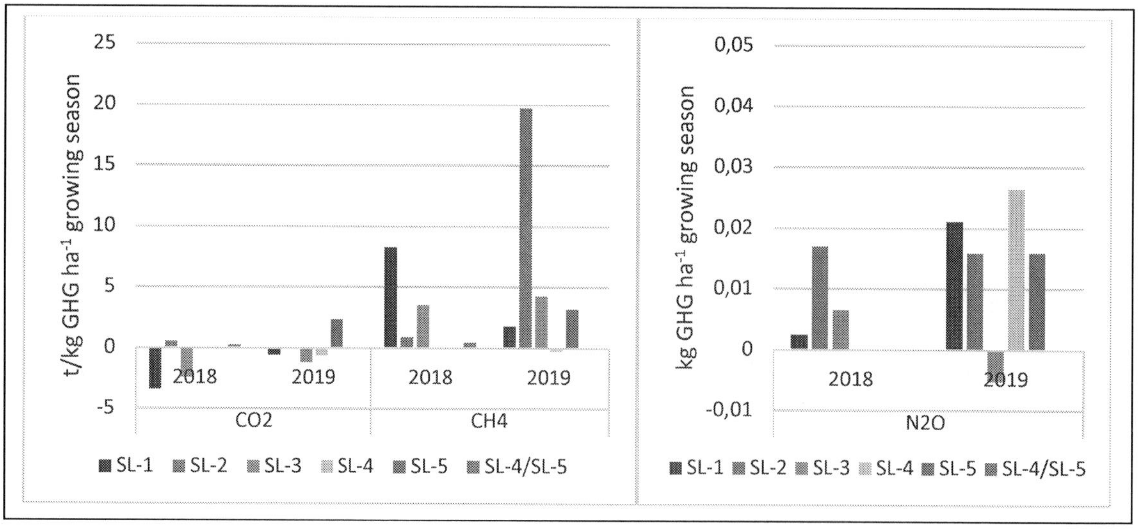

Figure 3: Reconstructed growing season greenhouse gas (GHG) fluxes of carbon ($CO_2$ and $CH_4$ on the left) and nitrous oxide ($N_2O$ on the right) in Suursoo-Leidissoo, Estonia. Please note that GHG fluxes for vegetation types SL-4 and SL-5 were reconstructed together in 2018 due to lower number of measurements in SL-5, and separately in 2019.

## DISCUSSION

The $CO_2$ emitting from SL-2 is probably a result of the extremely dry summer period of 2018, and Sphagnum is highly dependent of precipitation and sensitive to drying, while communities with higher abundance of vascular plants (e.g. SL-1, SL-3) can receive water also in case of deeper WL and are so more drought resistant. Importance of vascular plants in peatland drought response (Kuiper et al. 2014) and the significance of frequent precipitation to $CO_2$ sequestration into Sphagnum moss carpet (Nijp et al. 2014) have been reported before, so supporting our conclusions. Higher methane emissions are generally measured from sites or microtopographic zones with higher WL(Bubier et al. 1993; Saarnio et al. 1997; Chimner et al. 2017), especially in case of higher sedge cover (Saarnio et al. 1997; Li et al. 2016). This was also generally so in Suursoo-Leidissoo, whereas low $CH_4$ emissions in 2019 in SL-1 in comparison to other vegetation types and also year 2018 need further investigations. Nitrification is low on (relatively) undisturbed peatlands (Nykänen et al. 1995; Regina et al. 1996), and increases with drainage rather on nutrient-rich peatlands, especially if these are fertilized (Nykänen et al. 1995). So the low $N_2O$ emissions, or even $N_2O$ uptake were expected in Läänemaa-Suursoo.

## ACKNOWLEDGEMENTS

The study was funded by LIFE Climate Change project Life Peat Restore 2016-2021 (LIFE15 CCM/DE/000138). We thank the Estonian "Peat Restore" project team for their help during the measurements.

# REFERENCES


1. Barthelmes, A., Couwenberg, J., Risager, M., Tegetmeyer, C.,and Joosten, H. (2015): Peatlands and Climate in a Ramsar Context:A Nordic-Baltic Perspective, Nordic Council of Ministers, TemaNord, Rosendahls-Schultz Grafisk, Denmark,
2. Bubier J, Costello A, Moore T.R, Roulet N.T, Savage K. (1993) Microtopography and methane flux in boreal peatlands, northern Ontario, Canada. Canadian Journal of Botany, 71: 1056—1063
3. Chimner, R.A, Pypker T.G, Hribljan J.A, Moore P.A, Waddington J.M. (2017) Multi-decadal Changes in Water Table Levels Alter Peatland Carbon Cycling. Ecosystems, 20: 1042—1057
4. Kuiper J.J, Mooij W.M, Bragazza L, Robroek B.J.M. (2014) Plant functional types define magnitude of drought response in peatland $CO_2$ exchange. Ecology, 95: 123-131.
5. Leifeld, J. & Menichetti, L. (2018) The underappreciated potential of peatlands in global climate change mitigation strategies. Nature communications, DOI:10.1038/s41467-018-03406-6.
6. Li T, Raivonen M, Alekseychik P, Aurela M, Lohila A, Zheng X, Zhang Q, Wang G, Mammarella I, Rinne J, Yu L, Xie B, Vesala T, Zhang W. (2016) Importance of vegetation classes in modeling $CH_4$ emissions from boreal and subarctic wetlands in Finland. Science of the Total Environment, 572: 1111—1122.
7. Nijp J.J, Limpens J, Metselaar K, van der Zee S.E.A.T.M, Berendse F, Robroek B.J.M. (2014) Can frequent precipitation moderate the impact of drought on peatmoss carbon uptake in northern peatlands? *New* Phytologist, 203: 70—80
8. NIR_POL, Olecka, A., Bebkiewicz, K., Chłopek, Z., Doberska, A., Jędrysiak, P., Kanafa, M., Kargulewicz, I., Rutkowski, J., Sędziwa, M., Skośkiewicz, J., Waśniewska, S., Zasina, D., Zimakowska-Laskowska, M., Zaczek, M. (2020) Poland's National Inventory Report.
9. Nykänen H, Alm J, Lång K, Silvola J, Martikainen P.J. (1995) Emissions of $CH_4$, $N_20$ and $CO_2$ from a virgin fen and a fen drained for grassland in Finland. Journal of Biogeography, 22: 351—357.
10. Parish, F., Sirin, A., Charman, D., Joosten, H., Minayeva, T., Silvius, M. and Stringer, L. (Eds.) (2008) Assessment on Peatlands, Biodiversity and Climate Change: Main Report. Global Environment Centre, Kuala Lumpur and Wetlands International, Wageningen.
11. Regina K, Nykänen H, Silvola J, Martikainen P.J. (1996) Fluxes of Nitrous Oxide from Boreal Peatlands as Affected by Peatland Type , Water Table Level and Nitrification Capacity. Biogeochemistry, 35: 401—418
12. Saarnio S, Alm J, Silvola J, Lohila A, Nykänen H, Martikainen P.J. (1997) Seasonal variation in $CH_4$ emissions and production and oxidation potentials at microsites on an oligotrophic pine fen. Oecologia, 110: 414—422

13. Tiemeyer, B., Freibauer, A., Borraz, E.A., Augustin, J., Bechtold, M., Beetz, S., Beyer, C., Ebli, M., Eickenscheidt, T., Fiedler, S., Förster, C., Gensior, A., Giebels, M., Glatzel, S., Heinichen, J., Hoffmann, M., Höper, H., Jurasinski, G., Laggner, A., Leiber-Sauheitl, K., Peichl-Brak, M., Drösler, M. (2020) A new methodology for organic soils in national greenhouse gas inventories: data synthesis, derivation and application. Ecological Indicators, 109

ID 72848

# HOW MUCH DO PEATLANDS CONTRIBUTE TO ACHIEVING INDONESIA'S NDC TARGET

Nurul Silva Lestari[1], Nisa Novita[2], Mega Lugina[1], Subarno[3]

[1] Center for Research and Development of Socio-Economic Policy and Climate Change, Ministry of Environment and Forestry, Bogor, Indonesia
[2] Yayasan Konservasi Alam Nusantara (YKAN), Jakarta, Indonesia
[3] Daemeter, Bogor, Indonesia

*nisa.novita@tnc.org*

## SUMMARY

Land use change including peat fires is the main source of GHG emissions in Indonesia in the recent years, yet it is expected to contribute around 0.5 GT$CO_2$e to achieve its Nationally Determined Contribution (NDC) by 2030. We quantify the maximum potential of emission reduction and applying the emission factors and data activity at the country level from three Natural Climate Solution (NCS) pathways including avoided decomposition and vegetation loss, avoided emissions from peat fires and rewetting degraded peatlands. We compiled the most recent comprehensive dataset of Indonesia's peat deforestation areas and relevant emission factors to support the policy makers based on scientific evidence to determine the mitigation and adaptation opportunities from peat conservation and restoration. We applied 2009-2019 as a baseline year for the three NCS pathways from peatlands. Avoided emissions from peat decomposition and vegetation loss due to peat conversion have the highest emission reduction potential approximately to be 511.8 Mton$CO_2$e $yr^{-1}$. The average annual peat fire emissions are estimated to be 217.7 Mton$CO_2$e $yr^{-1}$, where peak emissions are recorded in 2014-2015. By applying a realistic scenario based on current degraded peat condition in the country, peat rewetting potentially reduce GHG emissions up to 204.2 Mton$CO_2$e $yr^{-1}$. To sum up, combined NCS pathway from peatlands in Indonesia were estimated to provide GHG emissions reductions of 933.7 Mton$CO_2$e, exceeding the target set by Indonesia's government to reduce emissions as much as 497 Mton$CO_2$e from the forestry sector by 2030. Hence, peatlands is the most effective and powerful natural climate solution pathway to achieve Indonesia's NDC target.

***Keywords**: Peatlands, emission, NDC, Indonesia, natural climate solutions*

## INTRODUCTION

Tropical peat swamp forests play substantial roles in the global carbon cycle and can be an important component of climate change mitigation strategies. This is because they comprised 11% of all global peatlands area yet they store 15 - 19% of the total global peat carbon pool (Page et al. 2011)[6]. Indonesia covers 14.9 million ha of peatlands (Ritung et al, 2011)[7]. Given their significance of areas and carbon storage, preventing peat loss from deforestation and rewetting degraded peatlands would be prominent natural climate solution pathways to achieve Indonesia's NDC emission reduction target by 2030. Based on Indonesia's 2[nd] Biennial Update Report (MoEF, 2018)[5], peat decomposition and peat fires have contributed as much as 358 Mton$CO_2$ $yr^{-1}$ and 90 Mton$CO_2$ $yr^{-1}$ respectively from forestry sector emissions (635 Mton$CO_2$ $yr^{-1}$) in 2016. This data clearly showed that conserving remaining forested peatlands and peat fire suppression are the main key to lowering national greenhouse gas emissions. Restoring at least two million hectares of degraded peatlands is included as one of four main NDC's strategies. Griscom et al (2020)[1] estimated that maximum mitigation potential from Indonesia's peatlands is up to 878 Mton$CO_2$e $yr^{-1}$ using global/regional datasets. Here, we refined the estimated maximum potential emissions reduction from three main sources on peatlands including avoided emissions from land cover change (vegetation loss and soil decomposition), avoided peat fire emissions, and reduction emissions from rewetting degraded peatlands. Tier-2 emission factor were used based on meta-analysis from each greenhouse gas emissions source from peatlands.

## MATERIALS AND METHODS

There are three peatland pathways to be calculated for each maximum potential emission reduction, including avoided peat conversion, rewetting, and avoided peat fire emissions. The GHG type counted from avoided peat conversion is $CO_2$, while for peat rewetting and avoided fire emissions are $CO_2$ and $CH_4$. Land cover change data from 2009-2019 was used as the baseline to project emission level in 2030. A literature review was carried out to derive a database of emission factors of $CO_2$, $N_2O$ and $CH_4$ emission factors to obtain a higher tier. Then the database was classified based on Indonesia's land cover classes. Calculation of emissions that can be avoided from peat conversion comes from the amount of carbon stored in vegetation and the avoidable peat decomposition. Mitigation potential from rewetting was estimated based on the current status of degraded peat areas. It is assumed that during the projection year, there will be no additional degraded peat in other places except the degraded peat that occurred in 2009-2019. The potential mitigation from peat fires was estimated from emissions of the soil burnt. Indonesia's peat map and burn scars from MODIS were used to attain activity data of peat fire. A stoichiometric factor of 0.47 was used to convert biomass to carbon stock values and the conversion of 28 is applied for global warming potential for $CH_4$ in peat fire emissions and rewetting.

## RESULTS

### 1. Avoiding peat conversion

Mitigation potential from peat conversion consists of mitigation potential from avoiding peat decomposition and vegetation loss. Based on 2009-2019 land cover maps, annual peatland deforestation (forest to non-forest conversion) and peat degradation (primary to secondary forest) are 167,218 ha $yr^{-1}$ and 17,199 ha $yr^{-1}$, respectively. The highest deforestation rate is observed in 2014-2015, which was affected by El-Nino year. Degradation is relatively low every year, and has the highest rate in 2015-2016 at 45,000 hectares.

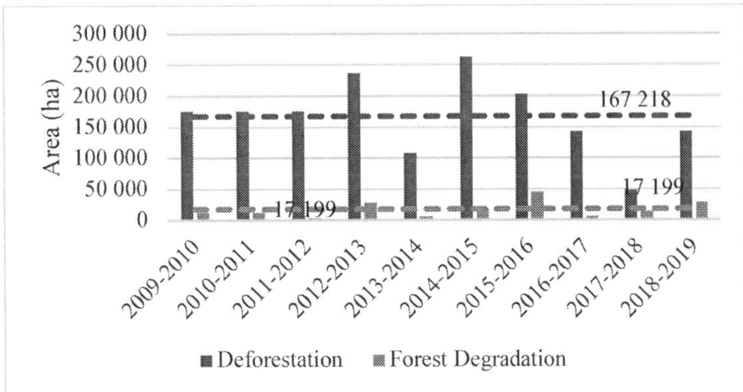


Figure 1. Peat deforestation and degradation in 2009-2019

We refer to emission factors from FREL (2006) to estimate emissions aboveground vegetation loss on peatlands (Table 1), which based on main islands and land cover types. Moreover, peat decomposition emissions due to land cover change is estimated using Tier-2 emission factors derived from a meta-analysis based on 32 publications in Indonesia.

Table 1. Emission factor for vegetation loss

| Activity | Land cover type | Emission factor ($MgCO_2$ $ha^{-1}$) |
|---|---|---|
| Deforestation | Primary peat swamp forest | 474 (Kalimantan), 308.4 (Papua), 380.9 (Sumatra) |
| | Secondary peat swamp forest | 294.1 (Kalimantan), 251.3 (Papua), 261.1 (Sumatra) |
| Degradation | Primary peat swamp forest | 179.9 (Kalimantan), 57.1 (Papua), 119.7 (Sumatra) |

Source: MoEF (2016)[4]

Table 2. Emission factor for peat decomposition

| Land cover class | n | Total $CO_2$ emissions (mg $CO_2$ $ha^{-1}$ $y^{-1}$) | | |
|---|---|---|---|---|
| | | Mean | SE | 95% CI |
| Bare ground | 3 | 62.7 | 3.5 | [47.5, 78.0] |
| Estate crop | 41 | 47.5 | 5.2 | [37.1, 58.0] |
| Mixed dry agriculture | 6 | 79.3 | 10.5 | [52.3, 106.2] |
| Paddy field | 4 | 47.8 | 14.2 | [2.6, 93.0] |
| Plantation forest | 13 | 84.5 | 10.8 | [61.0, 108.1] |
| Primary swamp forest | 14 | 35.6 | 2.9 | [29.2, 41.9] |
| Pure dry agriculture | 8 | 70.3 | 11.8 | [42.2, 98.3] |
| Secondary swamp forest | 33 | 44.4 | 4.5 | [35.3, 53.5] |
| Wet shrub | 10 | 53.2 | 10.9 | [28.4, 77.9] |

Source: Meta-analysis from 32 publications

Mitigation potential from vegetation loss and peat decomposition in peat swamp forest are 52.7 Mton$CO_2$e $yr^{-1}$ and 459.1 Mton$CO_2$e $yr^{-1}$. By combining both source of emissions, avoiding forest conversion can potentially reduce 511.8 MtonCO2e $yr^{-1}$.

2. Peat rewetting

Based on the current extent of degraded peatland areas, we assumed the potential peat rewetting area is similar with non-forested peatlands of 8,761,242 ha. To estimate mitigation potential from peat rewetting, we assumed that this area will be gradually rewetted by 2030. Compared to the baseline emission from degraded peatland (385.8 Mton$CO_2$e $yr^{-1}$), emission from rewetting activity is estimated to be 181.6 Mton$CO_2$e $yr^{-1}$. Hence, the potential emission reduction from rewetting in peatland is about 204.2 Mton$CO_2$e $yr^{-1}$.

3. Peat fire

Based on MODIS burnt areas on peatlands, the annual average of peat burnt areas in the period of 2009-2019 is 308,019 ha $yr^{-1}$. The highest peat burnt area occurred in 2014-2015 which accounted for 757,984 ha, which is related to El Nino event in this period. The lowest peat burnt areas occurred in 2017-2018, which accounted for 10,413 ha.

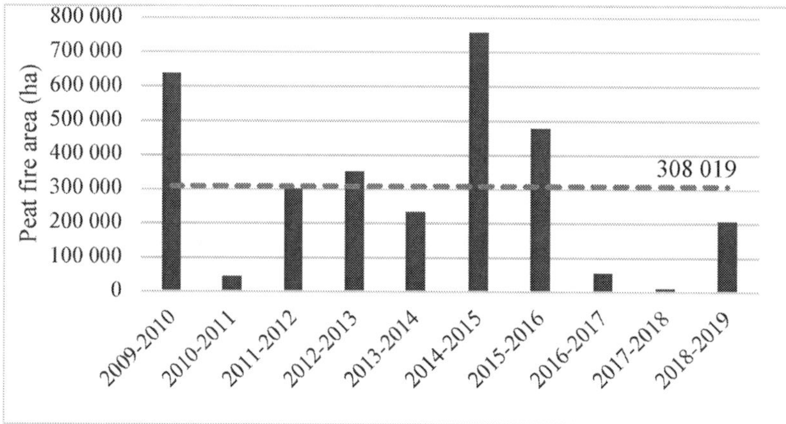


Figure 4. Peat fire area in 2009-2019

Peat fire emissions are quantified from several variables including peat burnt depth, bulk density and emission factor for each gas. The values used to estimate peat fire emission derived from a systematic review based in recent literatures in Indonesia which are presented in the following table.

Table 3. Variables used to estimate peat fire emission

| Variables | Mean ± SE |
|---|---|
| EF $CO_2$ (g/kg burnt mass) | 1673.2 ± 38.6 |
| EF $CH_4$ (g/kg burnt mass) | 11.8 ± 1.99 |
| Peat burnt depth (cm) | 0.29 ± 0.12 |
| Bulk density (t/$m^3$) | 0.12 ± 0.01 |

We estimate that mitigation potential from avoiding peat fire emissions is 217.7 Mton$CO_2$e $yr^{-1}$. Peak emission was observed in the period of 2014-2015, which accounted for 535.8 Mton$CO_2$e.

## DISCUSSION

Forest conversion on peatlands is a significant contributor to national GHG emissions from land sector in Indonesia. Based on our land cover change analysis data, natural peat swamp forests have been converted into shrubs, estate crops, plantation forests and agriculture. Compared to other forest types, forest conversion on peatland contributes higher emissions because the source is not only from biomass loss, but also from peat soil decomposition. The increase in aeration in degraded peatland leads to higher soil decomposition (Hooijer et al., 2012)[2]. This study shows that avoiding peat swamp forest conversion is an effective mitigation strategy to support emission reduction from forestry sector as pledged by the government in Indonesia's NDC. Even though vegetation loss from peat swamp forest conversion only resulted small amounts of emissions, avoiding emission from peat soil decomposition should be seriously considered as an important nature climate solution pathway as the latter produce significant emissions. Combining emissions from vegetation loss and peat decomposition, the mitigation potential of conserving remaining peat swamp forests is about 511.8 $MtCO_2e\ yr^{-1}$, exceeding emission reduction target from the forestry sector.

The intervening degraded peatland is assumed to an area that has repeatedly experience fires so that the condition is bare ground. Through rewetting, the water table in peatland is maintained at or near the peat surface throughout the year (Hooijer et al., 2012)[2]. Rewetting of degraded peatlands will reduce emission, where in tropical peat forests the amount of $CO_2$ and $CH_4$ fluxes on the peat surface is not influenced by vegetation but is determined by the water table (Hoyos-Santillan et al., 2019)[3]. The low groundwater level results in reduced $CH_4$ emissions, while a different response is shown in the $CO_2$ flux, which increases with the decreasing groundwater levels (Sakabe et al., 2018)[8]. From this study, it is identified that rewetting can reduce by more than half of the annual degraded peatland emissions.

We also have refined parameters used to estimate peat fire emissions including the peat burnt depth, bulk density, and emission factors for $CO_2$ and $CH_4$ gases based on recent literatures in Indonesia. Using Tier-2 data, we calculated that avoided peat fires emissions are critical to achieve emission reduction target by 2030 in Indonesia. The average annual emissions in the last decade was 217 $MtonCO_2e\ yr^{-1}$ which can be doubled during the extreme drought years. Referring to the Indonesia's NDC document, emission reduction from forestry sector is expected to be 497 $MtonCO_2e$ in 2030. Based on historical data from 2009-2019, by assuming peat fire emissions is 100% suppressed, it can contribute up to 44% of the emission reduction target by 2030.

## CONCLUSION

This study finds that conserving peat swamp forests and restoring degraded peatlands can potentially contribute to Indonesia's GHG emission reduction by 933.7 $MtonCO_2e$ in 2030. This amount is almost doubled compared to the emission reduction target in Indonesia's NDC from the forestry sector. Peatland conservation and restoration are the most effective and powerful natural climate solution pathways to fulfill emissions reduction target stated on Indonesia's NDC. The climate benefit opportunities from managing and restoring peatlands should be should be translated into climate actions at the site levels which requires a strong and collaborative effort among relevant stakeholders.

## ACKNOWLEDGEMENTS

This study is a collaborative work between P3SEKPI (Center for Research and Development of Socio-Economic Policy and Climate Change) of MoEF and Yayasan Konservasi Alam Nusantara under Natural Climate Solution in Indonesia program.


## REFERENCES


1. Griscom, Bronson W., et al. (2020) "National mitigation potential from natural climate solutions in the tropics." *Philosophical Transactions of the Royal Society B* 375.1794: 20190126
2. Hooijer, A., Page, S., Jauhiainen, J., Lee, W. A., Lu, X. X., Idris, A., & Anshari, G. (2012) Subsidence and carbon loss in drained tropical peatlands. *Biogeosciences*, *9*(3), 1053-1071.
3. Hoyos-Santillan, J., Lomax, B. H., Large, D., Turner, B. L., Lopez, O. R., Boom, A., ... Sjögersten, Sofie. Evaluation of vegetation communities, water table, and peat composition as drivers of greenhouse gas emissions in lowland tropical peatla, 1193–1204. doi:10.1016/j.scitotenv.2019.06.366. (2019). Evaluation of vegetation communities, water table, and peat composition as drivers of greenhouse gas emissions in lowland tropical peatlands. *Science of The Total Environment*, *688*, 1193–1204. https://doi.org/10.1016/j.scitotenv.2019.06.366
4. MoEF. (2016) National Forest Reference Emission Level for Deforestation and Forest Degradation: In the Context of Decision 1/CP.16 para 70 UNFCCC (Encourages developing country Parties to contribute to mitigation actions in the forest sector), Directorate General of Climate Change. The Ministry of Environment and Forestry. Indonesia
5. MoEF. (2018) Indonesia Second Biennial Update Report under The UNFCCC. Republic of Indonesia
6. Page, S. E., J. O. Rieley, and C. J. Banks. (2011) Global and regional importance of the tropical peatland carbon pool. Global Change Biology 17: 798-818.
7. Ritung, S., Wahyunto, K. Nugroho, Sukarman, Hikmatullah, Suparto, dan C. Tafakresnanto. (2011) Peta Lahan Gambut Indonesia Skala 1:250.000. Balai Besar Litbang Sumberdaya Lahan Pertanian. Bogor, Indonesia.
8. Sakabe, A., Itoh, M., Hirano, T., & Kusin, K. (2018). Ecosystem-scale Methane Flux in Tropical Peat Swamp Forest in Indonesia. Global Change Biology, 24(11), 5123–5136. https://doi.org/10.1111/gcb.14410

ID 72997

# ECOLOGICAL THRESHOLDS IN HIGH ANDEAN PEATLANDS ALONG A GRADIENT OF LIVESTOCK USE IN EL COCUYNATIONAL PARK (COLOMBIA)

Violeta Martínez-Amigo and Juan Benavides

Department of Ecology and Territory, Pontificia Javeriana University, Bogotá D.C., Colombia

*martínez_v@javeriana.edu.co*

**SUMMARY**

High elevation cushion peatlands are typical ecosystems above 4000 m of altitude in the tropical Andes, with an important role in hydrology and global carbon sequestration. Peatlands in the Andes are affected by multiple human factors, predominantly by grazing. Disturbances brought by grazing activity are expected to have large impacts on the vegetation and the $CO_2$ fluxes and soil organic carbon content. Our research was focused on analyzing how environmental and plant composition variables along a grazing gradient influence peat accumulation process of high elevation Andean peatlands, and at what point of environmental change or ecological threshold the peat forming ecosystem switches from a net carbon sinkto a net carbon emitter. The research in a tropical high elevation range above 4100 masl, showed that disturbances by grazing have a negative effect on vegetation cover, water table, net primary production, and net ecosystem carbon exchange. We hypothesize that the drawdown of the water table favors the colonization of grasses over the cushion plants, changing aeration of the superficial peat layers and increasing decomposition and net CO2 efflux. We determined the threshold of disturbance at which the system switches from a net carbon sink to source identifying that over a 19% of grass cover and over 8% of exposed soil cover the system becomes a net CO2 emitter. Our results have large scale implications to direct management decisions since the grass and bare soil cover can be easily measured over large areas using high resolution remote sensing.

**Keywords:** Carbon balance, grazing, high Andean peatlands, ecological thresholds, livestock use.

## INTRODUCTION

Peatlands in the tropical Andes are heavily used by the society since they offer a steady water supply and can be easily transformed in suitable environments for cattle grazing. Disturbance by grazing on peatlandshave lasting effects on plant composition, ecosystem functioning and hydrology (Benavides, 2013).Peatlands dominated by vascular cushion plants are common in the tropical Andes above 4000 masl. Peatlands in the Andes develop in specific geomorphic settings with a positive water balance and a stable water table. Peatlands at very high elevation in the Andes are dominated by cushion forming vascular plantssuch as Distichia muscoides (Juncaceae) and Plantago rigida (Plantaginaceae). Cushion plants are ecosystem engineers that play a key role in the functioning of the ecosystem since the rigid structure of theburied cushions have an effect in plant composition, in hydrology, and in the carbon sequestration process(Jones et al., 1994).

In peatlands, the carbon sequestration process is controlled by an imbalance between the amount of $CO_2$ assimilated by the vegetation and the $CO_2$ lost by the ecosystem respiration, resulting in a net carbon gain or net ecosystem exchange (NEE) (Clymo 1984). Plant composition and water table influence primary production and decomposition rates having a direct influence on the carbon balance of the ecosystem (Belyea and Malmer, 2004; Moore and Dalva, 2006). Changes in the vegetation or the hydrology of peatland ecosystems could result in the alteration of decomposition rates, which could rapidly alter the carbon balance from a sequestering system to a net emitter of greenhouse gases (Turetsky et al. al., 2002; Eppinga et al., 2007). In a particular ecosystem, the change from carbon sink to emitter can be understood as an ecological threshold (Toms and Villard, 2015). Although studies dedicated to understanding ecological thresholds in natural systems are limited, this approach can be useful to identify at what point the changes in a net carbon sink ecosystem such as peatlands switch the system to a net carbon emitter (Eppinga et al., 2007; Toms and Villard, 2015).

In the Andes, grazing disturbance is one of the main threats to cushion peatlands because they affect the hydrology, soil conditions, the composition of the peat forming vegetation, and lead to a significant change in the ecological functions of the ecosystem (Benavides, 2013; Salvador et al. 2014). The effect of grazingpressure on the functioning of high Andean peatlands is still poorly understood and, even less is known about the ecological limits that control the carbon balance of peat forming ecosystems. Therefore, the purpose of this study was to better understand how livestock use influences the functioning ofhigh elevationAndean peatlands by 1) comparing environmental and vegetation patterns along a gradient of livestock use,
2) determining how environmental and plant composition variables influence peat accumulation process, and 3) at what point of environmental change or ecological threshold the peat forming ecosystem switchesfrom a net carbon sink to a net carbon emitter.

## MATERIALS AND METHODS

The study was carried out in four peatlands in El Cocuy National Park, in the northern part of the Eastern mountain range in Colombia. The protected area shares its jurisdiction with an indigenous preservation belonging to the U'wa indigenous people, as well as with private lands owned by farmers that use the land for livestock grazing within the protected area (Ordóñez-Pachón, 2016). The peatlands were selected acrossa disturbance gradient regardless of the land ownership. At each study site, 4 to 10 plots of 1 $m^2$ were randomly established depending on the peatland area and variation on plant composition. The study sites were visited five times between January 2019 to February 2020.

Vegetation cover of the different plant species were registered using a 1 $m^2$ quadrant with 20 x 20 cm sub- quadrants (Mueller-Dombois and Ellenberg, 1974). For each quadrant, the percentage of Distichia muscoides, mosses, grasses, and exposed peat was also recorded. In order to determine a gradient of disturbance intensity within the sampled peatlands, exposed peat data and disturbance type present in everyquadrant were combined to obtain the variable "disturbance categories". The water table level was measuredusing monitoring wells made with PVC slotted pipes, and monitored for each plot during each visit. The $CO_2$ flux was measured using an infrared gas analyzer (EGM-4, PP Systems, Amesbury, USA) connected to a cylindrical closed static chamber with a diameter of 40 cm and height of 50 cm. For each measurement, soil temperature was taken, as well as air temperature, relative humidity, atmospheric pressure, and photosynthetically active radiation using a PAR sensor coupled to the camera. Each measurement lasted 124 seconds and was performed in two consecutive phases: a phase where the chamber receives natural solar radiation, registering net exchange of the ecosystem (NEE), and a second phase where the chamber iscovered by a shade-tarp, and registers ecosystem respiration (RE).

For the Statistical analysis, a Principal Components Analysis (PCA) was performed to determine which variables best explain the variance of the data, and an MDS analysis to interpret the homogeneity of the plots. To determine the influence of the most relevant explanatory variables to the carbon balance, linear regression models were used. To identify ecological thresholds, the relationships between the variables andNEE were analyzed using binomial logistic regression analysis (McCullagh and Nelder, 1989) (Toms and Villard, 2015). The NEE was coded as a binary variable, converting negative values to values of 0 when thesystem accumulated carbon, and positive values to values of 1 when the system emitted carbon. The threshold was determined when the probability of the system going from sink to emitter crossed 0.5 probability (Toms and Villard, 2015).

## RESULTS

The studied peatlands presented a variation on $CO_2$ fluxes related to changes in air humidity, air temperature, solar radiation, and water table level. During the hours of highest radiation and air temperature,the NEE values were higher and negative indicating strong assimilation rates, while without solar radiation(PAR= 0) the NEE values were positive. Ecosystem respiration rates showed a significant positive relationship with soil temperature ($F_{1,78}$= 1.2, p = 0.04). Water table data showed a significant relationshipwith Distichia muscoides cover ($F_{1,28}$= 10.9, p = 0.002), grasses, and exposed peat the $CO_2$ flux data. Linearregressions showed an increase of Distichia muscoides cover when the water table was closer to the surface and, conversely, and increase of grasses and exposed peat cover when the water table was longer to the surface. In plots where the water level was above 20 cm depth, Distichia muscoides cover was above 50%.In plots where the water table was below 20 cm from the surface, an increase of 15% in grasses was observed ($F_{1,28}$= 3.6, p = 0.06). In plots where the water table was found further from the surface, lower NEE and GPP values were obtained and, when the levels were closer to the surface, NEE and GPP valueswere higher ($F_{1,106}$= 4.0, p = 0.04 and $F_{1,108}$ = 4.0, p = 0.04 respectively). In contrast, ER values increased when water table was found further from the surface ($F_{1,108}$ = 5.4, p = 0.02). Also, Distichia muscoides andgrass covers showed a significant relationship with NEE values ($F_{1,108}$ =12.4, p = 0.00 and $F_{1,108}$= 8.2, p = 0.00 respectively). When the percentage of grasses increased, the NEE values tended to

become positive and, when the percentage of Distichia muscoides increased, the NEE values tended to become negative.
Logistic regression models for the NEE data showed that in plots with a Distichia muscoides cover less than 33%, there is a high probability of a net carbon emission, reaching a probability of 0.78 when Distichiamuscoides cover is completely lost. Although this is not a tipping point, these results show a change in the$CO_2$ balance, from which respiration exceeds assimilation (Figure 1). The increase in the disturbance category also showed a significant change in carbon balance behavior. The logistic model showed that NEEvalues decreased as the disturbance category increased. From category 6 a 50% probability of presenting net carbon emission was obtained (Figure 2). Category 6 corresponds to dis trampled and chewed plots andwith a percentage of exposed peat of 8-44%. By incorporating the interaction between grass cover and disturbance category into the logistic model, an increase of the probability of obtaining a positive NEE balance was observed in plots with 19% grass cover and a disturbance category of 5 (Figure 3).

**DISCUSSION**

The results confirm the hypothesis that the water table is the environmental variable that best explains the variation in the dominant vegetation, which is consistent with results obtained in other studies in the Andeanregion (Buytaert et al. 2006[a]; Benavides 2013; Salvador et al. 2014; Ruthsatz, 2012). Although this researchdoes not allow us to explain the variability of the process at large temporal scales, it does allow us to understand the influence of water level fluctuations on the instantaneous $CO_2$ fluxes.

The disturbance category was an adequate explanatory variable to reflect the degree of deterioration of theplot and allowed to analyze the influence of the livestock disturbance in the $CO_2$ flux within the peatland. This suggests that the signal for livestock disturbance is not homogeneous in the peatlands and it is evidentat a smaller scale, on the specific sites where the measurement was made, rather than on the whole peatlandas a unit. Livestock disturbance influenced the dominance of Distichia muscoides and the diversity and abundance of species associated with grazing pressure, replacing cushion species by graminoid species as an indicator of ecosystem degradation (Loza-Herrera et al. 2015; García et al., 2014). The relationship between low water table and increased grass cover generates a dilemma as to whether the presence of grasses is explained, to a greater extent, by livestock disturbance or by the low water table, and opens a new question to future studies. Both the decrease in Distichia muscoides cover and the increase in disturbance category had an effect on the NEE, altering the carbon balance to the point where it became a net carbon emitter. The high probability obtained in the models of net carbon emission suggests that there are areas of the peatland where the ecological threshold has been crossed and are losing the stored carbon, which compromises the peat accumulation process and the persistence of the ecosystem. The interaction between disturbance category and grass cover demonstrates synergies between stressors that impair the ability to store $CO_2$ and increase the probability of crossing the threshold. Little is known about how vegetation and ecological processes respond to ecological thresholds or what the alternative states might be (Belyea and Malmer, 2004; Benavides et al., 2013). However, smaller spatial and temporal scale processessuch as NEE could be indicators that anticipate responses in vegetation and larger-scale processes (Eppinga et al., 2007). According to Keddy (2010), when enough peat accumulates so that plant roots cannot reach the mineral soil, the system rapidly changes from a swamp to a peatland. This suggests that, in the oppositecase, when peat decomposition allows vegetation to reach the mineral soil, a change to an alternative statecould occur.

## CONCLUSION

This study provides information for a better understanding of the functioning of high Andean peatland ecosystems, crucial in $CO_2$ storage and water regulation (Salvador et al., 2014), and underlines the key role of Distichia muscoides cushions and the water table in the peat accumulation process. Considerable variation in the conservation status of Distichia muscoides cushions was found within the sampled peatlands, reflecting a signal of livestock disturbance at the plot-specific level. This shows that disturbanceis not homogeneous across the peatland and is evident on a smaller scale. Also, the combined influence ofenvironmental stress and disturbance by livestock use is shown. The results show that the peat accumulation rate, intrinsically related to cushion plant characteristics, is highly dependent on the water table. A greaterdistance of the water table from the surface has a negative effect on the Distichia muscoides cover and, onthe contrary, a positive effect on the increase of grasses and exposed peat. The research explores changes in the carbon imbalance, where two thresholds were found through the probability of obtaining net carbonemissions. The first corresponds to the percentage of Distichia muscoides cover (below 33%), and the second corresponds to the disturbance category. The disturbance category can be even lower in presence ofgrasses since the interaction effect model showed that there is a high probability of a net carbon emission at a lower category when there is grass cover.


## ACKNOWLEDGEMENTS

We thank Marcos Correa, and A. Rozo and L. Merchán for their assistance in the fieldwork. We also thankOctavio Eraso and El Cocuy National Park institution for site access, transport and accomodation. This research was funded by Ditter Mosquera grant from the Pontificia Universidad Javeriana.


## REFERENCES


Belyea, L. R. y Malmer, N. (2004). Carbon sequestration in peatland: patterns and mechanisms of responseto climate change. Glob Change Biol. 10,1043–1052.

Benavides, J.C., Vitt, D. H. y Wieder, R. K. (2013). The influence of climate change on recent peat accumulation patterns of Distichia muscoides cushion bogs in the high-elevation tropical Andes ofColombia. Journal of Geophysical Research: Biogeosciences, 2013. 118(4), 1627-1635.

Buytaert, W., Celleri, R., De Bievre, B., Cisneros, F., Wyseure, G., Deckers, J. y Hofstede, R. (2006a). Human impact on the hydrology of the Andean paramos. Earth Science Reviews. 79, 53-72.

Clymo, R. S. (1984). The limits to peat bog growth. Philosophical Transactions of the Royal Society of London B. 303, 605–654. Clymo, S. R. 1970. The Growth of Sphagnum: Methods of Measurement. The Journal of Ecology. 58. 13. 10.

Eppinga, M. B., Rietkerk, M., Wassen, M. y De Ruiter, P. C. (2007). Linking habitat modification to catastrophic shifts and vegetation patterns in bogs. Plant Ecology. 200, 53–68. Florez-López, F., Galaitsi,

S. E., Escobar, M. y Purkey, D. (2016). Modeling of Andean Páramo Ecosystems' Hydrological Responseto Environmental Change. Water. 8, 94.

García, M. C., Meneses, R. I., Naoki, K. y Anthelme, F. (2014). Métodos para evaluar el efecto de pastoreosobre las comunidades vegetales de bofedales. Ecología en Bolivia. 49, 91–103.

Jones, C. G., Lawton, J. H. y Schachak, M. (1994). Organisms as ecosystems engineers. Oikos.69,373- 386.

Keddy, P. (2010). Wetland Ecology: Principles and Conservation. Cambridge: Cambridge University Press.

McCullagh, P. y Nelder, J. A. 1989. Generalized Linear Models. Chapman and Hall. London.
Moore, T. y Dalva, M. (2006). The Influence of Temperature and Water Table Position on Carbon Dioxideand Methane Emissions from Laboratory Columns of Peatland Soils. Journal of Soil Science. 44, 651-664.Mueller-Dombois, D. y Ellenberg, H. (1974). Aims and Methods of Vegetation Ecology. The Blackburn Press.
Ruthsatz, B. (2012). Vegetación y ecología de los bofedales altoandinos de Bolivia. Phytoecologia 42, 133-179.
Salvador, F., Monerris, J. y Rochefort, L. (2014). Peatlands of the Peruvian puna ecoregion: Types, characteristics, and disturbance. Mires and Peat. 15.
Toms, J. D. y Villard, M. A. (2015). Threshold detection: matching statistical methodology to ecological questions and conservation planning objectives. Avian Conservation and Ecology. 10(1), 2.
Turetsky, M., Wieder, K., Halsey, L. y Vitt, D. (2002). Current disturbance and the diminishing peatland carbon sink. Geophysical Research Letters. 29, 1526.

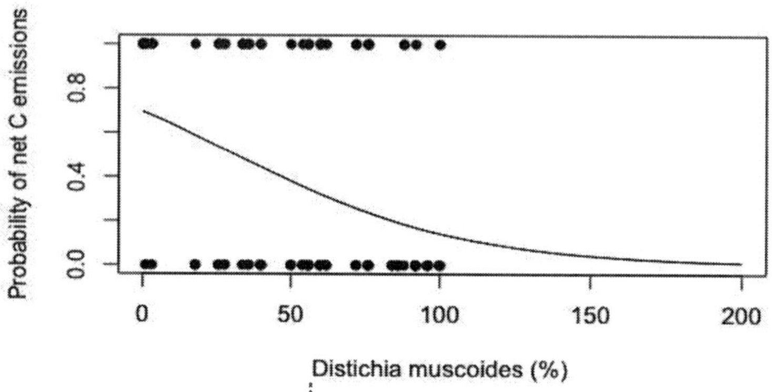


Figure 5. Logistic regression of net carbon emission according to Distichia muscoides cover. Red line represents the ecological threshold where there is a 50% probability of a positive carbon balance.

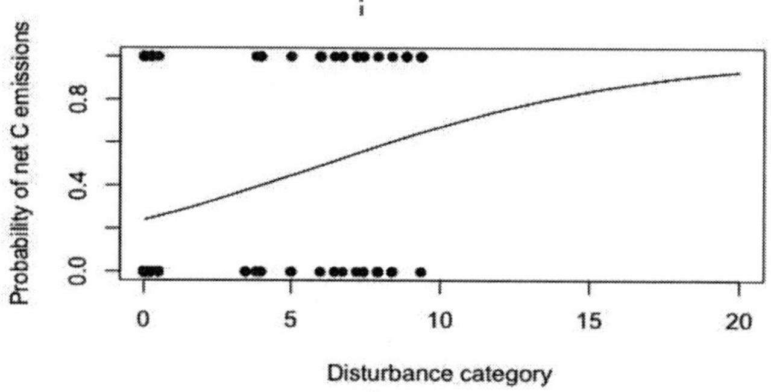


Figure 4. Logistic regression of net carbon emission according to disturbance categories. Red line represents the ecological threshold where there is a 50% probability of a positive carbon balance.

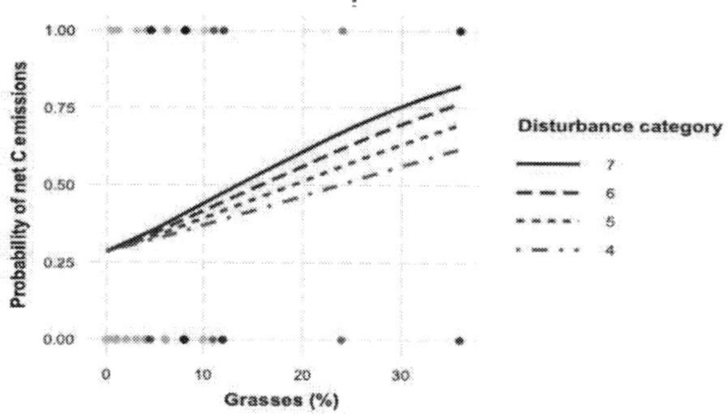

Figure 5. Logistic regression of net carbon emission according to the interaction effect between grass and disturbance. Blue lines represent disturbance categories 4, 5, 6, and 7 for a given grass cover. Red line represents the ecological threshold where there is a 50% probability of a positive carbon balance.

ID 62276

# HOW TO MAKE INTENSIVELY USED PEAT MEADOWS SUSTAINABLE FOR THE FUTURE? THREE MITIGATION OPTIONS TO POTENTIALLY REDUCE PEAT OXIDATION

*Merit van den Berg[1], Christian Fritz[1], Bas van de Riet[2], Stefan Weideveld[1], Thomas Gremmen[2], Eva van den Elzen[1], Renske Vroom[1], Jeroen Geurts[1], Leon Lamers[1]

[1] Radboud University Nijmegen, Aquatic Ecology and Environmental Biology, The Netherlands
[2] B-WARE Research Centre, The Netherlands

*merit.vandenberg@science.ru.nl*

Almost all peatlands in the Netherlands are drained for agricultural purposes or in the past for peat extraction. What remains is a peatland area of about 300.000 ha of which 85 % is used for agriculture. As a result of peat oxidation, these areas are still subsiding by about 1 cm per year. Another effect is the enormous emission of $CO_2$, which contributes to about 4% of total Dutch greenhouse gas emissions. With the awareness of a changing climate and the need for protection against flooding of coastal areas, solutions are being searched to reduce or stop peat oxidation and coinciding land subsidence and $CO_2$ emission.

In this presentation we will show different management options (submerged drainage, pressurized submerged drainage, paludiculture) which are currently being tested in the Netherlands. These options all focus on increasing the groundwater table to lower oxygen intrusion and consequently lower aerobic decomposition. Depending on crop choices water levels may need to stay 40 cm below the surface to maximize fodder plant yields, or go to surface level to increase peat ecosystem functions like C-sequestration. We expect a trade-off between land-use intensity (yields) and $CO_2$ emission reduction. The management options range from maintaining the current land-use by elevating summer water levels with submerged drainage pipes to the development of peat-forming plant species by complete rewetting. Data of the effects of these management options on $CO_2$ emission show that Sphagnum farming is the most promising mitigation option to reduce greenhouse gas emission from drained peatland in the Netherlands. It turned the land from a carbon and greenhouse gas source into a sink.

# AMAZONIAN OPEN PEATLANDS: A PALYNOLOGICAL INVESTIGATION OF LATE HOLOCENE VEGETATION SUCCESSION AT VEINTE DE ENERO, PASTAZA- MARAÑÓN FORELAND BASIN, PERU

*Dael Sassoon[1], William Fletcher[1], Peter Ryan[1], Katherine Roucoux[2], Ian Lawson[2]

[1] University of Manchester, United Kingdom
[2] University of St Andrews, United Kingdom

*dael.sassoon@manchester.ac.uk*

The Pastaza-Marañón Foreland Basin (PMFB), a globally important peatland complex, comprises a mosaic of various types of swamp and flooded forest, interspersed with treeless, 'open' peatlands. Most previous work has focused on palm swamps and pole forest, while open peatlands remain comparatively understudied. This project aims to understand the formation of open peatlands in the PMFB, identify drivers of vegetation change, and determine the spatial and temporal relationship between the vegetation succession pathways of open peatlands and other peatland vegetation types. To meet these aims, fieldwork in the PMFB was carried out in 2019 near the village of Veinte de Enero, north-eastern Peru. Two peat cores were collected from an area of open peatland (VEN_OP) and palm swamp (VEN_PS). Downcore palynology revealed a transition from a lake scenario to a transitional phase with herbaceous swamp plants, and finally to a palm swamp forest dominated by the flood-tolerant palm Mauritia flexuosa. Radiocarbon dates from VEN_OP (1500 cal yr BP) and VEN_PS (990 cal yr BP) also indicate that peat first began to accumulate at the centre of the peatland and more recently towards the margins, in the palm swamp. This suggests that the site of VdE is undergoing terrestrialisation. Thanks to the rangefinder dates and preliminary statistical analysis, we found that the beginning of the VEN_PS record, before the transition to palm swamp, closely resembles the changes observed throughout the VEN_OP record. Thus, we suggest that open peatlands at Veinte de Enero represent an early stage of succession. Further work will involve comparing these results with another open peatland site in the PMFB, San Roque. The two sites are hydrologically separate, but they may have been affected by the same climatic changes and vegetation succession phases. Comparison will help unify a model about the formation of open peatlands in the PMFB.

# IV CULTURAL AND SOCIAL SERVICES

ID 62785

# MAINTENANCE AND/OR SUSTENANCE OF HERITAGE IN MIRE LANDSCAPES IN ESTONIA

Piret Pungas-Kohv

Estonian Fund for Nature, Estonia

*piretpk@elfond.ee*

Peatland is an area covered with at least ca 1 cm of peat and mires are peatlands with at least 30 cm of peat and ongoing peat formation. Among scientists related with natural studies, it is well-known definition about mires. Scientists related with cultural studies could use the proverb as a mire-determination „There is land, but it is not walkable, there is water, but not navigable". Thus, it would be more suitable to use mire-landscape as a concept if we need to intertwine ecological definition of mires with human-centred proverb.

Estonian landscape had historically lots of (22%) different wetland types and sites but nowadays various mires cover only ca 8% of Estonia's territory. The huge change in the amount of mire-landscape is mainly related to human activity – mainly drainage – as it is determined in many parts of the world and Estonia is not an exception in this perspective. Current status of mires as landscape cannot be understood without heritage as a meaningful intertwining of space and time, which is constantly in changing position. "Draining the swamp" became one of the most prevailing practices during the second half of the 20nd century but many older (and contradictory) activities remained and new ones, like tourism emerged.

The presentation will talk about the findings and peculiarities of mire-heritage in Estonia. How people preserve the heritage in mires – is it rather related with maintenance or sustenance? How the meaning of heritage in mires is changing during preservation process?

ID 61302

# RE-BUILDING THE CULTURAL HERITAGE OF MIRES:NEW MIRE TRENDS IN FINLAND

Kirsi Laurén[1] & Pauliina Latvala-Harvilahti[2]

[1]University of Eastern Finland, Finland

[2]University of Eastern Finland, Finland

*kirsi.lauren@uef.fi*

**SUMMARY**

Over the past decades, various open-air activities have been organized on mires by both athletes and artists. While sports events have an entertainment function, art installations and performances are usually motivated by an environmental concern. Other than traditional mire activities, these events have become more and more common in Finland, indicating a change in the human-nature relationship and attitudes towards mires. That change in attitudes reflects everyday narratives and cultural products such as media and literature. It is argued inthis paper that there is now a new mire trend that affects the cultural heritage of mires today.

This paper introduces a multidisciplinary Mire Trend research project that focuses on new practices and representations of mires and peatlands. The aim is to find out how these new uses modify the intangible culturalheritage of mires. This understanding is a vital tool by which to pursue a sustainable future and look for solutions to environmental challenges. Two main research questions are posed: What is the contemporary mire trend like, and how does it influence the construction and re-building of a new cultural heritage? The empirical research material of the project consists of interviews, ethnographic observations, and various cultural texts and images found in literature and media. These will be analyzed by using diverse methods of cultural research.
Although the study is conducted in Finland, the phenomena of a new mire trend is acknowledged to be global.

***Keywords**: mire, trend, intangible cultural heritage, human-nature relationship, environmental concern.*

## INTRODUCTION

Culture refers to everyday life, beliefs and practices, and shared and often negotiated values and meanings (Hall 1997, 1–2). Hence, culture determines how people evaluate nature and what practices are considered appropriate.It is therefore extremely important to study the cultural aspects of various nature areas, alongside ecological, economic and social aspects. Because of the increasing global environmental awareness and the current problem of climate change, more attention is being paid to the protection of pristine mires and the possibilities to restore former peatlands. The relationship between human and nature thus plays a key role in finding answers to environmental challenges.

This research paper gives an example of how contemporary mires and wetlands can be studied from the perspective of cultural research. The text is based on the Mire Trend research project (Uef//Connect) that concentrates on contemporary mire culture in Finland. Finland is one of the most wetland-rich countries in the world, and for centuries Finns have utilized mires as both livelihood and recreation. However, the starting pointfor the study is the notion that alongside the old familiar uses of mires, new ways of understanding them have emerged in the 2000s. For example, the environmental art and various culture and sport events related to mires have increased. (Laurén 2006; see pictures 1. & 2.)

**Picture 1:** Shooting the video of Annatuuli Saine's MireSong (SuoLaulu) project in Seinäjoki 2017. Photo: KirsiHaapamatti.

**Picture 2:** Floral dress high heels swamp skiers in Kapustasuo, Pudasjärvi, 2020. Photo: Noora Vikman.

It is noticeable that new kinds of mire events are constantly emerging in Finland, and this also affects the culturalheritage associated with mires. The construction of cultural heritage is considered as a dynamic act. It is a view from the present, either backwards to a past or forwards to a future (Graham & Howard 2008; Graham, Ashworth & Tunbridge 2000). The cultural heritage of mires stems from their past uses and images, but the imagery is renovated today for instance by media, officials, artists, tourists, and researchers.

The aim of this study is to identify a contemporary mire trend that has transformed the human-nature relationshipof mires. The focus of identifying the mire trend is especially on people who use and act on mires, mire-related social relationships, as well as the affect these relationships have on the cultural heritage of mires. (See Gomes, Mendonça Cohen & Flores 2018, 86.) Importantly, examining mire trends means that we are dealing withpeople's notions of the past, the present, and the future (Dragt 2018, 18).

Unconventional uses of mires like mire art, sports and fitness have grown in popularity in several European countries, but especially in Finland over the past 20 years (Laurén 2006; Laurén 2008; Nikkilä & Korhonen 2008; Wulff 2008). There are several reasons behind this. Mires are no longer an everyday environment for mostpeople because people are living in urbanized societies, and in most cases far from mires. Only a few need to go to nature to make a living, and the work in nature has become more and more specialized. (Laurén 2011, 115.) However, leisure time has increased, as has the recreational use of nature. In order to investigate this phenomenon, we ask: What is the contemporary mire trend like, and how does it influence the construction and re-building of a new cultural heritage?

## MATERIALS AND METHODS

The research of the Mire Trend project is based on qualitative methods, and its empirical research material consists of thematic research interviews, ethnographic observations, and various cultural texts and images foundin literature and media. In this paper, we concentrate on 42 interviews conducted with mire artists (dancers, photographers, singers) and athletes (swamp skiers, swamp soccer and swamp volley players). The intervieweeswere women and men from all over Finland who have participated in the research after noticing the published study/interview request in various online communities and newspapers. They were aged from 28–83 years old and represent different social backgrounds. Among them were 29 visual artists, photographers, dancers, singers and performance artists, and 13 who had participated in swamp skiing, swamp soccer and swamp volley events.

The thematic, semi-structured open interview is a data collection method in which a researcher participates interactively in the production of the research material. The aim of an interview is to obtain information and to understand the specific questions of the research. (Gillham 2000, 1.) The interviews in the Mire Trend project were audio-recorded. The purpose of the artist interviews was to examine e.g. in what ways mires inspire artists,as well as to gain the interviewees' views on the impacts of mire art on the human-nature relationship. From thispoint of view, the research takes a closer look at mire sites as political, artistic, and affective landscapes, and examines the questions of power, symbols, and emotions. When the athletes were interviewed, the main purposewas to find out what motivates them to play on the mire, what is the role of bodily senses (Bendix 2005, 3) in mire experiences, and what mires mean to players as landscapes and natural areas.

Content analysis and a close reading method of analyzing the interview data allowed us to discover the themes and aspects regarding mires that are being repeated by interviewees, and why they are important to them. The analysis reveals what is considered to be common or suitable behavior on mires, and what is not. In the analysis,attention is also paid to weak signals, pointing to possible emerging new issues that can be perceived through allfive human senses (Heinonen & Hiltunen 2012). Here, the study highlights new kinds of thoughts about mires that anticipate changes in attitudes, agencies, and actions. These weak signals are relevant because they may intensify and come to form a shared cultural element of the new mire trend.

## RESULTS

Heritage is often seen as both a cultural practice and a conscious act. From that point of view, art provides an instrument for gaining knowledge on related environmental issues. The artists represent a group of professionalswho collaborate with NGOs and other organizations, and who wish to strengthen an awareness of mires as carbon sinks. For the artists, mires represent communal landscapes that are possible to experience together (cf. Bender 2006, 303; Gruppuso 2017). By taking art and people to the mire, the artists raise people's awareness of the endangerment of pristine mires. The interviewees highlighted that 'being' and 'acting' on the mire mphasizes the close relationship between human and nature, evokes a sense of freedom, and inspires humancreativity.

Mire sport events are usually team sport festivals which are held once a year during the summer. It is typical that players do not train in advance for a tournament. Teams consist of women and men who know each other beforehand, such as co-workers or friends. The humorous nature of the games is emphasized with special and unusual costumes. The sport events on mires are somewhat boisterous and carnivalistic in nature. According to the interviewees, the most important thing is a good, relaxed team spirit with a sense of humor. Being together and having fun is paramount in swamp events. In addition, it is essential that players soil themselves with peat. Various bodily sensory experiences emerge as essential, including the visual landscape, the smell of the swamp,and the touch of cool peat on skin. All of these are a part of the mire experience that is both expected and hopedfor. However, the mire is the background for sports and social interaction, rather than a target, and the activities offer a physical challenge but without any serious competition or compulsion. The players participate in the events year after year because of their social atmosphere and the sense of community. A special quality of the mire is that it makes a unique place for an annual wacky carnival, where everyday life can be forgotten.

## DISCUSSION

Environmental concerns have grown dramatically during the current millennium, alongside the shadow of globalwarming. Mires are crucial in public discussions of the future and climate. In Finland, as in some other countries,mires are landscapes which are progressively being transformed into arenas and stages for sports and art performances. At the same time, they still provide a livelihood for many who live in the countryside, and are alsoused in traditional recreation activities such as hiking and nature spotting. Sport festivals, art installations and performances offer a way to facilitate social encounters on mires. In that sense they represent a new trend to relax in nature. The personal attachment given to mires is rooted in a sense of place, where the recognizable and intangible cultural heritage of communities and individuals is passed on, for example, through representations, expressions and cultural spaces, as well as knowledge and practices concerning nature (cf. Smith & Akagawa 2009; 7; Schofield & Szymanski 2010).

The research shows that the new mire trend seems to be hybrid, including many different elements, and fulfillingboth individual and collective needs. Open sports and artistic events organized on mires are of growing interest. Cultural significance is also embodied in mires and their political context. Furthermore, mires form a cultural resource for people, as well as being an environment for flora and fauna. These aspects bring together the physical and the cultural, as well as introducing mental and material elements to the use of the mire landscape asa stage for varied communal action. (Cf. Harvey & Wilkinson 2019, 187.)

## CONCLUSION

The study suggests that in the future research should carefully monitor the development of mires as culturally significant places, and examine whether it is possible to utilize them more for exercise and sports in the future,and whether sports are a sustainable use of nature. It is also worth considering if mires will be the next tourist attraction in Finland that pass on a message of the vulnerability of nature, and the responsibility of individuals and communities that can’t wait for the next generation to act in the favor of the Earth.

## ACKNOWLEDGEMENTS

The research has received support from the Kone Foundation and the University of Eastern Finland.

## REFERENCES

Bendix, R. (2005) Introduction: Ear to ear, nose to nose, skin to skin: the senses in comparative ethnographic perspective. In Bendix R. & Brenneis, D. (eds) *The Senses.* Etnofoor 18:1. Anthropological-Sociological Centre:Amsterdam: 3–14.

Dragt, E. (2018) *How to research trends. Move beyond trend watching to kickstart innovation.* Amsterdam: BIS

Publishers: 199 pp.

Gillham, B. (2000) *The research interview.* London: Continuum: 96 pp.

Gomes N. P., Mendonça Cohen S.A., Flores A. M. M. (2018) Trend Studies: an approach for analyzing and managing culture. *ModaPalavra e-periódico /DOSSIÊ*, Vol. 11, 82–112. DOI: https://doi.org/10.5965/1982615x11222018

Graham, B., Howard P. (2008) Heritage and Identity, in *The Ashgate Research Companion to Heritage and Identity.* Brian Graham and Peter Howard (eds.) Ashgate Publishing: 1–18.

Graham, B., Ashworth, G. J., Tunbridge J. E. (2000) *A Geography of Heritage. Power, Culture and Economy.* London and New York: Routledge. 288 pp.

Gruppuso, P. (2017) Geologic and Historical, Surface and Depth. Entanglement of Water and Temporality in a contested Wetland of Agro Pontino. *Archivio Antropologico Mediterraneo* (19) 2, 69–79. Università degli Studi di Palermo, Dipartimento Culture e Società.

Hall, S. (ed) (1997) Introduction. In Hall S. (ed) *Representation: cultural representations and signifyingpractices.* London: Sage: 1–12.

Harvey, D., Wilkinson, T. J. (2019) Landscape and heritage: emerging landscapes of heritage. In Howard P,Thompson I, Waterton E, Atha M. (eds) *The Routledge Companion to Landscapes Studies.* 2nd edition. New York: Routledge: 176–191.

Heinonen, S., Hiltunen, E. (2012) Foresight Space and the Futures Window: Using visual weak signals to enhance anticipation and innovation. *Futures*; 44:3: 248–256.

Laurén, K. (2011) Writing the environment: Finnish written nature narratives. In Peil T. (ed) *The Space in Culture – the Place of Nature in Estonia and Beyond.* Approaches to Culture Theory Series, Vol. 1. Tartu: TartuUniversity Press: 107–119.

Laurén, K. (2008) Mires in Finnish Art. In Korhonen R, Korpela L, Sarkkola S. (eds) *Finland – Fenland. Research and Sustainable Utilisation of Mires and Peat.* Finnish Peatland Society: Maahenki Ltd: 272–277.

Laurén, K. (2006) *Suo – sisulla ja sydämellä. Suomalaisten suokokemukset ja -kertomukset kulttuurisen luontosuhteen ilmentäjinä* [Putting one's heart and soul into mire: The Finnish people's mire experiences and narratives as indicators of a cultural relationship to nature]. Helsinki: Finnish Literature Society: 243 pp.

Nikkilä, L-E., Korhonen, R. (2008) Tourism and Sports on Mires in Finland. In Korhonen R, Korpela L, Sarkkola S. (eds) *Finland – Fenland. Research and Sustainable Utilisation of Mires and Peat.* Finnish PeatlandSociety, Maahenki Ltd: 252–256.

Smith, L., Akagava, N. (2009) Introduction. In Smith, L., Akagawa, N. (eds) *Intangible Heritage.* Milton Park,Abingdon, Oxon, New York, NY: Routledge: 1–9.

Schofield, J., Szymanski, R. (eds) (2010) *Local Heritage, Global Context. Cultural Perspectives on Sense of Place.* London: Routledge.

Uef//Connect: Mire Trend research project. Online at: https://uefconnect.uef.fi/en/group/mire-trend-research-project/ [Checked 19th March 2021.]

Wulff, H. (2008) *Dancing at the Crossroads. Memory and mobility in Ireland.* Dance and Performance Studies.New York: Berghahn Books. 184 pp.

# ID 62540

# EXAMINING HUMAN-PEATLAND RELATIONSHIPS THROUGH PARTICIPATION SPACE: A CASE OF SUNGAI TOHOR, INDONESIA (1985-2019)

*Yuti A. Fatimah[1], Zaenuddin Hudi Prasojo[2], N. Estya B. Rahman[1], Stuart W. Smith[1], David A. Wardle[1], Kwek Yan Chong[3], Asmadi Saad[4], and Janice S. H. Lee[1]

[1] Asian School of Environment, Nanyang Technological University, Singapore
[2] Department of Religious Studies, Pontianak State Institute of Islamic Studies, Indonesia
[3] Department of Biological Sciences, National University of Singapore, Singapore
[4] Department of Soil Science, Universitas Jambi, Jambi, Indonesia

*yuti.ariani@ntu.edu.sg*

The Indonesian government targeted to restore at least 2 million hectares of peatland by 2020. Community participation was adopted by the government as a key element of obtaining local people's support. However, despite the involvement of communities in many peatland restoration activities, the continuity of these activities faced many challenges, including: land tenurial conflict between the local community and companies, lack of market for peatland products, mismatches between the designated and actual locations for canal blocking, and limited funding.
These challenges indicate that participation success is not only determined by the process of including heterogenous actors in peatland-related meetings but also on how participation supports or challenges the existing socio-ecological structure. Here, we propose a framework which we call 'participation space', which is defined as a set of practices embedded in a specific time and place in which heterogeneous actors are included in (i) defining the problem, (ii) constructing procedures to solve the problem, (iii) deciding the type of resources to be mobilized for implementing the procedure and (iv) maintaining the new procedure.

We apply the participation space framework in our ethnography in Sungai Tohor village, Riau, Indonesia where we combine observation, snowballing interviews and secondary data to construct how participation spaces has been constructed, destructed and reconstructed. The framework allows to capture three types of participation space: (i) an unintended space where local people relationship with peatland was formed by altering the government's rice intensification program into sago cultivation, (ii) a contested space where sago entrepreneurs, villagers and NGOs collaborated in rejecting pulpwood plantations in the area and (iii) a protective space where NGO, local community, sago entrepreneurs and scientists collaborated in peatland restoration activities. Our study shows that sustainability of these spaces is determined by actors' ability in maintaining their resources and adjusting the space against external pressure.

ID 62749

# PEAT, PALMS AND PEOPLE: HUMAN IMPACTS ON AMAZONIAN PEATLANDS

*Anna Macphie[1], Katherine Roucoux[1], Nina Laurie[1], Althea Davies[1], Lera Miles[2]

[1] University of St Andrews, UK
[2] UN Environment Programme World Conservation Monitoring Centre, UK

*ajm50@st-andrews.ac.uk*

Globally, lowland tropical peatlands are estimated to cover 441,000 km2. The peatlands of North Peru's Pastaza-Marañón Foreland Basin account for 35,600 ± 1088 km2 of this area with peat deposits recorded up to 7m thick. Tropical peatlands play a vital role in the global carbon cycle as carbon sinks but, despite their importance, they are often overlooked in conservation plans due to their relatively low floristic diversity compared to terra firme forest. Amazonian peatlands are also important for local forest-dwelling communities as they provide a wide range of natural resources and ecosystem services such as food, timber, hydrological regulation, and socio-economic benefits.

This interdisciplinary project uses a combination of social and natural science methods to investigate the ways in which the management and utilisation of natural resources in the peatlands of North Peru's Pastaza-Marañón Foreland Basin impact these ecosystems. By comparing social, ecological and palaeoecological indicators of ecosystem use, the project looks at how degradation is understood from different disciplinary approaches. From the social science perspective, this involves ethnographic study and observations in rural communities and interviews with key stakeholders from in-country NGOs to understand the political and legal frameworks within which conservation and sustainable development efforts are able to operate. From the natural science perspective, this involves identifying indicators of degradation visible both in the current surface vegetation and within the palaeo record preserved within the peat, which enables the reconstruction of historical usage of these areas and aids our understanding of how tropical peatlands can be impacted by human activity, and if/ how they are subsequently able to regenerate.

ID 62642

# CHANGES IN VIEWS AND MANAGEMENT OF PEATLAND IN INDIGENOUS VILLAGES IN INDONESIA: INSIGHTS FROM MENTAL MODEL STUDY

*Willy Daeli, Dean Affandi

World Resources Institute Indonesia, Indonesia

*willy.daeli@wri.org*

The government of Indonesia's commitment to reduce greenhouse gases emissions by 29% from a projected business-as-usual baseline by 2030 depends on the country's ability to curb deforestation, particularly on peatlands. Managing peatland as part of sustainable peatland management is fundamental to prevent wildfires, and many studies have put emphasis on policy and governance issues that argue both have a major role to manage peatland ecosystems sustainably. However, there is still limited study that offers insights on how indigenous people and local communities' views could contribute to this effort. This study uses a mental model approach and 3CM (Conceptual Content Cognitive Map) method to understand factors that shape the behavior of local communities towards the national government's peatland restoration program. The insights from this study would be beneficial to generate behavioral change and policy uptake by the local and indigenous communities. As this is crucial for the sustainability for peatland management in the long run. This study reaffirms that market opportunities have influenced a shift in environmental and socio-cultural landscape. In addition, local and indigenous people are quite open in negotiating their values when confronted by economic gains. This mental model study contributes to identify which solutions are prevalent and how do the local communities relate to the interventions and what are the barriers to more successful peat management interventions. Future programs should have a more integrated sustainable peat management program where it is important to examine the connection between livelihood decisions and cultural reality that shape the mental model of indigenous communities.

ID 62637

# GENDER ROLE IN HOUSEHOLD LIVELIHOOD STRATEGIES: A CASE FROM PEATLAND COMMUNITY IN OGAN KOMERING ILIR AND TUMBANG NUSA, INDONESIA

*Sri Lestari, Bondan Winarno

Environment and Forestry Research and Development Institute of Palembang, Indonesia

*lestari@iuj.ac.jp*

Women and men have different strategies to improve their livelihood options in relation to peatland management. This research focused on gender issues and household livelihood strategies in managing peatland area in Ogan Komering Ilir (OKI), South Sumatra and Tumbang Nusa, Central Kalimantan. The data was collected through survey, in-depth interviews to the key stakeholders, and Focus Group Discussion. It was found that there is a very striking difference between community livelihood options in OKI and Tumbang Nusa. Communities in OKI have livelihood options in peatland agriculture, while in Tumbang Nusa the community is more focused on utilizing river resources around peatlands. In agricultural activities gender roles are significantly dominated by men while in the river activities there are many husbands and wives working together as a partner, fishermen and fish traders.In OKI, men's access to the natural resources and information was higher than women. Men have important role in managing their agricultural land and selling the products. In this area women have a significant role in domestic activities. Although there are also some women who carry out economic activities by making handicrafts from purun materials or helping their husbands in the fields after their domestic work is finished. Meanwhile in Tumbang Nusa, Men and women delegate responsibilities based on gender roles, men as fishermen will collect fish from the river, while women will play the role of selling fish or processing the fish so that it has added value. The research indicated that there is a community where men play an important role in livelihood strategies, while there are also communities that implement the division of labor based on gender. This strategy is important for household survival, especially if there is a change in season, and a decrease in harvest or market prices.

ID 62754

# TOWARDS ESTIMATING TOTAL ECONOMIC VALUE OF PEATLANDS IN KAHAYAN-SEBANGAU PEAT HYDROLOGICAL UNIT, CENTRAL KALIMANTAN PROVINCE

*Eli Nur Nirmala Sari[1], Rizky Januar[1], Albertus Sulaiman[2], Arief Darmawan[2], Awaluddin[2], Riissiyani[2], Doni Fernando[2], Nugraheni Setiyaningrum[2], Wisnu Ali Martono[2], Yusurum Jagau[3], Kitso Kusin[3]

[1] World Resources Institute (WRI) Indonesia, Jakarta, Indonesia

[2] Regional Resources Development Technology Center, Agency for the Assessment and Application of Technology (BPPT), Serpong, Indonesia

[3] Center for International Cooperation in Sustainable Management of Tropical Peatland (CIMTROP), Palangka Raya, Indonesia

*Corresponding author: eli.sari@wri.org*

## SUMMARY

Indonesia has 13.43 million ha of peatlands spread in 8 provinces. Among them, Central Kalimantan province, Indonesia, has approximately 2.7 million hectares of peatland; spread within 18 Peat Hydrological Unities (PHU). Within the last two decades, the local peatland ecosystems are significantly degraded by land-use change for agriculture, including the construction of drainage canals, making the peatlands dry and prone to fires. Severe peat fires occurred in 1997, 2015, and 2019, leading to massive peat loss. Such loss threatens its provision for carbon storage, microclimate, water-saving, and economic benefits such as non-timber forest products, among others. Failure to account for such negative externalities may lead to persisting unsustainable peatland use. This study is designed to estimate the total economic value (TEV) of local peatlands. Case study is committed in peat hydrological unit (PHU) of Kahayan-Sebangau, which has 338,155 hectares of peatland ecosystem. Accordingly, the economic value of market and non-market benefits is derived by integrating the calculation of three aspects: direct use value, indirect use-value, and non-use value. A household survey was conducted in October 2019 toward a sample of 410 respondents for use-value and 280 respondents for non-use value within the PHU environment, supported by spatial analysis and desk research. Thus, the overall approximation of the existing market and non-market values of the peatlands is provided. The results show that TEV of peatlands in PHU of Kahayan-Sebangau is on the order of IDR 350 trillion/year, whereas the most significant proportion of the TEV coming from the functional values of carbon cycling, which is IDR 340 trillion/year. This result implies that peat ecosystems have significantly high value to remain protected, in contrast to conversion for extractive purposes.

***Keywords**: Total Economic Value (TEV), peatlands, conversion, conservation, Central Kalimantan*

## INTRODUCTION

Indonesia has 13.43 million ha of peatlands spread in 8 provinces. Among them, Central Kalimantan province, Indonesia, has approximately 2.7 million hectares of peatland; spread within 18 Peat Hydrological Unities (PHU) (Suwarno, et al., 2016). Within the last two decades, the local peatland ecosystems are significantly degraded by land-use change for agriculture, including the construction of drainage canals, making the peatlands dry and prone to fires. Severe peat fires occurred in 1997, 2015, and 2019, leading to massive peat loss. Such loss threatens its provision for carbon storage, microclimate, water-saving, and economic benefits such as non-timber forest products, among others. Failure to account for such negative externalities may lead to persisting unsustainable peatland use. Peatland conversion to plantation, logging activities, drainage, peat fires, and expansion of small-holder have rapidly increased in peatland areas since the 1980s (Silvius and Diemont 2007) which lead to peatland degradation.

Undervaluation of peatland ecosystem goods may lead to peatland degradation which if not abated may threaten future survival of local communities whose livelihoods revolve around peatlands functions and services. The use of economic values is attractive as it enables environment to be taken into account in sustainable use of natural resources, landscape conservation and restoration (Admiraal, et al., 2013). Total economic value assessment is the most inclusive way for economic evaluation of peatland ecosystem.

## MATERIALS AND METHODS

### Study Area

This study is conducted in peat hydrological unit (PHU) of Kahayan-Sebangau, which has 338,155 hectares of peatland ecosystem. The PHU of Kahayan-Sebangau is located in Central Kalimantan Province, Indonesia.

### Research Design and Data Collection

Accordingly, the economic value of market and non-market benefits is derived by integrating the calculation of three aspects: direct use value, indirect use-value, and non-use value. A household survey was conducted in October 2019 toward a sample of 410 respondents for use-value and 280 respondents for non-use value within the PHU environment, supported by spatial analysis and desk research. The component classification for measuring the economic value of peatlands is presented in the Table 1.

Table 1. Methods for measuring economic value on peatlands

| Value | Variable | Measured Component | Referred Value |
|---|---|---|---|
| Direct Use Value | **Extractive Direct Use Value** | | |
| | *Plantation company | Value from company level oil palm plantation | Market price method |
| | *Smallholder plantation | Value from smallholder level oil palm plantation | Market price method |
| | *Rubber plantation | Value from smallholder level rubber plantation | Market price method |
| | *Coconut plantation | Value form smallholder level coconut plantation which represent also mixed plantations | Market price method |
| | *Rice cultivation | Value from smallholder rice cultivation in peatlands | Market price method |
| | *Crops | Value from smallholder vegetable cultivation | Market price method |
| | *Multi-cropping | Value from smallholder fruits plantation | Market price method |
| | *Dry fields | Value from smallholder corn plantation | Market price method |
| | *Fishing & fish trap pond practice | Value from all fishery practice in open area and forest, including fishing and fish trap pond practice | Market price method |
| | *Forest | Value from collecting timber, rattan, honey, non-timber forest products from drained forest | Market price method |
| | *Swamp forest | Value from collecting timber, rattan, honey, non-timber forest products from un-drained forest | Market price method |
| | **Non-extractive Direct Use Value** | | |
| | *Ecotourism | Value from ecotourism from Sebangau National Park | Market price method |
| Indirect Use Value | *Carbon storage (below ground) | Value from above ground carbon content, based on the vegetation volume | Replacement cost method |
| | *Carbon storage (above ground) | Value from peat carbon content, based on peat maturity and peat volume | Replacement cost method |
| Non-Use Value | **Bequest value** | | |
| | *Biodiversity service value | Willingness to provide compensation if biodiversity is lost | Contingency valuation method (CVM), Willingness to pay (WTP), and Willingness to Accept (WTA) |
| | **Existence value** | | |
| | *Social cultural service value | Willingness to pay (WTP) if there is a sacred place/place of worship on peatlands is removed | Contingency valuation method (CVM), Willingness to pay (WTP), and Willingness to Accept (WTA) |
| | *Nature reserve value | Willingness to pay (WTP) if the nature reserve on peatlands is removed | Contingency valuation method (CVM), Willingness to pay (WTP), and Willingness to Accept (WTA) |
| | *Aesthetic value | Willingness to pay (WTP) if the peatlands had to be removed so that the natural landscape changed | Contingency valuation method (CVM), Willingness to pay (WTP), and Willingness to Accept (WTA) |

## RESULTS AND DISCUSSION

### Goods and Services from Peatlands

The concept of total economic value can be illustrated by comparing two scenarios (Adger et al., 1995). The first scenario, peatland ecosystem is conserved at the present level, and provide a stream of goods and services including timber and non-timber forest products, recreation, climate regulation, carbon sequestration, existence value and so forth. In an extreme alternative scenario, peatland ecosystem and the above benefit streams are absent (Adger et al., 1995). Indonesian tropical peatlands have substantial number of goods and services which give benefits for surrounding people. The values from peatlands is measured from willingness to pay from people who get direct benefit or indirect benefit (Pierce, 2001). These values are classified as follows:

- Direct use value is the economic or social value of the goods or benefits derived from the services provided by a peatland ecosystem that are used directly by beneficiaries. These include consumptive uses (e.g., harvesting goods) and non-consumptive uses (e.g., enjoyment of peat nature beauty);
- Indirect use value is the benefits derived from the goods and services provided by a peatland ecosystem that are used indirectly by beneficiaries;
- Non-use value is the value that is placed on private willingness to pay for the peatland ecosystem in a conserved or sustainable use state, but the willingness to pay is unrelated to current of planned use of the peatland ecosystem.
-

### Direct Use Value

Direct use value is classified into extractive direct use value and non-extractive direct use value. Extractive direct use value is the economic value obtained from the direct use of a resource from peatlands or peatland ecosystem that results in a reduction in the amount of natural resources. In the case of the Kahayan-Sebangau Peat Hydrological Unit, the extractive direct use value is classified into: a) values from plantations; b) values from agriculture; and c) values from forests. Non-extractive direct use value is all direct use of peatland resources which does not cause a reduction in the amount of peatland resources. In this research, the value from eco-tourism is generated as non-extractive direct use value. The direct use value is presented in the Table 2.

Table 2. The extractive direct use value in Kahayan-Sebangau Peat Hydrological Unit

| No | Direct Use Value | Economic value (IDR) |
|---|---|---|
| 1 | Extractive Direct Use Value | 1,641,961,783,099.95 |
| 1.1. | Plantations | 144,938,702,763.76 |
| | Plantation company | 62,628,424,219.72 |
| | Smallholder plantation | 11,460,153,223.72 |
| | Rubber plantation | 23,375,169,280.19 |
| | Coconut plantation | 47,474,956,040.13 |
| 1.2. | Agriculture | 84,702,244,121.19 |
| | Rice cultivation | 2,456,770,245.32 |
| | Crops | 19,953,503,637.00 |
| | Multi-cropping | 62,176,154,718.13 |
| | Dry fields | 115,815,520.74 |
| 1.3. | Fishery | 86,770,809,000.00 |
| 1.4. | Forest | 1,325,550,027,215.00 |
| | Forest | 781,507,636,553.72 |
| | Swamp forest | 544,042,390,661.28 |
| 2 | Non-extractive Direct Use Value | 5,936,864,761.90 |
| 2.1. | Ecotourism | 5,936,864,761.90 |

As a result, forests provide the highest value through their function in delivering economic value products, for example in the supply of non-timber forest products. This value is felt most highly by the community.

## Indirect Use Value

In this study, the total carbon storage from below ground and above ground are generated as indirect use value, which is presented in the Table 3.

Table 3. Indirect use value in Kahayan-Sebangau Peat Hydrological Unit

| Indirect Use Value | Economic value (IDR) |
|---|---|
| Total Carbon Storage | 341,734,865,436,403.00 |
| Carbon storage (below ground) | 226,170,076,366,735.00 |
| Carbon storage (above ground) | 115,564,789,069,668.00 |

The value of the benefits of peat as a carbon sink is very high. peatlands are ideally wet, and in these ideal conditions, peatlands store a lot of carbon, which has accumulated over thousands of years. when peatlands dry up, peatlands expose carbon emissions to the air. therefore, peatlands should ideally be wet (Page et al. 2009, Dommain et al. 2010, Evers et al. 2017).

## Non-Use Value

In this study, the non-use value is classified into bequest value and existence value. The bequest value is the value of satisfaction from preserving a natural peat environment or a historic peat environment, in other words natural heritage or cultural heritage from peatland ecosystem for future generations. The data of biodiversity service is generated as bequest value. The existence value is the value of the benefits derived from the peatland ecosystem's existence alone. The result of non-use value is presented in the Table 3.

Table 4. Non-use value in Kahayan-Sebangau Peat Hydrological Unit

| No | Non-Use Value | Economic value (IDR) |
|---|---|---|
| 1 | **Bequest value** | **1,837,960,461,169.41** |
| | Biodiversity service value | 1,837,960,461,169.41 |
| 2 | **Existence value** | **10,926,071,176,686.00** |
| | Social cultural service value | 2,592,505,556,700.00 |
| | Nature service value | 5,504,377,739,950.00 |
| | Aesthetic value | 2,829,187,880,036.00 |

## CONCLUSIONS

The results show that TEV of peatlands in PHU of Kahayan-Sebangau is on the order of IDR 350 trillion/year, whereas the most significant proportion of the TEV coming from the functional values of carbon cycling, which is IDR 340 trillion/year. This result implies that peat ecosystems have significantly high value to remain protected, in contrast to conversion for extractive purposes.

## ACKNOWLEDGEMENT

This research was funded by World Resources Institute (WRI) Indonesia.

## REFERENCES

Adger N, Brown K, Cervigni R, Moran D. (1995) Towards Estimating Total Economic Value of Forests in Mexico. Centre for Social and Economic Research on the Global Environment, University of East Anglia and University College London.

Admiraal, J F, Wossink A, Groot WT, Snoo GR. (2013) More than Total Economic Value: How to Combine Economic Valuation of Biodiversity with Ecological Resilience. Ecological Economics 89 (2013) 115-122.

Dommain, R., Couwenberg J, and Joosten H. (2010) Hydrological self-regulation of domed peatlands in south-east Asia and consequences for conservation and restoration. Mires and Peat, Volume 6, article 5:1–17.

Evers S, Yule CM, Padfield R, O'Reilly P, Varkkey H. (2017) Keep wetlands wet: the myth of sustainable development of tropical peatlands – implications for policies and management. Global Change Biology, 23:534–549, doi: 10.1111/gcb.13422.

Page S, Hoscilo A, Wösten H, Jauhiainen J, Silvius M, Rieley J, Ritzema H, Tansey K, Graham L, Vasander H, Limin S. (2009) – Restoration Ecology of Lowland Tropical Peatlands in Southeast Asia: Current Knowledge and Future Research Directions. Ecosystems (2009) 12: 888–905. DOI: 10.1007/s10021-008-9216-2

Pierce DW. (2001) The Economic Value of Forest Ecosystems. CSERGE-Economics, University College London, UK.

Silvius M, Diemont H. (2007) Deforestation and degradation of peatlands. Peatlands International 2: 32–34.

Suwarno Y, Purwono N, Suriadi AB, Nahib I. (2016) Study of Peat Hydrological Unit at Central Kalimantan Area. Seminar Nasional Peran Geospasial dalam Membingkai NKRI, 2016: 233-242.

ID 62348

# COOPERATION IN MIRE ECOSYSTEM STUDIES BETWEEN FINLAND AND RUSSIA

Tapio Lindholm[1], *Harri Vasander[2], Raimo Heikkilä[3], Oleg Kuznetsov[4],

[1] Finnish Environmental Institute, Finland
[2] University of Helsinki, Finland
[3] Välppätie 5, Turku, Finland
[4] Karelian Research Center, Russia

*harri.vasander@helsinki.fi*

When Finland was a part of Russia as the Grand Duchy of Finland (1809-1917) Finnish botanists and mire specialists could well study mires and peatlands in the huge Russia. There was even a wish from the scientific advisors of the Emperor that Finnish mire scientists could work near the border that has similar natural conditions on both sides of the border. Also during the Second World War there were Finnish researchers and many studies in Olonets Karelia. We Finns born in 1950's started to get contacts in the final phases of the USSR. First we found there Marina Botch, Tatyana Yourkovskaya and their student Olga Galanina in Leningrad and next a young and enthusiastic mire specialist Oleg Kuznetsov in Petrozavodsk. This was a good start. After the collapsing of the USSR, there was a big interest in cooperation on both sides of the former iron curtain. There were several smaller and bigger projects, which have given option to versatile mire studies. Due to joint excursions, targeted research, and good contacts with the administration, many new nature protection areas have been established on both sides of the border. Excellent support to all this has been the Finnish-Russian Nature Conservation Working Group between Russian Ministry of Natural Resources and the Environment and Finnish Ministry of Environment from the year 1985, when professor Rauno Ruuhijärvi from Finland started that. Here we tell what has been done in mire study cooperation before us and during our time. Now it is time for the future work!

# V PEATLAND AND PEAT RELATED ECONOMIC SERVICES

IPC2021

ID 61288

# ALTERNATIVE FARMING PRACTICES FOR LONG TERM RESILIENT LAND USE IN PEATLAND REGIONS IN THE NETHERLANDS; A COST BENEFIT ANALYSIS

Jos Schouwenaars

Water Authority Fryslân, Leeuwarden, The Netherlands

*jschouwenaars@wetterskipfryslan.nl*

## SUMMARY

Climate change, sea level rise, weather extremes, soil subsidence and declining biodiversity are reason to try to develop a sustainable water system and land use for the peatland regions in the Netherlands. The main research and design question was: are profitable systems of agricultural land use possible based on a sustainable water system. For different types of peatland regions with different water systems alternative farming practices are designed aiming to reduce emission of CO2 and guaranteeing a good income for farmers. These alternative agricultural land use types are evaluated using a cost-benefit analysis.
Results show that transition to alternative farming practices has the potential to be very cost effective for the society as a whole. The most important benefits are related to the reduction of greenhouse gas emissions.
It is important to start pilots for transition at a local farm level. Different supporting mechanisms for the transition to less intensive, nature-inclusive farming should be applied. These can partly be technical such as subsurface drainage and infiltration techniques, but probably other mechanisms like adding extra land to farmers or financial compensation for loss of yields are of greater importance.

***Keywords**: water management, reduction CO2 emission, cost benefit analysis, agricultural transition*

# INTRODUCTION

In the province of Fryslân, situated in the northern part of the Netherlands ( see Fig.1), peatland is dominantly use for intensive dairy farming. The rate of land subsidence is ca. 0.5 – 1.0 cm per year. Based on recent flux measurements yearly CO2eq. emissions are estimated between 15 and 40 ton per ha.

Distribution of the different peat soil types are presented in Fig.2. Types of peat soils and their areas are presented in Table 1.

*Fig. 1 Location of the peatland district of Fryslân*

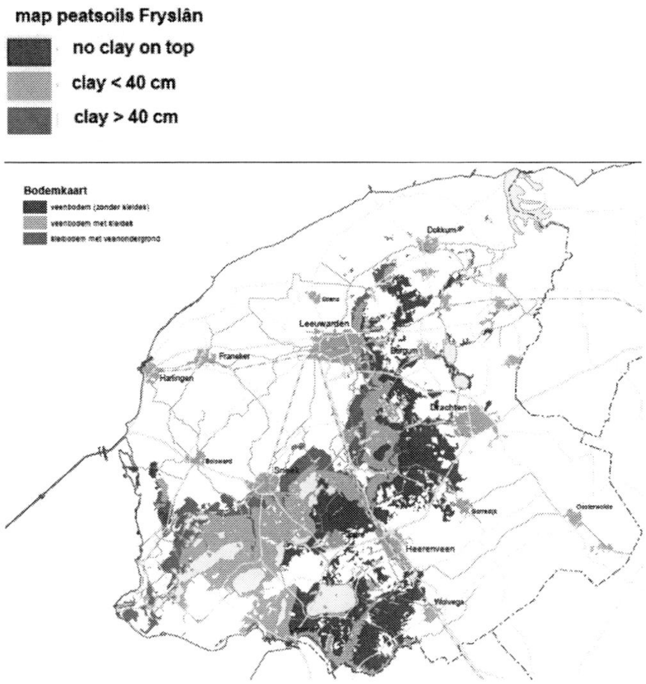


*Fig.2 Peat soil types and distribution in the peatland district of Fryslân*

Table 1 Distribution of peat soil types

| | ha | % |
|---|---|---|
| Total peatland area | 60.000 | |
| ***With toplayer of clay*** | | |
| clay > 40 cm | 16.000 | 27 |
| clay < 40 cm | 8.500 | 14 |
| ***no clay on top*** | | |
| peat > 80 cm | 12.000 | 20 |
| peat 40-80 cm | 7.500 | 13 |
| peat < 40 cm | 16.000 | 27 |

To comply with the objectives of the Paris Agreement on Climate Action, the Dutch Government aims to reduce CO2 emissions from peatlands under agricultural use with ca. 30% in 2030.
Therefore regional authorities develop planning strategies for the period 2020-2030. As part of the planning process in 2019 a cost benefit analysis was made of alternative farming systems in combination with reduced drainage levels. Results serve to facilitate discussions with the boards of the provincial authority and the regional water authority and with stakeholders, in particular the different farmer associations.

## MATERIALS AND METHODS

In the cost benefit analysis 3 different farming systems were studied, which vary in intensity of land use ( intensive versus extensive) and rate of circularity ( common versus circular system partly using paludiculture ).
In Table 2 the features of the studied farming systems are presented.

Table 2. Characteristics of the 3 farming systems analysed in the cost benefit analysis.

| | **dairy farming system** | | |
|---|---|---|---|
| | intensive | extensive | circulair |
| | *area / kg. dry matter per ha per year* | | |
| *gras* | 60 ha / 11.000 | 70 ha / 8.000 | |
| *maize* | 10 ha / 16.000 | | |
| *azolla* | | | 30 ha / 20.000 |
| *wheat* | | | 40 ha / 10.000 |
| *number* of cows | 110 | 90 | 105 |
| milk production per cow *in liter per year* | 9.700 | 6.000 | 11.000 |
| | *Euro per year* | | |
| total added value | 475.000 | 353.000 | 475.000 |
| total costs | 372.000 | 288.000 | 410.000 |
| income family ( labour input 1.6 persons) | 103.000 | 65.000 | 65.000 |

Also different scenarios for rewetting were used, varying in the relative distribution of (1) reduced drainage with subsurface infiltration by drains, (2) limited drainage without subsurface drains and (3) complete rewetting.
Calculations of costs and benefits for society for different scenarios for rewetting and corresponding farming systems were calculated in terms of Net Present Value (NPV) over a period of 100 years ( 2020-2120) using an interest rate of 3% per year.

## RESULTS

Results of the cost benefit analysis are presented in Table 3.

Table 3. Most cost effective farming system for different soil types and its difference with the actual dairy farming system ( intensive, deep drainage ), expressed in Net Present Value. (negative value indicate higher costs or reduced benefits, positive values indicate lower costs or higher benefits )

| | **most cost effective farming system** | **differences in Net Present Value (NPV) for alternative farming systems when compared to actual dairy farming over the period 2020 – 2120** | | | |
|---|---|---|---|---|---|
| ***toplayer of clay*** | | **water management** | **agri-culture** | **climate*** | **total*** incl. other aspects |
| clay > 40 cm | extensive, nature inclusive | -5 | 3 | 28 - 81 | 124 - 177 |
| clay < 40 cm | extensive, nature inclusive | -5 | -70 | 147 - 280 | 190 - 323 |
| ***no clay on top*** | | | | | |
| peat > 80 cm | intensive with subsurface irrigation/drainage | -23 | 30 | 28 - 152 | 274 - 149 |
| | extensive, nature inclusive | -3 | -50 | 145 - 237 | 209 - 301 |
| peat 40-80 cm | intensive with subsurface irrigation/drainage | -19 | 19 | 42 - 104 | 147 - 209 |
| | extensive, nature inclusive | -4 | -53 | 100 - 238 | 153 - 291 |
| peat < 40 cm | intensive with subsurface irrigation/drainage | -24 | -29 | 48 - 185 | 53 - 190 |
| | circulair | -1 | -287 | 71 - 381 | -150 - 160 |

## DISCUSSION

Based upon the results of the cost benefit analysis the most promising ( or cost-effective) farming systems for the different soil types can be derived. The preferred farming system for a given soil type is closely related to its drainage level. The latter determines CO2 emission.

The costs for investments in the water infrastructure for partial rewetting and for transition in farming systems were part of the cost benefit analysis.
In Table 4 an overview is given of these interrelated aspects.

Table 4. Overview of preferred farming systems per soil type and corresponding costs and benefits

| | **most cost effective farming system** | **drainage level**<br>% area in cm below surface | **initial investments for transition**<br>in Euro per ha | **yearly reduction emission $CO_2$ eq.**<br>in ton per ha* | **costs per ton $CO_2$ eq. Reduction**<br>in Euro |
|---|---|---|---|---|---|
| ***toplayer of clay*** | | | | | |
| clay > 40 cm | extensive, nature inclusive | 40% 0-30<br>60% 30-60 | ca. 1.000 | 0,9 – 2,7 | 15 - 40 |
| clay < 40 cm | extensive, nature inclusive | 40% 0-30<br>60% 30-60 | ca. 9.000 | 8,8 – 17,8 | 20 - 40 |
| ***no clay on top*** | | | | | |
| peat > 80 cm | intensive with subsurface irrigation/drainage | 100% 30-60 | ca. 2.000 | 1,3 – 6,2 | 15 - 60 |
| | extensive, nature inclusive | 40% 0-30<br>60% 30-60 | ca. 4.000 | 6,2 – 10,7 | 15 - 25 |
| peat 40-80 cm | intensive with subsurface irrigation/drainage | 100% 30-60 | ca. 3.000 | 3,2 – 6,8 | 20 - 40 |
| | extensive, nature inclusive | 40% 0-30<br>60% 30-60 | ca. 7.000 | 6,8 – 17,1 | 20 - 40 |
| peat < 40 cm | intensive with subsurface irrigation/drainage | 100% 30-60 | ca. 3.000 | 1,5 - 6,5 | 20 - 80 |
| | circulair | 100% 0-30 | ca. 15.000 | 2,3 – 12,9 | 50 - 250 |

## CONCLUSION

Results show that transition to alternative farming practices has the potential to be very cost effective for the society as a whole. The most important benefits are related to the reduction of greenhouse gas emissions.
It is important to start pilots for transition at a local farm level. Different supporting mechanisms for the transition to less intensive, nature-inclusive farming should be applied. These can partly be technical such as subsurface drainage and infiltration techniques, but probably other mechanisms like adding extra land to farmers or financial compensation for loss of yields are of greater importance.

## ACKNOWLEDGEMENTS

Several components of the work presented in this study were carried out by colleagues participating in the Peatland Program Fryslân. The cost benefit analysis was carried out by Elisabeth Ruijgrok of Witteveen en Bos Consultancies.

# REFERENCES


1. Ruijgrok E.C.M., van Tuinen E.J. (2019). Cost benefit analysis of alternative farming systems in the peatland district Fryslân (in Dutch). MKBA remming bodemdaling in het Friese veenweidegebied. Provincie Fryslân, Witteveen+Bos, Rotterdam.
2. De Ruyter P., van Rijen J. , Schouwenaars J., Vogelzang, T. (2019) Alternative farming in sustainable Frisian peatlands. (in Dutch). Anders boeren in een weerbaar en volhoudbaar Fries laagveenlandschap. *De Levende Natuur*; 120: 149-152
3. Gielen, J.C.A. (2019) Findings on Places of Hope concept for farming systems in the peatland district Fryslân. (in Dutch). Rapport van bevindingen Places of Hope; bedrijfssystemen voor het veen in het Lage Midden van Fryslân. Provincie Fryslân, Countus Accountants and Consultancies, Zwolle.

ID 61776

# SMALLHOLDER AGRICULTURE ON PEATLAND IN INDONESIA: BALANCING LIVELIHOOD AND CLIMATE SECURITY

*Susan Page[1], Patrick O'Reilly[1], Caroline Upton[1], Sara Thornton[1], Gusti Anshari[2], Adi Jaya[3], E. Antang[3], C. Entang[3], Jonay Jovani Sancho[4,5], Sofie Sjogersten[4], Chris Evans[5]

[1] School of Geography, Geology & the Environment, University of Leicester, Leicester, UK
[2] Magister of Environment and Soil Science Department, Universitas Tanjungpura, Pontianak, Indonesia
[3] Faculty of Agriculture, Universitas Palangkaraya, Palangkaraya, Indonesia
[4] School of XXXX, University of Nottingham, Nottingham, UK
[5] UK Centre for Ecology & Hydrology, Bangor, Wales, UK

*sep5@le.ac.uk*

## SUMMARY

Tropical peatlands are 'marginal to poor' for agricultural production, yet 5-7 million ha in SE Asia have been cleared and drained for production of plantation and food crops. Adverse environmental impacts associated with land use change include increased greenhouse gas (GHG) emissions, soil degradation, land subsidence and fire which have negative influences on climate, livelihoods and health. Peat oxidation emissions of 64 Mt C $yr^{-1}$ are attributable to large-scale plantations, but a further 49 Mt C $yr^{-1}$ have been ascribed to smallholder agriculture (SHA). Moreover, peat fires, often associated with land management for SHA, cause additional GHG emissions and significant health and socio-economic burdens. Within Indonesian peatland SHA communities, undesirable environmental impacts are exacerbated by inefficient markets, unsustainable production systems, absence of secure land tenure, and limited access to alternative food systems and income sources. It can be argued that these factors drive SHA farmers to adopt short term, environmental and/or social strategies to secure livelihoods that may be regarded as suboptimal. This complex situation has gained some international attention, although this has been less intensive than that directed at large industrial plantations, and there remain important gaps in our understanding of the functioning of SHA landscapes as linked socio-ecological systems. This has not prevented multiple proposals for new economic practices that are claimed to be environmentally sustainable and financially viable (from a farmer's perspective) alternatives to drainage-based cultivation in SHA peat systems. We contend that this question must be addressed through a multidisciplinary approach that incorporates an understanding of the environmental impacts of peatland SHA practices, alongside detailed analysis of SHA livelihood practices. This paper considers to what extent new forms of SHA land management could provide viable alternatives to drainage-based agriculture, whilst recognizing the need for co-produced solutions that are credible and take account of farmer's livelihood needs, understandings and aspirations.

***Keywords**: Tropical, Peatland, Smallholder, Agriculture, Livelihoods*

## INTRODUCTION

Since the latter half of the 20th century, socio-technical innovations in agriculture, engineering and construction have significantly increased the scope and intensity of human activities in many landscapes. This has resulted in the conversion of land previously considered of limited value in relation to human development for multiple agricultural and non-agricultural uses, including significant areas of tropical peatland. While recognised as being sub-optimal for agricultural production, a combination of push factors including expanding populations and expectations regarding food security and development, and pull factors such as economic opportunities and increased availability of investment funds have led to rapid land use change on the tropical peatlands of SE Asia.

By 2018, it is estimated that ca. 242,000 km$^2$ of tropical peatlands (i.e. nearly half of the area of degraded peatland globally) had experienced some degree of degradation due to human activities, with the majority concentrated in SE Asia (Leifeld & Menichetti, 2018). The negative environmental implications of this trend require little further elaboration. Over the past two decades, attention has been drawn to the very significant role that tropical peatlands play in carbon sequestration and their consequent role in increasing greenhouse gas (GHG) emissions when converted in ways that change the basic characteristics of the peatland ecosystem. Of particular note in this respect has been the drainage of large areas for agricultural crops, involving a combination of large companies producing commodities such as timber, wood pulp and palm oil, and the production of both commodities and food crops by a variety of smaller-scale producers. Drainage required to facilitate these activities directly contributes to an increase in GHG emissions as the dry peat is oxidised. Various soil management and agronomic practices employed by large- and small-scale producers exacerbate this problem. Activities such as controlled burning, removal of biomass and application of various soil treatments such as lime, chemical fertilizers and mineral soil may have a significant (and arguably under researched) impact on tropical peatland, altering both soil chemistry and microbial communities in ways which contribute to accelerating GHG emissions. Other negative environmental impacts associated with peatland agriculture include subsidence, flooding, heavy metal mobilization, and increased risk and intensity of major fires. These negative impacts have generated intense disputes concerning the future of these areas, leading to widespread calls for national and global measures to protect remaining intact tropical peat swamps and to rehabilitate or restore degraded systems.

While large scale plantation companies are widely seen as the drivers of peatland conversion in SE Asia, small-scale producers are said to account for a substantial (though by no means dominant) proportion of the area converted. In relation to oil palm for example, some industry sources state that smallholders account for 40% of total production in Indonesia and at least 11% of total production in Malaysia (RSPO, n.d.). Other commentators suggest that the total figure may be as much as 40% of the total production of both countries (Aubert et al., 2017). While little data exist, it is undoubtedly the case that these figures include many smallholders who live and work on tropical peatland and whose activities have significant impacts (see for example Jewitt et al., 2014; Nath et al., 2016). Smallholders have been implicated in peatland conversion and also in the regular fires which affect peatlands in both Malaysia and Indonesia (e.g. Aubert et al., 2017; Gaveau et al., 2014).

At the same time, however, the movement of smallholders into peatlands is widely presented in positive terms. The cultivation of oil palm and other crops on peatland is claimed to significantly improve income and expand life chances for small-scale producers and their children. As a consequence, and not without some justification, the position of smallholders is often mobilised in support of the continuation of peatland agriculture in public debate (e.g. see Hii, 2017). Such views are in keeping with popular political discourse in the region championing the rights of nations to pursue a modernising agenda (Varkkey & O'Reilly, 2019). In this context, the conversion of peatlands is portrayed as a necessity if the countries where they are found are to achieve a greater degree of development. The conversion of "unproductive" peatlands into economically productive smallholder landscapes has become intimately associated with narratives of development and progress (ibid).

Given that smallholder agriculture (SHA) has come to hold such an important place in policy debates concerning the fate of tropical peatlands in SE Asia, it is scarcely surprising that significant attention has been paid to the plight of "smallholders" in popular discourse concerning the current and future status of these locations. This is also reflected in ongoing academic discussion and research concerning the role and condition of smallholders in tropical peatlands, much of which has sought to assess the relative costs and benefits of the adoption or non-adoption of specific crops and farming practices (most notably oil palm). A key element of such approaches appears to be the assumption that small-scale production involves a relatively homogenous population of "smallholders" choosing between a limited range of options. Furthermore, in many instances the basis of decision making in this research and subsequent policies draws on concepts that equate and/or evaluate decision making in terms of utility maximisation equated to income. Such framings and the analysis they produce embody ideas about the nature of decision making, farming systems, knowledge transfer and agency that have significant implications for the design and implementation of policies to promote the more "sustainable" use of peatlands.

A number of studies have raised questions concerning this perspective by drawing attention to the considerable variation which exists within SHA communities along with its implications for peatland management policies. Santika et al. (2019a, 2019b) demonstrate that the outcomes of oil palm adoption are more mixed than previous studies suggest and not universally beneficial. She draws attention to variations in performance and the fact that such differences cannot be ascribed simply to agronomic and/or economic factors but also to a combination of social, historical and cultural issues. Work by Jelsma et al. (2016, 2017) and others also draws attention to the existence of a range of different small-scale production systems with different characteristics concerning such factors as labour organisation, capitalisation, crop selection and relationships to market. It largely remains the case that geographers, agronomists and other researchers who refer to the "smallholder mosaic" are primarily referring to morphological characteristics reflecting crop choices and property demarcations of actors involved in what continues to be largely framed as a smallholder system. However, a critical question concerns the capacity of current research approaches to provide in depth understanding of the variations within the generic of different farming approaches that make up the smallholder sector.

The recent Sustainpeat project and other initiatives in which the authors are involved, are attempting to begin to address this question. Rather than embarking from either an agronomic or an environmental basis these projects have sought to centre their analysis around the livelihood practices of small-scale producers living in peatland areas in Indonesia and Malaysia. In particular, our work seeks to explore how livelihood practices emerge within wider socio-ecological assemblages of human and non-human objects and processes. Our approach is interdisciplinary, involving both natural and social scientists, and multi-perspectival rather than integrative, recognising the existence of multiple, valid knowledge framings and the need to treat them holistically rather than seeking to incorporate them into a single frame of meaning. Our aims are to i) examine the range of practices that are currently being undertaken in peatland SHA areas and to assess which of these practices are least environmentally damaging, thereby offering clues to ways in which small-scale production on peatland can be made more 'responsible' (see Clarke & Rieley, 2019); and ii) to consider to what extent new forms of SHA land management could provide viable alternatives to drainage-based agriculture, whilst recognising the need for co-produced credible solutions that take account of farmer's livelihood needs, understandings and aspirations.

## MATERIALS AND METHODS

Our research was undertaken within a number of peatland SHA communities in Selangor (Peninsular Malaysia) and in West and Central Kalimantan (Indonesian Borneo). At these locations, we obtained both biophysical data from a representative range of crops along with socio-economic data from SHA households and communities. We collected peat surface GHG emissions ($CO_2$, $CH_4$, $N_2O$) along with peat samples (surface and down core) and water samples for determination of physical and chemical characteristics. On the socio-economic side, we used interviews and workshops to obtain data on the types of crops being grown and their contributions to household incomes, agronomic and other land management techniques, livelihood strategies and so on. We present an overview of some of our key findings to date in relation to the aims of this paper.

## RESULTS

Our original intention was to seek to identify crops that may be less environmentally harmful, but our results indicate that there is little evidence that any of the practices and crops currently employed in these areas provide a good basis for more responsible SHA peatland production systems. Indeed, the level of microvariation in the results indicate that at farm level a number of factors beside the crop, in particular water management (intensity of drainage, use of surface irrigation), burning practices, and soil treatments have as much to do with the environmental consequences as the choice of crops and cropping practices. Across a range of crops and agronomic practices, we observed maximal heterotrophic (Rh) $CO_2$ emissions at a water table of 60 cm below the peat surface and decreasing Rh emissions with both shallower and deeper WTDs. Rh emissions for an average WTD of 60 cm were typically in the range 25 – 45 t $CO_2$ $ha^{-1}$ $yr^{-1}$, in line with IPCC Tier 1 emission factors for cropland and oil palm (IPCC, 2013). Peat surface $CH_4$ emissions were negligible except during short periods of flooding. The application of organic manure and inorganic fertilizers were important in determining the scale of $N_2O$ emissions. We measured highest emissions (typically around 17.5 kg $ha^{-1}$ $yr^{-1}$) for crops being grown with a water table close to the peat surface, at around 20 cm, and where there was regular fertilizer application. There have been few previous studies of $N_2O$ emissions from tropical peatland under SHA, and our results indicate that this land use is likely a strong regional source for this GHG (for comparison, the IPCC Tier 1 emission factor for tropical cropland is 7.9 kg $ha^{-1}$ $yr^{-1}$; IPCC 2013). On shallow peats, our data indicate a heightened risk of mobilisation of potentially phytotoxic levels of heavy metals in the soil solution resulting from exposure and oxidation of underlying potential acid sulphate (PAS) substrates through peat degradation. For SHA on shallow peats, peat subsidence incurs not only an increased risk of flooding but also of reduced fertility which may ultimately limit on-going, drainage-based agricultural production.

The socio-economic results in many ways echo those of the natural science research with high levels of variation between the environmental awareness and land management strategies adopted by different farmer households. Farmers stated that soil productivity was a principal concern, key issues being drainage/irrigation and pH/fertility. Many farmers had limited control over the level of drainage on their land, and limited opportunities to irrigate (e.g. using small pumps). Application of and knowledge of fertilizers and other soil amendments was variable, with cost the main factor determining their use. Fire was used by more than 68% of farmers, both as a source of cheap ash fertilizer, and to clear crop residues and scrub. Most farmers demonstrated some awareness of the environmental consequences of their land management but continued to prioritize their short-term economic objectives over longer-term concerns. There was patchy awareness of less environmentally damaging practices, and willingness to adopt these was driven by both financial concerns and previous farming knowledge. Farmers often failed to link their own activities to wider environmental degradation – e.g. air pollution and health problems caused by wildfires were not linked to on-farm fire use. Significantly, there was little penetration of state interventions aimed at improving environmental practices, e.g. in terms of reduced use of fire or maintaining high(er) water levels.

The farmers employed heterogenous household strategies. Rather than solely being dependent on agriculture, multiple income sources were the norm with, at the Indonesian study sites, an average of 2.1 income sources per family. From interviews it was clear that small-scale producers did not see this situation as incompatible with their self-identification as farmers and it may be reasonable to assume that multiple income sources are an established feature of SHA livelihoods on peatland. In the communities we examined small-scale producers generally practiced multi-cropping. In total, 55 crops were identified across our study communities, the choice of crops reflecting the natural characteristics of the area, the previous experience of the producers themselves, market intelligence gathered via traders, neighbours and family and in some cases access to government support. Crop selection was largely driven by commercial rather than subsistence concerns with none of the areas producing sufficient staple foods and all the areas producing mainly for market. The activities of producers also appeared to be primarily entrepreneurial; they were willing to take risks, make investments and enter financing arrangements with a view to generating profits.

## DISCUSSION

Our results indicate that within peatland SHA communities there is at best a weak association between the crops grown and the level of income generated by individual farmers. Equally there is no clear evidence of a relationship between the crops grown and environmental impacts, with average water level and amount/type of fertilizer application providing the strongest controls on $CO_2$ and $N_2O$ emissions, respectively. These observations are in line with studies of northern peatlands under intensive agricultural production, e.g. Evans et al. (2016), which demonstrate that the average position of the water table, rather than crop type or other aspects of agronomic management, exerts an over-riding influence on the scale of $CO_2$ emissions, whilst fertilizer application is the key determinant of $N_2O$ emissions (e.g. Taft et al., 2017). Where SHA crops were being grown at high(er) water levels, the level of fertilizer application required to maintain production invariably resulted in high $N_2O$ emissions, thereby limiting, in climate terms, the benefits of reduced $CO_2$ emissions. Strategies aiming to balance livelihood and climate security by SHA communities need to take account of these environmental trade-offs which reflect pragmatic decisions by farmers to maximize production and hence income. This is despite the known medium to longer-term risks posed by high rates of peat mineralization, which result in increased risks of flooding and PAS exposure that ultimately threaten the longer-term economic viability of SHA farming. Any moves towards high(er) water table agriculture that also involve reduced or no fertilizer use will need to take account of the limitations that these changes will place on farmers' economic prospects.

In relation to income, a range of factors appear to be associated with better income which are in many cases only indirectly related to cropping practices. These include social attributes such as the level of education achieved and the availability of social capital, particularly in the form of relationships with the village government which enabled certain people to adopt improved livelihood strategies (O'Reilly et al., 2020). Many of the SHA farmers were responsive to changing markets, i.e. they were willing to be versatile in their choice of crop, indicating that they could be responsive to new crops or new ways of farming. Local governance and SHA community characteristics could offer the capacity to implement innovative responses, if managed appropriately.

## CONCLUSION

In summary, and when examined in detail, different small-scale producers within peatland communities in Indonesia and Malaysia exhibit a high level of variation in relation to the practices they adopt. This includes the type of crops they choose to grow, the ways in which they grow them, how they are traded and what other ways they generate income. While this to a certain extent confirms the need for greater granularity in the analysis of small-scale producers suggested by Jelsma et al. (2017) and others, it also points to the limitations of any typology based on the morphological features of different small-scale producers and to the need for an in depth exploration of smallholder practices. It may be the case that such in depth work is the best means for designing interventions, such as those aimed at reducing GHG emissions, subsidence, fire use etc., that are suited to local biophysical conditions, relevant to local community skills and interests, and appropriate to local markets and governance arrangements. Such tailored local solutions would imply that livelihood may represent an important framing for policy questions, particularly in relation to more responsible peatland management; that the household is an important unit for policy analysis (although not discounting the critical significance of intra-household issues); and the village an important unit for policy action. Our data suggest that SHA communities are highly heterogenous, therefore efforts to introduce more environmentally responsible land management practices will likely need to be individually tailored to suit local socio-ecological conditions. A 'one size fits all' response to is unlikely to be effective.

## ACKNOWLEDGEMENTS

The authors acknowledge funding from BBSRC for the Sustainpeat project. We also wish to thank the smallholder communities in which the studies were undertaken and several colleagues at Universiti Palangkaraya and Universiti Tanjungpura for their invaluable assistance with field work.

## REFERENCES


Aubert, P., Chakib, A., & Laurans, Y. (2017) Implementation and effectiveness of sustainability initiatives in the palm oil sector: a meta-analysis, Studies N° 11/17, IDDRI, Paris, France, p. 56.

Clarke, D. & Rieley, J. (2019) *Strategy for responsible peatland management.* 6th edition, International Peatland Society, Jyväskylä, Finland.

Euler, M., Hoffmann, M. P., Fathoni, Z., & Schwarze, S. (2016) Exploring yield gaps in smallholder oil palm production systems in eastern Sumatra , Indonesia. *Agricultural Systems;* 146: 111–119.

Euler, M., Krishna, V., & Schwarze, S. (2017) Oil palm adoption, household welfare and nutrition among smallholder farmers in Indonesia. *World Development*; 93: 219–235.

Evans, C., Morrison, R., Burden, A. et al. (2016). *Final report on project SP1210: Lowland peatland systems in England and Wales – evaluating greenhouse gas fluxes and carbon balances.* Centre for Ecology and Hydrology, UK.

Gaveau, D. L. A., Salim, M. A., Hergoualc'h, K., Locatelli, B., Sloan, S., Wooster, M., ... Sheil, D. (2014). Major atmospheric emissions from peat fires in Southeast Asia during non-drought years: Evidence from the 2013 Sumatran fires. *Scientific Reports;* 4: 1–7.

Hii, R. (2017). Indigenous Palm Oil Farmers Issue Open Letter to EU MEPs. *Huffpost*, p. 1. Retrieved from https://www.huffingtonpost.com/entry/indigenous-palm-oil-farmers-issue-open-letter-to-eu_us_5a034985e4b055de8d096a01

IPCC (2013) *Supplement to the 2006 IPCC guidelines for national greenhouse gas inventories: Wetlands.* Intergovernmental Panel on Climate Change.

Jewitt, S., Nasir, D., Page, S., Rieley, J. & Khanal, K. (2014) Indonesia's contested domains : deforestation, rehabilitation and conservation-with-development in Central Kalimantan's tropical peatland. *International Forestry Review*; 16(4): 405–420.

Jelsma, I. & Schoneveld, G.C. (2016) *Towards more sustainable and productive independent oil palm smallholders in Indonesia: Insights from the development of a smallholder typology* (Vol. 210). CIFOR.

Jelsma, I., Slingerland, M., Giller, K. E. & Bijman, J. (2017) Collective action in a smallholder oil palm production system in Indonesia: The key to sustainable and inclusive smallholder palm oil? *Journal of Rural Studies*; 54: 198-210.

Leifeld, J. & Menichetti, L. (2018) The underappreciated potential of peatlands in global climate change mitigation strategies. *Nature Communications*; 9: 1071.

Nath, T. K., Puat, M., Dahalan, B., & Parish, F. (2016) Local peoples' appreciation on and contribution to conservation of peatland swamp forests: Experience from Peninsular Malaysia. *Proceedings of the 15th International Peat Congress, Kuching.* International Peatland Society, pp. 577-581.

O'Reilly, P. et al. (2020) Palm oil governance in different locations: Using an assemblage approach to understand a complex sector. *International Review of Modern Sociology*; 46 (1-2): 1-17.

RSPO (n.d.). An overview: oil palm smallholders. *Presentation downloaded from https://www.rspo.org/file/Annex2%2020An%20Overview%20of%20Palm%20Oil%20Smallholders.pdf*

Santika, T., Wilson, K.A., Budiharta, S., Law, E.A., Poh, T.M., Ancrenaz, M., Struebig, M.J. & Meijaard, E. (2019a) Does oil palm agriculture help alleviate poverty? A multidimensional counterfactual assessment of oil palm development in Indonesia. *World Development*; 120: 105-117.

Santika, T., Wilson, K.A., Meijaard, E., Budiharta, S., Law, E.E., Sabri, M., Struebig, M., Ancrenaz, M. & Poh, T.M. (2019b). Changing landscapes, livelihoods and village welfare in the context of oil palm development. *Land Use Policy*; 87: 104073.

Taft, H.E., Cross, P.A., Edwards-Jones, G, Moorhouse, E.R. & Jones, D.L. (2017) Greenhouse gas emissions from intensively managed peat soils in an arable production system. *Agriculture, Ecosystems & Environment*; 237: 162-172.

Varkey, H. & O'Reilly, P. (2019) *Socio-political responses towards transboundary haze: The oil palm in Malaysia's development discourse.* Southeast Asia and Environmental Sustainability in Context, Lanham, Lexington Books.

ID 62593

# POTENTIALS AND CAPACITIES OF CLIMATE CHANGE MITIGATION BY PEATLAND REWETTING AND WET AGRICULTURE ON PEATLANDS (PALUDICULTURE) IN THE BALTIC COUNTRIES

Jüri-Ott Salm[1], Andreas Haberl[5], Janis Ivanovs[3], Leonas Jarasius[4], Ilze Ozola[2], Jan Peters[5], Kristian Piirimäe[1], Normunds Stirvins[2], Nerijus Zableckis[4]

[1] Estonian Fund for Nature ELF, Estonia
[2] Lake and Peatland Research Center, Latvia
[3] Latvian State Forest Research Institute "Silava", Latvia
[4] Lithuanian Fund for Nature LFN, Lithuania
[5] Michael Succow Stiftung, Partner in the Greifswald Mire Centre, Germany

*jott@elfond.ee*

While peatlands only cover ~10% of land in Europe, they comprise Europe's largest terrestrial carbon stock. Drained peatlands are major sources of greenhouse gases and nutrients (nitrogen, phosphorus). In the Baltic countries (Estonia, Latvia, and Lithuania) >50% of the 21,602-24,646 km2 total peatland area are drained and degraded for agriculture, forestry, and peat extraction. Hence Baltic countries rank among the EU's Top 10 of greenhouse gas emitters from drained peatlands (LV 5th, EE 8th, LT 9th).

Rewetting of drained peatlands and use with close-to-surface groundwater levels (paludiculture) could reduce or even stop emissions and considerably contribute to reach Baltic Countries' climate mitigation targets. However, adaptation of peatland agriculture to higher water levels is challenging for society and needs to tackle physical, social, legal, and technologic obstacles.

Therefore, we conducted feasibility studies on the use of peatlands in Estonia, Latvia, and Lithuania. Assessed suitability of peatlands for paludiculture and integrated the results in national and Pan-Baltic maps considering physical, social, and economic criteria. GIS analysis shows that in total 450,668 ha (~1/4 of suitable peatlands) are available for paludiculture in the near-term. As agriculture and forestry are the main driving factors for peatland drainage we analysed legal frameworks for, and the impact of the EU's Common Agricultural Policy (CAP) on peatland utilisation in the Baltic states. Whilst the CAP supports drainage-based peatland use with payments from the 1st and 2nd pillar it neglects the special properties of peat soils. Lacking incentives for raising water levels it subsequently frustrates implementation of paludicultures. To incorporate our results into national and regional strategies for steering spatial and rural development planning we: started a multi-level stakeholder dialogue on CAP and National Energy and Climate Plans; promoted wet peatland management and paludiculture; selected auspicious sites for paludiculture; and preplanned a paludiculture pilot, in each Baltic state.

ID 62699

# ECOLOGY DRIVEN INNOVATIONS REDUCE GHG EMISSIONS AND SUPPORT MIXED AGRICULTURAL LAND-USES OVER TROPICAL PEATLAND

*Shailendra Mishra[1], Jyrki Jauhiainen[2], Hanna Silvennoinen[3], Shivshankar Umashankar[4], Peter I Benke[4], Aswandi Idris[5], Romy Chakraborty[6], Lee Ser Huay Janice Teresa[1], David Wardle1

[1] Asian School of the Environment, Nanyang Technological University, Singapore
[2] Department of Forest Sciences, University of Helsinki, Finland
[3] NIBIO - Norwegian Institute of Bioeconomy Research, Norway
[4] NUS Environmental Research Institute, National University of Singapore, Singapore
[5] LPPM, University of Jambi, Indonesia
[6] Ecology Department, Lawrence Berkeley National Lab, Berkeley, USA

*shailmishra@gmail.com*

Unprecedented drainage and burning of tropical peatlands in Southeast Asia for commercial agro-industrial plantations lead to nearly 12% in global $CO_2$ emissions. Hydrological restoration of drained peatlands by rewetting them is being planned on a large scale, as a strategy to reduce fire incidences as well as mitigate $CO_2$ emissions. However, the immediate consequences of saturating dry peat on greenhouse gas emissions that result from carbon decomposition are not well understood.

We conducted this study to unravel the consequences of drying and wetting on peat carbon decomposition. We show from both controlled microcosms and field studies that anoxic decomposition from water-saturated peat is the major source of $CO_2$ production. Also, corroborating field data showed that rainfall inundations do not reduce peat decomposition rates and loss of carbon continues during wet periods. The mechanistic basis of the continued peat decomposition even in the wet period, which results in high anoxia, was linked with increased nutrient availability (of both carbon and nitrogen) due to the priming effect. The solubilization of nutrients due to priming resulted in extensive changes in >360 different organic molecules from carbon-nitrogen metabolism. This coupled carbon-nitrogen metabolism is also explained from high $N_2O$ and $CO_2$ release from anoxic zones in the field. Towards revegetation efforts, we found that plantations with mixed cropping had the least subsidence rates (a proxy for peat oxidation) when compared to monoculture plantations. This pattern is linked with the release of diverse exudates from different crops, supporting high below-ground and metabolic diversity in mixed crop plantations. Overall, by adopting these technological solutions, we aim to perform socio-economic analysis in the future that can reveal the benefits for the livelihood of people affected by land-use change in the region.

ID 62715

# ECONOMIC VIABILITY OF SPHAGNUM FARMING ON FORMER BOG GRASSLAND

*Sabine Wichmann[1], Silke Kumar[2], Matthias Krebs[1], Greta Gaudig[1]

[1] Institute of Botany and Landscape Ecology, University of Greifswald, Germany
[2] Torfwerk Moorkultur Ramsloh (MOKURA), Germany

*wichmann@uni-greifswald.de*

Sphagnum farming on formerly drained bog grassland combines a low GHG emission agriculture with the production of a renewable growing media constituent. *Sphagnum* biomass has been acknowledged as high-value raw material for professional horticulture. In contrast to other alternatives, *Sphagnum* biomass is suitable to replace peat in growing media with a share of up to 100 %. While the qualitative competitiveness with peat has been shown, we examine the current competitiveness in price and discuss market prospects. Our calculations are based on the first five years of field experience on former bog grassland in North West Germany and anticipate costs and revenues for a total cultivation time of 20 years. Sensitivity analysis encompasses costs, yields, prices and the effect of public non-market payments. We found that the cultivated Sphagnum biomass can not compete with current market prices of peat, whereas it is economically viable for orchid cultivation in case of medium to high Sphagnum productivity. Selling Sphagnum shoots as founder or "seeding" material is profitable even in pessimistic scenarios with high costs and low yields. Cost-covering prices for Sphagnum biomass substituting peat seem achievable, if end consumer pay a top up of 10 % for peat free cultivated plants. A commercial-scale implementation, an increasing market demand for renewables and setting climate targets for the agricultural and horticultural sectors will accelerate the development of Sphagnum farming as a profitable alternative to drainage based peatland agriculture and peat extraction.

ID 62643

# EFFECT OF PADDY LAND USE ON MITIGATION OF PEAT SUBSIDENCE

Minoru Yokochi[1], Koichi Sekimoto[2], Takashi Inoue[3, 4]

[1] Graduate School of Global Food Resources, Hokkaido University, Sapporo, Japan
[2] Graduate School of Agriculture, Hokkaido University, Sapporo, Japan
[3] Research Faculty of Agriculture, Hokkaido University, Sapporo, Japan
[4] Global Station for Food, Land and Water Resources, GI-CoRE, Hokkaido University, Sapporo, Japan

*mino_violalala@eis.hokudai.ac.jp*

## SUMMARY

Agricultural land use on peatlands inevitably causes ongoing land surface subsidence resulting in the reduction of productivity. Also, oxidation of peat substrate associated with subsidence is responsible for greenhouse gas emission. A concept of "Paludiculture", the utilization of wetted peatlands for agriculture, has been proposed in Europe to avoid further subsidence and carbon loss. However, few studies have documented long-term records of subsidence through agriculture in wet peatlands such as paddy fields for rice cultivation. In this study, we clarified the subsidence rates of peatland in rice paddy use and compared them to the rate in peatland with upland crop cultivation. In our study region, Shinotsu Peatland, central Hokkaido, Japan, the land has been used as multi-use paddy fields (rotational cultivation of paddy rice and upland crop) for more than a half-century. Using topographical maps and digital elevation models, the rates of subsidence were calculated in several tens of field plots during the two periods of 1998-2017 and 2006-2017. For all the plots, the land use (paddy or upland) in each year was reconstructed using optical satellite imagery to assess the effect of land use on the dynamics of peat subsidence. The average rate of subsidence was 14.6 and 13.6 mm $yr^{-1}$ during 1998-2017 and 2006-2017 respectively, suggesting a slight decrease as time advances. In both observation periods, the rate of subsidence of the upland-use plots was higher than that of the paddy-use plots. The rates decreased as the period of paddy use increased. These results suggest that paddy use of peatlands can effectively reduce subsidence. Less subsidence through the paddy use was attributed to the reduction of oxidation of peat due to the high water table in the paddy during the irrigation period. Our study suggested that wet use of peatland would be an effective option for the mitigation of subsidence.

***Keywords**: Subsidence, Paludiculutre, Rice paddy, Airborne Laser Survey, Satellite image*

## INTRODUCTION

Drainage and land reclamation for agricultural use of peatlands inevitably causes ongoing land surface subsidence. Many studies of subsidence thorough agricultural use of peatlands have reported all over the world (Leifeld et al., 2011; Pronger et al., 2014; Schipper and McLeod, 2006; Zanello et al., 2011). Subsidence in farmlands with peat often lead to social, economic, and environmental troubles including reduction of agricultural productivity due to relative groundwater level rise, increased risks of inundation combined with sea-level rise (Zanello et al., 2011), and increased cost to maintain farmland productivity (Gambolati et al., 2006; Wösten et al., 1997). Additionally, drained boreal peatlands are estimated to be causing more than $8.5 \times 10^{12}$ g・$yr^{-1}$ of carbon emission through oxidation process of peat substrate (Gorham, 1991), with ensuing indispensable consequences to global climate stability (Parish et al., 2008). Without appropriate management, not only will the agricultural economic value of cultivated peatlands be lost, but also the whole society will be adversely affected by the subsidence related problems. Hence, appropriate land use management on agricultural peatlands is strongly required.

Recently several techniques of land use management on cultivated peatlands has been proposed to mitigate further subsidence and greenhouse gas emission. Higher groundwater level generally reduces decomposition of peat substrate, and therefore, maintenance of high water table with rewetting and submerged infiltration of water has been regarded as a promising option (Hendriks et al., 2007). Paludiculture, the agricultural use of wet or rewetted peatlands, has been discussed as a solution to the subsidence related problems in peatlands. It may effectively reduce the decomposition of organic material and, is acknowledged as a possible land use option on organic soils. However, few studies have documented long-term records of peat subsidence and peat loss through agriculture in wet peatlands because the implementation of paludiculture has evolved only in recent years.

In Hokkaido, northern Japan, peatlands have been used as multi-use paddy fields (rotational cultivation of paddy rice and upland crop), one form of palidiculture, for more than a half-century. In paddy fields, the groundwater table maintains near the ground surface or above during the summer irrigation period, so the subsidence in paddy is expected to slow due to reduction of decomposition of peat substrate. Some studies, indeed, suggested the possibility of the lower rate of peat subsidence in paddy fields compared to upland fields in Hokkaido (Kasubuchi et al., 1998; Miyaji et al., 1995), yet the number of observation in those studies was not sufficient to statistically conclude.

Here, we present the quantitative comparison of the long-term peat subsidence rates between paddy and upland fields in Hokkaido to assess the potential of agricultural use of wet peatlands as a solution of peat subsidence-related problems. Firstly, we investigated the long-term subsidence rates in dozens of field plots using elevation data measured by ground-based survey and digital elevation models constructed by airborne laser survey. Then, the history of land use form (paddy or upland use) was assessed using satellite imagery. Finally, the relationship between the land use form and the subsidence rate was discussed to evaluate the effect of paddy use on the reduction of peat subsidence. This study will provide an essential suggestion for future land use in peatland in Hokkaido and also key knowledge for the attempt of the paludicultural use of peatlands worldwide as well.

## MATERIALS AND METHODS

The investigation of peat subsidence was conducted in Shinotsu Peatland (Fig. 1; 43°15′ N, 141°30′ E), central Hokkaido, Japan, covering 12,000 ha, located at 5-20 m above sea level. Currently, almost all area was converted into cultivated land for rice, wheat and other crops in the early last century. The mean annual temperature is 7.0 °C, and the mean annual precipitation is 1,105 mm at Shin-Shinotsu Weather Station of Japan Meteorological Agency. Peat deposited 6 to7 m thick on alluvial sediment. The both of bog-type peat and fen-type peat are distributed all over the area, and generally, the fen-type peat is surrounding the bog-type

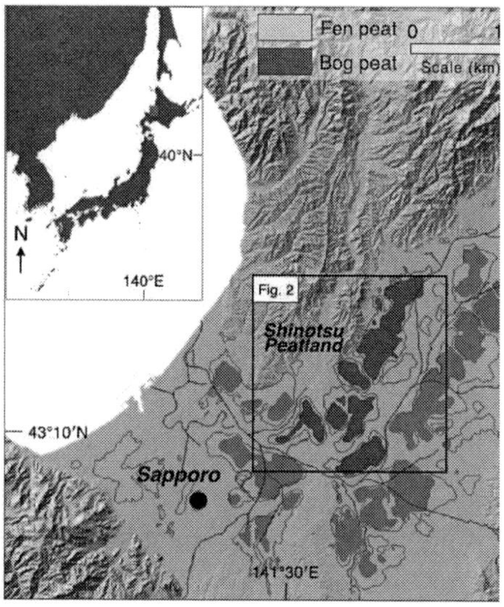


area in Shinotsu, Hokkaido. An inset map in the upper left

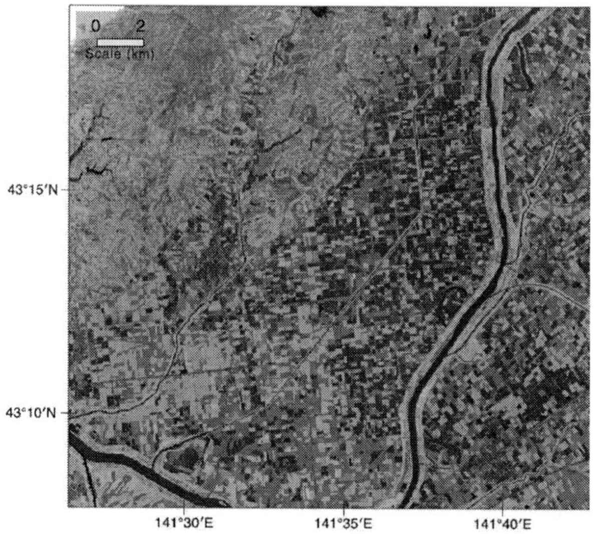


infrared (NIR) and short-wave infrared (SWIR), of Sentinel-2 taken on 28th May 2016 covering Shinotsu Peatland. RGB = (SWIR, NIR, R). Green, pink and blue coloured area represent upland fields with vegetation, upland fields with no vegetation, and paddy fields, respectively.

The peatland has been used as multi-use paddy fields (rotational cultivation of paddy rice and upland crop), and the main crops in this area are currently paddy rice, wheat, soybean, and vegetables. Initially, the area converted to paddy for rice, but the area that is producing upland crop such as wheat have been increasing under the situation of overproduction of rice and the implementation of the set-aside policy by the government since 1971. In the paddy fields, the ground surface is always saturated with irrigation water between middle May and middle August. Both of the paddy and the upland fields has drainage ditches and subsurface drainage systems to maintain a suitable groundwater table for the crops, so either paddy rice and upland crops can be grown with the combination of irrigation and drainage systems.

Subsidence measurement was conducted at 46 field plots on a 2.5 × 2.5 km area in Shinotsu Peatland. The surface level of each field plot in the area was measured in 1998 by ground-based survey and is available in the National Fundamental Terrain Map. In 2006 and 2017, the surface level measurements were done with airborne laser survey by Hokkaido Development Bureau in Ministry of Land, Infrastructure, Transpiration and Tourism, and the digital elevation models (DEMs) based on the survey are available with 1 × 1 m of spatial resolution. Subtracting those elevation data, the subsidence rates were calculated. However, the airborne laser survey in 2006 was conducted in crop growing season, so the elevation data in some of the field plots including the plots where the level data is available in 2006 contains error associated with vegetation height. With this reason, the evaluation of the subsidence was conducted as follows: 1) the subsidence between 1998 and 2006 was not calculated due to the error in the DEM in 2006; 2) the subsidence between 1998 and 2017 was calculated in the 46 field plots; 3) the subsidence between 2006 and 2017 was calculated in the 50 field plots which did not have vegetation cover in 2006. Note that the field plots which were employed in the subsidence analysis in 2) and 3) were not the same.

We reconstructed the land use form (paddy or upland field) of the field plots for each year between 1998 and 2017 to examine the relationship between the peat subsidence and the land use form. We used satellite images which were taken by the optical sensor to assess the land use form of each year. The satellite included Landsat-5 TM, Landsat-8 TM, and Sentinel-2. We employed the bands of visible red (R), near-infrared (NIR), and short-wave infrared (SWIR). The reflection of each band of the electric wave on the ground surface varies depending on the land cover because each land cover has different spectral reflection characteristic. Water can absorb all bands, so reflectance of R, NIR and SWIR are generally low. The plant vegetation highly reflects NIR, but less for R and SWIR. Soil can highly reflect SWIR, but less for R and NIR. During the rice transplanting period (May to early June), the paddy fields are filled by irrigation water whereas the upland fields are covered by vegetation or bare lands. Based on the land covered difference, we distinguished the land use forms using a colour composited image of the R, NIR, and SWIR bands (Fig. 2). This remote sensing technique is often used in crop classification (Liu et al., 2005). We reconstructed the land use form in the 53 field plots between 1998 and 2017, excluding 1998, 2001, 2003, and 2012 in which the satellite images were not available due to cloud cover. Based on the land use form reconstruction, the relationship between subsidence and land use was examined.

## RESULTS

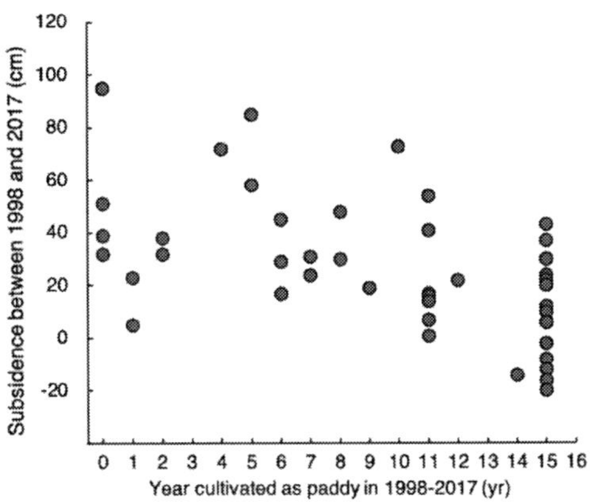


**Fig. 3**: The relationship between the total subsidence in 1998-2017 and the period during which each field was used as paddy field.

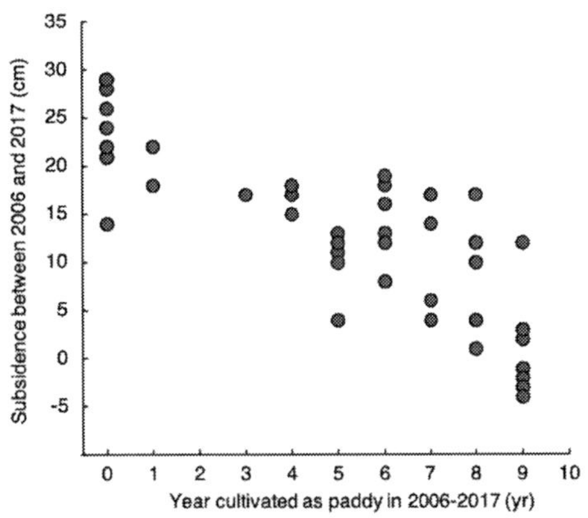


**Fig. 4**: The relationship between the total subsidence in 2006-2017 and the period during which each field was used as paddy field.

The average subsidence between 1998 and 2017 in the 46 field plots was 27.8 cm, equivalent to 14.6 mm $yr^{-1}$. On the other hands, the subsidence between 2006 and 2017 in the 50 field plots was 13.6 cm, equivalent to 13.6 mm $yr^{-1}$. Subsidence in the peatland has been still ongoing although it has been more than a half-century since the onset of the cultivation. The assessment of the land use form showed the existence of various practices of agricultural land use management. Some of the field plots were permanently used as paddy and some were permanently used as upland field. Also, rotational use of paddy and upland were conducted in the majority of the plots, and the interval of the rotation of paddy rice and upland crops was generally 3 or 4 years in such plots. Fig. 3 and Fig.4 show that the relationship between the subsidence and the period during which each field plot was cultivated as paddy out of each observation period. The subsidence tended to be reduced as the period of the paddy use increased in both of the observation periods. This tendency was clearer in the observation period between 2006 and 2017 than that in the period between 1998 and 2017. The variability of subsidence within the same period of the paddy use was much larger in the period between 1998 and 2017 than that in the period between 2006 and 2017.

## DISCUSSION

The total subsidence in the paddy plots was significantly smaller than that of the upland field plots. From 2006 to 2017, the subsidence was almost zero in the permanent paddy plots. The average subsidence rates the permanent paddy plots in both observation periods were extremely low value compared with globally reported values of the peat subsidence through agricultural exploitation (Pronger et al., 2014). Whereas, the average subsidence rate in the upland plots was well consistent with the globally reported values. The global comparison also showed that the peat subsidence through paddy use was smaller than through upland use.

The larger variability of the subsidence in the period between 1998 and 2017 indicated that the subsidence rate is not predominantly controlled by the duration of paddy use in long terms. Other agricultural practices such as intensification of the drainage and artificial soil adding for soil improvement might have impacts on the subsidence in long terms.

The possible reason for the reduction of subsidence in the paddy may have been high groundwater table which inhibits oxidation of peat substrate. Previous studies have reported that high groundwater table reduced decomposition of peat substrate (Hendriks et al., 2007; Kim and Verma, 1992). In the paddy plots, the water table was always maintained above the ground surface in cultivate period in summer, which kept the peat layer in anaerobic condition. Although the groundwater is drained and lowered from autumn to early spring, the temperature is generally low, and much snowfall occurs in the season without irrigation, which restrain the microbe activity of the decomposition of the peat. This implies that the maintenance of wet condition only in the summer season can sufficiently reduce peat subsidence.

## CONCLUSION

We assessed the subsidence rates in different agricultural land use form, i.e., rice paddy or upland field. The subsidence rate in the rice paddy had significantly lower than that in the upland field. This suggested that paddy or wet use of peatland for agriculture can prevent from causing subsidence. Our results will encourage the agricultural use of wet or rewetted peatlands as one of the valid options for future peatland management in terms of mitigation of land subsidence and peat loss.

## ACKNOWLEDGEMENTS

We express our sincere thanks to Shinotsu Chuo Land Improvement District (Farmers' water use association) and Hokkaido Development Bureau for providing us airborne laser survey data. This study was funded by the Land Improvement Construction Association of Japan, and we appreciate their grateful support.

## REFERENCES

Gambolati, G., Putti, M., Teatini, P., Gasparetto Stori, G., 2006. Subsidence due to peat oxidation and impact on drainage infrastructures in a farmland catchment south of the Venice Lagoon. Environ. Geol. 49, 814–820. https://doi.org/10.1007/s00254-006-0176-6

Gorham, E., 1991. Northern Peatlands: Role in the Carbon Cycle and Probable Responses to Climatic Warming. Ecol. Appl. 1, 182–195. https://doi.org/10.2307/1941811

Hendriks, D.M.D., Van Huissteden, J., Dolman, A.J., Van Der Molen, M.K., 2007. The full greenhouse gas balance of an abandoned peat meadow. Biogeosciences 4, 411–424. https://doi.org/10.5194/bg-4-411-2007

Kasubuchi, T., Yoshida, C., Kudo, S., Miura, K., 1998. Prevention of peat subsindece in enlarged paddy fields and cycle irrigation. Water, land, Environ. Eng. 66, 177–182. https://doi.org/https://doi.org/10.11408/jjsidre1965.66.2_177, *in Japanese with English abstruct*

Kim, J., Verma, S.B., 1992. Soil surface CO2 flux in a Minnesota peatland. Biogeochemistry 18, 37–51. https://doi.org/10.1007/BF00000425

Leifeld, J., Müller, M., Fuhrer, J., 2011. Peatland subsidence and carbon loss from drained temperate fens. Soil Use Manag. 27, 170–176. https://doi.org/10.1111/j.1475-2743.2011.00327.x

Liu, J., Liu, M., Tian, H., Zhuang, D., Zhang, Z., Zhang, W., Tang, X., Deng, X., 2005. Spatial and temporal patterns of China's cropland during 1990-2000: An analysis based on Landsat TM data. Remote Sens. Environ. 98, 442–456. https://doi.org/10.1016/j.rse.2005.08.012

Miyaji, N., Kohyama, K., Hiroo, O., Kasubuchi, T., 1995. Surface Subsidenee of Peatland in Bibai, Central Hokkado. Japanese J. Soil Sci. Plant Nutr. 66, 465–473. *in Japanese with English abstruct*

Parish, F., Sirin, A., Charman, D., Joosten, H., Minayeva, T., Silvius, M., Stringer, L., 2008. Assessment on Peatlands, Biodiversity and Climate change.

Pronger, J., Schipper, L.A., Hill, R.B., Campbell, D.I., McLeod, M., 2014. Subsidence Rates of Drained Agricultural Peatlands in New Zealand and the Relationship with Time since Drainage. J. Environ. Qual. 43, 1442. https://doi.org/10.2134/jeq2013.12.0505

Schipper, L.A., McLeod, M., 2006. Subsidence rates and carbon loss in peat soils following conversion to pasture in the Waikato Region, New Zealand. Soil Use Manag. 18, 91–93. https://doi.org/10.1111/j.1475-2743.2002.tb00225.x

Wösten, J.H.., Ismail, A.., van Wijk, A.L.., 1997. Peat subsidence and its practical implications: a case study in Malaysia. Geoderma 78, 25–36. https://doi.org/10.1016/S0016-7061(97)00013-X

Zanello, F., Teatini, P., Putti, M., Gambolati, G., 2011. Long term peatland subsidence: Experimental study and modeling scenarios in the Venice coastland. J. Geophys. Res. Earth Surf. 116, 1–14. https://doi.org/10.1029/2011JF002010

ID 72840

# REGIONAL DEVELOPMENTS AND PERSPECTIVES IN AGRICULTURAL USE OF PEATLANDS AS IDENTIFIED BY DIFFERENT STAKEHOLDERS

*Schouwenaars, J.M.[1], Akker, J.J.H. van den [2], Buschmann, C. [3], , Krigere, I. [4], Page, S. 5, Silvius, M. [6], Tata, H. [7], Tiemeyer, B. [3], Kalisz, B. [8]

[1] IPS Expert Group Peatlands and Agriculture, The Netherlands
[2] Wageningen University & Research, Wageningen Environmental Research, The Netherlands
[3] Thuenen Institute, Coordination Unit Climate Protection, Braunschweig, Germany
[4] Latvian Peat association, Latvia
[5] School of Geography, Geology & the Environment, University of Leicester, UK
[6] Global Green Growth Institute, Indonesia
[7] Forest Research and Development Center, Bogor, Indonesia
[8] University of Warmia and Mazury, Department of Soil Science and Microbiology, Poland

*josschouwenaars@kpnmail.nl*

Recently, the IPS Expert Group on Peatlands and Agriculture made an inventory of current debates and challenges related to the agricultural use of peatlands in different regions/countries.

The results of this survey offer a global picture of regional differences and similarities in:

1) regulations and policies for responsible peatland use and related challenges and incentives for transitions in land use.

2) corresponding challenges and perspectives for agricultural enterprises, smallholder farmers and local communities.

In this paper, preliminary results are presented and discussed. Also, an attempt is made to indicate relevant and priority topics for future activities of the International Peatland Society.

ID 73535

# DOC IN SOIL OR WATER, WHAT IS MORE SEASONALLY DEPENDABLE? – A CASE STUDY OF SHORT-TERM AGRICULTURAL PEATLAND MONITORING IN CENTRAL POLAND

*Bartłomiej Glina, Łukasz Mendyk, Agnieszka Piernik, Stephan Glatzel

Poznań University of Life Sciences, Poland

*bartlomiej.glina@up.poznan.pl*

Temperate minerotrophic peatlands in the mid-latitudes are mostly used for intensive agriculture due to their fertile organic soils. Drainage for agricultural use is the most common cause of peatland degradation, especially noticeable in relation to the transformation of soil organic matter, and by the elevated dissolved organic carbon (DOC) concentrations in the soil and pore water. The aim of this study was to analyse the spatial and temporal distribution of DOC in soil and water of agro-managed minerotrophic peatland adjacent to open-pit lignite mines in the central part of Poland (Grójec Valley). Additionally, we determined factors controlled DOC production, as this issue in degraded fen peatlands remains largely equivocal. The study was conducted in the growing seasons (from 1 March to 31 October) in the period 2017–2019, within the research transect consisted of six study sites, among which site B and D were located within depression cones (the effect of open-pit lignite mining). DOC concentration in soil (0–30 cm layer) and water samples, as well as selected environmental parameters (e.g. water table depth, soil moisture, pH, redox potential, soil/water temperature, soil organic carbon) were measured monthly during study period. We found that the most critical environmental factors that shape DOC concentration in soil and water are air temperature and precipitation, which all together explained 59.9% of the variability. Moreover, significant positive correlations with soil organic carbon content ($r=0.944$, $p< 0.01$), C/N quotient ($r=0.766$, $p< 0.01$) and pH ($r=0.521$, $p< 0.01$) was found. The seasonal dependency was confirmed only for DOC in water, as the statistically higher concentrations in summer period than in spring and autumn was observed in the consecutive study years. The potential impact of lignite open-pit mining on the short-term variability of DOC was not confirmed in our study.

ID 62398

# EFFECTS OF CROP RESIDUE AND ALTERED WATER TABLE ON CARBON DIOXIDE, METHANE AND NITROUS OXIDE EMISSIONS ON CULTIVATED PEAT SOILS

*Samuel Musarika[1,2], Dave Chadwick[2], Niall McNamara[1,3], Davey Jones[2], Chris Evans[1]

[1] UK Centre for Ecology and Hydrology, Environment Centre Wales, United Kingdom
[2] School of Natural Sciences, Bangor University, United Kingdom
[3] Lancaster Environment Centre, United Kingdom

*smusarika@ceh.ac.uk*

Globally peatlands cover ~400 Mha (3%). However, they account for 30% of global carbon (C) storage. Due to agriculture, peatlands are drained to support horticultural production. It is estimated agriculture exploits over 20% of peatlands worldwide. Exploited peatlands are no longer capable of storing C and have become significant carbon dioxide ($CO_2$) and nitrous oxide ($N_2O$) emitters. In Europe, agriculture is the second largest contributor of greenhouse gas (GHG) emissions. In addition to being large contributors of GHGs, we are fast losing productive peatlands; it is estimated that by 2050, a third of these productive peatlands will be lost. Loss of productive peatlands will affect productivity and food security. An increasing practise to prevent soil loss, is crop residue management, which involves crop residue from previous growing season being left to provide cover then ploughed in next season. Alternatively, specially selected cover crop can be grown. Nevertheless, there is concern that ploughed in fresh organic matter (FOM) might accelerate decomposition of existing organic matter in cultivated peat soils.

Aims of this study were to assess effects FOM and water table (WT) alteration on $CO_2$, methane ($CH_4$) and $N_2O$ in a cultivated peatland. An experiment was conducted using intact cores for 27 weeks. The cores were divided into two WT regimes (-50 cm and -20 cm). Half of each WT treatment had barley residue added.

There was an effect of both WT manipulation and FOM. $CO_2$, $CH_4$, and $N_2O$ emissions were different in WT treatments. Effect of FOM was observed between. -20 cm cores were shown to produce $CH_4$ whilst -50 cm cores sequestered $CH_4$.

Evidence shows that ploughing in crop residue does not have the desired effect as it led to increased emissions.

ID 62689

# SPHAGNUM FARMING UK: EFFICIENT AND HIGHLY PRODUCTIVE METHODS FOR SPHAGNUM AS A PEAT ALTERNATIVE

*Neal Wright[1], Simon Caporn[2], Anna Keightley[2], Chris Field[2], Richard Lindsay[3], Jack Clough[3], Paul Thomas[4], Catharine Dawson[5], Ben Clutterbuck[6]

[1] Micropropagation Services Ltd, United Kingdom
[2] Manchester Metropolitan University, United Kingdom
[3] University of East London, United Kingdom
[4] Natural England, United Kingdom
[5] Melcourt Industries Ltd, United Kingdom
[6] Nottingham Trent University, United Kingdom

*neal@microprop.co.uk*

Farmed Sphagnum could replace peat in growing media, but there are barriers to overcome before it can reach the scale required to offer the proven at-scale alternative necessary to meet the need posed by the likely UK peat ban in 2030. There needs to be: a sustainable source of starting material, rapid establishment, an efficient way to irrigate without flooding adjoining land, high biomass volume growth and a proven product for growing a wide range of horticultural plants. All of these were achieved and are reported here using patent pending techniques following trials on two sites in England, a cut-over lowland peatbog and an ex-agricultural pasture of very shallow peat (organo-mineral) soil. On both sites, micropropagated Sphagnum palustre (high productivity clone) was planted, as BeadaHumok™ and BeadaGel™. BeadaHumok™ proved more resilient on the organo-mineral site, but the planting of BeadaGel™ was less labour intensive being mechanically applied and provided rapid cover on cut-over peat. Different irrigation systems were tested (spray and drip), without controlling the water table, along with different covers (straw, plastic mesh, plastic sheet (permeable) and no cover). The sustainably produced Sphagnum yielded almost 100% cover within <10 months of planting, showing very high-volume productivity. Growth data from Terrestrial laser scanning (FAROx330), volume productivity measurements and the economics of Sphagnum farming UK will be presented. Extensive commercial nursery trials of Sphagnum in growing media of a wide range of horticultural plants proved its suitability as peat replacement, achieving equal quality & saleability and all growers taking part wanted more of the product. These methods will enable farmers to produce an economic, high value crop, allowing the rapid scale up of Sphagnum farming to the extent required for peat replacement. The carbon losses associated with drained peatland were prevented and carbon sequestration was achieved approx. 10 months (presented elsewhere).

ID 62735

# THE EFFECT OF PLANTATION DEVELOPMENT ON KEY SOIL PARAMETERS: A CASE STUDY IN SOUTH SUMATRA

Klaas Metselaar, *Thomas Westhoff

Wageningen University, The Netherlands

*thomas.westhoff@wur.nl*

Plantation developments have played a key role in land management of peat in Indonesia. 27,8% of the province of South Sumatra, where this research takes place, consists out of plantations. Agricultural production creates new activities on peat, including drainage, the use of fertilizers, and machinery.

This research focuses on the effect of plantation developments on different key soil parameters. Knowing the outcome allows for evaluating the impact of plantation developments. This case study takes place in South Sumatra and compares a forest and plantation. The plantation is drained and used for the production of one single crop, which is oil palm (*Elaeis guineensis*).

Differences are found in key soil parameters between the forest and plantation. The plantation has a higher bulk density, which can be explained by more decomposition activities. A lower hydrophobicity was observed in the plantation, which may be linked to recent research that showed that peat could become hydrophilic again after it was heated for a long time. A few weeks before the study, fires took place, which may have caused this heating and change in hydrophobicity. No statistically significant differences were observed for the organic carbon content, infiltration rate, soil moisture, and the degree of decomposition.

To conclude, plantation development affects key soil parameters. Differences have been found for the bulk density and hydrophobicity. For the other parameters, especially the organic carbon content, more monitoring, and a larger dataset are needed to draw conclusions.

ID 62681

# LAND USE PATTERN IN THE PEATLAND HOME YARD OF RURAL COMMUNITIES AND FARM INCOME

Niken Sakuntaladewi[1], Dony Rachmanadi[2], Daniel Mendham[3], Dian Charity Hidayat[1], Rama Wati[1], Kushartati Budiningsih[1]

[1] Centre for Research and Development on Social, Economy, Policy, and Climate Change, Indonesia
[2] Banjarbaru Environment and Forestry Research and Development Agency, Indonesia
[3] Commonwealth Scientific and Industrial Research Organization (CSIRO), Australia

*niken_sakuntaladewi@yahoo.co.uk*

## SUMMARY

Utilization of peatlands is intended to provide benefits for life. However, the use of peatlands creates environmental problems in the form of peatland damage and fires, health problems, and economic losses. This study analyzes the use of peat land in the community's home yards, farm income, and challenges. The research was conducted in the village of Tumbang Nusa. Data were collected from 20 households using field observations and in-depth interviews. Data analysis was carried out descriptively and analysis of farmers' income. The research found that there are several forms of peat land use in the community yard, namely a mixture of nurseries, agricultural crops, fruit trees, plantations, and livestock. Nurseries and plantation crops are for commercial purposes, while agricultural crops and fruit trees are for subsistence needs and for sale when there is excess (Table 1). They adopt the technology of digging canals to drain peatlands, making mounds, and providing agricultural inputs, as well as using polybags. The choice of land use patterns takes into account the capital, family labor, agricultural knowledge, and potential income to be obtained. The nursery business requires less than 0.25 ha of land but has the potential to earn promising income to meet family needs ranging from tens to hundred of millions of rupiah per year, but the payback period is uncertain for small-scale nursery entrepreneurs due to business competition. Other forms of land use can provide short, medium and long-term income, but require land up to 1-8 ha, with fluctuating incomes and a greater risk of failure. In Tumbang Nusa village, the use of peat land in the yard faces various challenges, namely fire, soil acidity, inundation, infertile soils, and a limited selection of species suitable for cultivation on peatlands. Government assistance and community empowerment are needed to get economic and ecological improvements.

**Key words:** peat-land, land-use, rural community, farm-technology, farm-income

## INTRODUCTION

The use of peatlands for economic development is prevalent in Indonesia. This condition was triggered by, among other things, population growth which had an impact on increasing the need for food, shelter, and cash for education, health, and other family needs. Massive use of peatlands in Pulang Pisau Regency, Central Kalimantan Province, occurred in 1995 in the form of the construction of one mega rice project for the purpose of food self-sufficiency (Mawardi, 2007). Many canals were constructed to drain the peat so that it could be planted with paddy rice (Notohadiprawoto, 1998). The government also brings in people from various regions to make the program a success. Three to four years later this activity was stopped because the program was not successful (Mawardi, 2007). Oil palm plantations are also commonly found on peatlands in Pulang Pisau Regency. Oil palm plantations also require draining the peat with trenching technology. The dryness of the peat makes it flammable, especially during the dry season (Novitasari et al. 2018).

The Indonesian government recognizes the importance of preventing fires and restoring damaged peatlands. Various policies related to peat management were issued, including prohibiting burning, stipulating deep peat for protection, and shallow peat for cultivation, and provisions to maintain the water level of peat at least 40 cm above the ground. Peatland restoration is carried out through rewetting, replanting and economic revitalization activities, which are coordinated by the Peat Restoration Agency established by the Government in 2016 (now called the Peat and Mangrove Restoration Agency). Although the Government has imposed various provisions on peatlands, the use of deep peatlands continues, peat fires and floods often occur, among others, in Tumbang Nusa village, Pulang Pisau Regency.

Tumbang Nusa Village is one of 95 villages in Pulang Pisau Regency. Some people build houses on peat land and use their yards for various types of business. This paper will present the pattern of land use in the yard with various challenges, and the income earned from the yard.

## MATERIAL AND METHODS

The research was conducted in the village of Tumbang Nusa, Pulang Pisau Regency, Indonesia. Only a part of the villagers lives on peat land and get a portion of their income from the peat land. Data were collected by stratified random sampling from 20 households who live on peatland and cultivate their home yards. Data collection was carried out by means of in-depth interviews and by using field observations. The data collected included reasons for living on peatlands, reasons for using their home yard, patterns of land use in their yards, income from home yards, and challenges faced by the community in managing peatlands. The data were analyzed using descriptive analysis and the farmers' income from their yards.

## RESULTS

1. The reason why people live on peat land

Tumbang Nusa Village, Pulang Pisau Regency, has an area of 200 km2 (BRG., 2020). The potential in this village is the Kahayan river which is the second largest river in Central Kalimantan Province and flows in the village, peatlands which cover 90% of the area of Tumbang Nusa with peat depths varying from 3 m to 8 m (BRG., 2020), mineral lands that are planted with rubber and rattan, and tidal marshes where purun grass (**Lepironia articulata**) is growing.

The village of Tumbang Nusa has a population of around 286 households. Initially they lived along the Kahayan river and lived from various natural resources, namely fishing in the Kahayan river and in peat swamps, tapping rubber, harvesting rattan and purun grass. Their livelihood is seasonal, that's why each family has more than one source of income. They generally take just enough natural resources for family life.

The life of the Tumbang Nusa village community changed after development of the 1 million ha mega rice project in Pulang Pisau Regency, and the construction of a trans Kalimantan road in the late 1990s connecting Palangkaraya, the capital of Central Kalimantan Province, with the city of Banjarmasin, the capital of South Kalimantan Province. This road passes through the village of Tumbang Nusa, built on peat land and is located about 3 km away from the Kahayan river/the settlement. The road construction has resulted in around 40% of the families moving to live along the Trans Kalimantan road. They occupy the peatland given by the village head.

The reasons for them moving and occupying peatlands along the trans Kalimantan road included the desire to change their lives, to get better family livelihoods, and to get good access to the cities of Palangkaraya and Banjarmasin. They wanted to get a new source of income because they could not rely anymore on rubber latex and rattan that were low in price. They also wanted to get better access to Palangkaraya for marketing their farm products and buying family needs.

2. Utilization of peat land in the home yards

The people of Tumbang Nusa village who live on peatlands along the Trans Kalimantan road have more than one livelihood. Some of them still catch fish, but many leave their rubber and rattan plantation because the price of rubber latex and rattan has dropped dramatically. One of the different sources of income for people living in the old village and in the new village along the Trans Kalimantan road is the use of the peat land around the house for food and drink stalls, motorcycle repair shops, and agricultural practices. From the agricultural aspect, there are many patterns of the use of peat land in the respondents 'home yard. They are:

- Livestock, nurseries, perennials
- Food and drink stalls, fruit trees and perennials
- Livestock, vegetable crops, plantation crops
- Fruit crops, perennials, tubers

There are no rules in the use of the house yard. Some respondents organize their plants in the form of clusters (clusters of vegetable crops, plantation crops, perennials) or plant vegetable crops under plantation crops. Some respondents use polybags or other used items (plastic buckets, sacks, even bathtubs) to grow vegetables. Utilization of house yard is intended to fulfill family nutrition and to earn daily, weekly, monthly, seasonal/annual cash income, to long-term income (Table 1). The fruits and vegetables are only sold when there is leftover after the family's needs have been fulfilled

Table 1. Use of house yard

| pes of use of the yard | Family nutrition | Cash income | | | | |
|---|---|---|---|---|---|---|
| | | Daily | Weekly | Monthly | Seasonal/ Annually | Long-term |
| rsery | | | | | ■ | |
| estock | | | | | | ■ |
| ennial crops*) | | | | | | ■ |
| m oil plantation**) | | | | ■ | | |
| bber plantation**) | | | ■ | | | |
| it trees | ■ | | | | ■ | |
| getables | ■ | ■ | | | | |

Note: *) Timber are harvested at least after they are more than 10 years old
**) Rubber and oil palm are harvested after the plants are 5 years old

The types of plants cultivated by the community vary according to the knowledge they have and the ease with which they cultivate the plants. The cultivated area also varies according to the availability of capital and family labor to maintain the plants. Of the various types of plants cultivated in the yard, the nursery does not require a lot of land. Respondents made beds for nurseries with capacities ranging from 3,000 seedlings to 200,000 seedlings with a required land area of less than 0.25 ha. Meanwhile, plantations and vegetables require a large area of land, varying from 1 to 8 ha of peat land. The types of plants cultivated on peatlands and their yields are presented in Table 2.

Table 2. Respondent's type of business, species, and yields

| Type of business | Species | The income *) |
|---|---|---|
| Nursery | Belangiran (*Shorea balangeran*), sengon (*Paraserianthes falcataria*), jelutong (*Dyera costulata*), pulai (*Alstonia scholaris*), agarwood | IDR 1,5 million/month to IDR 10 million/month |
| Livestock | goats and cows | Goat manure IDR 200,000/month |
| Palm oil plantation | Palm oil | IDR 390,000 /month |
| Rubber plantation | Rubber | IDR 1.8 million/month to IDR 2.9 million/month |
| Fruit | Rambutan (*Nephellium lappaceum*), pineapple, mango, water apple, guava | Rambutan: around IDR 2.5 million/harvest |
| Vegetable | Chili, corn, eggplant, cassava, tomato | IDR 4.25 million/month |

Note: Income of each business is gross income, not yet deducted by the production cost
1US$ = IDR 14,500

The income from the nursery is quite large, but the competition in this business is quite fierce. In the village, there is a government-owned nursery that distributes free seedlings. Respondents who already have 'regular buyers' can still benefit, but respondents with small businesses have to fight hard to be able to sell them. Income from peatlands fluctuates due to the considerable risk of failure

The Peat Restoration Agency provided assistance in the form of cattle and goats to several villagers. Cows are raised by releasing them in nature. Respondents make a goat pen in their yards. Husband, wife, or children take turns looking for animal feed every two days and cleaning the pen 2 to 3 times per week. Raising cows and goats is something new for the respondents.

Blangiran, pulai, and jelutong are endemic plants. They grow naturally in the yard, but many are also planted. The respondents have known this plant quite well. They have not yet sold these plants.

Utilization of peat for farming like planting vegetables, fruits and plantation crops (oil palm, cacao, sengon, rubber) is relatively new for them. The respondents stated that knowledge about farming on peatlands was obtained from neighbors, friends, relatives, or seeing plants thriving in neighboring villages. The knowledge they obtained includes canal construction, agricultural land preparation, agricultural inputs, planting crops on relatively acidic and inundated peatlands. Knowledge about the nursery is obtained from working as a laborer in the government's owned nursery in Tumbang Nusa village. This knowledge includes preparing planting media, filling polybags, sowing seeds, watering seedlings, etc.
After cultivating the yards for a number of agricultural businesses, respondents considered that sengon plants are not good for planting on peatlands because many of the leaves turn yellow after 2 years of age, the rootstock of palm trees are bent, rubber plants do not produce much latex, but vegetables grow well and the fruit of the rambutan plant is abundant so it is an important investment. The challenge faced is that when the main harvest arrives, the price of rambutan fruit drops. At the end of 2019 there was a large and prolonged flood which resulted in crop failure and many rambutan plants died. Floods occur regularly in Tumbang Nusa every two years with varying intensity and duration of inundation.

3. Challenges in utilizing peatlands

Peat fires often occur in Pulang Pisau Regency. The fire is very worrying for the residents of Tumbang Nusa Village because the impact is very wide. The haze is not good for health, interferes with the learning process of students, even the people of Tumbang Nusa village cannot catch fish in the river because of the very close visibility. Peat fires also could destroy community crops

Despite realizing that the construction of canals can dry peatlands, the practice of constructing canals is still happening in Tumbang Nusa village. The construction of canals is intended as access for residents to agricultural land and for the purpose of drying peat so that it can be planted with oil palm.

Even though the community no longer burns during the land preparation, fires still occur in the village of Tumbang Nusa. The fire can come from the negligence of outsiders who carry out activities in Tumbang Nusa village or from neighboring villages. The challenges faced by respondents in managing peatland are presented in Table 3.

Table3. Challenges in utilizing peatlands

| Type of business | Challenges |
|---|---|
| Nursery | Leaf-eating pests, very high mortality (up to 20%), uneven seedling growth, |
| Livestock | Goats often get bloated and die, skin diseases, flood |
| Perennial crops | It takes a long time before it can be harvested |
| Palm oil plantation | Plants grow less well, curved stems, expensive |
| Rubber plantation | Prone to burns in the dry season, pests and diseases, not much latex, and rainy season cannot tap latex |
| Fruit trees | It takes a lot of fertilizer, the selling price fluctuates, floods in the rainy season, fires |
| Vegetables | Acidic soils, need a lot of dolomite lime and fertilizer, the selling price fluctuates, floods in the rainy season, fires |

## DISCUSSION

Peatlands are fragile ecosystems. This is realized by the people of Tumbang Nusa village. They used to only use mineral land for farming and fishing in the river. Fish is a source of protein as well as a source of daily income. Rubber is a weekly income, purun is a seasonal income, and rattan is a savings for them. They use the peatlands to catch fish and cut wood as needed. No one lives / builds a house on peat land, let alone drain it for farming. This is their local wisdom.

The major change in peatland use in Tumbang Nusa village occurred after the construction of the Trans Kalimantan road. They move and settle along the road and start cultivating the peatland by making canals to drain it, as seen in the mega rice project and oil palm plantations. They also get the knowledge of farming from various sources and practice it on peatlands. Even though they know that draining the peat will make it prone to burning, they still do it to earn cash income. They did this because the rubber and rattan gardens could no longer be relied on. What they do not realize is that they are planting various types of suitable crops on mineral soils to be cultivated on peatlands. They have to do more work and spend extra money for drying the peat (digging canals), making soil mounds so that the plants are not flooded, buying dolomite lime to increase the soil pH, and fertilizer. For respondents, as long as the business they are going to do, according to their calculations or according to the information they get from people they trust, will generate a lot of money, they are willing to do it even though it requires a lot of capital. Respondents do not dare to use fire during land preparation because there are regulations from the government and sanctions for burning.

The vegetables and fruit plants that they cultivate in their yards are few for various reasons, including the cost for farming and availability of family labor. Labor is quite expensive because the work on the peatlands is quite heavy. Preparation of agricultural land can take years to be ready for planting. Respondents must also continue to experiment with various agricultural inputs in order for their yields to be viable. In the dry season, they have to keep their gardens from burning down, and in the rainy season they can only hope that their crops don't get flooded.

Of the various farming technologies applied, the use of polybags or other used materials for growing vegetables is more suitable for peatlands. This simple technology allows respondents to move the plants to a place that is safe from flooding and the fertilizer does not dissolve during the flood. With this technology, plants that need shade can be placed under trees without competition for plant nutrition. They do not have to spend a lot of money to build canals to drain the peatlands.

Of the various types of businesses conducted by the respondents, the nursery requires the smallest area (less than 0.25 ha) and generates a lot of money. It is because they live along the Trans Kalimantan road, the vehicle for transporting seedlings can stop in front of the house so that loading costs are cheap and transportation is not a problem. However, the risks faced are quite large due to the high mortality rate and competition in marketing.

The respondents finally realized that cultivating peatland for agriculture is quite expensive and the risks they face are quite high. The only livelihood that they can rely on at all times is fishing in the river. That is why even though the respondents change the profession to do farming on peatlands, they still do fishing to cover their household needs.

To overcome something that has already happened where many farmers live on peatlands and cultivate peatlands for agricultural activities at high costs and risks, the Government feels the need to step in to assist farmers in providing a decent source of income while maintaining environmental quality. This is a big challenge. Moving them back to their original village along the river is impossible, getting cheap but environmentally friendly peatland farming technology is not yet available. Providing livestock (cows and goats) assistance is one way of helping the community's economy. The cows thrive there. The respondents like raising cows because they don't have to look for cow feed. Cattle feed is widely available in Tumbang Nusa and the cows feed themselves. However, no one sell their cow nor goat yet, but the goat manure with the price of IDR 50,000/week or around IDR 200,000/month. They sell the manure to their neighbors. But this assistance cannot generate daily income.

The types of crops cultivated and the yields obtained (Table 2) as well as the various challenges faced by respondents (Table 3) can be used as considerations in determining development programs to help overcome challenges or explore other, more environmentally friendly sources of income.

## CONCLUSION

- Choosing the right development programs is necessary because it can inspire village community to do the same. If the development program is successful and the community follows it, it will accelerate the achievement of development targets. However, if the opposite is the case, it will require considerable effort and expense to overcome it.
- Village community tend to listen information provided by someone they trust, or the examples of success they have seen. They don't even hesitate to spend money on trying and seek capital / borrow money to develop a business if according to their calculations it will provide large profits like nurseries. However, some of them cultivate peatlands with a capacity according to the costs they have and the available family labor.
- Village communities have many sources of income because they are very dependent on nature at considerable risks and results cannot always be expected. In utilizing peatlands in their home yards, they also tend to plant various types of plants for the same reasons, high risks and uncertain yields.

## ACKNOWLEDGEMENT

This research was funded by a collaborative research activity between the Indonesian government and the Australian government / ACIAR entitled 'Improving Community Fire Management and Peatland Restoration in Indonesia'.

## REFERENCES

[BRG] Badan Restorasi Gabut (2018) Profil desa peduli gambut. Desa Tumbang Nusa, Kecamatan Jabiren, Kabupaten Pulang Pisau. Provinsi Kalimantan Tengah (Peat care village profile. Tumbang Nusa Village, Jabiren District, Pulang Pisau Regency. Central Kalimantan Province). Deputi Bidang Edukasi, Sosialisasi, Pertisipasi dan Kemitraan. Badan Restorasi Gambut.

Mawardi, I. (2007) Rehabilitasi dan revitalisasi eks proyek pengembangan lahan gambut di Kalimantan Tengah (Rehabilitation and revitalization of former peatland development projects in Central Kalimantan). Jurnal Teknologi Lingkungan, Vol.8 No.3. pp. 287-297

Notohadiprawoto, T. (1998) Proyekpengembangan 'lahan gambut sejuta hektar' keinginan dan kenyataan (The 'million hectare peatland development project' whishes and realities. http://faperta.ugm.ac.id/download/publikasi_dosen/tejoyuwono/1991/1998%20proy.pdf

Novitasari, Sujono,J., Harto, S., Maas, A., Jayadi, R. (2018) The effect of degraded peat characteristic on peatland fire (A case study on peatland of block A, ex rice megaproject in Central Kalimantan). Prosiding seminar nasional lingkungan lahan basah. Vol. 3 No. 2 pp. 347-351.

ID 62753

# SUBSIDENCE MONITORING DURING 50 YEARS OF THE PEAT MEADOW PARCELS OF ZEGVELD EXPERIMENTAL FARM IN THE NETHERLANDS

*Jan J.H. van den Akker[1], Harry Massop[1], Karel van Houwelingen[2]

[1] Wageningen University & Research, Wageningen Environmental Research, The Netherlands
[2] KTC Zegveld, The Netherlands

*janjh.vandenakker@wur.nl*

The experimental farm Zegveld was founded in 1966 and one of the main goals was to study the effect on subsidence of lowering ditchwater levels from 35 cm minus surface to 70 cm minus surface. To do so the northern part of the experimental farm was divided in four blocks with each 4 to 5 parcels, in total 20 parcels. The ditchwater levels in the north-west block and south-east block were lowered from 35 cm minus surface to 70 cm minus surface. The ditchwater level in the remaining blocks stayed 35 cm minus surface. In time the ditchwater levels became minus 55 to 60 cm respectively 20 cm minus surface. As a start in 1966 an altitude map was created by measuring altitudes in a grid of about 100 points per parcel. The altitude measurements were repeated in 1992, 2003 and 2020. This made it possible to create altitude maps and subsidence maps over a period of almost 50 years and calculate the average subsidence per block and parcel. Moreover, in the period 1970 to 1973 four fixed points were installed existing of a steel pole hammered into the sand base of the peatsoil profile at a depth of about 6 meters. The altitude of 10 points around the fixed pole was measured each year in early spring until now. By measuring in early spring, we avoided to include in the measurements the temporarily subsidence by shrinkage. We have also some periods with measurements of the groundwater levels. The result of 50 year of subsidence measurements and derived relations between subsidence and ditchwater levels and relations between subsidence and groundwater levels show the strong relation between subsidence and ditchwater levels and groundwater levels. The last 20 years the subsidence diminished to about 70% of the subsidence in the first 30 years.

ID 61832

# IMPLEMENTING CLIMATE CHANGE IN A DECISION SUPPORT SYSTEM DESIGNED FOR THE MANAGEMENT OF IRELAND'S WESTERN PEATLAND FORESTS

Anders Lundholm, Corrigan, *Maarten Nieuwenhuis

University College Dublin, Ireland

*maarten.nieuwenhuis@ucd.ie*

Forest managers must comply with Sustainable Forest Management (SFM) practices, including considering the long-term impacts that Climate Change (CC) and the bioeconomy may have on their forests and their management. The aims of this study were: (1) to incorporate the effects of CC and Dynamic Prices (DP) in a Forest Management Decision Support System (DFMDSS) that was developed for Ireland's peatland forests, and (2) to analyse the impact of global climate and market scenarios on forest management and forest composition at the landscape level. A linear programming model was developed for Ireland's Western Peatland forests using Woodstock. Remsoft Woodstock is a strategic planning decision support system that is widely used for forest management around the world. Data from Climadapt, which is an expert-based decision support system that was developed in Ireland, were used to include CC effects on forest productivity and species suitability. Dynamic market prices were also included to reflect the changing demands for wood fibre as part of the European Union (EU) and global efforts to mitigate CC. The results showed that dynamic prices will likely have more impact on harvest patterns, volumes and net present value than CC. Higher assortment prices, especially for pulpwood, stimulate the harvesting of forests on marginal sites and off-set some of the negative CC growth impacts on forest profitability. Incorporating CC and bioeconomy prices in a forest decision support system was shown to be feasible, and foresters are recommended to incorporate the expected global changes in their long-term management planning to mitigate the negative effects that un-informed management decisions can have on the sustainability of their peatland forests.

ID 62459

# COSTING THE LEGACY OF FORESTRY ON A NORTHERN IRISH BLANKET BOG

*Raymond Flynn[1], Bryan Irvine[2], Kathryn Speers[1], Rebecca Pennell[1]

[1] Queen's University Belfast, Ireland
[2] Northern Ireland Department of Agriculture, Environment and Rural Affairs, Ireland

*r.flynn@qub.ac.uk*

Blanket bog dominates uplands across large areas of Great Britain and Ireland. Poor drainage and low fertility have limited bogs' value for conventional economic activity, leading to widespread reclamation. This has included drainage and conversion of blanket peat-covered areas to plantations of exotic coniferous forestry, often on relatively flat ground containing deep (>1m) peat. A more recent appreciation of ecosystems services provided by blanket bogs has led to a recognition of the need for a reappraisal of the wider impacts of forestry, including its impacts to water.

A study of two similarly-sized (~30ha) blanket peat-covered catchments on Glenwherry Hill Farm, Co. Antrim, Northern Ireland, examined the impacts of forestry, and associated recent clearing, on stream flow and water quality. Results from an afforested and partially cleared catchment were compared with those of an adjacent unplanted area of open moorland. Both of the monitored water courses contribute to Killylane Reservoir, Co. Antrim, supplying 12ML/day to a population equivalent of approximately 60,000 people (200l/person/day). Continuous monitoring, completed from October 2019 to the end of January 2020, aimed to assess the difference in water quality and flow regime between both catchments.

Preliminary findings reveal that over the monitoring period the moorland catchment supplied better quality (less coloured) water to the reservoir at a more consistent rate. Conversely, water from the forest-impacted catchment generated a significant supplemental drinking water treatment cost that must be considered against the value of timber yield in the forested catchment. Further monitoring is anticipated to permit evaluation of the longer term economic impact of felling on flow and water quality. Results to date effectively highlight the benefits of the ecosystem services provided by blanket bogs to water, while also providing further justification for Northern Ireland Forestry's policy of avoiding future planting on flatter upland areas underlain by deep peat.

ID 62480

# CHARACTERISTICS OF PROKARYOTIC COMMUNITY ASSEMBLY IN TROPICAL PEATLANDS: SPATIAL CONSTRAINTS DUE TO HETEROGENEITY OF OIL PALM PLANTATION IN BORNEO SARAWAK

Kim Yrjälä[1,2], Oili Kiikkilä[3], Jyrki Jauhiainen[3], Hanna Silvennoinen[4], Lip Khoon[5], Harri Vasander[1]

[1] Department of Forest Sciences, University of Helsinki, Finland
[2] Zhejiang Province Key Laboratory of Soil Contamination Bioremediation, Zhejiang A&F University, China
[3] Department of Forest Sciences, University of Helsinki, Finland
[4] Norwegian Institute for Bioeconomy Research, Norway
[5] Tropical Peat Research Unit (TROPI), Malaysian Palm Oil Board, Malaysia

*kim.yrjala@helsinki.fi*

Land use change is at the heart of global development to ensure living conditions and crop production for future generations. A very rapid land use change has taken place in Southeast Asia, especially in the countries of Indonesia and Malaysia, resulting in severe documented damage on quality of soil and living conditions experienced latest in 2019 by smog and smoke in affected region. We study peat quality in peatlands of Bintulu division in Sarawak, north Borneo, decomposition processes producing greenhouse gases (GHGs), and especially their microbial bases resulting in GHG emissions from differing land uses. The three peat ecosystems under study differ in their fertilization and water regimes affecting the microbial life and organic matter decomposition. The approach is elucidating the type of prokaryotes, the diversity and community structures in stratified tropical peat. The study takes use of 16S rRNA marker gene to elucidate the Bacteria, but also get some knowledge about the Archaea at different depths of the peat in three different types of land use: tropical forest, oil palm plantation and agricultural land. A clear trend was that the microbial community structure was dependent on depth from the peat surface in all land uses, and the forest was distinct from the managed land uses of oil palm plantation and small-scale agriculture evidenced by Nonmetric multidimensional scaling (NMDS). The Proteobacteria were highest in abundance in tropical peat of Sebungan area, but some forest samples had decreased relative abundance accompanied with higher abundance and diversity of Firmicutes. With respect to Archaea, the Thaumarchaeota were detected in all samples irrespective of land use and sample depth. Among methane producing Euryarchaeota the hydrogenotrophic Methanoregula genus was most common. Our study is first to study prokaryotic community assembly of different microsites in Oil palm plantations in the tropics.

ID 62680

# MITIGATION OF PHOSPHORUS, NITROGEN AND ORGANIC CARBON EXPORTS BY CONTINUOUS COVER FORESTRY ON DRAINED PEATLANDS

*Sakari Sarkkola[1], Kersti Haahti[1], Timo Penttilä[1], Kari Minkkinen[2], Paavo Ojanen[2], Mika Korkiakoski[3], Raija Laiho[1], Annalea Lohila[4], Mika Nieminen[1]

[1] Natural Resources Institute, Finland
[2] University of Helsinki, Finland
[3] Finnish Meteorological Institute, Finland
[4] Finnish Meteorological Institute, Finland

*sakari.sarkkola@luke.fi*

In peatland forestry, ditch network maintenance (DNM) and clear-cuttings are the most adverse measures inducing detrimental impacts on water quality. From this perspective continuous cover forestry (CCF) has been suggested as a feasible alternative to traditional even-aged management as clear-cuts will be avoided and the continuously maintained tree stand with significant evapotranspiration capacity would decrease the need for DNM. However, the positive impacts of CCF are still based on theoretical conjecture. This study elucidates the effects of CCF (release of undergrowth) on the exports of total nitrogen (TN), total phosphorus (TP) and total organic carbon (TOC) during three growing seasons in a nutrient-rich drained peatland forest in southern Finland. The stand supported a mature Scots pine (Pinus sylvestris L.) stand with total volume of ca 278 $m^3$/ha an abundant undergrowth of Norway spruce (*Picea abies* L. Karst.) and downy birch (*Betula pubescens* Ehrh.). In March 2016, three parallel sites were established: a CCF harvest area removing overstory pines resulting in a removal of 74% of the pre-harvesting stand volume (14 ha), a clear-cut area mounded and planted with spruce seedlings in 2017 (1.8 ha), and a non-managed control (3 ha). Water quality was monitored during 2015-2018. Continuous runoff estimates were based on manual and automatic monitoring, and hydrological modelling. During the three post-treatment years, the average annual element exports (kg/ha) were higher from the CCF-treatment (TN: 5.2, TP: 0.3, DOC: 197.3) than the control (TN: 3.6; TP: 0.12; DOC: 138.3). However, TOC, TN, and TP exports from the clear-cut were 63%, 140%, and 340% higher than from the CCF-treatment, respectively. The treatment effect was the largest during the second post-treatment year. Even though CCF increased element exports compared to the uncut forest, it was a significantly better option from water quality perspective than clear-cutting at least in the short term.

ID 62682

# COULD CONTINUOUS-COVER FORESTRY REPRESENT PALUDICULTURE IN BOREAL PEATLAND FORESTS?

*Sakari Sarkkola, Hannu Hökkä, Raisa Mäkipää, Päivi Mäkiranta, Mika Nieminen, Meeri Pearson, Timo Penttilä, Markku Saarinen, Raija Laiho

Natural Resources Institute Finland, Finland

*sakari.sarkkola@luke.fi*

Drainage for forestry, agriculture and peat extraction threatens the ecosystem services that peatlands provide in their pristine state. Land management increases the radiative forcing of peatlands, as the decreases in $CH_4$ emissions are more than offset by the increases in $CO_2$ and $N_2O$ emissions. Forestry results in less drastic changes in ecosystem greenhouse gas balance than other peatland use. For instance, in Finland, about 0.25 million hectares of drained peatland in agricultural use and 4.6 million hectares in forestry use are estimated to produce similar emissions. Soil emissions usually increase with more effective drainage, thus maintaining high water-table levels is considered the best way to protect the peat C stores. Since peatlands are in many regions important providers of livelihood, often through production of different biomasses, combining raised water-table levels with sustained sources of income is critical for successful mitigation. Different forms of paludiculture, production of crops that can be grown under high water-table levels, are gaining increasing interest. In northern Europe, e.g., Finland, Estonia and Latvia, forestry is a more important land use form of peatlands than agriculture, in contrast to the rest of Europe. Consequently, paludicultural or paludiculture-like options for peatland forests would be useful in this region. Boreal peatlands host several site types that are densely forested even without drainage. Such peatland forests could serve as a model for developing paludiculture-like management for peatland forests. In this presentation we explore the prospects for developing paludiculture-like forest management for boreal peatland forests, and the environmental benefits such management might provide. For this purpose, we first review the relationships between the tree stand and water-table level and the idea and feasibility of continuous cover forestry (CCF) as a paludiculture-like forest management in boreal peatland forests, and then present first results on the water-table levels and soil greenhouse gas exchange obtained under CCF.

ID 72852

# GROWTH CHARACTERISTICS OF ACACIA CRASSICARPA ON A PEAT DOME SLOPE IN TROPICAL PEATLANDS

*Sisva Silsigia, Tsuyoshi Kato

PT. Mayangkara Tanaman Industri/PT. Wana Subur Lestari, Jakarta, Indonesia

*sisva@wanasl.com*

## SUMMARY

Tropical peatlands are often composed of peat domes of varying sizes in area. However, even though they are called domes, the slopes are very gentle, with a gradient of only 0.6 m in 1 km. On this very gentle slope, industrial forest and palm plantations have been developed.

Despite the small difference in elevation and slope, there is a significant difference in the growth of the planted trees and the yield of fruit, so many companies have tried to increase the growth and yield by water drainage and applying large amounts of fertilizer. In order to identify the cause of this difference, the slope of a peat dome was divided into three zones from the top: Upper, Middle, and Lower. The growth of *Acacia crassicarpa* from 6 months to 48 months after planting in each zone was then compared. At the same time, peat depth, chemical characteristics of the peat, seasonal changes in groundwater level, and rainfall were compared in the three zones.

The results showed that the average DBH in the Lower and Middle zones was 11.3 cm and 11.2 cm, respectively, while in the Upper zone it was only 9.2 cm on average. On the other hand, the density of the Upper zone was about 1,032 trees per hectare, which was significantly higher than the others.

In this study, the causes of small DBH, while high density and low mortality of planted trees in the Upper zone will be examined in the perspective of slope, peat depth, peat soil characteristics, groundwater level fluctuation and precipitation.

***Keywords**: tree growth, groundwater level, Acacia crassicarpa, tropical peatland, water management*

## INTRODUCTION

Tropical peatlands are one of the most important soil carbon-rich ecosystems in the world (Page et al. 2011). Besides the function of storing carbon in the soil, tropical peatlands play an essential role in storing water in the soil from the abundant rainfall that characterizes the tropics (Rezanezhad et al. 2016). However, for more than two decades, peatlands in the tropics, especially in Indonesia, experienced degradation by peat fires and unwell-planned management (Miettinen and Liew 2010; Miettinen et al. 2016). Moreover, in 2015, Indonesia encountered massive fires that burned 4.6 million ha of forest and peat area (Lohberger et al. 2017), which were very detrimental economically and ecologically. More than two million ha of peatland were burnt (Presidential Decree 2016), causing severe smoke pollution and health hazards (Koplitz et al. 2016). As a result, about 2 million ha of peatlands degraded by fire need to be restored to reduce further degradation and the release of $CO_2$ into the atmosphere.

The Indonesian government has made efforts to prevent the occurrence of serious disasters by establishing laws and regulations. One of these regulations is that the groundwater level (GWL) should not be lowered more than 40 cm below the ground surface to prevent peat fires (Indonesian Government Regulation 2016). In response to the regulation, all companies utilizing peatlands must raise their GWLs higher than before and report their GWLs periodically.

Increasing the GWLs keeps the peat soil in moist condition and prevents peat fires (Frandsen 1987); on the other hand, there has always been a concern that a significant decline in the production of wood and oil palm might occur. Considering that the global demand for wood continues to increase (FAO 2018), sustainable land use that does not negatively impact the environment and effective utilization of already degraded land will be required for future wood supply. One of the challenges being faced is ensuring sustainable wood production and meeting the international demand for wood. Commercial tree planting on degraded peatlands after fires may be one solution for a stable supply of wood, not just vegetation restoration.

A study in 2015 revealed that 7.8 million hectares of the tropical peatland of Peninsular Malaysia, Sumatra, and Borneo were covered by land use where development has taken place (Miettinen et al. 2016). Meanwhile, the tropical peatlands are characterized by peat domes' formation, and peat domes' characteristics typically have high GWLs, a gentle slope, acidic soil, and extremely poor nutrients (Page et al. 1999). Therefore, many companies have drained the water from the peatlands and have tried to increase productivity by applying large amounts of fertilizer. These activities could degrade peatlands and lead to huge $CO_2$ emissions due to peat decomposition.

Best practices need to be considered for the sustainable use of already developed and degraded peatlands. Especially, it will be important to consider peat domes, a typical geomorphic feature in tropical Asia. In this study, tree growth under high GWL conditions was examined, considering the effects of topography.

## MATERIALS AND METHODS

### Site Description

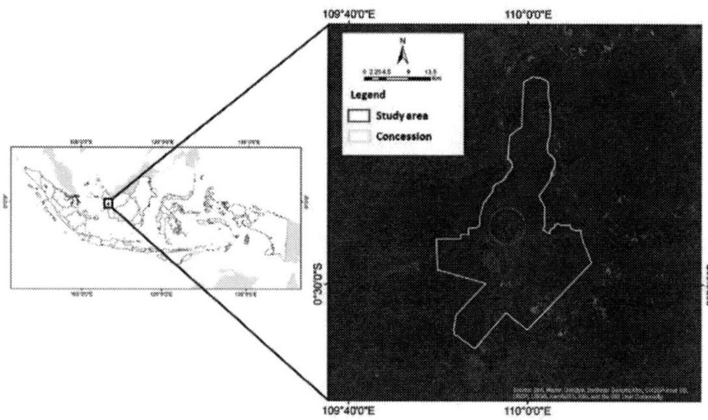


Figure 1. Location of the study area in West Kalimantan, Indonesia

The study was conducted in a coastal peatland in West Kalimantan, in an industrial forest plantation of wood fiber production, namely PT. Mayangkara Tanaman Industri (MTI) (Figure 1). Formerly, the area had been commercially logged by another company from the 1960s to

1990, and then severely degraded by illegal logging and slash-and-burn agriculture. As a result, it was predicted that if nothing was done, some of the remaining valuable natural forest would be lost, so MTI obtained a license for the forest plantation business in 2009.

The study site is located in the humid tropics, with annual precipitation for 2019-2020 is 2675 mm, and a generally distinct dry season occurring in July and August. The average monthly temperature varies from 27.4°C to 36.8°C, depending on the season. The plantation area was developed in a peatland dome with a very gentle slope with a gradient of only 0.6 m in 1 km. The study area's elevation is from 4.2 m, near the river, until 9.2 m adjacent to the conservation area that functions as a water reservoir. Peat depths are positively correlated with elevation, ranging from 3.2 m to 7.8 m. The site was then divided into three zones: upper, middle, and lower to examine the relationship between the effects of topography and tree growth. The value of organic carbon at the site is relatively equal, and total potassium and phosphorus available is relatively larger in the lower zone (unpublished data).

### Tree planting history and its treatments

The plantation of MTI is started in 2011 with *Acacia crassicarpa*. At first, the 6-year harvesting period was adopted, but fallen trees tended to occur after five years and yield to decrease. As a result, a 4-year harvesting period has recently been adopted.

The study area was the second rotation which was planted from March 2016 to March 2017 with 2.5 x 3-meter spacing. Although peat soils are poor in nutrients, MTI does not use fertilizers at all. Besides, some treatments were applied during the plantation period, such as manual weeding and singling. Weeding without herbicides is carried out four to five times. Singling is an activity of pruning branches or twigs carried out six months after planting. It aims to obtain a single, healthy, large, and straight stem.

### Water management for groundwater level of 40 cm

MTI conducted field surveys and peat depth studies inside and outside the concession, and based on the results, zoning for water management was developed (Kato et al. 2021). The water zones were divided by elevation at intervals of one meter and equipped with a peat dam and other water controls. The plantation area's water table was monitored every day to maintain the GWLs at 40 cm below the soil surface.

### Data collection

The diameter at breast height (DBH) and tree density data were collected from 68 plots from 6 to 48 months after planting. The GWLs and rainfall were collected from June 2018 to December 2020 using a sensor installed at the study site. Four sensors were installed in the upper zone, while the middle and lower zone was installed with three and two sensors.

## RESULTS

### Groundwater levels fluctuations and rainfall variation in each zone

The monthly rainfall in the upper, middle, and lower zone is shown in Figure 2 (a). There is no apparent difference between the upper, middle, and lower zone from June 2018 to December 2020. It is noted that drier months occurred in July to August with rainfall less than 100 mm.

The average GWLs of the upper, middle, and lower zone was 20.7 cm, 21.5 cm, and 23.6 cm, respectively. The GWLs of the upper zone were slightly higher during the monitoring period

(Figure 2(b)). It was also shown that there was a decrease in GWLs in all zones from July to September 2018 and 2019. However, there was no significant fluctuation of GWLs in the drier months in 2020.

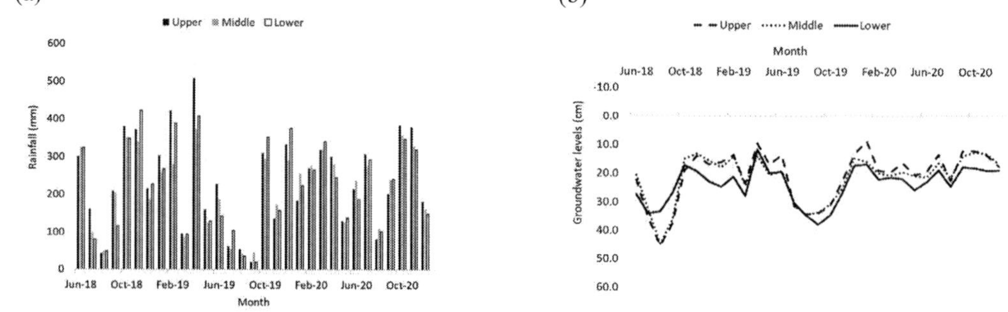


Figure 2. (a) Monthly rainfall and (b) GWLs in the upper, middle, and lower zone from June 2018 to December 2020

## The growth trend in the upper, middle, and lower zone

Figure 3 shows the DBH growth of *Acacia crassicarpa* in the second rotation from planting to the fourth year before harvesting. Initial growth of DBH is biggest in the lower zone, but there is no significant difference between the lower and middle zones in the year four prior to harvesting. In contrast, the planted trees in the upper zone clearly grew poorly from the beginning to before harvesting, with a high degree of variability. The average DBH of the planted trees before felling was 9.2 cm, 11.2 cm and 11.3 cm in the upper, middle and lower zones, respectively.

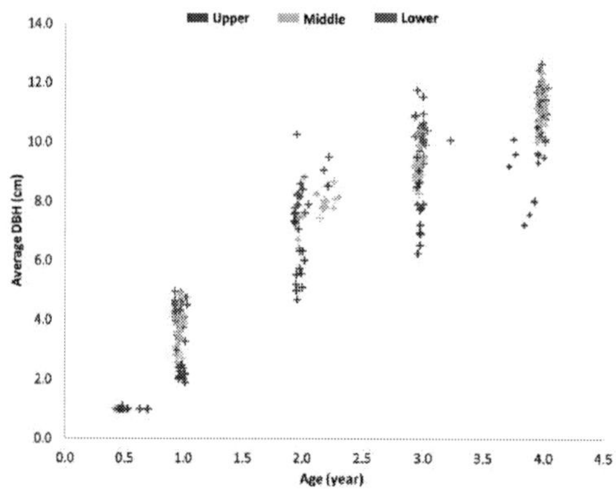


Figure 3. DBH growth of *Acacia crassicarpa* in the upper, middle, and lower zones

## DBH growth and tree density relationship in high GWLs condition

Figure 4 shows the relationship between average DBH and survival density of 4-year-old planted trees in the upper, middle, and lower zone. Since some of the sampling plots had slightly different measurement times, their average DBHs were adjusted to be 4 years old. The average survival densities in the fourth year were 1032, 900, and 947 in the upper, middle, and lower zones, respectively. Higher tree density and lower growth of DBH were recorded in the upper zone. Although survival density was lower in a few sampling plots in the lower zone, there was no distinct difference between the lower and middle zones. In the upper zone, several plots with high survival density but clearly small average DBH were observed. Based on the average DBH and survival density, the calculation of wood yield revealed that the yield in the upper zone was significantly smaller.

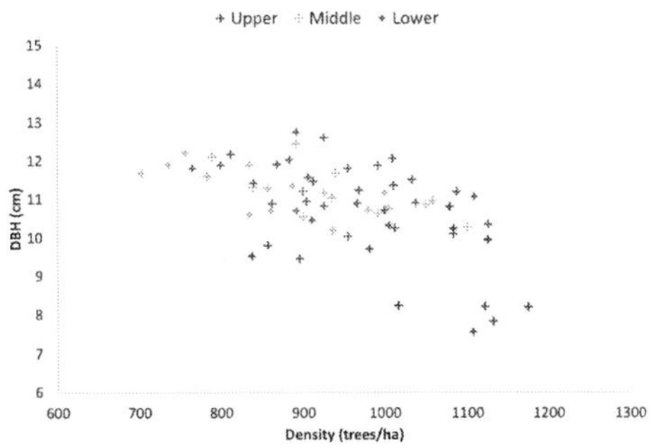


Figure 4. Relationship between average DBH and survival density of 4-year-old planted trees

## DISCUSSION

*Acacia crassicarpa* grows well on peat soils and has been planted in Indonesian peatlands as a raw material for wood fiber and pulp. The species is one of the legumes, which does not require nitrogen fertilizer because of its nitrogen fixing capabilities. However, a large amount of nitrogen fertilizer is still applied in most of the forest plantations. This is probably because plantation owners are unable to stop the application of fertilizer because, as the results of this study indicated, tree growth is clearly reduced depending on the topography. The application of nitrogen fertilizer stimulates microbial activity, which leads to the decomposition of peat soil and the release of $CO_2$. Since no nitrogen fertilizer was applied at this study site, it was possible to simply evaluate the impact of topography and GWLs on the growth of planted trees. The results showed that although the survival rate of planted trees was higher in the upper zone of the slope of the peat dome, the growth was significantly lower, and the wood yield was smaller. Meanwhile, as can be seen in the middle and lower zones, it is clear that planting of *Acacia crassicarpa* is possible even at high GWLs, which forest plantation companies had said was difficult in the past.

In the tropical regions, water in peat domes is supplied only by rain. As a result, the soil in the peat dome is extremely poor in nutrients. However, the lower zones have a higher average DBH than the others. According to the results of chemical analysis of peat soils, some elements, such as nitrogen, available phosphorus, and total potassium, tend to increase from the top of the slope to the bottom (unpublished data). It is quite possible that this trend is affecting the growth of trees. Nutrients generated by litter from the first planting rotation and residues after logging may have flowed over the soil surface and accumulated in the lower part of the slope.

A study in an ombrotrophic peatland in the Republic of Panama showed that total phosphorus in surface of peat soil decreased markedly along a 2.7 km transect from the marginal *Raphia taedigera* swamp (lower area) to the interior sawgrass swamp (higher area), with similar trends in total nitrogen and potassium (Sjogersten et al. 2011). Moreover, a study revealed that water flow across the peat dome must also be considered since this mass flow brings a constant supply of nutrients in low concentrations that the trees can use for their growth (Page et al. 1999). The lower zones are the final recipients of all the water flowing and this, in part, may explain the larger growth of DBH in these areas compared with the upper zones.

There was a trend of increasing number of trees per hectare from the lower to the upper zone of the peat dome in the study area. The same condition was also recorded in a study conducted in the peat swamp forest while the tree density per plot was increasing from the riverine forest, through mixed swamp forest to low pole forest which situated in a higher area (Page et al. 1999). It is very interesting that the trend of the natural vegetation was similar to the growth and density of the planted trees in this study. Further research is needed to clarify the factors that limit the growth and density of planted trees.

## ACKNOWLEDGEMENTS

This study was supported by Sumitomo Forestry, co., Ltd., Alas Kusuma Group, and The Sustainable Trade Initiative (IDH). We thank the entire staff of WSL-MTI for their efforts in field works, data collection, and continuous supports.

## REFERENCES

1. FAO (2018) Global Forest Products: Facts and Figures 2018. FAO Forestry Department
2. Frandsen WH (1987) The influence of moisture and mineral soil on the combustion limits of smoldering forest duff. Can. J. For. Res. 17: 1540-1544
3. Indonesian Government Regulation (2016) No. 57 of 2016 about the amendment of Indonesian Government Regulation no. 71 of 2014 about the protection and Management of Peatland Ecosystem
4. Kato T, Silsigia S, Yusup AA, Osaki M (2021) Large-Scale Practice on Tropical Peatland Eco-Management. Tropical Peatland Eco-management. Springer Japan
5. Koplitz SN, Mickley LJ, Marlier ME, Buonocore JJ, Kim PS, Liu T, Sulprizio MP, DeFries RS, Jacob DJ, Schwartz J, Pongsiri M, & Myers SS (2016) Public health impacts of the severe haze in equatorial Asia in September–October 2015: Demonstration of a new framework for informing fire management strategies to reduce downwind smoke exposure. Environmental Research Letters, 11(9), 094023
6. Lohberger S, Stängel M, Atwood EC, Siegert F (2017) Spatial evaluation of Indonesia's 2015 fire-affected area and estimated carbon emissions using Sentinel-1. Glob Change Biol. 2017;1–11
7. Miettinen J, Liew SC (2010) Status of Peatland Degradation and Development in Sumatra and Kalimantan. Ambio 39:394–401
8. Miettinen J, Shi C, Liew SC (2016) Land cover distribution in the peatlands of Peninsular Malaysia, 1126 Sumatra and Borneo in 2015 with changes since 1990. Glob Ecol Conserv 6:67–78
9. Page SE, Rieley JO, Banks CJ (2011) Global and regional importance of the tropical peatland carbon pool. Glob Chang Biol 17:798–818
10. Page SE, Rieley JO, Shotyk OW, Weiss D (1999) Interdependence of peat and vegetation in a tropical peat swamp forest. Phil.Trans. R. Soc. Lond. B: 354,1885-1897
11. Presidential Decree (2016) No.1 of 2016 about Badan Restorasi Gambut (National Peat Restoration Agency)
12. Rezanezhad F, Price J, Quinton W, Lennartz B, Milojevic T, Van Cappellen P (2016) Structure of peat soils and implications for water storage, flow, and solute transport: a review update for geochemists. ChemGeol 429:75–84
13. Sjögersten S, Cheesman AW, Lopez O, Turner BL (2011) Biogeochemical processes along a nutrient gradient in a tropical ombrotrophic peatland. Biogeochemistry (2011) 104:147–163

ID 62652

# EFFECT OF WATER LEVEL CHANGE ON RADIAL INCREMENT OF SCOTS PINE IN A RESTORED PEATLAND IN ESTONIA

*Kärt Erikson, Ain Kull, Alar Läänelaid, Kristina Sohar

Institute of Ecology and Earth Sciences, University of Tartu, Tartu, Estonia

*kart.erikson@ut.ee*

## SUMMARY

The study focuses on long term changes in annual radial increment of pines (*Pinus sylvestris*) at Laiuse Bog. This is an abandoned peat extraction site in East Estonia where an experiment of peatland restoration is going on since 2019. We studied effect of water regime change on tree growth along a gradient of water table from abandoned and restored peatland area to the pristine parts of the peatland. The peatland has been drained in its northern part for peat extraction. Mining activity was ceased in 1996 and the peatland was left for natural regeneration. Since 2019 water level was raised as a result of peatland restoration. Tree-ring samples were collected in autumn 2019 from five different sections of the peatland. At the former peat extraction area samples from stumps (cross sections) and living trees (by increment borer) were collected. The second sample set was collected from pines growing next to the ditch surrounding the extraction site. The third set was collected at distance of 150 m from the drainage ditch. Fourth sample set consists of cores collected from the pristine part of the peatland. An additional sample set represents a pine stand in the southern part of the peatland near the bog lake. This site was unaffected by peat extraction but should reflect a dated event of water level lowering in the lake. Tree-ring widths of pines were measured and the increment series were analysed to establish the effects of anthropogenous disturbances. The results show difference in reaction in annual increment to various kinds of manipulated water regime.

***Keywords***: *Climate, dendrochronology, water regime, tree ring, peat extraction site*

## INTRODUCTION

Peatlands provide many important ecosystem services such as carbon sinks, water reservoirs and habitats (de Groot et al. 2012, Taminskas et al. 2019, Edvardsson et al. 2019). It is estimated that about 22.3% of Estonia (Orru and Orru 2008) and 12.3% of the Baltics are covered with peatlands (Taminskas et al. 2019). Over the last century peatlands have been under heavy human influence, mainly by draining (Edvardsson et al. 2019). It is estimated that about 70% of peatlands in Estonia have been influenced by drainage or other activities (Vasander et al. 2003, Paal and Leibak 2011). The main activities influencing peatlands in Estonia have been forestry, agriculture and peat-harvesting (Vasander et al. 2003, Masing et al. 2010). Peat harvesting started in the 17th century. By the beginning of 19th century draining and burning mires were one of the most common agricultural practices (Vasander et al. 2003). Previous studies have shown that drainage increases tree growth and thus annual tree rings (Macdonald and Fengyou 2001, Choi et al. 2007). This study focuses on spatial and temporal relations between anthropogenic changes in water level and annual tree-ring growth in a raised bog covering full sequence from natural status to drainage and peat extraction, abandonment and restoration of the bog.

## MATERIALS AND METHODS

The study area is located in Laiusevälja Village in Jõgeva County in Eastern Estonia. The area is on the northern part of the old Kivijärve peat deposit in the Laiuse Bog. Mining activity was ceased there in 1996 and the peatland was left for natural regeneration (Ramst et al. 2006). The bog area is 1066 ha and of that37.38 ha was the former milled peat extraction area (Orru et al. 2020). Since 2013 there was a raise in water level in the southern part of the abandoned extraction site due to beaver activity. Since 2019 water level was raised because of the restoration of the peatland.

On the southern border of the study area lies Lake Kivijärv. The lake had its water level lowered in the 1920s and during the 1950s the lake almost overgrew (Kalapeedia). There was also a second attempt in lowering the lake's water level in 1973 (Maaparandussüsteemide register). Nowadays the lake has an area about 20 hectares (Otsmaa 2017). Since the 19th century the lake has lost most of its volume and nowadays only the former deepest part of the lake remain (Kalapeedia).

Tree-ring samples of pine trees (*Pinus sylvestris*) were collected in October 2019 from five different sites of the Laiuse peatland (Figure 1). At the former peat extraction area samples from stumps (cross sections) and living trees (by increment borer) were collected. Only core samples were collected from other study sites. The second sample set was collected from pines growing next to the ditch surrounding the extraction site. The third set was collected at a distance of 150 m from the drainage ditch. These three study sites were assumed to be most affected by the lowering of water level in the former peat extraction site. The fourth sample set consists of cores collected from the pristine part of the peatland. An additional sample set represents a pine stand in the southern part of the peatland near the bog lake. This site was unaffected by peat extraction but presumably reflects a dated event of water level lowering in Lake Kivijärv.

Figure 1. Study area in the Laiuse peatland and location of the sample sites (numbered).

Tree-ring widths of pines were measured and the increment series were analyzed to establish the effects of anthropogenic disturbances. Except for the tree stumps the samples were collected at about half a meter from the ground. The widths of tree rings in the samples were measured with a LINTAB measuring device and Leica S4E microscope. Each sample was measured from two opposite radii – from bark to pith. The TSAP-Win™ program was used for recording the tree-ring widths. From each site at least 12 samples were collected. For every study site a synchronized tree-ring chronology was composed with at least two trees (Figure 2). These chronologies were later compared with each other and analysed using historical records about water level manipulations in the area.

## RESULTS

In the first site the seven samples collected with increment borer were up to 15 years long (Figure 2). The trees started to grow randomly in that area after the peat extraction stopped on the site in the 1990s (Figure 1). The average tree-ring width in sample site was 3.37 mm.
In the second site the chronology consists of seven increment borer samples and is 43 years long. Average tree-ring width for the samples was 2.06 mm. The average tree-ring width in the site is declining since the 1990s (Figure 2).
The tree-ring width chronology for the third study area consists of seven tree-ring width chronologies. The length of the chronology is 172 years, with the average tree-ring width of 0.61 mm. Trees from that site show an increase in tree-ring widths from the middle of 1970s till the middle of 1980s (Figure 2).
The fourth study site tree-ring chronology consists of nine samples and the length of that chronology is 157 years. The average tree-ring width for the area was 0.47 mm. An increase in tree-ring growths is visible between the years 2011-2015 (Figure 2).
The fifth site's synchronised and averaged chronology consists of eleven tree-ring chronologies. The chronology is 115 years long. The average tree-ring width for the samples was 1.31 mm. The results show an increase in tree-ring widths in 1930s and in 1970 and followed by steady decreases shortly after that. Small peaks in 1980s and 1990s are also clearly visible (Figure 2).

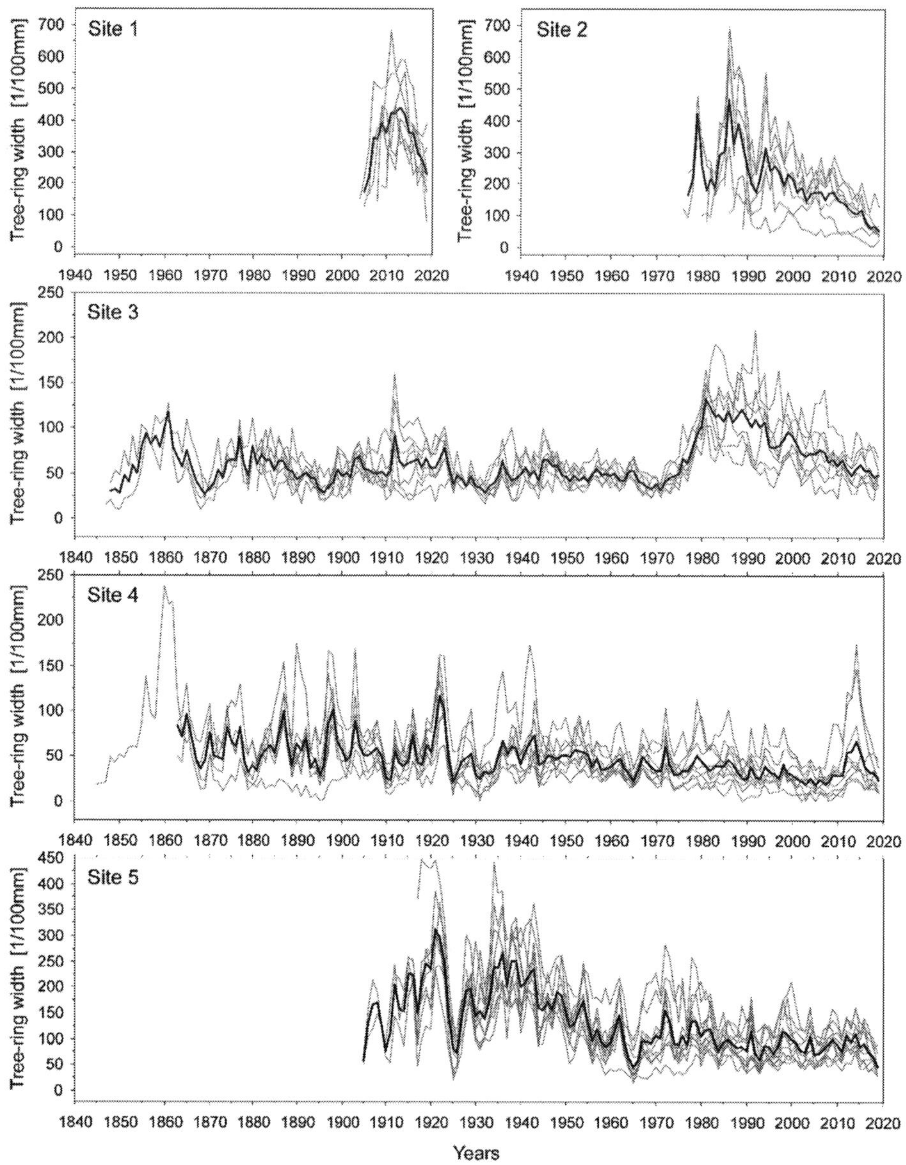

Figure 2. Tree-ring widths of pines (gray lines) and the average chronologies (black lines) in the study sites.

## DISCUSSION

In the first study area there is no visible correlation between the individual samples collected in the area (Figure 2). That is because of the young age of the sample pines and differences in their individual growth sites. Because of the short age of the sample trees the study area can also not be compared with other study sites.

There is no correlation between second study site and the other sites average chronologies. The samples show a decrease in average tree-ring widths since the 1990s that coincides with the abandoning of the peat extraction site and end of the drainage system functioning. Also, the effect of flooding due to beaver activity in the area can be seen on the last tree-ring widths (Figure 2).

The third study area shows an increase in tree-ring widths from the middle of 1970s till the middle of 1980s (Figure 2). The reason for that increase is the lowering of water level for peat extraction in the nearby area (150–200 meters) (Figure 1). After that, a slow and steady

decline in tree-ring widths can be seen which is consistent with raising of the water level due to leaving the former peat extraction site to recover on its own (Figure 2).
The fourth study area was located in the wettest part of the peatland and should not have been influenced by the peat extraction. Growth of pines in this study area should therefore reflect the influence of climatic variables. The tree-ring chronology from that area shows quite steady tree-ring growth. The increase in tree-ring growth in the 2011–2015 period can be explained by warmer seasons (Kotta et al. 2018) (Figure 2).
The chronology from the fifth study site shows the effects of lowering the water level in Lake Kivijärv in the 1928–1929 and the 1973. There can be seen an abrupt increase in tree-ring growth in the 1930s and after that a steady decline. That is due to the lowering of water level by one meter in nearby Lake Kivijärv (Figure 1). The short-lasting decline in growth after 1928 can be explained by the trees' shock to that change. The small peaks in the 1970 and 1980 can be explained by secondary drainage and extensive use of fertilizers and aerial fertilization in the nearby fields (Sults 2003) (Figure 2).
Comparing the site chronologies with each other shows a noticeable correlation between the chronologies of the study areas 3 and 4 (Figure 2). Nevertheless, there is a big difference starting in the middle of 1970s and coinciding with the lowering of the water level in the former peat extraction site. Lowering of the water level affected the third study area by increasing the annual tree-ring growth.
The third, fourth and fifth study area have a common increase in radial growth in the 1920s and a sharp decline shortly after that. This change is to be attributed to climatic effect while the prolonged increase of tree-ring width at fifth study area since 1928 is due to the lowering of water level in the nearby Lake Kivijärv by one meter. All five study sites showed that in the recent years annual tree-ring growth decreased (Figure 2). While decrease is common for all study sites it is more pronounced for sites affected by drainage system of former peat extraction area. The study also indicates that the pines in Laiuse peatland may have a quicker reaction to the lowering of the water level than to the rise. However, that aspect should be further investigated.

## CONCLUSION

The study in Laiuse peatland shows that changes in water level influence tree growth substantially. In the first two study sites the influence of drainage from the peat extraction was the most considerable. The third study area was also influenced by drainage in the peat extraction site but with considerable delay due to larger distance. The fourth study site serves as a natural reference with minimal long-term growth variation but revealing climate induced peaks in 1920s and 2011-2015 reflected also in other chronologies. The fifth study site was mostly influenced by changes in water level in Lake Kivijärv. The biggest similarity lay between the tree-ring width patterns of the third and fourth study areas. All five study areas showed a steady decrease in tree-ring growth over the recent years.

## ACKNOWLEDGEMENTS

This study was supported by the Estonian State Forest Management Centre (project LLTOM17250 "Water level restoration in cut-away peatlands: development of integrated monitoring methods and monitoring", 2017–2023), by the Estonian Research Council (PRG352), and by the Mobilitas Pluss project MOBTP35 financed from the European Regional Development Fund.

## REFERENCES


Choi, W.-J., Chang, S.X., Bhatti, J.S. (2007) Drainage affects tree growth and c and n dynamics in a minerotrophic peatland. Ecology, 88(2): 443–453. https://doi.org/10.1890/00129658(2007)88[443:DATGAC]2.0.CO;2

de Groot, R., Brander, L., van der Ploeg, S., Costanza, R., Bernard, F., Braat, L., Christie, M., Crossman, N., Ghermandi, A.N., Hein, L., Hussain, S., Kumar, P., McVittie, A., Portela, R., Rodriguez, L.C., ten Brink, P., van Beukering, P. (2012) Global estimates of the value of ecosystems and their services in monetary units. Ecosystem Services, 1(1): 50–61. https://doi.org/10.1016/j.ecoser.2012.07.005

Edvardsson, J., Baužienė, I., Lamentowicz, M., Šimanauskienė, R., Tamkevičiūtė, M., Taminskas, J., Linkevičienė, R., Skuratovič, Ž., Corona, C., Stoffel, M. (2019). A multi-proxy reconstruction of moisture dynamics in a peatland ecosystem: A case study from Čepkeliai, Lithuania. Ecological Indicators, 106. https://doi.org/10.1016/j.ecolind.2019.105484

Kalapeedia. Eesti kalastuse entsüklopeedia. Kivijärv (Laiuse Kivijärv, Kibijärv). https://www.kalapeedia.ee/kivijarv-laiuse-kivijarv-kibijarv.html. (29.03.2021)

Kotta, J., Herkül, K., Jaagus, J., Kaasik, A., Raudsepp, U., Alari, V., Arula, T., Haberman, J., Järvet, A., Kangur, K., Kont, A., Kull, A., Laanemets, J., Maljutenko, I., Männik, A., Nõges, P., Nõges, T., Ojaveer, H., Peterson, A., Reihan, A., Rõõm, R., Sepp, M., Suursaar, Ü., Tamm, O., Tamm, T., Tõnisson, H. (2018). Linking atmospheric, terrestrial and aquatic environments in high latitude: Regime shifts in the Estonian regional climate system for the past 50 years. PLoS ONE, 13 (12), ARTN e0209568–20. https://doi.org/10.1371/journal.pone.0209568

Maaparandussüsteemide register (Register of Land Amelioration Systems) https://portaal.agri.ee/avalik/#/maaparandus/systeem/2020552000020 (30.03.2021)

Macdonald, S.E., Fengyou, Y. (2001) Factors influencing size inequality in peatland black spruce and tamarack: evidence from post-drainage release growth. Journal of Ecology, 87(3): 404–412. https://doi.org/10.1046/j.1365-2745.1999.00370.x

Masing, V., Botch, M., Läänelaid, A. (2010) Mires of the former Soviet Union. (2010) Wetlands Ecology and Management, 18: 397–433. https://doi.org/10.1007/s11273-008-9130-6

Orru, M., Orru, H. (2008). Sustainable use of Estonian peat reserves and environmental challenges. Estonian Journal of Earth Sciences, 57(2): 87–93. https://doi.org/10.3176/earth.2008.2.04

Orru, M., Aarniste, M., Mustonen, E., Hints, O. (2020). Eesti turbauuringute andmebaas https://doi.org/10.15152/GEO.487 Kivijärve turbaala. https://turba.geoloogia.info/turbaala/52 (29.03.2021)

Otsmaa, M. (2017) Eesti järvemuda isesugustes järvenõgudes. (Estonian lake mud in unique lake basins) Eesti Loodus, 10: 18-24

Paal, J., Leibak, E. (2011). *Estonian mires: inventory of habitats*. Regio Ltd, Tartu: 173 p. https://issuu.com/elfond/docs/estonian_mires_inventory (30.03.2021).

Ramst, R., Orru, M., Salo, V., Halliste, L. (2006) Eesti mahajäetud turbatootmisalade revisjon. 2. etapp. Ida-Viru, Lääne-Viru, Jõgeva, Järva ja Tartu maakond. (Revision of abandoned peat production areas in Estonia. Stageep 2. Ida-Viru, Lääne-Viru, Jõgeva, Järva and Tartu counties) OÜ Eesti Geoloogiakeskus, rakendusgeoloogia ja maavarade osakond.

Sults, Ü. (2003) *Rohke- ja liigtoitelisus: veekogude loomuliku vananemise kiirendaja. Käsiraamat eutrofeerumise mõjudest pinnaveekogudele.* (Eutrophication and supertrophication: accelerator of natural aging of water bodies. Handbook on the effects of eutrophication on surface waters). Peipsi Koostöö Keskus, Tartu: 32p.

Taminskas, J., Edvardsson, J., Linkevičienė, R., Stoffel, M., Corona, C., Tamkevičiūtė, M. (2019) Combining multiple proxies to investigate water table fluctuations in wetlands: A case study from the Rėkyva wetland complex, Lithuania. Palaeogeography, Palaeoclimatology, Palaeoecology, 514: 453–463. https://doi.org/10.1016/j.palaeo.2018.11.004

Vasander, H., Tuittila, E.-S., Lode, E., Lundin, L., Ilomets, M., Sallantaus, T., Heikkilä, R., Pitkänen, M.-L., Laine, J. (2003) Status and restoration of peatlands in northern Europe. Wetlands Ecology and Management, 11: 51–63.

ID 62682

# BOREAL PEATLAND FORESTS: DITCH NETWORK MAINTENANCE EFFORT AND WATER PROTECTION IN A FOREST ROTATION FRAMEWORK

*Jenni Miettinen[1], Markku Ollikainen[1], Jukka Aroviita[2], Soili Haikarainen[3], Mika Nieminen[3], Jarno Turunen[2], Lauri Valsta[1]

[1] University of Helsinki, Finland
[2] Finnish Environment Institute, Finland
[3] Natural Resources Institute Finland, Finland

*jenni.miettinen@helsinki.fi*

Ditch network maintenance promotes forest growth in drained peatland forests but increases nutrient and sediment loads, which are detrimental to water quality. Society needs to balance the harvest revenue from improved forest growth against deteriorating water quality. We examine socially optimal even-aged forest management in drained peatlands when harvesting and ditch network maintenance cause nutrient and sediment loading but can be reduced using water protection measures. The means to reduce loading include establishing overland flow fields, and abstaining from ditch network maintenance. We characterize this choice analytically in a rotation framework and examine, in a numerical model, the key factors affecting the choice of optimal forest management and water protection measures. We choose a drained peatland forest site located in northeastern Finland in the vicinity of ecologically vulnerable forest headwater streams. We use field data from 33 forest streams to determine the sediment load damage and data on nutrient and sediment loads from Finnish peatland sites. On the given drained forest site, we find a set of parameters under which implementing ditch network maintenance is privately but not socially optimal. When ditch network maintenance is implemented, the optimal size of overland flow fields depends highly on the establishment costs and the values of sediment load damage.

ID 72870

# CARBON STOCK IN OLD-GROWTH SCOTS PINE (PINUS SYLVESTRIS L.) FORESTS ON WET PEAT SOILS IN LATVIA

Laura Ķēniņa, Ieva Jaunslaviete, Āris Jansons

Latvian State Forest Research Institute Silava, Salaspils, Latvia

*laura.kenina@silava.lv*

## SUMMARY

Assessments of carbon storage capacity in different ecosystems is essential to guide the decisions on effective climate change mitigation. In Latvia, 22% of the total forest area are located on peat soils and among them 9%, i.e. 352,650 ha, are classified as naturally wet peatland forests according to the National forest inventory (NFI). Old-growth forests are recognised as major carbon pool for a certain period of its development, although there are no data available from stands on wet peat soils to evaluate the influence of increased share of unmanaged areas on progress towards climate change mitigation targets. Large, changing and manageable carbon pools in forests are tree biomass, therefore we aimed to evaluate carbon stocks in tree biomass and deadwood in old-growth and mature Scots pine (*Pinus sylvestris* L.) stands on wet peat soils.

Four Scots pine stands in *Caricoso-phragmitosa* forest type at the age of 167 to 187 years were measured. The methodology used for the fieldwork and the data analysis is the same as was published in Ķēniņa et al. (2018). Values from old-growth forests were compared to NFI data.

Old-growth stands on wet peat soils had similar carbon stock in tree biomass compared to mature stands, 106 ± 11.8 t C $ha^{-1}$ and 102 ± 33.1 t C $ha^{-1}$, respectively. The total deadwood carbon pool was highly variable among the sample plots, ranging from 1 t C $ha^{-1}$ to 53 t C $ha^{-1}$ (mean 19 ± 4.5 t C $ha^{-1}$). Also mean deadwood carbon of old-growths pine stands was higher compared to mature stands. The mean annual rate of changes in the tree biomass and deadwood carbon pool is gradually decreasing over time, still old-growth stands can be a notable carbon storage in absence of intensive disturbances. Further studies shall address the long-term influence of natural disturbances on carbon pools in old-growth forests.

***Keywords***: *hemiboreal forests, carbon pools, organic soils, above- and below-ground biomass, semi-natural forest*

## INTRODUCTION

Assessments of carbon storage capacity in different ecosystems is essential to guide the decisions on effective climate change mitigation. Increasing awareness to achieve carbon neutrality targets requires accurate carbon stock data of un-managed forests, as they may represents the reference level of carbon carrying capacity. Old-growth forests are recognised as major carbon pool for a certain period of its development, although there are no data available from stands on wet peat soils to use this information in decision support tools to evaluate the influence of increased share of unmanaged areas on progress towards climate change mitigation targets.

Old-growth forests are highly variable due to large heterogeneity of these forests according to the climate, site type, stand structure and other factors (Jacob et al., 2013). Beside regional differences, natural disturbance has a great impact on carbon storage in old-growth forests, impacting live tree biomass and deadwood proportion in such forest.

Latvia is situated in the hemiborial zone. According to National forest inventory (NFI), Scots pine (Pinus sylvestris L.) is most widespread and economically important coniferous tree species in Latvia (27% of total forest area) and Northern Europe. Yet, knowledge of carbon storage in old-growth forests is scare, but there are few studies in hemiboreal region assessing Scots pine and Norway spruce (Picea abies (L.) Karst) stands growing on mineral soils (Ķēniņa et al., 2018; Ķēniņa et al., 2019). In Latvia, 22% of the total forest area are located on peat soils and among them 9%, i.e. 352,650 ha, are classified as naturally wet peatland forests according to the National forest inventory (NFI). Although, forests older than 120 years in Latvia are rare and scattered, due to decrease of forest management activities and increase of protected areas, especially on peat soils (mainly unmanaged due to low soil capacity), area of old-growth forests in Europe continue to growth (Badalamenti et al., 2019).

Large, changing and manageable carbon pools in forests are tree biomass (Jacob et al., 2013). The few remaining old-growth forests on natural organic soils represents an exclusive opportunity to study forests carbon stock. Soil, especially organic soil is one of the main carbon pools in forest ecosystem, although, estimated are highly uncertain, especially in old-growth forests (Bradshaw et al., 2015). Therefore, we aimed to evaluate carbon stocks in tree biomass and deadwood in old-growth and mature Scots pine stands on wet peat soils.

## MATERIALS AND METHODS

Four Scots pine stands in *Caricoso-phragmitosa* forest type (wet peat soil - peat layer exceeds 30 cm) at the age of 167 to 187 years were measured. The methodology used for the fieldwork and the data analysis is the same as was published in Ķēniņa et al. (2018). Namely, forests stands were pre-selected and checked in field for actual occurrence of a chosen forest type, age group (>160 years), dominance of Scots pine (>60% from basal area), old trees, no human intervention. Only stands, where old trees are still dominant cohort were measured. Altogether, 30 sample plots (6-8 sample plots in each stand) of 500m$^2$ were systematically established.

The diameter of the breast height of all live trees and standing dead trees (≥6.1 cm) was measured in each sample plot. Tree height of three to five live trees in each canopy layer and all standing dead trees were measured. The diameter (≥14.1 cm) in both ends and length of the downed logs, decay stage in five classes (fresh to almost complete decay) and tree species (if possible) were recorded within the sample plot. Soil samples were taken outside the sampling plot at three systematically located points from each stand. Soil and forest floor samples were taken.

The live tree biomass (above- and below-ground) was estimated from diameter at breast height

and calculated tree height for individual trees based on the biomass equations for the main tree species in Latvia (Liepiņš et al., 2017). The carbon content of 50% was used for the tree biomass carbon stock estimation. The volume of downed logs and dead standing trees with broken tops was calculated according cylinder formula and converted to biomass using decay class-specific density. Decay class-specific density and carbon content for the main tree species for deadwood carbon stock estimations were applied after the testing from Köster et al. (2015).
Obtained carbon stock results from old-growth Scots pine stands in Caricoso-phragmitosa forest type were compared to National forest inventory (NFI) sample plots – field data from 12 NFI mature (on average 102 years old) Scots pine sample plots in Caricoso-phragmitosa forest type were used.

## RESULTS

The mean standing volume of old-growth pine stands in Caricoso-phragmitosa forest type was 304.3 ± 35.47 $m^3$ $ha^{-1}$ (ranging from 107 to 441 $m^3$ $ha^{-1}$) and mean basal area was 32 ± 3.2 $m^2$ $ha^{-1}$. The mean basal area in the upper layer was 26.1 ± 3.09 $m^2$ $ha^{-1}$, of which 18.1 ± 2.42 $m^2$ $ha^{-1}$ were Scots pine. In the second tree layer, the mean basal area was 5.3 ± 0.87 $m^2$ $ha^{-1}$ and it was dominated by Norway spruce (5.0 ± 0.87 $m^2$ $ha^{-1}$). The mean stand density was 1509 ± 273 trees $ha^{-1}$, of which 489 ± 62 trees $ha^{-1}$ was in the upper layer. The mean deadwood volume was 120.3 ± 28.94 $m^3$ $ha^{-1}$ (ranging from 8 to 337 $m^3$ $ha^{-1}$).
Stand basal area, as well as tree density and tree height in upper layer had a significant effect (all $p> 0.0001$) on live tree biomass carbon stock and less, but still significantly (all $p>0.05$) on carbon stock in deadwood. Neither stand age and tree diameter at breast height had an effect on live tree biomass and deadwood carbon pools.
The carbon in above-ground biomass accounted for 78% (83 ± 9.3 t C $ha^{-1}$) of live tree biomass. The mean carbon stock in live tree biomass was 106 ± 11.8 t C $ha^{-1}$ (ranging from 36 to 149 t C $ha^{-1}$) in old-growth Scots pine stands on wet peat soils. More than 90% of live tree biomass carbon in upper layer was stored in Scots pine trees with diameter 20-40 cm. More than half (62%) of the second layer's live tree biomass carbon was stored in Norway spruce trees with diameter up to 20 cm. Only 25% of the second layer carbon storage of live tree biomass formed Scots pine.
The mean total deadwood carbon pool of old-growth forests was highly variable among the sample plots, ranging from 1 t C $ha^{-1}$ to 53 t C $ha^{-1}$ (mean 19 ± 4.5 t C $ha^{-1}$). The deadwood carbon pool was significantly ($p=0.002$) different between deadwood types – downed logs, dead standing trees and dead standing trees with broken tops. Dead standing trees constituted the significantly ($p=0.001$) greatest share (on average 10 ± 3.4 t C $ha^{-1}$; 51%) of the total deadwood than downed logs (on average 3 ± 0.9 t C $ha^{-1}$; 17%) (Figure 1).

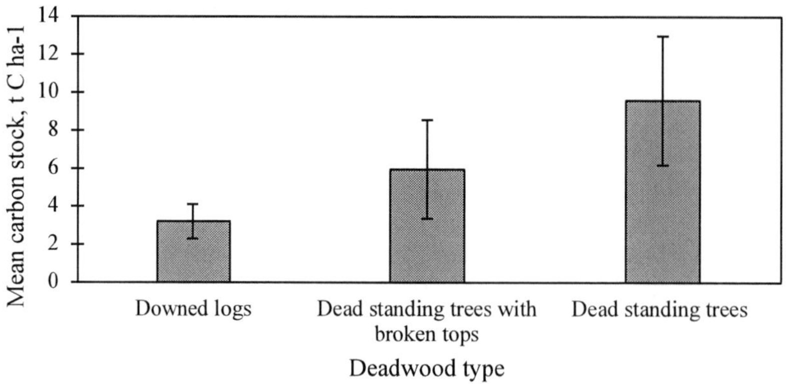

Figure 1. Deadwood mean carbon stock in three deadwood types – downed logs, dead standing trees, dead standing trees with broken tops of old-growth Scots pine stands in Caricoso-phragmitosa forest type. Error bars show 95% confidence intervals

Most of the deadwood carbon consisted of moderately decomposed Scots pine (mean 14 t C $ha^{-1}$), followed by birch (mean 3 t C $ha^{-1}$) and Norway spruce (mean 2 t C $ha^{-1}$) debris.
The mean live tree biomass and deadwood carbon stocks in mature Scots pine stands in Caricoso-phragmitosa forest type were found 102 ± 33.1 t C $ha^{-1}$ and 3 ± 1.9 t C $ha^{-1}$, respectively. The live tree biomass carbon pool size was similar between mature and old-growth stands, but deadwood carbon pool size differed significantly ($p=0.001$). Mean annual difference of live tree biomass and deadwood carbon stock was gradually ($p=0.01$) decreasing over time from mature to old-growth stage, 1.1 ± 0.39 t C $ha^{-1}$ $year^{-1}$ and 0.7 ± 0.08 t C $ha^{-1}$ $year^{-1}$, respectively.

## DISCUSSION

Carbon storage of old-growth forest stands depends on a set of many factors (i.e., climate, natural disturbance regime, dominant tree species, stand structure and soil type) (Jacob et al., 2013; Blaško et al., 2020). Stand age is main factor affecting carbon stock dynamics in stand (Lee et al., 2016). Our data is obtained in on average 177 ± 13 years old old-growth stands. There are only few older studies in Europe of carbon storage in Scots pine stands older than 120 years (Lee et al., 2016; Vucetich et al., 2000). We found that large upper layer's Scots pines formed the majority of carbon stock of live tree biomass, but Norway spruce are the dominant in second layer.
Live tree biomass carbon pool in old-growth Scots pine stands on wet peat soil is considered important carbon stock (mean 106 ± 11.8 t C $ha^{-1}$), but it is smaller as observed in old-growth Scots pine stands on mineral soils (171± 6.1 t C $ha^{-1}$) (Ķēniņa et al., 2019). Although, we failed to obtain reliable soil carbon pool data due to too small data set. Despite, trend showed that soil is the main carbon pool in old-growth Scots pine stands in Caricoso-phragmitosa forest type. following the general patter that organic soils in Norther hemisphere store large carbon stock (Bradshaw et al., 2015; Beaulne et al., 2021). Our estimated mean deadwood carbon storage was 19 ± 4.5 t C $ha^{-1}$, of which dead standing trees formed the greatest share (51%). Several previous studies have reported downed logs (~50-70%) as main deadwood type (Siitonen et al., 2000; Ķēniņa et al., 2018)
Although, the live tree biomass carbon pool size was similar between mature and old-growth stands, the deadwood carbon stock in old-growth stands was sixfold compared to mature stands and was comparable to obtained results in Finland (Siitonen et al., 2000). Nevertheless, the mean annual difference of live tree biomass and deadwood carbon stock was decreasing from mature to old-growth stage. Obtained results coincide with previously published that old-growth stands despite that it is a large carbon pool, become weaker carbon sink with increasing age (Bellassen & Luyssaert, 2014).

## CONCLUSION

Old-growth stands on wet peat soils had similar carbon stock in tree biomass compared to mature stands in same forest type, but overall smaller carbon stock compared to forest stands on mineral soils. The mean annual rate of changes (growth) in the tree biomass and deadwood carbon pools is gradually decreasing over time, thus making retention of old-growth stands not very efficient as mean for carbon sequestration. The influence of natural disturbance over longer period and forest landscape scale needs to be added in furthers studies for more complete understanding of role of old-growth forest in context of climate-change mitigation targets.


## ACKNOWLEDGEMENTS

Project: Development of a decision support tool integrating information from old-growth semi-natural forest for more comprehensive estimates of carbon balance (ERDF No. 1.1.1.1/19/A/130)


## REFERENCES


1. Beaulne J, Garneau M, Magnan G, Boucher E. (2021) Peat deposits store more carbon than trees in forested peatlands of the boreal biome. *Scientific Report*; 11: 2657
2. Bellassen V, Luyssaert S. (2014) Carbon sequestration: managing forests in uncertain times. *Nature*; 506: 153–155
3. Bradshaw C, Warkentin I. (2015) Global estimates of boreal forest carbon stocks and flux. *Global and Planetary Change*; 128: 24–30
4. Blaško E, Fors,arl B, Gundale MJ, Lundmark T, Nordin A. (2020) Impacts of tree species identity and species mixing on ecosystem carbon and nitrogen stocks in a boreal forest. *Forest Ecology and Management*; 458: 117783
5. Jacob M, Bade C, Calvete H, Dittrich S, Leuschner C, Hauck M. (2013) Significance of over-mature and decaying trees for carbon stocks in a Central European natural spruce forest. *Ecosystems*; 16: 336–346
6. Ķēniņa L, Elferts D, Bāders E, Jansons Ā. (2018) Carbon pools in a hemiboreal over-mature Norway spruce stands. *Forests*; 9: 1–10
7. Ķēniņa L, Jaunsaviete I, Liepa L, Zute D, Jansons Ā. (2019) Carbon pools in old-growth Scots pine stands in hemiboreal Latvia. *Forests*; 10: 911
8. Köster K, Metslaid M, Engelhart J, Köster E. (2015). Dead wood basic density, and the concentration of carbon and nitrogen for main tree species in managed hemiboreal forests. *Forest Ecology and Management*; 354: 35–42
9. Liepiņš J, Lazdiņš A, Liepiņš K. (2017) Equations for estimating above- and belowground biomass of Norway spruce, Scots pine, birch spp. and European aspen in Latvia. Scand. *Scandinavian Journal of Forest Research*; 33: 58–70
10. Lee J, Tolunay D, Makineci E, Çömez A, Son YM, Kim R, Son Y. (2016) Estimating the age-dependent changes in carbon stocks of Scots pine (Pinus sylvestris L.) stands in Turkey. *Annals of Forest Science*; 73: 523–531
11. Vucetich JA, Reed DD, Breymeyer A, Degórski M, Mroz GD, Solon J, Roo-Zielinska E, Noble R. (2000) Carbon pools and ecosystem properties along a latitudinal gradient in northern Scots pine (Pinus sylvestris) forests. *Forest Ecology and Management*; 136: 135–145
12. Siitonen J, Martikainen P, Punttila P, Rauh J. (2000) Coarse woody debris and stand characteristics in mature managed and old-growth boreal mesic forests in southern Finland. *Forest Ecology and Management*; 128: 211–225

ID 61470

# THE PEATLANDS OF LOWLAND PERU: AN EXPLORATION OF THE ECOLOGICAL AND SOCIO-ECOLOGICAL VALUE OF THESE 'SUCKING' SWAMPS

*Lydia Cole[1], Luis Andueza[1], Katy Roucoux[1], Ian Lawson[1], Nina Laurie[1], Althea Davies[1], Charlotte Wheeler[2], Ed Mitchard[2], Nállarett Dávila[3], José Reyna[3], Margarita del Águila Villacorta[3], Wendy Darlyn[3], Manuel Martín Brañas[3], Cecilia del Carmen Nuñez Perez[3], Euridice Honorio Coronado[3]

[1] University of St Andrews, United Kingdom
[2] University of Edinburgh, United Kingdom
[3] Instituto de Investigaciones de la Amazonía Peruana, Peru

*lesc1@st-andrews.ac.uk*

The tropical peatlands of Peru are mostly found within the subsiding Pastaza-Marañón Foreland Basin (PMFB) of the western Amazon. Their full geographical extent, role in global carbon cycling and suite of ecological and socio-ecological values are still largely unknown. Our Leverhulme Trust-funded project aims to address knowledge gaps on: (i) the types of peat-forming ecosystems that exist in the PMFB; and, (ii) the ways in which local people use and value the different types of wetlands present there, in order to understand the local basis for protecting these globally important ecosystems. During four months in 2019, a team of ecologists and social scientists performed field surveys and a range of interviews in four communities living in the proximity of peat-forming ecosystems within the PMFB. After a process of participatory mapping and key informant interviews within each community, plots of 0.1ha were set-up in the range of wetland forest types used by community members, and above- and belowground characteristics sampled. The ecological survey data demonstrate that peat is forming under a wide range of forest types and hydrological conditions. Results from the social surveys show that peatland ecosystems have several, specific uses for people living locally, e.g. for the harvesting of aguaje fruit (from the Mauritia flexuosa palm), but otherwise are avoided where possible. Initial conclusions from our interdisciplinary study suggest that, although these ecosystems form an important part of the geography and socio-ecological dynamics of these communities, their use in local livelihood acquisition does not threaten their status as intact ecosystems. Further, the threats to the wetlands of the PMFB are arriving from extra-local sources, and their impacts on the resident ecological and socio-ecological systems are starting to unravel.

ID 73114

# THE EUROPEAN MARKET FOR GROWING MEDIA

Gerald Schmilewski[1], Lambert van Horen[2], *Cecilia Luetgebrune[1]

[1] Growing Media Europe, Belgium
[2] RaboResearch Food & Agribusiness, The Netherlands

*cecilia.luetgebrune@growing-media.eu*

The objective of this study is to give insights on the size of the growing media industry in Europe (European Economic Area) for horticulture, landscaping and hobby gardening. We try to estimate the economic value of the industry in terms of added value and/or employment. We try to elaborate on and discuss developments which will influence these parameters in the next five years. Important developments could be the trend towards more intensive growing systems (e.g. protected cropping), different crops in future crop plans and discussions on environmental footprints. All these topics will influence the future demand for growing media. Altough the main focus will be on the peat market, the study takes other constituents like coir pith, mineral wool, wood fibres into account. Trends and developments with large impact on the European growing media supply chain for the next five years will be discussed. These will include the raw material extraction and the raw material consumption. The study also refelcts on the type of end products manufacturesd, the market segments they are supplied to and the respective purpose they are used for.

ID 62734

# TOWARD THE DEVELOPMENT OF A NEW GENERATION OF GRANULAR PEAT PRODUCTS FOR WASTEWATER REMEDIATION: REACTION MECHANISMS OF PEAT SURFACES WITH HEAVY METAL CATIONS

*Igor V. Kolomitsyn, Ph.D.[1], Vitaliy Goncharov[2], Hannah Leopold[2], Liudmyla Kildyshova[1]

[1] Natural Resources Research Institute, University of Minnesota Duluth, USA
[2] Department of Chemistry & Biochemistry, University of Minnesota Duluth, USA

*ikolomit@d.umn.edu*

Recently, we reported the development of three granular peat media, APTsorb IITM, APTsorb II*Na™, and APTsorb III™, which have breakthrough capacities for $Cd^{2+}$ of 13 mg/g, 16 mg/g, and 22 mg/g respectively. These peat products are designed to remove toxic heavy metals from wastewater streams such as mine water and stormwater. It is important to understand the distribution of cation exchange sites in comparison to the total number of sorption sites in different types of peats. Seven peat samples were obtained from different geographical areas in Minnesota, USA. Each peat sample was subjected to a series of chemical treatments: *i*-PrOH, 4% HCl, 0.25N NaOH, and 72% $H_2SO_4$. Consequently, six different fractions were obtained: raw peat, extracted peat, hemicellulose, humic acids, cellulose, and peat Klason lignin. Each fraction was measured for cation exchange capacity (CEC) using a $Ba(AcO)_2$ test, which is designed to measure the number carboxylic acid groups, and for copper sorption capacity (CSC), using a solution of $Cu^{2+}$ at pH=4.4, which measures the total amount of $Cu^{2+}$ that was sorbed by the material. The difference between CEC and CSC indicates the number of complexation and other sites available for metal sorption. All the fractions exhibited both CEC and CSC. The highest CEC (161 mEq/100 g) and CSC (197 mEq/100 g) was found for woody reed-sedge peat collected near the city of Boy River, Minnesota, USA. Moreover, the CSC of the Klason lignin fraction of Sphagnum peat was twice the CEC of the same fraction, with a value of 209 mEq/100 g CSC compared to 110 mEq/100 g CEC. This data also suggests that Klason lignin from peat is different from wood lignin.

ID 62764

# MINERALISATION OF ORGANIC FERTILIZERS IN GROWING MEDIA

Hein Boon

Foundation RHP, The Netherlands

*boon@rhp.nl*

Nowadays more and more growers are aiming for organic farming which implies the use of organic fertilisers. However, a change from mineral fertilisers to organic ones, demands attention on several aspects. As basic fertilisation in substrates, organic fertilisers or mineral fertilisers (direct soluble or controlled-release fertilisers -CRF-) can be used. However, there are important differences between the composition and effects of these fertilisers. The mineralisation of organically bound nitrogen (N) takes place because of bacteria in a dynamic process that follows certain steps. Fundamentally ammonification takes place first, followed by nitrification. Whether or not these processes start, depends on different factors and circumstances.

When using organic fertilisers, the pH may initially -because of ammonification- strongly increase and then -because of nitrification- strongly decrease. The buffering capacity for pH of growing media does play an important role. A growing medium with a large pH buffering capacity can avoid the pH from rising too high, which subsequently can cause appearance of plant toxic ammonia. Especially growing media with little or no peat, often have a low pH buffering capacity, this is an important aspect to be aware of. With a mineralisation test, which was especially developed for organic fertilisers, RHP provides insight in the behaviour of organic fertilizers in growing media. Growing trials at RHP do show the effect of the dynamics of the mineralisation on seedling crops grown in various growing media.

ID 72771

# THE PARTICLE SHAPE OF PEATS: A COMPLEMENTARY ANALYSIS FOR THEIR CHARACTERIZATION

Stan Durand, *Jean-Charles Michel

*EPHOR, L'INSTITUT AGRO, 49045, ANGERS, France*

*jean-charles.michel@agrocampus-ouest.fr*

## SUMMARY

As for other substrates' components, peats are classified and selected for mixes from their particle size through sieving processes. However, sieving tools and methods are often different, and, moreover, do not consider particleshape. These irregular shapes and sizes fall together to create a large pore size distribution (over 85% by volume),so that the shape and size of particles greatly influence the resulting matric structure of the materials, and therefore their physical properties (water retention, drainage).
Particle size and shape of two types of *Sphagnum* white and black peats were studied using a dynamic image analyzer, QicPic. Shape parameters (elongation, sphericity, roundness and straightness) of both peats were determined, and analyzed related to their particle size distribution.
Results showed a similar PSD for both peats, but the particle shape was different: white peat was more elongated,angular and exhibited the largest diversity of shapes, whereas black peat is more rounded and regular. Moreover, particle shape varied according to particle size: larger particles were more elongated and curved, but less straight and circular.

***Keywords***: *QicPic, dynamic image analysis, shape analysis*

## INTRODUCTION

Substrate manufacturers engineer the particle size of growing media constituents to provide to the plant root system the most suitable physical environment. Particle analysis of growing media constituents is a main factor explaining physical properties. From the particle size distribution (PSD) will depend their arrangement and consequently water and air retention and flow properties of substrates. Several authors have already described relationships between PSD and some physical properties. Showing the larger the particle size, the greater the air-filled porosity (AFP), and the lower the water retention properties (Bunt, 1983; Hendreck, 1983; Abad et al., 2005; Caron et al.,2005; Jackson et al., 2010; Fields et al., 2015). Conversely, the smaller the particle size, the smaller the pore size distribution (Owen & Altland, 2008), and the higher the bulk density of the substrate (Rezanezhad et al., 2010). Until now, the PSD study is restricted to sieve analysis, and is mainly used for a control of raw materials. But theresults obtained should be analyzed cautiously. Sieve analysis is indeed clearly relevant for granular particles, butthe large diversity of particle shapes of raw materials makes this method less suitable for substrates containing fibers, chips, and plates, which are far from spherical. Bartley (2019) demonstrated that the higher the particles elongation, the smaller is the accuracy of the PSD.
Computerized tools have been developed since the 90's for a more detailed analysis of PSD

in many research fields and industries. Significant improvement in dynamic image analysis in the past years has also helped for particle shape analysis, like recent works developed on dry materials by Bartley (2019) using the CPA (W.S. TylerGroup). Our study was based on the use of another device called QicPic (Sympatec GmbH) allowing particle size and shape analysis from wet materials for a finer and more representative knowledge of particle size and shape distribution of growing medium constituents.

## MATERIALS AND METHODS

Works were carried out on two types of *Sphagnum* peat moss (Fig. 1) provided by the Klasmann-Deilmann and Floragard companies: a 0-25 mm white milled peat (H3-H6 Von Post index) processed by sieving, and a 0-7 mm black peat (H5-H8 Von Post index) processed though star screen, harvested in Lithuania and Germany, respectively.

(a) (b)

*Figure 1: Study materials: Sphagnum (a) white peat and (b) black peat.*

Two grams of peat at 60% mass moisture content were stirred with ~10-15 L water in a tank passed through the QicPic (Sympatec GmbH) with a constant flow controlled by a peristaltic pump, and circulated through a flow cell equipped with a camera for a continuous image recording. Particle size and shape were then analyzed with the associated software, PAQXOS, creating 3D images from 2D images recorded by the camera. The device is able to detect size and shape in a range from 50 µm to 33,8 mm.

Some distances, called diameters in this context, like particle length, width, and skeletonized length are calculated using PAQXOS (Fig. 2): FeretMAX is the maximal distance between two parallel tangents of the particle contour; EQPC (EQuivalent Projection area Circle) is the diameter of a circle having the same area of the projection area of the particle; CC (circumscribed circle) is the diameter of the circle than encloses the particle contour; LeFi (Length of Fibre) is the distance between the farthest extremities of a particle within its contour. LeFi diameter was chosen for assessing the particles size, considering the particle shapes of peats containing +/- curved fibers.

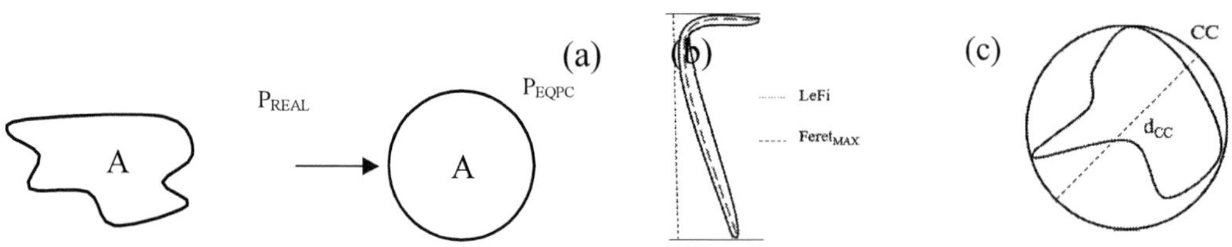


*Figure 2: Diameters used for particle shape calculation: (a) $P_{EQPC}$ for circularity calculation, (b) LeFi and $Feret_{MAX}$ for elongation and straightness (c) Diameter of the circumscribed circle for roundness*

Four main shape descriptors, usually used in the literature (Blott & Pye, 2008) were determined using PAQXOS:

- The elongation, which is the ratio of the width to the length of a particle.
- The roundness, which is the ratio of the averaged radius of curvature of all convex regions to the circumscribedcircle of the particle, according to Wadell (1932). The roundness refers to the relative sharpness of corner andedges of a particle.
- The straightness, which is the ratio of the Feret$_{MAX}$ to the LeFi diameter. The straightness is used to represent the degree of curvature of curled fibers.
- The circularity, which is the ratio of the perimeter of a circle having the same area of the projection area of theparticle (known as EQPC) to the real perimeter of the particle according to Wadell (1933). That shape descriptor does not refer to the circular shape like of a particle, but to the regularity of the particle contour andthe its elongation (Fig. 2). Indeed, the circle is the shape having the smallest perimeter for a given area. As an example, a square is considered to have a high circularity (=0,89).

The class designation for shape descriptors were defined from the referential proposed by Powers (1953) and Blottand Pye (2008). However, because circularity and roundness were calculated from other formulas than the one used by Blott and Pye (2008), the class limits have been changed but fit the same geometrical dimensions.

Cumulative PSD was obtained by fitting experimental data with the Rosin-Rammler distribution function (Perfect et al, 1998; Allaire & Parent, 2003). Characteristic distribution parameters (Kuchenbecker et al., 2012; Videc et al., 2020) D10, D50, D90 corresponding to the size of the 10th, 50th and 90th percentile of the cumulative PSD were determined (Table 3). The relative span factor (RSF), a dimensionless indicator of distribution width (Bitra *et al.,* 2009), was also calculated to analyze the size uniformity/diversity (Eq. 1), knowing that the lower the RSF, the smaller the distribution width.

$$RSF = \frac{(DD90 - DD10)}{DD50} \qquad \text{[Eq. 1]}$$

where $D10$, $D50$ and $D90$ correspond to the interpolated particles size and shape descriptor values at 10th, 50th, and 90th percentiles of cumulative size distribution and shape distribution, respectively.

## RESULTS

Particle shape

Illustration of particle shape factors are given Figure 3 from images database extracted using PAQXOS for the white milled peat. description and distribution from DIA are available Figure 3 and Table 1 to illustrate this point.

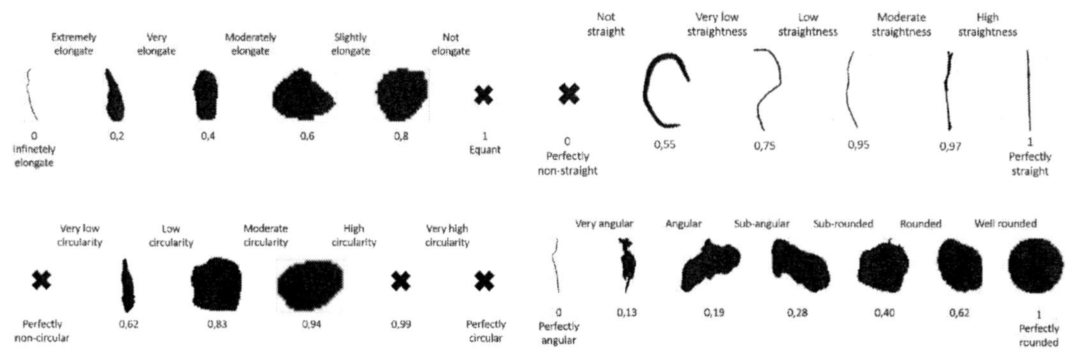


*Figure 3: Examples of particles corresponding to the shape descriptor classes. Images obtained with the QicPic device on white peat, extracted from the PAQXOS database.*

White peat is mainly composed by moderately to extremely elongated particles (93%). Most of the white peat particles are also highly straight (70%) and angular (75%), with a low to very low circularity (71%). Black peat mainly presented moderate and very elongate particles (63%). Most of the black peat particles are also highly straight (72%), with a low to moderate circularity (88%), without preferential roundness. (Table 1).

*Table 1: Distribution of particle's mass proportion according to their shape*

| Shape descriptors | Classe | | White peat | Black peat |
|---|---|---|---|---|
| | Designation | Value of shape descriptor | Mass proportion (%) | |
| Elongation | Extremely elongate | [0 - 0,2[ | 25,1 | 14,2 |
| | Very elongate | [0,2 - 0,4[ | 35,7 | 31,4 |
| | Moderately elongate | [0,4 - 0,6[ | 22,7 | 31,6 |
| | Slightly elongate | [0,6 - 0,8[ | 13,7 | 19,9 |
| | Not elongate | [0,8 - 1[ | 2,7 | 2,9 |
| Straightness | Not straight | [0 - 0,55[ | < 0,1 | < 0,1 |
| | Very low straightness | ]0,55 - 0,75[ | 1,2 | 0,7 |
| | Low straightness | ]0,75 - 0,95[ | 20,7 | 19,3 |
| | Moderate straightness | ]0,95 - 0,97[ | 7,6 | 7,8 |
| | High straightness | ]0,97 - 1] | 70,5 | 72,2 |
| Roundness | Very angular | [0 - 0,13[ | 44,5 | 23,2 |
| | Angular | ]0,13 - 0,19] | 17,5 | 12,2 |
| | Sub-angular | ]0,19 - 0,28[ | 15,4 | 16,4 |
| | Sub-rounded | ]0,28 - 0,40] | 11,1 | 17,9 |
| | Rounded | ]0,40 - 0,62] | 8,3 | 20,8 |
| | Well-rounded | ]0,62 - 1] | 3,2 | 9,5 |
| Circularity | Very low circularity | [0 - 0,62[ | 19,0 | 9,8 |
| | Low circularity | ]0,62 - 0,83[ | 52,4 | 46,4 |
| | Moderate circularity | ]0,83 - 0,94[ | 26,2 | 41,9 |
| | High circularity | ]0,94 - 0,99[ | 2,3 | 1,9 |
| | Very high circularity | ]0,99 - 1] | 0 | 0 |

*Table 2: Values of shape factor interpolated from cumulative particles shape distribution for the 10th, 50th and 90th percentile. Relative span factor (RSF) calculated from Eq. 1.*

| Shape descriptors | White pe | | | | Black peat | | | |
|---|---|---|---|---|---|---|---|---|
| | Percentile of the cumulative shape distribution | | | RSF | Percentile of the cumulative shape distribution | | | RSF |
| | 10 % | 50 % | 90 % | | 10 % | 50 % | 90 % | |
| Elongation | 0,12 | 0,33 | 0,68 | 1,7 | 0,17 | 0,43 | 0,71 | 1,3 |
| Straightness | 0,90 | 0,99 | 1,00 | 0,1 | 0,91 | 0,99 | 1,00 | 0,1 |
| Roundness | 0,04 | 0,15 | 0,43 | 2,6 | 0,07 | 0,27 | 0,61 | 2 |
| Circularity | 0,54 | 0,76 | 0,90 | 0,5 | 0,63 | 0,82 | 0,90 | 0,3 |

In comparison, white peat showed less elongated and more rounded particles, with a little bit higher circularity forblack peat than for white peat, whereas both of them presented high straightness. The lower RSF for elongation, roundness and circularity calculated for black peat indicated that particles shape was more homogenous than those observed for white peats (Table 2).

Particle Size Distribution

Samples of *Sphagnum* white and black peats analysed here showed quite similar PSD: $D_{10}$ and $D_{90}$ varying from 84 to 2007 μm, and from 116 to 2053 μm, with a $D_{50}$ values of 582 and 670, respectively. RSF calculation also indicated a little bit more homogeneous particle size for black peat (RSF=2,9) than for white peat (RSF=3,2).

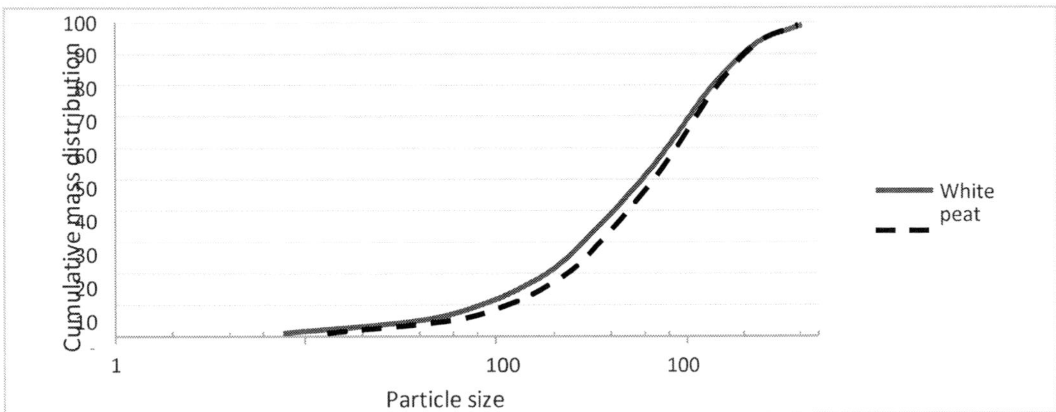


*Figure 4: Cumulative mass distribution of Sphagnum white and black peat particles size, determined from QicPic.*

Evolution of the shape descriptor as a function of size

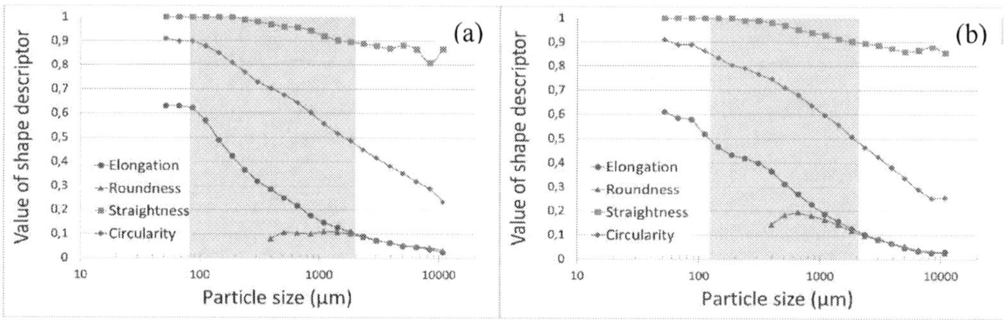


*Figure 4: Values of shape descriptors for Sphagnum (a) white and (b) black peat related to the particle size distribution. Grey sector indicates the diameters of particles corresponding to the intervals [$D_{10}$; $D_{90}$].*

Figure 4 showed a tendency to decrease all shape descriptor values related to the increase in particles size for bothpeats. Thus, an increase in particle size led to more elongated (from moderately to extremely), more curled, less straight (from high to low) and less circular (from high to low) particles. White peat particles remained very angularwhatever the size, whereas black peat changed from angular to very angular particles.

## DISCUSSION & CONCLUSION

Our work here showed the contribution and the high potential in the use of the QicPic tool based dynamic image analysis for a finer particle analysis, describing some shape parameters, also depending on the particles size. The influence of the degree of decomposition, peat species, extraction techniques, etc. could be analyzed in the future. Also, the use of this technique could be envisaged for a better control and selection of raw materials.
Comparison between our two peat samples here (*Sphagnum* white and black peats) is of limited scope, knowing that: (1) samples did not come from the same peatland, (2) white peat was extracted by milling, and (3) its particleshigher than 25 mm were previously removed. However, results obtained here gave a lot of and more detailed information about their particle size and shape, compared to those from observations with the naked eye, and fromsieving methods. In particular, our work showed that particle shape varied in function of size. Knowing the influence of particle size on the physical properties of peats (and other materials) used in soilless culture, segregating particles from their size (and then from their shape) would be possible to a better selection of fractions,and for a possible engineering of materials in order to meet to the desired properties.

## REFERENCES


1. Abad M, Fornes F, Carrion C, Noguera V. (2005) Physical properties of various Coconut coir compared to peat.
   *HortScience*; 40(7): 2138–2144
2. Allaire SE, Parent LE. (2003) Size Guide Number and Rosin–Rammler Approaches to describe particle sizedistribution of granular organic-based fertilisers. *Biosystems Engineering*; 86(4): 503–509
3. Bartley PC. (2019) Multidimensional characterization of horticultural substrates. Ph.D. Thesis, North CarolinaState University. 2019. 160 p.
4. Bitra VSP, Womac AR, Yang YT, Igathinathane C, Miu PI, Chevanan N, Sokhansanj S. (2009) Knife milloperating factors effect on switchgrass particle size distributions. *Bioresource Technology*; 100(21): 5176-5188.
5. Blott SJ, Pye K. (2008) Particle shape: a review and new methods of characterization and classification.
   *Sedimentology*; 55(1): 31–63
6. Bunt AC. (1983) Physical properties of mixtures of peats and minerals of different particle size and bulk densityfor potting substrate. *Acta Horticulturae*; 150: 143–145
7. Caron J, Rivière LM, Guillemain G. (2005) Gas diffusion and air-filled porosity: Effect of some oversize fragments
   –in growing media. *Canadian Journal of Soil Science*; 85(1): 57–65
8. Fields JS, Owen JS, Scoggins HL. (2015) Exploring the influence of particle size on plant water availability in pine bark substrates. In: Proceeding of the 60$^{th}$ SNA Research Conference. McMinnville, Tennessee, 2014. 20–27
9. Jackson BE, Wright RD, Barnes MC. (2010) Methods of constructing a pine tree substrate from various wood particle sizes, organic amendments, and sand for desired physical properties and plant growth. *HortScience*; 45(1): 103–112
10. Kuchenbecker P, Gemeinert M, Rabe T. (2012) Inter-laboratory study of particle size distribution measurements by laser diffraction. *Particle & Particle Systems Characterization*; 29(4): 304–310.
11. Owen JS, Altland, JE. (2008) Container height and Douglas fir bark texture affect substrate physical properties.
    *HortScience*; 43(2): 505–508
12. Rezanezhad F, Quinton WL, Price JS, Elliot TR, Elrick D, Shook KR (2010) Influence of pore size and geometryon peat unsaturated hydraulic conductivity computed from 3D computed tomography image analysis. *Hydrological Processes*; 24(21): 2983–2994
13. Rosin P, Rammler E. (1933) The laws governing the fineness of powdered coal. *Journal of the Institute of Fuel*; 6: 29–36
14. Videc D, Planinšek O, Lamešić D. (2020) Design of experiments for optimization of the lactose spherical crystallization process. *Journal of Pharmaceutical Sciences*; 109(9): 2774–2786
15. Wadell H. (1932) Volume, shape, and roundness of rock particles. *The Journal of Geology*; 40(5): 443–451
16. Wadell H. (1933) Sphericity and roundness of rock particles. *The Journal of Geology*; 41(3): 310–331

ID 72854

# COST-BENEFIT ANALYSIS OF PEATLAND MANAGEMENT IN INDONESIA: CASE STUDY IN KAHAYAN-SEBANGAU PEAT HYDROLOGICAL UNIT, CENTRAL KALIMANTAN

*Rizky Januar, Eli Nur Nirmala Sari, Surahman Putra

World Resources Institute, Indonesia

*rizky.haryanto@wri.org*

The unsustainable management and use of peatlands in Central Kalimantan, Indonesia had caused peatland damage and fires. Despite existing restoration and conservation efforts, challenges remain on promoting profitable livelihood sources and more environmentally friendly utilization of peatlands. There is limited knowledge on the economic potential of best practices in peatland management and use at landscape level. This research aims to provide such reference, with case study in Kahayan-Sebangau peat hydrological unit, comprising 278,714 hectares of peatland ecosystem.

Using cost-benefit analysis approach, economic benefits and costs are estimated for two scenarios: 1) business-as-usual (current scenario); and 2) hypothetical best practice application (policy scenario). The latter includes paludiculture, full rewetting, and halt of logging & oil palm cultivation, among others. Spatial analysis, field survey, and desk research are committed to develop a database of modeled land transition and to estimate the economic values. Accordingly, the net present value (NPV) and benefit-cost ratio (BCR) can be calculated.

With baseline assumption of 10-year land-use change time requirement and 12% discount rate; simulation of direct use value for a 25-year period (2019 prices) shows the NPV: USD 230.9 - 787.83 million (BCR: 1.29-1.97) for BAU scenario, and USD 75.89 - 122.74 million (BCR: 1.15-1.25) for policy scenario. For a 50-year period, the simulation shows NPV: USD 242.95 - 828.93 million for BAU scenario, and USD 95.08 - 146.83 million (BCR: 1.17-1.28) for policy scenario. 15% increase of benefit values in policy scenario within 50-year simulation leads to NPV: USD 193.9 - 248.55 million (BCR: 1.34-1.47); suggesting policy importance to improve value chain within sustainable peatland use. Meanwhile, a 50-year simulation of policy scenario leads to avoided social cost of carbon of at least USD 1.25 - 35.52 million higher than BAU (depending on unit value assumption). Peatland restoration costs will be further incorporated, and multiple scenarios and parameter sensitivity will be explored.

# ID 62578

# METHODOLOGY BASIS OF PEAT SELECTION FOR USE IN LIVESTOCK IN ORDER TO IMPROVE THE ECOLOGICAL AND BIOLOGICAL SAFETY OF ANIMAL PRODUCTS

Lilia Stepchenko

Dnipro State Agrarian and Economic University, Ukraine

*stepchenko2@gmail.com*

In recent decades, the use of peat as a source of biologically active compounds (BAC) with unique regulatory, adaptogenic and immunomodulatory properties in the production of animal products has expanded significantly. However, the range of biologically active compounds in peat is quite wide, heterogeneous, and substantially depends on many geobotanical, physicochemical, environmental, and biological factors. Therefore, the use of peat in livestock production without a preliminary assessment of biological effects is unreasonable, which often does not give the expected results.

We have created a new integral information base, which is called the "Biocadastre of Ukrainian Peat". This base was created using the peat screening system developed by us. It's based on the assessment of a wide range of biological effects of both peat and BAC, that are extracted from it by various methods. As well as taking into account the correlation between peat physicochemical properties and its toxicity level, botanical composition, and biological activity.

Currently, in the research laboratory named after Prof. L.A. Khristeva in Dnipro State Agrarian and Economic University, we developed feed additives of humic nature from selected Ukrainian peats in accordance with the screening system for its evaluation developed by us. Experiments on the use of the obtained feed additives were carried out on the basis of enterprises for the breeding and raising of farm animals. As a result, were developed technological schemes for the application of feed additives from peat as Huminate, Hydrohumate, Humilid for broiler chickens, laying hens, ostriches, pheasants, turkeys, rabbits, pigs of various technological groups, as well as Holstein cows, to increase quantitative and qualitative characteristics of obtained biological products and to improve their ecological safety.

The report will also consider the regulatory mechanisms of BAC action of a humic nature from peat that has immunomodulating, adaptogenic, anti-stress, hepatoprotective and enzyme-stimulating effects on the various types of farm animals body and birds.

# ID 62766

# TESTING OF PROCESSES IN GROWING MEDIA PRODUCTION ON SANITATION EFFECTIVENESS WITH BACILLUS GLOBIGII AS A TEST ORGANISM

Ruth Sjoukes

Foundation RHP, The Netherlands

*boon@rhp.nl*

Raw materials for producing growing media for horticultural purposes must be free of contaminants like pests. Some raw materials need to be treated to eliminate pests that could be present. The effectiveness of the sanitation process (hygienisation) depends on pest-related aspects as the type of organism and infestation level, on the one hand, and the treatment chosen, on the other. There is a need for a test to assess the effectiveness of such a process in a simple way with minimal sanitary and phytosanitary risks. For this reason, a test was developed using Bacillus globigii as an indicator organism. Spores are counted before and after application of three different treatments that are used by the growing media industry: steaming, irradiation and friction heat. The materials tested were peat, wood fibre and sphagnum. The results of experiments using Bacillus globigii as a test organism were compared with existing tests using tomato mosaic virus and tomato seeds.

Bacillus globigii appeared to function well as a test organism. The results were related to the existing tests. The levels of decreased contamination (biological log reduction) could be estimated easily with a high distinction depending on the treatment. This makes the test valuable for certification purposes.

ID 72859

# HORTICULTURAL ADDITIVES INFLUENCE SOIL BIOGEOCHEMISTRY AND INCREASE GREENHOUSE GAS EMISSIONS FROM PEAT

*Bidhya Sharma, Nigel Roulet, Tim Moore, Isabel Strachan

Department of Geography, McGill University, Canada

*bidhya.sharma@mail.mcgill.ca*

Peat is used as the chief ingredient of growing media in horticulture. The high cation exchange capacity, water retention capacity, low bulk density, and appropriate physical properties make peat-based growing media desirable for horticulture. Peat in its natural form is acidic and low in nutrient compositions. Therefore, for suitability as a growing media, peat is mixed with liming agents, nutrients, surfactants, perlite among several other additives.

We assessed the change in soil biogeochemistry and Greenhouse Gas (GHG) fluxes because of horticultural additives. We obtained samples of raw peat and additive mixed growing media (n=52) from four different peat producers in Canada. Our analysis shows that the key soil biogeochemical parameters Carbon : Nitrogen ratio, pH, dissolved organic carbon, bulk density, and Carbon (C) content vary significantly ($p<0.01$) between raw peat and growing media. There is a two-fold increase in $CO_2$ and higher N2O fluxes from growing media as compared to raw peat. A further experiment is being done to isolate the importance of additives.

IPCC (2007) calculates that all C from harvested peat is lost in the atmosphere in the first year. However, from our initial results, we estimate 5% of C loss in the first year from growing media as compared to 2.5% for raw peat. Although the influence of additives in C loss from peat is significant, the current accounting from IPCC in terms of C loss is clearly an overestimation.

ID 61370

# COULD COMPROMISED PALUDICULTURE MANAGE TRADE-OFFS ON PEATLAND RESTORATION?

Bastoni Brata[2], *Ibnu Budiman[1], Eli N N Sari[1], Etik E Hadi[2], Asmawati Ahmad[2], Hengki Siahaan[2], Rizky J Haryanto[1], Rahmah D Hapsari[1]

[1] WRI Indonesia, Indonesia

[2] Balitbang LHK Palembang, Indonesia

*ibnu.budiman@wur.nl*

Sustainable peatland management practices are crucial to support restoration of degraded peatland ecosystems. Scholars argued that paludiculture as plant cultivation practices in wet conditions is considered as the practice that maintains the peat body and sustain ecosystem services on peatland. Yet, little is known about effectiveness of its implementation on tropical peatland. This research analyses the effectiveness of paludiculture implementation in supporting peatland ecosystem restoration, to what extent it fits with purpose of ecosystem restoration activities (soil rewetting, revegetation, and revitalization of people livelihood around peatland). This research draws on both qualitative and quantitative data from field measurement, observation, document reviews, and interviews with key stakeholders in two implementations of paludiculture (agrisilviculture and agrosilvofishery) in South Sumatra province, Indonesia. This study found that among two paludiculture implementations that are observed, there is only one namely agrisilviculture that supports soil rewetting and revegetation purposes. This agrisilviculture project utilised jelutung (Dyera polyphylla), ramin (Gonystylus bancanus), meranti (Shorea balangeran) that are three of the 534 species considered for supporting peatland restoration principles. These species are adaptive to peat soils and tolerant of acid conditions and inundation. Another paludiculture implementation namely agrosilvofishery that is mixed with fishery practices is found unsuccessful yet to support peatland restoration. The involvement of drainage activity in the implementation contributes to lower water table on peatland ecosystem. There is a trade-off between maintaining high peat water table for rewetting and fishery practice that aims to provide short-term economic benefits.

ID 62694

# SPHAGNUM MOSS HARVESTING WITHIN SUSTAINABLE BOG BIOMASS UTILISATION AND HIGH VALUE PRODUCT MANUFACTURING

Petri Konttinen[1], Teppo Rantanen[1,2], Heikki Rantanen[3], Janne Pitkänen[2, 3], Hannamaija Fontell[2]

[1]Novarbo Oy, Eura, Finland

[2] Biolan Oy, Eura, Finland

[3] EcoMoss Oy, Kihniö, Finland

*petri.konttinen@novarbo.fi*

## SUMMARY

Biolan Group of companies (Biolan Oy, EcoMoss Oy and Novarbo Oy) have developed a sustainable sphagnum moss harvesting, utilisation and high value product manufacturing value chain.

Our top layer moss harvesting revolutionises the use of bogs in a fully sustainable way. After 10 years of development, EcoMoss Oy has commercialised a new Light Sphagnum Removal technique (LSR) preserving the ecological and hydrological balance of bogs. LSR is based on special equipment that extracts only a partial layer of the living moss, squeezes out 30% of water in moss upon harvesting and returns this water back to the bog ecosystem, which also reduces the transportation and storage costs. Moss harvesting does not require the establishment of expensive ditching, field preparation or road construction. Bogs can be re-harvested within 20- 30 years, which is faster than forests.

Novarbo Oy has developed a sustainable and cost-effective way to manufacture hydroponics growth medium Mosswool® as a sustainable and compostable drop-in replacement for the non-biodegradable stone wool growth media for the hydroponic cultivation of vegetable crops. Mosswool® is based on the moss foam forming patents by VTT and Luke, which Novarbo have licenced exclusively. Novarbo has further developed Mosswool® manufacturing to a mass-production stage with a grant from the EU Horizon 2020 programme in 2017-19.

Based on an LCA study by National Resources Institute Finland (Luke)[1], the $CO_2$ climate impact of manufacturing a 14 litre Mosswool® substrate was significantly lower compared to a peat substrate; 2.20 and 3.63 kg$CO_2$-eq., respectively. Mosswool® water footprint was 14 litres per slab calculated with the AWARE method. Mosswool® stores water evenly and reserves water as a buffer if there are problems with the irrigation cycle or fertilization. With the internal water buffer capacity Mosswool® reduces water usage compared to stone wool.

Novarbo and Biolan are actively developing also other high-value sphagnum moss-based products. Novarbo MossCube is a sustainable propagation cube for vegetable seedling production. Biolan Moss Pellets are limed and fertilised substrates for germination of seeds for consumers.

***Keywords***: *Sphagnum moss, sustainable moss harvesting, hydroponics, growing medium, paludiculture*

## INTRODUCTION

Biolan Group of companies (Biolan Oy, EcoMoss Oy and Novarbo Oy) have developed a sustainable sphagnum moss harvesting, utilisation and high value product manufacturing value chain.

Biolan Oy (www.biolan.fi) is a Finnish family business specialising in developing, manufacturing and marketingproducts that help reduce the environmental impact of daily human activities. Biolan manufactures and sells products for ecological gardening as well as environmental products. Biolan has its own production facilities in Finland, Estonia and China.

Novarbo Oy (www.novarbo.fi) is a daughter company of Biolan founded in 2010. Currently Novarbo's main products are peat moss -based growth substrates for professional cultivation. Peat has traditionally been the most commonly used substrate in greenhouse cultivation. However, greenhouse cultivation is undergoing a transition from soil-based cultivation to hydroponic cultivation. Hydroponics means growing plants without soil in a liquid or soilless media with mineral nutrient solution addition. Novarbo has identified already a long time ago sphagnummoss as a potential raw material, but the economical and eco-friendly method to harvest moss and suitable production technology for growing media was until now lacking for us.

EcoMoss Oy is another daughter company of Biolan. After 10 years of development, EcoMoss Oy has commercialised a new Light Sphagnum Removal technique (LSR) preserving the ecological and hydrological balance of bogs. EcoMoss supplies sphagnum moss for Novarbo and Biolan for their high value products such asMosswool®, MossCube and Moss Pellets.

The purpose of this paper is to demonstrate how sphagnum moss can be sustainable harvested and utilised for highvalue product manufacturing by Biolan Group of companies.

## MATERIALS AND METHODS

In this paper we go through the whole sphagnum moss value chain from bog biomass to high value end products.

We demonstrate the new Light Sphagnum Removal technique (LSR technique) that skims only a top layer ofmoss.

We compare renewable and compostable Mosswool® hydroponic cultivation slab manufacturing and recycling tonon-renewable stone wool. We have analysed the needed recycling steps for both materials.

National Resources Institute Finland (Luke) has done a life-cycle analysis (LCA) study of Mosswool®. The $CO2$ climate impact was calculated for Mosswool®, and the results were compared to peat, stone wool and coir.

Luke also calculated Mosswool® water footprint with AWARE-methodology, which takes into account differences on water resources in different countries. Manufacturing process, packaging and water savings when irrigating cucumbers were included in the study.

Novarbo and Luke have performed growing tests for Mosswool® slabs with cucumber and tomato and we presentthe results of these tests.

## RESULTS

After 10 years of development EcoMoss Oy commercialised in 2014 a new Light Sphagnum Removal technique(LSR technique) that skims only a top layer of moss. In Finland bogs have been exploited in peat extraction thattypically requires cutting 2 meters long/deep/wide drainage channels prior to full removal of the peat bog resulting irreparable ruin of the ecosystem. Top layer moss harvesting (instead of deep peat extraction) revolutionises the use of bogs in a fully sustainable way.

The LSR technique is based on special equipment that extracts only a partial layer of the living moss, squeezes out 30% of water in moss upon harvesting and returns this water back to the bog ecosystem. The reduction of water content also reduces the transportation and storage costs. The LSR technique has been developed for over10 years in order to achieve economical and ecological method to harvest moss.

After LSR harvesting, the bogs return to their former moss state within a few years. Statistically significant effects on watercourses have not been observed[2]. Bog landscapes after our sustainable LSR harvesting are shownin Figure 1. After 1 year cotton grass and sphagnum moss have already started to spread back (Figure 1B), and after 2 years regeneration has been further accelerated (Figure 1C).

Figure 1. LSR moss harvesting (A) and bog landscapes 1 year (B) and 2 years (C) after harvesting.

The LSR moss harvesting technique is based on a timber forwarder combined with a clamshell grapple. From the grapple moss is guided to a press line and subsequently to an exchange container. The local logistics is done with a crawler dumper, which transports the container from the bog to the roadside. Special emphasis has been put on minimising the surface pressure on the bog. Only the top layer of living moss is extracted at maximum 25cm depth, thus ensuring regrowth of living moss, preserving deeper layers and ensuring water balance. A pictureof the moss harvesting equipment and harvesting depth is shown in Figure 2.

Figure 2. EcoMoss LSR moss harvester on the left and harvesting depth described on the right. The clamshell grapple extracts only the top layer at maximum 25 cm depth ensuring regrowth of living moss, preserving deeperlayers and ensuring water balance.

Technical Research Centre of Finland (VTT) and Natural Resources Institute Finland (Luke) have developed theoriginal proof of concept (at laboratory scale) and patented the method to produce porous media from moss.

This technology was transferred exclusively to Novarbo (under license). Novarbo scaled-up the technology to aMosswool® mass-production stage with a grant from the EU Horizon 2020 programme in 2017-19. Novarbo's Mosswool® slabs (Figure 3) are used in hydroponic cultivation as a drop-in sustainable replacement for stone wool.

Figure 3. Mosswool® slabs are used as a drop-in sustainable replacement for stone wool growing media in hydroponic cultivation.

Main benefits of Mosswool® are renewable and compostable raw materials (Figure 4).

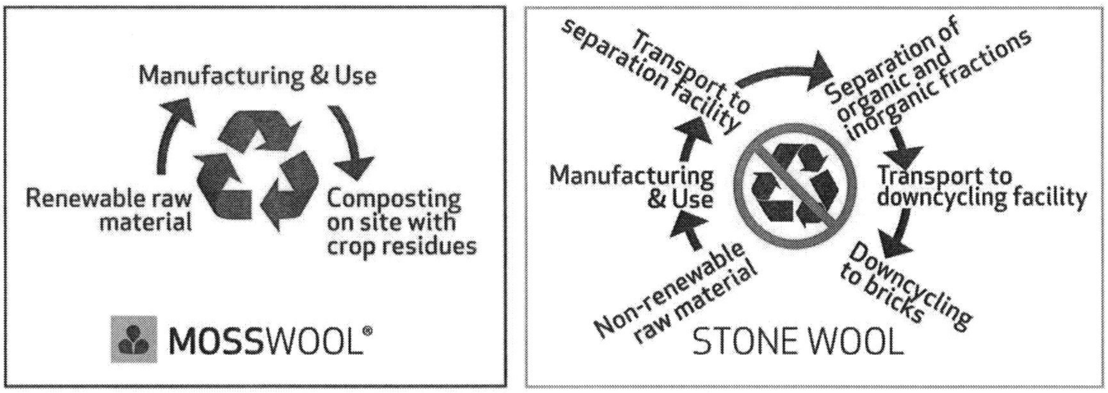


Figure 4. Mosswool® main benefits compared to stone wool are rapidly renewable raw material and compostability on site with normal greenhouse crop residues.

Novarbo and Luke have performed growing tests for Mosswool® slabs with cucumber and/or tomato. Both Novarbo and Luke growing tests show that Mosswool® yielded equal or better results compared to stone wool(Figure 5).

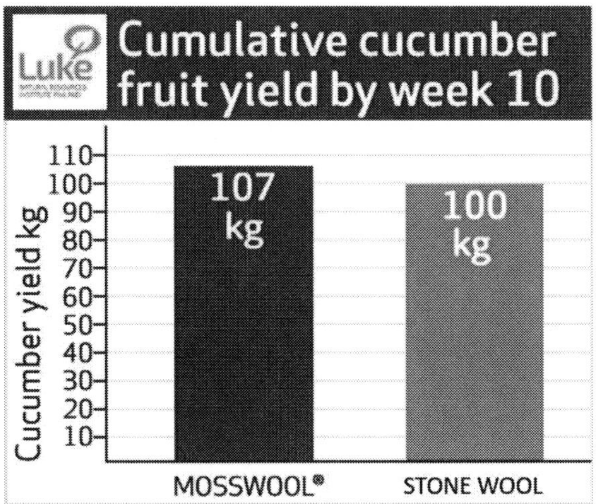


Figure 5. Cumulative cucumber fruit yield for Mosswool® and stone wool at National Resources InstituteFinland (Luke) test.

In addition, Mosswool® has the ability to reserve water, which works as a buffer if there are problems with the irrigation or fertilization. Figure 6 shows a comparison in cucumber roots growth in Mosswool® and stone wool.Roots have grown evenly on all sides of Mosswool® slab due to more even water distribution compared to stonewool, where water runs to the bottom of the slab.

Novarbo's and Luke's growing tests also showed that the main adaptation adjustment for the greenhouse groweris to adjust irrigation interval and length to suit Mosswool's better water reserving capacity compared to stone wool.

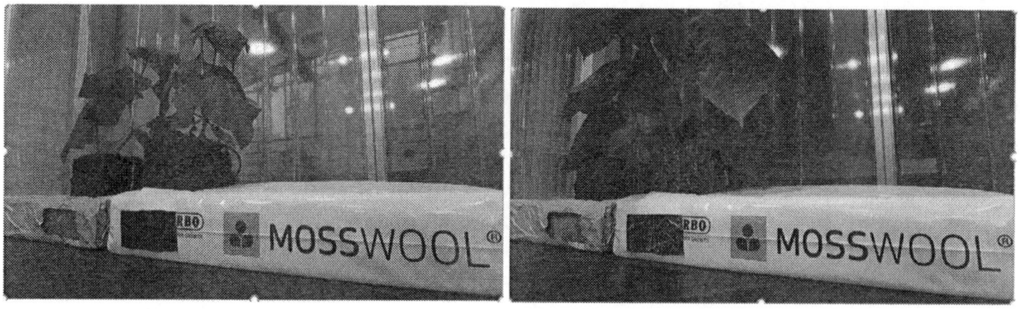


Figure 6. Cucumber roots grow evenly on all sides of Mosswool® slab.

Based on an LCA study by Luke[1], the CO2 climate impact of manufacturing a 14 litre Mosswool® substrate was significantly lower compared to a peat substrate; 2.20 and 3.63 kgCO2-eq., respectively. Mosswool® water footprint was 14 litres per slab calculated with the AWARE method. In use, Mosswool® reduces water usage compared to stone wool, since it withholds water and requires much less over-irrigation than stone wool.

## DISCUSSION

There is a need on the market for sustainable and recyclable growing medias. Hydroponic cultivation is a growing business area both globally and in Europe. At the same time there is an increasing demand for companies to transfer their businesses towards circular economy. At Biolan Group of companies, circular economy has been – and still is – the core essence of our business model since the 1960's. As part of this, webelieve that this trend to replace peat with sustainably harvested moss will continue.

Novarbo and Biolan are actively developing also other high-value sphagnum moss based products. Novarbo MossCube is a sustainable propagation cube for vegetable seedling production. Biolan Moss Pellets are limed andfertilised substrates for germination of seeds for consumers.

## CONCLUSION

We have demonstrated that sphagnum moss can be harvested in a sustainable way to utilise bog biomass. Moss harvesting does not require the establishment of expensive ditching, field preparation or road construction. Bogscan be re-harvested within 20-30 years, which is faster than forests.

We have developed and commercialised high value sphagnum moss hydroponics growth medium Mosswool® as a sustainable and compostable drop-in replacement for the non-biodegradable stone wool growth media for the hydroponic cultivation of vegetable crops.

Based on an LCA study by National Resources Institute Finland (Luke)[1], the CO2 climate impact of manufacturing a 14 litre Mosswool® substrate was significantly lower compared to a peat substrate; 2.20 and

3.63 kgCO2-eq., respectively. Mosswool® water footprint was 14 litres per slab calculated with the AWAREmethod.

Mosswool® stores water evenly and reserves water as a buffer if there are problems with the irrigation cycle orfertilization. With the internal water buffer capacity Mosswool® reduces water usage compared to stone wool.

## ACKNOWLEDGEMENTS

We thank Natural Resources Institute Finland (Luke) for their research.

## REFERENCES

- Natural Resources Institute Finland (Luke) (2019) The carbon and water footprint of Mosswool substrate
- Silvan N, Silvan K, Näkkilä J, Tahvonen R, Reinikainen O. (2012). Renewability, use and properties of Sphagnumbiomass for growing media purposes. *14th International Peat Congress, Stockholm*

ID 62663

# FROM ENERGY TO HORTICULTURE: TRENDS OF PEAT EXTRACTION IN LATVIA

Ingrida KRIGERE

University of Latvia, Faculty of Geography and Earth Sciences, Latvia

*ingrida.krigere@gmail.com*

## SUMMARY

Peat extraction in Latvia has increased from 1960s to 1990ties, when the use of energy peat for energy and agricultural use were rapidly developing. After 1991, peat industry suffered a major decline due to changes in socio-economic system, and gradually shifted to horticulture while the extraction of energy peat dropped. Now, almost all peat is extracted for horticultural use. Compared to other peat producing countries, Latvia was one of the first where peat extraction sector was restructured from energy to horticulture. In 2019, 97% of the extracted peat in Latvia was used for horticulture, 2% for energy, 1% for other purposes. Countries are rapidly reducing their peat extraction for energy use with the aim to reduce GHG emissions and to move towards climate neutrality. Demand for food and ornamental plants is increasing. The industry needs to refocus on horticultural products. As the planet 's population grows, global demand for substrates will increase rapidly. GHG emissions are created during peat extraction and storage. However, the use of peat in horticulture attracts GHG; 6000 tree seedlings can grow from 1m$^3$ of peat, 3 ha of forest can be established with these seedlings, which will absorb 1110 tons of $CO_2$ in 50 years. Probably, the high proportion of energy peat which has until now prevailed in peat producing countries, may also be the reason: 1) for the shortcomings regarding the statistics on foreign trade in goods under the Combined Nomenclature (CN), where peat is considered as an energy product. In result, an incorrect image on the use of peat is developing in international statistics. 2) for the GHG emission accounting methodology set out in the IPCC guidelines and the accepted immediate oxidation of peat (100% oxidation during extraction).

***Keywords**: peat, horticulture, agriculture, energy, growing media*

## INTRODUCTION

Peat is one of the national resources of Latvia, peat resources in the country are reaching 1.5 billion tons. Peat in Latvia is widely used for energy (as a fuel), for agricultural and for horticulture purposes. It was an important part of the national economy during the 20th century. To date, only 4% of all peatland areas in Latvia have been used for peat extraction, because of social, economic and political processes in the period between 1920 and 2020.
Peat became an energy source in Europe during the $12^{th}$ century. It is still used in industrial volumes to generate electricity and heat. Currently, the extraction and use of energy peat is declining due to climate considerations. In result, there is an impression that peat is mainly a component of energy production systems, and that it should be treated as a fuel. Many policy documents both in Latvia and in Europe are based on this assumption, but it has not been taken into account that peat today is an irreplaceable substrate for growing vegetables and ornamental plants, as well as landscaping and forestry. Two different objectives for peat extraction should be clearly defined: peat as an energy source and peat as an essential basis for horticultural development. Both of these require conditions and regulations of their own. Development of such regulations and documents for the peat industry is especially important for Latvia, where 97% of peat is harvested for horticultural needs.
Currently, the peat extraction sector in EU is most affected by the transition to a "green economy" and the introduction of climate change mitigation measures. The EU's Paris Climate Agreement sets a target of at least a 40% reduction from 1990 levels of greenhouse gas (GHG) emissions by 2030. Within the framework of European Green Deal, emissions are set to be reduced by 55% by 2030, and to become completely climate-neutral in 2050.
The peat extraction industry is emission-intensive, and particular attention is paid to the extraction of energy peat. There is a global tendency to discontinue the extraction of peat for the needs of the energy sector and to extract peat only for horticultural purposes and for the production of high value-added products. A lot of countries that have so far mainly extracted peat for energy purposes, have to reorganize and restructure their production.
This study aims to find out how the Latvian peat industry has developed over the last 100 years during the changing social and political conditions.
The study was carried out by collecting and analyzing historical data, focusing on various purposes for peat use, determining factors in the peat industry.

## MATERIALS AND METHODS

The information was collected and compiled using various literature sources, both published and unpublished. The study uses data published in: [1, 2, 3, 4, 5, 6, 7, 8, 9]; data collected by the Central Statistical Bureau for the period from 2000 to 2018 [10], as well as information from the State Geological Fund and materials from Meliorprojekts [11, 12, 13]; the project "Innovation in Peat Research and Development of New Products Containing It"; and the project "Preparation of Recommendations on Latvian Peat Deposit Data Quality for their Improvement and Use in the Preparation of the Basic Documents of the National Strategy"; as well as data from the Latvian Peat Association and data from the International Peatland Society (IPS).

## RESULTS AND DISCUSSION

In total, 9.9% of the territory of Latvia is covered by peatlands, where 11.3 billion m³ or 1.7 billion tons of peat have accumulated [1]. By comparison, peatlands cover about 20% of the total area of Estonia, and 5% of Lithuania [8].
The average accumulation rate over the last 200 years has been about 2mm per year [14]. This allows us to calculate that in the peatlands of Latvia, approximately 1.6 million tons of peat accumulates annually, while an average of 0.81 million tons of peat are being extracted per year (1991-2019). This means that peat resources in the country are increasing by 0.79 million tons per year on average and by approximately 22.91 million tons since 1991.
The origins of peat use in Latvia can be traced back to the 16th century; written evidence reveals its development and use at that time in heating, bedding, dry toilets, product storage, insulation materials and agriculture [15, 16].
Industrial-scale peat extraction started at the beginning of the 20th century for the needs of heating and bedding [17]. In 1912, the establishment of litter peat and litter production companies began, and the cutting of peat for litter production developed [18] In 1918, the Peat Utilisation Board was established, which began to produce peat for energy purposes on a large scale (Figure 1).

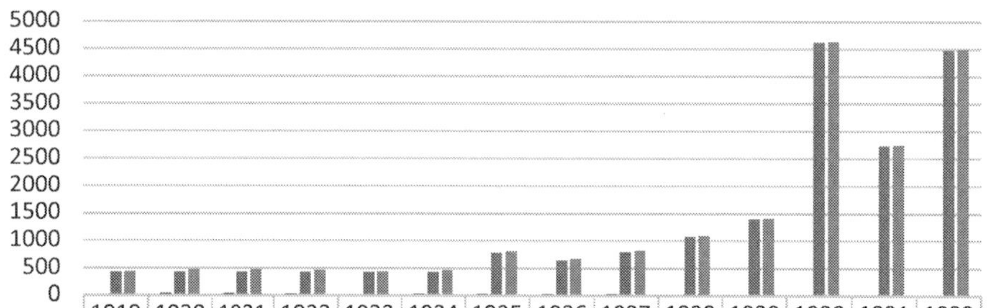


| | 1919 | 1920 | 1921 | 1922 | 1923 | 1924 | 1925 | 1926 | 1927 | 1928 | 1929 | 1930 | 1931 | 1932 |
|---|---|---|---|---|---|---|---|---|---|---|---|---|---|---|
| Energy peat t | 11 | 47 | 40 | 29 | 12 | 26 | 29 | 27 | 26 | 15 | 16 | 20 | 20 | 22 |
| Bedding peat t | 430 | 430 | 430 | 430 | 430 | 430 | 780 | 644 | 792 | 1075 | 1398 | 4616 | 2735 | 4474 |
| Total t | 441 | 477 | 470 | 459 | 442 | 456 | 809 | 671 | 818 | 1090 | 1414 | 4636 | 2755 | 4496 |

■ Energy peat t ■ Bedding peat t ■ Total t

Figure 1. Peat extraction and use in Latvia in the years 1919–1932, tonnes.

Peat extraction at larger volumes began after 1924. At that time, the state was practically the only owner of Latvian mires. It leased mires to companies and private individuals on long-term or annual leases. In the years up to 1940, the most common use for peat was bedding, with fuel peat in second place [19].
Peat extraction volumes grew in particular in the period from 1960 to 1990, when demand for energy peat and agricultural peat increased significantly (Figure 2). In 1958, a peat-fired thermo power plant TEC-1 was built in Rīga. To ensure its operation, peat extraction developed rapidly, and several peat factories were constructed. In the early 1960s, the extraction of agricultural peat for bedding and fertilizer also increased. By the 1970s, peat extraction was taking place in more than 100 deposits. Around 4.9 mln. tons of peat were extracted annually, and used for bedding, compost and as fuel.
The Latvian peat extraction industry experienced a sharp decline in 1991, when the largest peat consumers, state farms and collective farms were gradually eliminated. The state structure changed, and peat companies were privatized. In the late 1990s, the industry began to restructure and switch to peat extraction for horticultural purposes. During this time, many

foreign investors came to Latvia, they had experience in trading horticultural peat and had outlets to sell it at, as well as the opportunity to invest, and to start extracting and processing agricultural peat.

In 1993, volumes of extracted peat started to increase, and export of peat developed, exceeding domestic consumption by 2003.

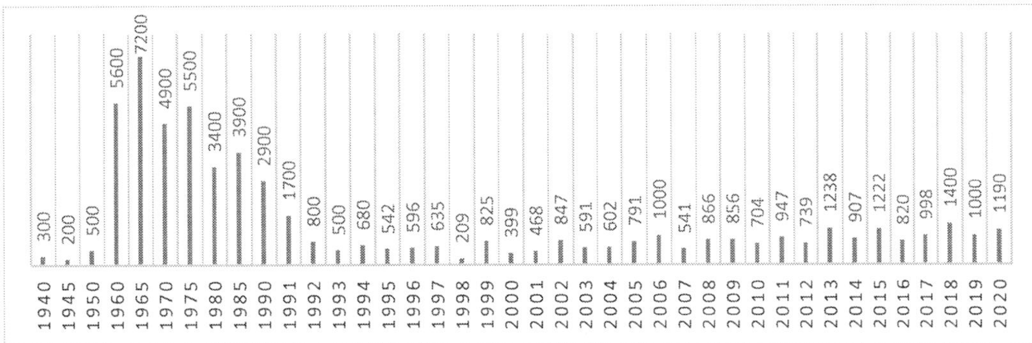


Figure 2. Amounts of peat extracted in Latvia from 1940 to 2020, thousand tons per year.

In the last 20 years, the industry has stabilized, and now ups and downs in peat extraction depend mainly on weather conditions and the amount of precipitation in the peat extraction season. The use of peat for energy experienced a dramatic decline in 2003, due to TEC-1 no longer using peat. Since 1998, peat extracted in Latvia was almost exclusively used for horticultural purposes. (Figure 3).

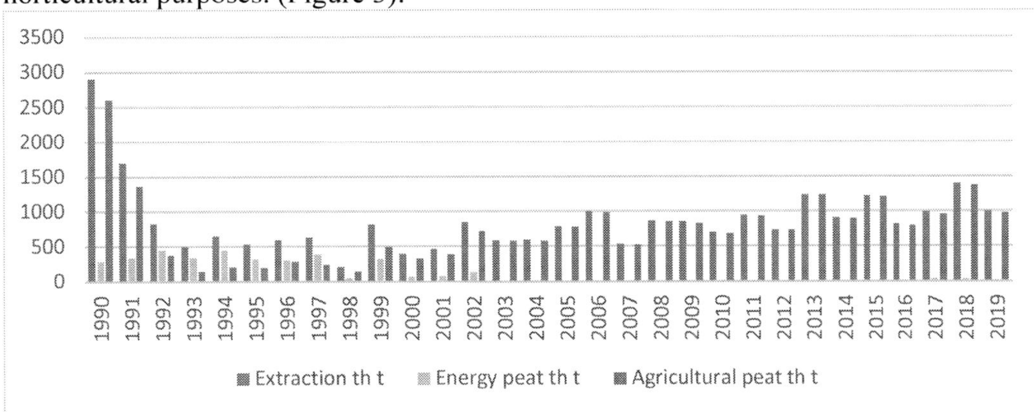


Figure 3. Volumes of peat extraction and types of use from 1990 to 2019, thousand tons.

Along with the reorientation of the industry, the market for peat consumption also changed. Until 1991, the extracted peat was used in the local market. After 1993, the export market started to develop. Starting from 2000, more than 90% of the peat resources extracted in Latvia were exported (Figure 4).

From 2003, export volumes started to increase, indicating an increase in the production of growing media. Statistics on exports comprise all peat products, including pure raw materials and various peat products. Latvia, in contrast with other peat-extracting countries, was the first to restructure its peat extraction industry from energy peat extraction to horticultural peat extraction.

According to data from the IPS, in 2017, 55% of peat extracted in the European Union was used for energy production, 37% for horticulture and 8% for other purposes. In Latvia in 2017, 95% of peat obtained was used for horticulture purposes, 4% for energy production and

1% for other needs. The situation is changing and it is expected that more than half of the peat extracted in the EU in 2019 will be used for horticulture.

The historical situation is favourable for Latvia's peat extraction sector, as the prevailing global trend in reducing GHG emissions directly affects the use of peat for energy purposes. According to the energy Regulations of the European Union, peat is considered a fossil resource. Consequently, in order to move towards climate neutrality and mitigate climate change, countries stipulate that the extraction and use of peat for energy must be reduced and gradually stopped. This has a major impact on peat-producing countries where the main use of peat is for energy.

Latvia is the most favourably situated peat-producing country, due to the reorientation of its industry at the very beginning of this century. Now we only extract horticultural peat, which is used for growing food, ornamental plants etc. GHG emissions also result from this kind of peat use; however, the cultivation of plants in peat substrates (peat-growing media) later results in the capture of GHG emissions. For example, 6,000 pine tree seedlings can be grown in 1 m³ of peat; with this three hectares of pine forest can be planted, and this in turn will capture 1110 t of CO2 in 50 years.

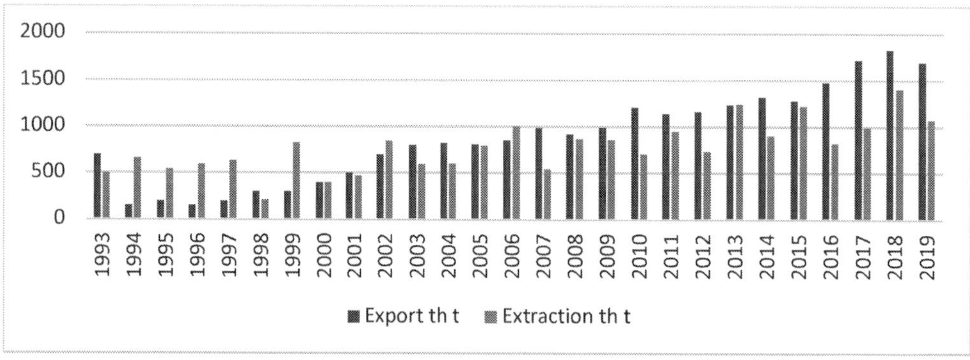


Figure 4. Peat extraction volume and export of peat products 1993-2018, thousand tonnes.

The large volumes of energy peat, which so far dominated in peat-extracting countries, may be the reason for shortcomings in statistical accounting, which have had and might continue to have consequences for European Union member states, as well as for the regulations of the EU and international regulations. In particular, this affects climate policy documents, where peat currently is considered primarily as an energy resource.

In the statistics on external trade in goods, within the meaning of the Combined Nomenclature (hereinafter – CN), peat is considered to be an energy product ("Chapter 27. Mineral Fuels, Mineral Oils and Products of Their Distillation; Bituminous Substances; Mineral Waxes", code 2703). In the description of the CN, peat is mentioned alongside coal products. There is no other place for peat and peat products (substrates) in this nomenclature, so for companies exporting peat and peat substrates, this is the only way to report these exports. Currently, Latvian, EU and international statistics are misleading about the use of peat. Consequently, the goal of introducing the CN – to provide internationally comparable statistics on foreign trade – is not being fulfilled.

For the implementation of Latvia's National Peat Strategy, the "Guidelines for the Sustainable Use of Peat 2020-2030" (Cabinet Regulation No. 696) were adopted in November 2020. This is the first sustainable planning document for peat in Latvia. The guidelines cover comprehensively the use of peat – the management and use of resources in a way and to an extent that preserves their potential to maintain environmental, economic and social functions at local, national and global levels, now and in the future, and does not pose a threat to other ecosystems.

## CONCLUSION

Political, economic and ideological factors have affected the development of the peat extraction industry in Latvia. Extraction objectives in Latvia have changed several times, and unlike in other European countries, the use of peat for energy played a key role in Latvia only for 30 years (1960-1990).

The peat industry in Latvia has been influenced by various kinds of peat use: the development of bedding peat, its use as fuel for home heating, its use as a fuel for TEC-1 power plant and its use in horticulture.

Determining factors in the peat industry in Latvia:

Political factors – establishment of the peat industry before the First World War, Latvia's first period of independence, the period of Soviet occupation, Latvia's second period of independence (starting in 1991), foreign investors. Social factors – the development of workers' skills and the development of technique.

For the last 19 years, peat has been extracted in Latvia primarily for horticultural needs (97%) and not for energy production. Thus, the Latvian peat extraction industry has already been restructured, and it significantly better than other countries can meet the climate requirements.

The high consumption of peat for energy use in the European Union has determined the political attitude towards peat resources. In the energy sector, it is classified in the category of fossil resources. There should be different approaches and regulatory frameworks for horticultural and for energy peat.

The structure of the peat market has changed over time. Until the end of the 20th century, peat was used for domestic consumption in Latvia, but since the beginning of the 21st century it has generally been exported. Currently, 93% of peat extracted in Latvia is exported. Peat products are an important part of Latvia's exports and make up 1.44% of the country's total export volume (in 2018) [10].

Currently, climate and nature conservation aspects are the main factors influencing peat extraction. Starting from 2026, countries will be required to report GHG emissions from economically used wetlands. In order to maintain the sustainability of peat extraction, compensatory measures in the field of GHG emissions must be developed for the industry. Scientific research is needed to create peat products with higher added value, thus making a greater contribution to the national economy per tons of GHG emissions created by peat extraction. In Latvia, only the export of processed peat should be promoted, and favorable conditions for local consumption should be created. At a national level, measurements of GHG emissions and research must be continued, in order to find the most efficient and emission-friendly way of peat resource management.

The Peat Guidelines, which are a policy planning document in Latvia, stipulate that peat extraction areas and peat volumes available for extraction must be maintained at the existing volumes until 2030. This ensures the predictability of the peat extraction industry, as well as the desire to invest in the establishment of production facilities, resulting in the creation of added value to peat, and more efficient resource management. At the current extraction volumes, peat resources in the country are not decreasing, because the average growth of peat in ten years' time is higher than the extraction volume. Protected nature areas must be maintained at the current level.

In the near future, peat industry may be affected by the creation of a new European framework for peat extraction, GHG emissions taxation, Taxonomy Regulation, or similar.

# REFERENCES


1. Latvijas valsts meliorācijas un projektēšanas institūts, 1980. Latvijas PSR kūdras fonds uz 1980. gada 1. janvāri (Latvian Peat Fund on 01.01.1980, *in Latvian).* Rīga, 1980., 716
2. Свиклис Л. (1970). Торфяная промышленность Латвийской ССР (Peat sector in Latvian SSR, *in Russian*), Рига, Латвийский республиканский институт научно технологической информации и пропаганды 7-21
3. Grosvalds I. (1970). Latvijas dzīļu bagātības (Riches of Latvian subterranean depths, *in Latvian*), Izdevniecība "Zinātne", Rīga, 123-125
4. Brakšs N. (1961). Purvi un kūdra (Mires ad peat, *in Latvian*). LPSR ZA izdevniecība, Rīga. 59-61
5. Eiduks J, Kalniņš M. (1961). Latvijas PSR derīgie izrakteņi un to izmantošana (Minerals of Latvian SSR and their use, *in Latvian*), Latvijas valsts izdevniecība, Rīga, 398-404
6. Clarke D., H.Josten. W wise use of mires and peatlands, (2002), International Mire Conservation Group and International Peat Society, Saarijerven Offiset Oy, Finland 45-65
7. Karnups. J. P., (2016) Kūdra Latvijā 1918.-1940. gadā (Peat in Latvia, 1918 – 1940, *in Latvian*). Akadēmiskā dzīve nr. 52. Akadēmiskās Dzīves Tēvzemes apgāds, Latvijas Universitāte, Rīga, 43.–50
8. Lappalainen, E. (ed.), 1997. Global peat resources. Finland: International Peat Society, Geological Survey of Finland, Saarijerven Offiset Oy, Finland 359
9. Korhonen R., Korpela L., Sarkkola S.(eds) (2008). Finland – Fenland, research and sustainable utilisation of mires and peat, Finnish Peatland Society, Finland, Maahenki Ltd 176-195
10. CSB 2020, Centrālās statistikas birojs. Tirdzniecība. (Trades, *in Latvian*) https://data1.csb.gov.lv/pxweb/lv/atirdz/atirdz__detalizeta__4zim/?tablelist=true&rxid=81da855b-f173-49db-9ad9-caaa04ab1d5c (05.04.2020)

9. LVĢMC Zemes dzīļu resursi. Kūdra. (Resources of subterrain depths, Peat, *in Latvian*) https://www.meteo.lv/lapas/geologija/zemes-dzilu-resursi/derigie-izrakteni-buvmaterialu-izejvielas-kudra-un-sapropelis-/kudra/kudra?id=1242&nid=594 (05.04.2020)
10. LVĢMC Ģeoloģija, derīgo izrakteņu krājumi (Geology, Mineral resources, *in Latvian*).
11. https://www.meteo.lv/lapas/geologija/derigo-izraktenu-atradnu-registrs/derigo-izraktenu-krajumu-bilance/derigo-izraktenu-krajumu-bilance?id=1472&nid=659 (05.04.2020)
12. Stivrins N., Ozola I., Gałka M., Kuske E., Alliksaar T., Andersen T. J., Lamentowicz M., Wulf S., Reitalu T. 2017. Drivers of peat accumulation rate in a raised bog: impact of drainage, climate, and local vegetation composition. Mires and peat, 19.
13. Šnore, A. 2013. Peat extraction. Nordik, Rīga, 452
14. Ozola, I., 2016. Kūdras ieguves un izmantošanas ekonomiskie un sociālekonomiskie aspekti (Economic and socioeconomic aspects of peat extraction and use, *in Latvian*). Akadēmiskā dzīve Nr. 52. LU, Rīga, 51.– 64.
15. Lācis, A. 2010. Purvu apzināšana un izpēte Latvijā, pielietotās metodes un sasniegtie rezultāti (Identification and research of mires in Latvia, methods and results, *in Latvian*). Latvijas universitātes raksti, zemes un vides zinātnes. 752. sēj. LU, Rīga, 106–115
16. Druvietis R. (1957). Kūdras pakaiši (Peat litter, *in Latvian)*, Latvijas valsts izdevniecība, Rīga, 5-9
17. Greste J. (1948). Latvijas PSR derīgie izrakteņi (Minerals of Latvian SSR, *in Latvian*), Latvijas valsts izdevniecība, Rīga, 53-56

# ID 62698

# SUSTAINABLE PEAT INDUSTRY (?)

*Jan Köbbing, Bert von Seggern, Sjanie Hindenberg

Klasmann-Deilmann GmbH, Germany

*jan.koebbing@klasmann-deilmann.com*

Even though there are still different opinions, peat is increasingly being classified as a fossil raw material on a social and political level. In view of the clear commitment of the international community, stated in the Paris agreement, to reduce carbon dioxide emissions to zero, peat extraction and use must be stopped until 2050. A peat ban is therefore being called for in many countries and even at European level. At the same time, the global population is growing and with it the demand for substrates for the use in commercial horticulture – especially for the growing of vegetables.

What does this mean for peat and substrate producers and the main peat-producing countries? The transformation to a $CO_2$-free economy contains both risks and opportunities for the industry.

How can a producer of growing operate sustainably? Klasmann-Deilmann has set the following course for the future:

- Increase the proportion of alternative raw materials to 15% by 2020 and 30% by 2025
- Major investments in research and development of new growing media constituents and propagation systems
- Strong commitment to bog restoration and research for further improvement (Sphagnum restoration)
- Certification of the peat resources used according to the Responsible Produced Peat (RPP) scheme, to minimize ecological impact

ID 63094

# CONCEPT OF ROBOTIC PEAT EXTRACTION

*Riho Kägo[1,2], Priit Vellak[2], Elar Abram[3], Bert Ruiters[4], Edgar Karofeld[5], Mart Noorma[2,6], Jüri Olt[1]

[1]Estonian University of Life Sciences, Institute of Technology, Tartu, Estonia
[2]Milrem Robotics, Estonia
[3]Kraver AS, Estonia
[4]Jiffy International, Netherlands
[5]Institute of Ecology and Earth Sciences, University of Tartu, Estonia
[6]Tartu Observatory, University of Tartu, Tõravere, Estonia

*riho.kago@emu.ee*

**SUMMARY**

In this article a concept for the extraction of milled peat based on centrally controlled unmanned ground vehicles (UGV) is presented. The concept is based on the replacement of traditional tractors with UGV-s with the objective to reduce operational costs in terms of human labour, fuel consumption and ecological footprint. A robotic system architecture has been developed and validated based on the comparative analysis with the following steps:

1) peat fields with surface areas of 140 ha and 280 ha were selected as bases for the case study;
2) Milrem Multiscope, a 1.6-ton diesel-electric semi-autonomous UGV was used to present the robotic system;
3) the robotic system was characterised during a field measurement campaign on the peat fields;
4) the collected data was analysed to compere the life-cycle operating costs of a traditional and robotic peat extraction processes.

As the result, it is demonstrated that by using currently available robotic technology for milled peat extraction, either with the Haku method or the vacuum harvester method can reduce production-related human work-hours by 34-43% and fuel consumption by 21-26% with respective reduction of $CO_2$ emissions. Further advancements of UGV technology will increase the positive impact of robotic technology in the future through reduction of required human intervention as well as using green energy in fully-electric UGV-s.

***Keywords***: *automation, autonomy, peat extraction, robotic and autonomous systems, unmanned ground vehicle*

## INTRODUCTION

As peat extraction costs today depend on the costs of conventional diesel-engine tractors carrying out all operations on standardised peat fields (Pakere & Blumberga, 2017), the only option to address the reduction of the peat extraction costs must challenge the limits of the diesel-tractor fleet. Most of the attempts to reduce the costs of the diesel-tractor fleet have resulted in successful but nevertheless incremental improvements, e.g. employment of algorithms to improve the performance of the tractor fleet (Johnson, Naffin, Puhalla, Sanchez, & Wellington, 2009; John Deere, 2017; John Deere, 2018). A feasible alternative to incremental improvements in the cost-effectiveness of the tractor fleet would mean introduction of the UGV fleet. The aim is not to alter the technical characteristics of the established tractor fleet but usher in cost-reducing changes to the architecture of the peat extraction process.

Depending on the weather (Gregow, Lehtonen, Pirinen, Venäläinen, Vajda, & Koskiniemi, 2019), the summer extraction season can last for about four-five months. For every 1000 ha of peat field a fleet of 25 tractors with at least one human operator per tractor is needed (Alakangas, Hölttä, Juntunen, & Vesisenaho, 2012; Ministry of Peat Industry of the RSFSR, 1986). Outside the extraction season, also in the case of unfavourable weather, the need for operators can be reduced by a half. As it is challenging to sufficiently cover the need for qualified seasonal operators, peat producers have to accept the costs of keeping their teams over the winter. Besides, the shortage of manpower keeps constantly growing (Baltic Peat Producers Conference, 2018). Furthermore, the diesel-tractors are often over-dimensioned and consume large quantities of fuel, making the extraction process harmful for the environment (Casals, Martinez-Laserna, Garcia, & Nieto, 2016; He, Li, Fang, deVoil, & Cao, 2019).

To sum it up, the authors of this article identify three major problems regarding the current state of milled peat extraction:

1) The labour problem.
2) The machine and the fuel efficiency problems.
3) The extraction environmental footprint problem.

In this paper all these problems are addressed by the proposal of a novel concept for the milled peat extraction based on centrally controlled UGV-s.

## MATERIALS AND METHODS

Depending on various factors (quality of the peat, extraction area size, etc.), the extraction of milled peat can be carried out differently (Alakangas, Hölttä, Juntunen, & Vesisenaho, 2012):

1) re-ridging (Peco) method;
2) conveyer belt (Haku) method;
3) mechanical harvesting method;
4) vacuum harvesting method.

By now, this system is entirely based on diesel-engine tractors. Since all methods are based on milling and harrowing of the peat fields, it is rational to automate these two operations first. This extraction system will partially base both on diesel-engine tractors and on centrally controlled UGV-s. This system is the subject of this article and is discussed in more detail. Once the concept is validated, the complexity of the extraction system can be increased by automating all the operations. In addition, in temperate regions, with the respective infrastructure (solar station and charging docks) solar energy can be harvested for powering the extraction system (Redpath, McILveen-Wright, Kattakayam, Hewitt, Karlowski, & Bardi, 2011). However, the peat extraction system architecture which is entirely based on UGV-s is not in the scope of this study and is not discussed further.

The robotic milled peat extraction solution consists of these building blocks:

1) Central Control System (CCS);
2) communication network;
3) UGV platform (or the UGV fleet);
4) digital twin;
5) fleet maintenance;
6) fleet logistics.

The fleet of UGV-s can be monitored (Gené-Mola, et al., 2020) and controlled by the fleet operator from a central control station by using the CCS. The central control station can be a stationary or a mobile workstation. Outgoing and incoming data is transmitted in two ways: a) directly (LOS) or b) indirectly (BLOS) using the communication network. GNSS/RTK/DGNSS is used for the positioning of the fleet (Valente, Momin, Grift, & Hansen, 2020; Kelc, Stajnko, Berk, Rakun, Vindiš, & Lakota, 2019). In case of an emergency and in cases where single UGV-s have to be operated directly, manual remote control can be used. The production and fleet data can be collected and stored as a digital twin (Qi, et al., 2019), whereas the data can be used by the production management executives for further decision-making. The system also consists of a maintenance component which includes a workshop for servicing the machines. The transportation of the UGV-s is carried out by the logistics component.

For current and future UGV applications, the Multiscope (Figure 1) by the Estonian UGV-manufacturer Milrem Robotics can be used (Milrem, 2019). The platform consists of two crawler modules which are mechanically and electrically connected to each other. Due to the tracks, the UGV has excellent properties for moving in wetlands. The Multiscope UGV is capable of ascending-descending gradients of up to 60% and driving sideways along the gradients of up to 30%. It has a low specific ground-pressure: 0.17 kgf $cm^{-2}$ with full load—which is less than one third of the specific ground-pressure exerted by the foot of a human. The UGV has a turning radius of 0 m, i.e. the machine can turn itself on the spot. The UGV has net weight of 1630 kg and payload capacity of 1200 kg. The maximum traction force is, depending on the ground, in the order of 21 kN. The UGV is powered by electric motors (2 x19 kW). The vehicle can be controlled manually via VLOS (Visual Line of Sight) or BVLOS (Beyond Visual Line of Sight).

Figure 1. The unmanned ground vehicle Multiscope by Milrem Robotics towing a harrower.

The assessment of possible resource savings (fuel, human resources, operating costs, $CO_2$) is based on a validated case study. The analysis is based on the comparison of milled peat extraction using diesel-engine tractors and centrally controlled UGV-s by the fleet's seasonal

a) volumetric fuel consumption;
b) human work-hours;
c) purchase price of fuel;
d) average salaries in Estonia and in Canada.

Canada is selected for the comparison because it is one of the world's leading producers of milled peat. The objects under study are peat fields with surface areas of 140 and 280 hectares.

First the size of the fleet is determined for two different extraction methods—for the Haku method and for the vacuum harvester method. The number of towing vehicles is derived from the extraction capacities of the peat extraction implements (Alakangas, 1995; Alakangas, Hölttä, Juntunen, & Vesisenaho, 2012).

Depending on the size of the fleet, the method of extraction and the country of origin, both volumetric fuel consumption and human work hours with fuel and labour costs for one extraction season are determined. According to the amount of fuel used, it is possible to evaluate $CO_2$ emissions.

## RESULTS

Depending on the extraction surface area, the size of the extraction fleet and on the method of extraction, the fuel consumption and human work hours for one season can be determined (Table 1). The calculations were carried out for two different extraction areas that take into account the purchase price of fuel and the average salaries for Estonia and Canada.

Table 1. Volumetric fuel consumption and human work-hours for the Haku method and the vacuum harvester method for peat fields with surface areas of 140 and 280 hectares. The values in parentheses represent the changes when comparing traditional tractor-based extraction with the extraction based on centrally controlled UGV-s.

| | **Haku method (milling, harrowing, ridging, harvesting)** | | | | **Vacuum harvester method (milling, harrowing, vacuuming)** | | | |
|---|---|---|---|---|---|---|---|---|
| | Field surface area $S$ = 140 ha | | Field surface area $S$ = 280 ha | | Field surface area $S$ = 140 ha | | Field surface area $S$ = 280 ha | |
| | Tractors | UGV-s | Tractors | UGV-s | Tractors | UGV-s | Tractors | UGV-s |
| Fuel consumption (kL) | 44.8 ± 5 | 33.3 ± 3 (-26%) | 70.4 ± 8 | 53.1 ± 5 (-25%) | 51.2 ± 6 | 39.7 ± 4 (-23%) | 83.2 ± 9 | 65.9 ± 6 (-21%) |
| Human work-hours (kh) | 15.0 ± 0.7 | 9.2 ± 0.3 (-39%) | 23.6 ± 0.7 | 13.5 ± 0.3 (-43%) | 17.2 ± 0.5 | 11.3 ± 0.3 (-34%) | 27.8 ± 0.8 | 17.8 ± 0.5 (-36%) |

The business impact is derived from the most notable operating costs of the peat industry: the fuel and labour costs (Pakere & Blumberga, 2017). Table 2 shows the difference in fuel and labour costs between a) the system under development and b) the currently available system—for the Haku method (milling, harrowing, ridging, and harvesting) and for the vacuum harvesting method (milling, harrowing, and vacuuming).

Table 2. Fuel and labour costs for one extraction season (18 weeks) for peat fields with surface areas of 140 and 280 hectares. The calculations take into account the purchase price of fuel and the average salaries for Estonia and Canada (as of 01.10.2019). The values in parentheses represent the change in costs when comparing traditional tractor-based extraction with the extraction based on centrally controlled UGV-s.

| | **Haku method (milling, harrowing, ridging, harvesting)** | | | | **Vacuum harvester method (milling, harrowing, vacuuming)** | | | |
|---|---|---|---|---|---|---|---|---|
| | Field surface area $S = 140$ ha | | Field surface area $S = 280$ ha | | Field surface area $S = 140$ ha | | Field surface area $S = 280$ ha | |
| | Tractors | UGV-s | Tractors | UGV-s | Tractors | UGV-s | Tractors | UGV-s |
| Fuel costs (Estonia) (k€) | 58 ± 7 | 43 ± 5 (-26%) | 92 ± 11 | 69 ± 7 (-25%) | 67 ± 8 | 52 ± 5 (-22%) | 108 ± 13 | 86 ± 9 (-20%) |
| Fuel costs (Canada) (k€) | 36 ± 4 | 27 ± 3 (-25%) | 56 ± 7 | 42 ± 4 (-25%) | 41 ± 5 | 32 ± 3 (-22%) | 67 ± 8 | 53 ± 5 (-21%) |
| Labour costs (Estonia) (k€) | 148 ± 10 | 96 ± 5 (-35%) | 232 ± 16 | 138 ± 8 (-40%) | 169 ± 11 | 117 ± 6 (-31%) | 273 ± 18 | 180 ± 10 (-34%) |
| Labour costs (Canada) (k€) | 256 ± 19 | 181 ± 9 (-29%) | 403 ± 30 | 254 ± 15 (-37%) | 293 ± 22 | 218 ± 12 (-26%) | 476 ± 36 | 328 ± 20 (-31%) |

The environmental impact can be evaluated through the reduced $CO_2$ emissions. In Table 3 a comparison of $CO_2$ emissions between the robotic milled peat extraction system with the current milled peat extraction system is given. As expected, as the fuel consumption of the fleet is reduced the $CO_2$ emissions decrease respectively.

Table 3. $CO_2$ emissions for one extraction season (18 weeks) for peat fields with surface areas of 140 and 280 hectares. The values in parentheses represent the change in fleet $CO_2$ emissions when comparing traditional tractor-based extraction with the extraction based on centrally controlled UGV-s.

| | **Haku method (milling, harrowing, ridging, harvesting)** | | | | **Vacuum harvester method (milling, harrowing, vacuuming)** | | | |
|---|---|---|---|---|---|---|---|---|
| | Field surface area $S = 140$ ha | | Field surface area $S = 280$ ha | | Field surface area $S = 140$ ha | | Field surface area $S = 280$ ha | |
| | Tractors | UGV-s | Tractors | UGV-s | Tractors | UGV-s | Tractors | UGV-s |
| Fleet size | 7 | 9 | 11 | 14 | 8 | 9 | 13 | 15 |
| $CO_2$ emissions (tonne) | 119 ± 15 | 88 ± 9 (-26%) | 186 ± 23 | 140 ± 14 (-25%) | 136 ± 17 | 105 ± 11 (-23%) | 222 ± 27 | 174 ± 18 (-21%) |

## DISCUSSION

Table 1 displays the difference in fuel consumption and in human work hours between a) the proposed system and b) the currently available system—for the Haku method (milling, harrowing, ridging, and harvesting) and for the vacuum harvesting method (milling, harrowing, and vacuuming). Based on the calculated data, it can be deduced that a reduction in fuel consumption and in human work hours can be expected. This is due to a) the lower specific fuel consumption of the UGV-s and b) the reduced need for labour to operate the fleet.

When taking into account the seasonal fuel and labour costs and the initial purchase cost of machinery, the yearly accumulating operational costs can be analysed. By doing this, the payback period for a milled peat extraction system that utilises centrally controlled UGV-s can be determined.

## CONCLUSION

The continuous advances of computer-assisted autonomy and unmanned ground vehicles have made it possible to take advantage of these developments for large-scale production. In this article, such possible developments were discussed in the context on using centrally controlled UGV-s for the extraction of milled peat.

Based on a validated case study, the main results found by this article are:

When comparing milled peat extraction that uses conventional tractors with milled peat extraction that uses centrally controlled UGV-s,

1) the fuel consumption and costs are noticeably lower by using UGV-s;
2) the human work-hours and labour costs are noticeably lower by using UGV-s;
3) the emissions of $CO_2$ are noticeably lower by using UGV-s.

Based on the case-study assessment, it can be noted that the robotic milled peat extraction system has a potential to be economically viable whereas at the same time being environmentally sustainable.

Rising from the results it becomes self-evident that further development efforts are justified and needed, such as:

1) robotic milled peat extraction system requirement analysis;
2) technical description of the system architecture and its components;
3) design modification of the current field implements to suit the needs of the proposed UGV solution;
4) system verification and concept validation based on long-term field measurements.

## ACKNOWLEDGEMENTS

The authors of this article would like to acknowledge and thank Mr Paul Elberg, Mr Henri Kuuste, Mr Janek Press and Mr Silver Lätt for their professional contribution.

## REFERENCES


Agriland (2019, January 15). *Fully electric Swiss tractor is now a reality.* Retrieved February 28, 2019, from https://www.agriland.ie/farming-news/fully-electric-swiss-tractor-is-now-a-reality/

Alakangas, E. (1995). *Bioenergy Research Programme, Yearbook 1995.* Technical Report, Vapo OY, Jyvaeskylae, Finland.

Alakangas, E., Hölttä, P., Juntunen, M., & Vesisenaho, T. (2012). *Fuel peat production technology.* Training material, JAMK University of Applied Sciences.

Baltic Peat Producers Conference. (2018). Retrieved 11 30, 2019, from https://balticpeatproducersforum.eu/bppf/bppf-2018

Casals, L. C., Martinez-Laserna, E., Garcia, B. A., & Nieto, N. (2016). Sustainability analysis of the electric vehicle use in Europe for $CO_2$ emissions reduction. *Journal of Cleaner Production, 127*, 425-437.

Gené-Mola, J., Gregorio, E., Cheein, F. A., Guevara, J., Llorens, J., Sanz-Cortiella, R., et al. (2020). Fruit detection, yield prediction and canopy geometric characterization using LiDAR with forced air flow. *Computers and Electronics in Agriculture, 168*: 105121.

Gregow, H., Lehtonen, I., Pirinen, P., Venäläinen, A., Vajda, A., & Koskiniemi, J. (2019). Preparing for peat production seasons in Finland and experimenting with long range impact forecasting. *Climate Services, 14*, 37-50.

He, P., Li, J., Fang, E., deVoil, P., & Cao, G. (2019). Reducing agricultural fuel consumption by minimizing inefficiencies. *Journal of Cleaner Production, 236*, 117619.

John Deere (2017) *Press Release, SIMA awards for innovation.* (2017). Retrieved February 28, 2019, from https://www.deere.co.uk/en/our-company/news-and-media/press-releases/2017/feb/sima-awards-for-innovation.html

John Deere (2018) *John Deere premiers electric tractor in action.* (2018). Retrieved March 1, 2019, from https://www.electrive.com/2018/12/12/video-john-deere-premiers-electric-tractor-in-action/

Johnson, D. A., Naffin, D. J., Puhalla, J. S., Sanchez, J., & Wellington, C. K. (2009). Development and implementation of a team of robotic tractors for autonomous peat moss harvesting. *Journal of Field Robotics, 26*(6-7), 549-571.

Kelc, D., Stajnko, D., Berk, P., Rakun, J., Vindiš, P., & Lakota, M. (2019). Reduction of environmental pollution by using RTK-navigation in soil cultivation. *International Journal of Agricultural and Biological Engineering, 12*(5), 173-178.

Milrem (2019). *Milrem Robotics Multiscope.* Retrieved 11 2019, from https://milremrobotics.com/multiscope

Ministry of Peat Industry of the RSFSR (1986). *Norms of technological design of peat extraction enterprises (Нормы Технологического Проектирования Предприятий По Добыче).* Technical Report.

Pakere, I., & Blumberga, D. (2017). Energy Efficiency Indicators in Peat Extraction Industry –A Case Study. *Energy Procedia, 113*, 143-150.

Qi, Q., Tao, F., Hu, T., Anwer, N., Liu, A., Wei, Y., et al. (2019). Enabling technologies and tools for digital twin. *Journal of Manufacturing Systems.*

Redpath, D. A., McILveen-Wright, D., Kattakayam, T., Hewitt, N., Karlowski, J., & Bardi, U. (2011). Battery powered electric vehicles charged via solar photovoltaic arrays developed for light agricultural duties in remote hilly areas in the Southern Mediterranean region. *Journal of Cleaner Production, 19*(17-18), 2034-2048.

Valente, D., Momin, A., Grift, T., & Hansen, A. (2020). Accuracy and precision evaluation of two low-cost RTK global navigation satellite systems. *Computers and Electronics in Agriculture, 168*, 105142.

# VI PROTECTION AND RECLMATION OF PEATLANDS

IPC 2021

ID 61527

# THE SOUTHERNMOST EDGE-OF-RANGE OF BLANKET BOGS IN EUROPE

*Guaduneth Chico, Ben Clutterbuck, Jillian Labadz, Nicholas G. Midgley

Nottingham Trent University, United Kingdom

*guaduneth.chicoleon@ntu.ac.uk*

Blanket bogs are a rare type of ombrotrophic peatland internationally recognised for long-term terrestrial carbon storage, the potential to serve as carbon sinks and habitat provision. These peatlands are mainly located in areas with an oceanic climate, and in Europe cover large areas of the United Kingdom, Ireland and Norway. Despite being protected under the European Commission Habitats Directive (92/43/ECC), many areas in north Spain are currently not recognised or protected and are exposed to anthropogenic pressures.

This research has developed a protocol to identify potential areas of unmapped blanket bog in the Cantabrian Mountains using climatic data, topography and aerial photography. Ground surveys were undertaken to record peat depth on a 15 m systematic grid across potential areas, and further GIS analyses were used to interpolate peat depth, define hydrological pathways and provide geo-hydromorphological assessment of blanket bogs identified.

Between 2017 and 2019 more than 2,500 peat depth measurements were collected and used to identify 15 currently unrecognised areas of blanket bog. A maximum peat depth of 3.78 m was recorded and the total extent of blanket bog (peat depth >30 cm) mapped covers 64.8 ha containing 555,000 m3 of peat.

The blanket bogs identified in this research represent the southernmost edge-of-range for this habitat in Europe and are also important nationally as these areas represent 10.5% of blanket bog currently recognised and protected in Spain. However, without protection these additional areas face threat of loss from high levels of anthropogenic pressures including livestock grazing and windfarm developments. Peat-forming species were observed at all sites and indicates the potential for blanket bogs in this region to act as carbon sinks, but urgent intervention is required. Assistance is needed to initiate designation of these areas under Natura 2000 and this would enable the European Union to provide financial support for restoration and long-term conservation.

ID 61487

# FIFTY-SIX YEARS OF VEGETATION CHANGE ON COOM RIGG RAISED BOG IN NORTH OF ENGLAND

Helen Adamson

Newcastle University, Newcastle-Upon-Tyne, United Kingdom

*helen.adamson@newcastle.ac.uk*

## SUMMARY

Raised bog is a priority habitat that would benefit from long-term monitoring to better understand drivers of change and inform its management. This 56 year study on the vegetation of Coom Rigg, an active raised bog, set within Kielder Forest in the north of England, provides detailed and robust data for this purpose.

Coom Rigg National Nature Reserve, part of Kielder Mires SSSI, has been mostly unmanaged since the planting of the surrounding forest in the mid-1950s. There has been some drain blocking and *Picea sitchensis* (sitka spruce) removal; the site is ungrazed apart from deer. Vegetation frequency data were collected in 1958, 1986 and 2014 in 10 quadrats at each of 33 locations at 100m grid intersections. A General Linear Model was constructed with year as the factor and the response variables: Ellenberg moisture, nitrogen, reactivity, light and Wet Bog Quality Index (WBQI; an ecological index devised specifically to measure vegetation quality on Kielder Mires).

The results reveal a reduction in WBQI, a decline in Ellenberg F and an increase in Ellenberg N suggesting the major drivers of vegetation change at the site are water levels and nitrogen deposition. Species adapted to acid conditions (Ellenberg R) increased after 1986 while the slight increase in species adapted to shade (Ellenberg L) was not significant. The decline in the bog quality despite its SSSI status is disappointing. Implications for management to restore high quality bog, include the need to block drains and remove trees to ensure a high water table. Light grazing or cutting to open the sward and remove nitrogen may be unnecessary if rewetting is successful. Long-term studies of this nature are rare, they are important to inform evidence-based policy and to provide robust evidence of long-term ecological change in these important habitats.

***Keywords**: Raised bog; Long-term; Vegetation; Ecological Indices; Kielder Forest*

## INTRODUCTION

The role of bogs for carbon sequestration, flood prevention and biodiversity is well-documented. Intact raised bogs of high quality have become increasingly rare in England, having been drained for peat-cutting, afforestation and agricultural practices (Rydin et al, 2013) thus it is a matter of some urgency that effective restoration is undertaken. Information from short-term studies that monitor response to conservation intervention can be misleading because direction and rate of change are not necessarily linear (Hancock et al, 2018) or unusual weather events may occur (Gunnarsson, 2007). Long-term studies can improve our understanding of long-term ecological processes (Frankl and Schmeidl, 2000) and are therefore invaluable to inform local conservation management (Chambers et al, 2013) and may also provide evidence to inform policy.

Long-term vegetation studies on raised bogs have been undertaken by Frankl and Schmeidl (2000) between 1957 and 1994 in South Germany; by Potocka (1999) between 1958 and 1994 in the Izera mountains, Russia and by Frankard and Hyndrck, (1998) between 1938 and 1995 in Belgium. In the UK, no studies on raised bogs were found, but Fojt and Harding (1995) surveyed valley mires (fen) in Suffolk between 1959 and 1991. The studies generally reported a reduction in bog quality and a loss of *Sphagnum* attributed to hydrology and tree invasion.

Kielder Mires Site of Special Scientific Interest (SSSI) includes 20 constrained mires plus Kielder Western Moorland which is blanket bog. Mostly located within the commercial Kielder Forest, is claimedto be the best series of mires in the British Isles outside the Flow Country (Lunn and Burlton, 2013). Prior to acquisition by the Forestry Commission, sheep grazed the bogs at low stocking rates, bogs were occasionally drained and some were planted with *Picea sitchensis* (sitka spruce) and *Pinus contorta* (lodgepole pine) (McIntosh, 1995). They are now grazed only by wild deer.

At Coom Rigg, one of the Kielder Mires, vegetation was first described in 1958 (Chapman, 1964), then again 28 years later in 1986 using the same technique and locations. This revealed considerable degradation in terms of loss of high quality bog indicator species (Chapman and Rose, 1991). This paper presents the results of a resurvey 28 years later in 2014, so providing an invaluable, long-term study (56 years) of this important habitat. The aim is to identify and given reasons for vegetation change and suggest management to protect the ecosystem.

## MATERIALS AND METHODS

Coom Rigg, a National Nature Reserve and part of Kielder Mires SSSI first notified 1959, is a constrained, raised peat bog 300m in altitude, located within Kielder Forest, Northumberland (BNG NY6979). Peat depths range between 3m and 6m and rainfall is between 890 and 1145mm/year (Lunn and Burlton, 2010). The vegetation is classified in the UK National Vegetation Classification (NVC) as M18 *Erica tetralix-Sphagnum papillosum* raised mire (Rodwell, 1991). The area surrounding Coom Rigg was planted with *Picea sitchensis* between 1954 and 1957. Agricultural grazers were removed, leaving only wild roe deer. The bog was too wet to be planted, but the surrounding area was ploughed to form ridges and furrows for tree planting. Drainage channels were dug along the eastern and southern edge of Coom Rigg. These remain active and the southern drain is particularly deep and eroded. Drains dug in the north-western corner were blocked in 1991-1994 with plywood or plastic piling. Trees were planted in 1974 south of the southern drain, but were felled in 2008 to improve status. The bog was recorded as ‘favourable’ according to Natural England Condition Standards Monitoring (JNCC, 2009). Invading trees were removed in 1994 and 2004 (Burlton, pers comm) (Figure 1).

Vegetation was surveyed in 2014 using methodology described in 1958 and 1986 (Chapman

and Rose, 1991). At each British National Grid 100m intersection, located by GPS in 2014, 10 125cm$^2$ diameter, circular 'quadrats' were randomly located using 8 random compass locations and 10 random distances between 1 and 10m. All species within the 'quadrat' were identified to give a species frequency. The 1958 survey included 58 locations, reduced to 33 for the current study, owing to tree planting in the south and tree encroachment on the eastern edge.
Ellenberg Moisture (F) Nitrogen (N), Reactivity (R) and Light (L) (Hill, 1999) and Wet Bog Quality Index (WBQI) (O'Reilly, 2015) were calculated for each location. WBQI is an ecological index designed to assess quality of the Kielder Mires with a single ecological index. A quality score between -1 and 4 was assigned to each species then multiplied by its frequency and totaled. For this study, the total was divided by the sum of the frequencies to give a score between -1 and 4 for each location. A quality below 0 is poor, usually grass dominated: 0-1 is fair; 1-2 good; 2-3 very good, likely to include *Andromeda polifolia, Drosera rotundifolia, Sphagnum magellanicum*; 3+ is unlikely. High WBQI implies functioning ecosystem services. All analysis was carried out in RStudio (R Core Team, 2020). Spatial interpretation was carried out on WBQI only using QGIS (QGIS Development Team, 2021).

**RESULTS**

WBQI was highest in 1958 at 1.95 dropped to 0.99 in 1986 and remained at 0.93 in 2014 ($P<0.001$). Ellenberg F values did not change between 1958 and 1986 at 8.11 to 7.89 then decreased to 7.53 in 2014 ($P<0.001$). Ellenberg N values increased a small but significant amount from 1.15 to 1.28 between 1958 and 2014 ($P<0.05$). Ellenberg R reduced from 1.86 to 1.92 between 1958 and 2014 ($P<0.01$) and Ellenberg L did not change (Table 1).

Table 1: Mean (SD) of Ellenberg and Wet Bog Quality Index (WBQI) values for 1958, 1986 and 2014 on Coom Rigg rasied bog. WBQI: 1 low, 4 high; Ellenberg Nitrogen:1 low 9 high; Moisture: 1 dry 9 wet; Light 1 shade 9 light; Reactivity: 1 acid 9 alkaline. Means with different letters are significantly different for that variable N=33

| **Response variable** | **Mean (Standard Deviation)** | | | **F (df=2,96)** | **P** |
|---|---|---|---|---|---|
| | 1958 | 1986 | 2014 | | |
| WBQI | 1.95 (0.55)$^a$ | 0.99 (0.48)$^b$ | 0.93 (0.35)$^b$ | 48.84 | 2.3x10$^{-15}$*** |
| Ellenberg Moisture | 8.11 (0.18)$^a$ | 7.88 (0.58)$^a$ | 7.53 (0.52)$^b$ | 13.19 | 8.7x10$^{-6}$*** |
| Ellenberg Nitrogen | 1.15 (0.10)$^a$ | 1.28 (0.32)$^{ab}$ | 1.32 (0.25)$^b$ | 4.284 | 0.017* |
| Ellenberg Reactivity | 1.86 (0.14)$^{ab}$ | 1.92 (0.22)$^a$ | 1.78 (0.15)$^b$ | 5.124 | 0.008** |
| Ellenberg Light | 7.54 (0.21) | 7.48 (0.35) | 7.41 (0.38) | 1.330 | 0.269n.s. |

Locations with a WBQI of 2-3 are frequent in 1958. These are typically high quality M18a (*Sphagnum magellanicum–Andromeda polifolia* sub-community) vegetation. The quality was much reduced by 1986 with more locations scoring 0-1; these resemble the M18b (*Empetrum nigrum* ssp *nigrum–Cladonia* spp sub-community). Locations scoring below zero, present in 1986 only, are grass dominated, similar to M25 (*Molinia caerulea-Potentilla erecta*) mire. The spatial change between 1986 and 2104 is not clear, there appear to be improvements in WBQI for some locations, but these are matched with declines elsewhere. There are no clear improvements near the drain blocking in the north-east corner or the tree removal below the southern drain. There may be a decline in WBQI near the tree encroachment on the western edge (Figure 1).

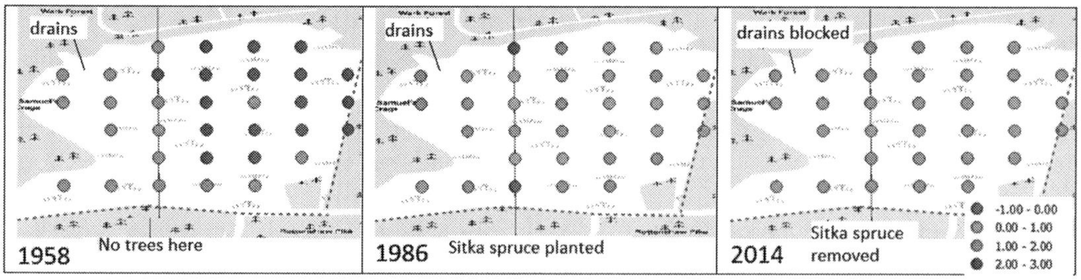


Figure 1: Wet Bog Quality Index (WBQI) at each location on Coom Rigg Raised Mire in 1958, 1986 and 2014. WBQI colours interpreted on key: -1 low quality, 4 high quality. Perimeter drains as red dotted lines.

## DISCUSSION

Moisture is a major driver of biotic variation in bogs and also of quality (Rydin et al, 2013; Hancock et al, 2018; Stivrins et al, 2017) primarily because peat building species such as *Sphagna* are dependent on a high water table (Krebs et al, 2016; Paal et al, 2016). Forest can impact the hydrology of an adjacent bog up to 40m from the forest edge (Shotbolt et al, 1998), so it is likely that the planting of the forest reduced bog moisture and quality at Coom Rigg (Smith and Charman, 1988) as indicated by an overall decline in Ellenberg F and WBQI respectively. Drains can affect the bog ecosystem from up to 1km away (Stivrins et al, 2017), while *Sphagnum* can be sensitive within 400m from a drain (Paal et al, 2016), therefore reduction in Ellenberg F and WBQI over time is also attributed to the ploughing of the plantation furrows and the creation of two drains on the southern and eastern edges around 1957 (Lunn and Burlton, 2010). Drain blocking can raise the water table (Holden, 2011), and although the effect of drain blocking on vegetation recovery is unclear it is generally not detrimental. Komulainen et al (1999) and Hancock et al (2018) found drain blocking increased species indicative of wet conditions, while Green et al (2017) and Williamson et al (2017) found it had no effect. Bellamy et al, (2012) and Hancock (2018) both found positive effects of drain blocking on blanket bog vegetation quality. Despite drain blocking in the north-west corner, tree felling beyond the southern drain in 2008, and ongoing tree encroachment removal, Ellenberg F and WBQI have continued to decline since 1958, with localized WBQI decline apparent near the western forest edge.

Bogs are nutrient poor; an increase in nitrogen (N) is known to reduce bog quality (Bobbink et al, 1998; Stevens, 2016), and specifically to reduce *Sphagnum* growth (Gunnarson and Rydell, 2000). There is a small but significant increase in Ellenberg N at Coom Rigg, indicating an increase in fertility, and a corresponding decrease in WBQI, suggesting that N affects WBQI. The change is attributed to N deposition. Latest available N deposition figures for the region are estimated at 15.3kg N/ha/yr, (CEH, 2016) which is considerably higher than critical loads 5-10 kg/N/ha (Bobbink and Roelofs, 1995). Drying of the peat can also cause mineralization of N (Tomassen, 2004) although *Sphagnum* can immobilise N making it unavailable to vascular species up to a critical point (Malmer et al, 1994). The need for high peat moisture to prevent mineralization, and to maintain *Sphagnum* cover with its degree of resistance to N deposition, is evident. The negative effects of N deposition on bog communities have been reported elsewhere in the UK (Britton, 2017) and in Sweden (Gunnarson, 2007).

Ellenberg R, decreased at Coom Rigg between 1986 and 2014 suggesting a reduction in pH. The small but insignificant Ellenberg L decline, corresponding to a reduction in WBQI, could reflect an increase in *Calluna vulgaris* (heather) dominance caused by a lack of grazing, resulting in a reduction of quality (Smith et al, 2003). No comparable Ellenberg R or L data for raised bog were found, though long-term studies on Scottish blanket bog revealed increased Ellenberg R and a small reduction in Ellenberg L attributed to overgrazing (Britton 2017).

These long-term results can inform effective management on Coom Rigg. Despite SSSI designation and some intervention, WBQI and Ellenberg F showed an overall decline, while Ellenberg N increased since 1958. Drains to the south and east should be blocked and management of tree encroachment continued. Removal of trees on the adjacent peat input slopes could raise the water table and reduce encroachment. Further mapping of adjacent drains and their potential blocking is recommended. Nitrogen reduction is less immediately critical. Grazing is difficult in this remote environment but grazing animals could remove nitrogen (Groome and Shaw, 2015), open the sward, so reducing heather dominance, and increase *Sphagnum* cover thus improving quality (Smith et al, 2003). Sward cutting is a more practical option to achieve these goals, though rewetting the site and reducing mineralisation may be sufficient to ensure low N levels (Tomassen, 2004) and to reduce *Calluna* vigour and dominance (Gimmigham, 1960) without the need for nitrogen removal. Priority therefore is to rewet the peat in order to improve bog quality and therefore ecosystem services, A repeat survey in 2042 or sooner, using WBQI, which usefully incorporates moisture, nitrogen and light drivers into a single measure, is recommended.

The long-term nature of this study provides insight into the decline of an intact, active raised bog under SSSI designation, with condition recorded as 'favourable'. Although this is a case study, the findings and recommendations for management can be applied elsewhere. More analysis is planned and will provide further robust evidence to inform both management and policy.

## CONCLUSION

The long-term nature of this study provides robust evidence of long-term ecological change on this important habitat. The decline in quality on the bog since 1958 is predominantly attributed to a loss of moisture through afforestation and associated drainage. The decline was not reversed after 1986 despite SSSI designation and subsequent intervention, which is of concern. The recommended management is to identify and block all drains and to remove encroaching trees including those on the adjacent peat input slopes. This should raise the water table and restore the bog quality and ecosystem services. These results can be used to inform management elsewhere and to produce evidenced-based policy.

## ACKNOWLEDGEMENTS

John O'Reilly of Ptyxis Ecology for the idea; Dr Marjorie Davy and Ray Kidd of Natural England, Professor Mark Reed Scottish Rural College and Dr Janet Simkin of Newcastle University for comments on draft and support; Bill Burlton for historical information; Forestry England for access and permission.

## REFERENCES


1. Bellamy PE, Stephen L, Maclean IS, Grant MC. (2012) Response of blanket bog vegetation to drain-blocking. *Applied Vegetation Science*; 15 129-135
2. Bobbink R, Hornung M, Roelofs JGM. (1998) The effects of air-borne nitrogen pollutants on species diversity in natural and semi-natural European vegetation. *Journal of ecology*; 86 717-738.
3. Bobbink R, Roelofs JG. (1995) Nitrogen critical loads for natural and semi-natural ecosystems: the empirical approach. *Water Air and Soil Pollution;* 85 2413-2418
4. Britton AJ, Hester AJ, Hewison RL, Potts JM, Ross LC. (2017) Climate pollution and grazing drive long-term change in moorland habitats. *Applied Vegetation Science;* 20 194-203
5. CEH 2016 Air Pollution Information System [Online] Available from: http://wwwapisacuk/search-location (Accessed 15 January 2021)
6. Chambers FM, Cloutman EW, Daniell JRG, Mauquoy D, Jones PS. (2013) Long-term ecological study (palaeoecology) to chronicle habitat degradation and inform conservation ecology: An exemplar from the Brecon Beacons South Wales. *Biodiversity and Conservation;* 22 719-736
7. Chapman SB. (1964) The Ecology of Coom Rigg Moss Northumberland: I Stratigraphy and Present Vegetation. *Journal of Ecology;* 52 299-313
8. Chapman SB, Rose RJ. (1991) Changes in the vegetation at Coom-Rigg moss national nature reserve within the period 1958-86. *Journal of Applied Ecology;* 28 140-153
9. Fojt W, Harding M. (1995) 30 years of change in the vegetation communities of 3 valley mires in Suffolk England. *Journal of Applied Ecology;* 32 561-577
10. Frankard P, Hindryckx MN. (1998) Evolution of the vegetation in the southern part of the fagne Wallonne raised bog during the last 60 years (Hautes-Fagnes Belgium). *Belgian Journal of Botany;* 131 28-40
11. Frankl R, Schmeidl H. (2000) Vegetation change in a South German raised bog: Ecosystem engineering by plant species vegetation switch or ecosystem level feedback mechanisms. *Flora;* 195 267-276
12. Gimingham CH, (1960) Calluna Salisb. *Journal of Ecology; 48* 455-483
13. Green SM, Baird AJ, Holden J, Reed D, Birch K, Jones P. (2017) An experimental study on the response of blanket bog vegetation and water tables to ditch blocking. *Wetlands Ecology and Management;* 25 703-716
14. Groome GM, Shaw P. (2015) Vegetation response to the reintroduction of cattle grazing on an English lowland valley mire and wet heath. *Conservation Evidence;* 12 33-39
15. Gunnarsson U, Flodin LA. (2007) Vegetation shifts towards wetter site conditions on oceanic ombrotrophic bogs in southwestern Sweden. *Journal of Vegetation Science;* 18 595-604
16. Gunnarsson U, Rydin H. (2000) Nitrogen fertilization reduces Sphagnum production in bog communities. *New Phytologist;* 147 527-537
17. Hancock MH, Klein D, Andersen R, Cowie NR. (2018) Vegetation response to restoration management of a blanket bog damaged by drainage and afforestation. *Applied Vegetation Science;* 21 167-178
18. Hill MO, Mountford JO, Roy DB. (1999) *Ellenbergs Indicator Values for British Plants* Huntingdon: Institute of Terrestrial Ecology
19. Holden J, Wallage ZE, Lane SN, McDonald AT. (2011) Water table dynamics in undisturbed drained and restored blanket peat. *Journal of Hydrology;* 402 103-114
20. JNCC (2009) *Common Standards Monitoring Guidance for Upland Habitats* Version July 2009 Joint Nature Conservation Committee Peterborough
21. Komulainen VM, Tuittila ES, Vasander H, Laine J. (1999) Restoration of drained peatlands in southern Finland: Initial effects on vegetation change and CO2 balance. *Journal of Applied Ecology;* 36 634-648
22. Krebs M, Gaudig G, Joosten H. (2016) Record growth of *Sphagnum papillosum* in Georgia (Transcaucasus): Rain frequency temperature and microhabitat as key drivers in natural bogs. *Mires and Peat;* 18
23. Lunn A, Burlton B. (2010) *The Border Mires: a Conservation History* Mires TB and Committee Bellingham Available at: http://wwwiucn-uk-peatlandprogrammeorg/sites/wwwiucn-uk-peatlandprogrammeorg/files/borderMires_history_0pdf (Accessed: 19 January 2021)

24. Malmer N, Svensson BM, Wallén B. (1994) Interactions between *Sphagnum* mosses and field layer vascular plants in the development of peat-forming systems. *Folia Geobotanica et Phytotaxonomica*; 29 483-496
25. McIntosh R. (1995) The history and multi-purpose management of Kielder Forest. *Forest Ecology and Management;* 79 1-11
26. OReilly J. (2015) *Design of a* vegetation *monitoring scheme for the Border Mires* Improvement Programme for England's Natura 2000 Sites (IPENS) – Planning for the Future IPENS060 Available at: http://publications.naturalengland.org.uk/publication/5697380567482368 (Accessed: 26 March 2021)
27. Paal J, Jurjendal I, Suija A, Kull A. (2016) Impact of drainage on vegetation of transitional mires in Estonia. *Mires and Peat;* 18
28. Potocka J. (1999) The dynamics of raised bog vegetation in the Izera Mountains. *Izvestiya Akademii Nauk Seriya Biologicheskaya;* 6 664-671
29. Rodwell JS. (1991) *Volume 2 Mires and heath* Cambridge University Press
30. QGIS Development Team. (2020) QGIS Geographic Information System 34 Open Source Geospatial Foundation Project http://qgisosgeoorg
31. R Core Team. (2020) R: A language and environment for statistical computing R Foundation for Statistical Computing Vienna Austria URL https://wwwR-projectorg/
32. Rydin H Jeglum JK Bennett KD 2013 *The biology of peatlands* 2nd Ed Oxford University Press
33. Smith R Charman D (1988) The vegetation of upland mires within conifer plantations in Northumberland northern England. *Journal of Applied Ecology;*25 579-594
34. Smith RS, Charman D, Rushton SP, Sanderson RA, Simkin JM, Shiel RS. (2003) Vegetation Change in an Ombrotrophic Mire in Northern England after Excluding Sheep. *Applied Vegetation Science;* 6 261-270
35. Shotbolt L, Andersen A, Townend J. (1998) Changes to blanket bog adjoining forest plots at Bad a' Cheo Rumster Forest Caithness Forestry. *An International Journal of Forest Research;* 71 311-324
36. Stevens CJ. (2016) How long do ecosystems take to recover from atmospheric nitrogen deposition? *Biological Conservation;* 200 160-167
37. Stivrins N, Ozola I, Gałka M, Kuske E, Alliksaar T, Andersen TJ, Lamentowicz M, Wulf S, Reitalu T. (2017) Drivers of peat accumulation rate in a raised bog: Impact of drainage climate and local vegetation composition. *Mires and Peat;* 19
38. Tomassen HB, Smolders AJ, Lamers LP, Roelofs JG. (2003) Stimulated growth of *Betula pubescens* and *Molinia caerulea* on ombrotrophic bogs: role of high levels of atmospheric nitrogen deposition. *Journal of Ecology;* 91 357-370
39. Williamson J, Rowe E, Reed D, Ruffino L, Jones P, Dolan R, Buckingham H, Norris D, Astbury S, Evans CD. (2017) Historical peat loss explains limited short-term response of drained blanket bogs to rewetting. *Journal of Environmental Management;* 188 278-286

ID 61598

# ENGAGING WITH IRISH FARMERS MANAGING UPLAND BLANKET PEATLANDS THROUGH AGRI-ENVIRONMENT SCHEMES AND EUROPEAN INNOVATION PROJECTS TO EFFECT BIODIVERSITY PRACTICE CHANGE

*Catherine Keena[1], Jim Kinsella [2]

[1] Teagasc, Kildalton, Piltown, Co Kilkenny, Ireland
[2] University College Dublin, School of Agriculture and Food Science, Dublin, Ireland

*Catherine.keena@teagasc.ie*

## SUMMARY

There are approximately one million hectares of uplands in Ireland, 45% of which is blanket peatland. Some 340,000 hectares are farmed as commonages by up to 15,000 farmers, other areas are privately owned and farmed. Farming in these vast upland areas is experiencing socio-economic decline, presenting unique challenges including low farm incomes and an aging farming population. Issues of overgrazing, undergrazing and abandonment have resulted in some of these peatland areas failing to attain Favourable Conservation Status with reduced biodiversity including declines in iconic upland bird species such as red grouse and hen harrier, encroachment of Invasive Alien Species, and a reduction in high status water quality.

EU policies and in particular the Common Agriculture Policy (CAP), impact significantly on Irish uplands. This paper examines the evolution and interaction of these schemes. Current Pillar 1 schemes include the Basic Premium Scheme and the Areas of Natural Constraint. Pillar 2 agri-environment schemes have evolved since the 1990's and have always had a focus on upland peatlands. Of 23 European Innovation Projects in Ireland, seven are located in upland peatland areas throughout the country. These involve two large projects (worth €25m) targeting the Hen Harrier and the Freshwater Pearl Mussel Project (worth €10m). Five smaller projects (worth approximately €1m each) are focused on management of upland peatlands in diverse upland blanket peatland areas of Ireland.

In order to effect biodiversity practice change on farms, engagement with farmers is key. A study on biodiversity knowledge exchange with Irish farmers using face-to-face questionnaire-based interviews on-farm on concluded that while farmers were positive towards biodiversity, it was not a priority. There was a lack of understanding of biodiversity, requiring effective training. Farm advisors were identified as the key source of environmental information, and along with other farmers and family members were key influencers of farming decisions.

***Keywords***: *Blanket bog, grazed peatlands, farmed peatlands, knowledge exchange, European Innovation Programme.*

## INTRODUCTION

Biodiversity is declining globally at rates unprecedented in human history, with one million animal and plant species threatened with extinction (IPBES, 2018). The increasing importance of biodiversity can be seen in the EU 2030 Biodiversity Strategy 'Making nature healthy again is key to our physical and mental wellbeing and is an ally in the fight against climate change and disease outbreaks. This is at the heart of the EU's growth strategy, in the form of the European Green Deal that gives more back to the planet than it takes away' (EU, 2020).

Agriculture is the predominant land use in about half of Europe's land area (Delbaere, Mikos and Pulleman, 2014). In Ireland farmland habitats rich in biodiversity range from hedgerows, watercourses, species rich grassland and blanket bogland. NATURA 2000 is the centrepiece of EU nature and biodiversity policy, with Special Areas of Conservation (SAC's) comprising the most valuable habitats. In addition to raised bog sites, Ireland identified fifty SACs for the protection of blanket bogs with an estimated area of 150,750 ha (NPWS, 2015). Many of these sites include complexes of other habitats such as heaths, grasslands and aquatic habitats also listed for protection under the Habitats Directive. For thousands of years, blanket bogs have been used for grazing principally sheep. Headage payments under the Common Agriculture Policy (CAP), contributed to extensive overgrazing in certain areas which damaged peatlands. It is known, that providing stocking levels are appropriate, grazing on blanket bogland is a sustainable activity which does not inhibit peat accumulation and should be supported (NPWS, 2015).

There is also blanket bogland outside SACs. There are approximately one million hectares of uplands In Ireland, 45% of which is blanket peatland. Some 340,000 hectares are farmed as commonages by up to 15,000 farmers, other areas are privately owned and farmed. Under the CAP, there are requirements for farmers who are farming on blanket bogs – whether NATURA 2000 or not. Cross compliance requirements for Pillar 1 Basic Payment Schemes set down good agricultural and environmental practices (GAEC) and statutory management requirements (SMRs) which must be followed to ensure the sustainable management of all soils including peatland areas for the protection and maintenance of soil organic matter, avoiding the deterioration of habitats and water protection. Management of commonage lands is complicated with multiple farmers involved. Farmers participating in the current Green Low-carbon, Agri-environment Scheme (GLAS), must manage their commonages per a Commonage Management Plan, prepared by an advisor. This included a grazing plan with minimum and maximum Ewe Equivalents (EE) for each commonage – based on habitat type and condition.

Targeted support actions underpinning the sustainable use of farmland, taking into account the particular sensitivities of peatlands, uplands and NATURA areas are continuing through European Innovation Partnerships. The Department of Agriculture, Food and the Marine awarded €59m to 24 projects which aim to foster a bottom-up, locally led approach to the sustainable use of farmland. A number of them involve uplands and blanket bog. These include the Hen Harrier Project and Pearl Mussel Project. Five smaller projects in upland areas are: Sustainable Uplands Agri-environment Scheme (SUAS); Blackstairs Farming Futures (BFF); Inishowen Upland Farmers Project; Sustainable Agricultural Plan for the MacGillycuddy Reeks; and North Connemara Locally Led Agri-environmental Scheme.

Under Article 17 Report on the EU Protected Habitats in Ireland, the overall status of blanket bogs is 'Bad' (NPWS, 2019). Farmer engagement is crucial to effect practice change and return and maintain blanket peatlands in Favourable Conservation Status. Knowledge exchange is crucial to effect change. If farmers are to halt biodiversity loss from farmland, they must be adequately informed about biodiversity and its drivers according to Lusher et al. (2014).

The 'intellectual puzzle' in this study was to identify and understand farmers' motivations with regard to biodiversity management practices. Social research is 'the detective work of big questions' (Babbie et al., 2013). According to Van de Fliert (2003) sustainable agriculture is 'characterised by the abilities and behaviours that farmers display, including the knowledge and skills they possess, decision-making processes they apply, and individual and collective actions they take'.

## MATERIALS AND METHODS

The literature on biodiversity was reviewed to provide a better understanding of its importance and association with agriculture. There were found to be challenges on all farms in Ireland to maintain and improve biodiversity (DAFM, 2015; NPWS, 2017) and these vary with enterprise, intensity of farming, farmland type and geographical location. The focus of this study was on intensive grassland farms as represented by dairy farms, while the results can relate to all farmers.

A quantitative approach was undertaken in this study. The research design was cross-sectional, examining biodiversity management practices by dairy farmers at one point in time. The method of data collection used was a questionnaire administered to farmers on their own farms by the researcher. Face-to-face on-farm questionnaire based interviews were conducted with 149 dairy farmers in the spring of 2013.

Farmers' attitudes to biodiversity on their own farms as well as their attitude to environmental management in general were determined. In order to transfer biodiversity knowledge and affect biodiversity practice change, it is relevant to identify sources of such information and consider key influencers of farmers. Sources of information used by the farmers in their farming business were explored in order to understand the sources which influence biodiversity management practices. Consideration was given to whether key environmental information sources differed from key environmental influencers, as these are two distinct and different roles in knowledge exchange, which may or may not be filled by the same actors.

## RESULTS

Almost all farmers in the study (97%) said they would like to see wildlife co-existing with farming on their farms. Most farmers (79%) were satisfied with the level of wildlife on their farms; some (14%) would like to see more while others (7%) would like to see less. In terms of changes in wildlife levels: over half of the farmers (56%) believed that the level of wildlife on their farms had remained the same over the previous ten years; thirty one per cent of farmers believed the level had increased; and 12% of farmers believed the level of wildlife had decreased. Over half the farmers considered themselves as 'reasonable' caretakers of the countryside. Forty two per cent of farmers said they were 'good' while only three per cent admitted to feeling they were 'not great' as caretakers of the countryside.

When challenged as to why they were not doing more to encourage wildlife on their farms, only two farmers said they didn't want any more wildlife. Reasons given by the farmers as to why they were not doing more for wildlife were that: they had never thought about it (35%); they couldn't afford to lose land (33%); they couldn't afford to reduce profits (28%); encouraging wildlife wasn't a priority (28%); and they didn't have time (24%). A minority of farmers (7%) said that they didn't know how to encourage more wildlife.

Therefore, while almost all of the farmers would like to see biodiversity co-existing with farming, improving biodiversity was not a priority for them, as the importance of encouraging wildlife on their farms was ranked low. Most farmers were satisfied with the current level of biodiversity on their farm, implying there was no need to carry out additional work. Farmers were also acutely aware of financial implications as they believed that taking the environment into account would lower farm profits. Tidiness of their farms was important to the farmers.

In this study there was a relatively high level of engagement by farmers with the advisory services and in farmer discussion groups. These farmers also engaged with farming organisations but not so much with environmental organisations, of which they knew relatively little. Farmers mainly sourced environmental information from their traditional sources for agricultural information. It is noteworthy that other farmers, family and friends who were not seen as important sources of information were key influencers in the decision-making process.

## DISCUSSION

In general farmers in the study were interested in wildlife. Almost all would like to see wildlife co-existing with farming on their farm. A study in Iceland by Jóhannesdóttir *et al.* (2017), found the vast majority of farmers considered it important to have rich birdlife on their estate. These authors identified the fact that most farms are family owned and many farmers live their entire life on the same farm with such strong connections to the land as being beneficial for conservation. A "connection to nature" promotes pro-environmental behaviour (Mackay and Schmitt, 2019) and connecting people with nature may be a promising avenue for promoting action to protect the environment and prevent harm to nature. If people feel connected to nature, they will be less likely to harm it (Mayer and McPherson Frantz, 2004), but people are also at times simply unaware that their actions are destructive. In a speech made in 1968 in New Delhi to the International Union for the Conservation for Nature (IUCN), the Senegalese Environmentalist Baba Dioum said 'In the end we will only conserve what we love; we will love only what we understand; and we will understand only what we are taught' (Dioum, 1968).

While there was a positive attitude by farmers towards wildlife, problems caused by individual species such as foxes and badgers generated very strong negative reactions, where damage was caused to agricultural production. Farmers in this study (7%), who wanted less wildlife were generally thinking of a single species causing particular problems for them, such as: foxes taking lambs; deer intrusion from adjoining forestry; and badgers spreading TB. Redpath *et al.* (2012) recognised that conservation conflicts are increasing and need to be managed to minimise negative impacts on biodiversity, and human well-being by better integration of the underpinning social context with the material impacts and evaluation of the efficacy of alternative conflict management approaches.

In this study, encouraging wildlife was ranked relatively low by farmers, compared to 'protecting water quality' and 'having a tidy farm'. Farmers are likely to engage in conservation practices that make their farm appear well-managed (Ryan, Erickson and De Young, 2003). Egoz, Bowring and Perkins (2001) found landscapes which are tidy and cultivated reflected New Zealand's legacy of a hardworking settler mentality, while environmentally friendly landscapes can be interpreted by some as being indicative of laziness and neglect and by others as responsible and healthy'. This tension between landscape tastes is evident in this study and therefore being aware of how farmers and other stakeholders interpret the landscape is clearly critical to effect practice change. The legitimation of sustainable practices is highly contingent on localised cultural tradition and the social hierarchies associated with that tradition (Phillips, 2000).

Farmers in the study used a wide range of sources of general information. Their farm advisors were identified as key information providers. Only 3% of the farmers in the study did not use any advisor. The farmers got environmental management information from the same sources they used for technical advice and scheme assistance. Jacobson et al. (2003) recommended that innovations in current farming practices that could enhance bird populations should be disseminated through existing social networks. Involvement of the farmers in the study in discussion groups was relatively high at 53% and Bogue (2013) found that discussion group members were more likely to adopt technology.

This study showed that one key source of environmental information was the AES course, supporting the finding in an evaluation of the impact of the CAP on biodiversity, habitats and landscape that one of the successful approaches to delivering outcomes via the CAP instruments was making sure that schemes are supported by training and on-farm advisory facilitation that recognises and develops farmers' knowledge and skills in biodiversity management (EC, 2019).

This study found that while other farmers did provide some information, their importance was in their role as influencers. In a study of factors affecting farmers participation in AES in Italy, Defrancesco *et al.* (2008) concluded that farmers normative beliefs, namely the opinions of society as a whole, and even more so those of neighbouring farmers, are relevant for active adopters, but negligible for passive participants'. In addition to other farmers, family members were, along with the farm advisors, key influencers of farming decisions taken by farmers in this study. Advisors are key enablers of change and innovation, as they build bridges between research and farers and between businesses and advisory services (Van Oost, 2013).

## CONCLUSION

Biodiversity is a priority in the management of blanket peatland. As these areas are farmed, it is critical to engage farmers in order to achieve Favourable Conservation Status. Aricultural advisory services are key in effective knowledge exchange on best practice management of blanket peatland.

Farmers' attitudes were positive towards biodiversity, but it was not a priority for them. There is a need for more biodiversity knowledge transfer to farmers to inform their attitudes and actions. A general lack of awareness and concern among farmers for the decline in biodiversity contrasts starkly with the reality. This may be explained by the fact that while there may not be a 'silent spring' as predicted by Rachel Carson (1962), specialist species are being replaced by an increase in generalist species. Farmers' understanding of the broad concept of biodiversity was found to be poor. Many did not recognise the value for wildlife of common habitats such as hedges and watercourses. The saying in Irish 'An rud is annamh is iontach' meaning what is rare is wonderful reflects their attitudes towards common habitats. In support of biodiversity knowledge, 'we will only conserve what we love; we will love only what we understand; and we will understand only what we are taught' (IUCN, 1968).

The role and attitude of agricultural advisors is key to mainstreaming biodiversity issues on farms. The important role of agricultural advisors was underlined in this study. Farmers sourced environmental information from their traditional sources of agricultural information. In addition, advisors along with other farmers and family were identified as key influencers of environmental decisions. The resource of agricultural advisory could be utilised more to engage farmers in biodiversity management on their farms, as has been done in locally led projects such as the Burren Programme, the Pearl Mussel EIP Project and the Hen Harrier EIP Project. While specialist expertise could be used for upskilling and training on biodiversity, agricultural advisors can transfer clear simple directions on biodiversity management practices, engage farmers, exchange knowledge and ultimately influence attitudes and actions. This would enable biodiversity to become a priority.

## REFERENCES


1. Babbie E. (2013) *The practice of social research.* 13th Edition. California: Wadsworth Cengage Learning
2. Bogue P (ed.) (2013) 'Impact of participation in Teagasc dairy discussion groups', evaluation report. Oak Park: Teagasc.
3. Carson R. (1962) Silent Spring. London: Penguin.
4. DAFM (2015) '*Food Wise 2025: Strategic Environmental Assessment Environmental Report'.* Available at: https://www.agriculture.gov.ie/finalenvironmentalanalysisfoodwise2025
5. Defrancesco E *et al.* (2008) Factors Affecting Farmers' Participation in Agri-environmental Measures: A Northern Italian Perspective. *Journal of Agricultural Economics*; 59(1): 114-31
6. Delbaere B, Mikos V, Pulleman, M. (2014) European Policy Review: Functional agrobiodiversity supporting sustainable agriculture. *Journal for Nature Conservation*; 22: 193-194
7. Dioum B. (1968) Speech to the International Union for Conservation. New Delhi, IUCN.
8. EC (2019) '*Evaluation of the impact of the CAP on habitats, landscapes, biodiversity*'. Available at: https://ec.europa.eu/info/food-farming-fisheries/key-policies/common-agricultural-policy/evaluation-policy-measures/sustainability/impact-cap-habitats-landscapes-biodiversity-0_en
9. EC (2020) EU Biodiversity Strategy for 2030. Available at: https://ec.europa.eu/environment/nature/biodiversity/strategy/index_en.htm
10. Egoz S, Bowring J, Perkins H C. (2001) Tastes in tension: form, function and meaning in New Zealand's farmed landscape. *Landscape and Urban Planning;* 57: 177-196
11. IPBES (2018) *The IPBES regional assessment report on biodiversity and ecosystem services for Europe and Central Asia.* Bonn, Germany: Secretariat of the Intergovernmental Science-Policy Platform on Biodiversity and Ecosystem Services. Available at: https://ipbes.net/assessment-reports/eca
12. IUCN (1994) The economic value of biodiversity. London: Earthscan Publications Ltd.
13. Jacobson S K, (2003) Assessment of farmer attitudes and behavioral intentions toward bird conservation on organic and conventional Florida farms. *Conservation Biology*; 17(2): 595-606
14. Jóhannesdóttir L et al. (2017) Reconciling biodiversity conservation and agricultural expansion in the subartic environment of Iceland. *Ecology and Society;* 22(1): 16
15. Keena C E (2019) An examination of biodiversity management practices on Irish farms and how this can be measured: the case of dairy farmers in County Waterford. PhD thesis, NUI, Dublin.
16. Lüscher G. et al. (2014) Appropriate metrics to inform farmers about species diversity. Environmental Science and Policy; 41: 52-62
17. Mackay C M L, Schmitt MT. (2019) Do people who feel connected to nature do more to protect it? A meta-analysis, *Journal of Environmental Psychology;* 65: 101-323.

18. Mayer F S, McPherson Frantz C. (2004) The connectedness to nature scale: a measure of individuals' feeling in community with nature. *Journal of Environmental Psychology*; 24: 503-515
19. NPWS (2015) National Peatlands Strategy: Managing Ireland's Peatlands. Available at: https://npws.ie/sites/default/files/files/national_peatlands_strategy_progress_report_2018_and_2019_english.pdf
20. NPWS (2017) *National Biodiversity Action Plan 2017 - 2021*. Available at: https://www.npws.ie/legislation/national-biodiversity-plan
21. NPWS (2019) The Status of EU Protected Habitats and Species in Ireland. Available at: https://npws.ie/sites/default/files/publications/pdf/NPWS_2019_Vol1_Summary_Article17.pdf
22. Phillips E. (2000) Social and cultural factors that influence the adoption of sustainable farm practices. in Shulman A D, Price R, (eds.). Case studies in increasing the adoption of sustainable resource management practices. Land and Water Resources Research and Development Corporation, pp 33-46
23. Redpath S M *et al.* (2012) Understanding and managing conservation conflicts. *Trends in Ecology and Evolution;* 28(2): 100-109
24. Ryan R L, Erickson D L, De Young R. (2003) Farmers' motivations for adopting conservation practices along riparian zones in a mid-western agricultural watershed. *Journal of Environmental Planning and Management*: 46(1): 19-37
25. Van de Fliert E. (2003) Recognising a climate for sustainability: extension beyond transfer of technology. *Australian Journal of Experimental Agriculture;* 43(1): 29-36
26. Van Oost (2013) '*Opportunities provided by the European Innovation Partnership ''Agricultural Productivity and Sustainability'' and its Operational Groups', in Teagasc Knowledge Transfer Conference 2013 Future of Farm Advisory Services, Delivering Innovative Systems*. Available at: https://www.teagasc.ie/.../2013/knowledge-transfer-conference-2013- proceedings--presentations.php

ID 62431

# THE SUSTAINABLE WETLANDS ADAPTATION AND MITIGATION PROGRAM (SWAMP); INTEGRATING TROPICAL PEATLAND SCIENCE AND INTERNATIONAL DEVELOPMENT

*Randy Kolka[1], Daniel Murdiyarso[2]

[1] USDA Forest Service Northern Research Station, United States
[2] Center for International Forestry Research, Indonesia

*randall.k.kolka@usda.gov*

Carbon-rich tropical wetlands peatlands are important in climate change adaptation and mitigation strategies and provide numerous ecosystem services such as storm protection, nursery areas for fish, habitat for rare species, long-term storage of carbon, and food, fiber, and fuel for humans. Because of their importance we developed the Sustainable Wetlands Adaptation and Mitigation Program (SWAMP) to assist countries with their accounting and conservation of tropical wetlands. SWAMP is a collaborative effort between the Center for International Forestry Research and the USDA Forest Service through support from the US Agency for International Development. The goal of SWAMP is to provide policy makers and natural resource professionals with credible information and training to make sound decisions regarding the role of tropical wetlands in climate change adaptation and mitigation. The SWAMP objectives are to: (1) Quantify greenhouse gas emissions from intact and disturbed wetlands; (2) Quantify carbon stocks of representative tropical wetlands; (3) Develop carbon modeling tools and scaling approaches using remote sensing; (4) Define roles for tropical wetlands in climate change adaptation strategies; and (5) Promote capacity building and outreach as integral parts of all activities. Through integrating research, outreach and policy, SWAMP has led to many leveraged efforts both within and across participating countries leading to more accurate tropical wetland greenhouse gas accounting and governmental responses to changing climate.

ID 62303

# INTEGRATED MANAGEMENT OF THE SOUTH KETAPANG LANDSCAPE, INDONESIA

Faizal Parish[1], Serena Lew Siew Yan[1], *Mulyadi[2]

[1] Global Environment Centre, Malaysia

[2] Yayasan Gambut, Indonesia

*yayasangambut@gmail.com*

## SUMMARY

The South Ketapang Landscape covers about 750,000 hectares (ha) in the southern portion of Ketapang District, West Kalimantan, Indonesia. A quarter of the landscape is in formal conservation areas while 60% is managed by oil palm and forest plantation companies. The landscape contains significant forests and peatlands as well as extensive lakes, rivers, floodplains and grasslands. Many of the peatlands are riverine or basin peatlands which are quite rare in Indonesia and as such represent important ecological diversity. Endangered species such as the orangutan and sun bear are found in the landscape. The area is one of the most fire prone areas in West Kalimantan Province. This is caused by drainage within concessions as well as by intentional burning in conservation areas and community land. Fires threaten existing conservation areas such as the Muara Kendawangan Nature Reserve, forest and peat areas. In 2018, the South Ketapang Landscape Initiative (SKLI) was established through a partnership between IOI Corporation (which has nearly 40,000 ha of plantations in the landscape), Global Environment Centre and Aidenvironment, in association with the local government of Ketapang District and the Provincial Nature Conservation Agency. The initiative is still under development, but the local government and a majority of the oil palm and forest plantation companies have committed to the partnership in the Initiative. Initial priorities for collaborative activities between the stakeholders in the landscape include: (a) Conservation of the Cagar Alam Muara Kendawangan, a 150,000 ha nature reserve, the boundary of which is shared by seven different plantation companies; (b) Collaborative fire management including joint prevention, monitoring and control measures; (c) Sharing of experiences and lessons learnt in conserving and rehabilitating the valley peatland ecosystems; and (d) Collaborative measures to enhance community development for 53 villages in the landscape. The paper will provide an overview of this important model for integrated landscape approaches.

***Keywords**: Landscape approach, multi-stakeholder partnership, integrated management, South Ketapang Landscape Initiative*

## INTRODUCTION

### South Ketapang Landscape

The indicative area of the South Ketapang Landscape is approximately 751,741 hectares (ha). The Landscape comprises Cagar Alam Muara Kendawangan conservation area, Protected Forest (*Hutan Lindung*) as well as Gelinggang (*Danau Gelinggang*) and Belida Lakes (*Danau Belida*). Administratively, the Landscape comprises 53 villages in located in four (4) sub-districts of Ketapang District and land-use is mainly dominated by oil palm plantations of 262,358 ha (34.90%) and industrial tree plantations of 185,408 ha (24%), Conservation Area of 169,781 ha (22.59%) and Village/Other Land Uses of 134,194 ha (17.85%).

### Muara Kendawangan Nature Reserve

The Muara Kendawangan forest area was proposed as a Nature Reserve on 15 June 1981, based on a proposal of the Directorate General of Forestry – Number 2240/DJ/I/1981 with an area of 150,000 ha and subsequently on 12 October 1982, it was declared as a Nature Reserve through Decree of the Minister of Agriculture – Number 575/Kpts/Um/10/1982 with an area of 175,000 ha. In accordance with the Decree of the Minister of Forestry – Number 174/Kpts-II/1993 dated 4 November 1993, the boundary demarcation of an area of 149,079 ha was carried out.

Geographically, the Muara Kendawangan Nature Reserve is located between 2° 20’ to 3° 00’ South Latitude and 110° 05’ to 110° 35’ East Longitude. Based on the division of government administration included in the Kendawangan Sub-District, Ketapang District, West Kalimantan Province. Muara Kendawangan Nature Reserve is rich in flora species and has several types of ecosystem, some of which are quite unique. One of its unique features is a very wide expanse of semi-natural grassland covering thousands of hectares which are (mainly on low hills of podzolic soil where the hardpan restricts the growth of trees). These grasslands are an important habitat for deer and various other types of fauna.

Currently, the management of Muara Kendawangan Nature Reserve is facing various challenges, including in the form of forest fires that occur every year, especially during the dry season; animal hunting and community activities in the area. In addition, conditions of accessibility and richness of the natural resources in the form of potential minerals for mining, timber and animal diversity have been contributing to the increasing and widespread disturbance of the area.

### Potential Conservation Area within South Ketapang Landscape

Potential conservation areas within plantations and village land were identified using Landsat-8 satellite image with forest cover in 2016, reference to reports of IOI Group on conservation area and some High Conservation Value (HCV) assessments from plantation companies within the Landscape (Figure 1). Areas of remaining forest and wetland ecosystems were classified as potential conservation areas. Based on the results of the interim analysis of satellite images, a total of 86,000 ha of potential conservation areas were identified within plantations and village land. Administratively, the potential conservation areas within the South Ketapang Landscape are in 31 villages or 4 sub-districts; and an estimated 18,800 ha of the potential conservation areas are located outside the plantation concessions on village land, which have potential to be designated as village forest or village conservation area. An estimated 47,200 ha of potential conservation areas are located within four industrial tree plantation concessions and 20,000 ha within 16 oil palm plantations.

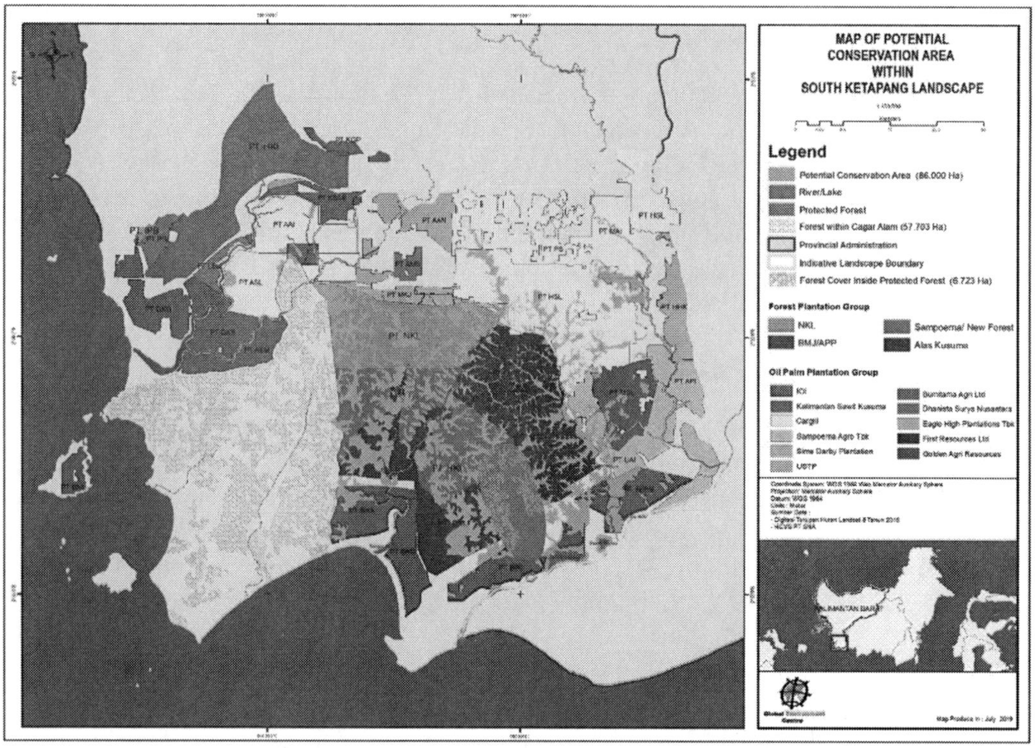


Figure 1: Map of potential conservation areas within South Ketapang Landscape

## Hotspot analysis

Fire hotspot data for the South Ketapang Landscape area from MODIS Terra and Aqua satellite imagery sourced from NASA[4], is an indicator of a fire occurrence in an area. Hotspot data is the result of detection of forest or land fires at a certain pixel size that may burn when the satellite passes in relatively cloud-free condition using a certain algorithm (Giglio L. et al., 2003). The confidence level indicates the level of likelihood that the hotspots monitored from remote sensing satellite data are real fire occurrences in the field – the higher the confidence level, the higher the potential that the hotspot is actually a land or forest fire that has occurred (LAPAN, 2016).

Based on data from a confidence level analysis above 70, there have been 3,733 hotspots in South Ketapang Landscape from 2008 to 2018, then based on BPS Administration data for 2014, these hotspots were located in 50 villages in the South Ketapang Landscape (Figure 2). A significant number have occurred in Muara Kendawangan Nature Reserve and other conservation areas in the landscape indicating further action on fire prevention is needed.

[4] https://earthdata.nasa.gov/earth-observation-data/near-real-time/firms/active-fire-data.

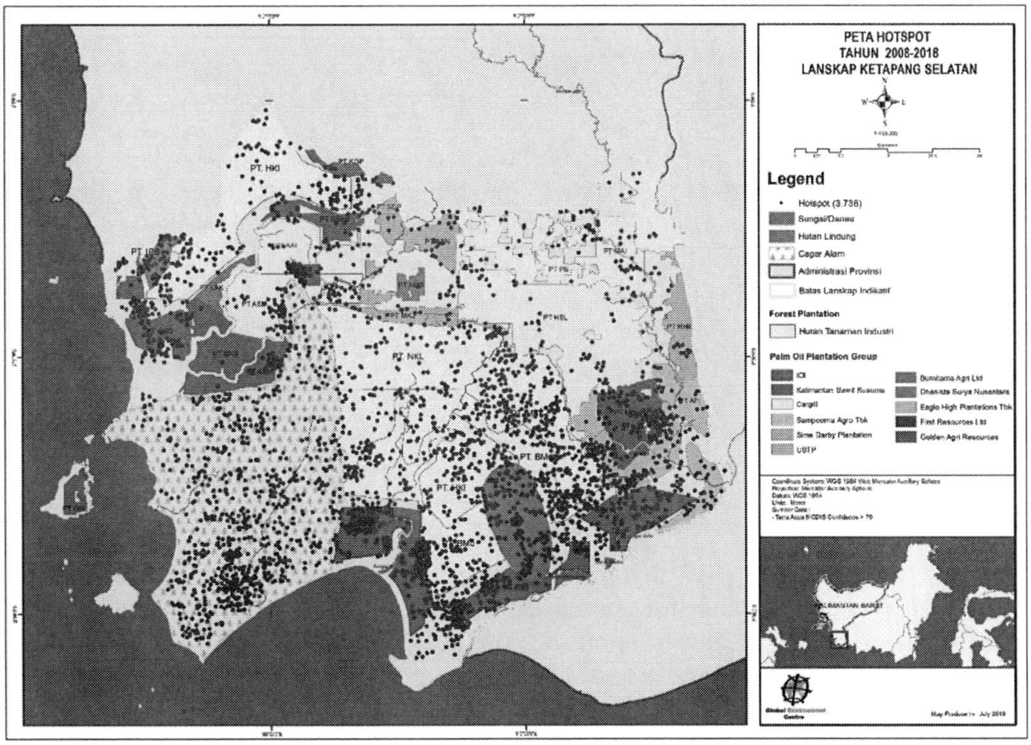


Figure 2: Map indicates hotspots captured in South Ketapang Landscape for the period of 2008 – 2018

## MATERIALS AND METHODS

### South Ketapang Landscape Initiative (SKLI)

The South Ketapang Landscape Initiative (SKLI) was first developed in 2017 by a small group of stakeholders, namely IOI Group and its arm in Indonesia PT Sawit Nabati Agro (SNA), Aidenvironment and Global Environment Centre (GEC). In 2018, the SKLI was approved with initial funding from IOI Group and through activities implementation to engage more stakeholders within the Landscape for a medium- and long-term commitment. Through consultation with government, companies, communities and NGOs, the vision has been sharpened, and initiatives have been identified. Concerns, needs, successes and impacts were shared through a stakeholder meeting in conjunction with the Conference of the Roundtable on Sustainable Palm Oil (RSPO's RTs) in 2018 in Kota Kinabalu, Sabah in Malaysia and 2019 in Bangkok, Thailand. This platform provided an opportunity to the stakeholders to share and contribute to sustainable development to the Landscape.

## RESULTS

### Stakeholder workshop to identify possible partnership

A series of meetings and workshops was conducted during an initial phase of the SKLI in late 2018 to 2019 to engage as many as possible partners from all sector, including government agencies, oil palm and industrial tree plantation companies, community-based organisations (CBOs), non-governmental organisations (NGOs) and local community groups from the villages to build multi-stakeholder collaboration in formulating development plan of the village areas and sustainable management of conservation areas in the Landscape. This development plan aligns with the vision and mission of the Ketapang District Government for period of 2016 – 2021 "Advancing Ketapang towards Prosperous Society". The vision and mission are guidelines for development that will be implemented in Ketapang District which is dominated by village areas. Most of the village land are areas which have been dominated by agricultural activity but included management of natural resources by farmers as well as by mining, forestry and plantation concessions holder companies.

Key elements are to provide opportunities for village areas development as well as support to conservation area management and sustainable use of natural resources. Equally important is building integrated effort and resources among various stakeholders in the Landscape in order to support the development planning in sustainable manner. A workshop on "Establishment of Multi-stakeholder Collaborative Forum for South Ketapang Landscape" was conducted in November 2019. Three Working Groups, i.e. Working Group for Forest and Land Fire Prevention and Mitigation, Working Group for Management of Muara Kendawangan Nature Reserve, and Working Group for Village Area Development were established to develop the initiative.

## DISCUSSION

### Input from stakeholder workshop

Proposed actions in the landscape were developed by respective Working Groups through meetings and workshop and the actions were presented at the multi-stakeholder Forum in November 2019, to be undertaken by relevant stakeholders. The proposed actions are listed as below:

### Collaborative Fire Prevention and Control

1. Reorganise fire management within the Landscape to optimise efforts and resources related to fire prevention rather than fire-fighting and control.
2. Document each fire prevention and control activity and resources by each stakeholder in the Landscape.
3. Analyse the main causes of causing fires and develop collaborative short-, medium- and long-term action strategies for fire prevention at the landscape level.
4. Increasing the dissemination of fire risk information and early warning of drought to all relevant stakeholders.
5. Take specific measures to reduce the risk of fire in fire-prone areas with partnerships between the government, plantation sector and local communities.
6. Empower and strengthen local community actions for fire prevention and control.

**Collaborative Community Development**

1. Completion of Village Boundaries in accordance with Permendagri No. 45/2016 (Ministry of Agriculture) concerning the determination and confirmation of the village boundaries.
2. Support community empowerment through formation of stakeholder clusters at the sub-landscape level to take coordinated action.
3. Establish collaborative programmes between plantation companies and the Government to increase investment in basic infrastructure for villages, including education, health and basic road facilities, and other water supplies.
4. Develop new products and options for livelihoods and related village markets for targeted village communities through partnerships with the private and government sectors.
5. Initiating pilot collaborative projects for community development and engagement in conservation, rehabilitation, utilization of forest areas and fire prevention.

**Enhancing Protection of Muara Kendawangan Nature Reserve and other conservation areas**

1. Review the input from the parties to support the management of the Nature Reserve and buffer zones including priorities for protection, fire prevention, ecosystem restoration, and long-term financing
2. Develop a collaborative program between the Nature Reserve / BKSDA and all concession bordering the Nature Reserve to enhance protection and conservation measures.
3. Clearly demarcate the boundary of the Nature Reserve and expand joint patrols (with companies and communities) for protection
4. Sustainable collaborative livelihood programs with all communities living around the Nature Reserve.
5. Legalisation of conservation areas within companies and wildlife corridors

## CONCLUSION

SKLI was first developed in 2017 and finalised for implementation since 2018 with initial phase of one year with potential active implementation by relevant stakeholders. However, the progress has been slow as there has been some limitations and challenges in particular financial support to execute proposed actions identified by the Working Groups members. Since February 2020, external access to the landscape has been limited by COVID-19 related travel restrictions. Despite the challenges, some actions have been undertaken by relevant government agencies and plantation companies as part of their sustainability activities with the government agencies and community groups nearby their concessions. Actions taken include rehabilitation of degraded conservation areas within plantations, collaboration between adjacent plantations on common issues, enhanced fire prevention and control measures.

## ACKNOWLEDGEMENTS

Appreciation to the government agencies involved such as Regional People's Representative Council of Ketapang Regency, Ketapang Regency Regional Apparatus Organisation, West Kalimantan Nature Conservation Agency (BKSDA), BKSDA Section I Ketapang Region, Manggala Agni Daops Ketapang, KPH Ketapang Selatan, Head of Kendawangan sub-district; plantation companies such as Cargill Group, Bumitama Gunajaya Agro Group, Sampoerna Group, Sinarmas Group; Global Environment Centre, Aidenvironment, Pongo Alliance; and the local community groups within the Landscape. Last but not least the heartfelt gratitude to IOI Group and its arm in Indonesia PT SNA) for financial support for the establishment the SKLI and support for the implementation of the initial phase of the SKLI (2018-2019). Support has also been provided for GEC involvement through the IFAD finance Technical Assistance and Knowledge Exchange for Sustainable Management of Peatland Ecosystems in Malaysia (TAKE-SMPEM).

## REFERENCES

1. Giglio, L., Descloitres, J., Justice, C. O. and Kaufman, Y. 2003. An enhanced contextual fire detection algorithm for MODIS. Remote Sensing of Environment 87:273-282. doi:10.1016/S0034-4257(03)00184-6
2. South Ketapang Landscape Initiative https://www.ioigroup.com/Content/S/S_Background_SKetapang

ID 73975

# RELATIONSHIP BETWEEN PEAT MOISTURE AND PHYSICAL PROPERTIES IN DIFFERENTLY AFFECTED PEATLANDS

*Laimdota Kalniņa[1], Māris Kļaviņš[1], Inese Silamiķele[1], Inārs Dreimanis[2], Ingrīda Krīgere[1,3], Jānis Krūmiņš[1], Karina Stankeviča[1], Annija Žentiņa[4]

[1] Faculty of Geography and Earth Sciences University of Latvia, Latvia
[2] SIA Laflora, Latvia
[3] Latvian Peat Association, 4SIA Hydrox, Latvia

*Laimdota.Kalnina@lu.lv*

**SUMMARY**

Peat is formed under conditions of excess water and are saturated or nearly saturated most of the time. It is known to be porous and to hold a large amount (90-96%) of water when saturated. Physical properties of peat are dependent to a large degree on porosity and pore-size distribution and both the particle size, peat structure and the resulting porosity is controlled primarily by the degree of decomposition degree. With the increasing peat decomposition, the size of organic particles and the size of pores decrease and increase the density of peat.
Drainage ditches in bogs are generally considered to have a significant effect on the hydrological regime of the bog, but there is no precise study of how far this effect extends and on what parameters it depends. It is believed that peat is dry and water levels are low in drained peatlands. We studied how peat moisture, water level and physical properties are closely related and affect each other in different peatlands and found that the moisture level in peat fields is different in comparison with natural bogs, however is higher than is often assumed.
The study aims to elucidate the relationship between moisture and other physical properties using a multidisciplinary approach, including the analysis of changes in moisture content and density in the peat section, taking into account the degree of decomposition and sphagnum pore size determined using a scanning electron microscope Phenom ProX.
The results of the research will be useful for understanding the formation and accumulation of peat, for more successful management of bogs and peat fields, including the assessment of the possibility of fire in the bog.

Keywords: **peat moisture, decomposition, density, pore size**

## INTRODUCTION

It is known that peat, especially raised bog sphagnum peat is porous and hold a large amount (90-96%) of water when saturated. The water storage characteristics at conditions other than saturation are equally important because they determine the quantity of water involved with a given water table fluctuation in the peat profile. Peat moisture, water level and physical properties are closely related and affect each other. Physical properties of peat are dependent to a large degree on porosity and pore-size distribution and both the particle size and structure and the resulting porosity is controlled primarily by the degree of decomposition. With increasing degree of peat decomposition, the size of organic particles decreases and increase the density of peat, as well as decrease size of sphagnum pores, which is an important factor for water level and moisture fluctuation in peat profile.

At least 2 types of water are distinguished in the sphagnum moss layer:

- osmotically bound inside plant cells;
- capillary water located in the pores between plant stems.

Capillary forces arise in small pores (capillaries) and move through them with meniscus force. The movement of water in both vertical and horizontal directions is affected by gravity. Its effect is relatively greater when water moves in the vertical direction than when it moves in the horizontal direction (Stewart, Durno, 1969).

The principal difference between the peat profiles in the distribution of plant remains, are not particularly noticeable in the upper horizons, where they are relatively undecomposed. Decomposition of plant remains down the profiles is paralleled by a decrease in fibrosity, the various components becoming finer with depth and more thinly dispersed through the amorphous material. It is related to a decrease of moisture content in the peat profile down and an increase in peat density. However, these processes are not always sequential and may fluctuate depending on the natural conditions that have determined peat formation over time. Therefore, it was important to conduct a complex study, which includes not only changes in peat moisture but also changes in other properties of peat in the section of the bog. Another important aspect is to identify and compare how the complexity of these properties changes in natural, affected bogs and peat extraction fields.

The study aims to elucidate the relationship between moisture and other physical properties using a multidisciplinary approach, including the analysis of changes in moisture content and density in the peat section of differently affected peatlands, taking into account the degree of decomposition and pore size determined using a scanning electron microscope Phenom ProX.

The results of the multidisciplinary detailed research will be useful for understanding the formation of bogs and changes in peat accumulation conditions and properties, as well as, how they behave in peat extraction field sections, what is important to know for more successful management of bogs and peat fields.

## MATERIALS AND METHODS

Sampling sites.

Peat samples for the study was sampled from three sites:

Sēme Bog (N 57o20'69381", E 22o17'35940") is located in Kursa Lowland, the northern part of Venta-Usma depression, north-western Latvia. It is raised bog which belongs to Stikli Mire complex. Peat was sampled from two locations a) in the natural bog (core Sēme1) and Sēme2) from probably slightly affected bog part due to closeness of drain age ditch (~100 m) (core Sēme 2) located 1750 m eastern from the sampling site Sēme1.

Lielsala peatland (N 57°20'67309", E 22 °19'12493") locates eastern from Sēme Bog and has common border. Sampling site Lielsala3 is located approximately 450 m from sampling site Sēme 2.

Drabiņas Bog ((N 57o47'88352", E 23o31'32978") is raised bog located in the north-western part of Tīreļi Plain, Middle Latvia Lowland. Peat was sampled both from the natural part of the bog (core Drab4) and from the peat field (core Drab5) approximately 400 m west from core location Drab4.

Sampling.

Geological coring was carried out using an Eijelkamp soft-sediment geological corer with a closed chamber. The core size was 5 cm in diameter and 50 cm in length with a sample volume of 10 ml/cm. The purpose of coring was to get peat samples for further investigation by laboratory methods and to find out how peat properties are changing if peatland influenced by drainage and significantly changed in peat in peat extraction fields.

Loss-on-ignition (LOI) analysis.

This method was applied to estimate the percentage of the peat moisture and dry matter, organic matter and ash, carbonates and mineral matter content in the studied sediments (Dean, 1974; Heiri et al., 2001). The moisture was determined for the peat after drying the sample at 105°C and was compared with results obtained by peat moisture measuring equipment ATS Max. The content of the organic and ash was estimated by incinerating the samples for 4 h at 550°C. Loss on ignition analysis has been carried out in special furnaces, according to internationally approved methodology (Heiri et al. 2001).

Determination of peat bulk density.

Density of peat is the volume unit of peat mass expressed as kg/m3 or g/cm3 (Päivänen 1969). It depends on the peat type, degree of decomposition, humidity and ash content. Ash content can increase not only due to natural processes but also due to human influence. Using the density as an indicator, it is possible to assess the depth of drainage influence in a bog.

Determination of peat pH value.

Peat acidity or pH value is an important parameter characterizing the peat environment, and it is usually related to a particular peat type. It is important to know peat pH value when choosing the reclamation method suitable for a particular peatland to know which plants can be reintroduced in the area, taking into account their habitat requirements. Peat pH value was determined in the laboratory of the University of Latvia, Faculty of Geography and Earth Sciences, in solution according to ISO 10390, 2005. For all boreholes studied, pH values were determined in the interval of 20-50 cm, by evaluating the changes in sediment composition after analysis of loss-of-ignition (Krūmiņš et al. 2012).

Determination of degree of decomposition and botanical composition.
Initially, the degree of peat decomposition was determined on the field, immediately after sampling, using the von Post scale. However, this method is approximate, so the degree of decomposition was also determined in the laboratory using a light microscope and standard GOST 28245-89 (Krūmiņš et al., 2012) which has been developed and accepted for this region.
Peat decomposition degree is closely related to the amount of humic matter in peat mass. According to peat decomposition degree, three types are distinguished: low decomposed (decomposition degree less than 20%); medium decomposed (20-30%); well-decomposed peat (higher than 30%) (Šnore 2013).

Scanning electron microscopy (SEM Phenom ProX).
In total seven peat samples from the entire Sēme Bog peat section was analysed by taking 2 to 5 images with up to 10 points for each sample. For each point, a chemical data graph was obtained. Electronic microscopy analysis was done using scanning electron microscope Phenom ProX. Images for viewing and morphology evaluation were based on 10kV mode. The size of the pore was measured and documented to compare their values with decomposition degree and moisture.

## RESULTS

The study analyzed peat sediments from five cores, three of which are from bog areas and two from peat extraction fields to compare peat properties in different environments. A study of the entire peat section from the Sēme Bog (core Sēme1 and Sēme2) was done. The evaluation of peat samples allows us to conclude that the accumulation of peat in Sēme Bog has mostly taken place in similar wet conditions, which has promoted the accumulation of low decomposed peat, however in some intervals appear darker peat interlayers with higher peat decomposition degree, while there almost were no observable changes in peat botanical composition.
However according to the data of LOI from the Sēme1 core section and the diagram compiled four zones (I-IV) can be distinguished based on the changes in the amount of ash and the amount of organic matter in the composition of the peat deposits, as well as fluctuations in moisture values.
The lower zone I of the section (380-400 cm) is characterized by the highest amount of minerals, reaching 95%, which indicates that the lower layer of the section consists of mineral sediments. In the upward direction, the amount of ash in the composition of sediments decreases rapidly and with the increase in the presence of organic matter, the beginning of peat accumulation and mire formation start can be determined before 7000 years (7000 yr.cal BP). Analyzing the botanical composition of peat and performing macroscopic residue analysis of plants, it was found that in this section interval (zone I) there is the highest concentration of carbon, which indicates the presence of charcoal and extensive fires in the area of the bog depression and its surroundings during the early stage of bog development. This is also confirmed by the results of the macroremain analysis. The highest pH value (5.5-6.1), the highest density and the lowest moisture content are determined in this depth interval. Zone II is determined in the interval 335-380 cm, in the lower part of which there is a small (5-7%) amount of ash, but in the upper part, it increases up to 25%. During this time the hydrological conditions in the area of the bog may have changed because charcoal presence has not been detected in this interval. The upper limit of this interval also marks marked changes in the botanical composition of peat.

Zone III divided in the peat section interval of 80-335 cm, in which no significant changes in the distribution of ash and organic matter were observed. Fluctuations in natural moisture are also small.
Zone IV is divided in the upper interval of peat section in the depth interval 0-80 cm, the lower limit of which indicates a marked decrease in the amount of minerals and natural moisture, but the zone as a whole is characterized by an increase in the proportion of minerals to 5%. The amount of charcoal dust in this interval is slightly higher than in the middle of the section (80-330 cm). Given that the site was hit by a fire in 2018, a significantly higher presence of coal was expected, but the fire may have flown over the site rapidly, leaving no significant amount of coal. There is a possibility that the coal dust was rinsed a little deeper through the sphagnum. This is suggested by a slightly increased amount of ash throughout the upper 70 cm interval.
Significant increases in pH values have been observed in the lower part of the section (330 - 392 cm) approaching the sandy bottom of the bog. Peat acidity or pH number usually characterizes the specific peat type formation environment, comparing the changes in the acidity of the studied Sēme Bog in the section, it can be concluded that there are no differences and deviations from the commonly observed indicators. Analysing the classical bog development cycle from fen to transition and raised bogs, the pH number varies from 5-7 in fen peat to 2.8 to 4 in raised bogs. The pH of the peat 0-0.05 has risen to 4.7, which is slightly higher than that of raised bog peat, which could probably be explained by the effects of fire.
Two distinct intervals can be distinguished in the studied composition of peat-forming plants of Sēme Bog. From the depth of 3.50 m upwards, there is a great uniformity in the composition of plant residues. The remains of sphagnum, pillows and cranberries predominate. The range from 0 to 60 cm from the sphagnum is dominated by Sphagnum magellanicum, which is replaced in the downward direction by brown sphagnum (Sphagnum fuscum), which dominates the peat composition to a depth of 3.4 m, where significant changes in the composition of peat-forming plants take place. This shows that at this depth the plants characteristic of the raised bog have begun to dominate in the bog - sphagnum, pillows, cranberries, which feed on precipitation water. According to the data obtained, including AMS 14C dating results, it can be concluded that raised bog started to develop before 6000 years.
In the frame of study of changes in peat structure and pore size by scanning electron microscope, Phenom ProX size of the pore was measured. It was found that their values vary from 17,70 μm in the upper depth interval 0.25 cm, decrease to 12,49 μm in depth 0.75 cm, where increase peat decomposition degree and density, but decrease moisture content. At the bottom of the section pore size again increase up to 16,52 μm, pointing at low decomposition degree at the level of raised peat formation start under high water level in the bog which is confirmed by the formation of low decomposed sphagnum peat. Due to the rather large pores in the sphagnum moss layer, the level of water capillary rise is low, but the rate of water rise is quite high. Therefore, capillaries can carry a very large amount of water to the top layer of the bog which affects both the water level in the bog and the moisture content of the peat.
The comparison of peat study results from both peat cores Sēme1 and Sēme2 indicate similar characteristics of peat sections, however, they are located in almost 2 km distance and peatland depression is uneven due to formation in the Baltic Ice Lake accumulative area. Some differences have been found in the course of peat moisture and density in the upper depth interval of 50 cm of core Sēme2 samples where appear slightly lower peat moisture (86-89%) and higher values of ash up to 3.8%.
Study of peat section from Lielsala peatland peat extraction fields located eastern from Sēme Bog and core Sēme2 was important to understand how peat characteristics are changed due to drainage and how it is influenced by removing of overlying peat layer. The obtained results

were surprising because taking into account that 2 m of peat has already been extracted in this place, it was expected that the peat moisture would below. However, its fluctuations in the lower part of the section were similar to those in the core Sēme2 section. The differences were only in the upper 50 cm, where the humidity gradually decreased from 85 to 73% at a depth of 10 cm from the top. Due to drainage and peat compaction, the ash content increases to 4.5% and the density reached 2.2 g / cm3.
Similar results show peat investigation results from Drabiņi peat extraction fields. Samples were taken the next day after sampling in Lielsala3. The difference in the results is slightly different mainly related to peat botanical composition with a higher presence of dwarf shrub (Oxiococcus and Calluna vulgaris) in core Drab5. However, these differences can be explained by the differences in the composition of peat-forming plants in Drabiņi Bog from Lielsala peatland. Also, peat moisture is slightly lower in core Drab2 and varied from 83 to 71% at a depth of 10 cm from the top, while the ash content increases to 15.2% and the density reached 3.8 g / cm3.
In the lDrabiņi Bog studied peat section a relatively high (10-25%) content of minerals uncharacteristic of high type peat was found. The changes in the composition of sediments in the section are relatively small and are associated with a significant amount of minerals throughout the analyzed section with a tendency to increase in the lower and upper part of the section. If higher amounts of minerals in peat can be attributed to the effects of drainage, then in the lower part their increase of up to 30% is difficult to explain.

## DISCUSSION

The results obtained in the multidisciplinary research carried out allow us to understand the relationship between peat moisture and other properties of peat and the processes taking place in bogs. It should be noted that the results of the research carried out in the bogs selected for the study, on the one hand, indicate how many Semes, Lielsalas and Drabiņi bogs are similar to each other, but still, detailed research can reveal such parameters that allow to find out the differences in the course of their development.
If it is classically assumed that the degree of decomposition of peat increases with increasing depth, then in our study it is marked that some peat layers whose properties do not obey the classical assumptions. In the study of Sēme Bog (core Sēme1), a 15 cm thick (0.75-0.60 cm) layer of medium decomposed peat was found under the low decomposed upper raised bog type peat. The significant difference between this layer and the overlay layer was also confirmed by the peat bulk density, moisture and ash data and decrease in sphagnum pore size. The fact that this layer is not a random lens in the peat section proves that the peat layer with very similar properties is also found in the Sēme2 section, which is located almost 2 km from Sēme1, and it reaches 0.25 cm at a slightly greater depth (0.9-1.10 cm). According radiocarbon dating it can be assume that in the period before 1012 to 1242 years there were drier conditions in Sēme Bog, which contributed to a better peat decomposition process. It is possible that this event can be related to the warm period at the end of the Iron Age and the beginning of the Middle Ages (Poschlod, 2015) because the features of such a thin layer of moderately distributed peat can also be observed in the other peatland sections, including the section of Drabiņi Bog.

Fluctuations in decomposition degree have been found also in the underlying Sphagnum fuscum and cottongrass – sphagnum peat indicating changing hydrological conditions (Romanov, 1968). Significant changes in the hydrological regime of the bog and the conditions of peat accumulation were found at a depth of 3.6 m, where the feeding conditions of plants change, plants that feed on precipitation water are rapidly introduced and a raised bog type or moss bog develops before 3300-3400 years.
Peat studies were carried out in the adjacent peat extraction fields close to natural and semi-natural bog areas to understand the changes in moisture regime and other peat properties due to drainage. In the vicinity of the studied sections of peat extraction fields, similar characteristics of peat properties were found in comparison with the adjacent bogs. The differences observed only in the upper 50 cm of the peat extraction field section, where the moisture decreases, the share of ash, which is related to the compaction of the peat and the increase of the density, increases. Besides, the tendencies of changes in peat properties in both studied peat extraction fields are similar. The differences depend on the nature of the peat properties of the adjacent bog.

## CONCLUSION

The results of the study confirm that the moisture and other physical properties of peat are dependent to a large degree on peat decomposition degree and sphagnum pore-size distribution in the section. With increasing peat decomposition, the size of organic particles, as well as the size of sphagnum pores decreases and increase the density of peat, which also causes a decrease in peat moisture.
The moisture content of peat significantly depends on other peat properties, including sphagnum pore size, peat density and the degree of decomposition of the peat.
Peat also retains its properties in the sections of peat extraction fields and they change significantly in the upper 50 cm, where the moisture decreases, but the density and ash content increase. However, the properties of peat change more sharply and vary more significantly in peatlands affected by drainage in comparison to natural bogs.

Sphagnum peat forms most of the peat layers in the studied sites and due to their unique structure, decomposition degree and density are closely related to the size of pores, studies of which reveal important information on processes in nature.

## ACKNOWLEDGEMENTS

This study was founded by projects of the University of Latvia "Climate change and its impacts on sustainability of natural resources" and "Studies of impact by peatland burning on the environment and bog recovery intensity" with partners JSC "Latvia's State Forest", The Nature Conservation Agency and Latvian Peat Association.

## REFERENCES

Heiri, O., Lotter, A. F., Lemcke, G. (2001) Loss on ignition as a method for estimating organic and carbonate content in sediments: reproducibility and comparability of results. *Journal of Paleolimnology*, volume 25, pp. 101-110.

Krūmiņš, J., Silamiķele, I., Purmalis, O, Stankeviča, K., Kušķe, E., Pujāte, A., Ozola, I., Ceriņa, A., Rūtiņa L., Stivriņš, N., 2012. "Kūdras un sapropeļa pētījumu metodes". L. Kalniņas un M. Kļaviņa red. LU Akadēmiskais apgāds, Rīga, pp. 132.

Päivänen J. (1969) The bulk density of peat and its determination. *Silva Fennica* vol. 3 no. 1 article id 4783. https://doi.org/10.14214/sf.a14569

Poschlod P. (2015) The Origin and Development of the Central European Man-made Landscape, Habitat and Species Diversity as Affected by Climate and its Changes – a Review. *Interdisciplinaria archaeologica natural sciences in archaeology*; VI: 197–221

Romanov, V.V. (1968) Hydrophysics of bogs. Kaner, N. (Translator); Heimann (ed), Israel program for scientific translations Ltd, Jerusalem. 1.–299.

Stewart, J. M., Durno, S. E. (1969) Structural variations in peat. *New Phytol.* 68, 167 – 83 pp

Šnore, A. (2013) Purvi un kūdra. Kūdras ieguve. Rīga, Nordik. pp.367.

ID 61326

# HOW TO IDENTIFY CULTIVATED PEAT SOILS SUITABLE FOR REWETTING

Kristiina Regina[1], Alina Oksala[2], Kersti Leppä[2], Hanna Kekkonen[3], Aleksi Lehtonen[2], Mikko Peltoniemi[2], Aura Salmivaara[2]

[1]Natural Resources Institute Finland, Jokioinen, Finland
[2]Natural Resources Institute Finland, Helsinki, Finland
[3]Natural Resources Institute Finland, Oulu, Finland

*kristiina.regina@luke.fi*

**SUMMARY**

More than half of agricultural greenhouse gas (GHG) emissions originate from cultivated peatlands in Finland. The most effective way to mitigate GHG emissions is to rewet the fields, i.e. to raise the water table level (WTL). Careful selection of the parcels for rewetting increases the success rate of such actions. Rewetting may be an especially acceptable option for the landowner if the field has lost its productivity due to peat subsidence and poor drainage. We hypothesized that readily available datasets can be used to produce a tool for agricultural advisors and policy planners to target incentives for GHG mitigation by rewetting.

A pilot study was done with the spatial software QGIS for one 37000 km$^2$ region in Finland. Extensive grasslands with a peat layer >60 cm were identified in order to find areas with high mitigation potential and low significance in food production. Water availability was first assessed based on the difference between precipitation and evapotranspiration. In two catchments (2068 ha and 11505 ha), Digital Elevation Model (DEM), Depth to Water (DTW) and Topographical Wetness Index (TWI) were used to estimate the variability of soil wetness due to topography.

For the two catchments studied in detail, 23% and 5% of the field area at least partly on deep peat in catchments 1 and 2, respectively, had been in extensive cultivation for more than 8 out of 10 years. As the poorest fields are often driven to extensive management, the most potentially rewettable fields are likely to be found among this area. The topographic analysis further reduced the proportions of rewettable area to 9% and 2%.

The results suggest that the difference between annual precipitation and potential evapotranspiration can be used for a first estimate of rewettability but additional information is required. The available topographical datasets allowed for a more detailed estimate of the adequacy of the water reserves for the WTL raise. This method allows for finding promising regions for initiating rewetting after which rewetting activities can be gradually expanded also to the surrounding fields to create dedicated larger areas for restoration or paludiculture.

***Keywords**: agriculture, ground water table, greenhouse gas, mitigation, GIS*

## INTRODUCTION

Finland strives for carbon neutrality by 2035 and it is likely that this goal will not be achieved without significant changes in the use of peat soils. GHG emissions from drained peat soils and energy use of peat are more than 20 Mt $CO_2$ eq. which is high compared to the total emissions of 50-60 Mt and net sink of the land use sector around 20 Mt. More than half of agricultural GHG emissions originate from cultivated peatlands in Finland which makes them a potential target for efficient mitigation measures. Rewetting to close to natural conditions or paludiculture are the most efficient options to slow down peat decomposition and to reduce GHG emissions.

As agricultural policy encourages maintaining the current field area and there are no incentives for giving up cultivation even on the poorest field parcels, there may be cultivated peatlands that are not essential for food production (Kekkonen et al. 2019). Rewetting may be an acceptable option for the landowner provided that the field has lost its productivity due to peat subsidence or poor drainage and suitable incentives are available.

The most effective way to mitigate GHG emissions is to raise the WTL but parcels for rewetting must be selected carefully. There must be water available, and rewetting must not interfere with surrounding agricultural or forestry activities. If the peat layer still is deep, the climate change mitigation effect will be long lasting and it may be worthwhile to invest mitigation actions in rewetting of such parcels.

We used readily available datasets to map cultivated peat soils (Oksala 2019). We hypothesized that most potential areas for rewetting activities consist of several field parcels that are 1) on deep peat, 2) in long term extensive use and 3) on low and flat terrain. The aim of this study was to develop a method for country scale mapping of cultivated peat soils to be used as a tool to target incentives for GHG mitigation by rewetting.

## MATERIALS AND METHODS

The feasibility of readily available spatial datasets in classifying field parcels was studied in a pilot study done with the spatial software QGIS for one 37000 km$^2$ region in Finland. Data from the Land parcel identification system from 2008 to 2017 was used to divide the field area of this region into three categories: parcels in long-term extensive use (80% of years in non-productive use like nature management field or fallow), long-term forage production (80% of years in forage production) and other use (mainly annual cropping or crop rotation). This information was combined with soil data to identify extensive grasslands with a peat layer >60 cm in order to find areas with high mitigation potential and low significance in food production (Fig. 1). However, forage areas were also considered potentially rewettable as it is known that some extensively managed parcels are recorded as forage parcels are in the register.

Climate and topographical data together with hydrological indices were used to estimate water availability for rewetting. Water availability was first assessed based on the difference between precipitation and evapotranspiration. In two catchments (2068 ha and 11505 ha), Digital Elevation Model (DEM), Depth to Water (DTW) and Topographical Wetness Index (TWI) were used to estimate the variability of soil wetness due to topography. DEM was used to detect elevation differences and flat parcels with slopes less than or equal to 2%. DTW values less than or equal to 1.5 m were considered rewettable. TWI was used to estimate accumulation of runoff; the higher the value the wetter the soil presumably gets after blocking of the drainage system.

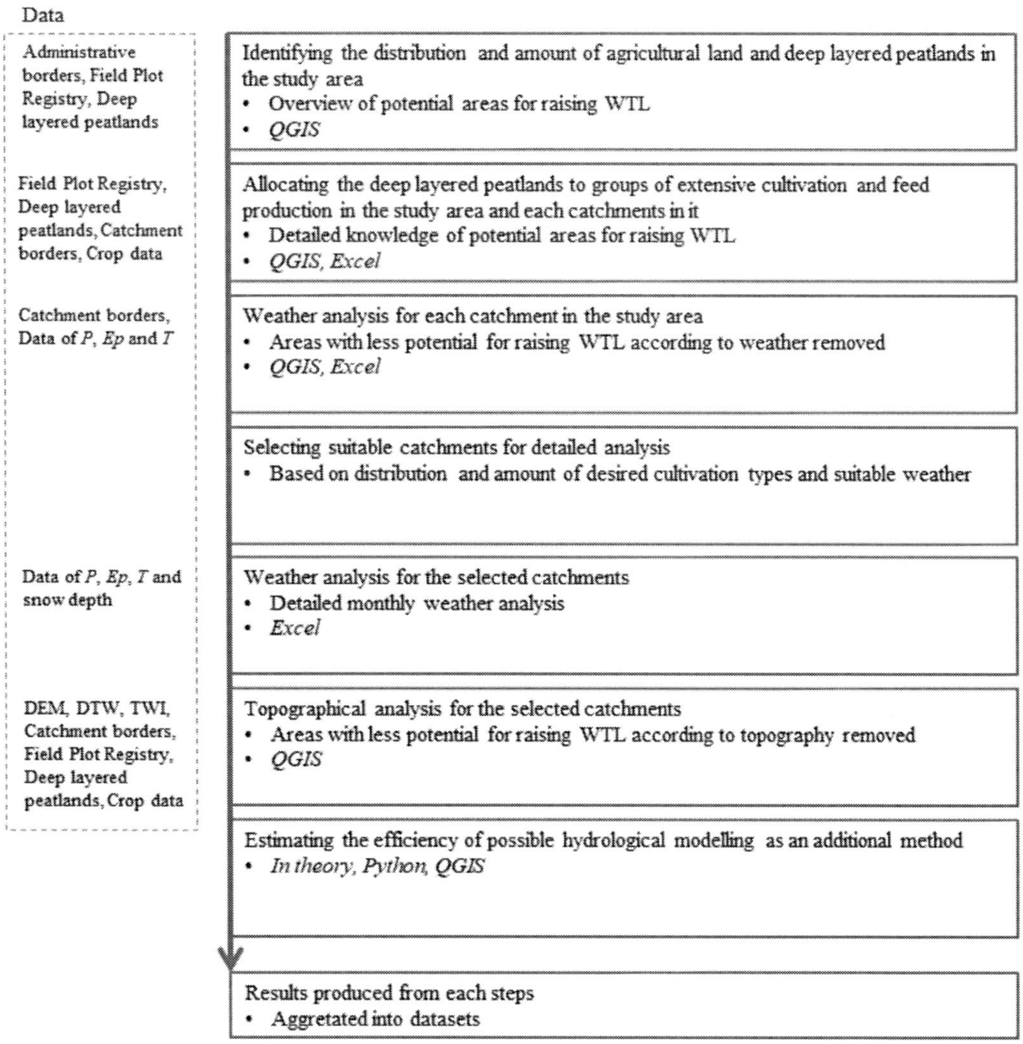


Figure 1 Scheme of the workflow

## RESULTS

The total area of field parcels at least partly on deep peat (>60 cm) was 67 000 ha in the studied region. Approximately 1550 ha or 2.3% of these parcels had been in extensive cultivation for at least 8 out of 10 years suggesting that some of these fields may have lost their productivity. An additional analysis using the self-evaluation of farmers regarding the drainage status of their fields indicated that the proportion of poorly drained parcels is higher among the extensively cultivated area (results not shown) suggesting that poorly functioning drainage may be a reason for giving up productive use of peaty field parcels. In addition to the extensive cultivation area, around 17 000 ha of forage area is also located on deep peat. This data was also analyzed on catchment level to reveal catchments with the highest density of extensively managed deep peat soils.

For the two catchments studied in detail, 23% and 5% of the deep-peated field area had been in extensive cultivation for more than 8 out of 10 years in catchments 1 and 2, respectively (Table 1). As the poorest fields are often driven to extensive management, the most potentially rewettable fields are likely to be found among this area. The topographic analysis further reduced the area potential for rewetting to 9 and 2%. The respective forage area with likely some additional GHG mitigation potential was 53 and 28 ha in these catchments.

Table 1 Areas (ha) of different field categories in two example catchments, C1 and C2

| **Land use** | **Area (ha)** | | **Area with slope ≤2%** | |
|---|---|---|---|---|
| | **C1** | **C2** | **C1** | **C2** |
| Total field area | 1740 | 204 | | |
| Parcels partly or totally on deep peat | 725 | 128 | | |
| Extensive 80% of years | 39 | 30 | 14 | 11 |
| Feed production | 182 | 67 | 53 | 28 |

The difference of precipitation and evapotranspiration for the study region showed considerable variation between the two years for which the data was available (data not shown) and it was concluded that a longer time series is needed for a reliable estimate.

DEM data showed that the parcels estimated as suitable for rewetting based on the cultivation type and peat depth usually were located at lower elevation than their surroundings (Fig. 2). The total field area on deep peat fulfilled the criterion of having DTW lower than 1.5 m. DTW was considered a better indicator of soil wetness than TWI.

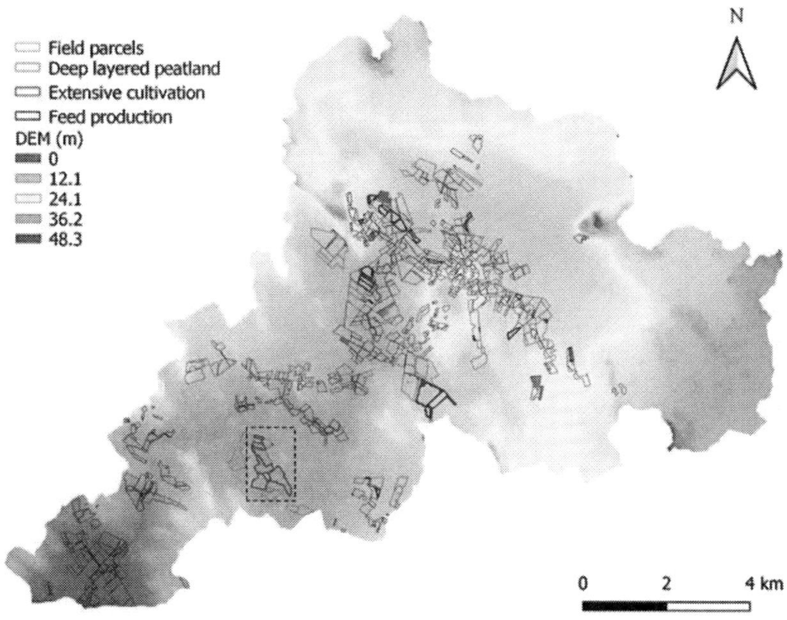


Figure 2 Map of catchment 2 showing the rewettable fields. The area surrounded by a dash line is an example of potentially rewettable area as there are several field parcels that fulfil the criteria set in this study.

## DISCUSSION

The results suggest that the difference between annual precipitation and potential evapotranspiration can be used for a first estimate of rewettability. However, in general the conditions in the boreal zone are favourable for wetland formation and thus additional information is required for a more site-specific estimate. The available topographic data allowed detecting areas with likely adequate water reserves for the WTL raise. TWI was found to be better suited for detecting locations of streams than wider wet areas like field parcels. Based on DTW, the total studied area of deep layered peat was rewettable. The use of DEM reduces the potentially rewettable area and thus can be considered a method for a conservative estimate and for selecting the primary targets for rewetting. After the potential areas are spotted using these coarse methods, hydrological modelling together with in situ studies can be used for the final decision on rewetting activities.

An earlier coarser analysis suggested that 13% of the area of cultivated peatlands could be available for the most efficient GHG mitigation measures like rewetting in the country scale (Kekkonen et al. 2010). In this work, we had much stricter criteria for rewettability but still the proportions ranged from 5 to 23% in the studied peat-rich catchments. This indicates that this "low-hanging fruit" of GHG mitigation exists and policy instruments for its utilization are urgently needed. Further work will extend this analysis for other parts of the country, and its usefulness for targeting rewetting will be estimated based on empirical rewetting experiments.

## CONCLUSIONS

The developed method can be used as a preliminary estimate of the area of rewettable fields in a region. However, it is clear that site characteristics must be more thoroughly investigated in situ before any concrete rewetting actions. This method could be used by authorities designing measures for rewetting and restoring. A well-structured selection system for parcels may ease the wide-spread application of rewetting and restoration activities as it communicates to the landowners that their poorly productive parcels can contribute to climate change mitigation. It may also decrease the possibility of unsuccessful rewetting cases or conflicts between landowners. This method allows for finding promising regions for initiating rewetting after which rewetting activities can be gradually expanded also to the surrounding fields to create dedicated larger areas for restoration or paludiculture.

## ACKNOWLEDGEMENTS

The study was funded by Suoviljelysyhdistys ry, Academy of Finland (project Novel soil management practices – key for sustainable bioeconomy and climate change mitigation) and EU Life (project Towards carbon neutral municipalities and regions; Life 17 IPC/FI/000002).

## REFERENCES

Kekkonen H., Ojanen H., Haakana M., Latukka A., Regina K. (2019) Mapping of cultivated organic soils for targeting greenhouse gas mitigation. *Carbon Management;* https://doi.org/10.1080/17583004.2018.1557990

Oksala A. (2019) Mapping suitable cultivated peatlands for mitigating greenhouse gas emissions by water table management. Master's thesis. Available at: https://aaltodoc.aalto.fi/handle/123456789/40928

ID 62303

# CONSERVATION OF PEATLAND LANDSCAPES IN MALAYSIA

*Faizal Parish, Serena Lew Siew Yan, Aida Hayati, Mohd Faizuddin, Mohd Faris Rabbani

Global Environment Centre, Malaysia

*fparish@gec.org.my*

## SUMMARY

Malaysia is a nature megadiverse country that contain approximately 2.56 million hectares (Mha) of peatlands which mainly covered in dense tropical peat swamp forest (PSF). PSF supports a high diversity of plant and animal species including more than 198 species of fish (Sule et. al., 2016), 181 species of plant (Giesen et. al., 2018), 57 species of mammals and 237 species of birds (Sebastian, 2002). However, over the past 50 years, more than 70% of peatlands in Malaysia have been developed for agriculture, plantations, housing and converted into other land-use. As a result, the remaining relatively intact peatlands have been fragmented and commonly occurred as part of a broader landscape with other uses. Since the management especially on water management, of the areas surrounded the remaining peat swamp forest have a major long-term impact through sub-surface drainage and subsidence – the natural hydrological regime of remaining peatlands has been disrupted, leading to increasing risk of fire and subsidence, and disruption of ecology. In order to address this challenge, it is necessary to develop an integrated landscape approach to peatland management – focusing on the management of the peatland hydrological unit or peat basin. A major peatland management initiative has been developed under Sustainable Management of Peatland Ecosystems in Malaysia (SMPEM) project financed by IFAD-GEF and the Government of Malaysia. This project focusses on five peatland landscapes covering more than 500,000 ha. The core of the landscapes are still covered with peat swamp forests with great significance for biodiversity conservation. Surrounding areas comprise agriculture, oil palm plantations, housing and mining land. Strategies have been developed to minimise the impact of the surrounding development on the peat swamp forest and reduce the occurrence of peatland fires and subsidence through better water and land management approaches. A multi-stakeholder approach is being used to bring together a broad range of government, private sector, community and civil society stakeholders to develop integrated management plans for these landscapes.

## INTRODUCTION

Malaysian peat soil covers an estimate total of 2.56 Mha, approximately 7.5% from the total land area of the country (Zakri, 2019). According to UNDP (2006), peat swamp forests are waterlogged forests growing on a layer of dead leaves and plant material up to 20 meters thick. The remaining peat swamp forest in Malaysia is estimated up to 1.6 Mha or 70% (1,120,000 ha) of total peatlands located in Sarawak (Melling, 2016); less than 20% in Peninsular Malaysia and the remaining (120,000 ha) in Sabah. Threats to peat swamp forest in Malaysia include logging, agriculture, industries, residential schemes and forest fires. 67% from 300,000 ha of peat swamp forest in Peninsular Malaysia have been gazetted under protected area (Musri I. et al., 2020), while the remaining were categorised as stateland. Most of the logging areas in stateland were seriously degraded, suffering from poor regeneration of peat swamp vegetation, and prone to repeated forest fires. Conservation of peat swamp forest is crucial to maintain environmental stability, slows down global warming by acting as carbon sink, and mitigate flood in water regulation. In order to address these challenges, it is necessary to develop an integrated landscape approach in peatland management which involving multi-stakeholder to widen conservation aspect. Case study in Southeast Pahang Peat Swamp Forest (SEPPSF) has shown an effectiveness of multi-stakeholder approach in combating peatland degradation and preventing forest fire. Major peatland management initiative has been developed under Sustainable Management of Peatland Ecosystems in Malaysia (SMPEM) project to focus on five peatland landscapes within the country, namely North Selangor Peat Swamp Forest, South Selangor Peatland Lanscape, Southeast Pahang Peatland Landscape, Klias Peninsular Peatland Landscape and Maludam Peninsular Peatland Landscape.

## MATERIALS AND METHODS

Implementation of peatland conservation initiated from imposing policies to strengthen the management and conservation effort of the peat swamp forest. Malaysia has recognised the significance of peatland ecosystems and has outlined a broad range of actions to maintain peatland through National Action Plan on Peatlands (NAPPs) which was developed and endorsed by the Malaysian Cabinet in 2011 (APFP, 2014). The NAPP has been guided by the regional ASEAN Agreement on Transboundary Haze Pollution (AATHP) which Malaysia signed in 2002 and ratified in 2003 and the associated ASEAN Peatland Management Strategy 2006-2020 (APMS).

Conservation of the peatland area has been included as one of key indicators for the National Policy on Biological Diversity 2016-2025 (CBD Report, 2019). A National Peatland Working Committee (NPWC) and a National Peatland Steering Committee (NPSC) have been established to coordinate and facilitate the stakeholders' efforts in sustainably managing the peatland ecosystems in Malaysia.

Malaysia has recognised the increasing extent and frequency of peatland fires as well as its associated smoke haze pollution and thus implementing a National Programme on Implementing Peat Fire Prevention to Combat Haze in Malaysia since 2009. Under the framework of this programme, the government adopted a Standard Operating Procedure (SOP) for Prevention of Peatland Fires (DOE, 2019) which is a component of the ASEAN Regional Haze Action Plan. The SOP outlines infrastructure support including construction of observation towers, check dams, tube wells and other facilities to prevent or control the peatland fires. Among others, the document provides guidelines relating to the responsibilities of various government agencies and chains of command in response to large scale forest and peatland fires.

A significant portion of the peatlands in Malaysia have been managed by the private sector in particular by oil palm plantations. All oil palm plantations, independent and organised smallholdings need to be certified by Malaysian Sustainable Palm Oil (MSPO) Standard to ensure its compliance to this mandatory standard. MSPO is a national commitment to enhance the sustainability of the oil palm sector in its production in all aspects include environment, human rights, safety and health, as well as land-use change. Plantations on peatland in Malaysia adopted zero burning policy, where open burning is not allowed in order to protect the environment and to avoid any uncontrolled burning. The implementation of certification on sustainable management practices is a feasible way to demonstrate good practices on peatland.

Public and private sectors are encouraged to involve through corporate social responsibility (CSR) activity by contributing to elements of peatland rehabilitation and conservation. Many private companies have been involved in peatland rehabilitation such as tree planting, rewetting degraded peatland areas and empowering the local community groups that are living on peatland areas. The involvement of private sector is commonly linked to Community, Education, Public Awareness (CEPA) activities as a key instrument to enhance knowledge and increase awareness on environmental management and protection, through programmes, corporate supported events and campaigns.

Malaysia has secured a national peatland project funded by the Global Environment Facility (GEF) through International Fund for Agricultural Development (IFAD) for "Sustainable Management of Peatland Ecosystems in Malaysia (SMPEM)" (GEF, 2020). The project will strengthen national policy and institutional capacity for implementing peatland related strategies and plans and to enhance integrated sustainable peatland management in five targeted peatland landscapes in Malaysia. State Action Plan for Peatlands (SAPP) will be developed under this project to complement new NAPP (2021-2030). Each SAPP will set down a vision, values and principles to guide state government for actions on peatlands in the respective state. The SAPP is aimed at policymakers from agriculture, forestry, plantation and urban sectors, as well as peatland managers, landowners and the community that are benefiting from the peatland ecosystem services. The SAPPs will give direction to each state's approaches on the peatland management, including ways to optimise the benefits derived from Malaysia's vast peatland resources over the coming decades.

Under the SMPEM framework, development of integrated landscape plan to manage the peatland which focusing on management of hydrological unit or peat basin has been initiated. The project also emphasises bottom-up approach to best use of existing consultative processes at the village level, to disseminate project-related information, promote discussions and solicit recommendations in a participatory and inclusive manner by the stakeholders.
In Southeast Pahang Peat Swamp Forest (SEPPSF) and South Selangor Peatland Landscape, indigenous community from Jakun and Temuan tribes, respectively, have been engaged for peatland rehabilitation in degraded landscapes within Pekan (Extension) Forest Reserve in Pahang and Kuala Langat PSF in Selangor. Engagement has been established with multi-stakeholder approach by linking the government, private sector and local community for a common goal. Several activites have been undertaken in conjunction to peatland rehabilitation through Free, Prior and Informed Consent (FPIC) process. These rehabilitation activties include blocking of abandoned logging canals, establish a community-based fire

patrolling team for prevention and supressing fire, initiate induced-natural regeneration by replanting forest tree species, introduce alternative livelihood options with socio-economic values and capacity building for the local community and relevant stakeholders.

**RESULTS**

GEC's involvement in rehabilitation of the peatland ecosystem in Southeast Pahang Peat Swamp Forest (SEPPSF), and North Selangor and Kuala Langat PSFs in Selangor, have shown successful case studies with multi-stakeholder approach in conserving and rehabilitating the degraded peatland landscapes. Peatland landscape in Pekan (Extension) Forest Reserve within SEPPSF has devastated with multiple fire incidents where the largest fire incident left enormous fire scars in 2018. Conservation effort started in 2019 and no fire incident has been reported since then. A total of ten canal blocks constructed within the fire incident area in Pekan (Extension) Forest Reserve (Figure 1) by multiple disciplinary sectors including government agencies namely Department of Irrigation and Drainage (DID), Pahang State Forestry Department and Department of Environment (DOE), and private sector with support of GEC and the local community. Canal block construction gave a positive impact on the peatland landscape in SEPPSF. Figure 2 shows a significant improvement from a 227 ha fire in 2018 that left a fire scar; and observation in 2020 after the hydrology restoration by canal blocks have encouraged natural regeneration at the area.
This effort of multi-stakeholder approach in preventing forest fire achieved successful outcome with anestimate of 1500 ha being rewetted. This has proven that rehabilitating hydrology regime in peatland is the most important aspect to be taken care in restoration effort.

Figure 1: Some of the canal blocks constructed by GEC within the landscape to rewet the degraded peat area

(a) (b) (c)

Figure 2: Photos showing changes from (a) forest fire occurred in 2018; (b) Fire scar observed in 2019 during initial stage of conservation effort; and (c) Rehabilitation in progress in 2020.

GEC also works with the local community groups to establish teams of community-based fire patrolling in both Pahang and Selangor states in Malaysia. A total of four patrolling teams were established of which each team consists of two to four members. Through close engagement with the local community groups, an early warning system tool such as Fire Danger Rating System (FDRS) signboards, water level markers and piezometers were installed. FDRS signboard provides information on near real-time condition of specific area on risk of forest fire prepared by Malaysian Meteorological Department. The community group were informed on the system from consecutive training session provided by GEC with collaboration of the villages leaders or village committee (*Majlis Pengurusan Komuniti Kampung* (MPKK)). The community understood the functions and aware of the upcoming dry day as indicated with colour code on the FDRS signboards. This allows the local community groups to do their daily activities with or without concerning on forest fire especially within the degraded peatland area.

In order to promote vegetation regeneration within the degraded peatland landscape, a series of replanting activities has been conducted after the rewetting process taken place. In the first phase, replanting activity has been conducted with nearby oil palm plantation stakeholders and community with fast growing pioneer forest tree species namely Mahang (*Macaranga pruinosa*). For the case in Pahang, engagement with the local community from Kampung Tanjung Kelapa to replant at buffer zone of Pekan (Extension) Forest Reserve, with initial planting of 140 wildings . After the rewetting effort, most areas were previously covered by grassess have been replaced by sedges and purun.

GEC also introduced alternative livelihood activities to the local community groups to reduce their dependency on the peatland. Among the activities are community nursery of forest tree species, stingless bee farming, catfish cultivation, straw mushroom cultivation, and *pandanus* weaving. A series of capacity building training sessions were conducted to empower the local community groups in undertaking the alternative livelihood activities. *Macaranga pruinosa* and *Melicope lunu-ankenda* are both native tree species that grow well in degraded peatland areas in Pahang and Selangor during rehabilitation programme. Stingless bee are a potential natural treasure with high socio-economic value living in smoke-free environment of peatland. Catfish and *pandanus* are a native species that can be found easily in peatland area. While the straw mushroom activity undertaken using empty fruit bunches (EFB), which is a by-product of crude palm oil production from a nearby mill, as one of stakeholders to be engaged to support providing alternative option to the local community. These activities have been significantly improving the community's household income.

(a (b (c (d

Figure 3: Alternative livelihood activities introduced to the local community groups, include: (a) Community nursery; (b) *Pandanus* weaving products; (c) Straw mushroom farming; and (d) Stingless bee honey in marketing-ready packaging.

## CONCLUSION

Malaysia has recognised the importance of the peatland ecosystems in the country and have been taking actions on improving the rehabilitation and conservation effort through better management practices, both on the cultivated peatland areas and the protecting of the peat swamp forests. The conservation effort includes strengthen national frameworks and capacities for the sustainable management of peatlands, multi-stakeholder approach, involvement of private sector especially through CEPA programmes as well as active engagement and partnership with the community. The multi-stakeholder approach which involves government, non-governmental or non-profit organisations, plantation sector and the local communities in rehabilitating the degraded peatland landscape and conserving the PSF is a must. Case studies from Pahang and Selangor have proven that all relevant stakeholders from different disciplinary need to joint hands in order to achieve the common objective and goal, especially on environmental management and protection including the peatland conservation in Malaysia.

## ACKNOWLEDGEMENTS

Global Environment Centre (GEC) as the implementer of the management and rehabilitation of the peatland landscapes with the local community groups in Selangor and Pahang States, Malaysia. Appreciation to the International Fund for Agricultural Development (IFAD) through Technical Assistance and Knowledge Exchange for Sustainable Management of Peatland Ecosystems in Malaysia (TAKE-SMPEM) Project, for providing support in peatland fire prevention, forest rehabilitation and community development activities within the Landscapes in Malaysia. Special thanks to all local community groups who have been actively supporting the programmes in preventing peatland fire and rehabilitating the degraded peatland areas within the Landscapes.

## REFERENCES


ASEAN Peatland Forests Project Malaysia Component Special Publication (2014). Gambut. https://ledsgp.org/wp-content/uploads/2015/12/Asean-Peatland-Forests-Management-Malaysia-Component.compressed.pdf. Access date: 3/1/2021

Giesen, W., Wijedasa, L.S. and Page, S.E. (2018). Unique Southeast Asian peat swamp forest habitats have relatively few distinctive plant species. Published at Mires and Peat, Volume 22. http://mires-and-peat.net/media/map22/map_22_01.pdf. Access date: 2/1/2021

Jabatan Alam Sekitar Malaysia (2019). Prosedur Tetap Operasi Melaksanakan Program Mencegah Kebakaran Tanah Gambut Untuk Mengatasi Jerebu.

Malaysia's Peat Swamp Forest Conservation and Sustainable Use (2006). Publication by United Nation Development Programme, Malaysia. https://www.my.undp.org/content/malaysia/en/home/library/environment_energy/EEPub_PeatSwamp.html#:~:text=Malaysia's%20Peat%20Swamp%20Forests%20Conservation%20and%20Sustainable%20Use,-Feb%2028%2C%202014&text=Peat%20swamp%20forests%20provide%20a,water%20supply%20and%20groundwater%20recharge. Access date: 2/1/2021

Melling L. (2016) Peatland in Malaysia. In: Osaki M., Tsuji N. (eds) Tropical Peatland Ecosystems. Springer, Tokyo. https://doi.org/10.1007/978-4-431-55681-7_4

Musri I., Ainuddin A. N., Hyrul M. H. I., Hazandy A.H., Azani A.M. & Mitra U. (2020) Post forest fire management at tropical peat swamp forest: a review of Malaysian experience on rehabilitation and risk mitigation. IOP Conf. Ser.: Earth Environ. Sci. 504 012017. https://iopscience.iop.org/article/10.1088/1755-1315/504/1/012017/pdf#:~:text=At%20present%2C%20some%20areas%20of,the%20National%20Forestry%20Act%2C%201984. Access date: 26/3/2021.

Sebastian, A. 2002. Globally threatened mammal and bird species in Malaysian peat swamp forests. In: Rieley, J. O. & Page, S. E. (eds) Peatlands for People: Natural Resources Management and Sustainable Management. Symposium Proceedings, Jakarta, august 2001. BPPT and IPA.

Sixth National Report Of Malaysia to the Convention on Biological Diversity (CBD) (2019). National report by Ministry of Water, Land and Natural Resources (KATS)

Sule, H. A., Ismail, A. and Amal, M. N. A. (2016). A Review of the Ichthyofauna of Malaysian Peat Swamp Forest. Published at Pertanika J. Trop. Agric. Sci. 39 (4): 421 - 458 http://psasir.upm.edu.my/id/eprint/49691/1/02%20JTAS%200765-2015%20-%20Review%20Article.pdf. Access date: 2/1/2021.

The Global Environment Facility (GEF) (2020) Sustainable Management of Peatland Ecosystems in Malaysia (SMPEM) Project. https://www.thegef.org/project/sustainable-management-peatland-ecosystems-malaysia-smpem. Access date: 26/3/2021

Zakri A.H. (2019). 'Peatland threatened' *New Straits Times.* 10/02/2019. Available at: https://www.nst.com.my/opinion/columnists/2019/02/459026/peatlands-threatened. Access date: 04/11/2020

# ID 62512

# UNDERSTANDING THE EFFECTS OF DRAINAGE AND FIRES ON HYDRAULIC CONDUCTIVITY TO SUPPORT TROPICAL PEATLAND RESTORATION

Adi Kunarso[1,3], Dony Rachmanadi[2], Tubagus Angga Anugrah Syabana[3], Samantha Grover[1]

[1] Applied Chemistry and Environmental Science, RMIT University, Australia
[2] Environment and Forestry Research and Development Institute of Banjarbaru, Indonesia
[3] Environment and Forestry Research and Development Institute of Palembang, Indonesia

*s3738965@student.rmit.edu.au*

Indonesian peatlands have been subjected to extensive logging and drainage for decades, resulting in recurrent fires in the prolonged dry season. Under natural forest conditions, tropical peat soil is characterized by high porosity, low bulk density, and high water content. The disturbances of fire and drainage have led to substantial alteration of peatland condition and affected the physical and chemical properties of the peat soil. Recently, peatland restoration has become an Indonesia Government priority, with programs to address the smoke haze issue which is a consequence of peatland fires. This study examines differences in the saturated hydraulic conductivity of the acrotelm layer in a secondary forest peatland and two drained and burnt peatlands in OKI District, South Sumatra, Indonesia. The soil samples were collected from four soil pits of each land cover type. Two replicate pits were located close to canals (100m), representing drained conditions, and two replicate pits were located far from the same canal (800m), representing wet conditions. Soil samples have been taken at 8 depths down to 100 cm in each pit, with 3 replicate samples at each depth, using cylindrical rings of length 5 cm and diameter 5.2 cm. Saturated hydraulic conductivity is measured using the constant-head method (Chameleon, Soilmoisture Equipment Corp, Santa Barbara). These results will yield a better understanding of tropical peat soil properties, that can be used to support the success of Indonesia's peatland restoration efforts.

Keywords: Tropical peatland, restoration, hydraulic conductivity

ID 62047

# RESTORATION OF EXTRACTED CENTRAL EUROPEAN PEATLANDS BY SPONTANEOUS SUCCESSION

*Karel Prach, Pospíšilová

Faculty of Science USB, Czech Republic

*prach@prf.jcu.cz*

Peatlands in central Europe represent an endangered habitat with the occurrence of many rare and relict species. We asked is there a potential for spontaneous restoration after peat extraction? The study was conducted at 17 peatlands in the Czech Republic mined either by the traditional block-cut method or industrially. Vegetation records of 5 × 5 m were carried out in representative parts of different successional stages. Vegetation records in undisturbed parts ofpeatlands represented the respective target stages. More than 200 records were analysed by the multivariate statistics. Age since peat extraction and environmental characteristics were assessed (position of water table, water pH, substratum chemistry, geographical area, altitude, average annual temperature and precipitation). Despite the great variability in vegetation, especially among industrially harvested sites, there is a general tendency for peatland vegetation to recover spontaneously, especially at traditionally harvested sites. All environmental variables investigated had at least some significant effect on the vegetation pattern, among them, soil pH, water table, nitrates, successional age and geographical location were most important. Abiotic site factors together and geographical location appeared to be more important in determining species composition than successional age. Generally, extracted peatlands can be successfully restored spontaneously but only under the assumption that water level is kept close to the peat surface. Artificial afforestation has detrimental effects on all biota typical for the peatlands.

ID 62118

# RESTORATION OF PEATLAND FORESTS IN SOUTH EAST ASIA

*Faizal Parish, Serena Lew, Nagarajan Rengasamy

Global Environment Centre, Indonesia

*fparish@gec.org.my*

There are about 25 million ha of peatlands in South east Asia - most of them being vegetated by peat swamp forests which are diverse forests with collectively more than 1,300 plant species recorded in the region. Many individual peat swamps forests may have up to 250 tree species and a total of 500 plant species many of which have important socio-economic or cultural values. Peat swamp forests in southeast Asia have been severely degraded by clearance, drainage, over-exploitation and fire over the past 30 years with less than 25% remaining in a relatively intact but degraded form. Work to actively rehabilitate or restore these forests have started mainly in the past 20 years supported initially by the forestry sector and more recently the plantation sector. The paper will share experience in peatland restoration and rehabilitation from a number of sites mainly in Indonesia and Malaysia as well as the key principles and guidance for restoration approaches and lessons learned. Initial attempts to rehabilitate peatland often failed - due to poor species selection and lack of attention to ecological or hydrological requirements. An important lesson learned is that the root causes of degradation especially disruption of the natural hydrology must be addressed as far as possible at the initial stage of restoration. Selection or planting of faster growing pioneer species is also important at the initial stages to create canopy cover and shade as well as increase humidity creating the conditions for a broader range of tree species to colonise sites. Prevention of fire and other disturbances in the restoration sites is also critical. While planting of saplings may be important in severely degraded sites with little remaining seed-bank, facilitating enhanced natural regeneration is more cost effective and may create more resilient habitats. Peatland restoration efforts need to be scaled up significantly and further degradation minimised.

ID 62363

# INTRODUCING BIOENERGY POTENTIAL PLANT AT RESTORATION OF DEGRADED TROPICAL PEAT SWAMPS WITH AGROSILVOFISHERY SYSTEM AND COMMUNITY PARTICIPATION

*Rujito Agus Suwignyo1, Himlal Baral2, Soo Min Lee3, Yusuf B Samsudin2, Erizal Sodikin1, Munandar4, Sarno5, and Budi Leksono6

1 Peatland Research Center (CoE PLACE) Sriwijaya University, Indonesia,
2 Center for International Forestry Research (CIFOR), Indonesia
3 National Institute of Forest Science (NIFoS), Republic of Korea
4 Department of Agronomy, Faculty of Agriculture Sriwijaya University, Indonesia
5 Department of Biology, Faculty of Mathematics and Natural Sciences Sriwijaya University, Indonesia
6 Center for Research and Development of Biotechnology and Forest Plant Breeding, Indonesia

*rujito@unsri.ac.id*

Indonesia has the largest tropical peatlands, but deforestation, drainage, and burning of peatlands have resulted in the loss of biodiversity and release of a large amount of carbon. Further, decades of such unsustainable practices have led to large areas of degraded peatlands which are highly susceptible to oxidation, dissolution, and fires. The long dry season in 2015 and 2019 caused many peatland fires in Indonesia. One of the factors causing land fires is the practice of land management for the cultivation of *sonor* rice which is carried out by burning land and rice seeds are broadcasted. This research has been carried out since 2018 on a shallow degraded peatland of farmers' land in Perigi Village, Ogan Komering Ilir Regency, South Sumatra Province, Indonesia. We aims to identify suitable tree species for bioenergy production with agrosylvofishery system and community participation to combat climate change while producing a variety of socio-economic and environmental benefits for rural communities. The species of plants can be used as a source of bioenergy, both wood or fruit that produces oil, i.e. *Calophyllum inophyllum, Cerbera manghas, Shorea belangeran, Dyera lowii, Shorea pauciflora, Alstonia pnumatophora*, and *Blumeodendron kurzii*. The results showed that *Calophyllum inophyllum* and *Cerbera Manghas* plants had the best growth compared to other types of plants that were tested. Both plants can grow well under degraded peatlands. The development of bioenergy-producing plants using the agrosilvofishery method turned out to be very effective to implement, because the landowner farmers guarded the land, for its brought value, so that it did not catch fire even though the surrounding land had a fire during the long dry season of 2019. Moreover, the agrosylvofishery technique will contribute to peat formation while producing commodities such as food, fish, fibre, bioenergy, and other Non-Timber Forest Products (NTFPs).

ID 62456

# ON THE RESTORATION OF EXTRACTED PEATLANDS IN ESTONIA – FROM THE TEST SITES TO THE ENVIRONMENTAL POLITICS

Edgar Karofeld[1], Kai Vellak[1, 2]

[1] Institute of Ecology and Earth Sciences, University of Tartu, Estonia
[2] Natural History Museum of the University of Tartu, Estonia

## SUMMARY

Estonia is still one of the most peatland rich countries in the world. Because of a of peatland drainage for centuries, the area of natural mires has decreased by 2/3, especially during last century. Currently, the mires in near natural state cover ~9 % of the territory. There are approximately 20,000 ha of active peat extraction areas and 9,800 ha of abandoned extracted peatlands in Estonia. Together with drained peatlands they have a strong negative effect on the environment also due to the replacement of carbon accumulation by the emission of greenhouse gases from peat decomposition. Therefore, there is obligation enforced by the legislation and urgent need to restore the extracted and drained peatlands. Here we report our results from the application of two techniques in experimental restoration of abandoned extracted peatlands. By the end of the 6$^{th}$ year after the application of the moss layer transfer technique, the plant cover dominated by *Sphagnum* mosses reached <80%. In restored areas water table depth higher than 20 cm is recommended to promote the revegetation. In restored areas with higher water table Sphagnum medium and Sphagnum fuscum and in drier areas S. fuscum gives the best results. Risen water table and re-vegetation have resulted in essential decrease in GHG emission and the area with higher water table have gained back the carbon accumulation ability. Good results to promote re-vegetation were also achieved with the application of oil shale ash and straw mulch. By the end of the 3$^{rd}$ year, the cover dominated by Polytrichum spp. and bog vascular plants reached over ca 60%.

**Keywords:** bog, MLTT, oil-shale ash, Sphagnum

## INTRODUCTION

In Estonia peatlands cover *ca* 22% of the territory (Orru, 1992), but the majority of them are affected by different human activities. Mires in a natural state are estimated to cover only one third of their initial area. Peatlands have been drained for centuries, mostly for forestry and agriculture, and in lesser extent for the peat extraction. As long as peat was hand-cut from the drenches at bog margins without drainage, this had only local impact and these areas revegetated spontaneously rather well. Situation changed drastically from 1950-s with the adoption of peat milling and vacuum-mining techniques which required large areas with deep drainage. There are ~9,800 ha of abandoned extracted peatlands in Estonia, left aside without any restoration mostly during or shortly after the end of Soviet period in the end of XX century (Ramst et al., 2006). Owing to their large areas, deep drainage, lack of viable propagules and hostile environmental conditions, the spontaneous revegetation of milled peatlands is very slow and uneven. Even after 30 years since abandonment the total plant cover can still be only few percentages. Poorly vegetated abandoned extracted peatlands are a threat to the environment locally and also globally, being a substantial source of greenhouse gas (GHG) emissions (Salm *et al*., 2009). Together with drained peatlands they are the second biggest GHG source in Estonia after oil shale mining and energetics.

Therefore, the restoration of extracted peatlands is crucial to stop their destructive environmental influences. Their restoration should support the vegetation succession towards the self-sustainable near-natural state resembling mire habitats, where the accumulation of peat could start again. The restoration of extracted peatlands in Estonia is speeding up thanks to the European Commission support to reduce the mineralization of residual peat and to create near-natural self-regulating ecosystems by restoring at least 2,000 ha by 2023. But the importance of extracted peatland restoration, their role in the national GHG budget and the need for active involvement of experienced peatland scientists in the restoration to achieve targeted results is still undervalued by the politicians and officials. Current overview is aimed to 1) summarise the results from the application of the Moss Layer Transfer Technique (MLTT) and oil-shale ash with straw mulch in the experimental restoration on three extracted peatlands, 2) to clarify main factors affecting on the growth of Sphagnum species under different conditions in restored sites, and 3) to find out which of the studied Sphagnum species are most promising in restoration areas with different water table depth.

## MATERIAL AND METHODS

The restoration experiment with the MLTT was done in spring 2012 at the edge of the Tässi peat extraction area in central Estonia where the peat milling was terminated ~30 years ago. The residual peat depth is ~2.5 m, of which the uppermost 1 m is Sphagnum bog peat. Water table depth (WTD) fluctuated greatly but during the vegetation season it was mostly 0.5−1 m below the peat surface. Spontaneous re-vegetation has been slow and total plant cover was still <1 %, consisting mostly of single Eriophorum vaginatum tussocks of and few Pinus sylvestris juvenils. For the restoration the topmost ~ 20 cm thick oxidized peat layer was stripped by bulldozer and surface was flattened. The surface of 1/3rd of the restoration area was levelled to be ca10 cm lower (wetter) than the rest (drier). Plant fragments for the restoration were collected from a donor site in Soosaare bog‒a typical hollow-ridge bog with sparse *P. sylvestris* trees on ridges and where in the ground layer Sphagnum mosses were dominating. We cut plant fragments from the topmost ~10 cm of *Sphagnum* hummocks with trimmers. Plant fragments collected from 1 $m^2$ in the donor site were spread over 10-15 $m^2$ in the restoration area and covered with straw mulch. The only outflow ditch from the restoration area was blocked with peat. WTD was measured mostly every few weeks during vegetation season from perforated plastic tubes. Ten 50x50 cm permanent plots were established at random locations in the restoration area on each treatment sites. The total plant cover (%) and the covers of every vascular plant and of bryophyte species were recorded in each plot. The length increment of Sphagnum medium, S. fuscum and S. rubellum shoots was measured with brush-wires in wetter and drier sectors in four sites with 3 wires per species. The length of wire above moss carpet was measured at the end of April and measurements were repeated in late October. Shortening of wire length gave the increment of Sphagnum shoots. For comparison, the same measurements were done in natural Parika and Männikjärve bog with hollow-ridge-pool complexes. More details in Karofeld et al., 2016, 2020.

To reveal the potential effect of oil-shale ash on the revegetation, the field studies were carried out in Tähtvere and Keressaare extracted peatlands in Central Estonia. Both peatlands were abandoned after peat milling ~30 years ago, but their total vegetation cover was still only a few percentages. In July 2009 two study sites were selected in both peatlands: one site at the edge and close to a forest and the second in the centre of extracted area. From the established permanent plots sparse vegetation and the topmost ~10 cm of the loose residual peat layer was peeled off. Thus, the spontaneous revegetation of the plots should start from a zero baseline. Every study site consisted of 40 permanent 1 $m^2$ sample plots; ten for each treatment: 1, plots without the treatment (control), 2, plots with straw mulch, 3, plots with oil-shale ash and straw mulch and, 4, plots with oil-shale ash. Plots treated with ash (3 and 4) received *ca* 350 g $m^{-2}$ of oil-shale ash consisting mainly CaO, SiO2, FeO, MgO, Al2O3, Fe2O3 and the pH of water solution ~12. Plots with treatments 2 and 3 were covered by a ~10-cm-thick fluffy layer of straw mulch. Drainage ditches alongside studied sites were blocked with peat dams. WTD was measured in the centre of each study site from perforated pipes during site visits in growing periods. In each plot the overall list of plant species, the total plant cover as well as the coverage of every species was estimated in the middle of vegetation periods. More details in Triisberg et al., 2018.

## RESULTS

Application of the MLTT. In restored area in Tässi peatland the mean WTD in the wetter area (23.5±0.1 cm) was in average by 7±4 cm higher than in the drier area (30.4±8,9 cm). Application of the MLTT had clearly positive effect on the revegetation of restored extracted peatland area. Higher WTD promotes especially the increase of the bryophyte species cover. The cover of the vascular plants and bryophyte species increased especially during the first years after the restoration. In the autumn of second year after the restoration the total plant cover reached 70-80 % and cover of bryophyte species over 60 % and most of it by Sphagnum mosses (Fig. 1 A). In restored areas all together 49 plant species were recorded, among them 34 bryophyte species, including five Sphagnum mosses. Already in the end of the second vegetation period the plant species composition became more similar to that in the natural bogs (Fig. 1 B).

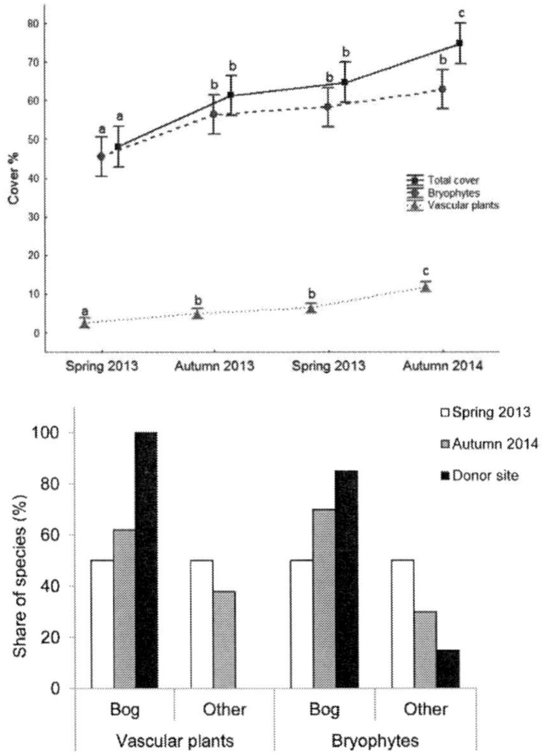


Fig 1. Total plant cover, cover of bryophytes and vascular plants in Tässi wetter area restored with MLTT (A) and changes on entire Tässi restored are in the share of vascular plant and bryophyte species characteristic (bog) and not specific (other) to natural raised bogs in Estonia (Karofeld et.al., 2016).

WTD had the significant effect on the Sphagnum cover in restored area. With six year their total cover reached 72 % in wetter and 52 % in drier sector of restored area. In wetter sector S. medium and S. fuscum attained higher coverage whereas in drier sector S. fuscum performed better than other species (Fig. 2). Difference in WTD caused also significant difference in Sphagnum shoots length increment being smaller in drier sector. No significant difference was revealed in the mean length increment between the studied species whereas weight of Sphagnum capitula was higher for all studied species in both restored sectors as compared to the natural bogs. The thickness of the newly formed Sphagnum layer reached in average 5.6±1 cm in wetter and 4.2±0.7 cm in drier restored sector in the autumn of 6 year after the restoration.

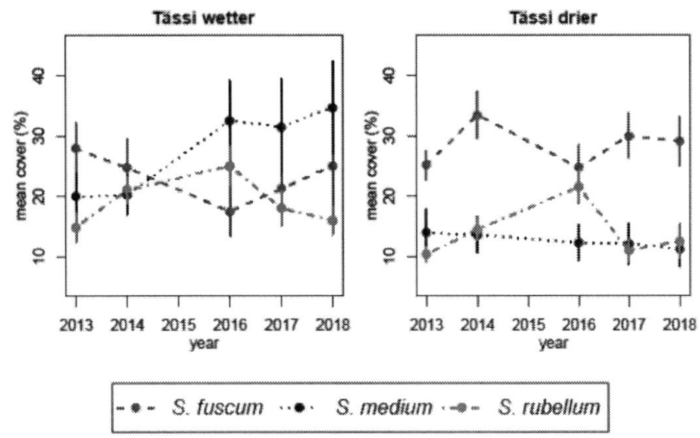


Fig. 2. Changes in the cover of Sphagnum species in Tässi restored wetter and drier sectors (Karofeld et al., 2020).

Treatment with oil-shale ash. In Keressaare and Tähtvere peatlands WTD varied from 14-42 cm. There was no significant difference between the locations on peatlands (edge or centre). Plots treated with oil-shale ash had slightly higher pH values (4.4-4.5) than in other plots. Four year after the treatments in total 32 vascular plant and 13 bryophyte species were registered in permanent plots. Treatments with oil-shale ash with straw mulch as well as with straw alone had significant positive effect on the total plant cover (Fig. 3A). The proximity to the vegetated peatland edge has also positive effect on the total plant cover (Fig. 3B). Especially in first years after the treatments mostly wind-spread plant species dominated. From bryophyte species several pioneer species arisen as Marcantia polymorpha, Dicarnella cerviculata, Funaria hygrometrica besides Polytrichum juniperinum and Pohlia nutans, which were most common. In plots treated with oil-shale ash alone the total plant cover remained low and similar to the control plots, but still also there P. juniperinum was dominating in vegetation.

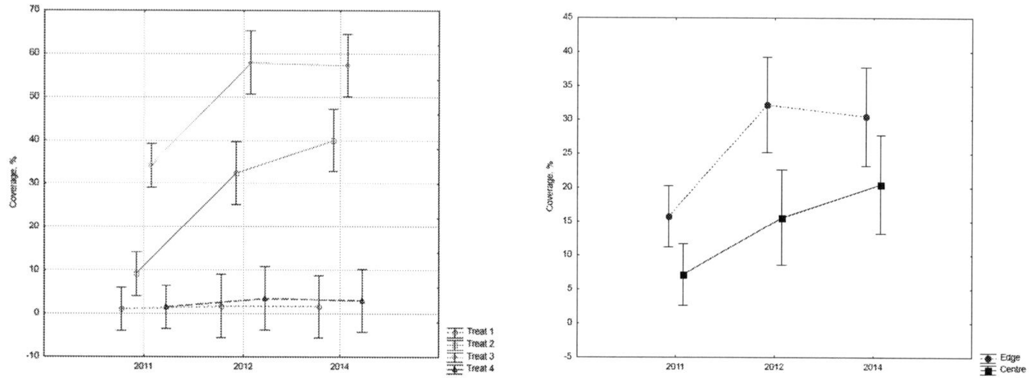


Fig. 3. Changes in the average total plant cover on the plots with different treatments (A) and the effect of the location on the plant cover (B) (Triisberg et al., 2018).

## DISCUSSION

As the main goal of the restoration of extracted peatlands is to convert them back to peat-forming and carbon accumulating ecosystems, it is paramount to restore Sphagnum cover and growth there. Because of very low ability of spontaneous revegetation the active restoration of abandoned extracted peatlands is necessary. Application of the MLTT gives good results in revegetation with Sphagnum mosses, especially when WTD was ~20 cm or higher Fig. 4). The cover of S. medium with wide ecological amplitude, growing in natural bogs in lawns and low hummocks, was significantly positively associated with higher WTD. S. fuscum, growing in bogs on hummocks and is better adopted to deeper WTD and desiccation, can therefore grow relatively well also in slightly drier restored areas. Smaller shoot length increment for all studied Sphagnum species in restored areas as compared to natural bogs is caused by the still relatively low WTD and pure capillary conductivity of residual peat. Therefore, shoots length increment depends also from the amount and regularity of precipitations and not solely from the WTD. The increasing thickness of newly formed Sphagnum layer combined with bigger capitula weight (branches and leaves thickness) allows to foresee improving moisture conditions for their growth. Risen WTD and revegetation mostly with Sphagnum mosses have caused big changes in GHG fluxes from Tässi restored area. The emission of N2O has decreased by 1-2 orders of magnitude and the emission of carbon cases (CO2 and CH4) by almost half as compared to unrestored control area and wetter restored area gained back its carbon accumulation ability (Järveoja et al., 2016).

Fig. 4. Edge of the Tässi abandoned extracted peatland before the restoration in the end of April 2012 (left) and on third summer after the restoration (right).

Application of oil-shale ash in combination with straw mulch promotes the re-vegetation of extracted peatlands and can be used on large areas to get results relatively fast. Although on treated areas there were also several plant species typical for raised bogs, the composition of vegetation in any study areas were not yet similar to that in the natural bogs. In time the alkaline effect of oil-shale ash decreases and established plant cover, including Polytrichum spp as nurse species can promote also the appearance of bog species, including Sphagnum mosses if the rise of WTD can also achieved. The positive effect of straw mulch alone showed the great importance of more stable and better moisture conditions for the spontaneous revegetation.

Although drained and extracted peatlands have big importance in the national GHG budget, their emission amounts and possibilities for the reduction by the restoration is not fully understood and often not accounted in scenarios for climate change mitigation. Since 2026 it becomes possible to take into the account and report the reduction of GHG emission and restarted carbon accumulation in restored extracted peatlands. But to do so, already now state financed long period projects to find out the best techniques for peatland restorations in different conditions and emission measurements should start. So far this, and the need for the involvement of experienced peatland scientists in every step of the extracted peatlands restoration is often neglected, leading to the poor restoration results.

## CONCLUSIONS

It can be concluded that the abandoned extracted peatlands revegetate spontaneously very slowly, but with human interference and restoration it is possible to accelerate this process remarkably. In good conditions and skilled application of different restoration techniques, only in few years the total plant cover ca 70-80 % and essential reduction in GHG emission can be achieved. Depending on the area, most appropriate restoration technique should be applied. The transplanting of plant fragments as well as fertilising with oil-shale ash, the plant cover and plants growth will be promoted, as shown by the results of our experiments. But the base knowledge is, that the water table should be high and stable for restarting paludification process henceforth.


## ACKNOWLEDGEMENTS

We thank Mari Müür, Triin Triisberg-Uljas and Ants Kaasik for their help in field works and data analyses.

## REFERENCES

Järveoja J, Peichl M, Maddison M, Soosaar K, Vellak K, Karofeld E, Teemusk A, Mander Ü. (2016) Impact of water table level on annual carbon and greenhouse gas balances of a restored peat extraction area. *Biogeosciences*; 13: 2637-2651.

Karofeld E, Müür M, Vellak K. (2016) Factors affecting re-vegetation dynamics of experimentally restored extracted peatland in Estonia. *Environmental Science and Pollution Research*; 23: 13706-13717.

Karofeld E, Kaasik A, Vellak K. (2020) Growth characteristics of three *Sphagnum* species in restored extracted peatland. *Restoration Ecology*; 28 (6): 1574-1583.

Orru M. (1992) Eesti turbavarud. Eesti Geoloogiakeskus (in Estonian) 146 pp.

Ramst R, Orru M, Salo V, Halliste L. (2006) Eesti mahajäetud turbatootmisalade revisjon. 2. etapp: Ida-Viru, Lääne-Viru, Jõgeva, Järva ja Tartu maakond. Eesti Geoloogiakeskus, Tallinn (in Estonian).

Salm J-O, Kimmel K, Uri V, Mander Ü. (2009) Global warming potential of drained and undrained peatlands in Estonia: a synthesis. *Wetlands*; 29(4): 1081-1092.

Triisberg-Uljas T, Vellak K, Karofeld E. (2018) **Application of oil-shale ash and straw mulch promotes the revegetation of extracted peatlands.** *Ecological Engineering*; 110: 99-106.

# ID 62515

# ENCOURAGING ECOTONE CREATION IN RESTORED PEATLANDS AT THE EASTERN EDGE OF CANADIAN PRAIRIES

*Pete Whittington[1], Line Rochefort[2], Marie-Claire LeBlanc[2], Michelle Mico[1], Richelle Bamber[1]

[1] Brandon University, Canada
[2] Peatland Ecology Research Group & Center for Northern Studies, Université Laval, Canada

*whittington.pete@gmail.com*

Restoration of peat extraction sites (in Canada) have typically been limited to the surfaces directly impacted by extraction, and thus in isolation from the surrounding landscape (i.e., not connected/integrated with the natural peatland around the site) leaving an abrupt change between the restored area and the surrounding natural peatland. In 2015 at the Elma North restoration site in Eastern Manitoba, we attempted to mitigate this issue by creating three slopes (North, South, West) along the 750 m periphery that were ~250 m long, ~20 m wide, ~1-2 m high connecting the natural peatland and the main restoration site to encourage ecotone creation. Peat surface elevation and peat depth were measured along 5 transects per slope. Two main transects per slope were established and instrumented with wells (3 per transect at low, mid, and high points along the slope) and tensiometers (mid and high points). Moisture content (every 0.5 m for 25 m) was also measured along these transects. Vegetation was also surveyed in three 25 cm square quadrats every 2.5 m along these transects. Results showed that slopes ranged between 5 cm/m (North) to 2 cm/m (West) with the South slope being 3.5 cm/m. Peat depths were variable, but averaged ~1 m. Water tables and moisture contents were relatively similar between the North and West slopes, decreasing in water content and water table with increased distance up-slope; the South Slope experienced flooded conditions from the mid-point down slope. Despite similarities between the slopes, early (<1 year restored) re-vegetation of non-vascular plants was significantly higher on the North and West slopes, likely due to better donor material from the healthier natural peatland found adjacent to the North and West slopes, that was "reworked" into the slope. Four year (2019) after restoration these differences appear to no longer exist, suggesting that exact slope dimensions are not critical to the ecotone creation/restoration efforts.

ID 62516

# HYDROLOGICAL TARGETS AND LESSONS LEARNED OF REWETTING EXPERIMENTS AT THE EASTERN EDGE OF THE CANADIAN PRAIRIES

*Pete Whittington[1], Line Rochefort[2], Marie-Claire LeBlanc[2]

[1] Brandon University, Canada
[2] Peatland Ecology Research Group & Center for Northern Studies, Université Laval, Canada

*whittington.pete@gmail.com*

The moss layer transfer technique is a well-established and successful technique for restoring Sphagnum peatlands after vacuum-extraction; it was established largely in Eastern Canada where precipitation often exceeds 1000 mm/year. However, as some bogs are extracted to fen-peat, with different peat chemistry, and thus, should these sites be restored to bogs? Eastern Manitoba receives only ~600 mm/year. And thus, would the techniques used in Québec be transferable to extracted sites in Manitoba? Three sites in eastern Manitoba were selected that were relatively isolated, hydrologically, from active operations. In 2015, we used a 'waffle-like' pattern (~10 m x 10 m grids), and a cascading crescent-shaped bund pattern, to retain as much snow/melt/rain as possible to try and achieve a water table just below the surface. Unfortunately, seasonal precipitation was anything but average, with > 300 mm of precipitation above average (May to Sept) in 2015 and 2016, functionally flooding the sites (water tables rose from <-100 cm to >+20 cm in the extracted sites, but only rose ~10 cm in the natural sites), showing the need for water control structures in restoration to remove excess water. With these lessons learned, in Sept 2019 we started restoration at Moss Spur 2 with fewer surface recontouring efforts with a 'less prescriptive/more adaptive' approach; but with > 100 mm surplus precipitation in September 2019, restoration efforts were halted. However, water tables appeared to be distributed evenly across the finished fields, and only 5-10 cm flooded, suggesting that gradual interventions might be the key.

ID 62514

# APPROACHES TO PEAT ECOLOGICAL RESTORATION IN INDONESIA: CHALLENGES, OPPORTUNITIES, AND FUTURE DIRECTIONS

*Eli Nur Nirmala Sari[1], Rizky Januar[1], Dede Sulaeman[1], Almag Fira Pradana[1]

[1] World Resources Institute (WRI) Indonesia, Jakarta, Indonesia

*eli.sari@wri.org*

## SUMMARY

Indonesia has 13.43 million ha of peatlands, approximately 13% of tropical peatlands worldwide. Since the last two decades, peatland conversion activities for plantation accompanied by the construction of drainage canals have been carried out on a large scale, which causes peatland degradation. Hence, peatlands have become dry and prone to fire hazards. After severe peatland fires in 2015, a nationwide peatland restoration effort to maintain a 0.4-meter groundwater level on peatlands is committed by the Indonesian government; involving NGOs, the private sector, and the community. However, severe peat fires still occur in several peat areas in 2019; indicating the need to intensify restoration efforts at these sites. This paper explores ideal direction, challenges, and opportunities for improving the restoration efforts onward. We collect and triangulate the required data through 1) FGD with multi-sectoral stakeholders in South Sumatra; 2) in-depth interviews with key stakeholders in Central Kalimantan; 3) systematic review of more than 40 scientific papers related to peatland restoration; 4) in-depth interviews with 6 peat-scientists. Our results show that to achieve peat ecological restoration close to its ideal condition, it is necessary to implement an ecological restoration effort consisting of three main approaches, namely: 1) performing a full rewetting with the right infrastructure; 2) carrying out vegetation restoration with paludiculture practices; 3) reducing pressure on peatland ecosystems. Accordingly, main challenges in implementing the ideal restoration effort in Indonesia are: 1) the lack of synchronization among programs and activities of national- and regional-level institutions in supporting sustainable peatland management; 2) substantial funds required to improve and sustain implementation of peatland restoration onward; 3) the need for improving awareness of all involved stakeholders regarding the benefits of wet and restored peatland ecosystems.

***Keywords**: peatland restoration, challenges, opportunities, full rewetting, paludiculture*

## INTRODUCTION

Indonesia has 13.43 ha of peatland (Ministry of Agriculture, 2019) which is formed from a collection of organic materials that are not completely decomposed. With a high content of organic matter, which is more than 65% (According to Driessen, 1978), peat in Indonesia has a very important role in carbon storage. Indonesian peatlands store large amounts of carbon, especially when in pristine conditions. Indonesian peat swamp forests store on average 220 ± 28 tons of carbon per hectare (t C / ha) in the phytomass (alive and dead vegetation) (Hergoualc'h and Verchot 2011) and 668 ± 20 t C / ha per meter depth of peat (Warren et al. 2012).

However, the conversion of peat forests to other uses, especially for plantations, which is accompanied by the construction of canals, has resulted in peatland degradation. Peat previously has a very good function in water regulation, which functions to store water during the rainy season so that floods do not occur, and release it during the dry season so that there is no drought. After peatland degradation occurs, the peat's ability to store water during the rainy season is reduced, so that flooding can occur during the rainy season. Likewise, during the dry season, peat will experience drought which then makes it prone to fires. Peat in Indonesia takes thousands of years to form. Based on research in peatlands in Central Kalimantan, Page et al. (2002) stated that to form peat with a depth of 200 - 300 cm takes 5,400 - 7,900 years, and a depth of 400 - 800 cm takes 9,400 - 13,000 years. However, peat that is formed over thousands of years can be lost in a relatively short time due to fire.

Historically, the peat formation started with the existence of water and organic matter, and from those components, then the peat is formed. If the peatlands are drained because of the establishment of the canal, the water in the peatlands will be drained, and destroy the peat which has irreversible drying characteristics. The drought that occurs, in addition to causing the release of emissions into the atmosphere, also causes subsidence. When the peat is drained, it shrinks, and this leads to initial peatland subsidence of around 1-1.5 m in the early years. Under dry conditions, biological oxidation will continue to occur causing subsidence at an average rate of 4 cm per year. Peat fires cause an increase in peatland subsidence by about 20-30 cm after the first fire and the subsidence rate will decrease in the following fires. In order to avoid the occurrence of more severe conditions due to the drying up of peatlands, the ecological restoration of peatlands in areas that have been degraded is very important, even though the challenges are enormous. Since 2016, peatland restoration activities using rewetting, revegetation and revitalization of livelihood approaches have been actively implemented in Indonesia. However, peatland fires still occur, especially in 2019. It is critical to evaluate the peatland restoration approach that has been implemented in order to conduct much better peatland restoration in the future.

## MATERIALS AND METHODS

In general, this research was conducted by reviewing scientific papers, discussions with key informants through Focus Group Discussions (FGD), and also direct interviews with peat experts. Data and information collection focused on the topic of peatland restoration in Indonesia, especially in South Sumatra and Central Kalimantan. The analysis was carried out from the information obtained after systematically reviewing more than 40 scientific papers. Data and information regarding peatland ecological restoration activities in the field were obtained through FGD activities with multi-sectoral stakeholders in South Sumatra as well as key stakeholders in Central Kalimantan. To strengthen data and information scientifically, interviews with peat experts and peat restoration experts have also been conducted. In addition, information about the concepts and practices of ecological restoration activities in several regions in Indonesia was also learned from various sources.

## RESULTS AND DISCUSSION

### Threats in Peatlands Ecologically

*Loss of land cover or vegetation*

Forest loss rates in Indonesia are among the highest globally. The loss of vegetation from the peat forests can be caused, among others, by rampant illegal logging activities in peat forests and also land conversion. In Kalimantan (Indonesian Borneo), loss and degradation of peatlands have been particularly acute, with only 426000 ha of the total 5.78 Mha of peatland in Kalimantan (7.4%) considered to remain in a "pristine" condition in 2015 (Harrison et al., 2019). In Indonesia, around 1.5 million - 2 million ha of peatland are converted into plantations (Noor, 2010). Species for plantation, such as oil palm and acacia, require dryland conditions for their growth. When converting peat forests, trees are cut down and this causes a loss of land cover function which then causes sunlight to penetrate directly to the surface and increase the rate of evapotranspiration (Limpens et al., 2014). An increase in surface temperature causes aerobic microorganisms to become more active and accelerates the rate of decomposition on the surface of peatlands, which then releases more emissions into the air (Batubara et al., 2019; Nakonieczna and Stepniewska, 2014). Another impact of the loss of land cover is the loss of opportunities for additional organic matter due to the loss of sources of organic matter from trees.

*Loss of water*

Peatland conversion activities are usually accompanied by the establishment of canals intended for draining the peatlands. Peatland drying occurs very quickly as a result of the establishment of this channel. When peat drainage occurs, microorganisms become more active, and the surface organic matter of the peat decomposes faster. Thus, the rate of subsidence will increase due to the process of consolidation, compaction, and oxidation (Jauhiainen et al., 2011). In addition, emissions that are exposed to the atmosphere are also increasing because of the drying up of peatland due to the construction of these canals. Dry conditions also make peatlands prone to fires. The ability of peat to store water also reduced in drained peatlands (Benavides, 2014). This means that drained peatlands will lose it's characteristics of high water holding capacity and will not act as a "sponge" to store large volumes of water in the rainy season and releasing this water gradually during the dry season. The impact of the loss of water, which is accompanied by the loss of land cover at the same time, causes the peatland draining to become even more severe.

*Loss of peat organic matters*
The loss of peat organic matter can be caused by drought, which causes the rate of decomposition of organic matter by microorganisms to accelerate. In addition, peatland fires can cause the loss of peat organic matter very rapidly. When peatland fires occur, it will be difficult to extinguish them because the embers occur below ground. Based on research conducted by Astiani and Fernando (2017) in Kubu Raya Regency, West Kalimantan, during peat fires, the weight of organic matter lost can be up to 39.14kg / m3 which has an impact on reducing peat depth to 0.621 m.

## Peat Ecological Restoration

Peat ecosystems have interrelated ecological and hydrological functions. Peat ecological restoration is an activity that aims to accelerate the sustainable restoration of the peat ecosystem, which focuses on restoring the ecosystem due to loss of water and loss of vegetation. The occurrence of fires in peatlands, of course, leaves damaged peatland due to the loss of large amounts of organic matter and changes of physical characteristics on peat soil which characterized by the decreasing of its water holding capacity, porosity, and permeability (Tahrun et al., 2015). Restoration of peatlands, in terms of restoring the volume of peat to what it was before the peat fires, will of course take a very long time, up to thousands of years. However, the peatland restoration efforts can be done so that at least, the condition of the peatland ecosystem can return to balance and can support the formation of natural peat.

## Challenge and Opportunities

*Hydrological restoration*
In natural conditions peatlands are waterlogged, and tropical peat contains more than 90 percent water. One of the parameters of degraded peatland is drying up of peatland. The surface of peatlands can become dry when the vegetation cover above is lost, which causes the evapotranspiration rate is high. Peat water becomes increasingly drained from the peatlands when canals are established. On peatlands that have been degraded due to draining due to canals, the canal blocking is critical to be established to re-wet the dry peatlands around them. The canal blocking activity is one of the steps for peatland restoration activities. The main purpose of establishing canal blocking is to minimize the potential for fires and facilitate restoration efforts by raising the water level and retaining water in the canal (Suryadiputra, et al., 2005). The activity of rewetting the peatlands is aimed at increasing the groundwater level in drained peatlands. In Indonesia, based on Government Regulation no. 57/2016 concerning Peat Protection and Management, peatland managers are required to maintain the water level at a level of 40 cm. The aim is to prevent fires by assuming that by maintaining a water level of 40 cm, the surface of the peatland remains moist. However, the regulation does not state that a water level of 40 cm must be maintained throughout the year. In fact, if the water level is kept at 40 cm only during the rainy season, then during the dry season, the water level will drop and the peat surface will dry out and remain prone to fires (Wösten et al. 2008). Moore and Dalva (1993) showed that, compared to emissions when the peat were saturated, water table at a depth of 40 cm increased $CO_2$ fluxes by an average of 4.3 times. Hydrological restoration by keeping the water level near the surface so as to ensure that the surface of the peatland remains wet is important because to keep peat sustainable, peatlands must be permanently saturated (Page et al., 2009; Evers et al., 2017).

*Vegetation restoration*

The existence of vegetation in peat forests functions to create a microclimate, one of which functions to maintain the surface moisture of the peatlands. The existence of this vegetation also functions to increase the accumulation of organic matter that forms peat. On tropical peatlands with normal rainfall, peat formation can increase by around 1 - 3 mm per year (Giesen and Sari, 2017). Logging of trees or land clearing on peatlands causes reduced humidity and the surface of the peat, which can lead to dryness on the surface of the peatlands. Thus, it is important to carry out vegetation restoration on peatlands that have lost their vegetation. Vegetation restoration is an important activity after hydrological restoration because it can support the re-creation of a microclimate, increase soil moisture, which has a positive impact on reducing the risk of fire occurrence. Vegetation restoration activities must consider the selection of native peat species, thereby increasing the chances of successful tree growth. The principle of vegetation restoration is to support the hydrology of wet peatland. These vegetation restoration efforts should also contribute to the accumulation of organic matter. According to Yule et al. (2016), the original type of peat which has a high polyphenol content will help accelerate the accumulation of peat, as these polyphenols can inhibit decomposition.

*Reducing pressure to peatlands*

To support hydrological restoration and vegetation restoration, any human activity that puts pressure on the peat ecosystem must be avoided. For example, the community's livelihood revitalization activities have been planned and done to support restoration. However, in practice, the implemented activities are contrary to the principle of restoration, for example, planting plantation crops that have economic value but require drying for their growth, such as pineapple, dragon fruit, coffee, and cocoa. This revitalization activity will in fact put pressure on the peatlands and cause the peatlands to be degraded. Activities to use peatlands for cultivation are still permitted, as long as they do not put pressure on the peat environment itself. Thus, peatland utilization activities must comply with the following principles: 1) Do not use fire at all or carry out activities that can trigger fires in peatlands; 2) The utilization of non-timber forest products (NTFPs) must be carried out in a peat-friendly manner, for example: not destroying or cutting down trees when taking NTFPs; 3) Do not conduct land clearing on peatlands that still have vegetation, even though they are in cultivated areas; 4) Utilization of land for plant cultivation by the community can be carried out on abandoned peatlands in the cultivated area, by considering the utilization of shallow peatland, considering the selection of species that can grow well in wet peatland conditions, not draining peatlands, and not using chemical substances excess which can poison the environment.

## CONCLUSION

Ecological restoration of peatlands can be successful if there is a balance in the peatland ecosystem. Proper hydrological restoration and vegetation restoration can create a peatland condition that is close to its naturally pristine condition. Hydrological restoration activities are implemented not only by maintaining a water level of 40 cm, but also by carrying out full hydrological restoration, by keeping the water level close to the natural groundwater level (near the surface). In addition to carrying out full hydrological restoration, vegetation restoration activities by planting trees in open peat areas, are important. If it is implemented continuously and it is ensured that these activities are not neglected, it will take at least 5 to 10 years to get the results of the peatland ecosystem with forest cover. As peat ecological restoration activities take a long time, to achieve full restoration results, a transition period is required, by carrying out partial hydrological restoration (for example, maintaining the water level up to 40 cm) and planting trees in some areas, especially in areas where there is no tree. Any activity that can give pressure to the peatland environment must be avoided to support the hydrological restoration process and vegetation restoration. Thus, gradually some functions of the peatland ecosystem will be recover, for example, as a function of storing and regulating water, carbon storage, the habitat for biodiversity, and creating a microclimate.

## REFERENCES


1. Astiani WD, Fernando T. (2017) Loss of peat biomass due to forest fires. Jurnal Hutan Lestari (2017) Vol. 5 (3):824-830
2. Batubara SF, Agus F, Rauf A, Elfiati D. (2019) Soil respiration and microbial population in tropical peat under oil palm plantation. IOP Conf. Series: Earth and Environmental Science 260 (2019) 012083.
3. Benavides JC. 2014. The effect of drainage on organic matter accumulation and plant communities of high-altitude peatlands in the Colombian tropical Andes. Mires and Peat 15(1):1-15
4. Driessen PM. (1978) Peat soils. pp: 763-779. In: IRRI. Soil and rice. IRRI. Los Banos. Philippines.
5. Evers S, Yule CM, Padfield R, O'Reilly P, Varkkey H. (2017) – Keep wetlands wet: the myth of sustainable development of tropical peatlands – implications for policies and management. Global Change Biology, 23:534–549, doi: 10.1111/gcb.13422.
6. Giesen W, Sari ENN. (2018) Tropical Peatland Restoration Report; The Indonesian Case. Berbak Green Prosperity Partnership. MCAI. 2018.
7. Harrison ME, Ottay JB, D'Arcy LJ, Cheyne SM, Anggodo, Belcher C, Cole L, Dohong A, Ermiasi Y, Feldpausch, et al. 2019. Tropical forest and peatland conservation in Indonesia: Challenges and directions. People and Nature. 1-25. doi: https://doi.org/10.1002/pan3.10060
8. Hergoualc'h K, Verchot LV. (2011) Stocks and fluxes of carbon associated with land-use change in Southeast Asian tropical peatlands: A review. Global Biochemical Cycles 25(2): GB2001. DOI:10.1029/2009GB003718.
9. Jauhiainen J, Hooijer A, Page SE. (2011) Carbon dioxide emissions from an acacia plantation on peatland in Sumatra, Indonesia. Biogeosciences Discuss., 8, 8269–8302, 2011; www.biogeosciences-discuss.net/8/8269/2011/ doi:10.5194/bgd-8-8269-2011.
10. Limpens J, Holmgren M, Jacobs CMJ, Van der Zee SEATM, Karofeld E, Berendse F. (2014) How Does Tree Density Affect Water Loss of Peatlands? A Mesocosm Experiment. PLoS ONE 9(3): e91748. https://doi.org/10.1371/journal.pone.0091748.
11. Moore TR and Dalva M. 1993. The influence of temperature and water table position on carbon dioxide and methane emissions from laboratory columns of peatland soils. Journal of Soil Science. 4465: 1-664

12. Nakonieczna AS, Stêpniewska Z. (2014) Aerobic and anaerobic respiration in profiles of Polesie Lubelskie peatlands. Int. Agrophys., 2014, 28, 219-229.
13. Noor M. (2010) Lahan Gambut, Pengembangan, Konservasi dan Perubahan Iklim. Gadjah Mada University Press. Yogyakarta. Hlm 212.
14. Page SE, Siegert F, Rieley JO, Boehm H-DV, Jaya A, Limin SH. (2002) The amount of carbon released from peat and forest fires in Indonesia during 1997, Nature, 420, 61-65.
15. Page S, Hosciło A, Wösten H, Jauhiainen J, Silvius M, Rieley J, Ritzema H, Tansey K, Graham L, Vasander H, Limin S. (2009) Restoration Ecology of Lowland Tropical Peatlands in Southeast Asia: Current Knowledge and Future Research Directions. Ecosystems (2009) 12: 888–905. DOI: 10.1007/s10021-008-9216-2
16. Suryadiputra INN, Dohong A, Waspodo SB, Muslihat L, Lubis IR, Hasudungan F, Wibisono ITC. (2005) A Guide to the Blocking of Canals and Ditches in Conjunction with the Community. Wetlands International – Indonesia Programme and Wildlife Habitat Canada, Bogor, Indonesia, 170 pp. ISBN: 979-99373-5-3. Also available in Indonesian as: "Panduan Penyekatan Parit dan Saluran di Lahan Gambut Bersama Masyarakat."
17. Tahrun M, Wawan, Amri AI. (2015) The change of physical peat soil characteristics caused by fire in Teluk Binjai Village, Teluk Meranti Sub-district, Pelalawan District. JOM FAPERTA Vol 2 No1, 1 February 2015.
18. Warren MW. 2012. A cost-efficient method to assess carbon stocks in tropical peat soil. Biogeosciences Discuss 9: 7049–7071.

# ID 62633

# WATER LEVEL AND CARBON EMISSION RATE IN RESPONS TO CANAL BLOCKING DEVELOPMENT

*Imam Basuki, Beni Okarda, Herry Purnomo

Center for International Forestry Research, Indonesia

*imambasuki1974@gmail.com*

This study aimed to examine water level and carbon emission rates in respons to canal blocking development. It was part of the larger research agenda in participatory action research to avoid peat fires and reduce GHG emissions at the village level. The study was situated on the peat landscape of both six action arenas and their control sites to test the impact of canal blockings on canal water level while considering the different environmental conditions (e.g., distance from primary canal, distance from canal block, slope, canal width, land use/cover types and management systems) that may affect the water level

Pair control and treatment design was applied in this study. The treatment was the development of canal blockings, while the control site was on the opposite or nearby site without canal blockings and their influence. Mean values of canal water level from 24 dipwells in six action arenas and their control sites was used, averaging 33 measurement weeks.

Canal blockings had increased the mean canal water level at 16.5 cm higher than that without the blockings (control) (paired t-test, $p = 0.01$). This means that on average, assuming that the ground water level will increase corresponding to the increase on canal water level, canal blockings may reduce carbon emission at about 32.4 $MgCO_2eq$/ha/yr. We found that areas managed by community showed significantly shallower canal water level (-105 cm) than those managed individually (-120 cm), only to those areas without canal blockings.

Based on our findings we recommend that to achieve effective rewetting activities and reduce fire risks, it is essential to Identify main outlets of water flow out from peat hydrological unit or peat dome and develop more canal blockings on those outlets, especially those with slope > 1%.

# ID 72715

# RECOVERY DYNAMICS OF VEGETATION IN MONTANE PEATLANDS IN THE FIRST TWO DECADES AFTER REWETTING

*Katharina Strobl, Timo Albrecht, Johannes Kollmann

Chair of Restoration Ecology, Dept Life Science Systems, Technical University of Munich, Freising, Germany

*katharina.strobl@tum.de*

## SUMMARY

Rewetting has become a common strategy for recovering biodiversity and ecosystem functions of degraded peatlands. It consists in blocking drainage ditches by wooden dams, or filling them with peat excavated in the direct surroundings, while expecting spontaneous recovery of hydrological conditions and characteristic peatland biodiversity. However, previous studies suggest, that vegetation recovers mostly during the first five years and within the restored drainage ditch. To prove this result, repeated sampling of peat mosses and typical vascular plants in- and outside former ditches is necessary. Thus, five years after a first survey of an 18-yrs chronosequence of montane transitional mires in NE Bavaria we again compared vegetation development in former drainage ditches with plots in 1, 2, 4, 7 and 11 m distance to the ditches. Results of this continued monitoring confirmed that specialist species as well as *Sphagnum* spp. achieve a large increase in the first five years; after that time, progress is slower. Older sites even seem to be moving back to the degraded state, particularly outside the restored drainage ditches. Thus, in montane transitional mires blocking of ditches restores vegetation only locally and for a limited time period. This also confirms, that long-term monitoring is essential after rewetting, since even after a first improvement there might be a return to unfavourable conditions, caused by a 'negative resilience' of the degraded system.

***Keywords***: *ditch blocking, plant specialists, recovery debt, transitional mires, tree removal*

## INTRODUCTION

Ecological restoration is aiming at reversing anthropogenic degradation and bringing an ecosystem back on a trajectory of recovery, for example in degraded peatlands (McDonald et al. 2016). Many montane transitional mires have been drained in order to increase forestry production leading to considerable ecological damage. There, a major restoration strategy consists in blocking ditches and removing trees to reverse the loss of rare and specialized species as well as ecosystem functions like carbon storage. Raising the water table to its original level should benefit peat and biodiversity. However, peatland recovery is complex and slow, and its long-term dynamics are poorly understood.

Previous studies suggest for fens (Hedberg et al. 2012) and boreal peatlands (Haapalehto et al. 2011), that there is significant recovery of peatland hydrology and vegetation during the first 8–10 years after restoration. However, in previous studies (Strobl et al. 2019a, b) we saw that progress might be spatio-temporally limited. Recovery was observed only in the direct surroundings of the blocked ditch, resulting from the fact that montane transitional mires have usually been drained by one or few ditches, and that rewetting effects are therefore limited to this area. Furthermore, there was a tendency of attenuated recovery after 10 years, while near-natural conditions had not yet been reached. These trends need further attention in order to understand if more time is needed for full recovery, if there remains a recovery debt (Moreno-Mateos et al. 2017), or the degraded ecosystem has reached an alternate state stabilized by 'unhelpful resilience' (Bauer et al. 2018).

Therefore, this study aims at analyzing the trajectory of vegetation recovery in rewetted montane transitional bogs and at disentangling recovery limitations. We wanted to know, if the previously observed recovery is actually stagnating, if the improved conditions inside the ditch are spreading towards the entire peatland, and if these tendencies are consistent for sites, that were restored at different points of time in the past 20 years.

## MATERIALS AND METHODS

The study was conducted in twelve montane peatlands in NE Bavaria (longitude E11°44'59''–12°5'5'', latitude N49°53'46''–50°5'45'', altitude 660–1000 m a.s.l.). They can be characterized as acidic transitional bogs with varying influence of surface and rain water, and some being entirely ombrotrophic. In the $19^{th}$ and $20^{th}$ century drainage and afforestation with spruce largely degraded the hydrological conditions of these peatlands with considerable losses of rare species. Since the late 1990s many drained peatlands within the region were successively restored by blocking ditches (approximately 1–2 m wide and 0.5–1 m deep) with wooden dams or peat, and removing unwanted trees nearby. Afterwards, the sites were left to natural succession. This specific setting allowed for assessing peatland recovery in a space-for-time substitution ('chronosequence') approach (Strobl et al. 2019a, b).

Five years later we repeated the sampling of vegetation and water table in ten transects within the restored sites, two within degraded sites, and one in a near-natural peatland. The former included three 'young' (restored 3, 5 and 6 years ago), four 'intermediate' (7 and 9 years) and three 'old' (13, 18 and 20 years). The transects were installed along former drainage ditches and included five randomly selected plots (0.5 $m^2$) within the ditch, and five plots in 1, 2, 4, 7 and 11 m distance from the ditch.

At each plot we sampled identified vascular plants and bryophytes to species level and visually estimated the cover of each species according to the Londo (1976) scale in July 2020. Plants were defined as peatland specialists of Bavarian montane peatlands according to Quinger und Siuda (2009) as in Strobl et al. (2019a). Additionally, we estimated the degree of peat decomposition following Post (1924). At eight transects automatic data loggers recorded the water table at the 4 m-plot every 12 hours since 2015. Data analyses were done in R version 3.5.3 (R Core Team 2015). We averaged the five plots inside and five plots outside the ditch prior to all analyses. We calculated a linear model to study the effect of the 5-year recovery (i.e. sampling year 2015 and 2020), the location (inside or outside the ditch) as well as time since restoration (i.e. degraded, young, intermediate and old sites) on plant specialist cover. We also assumed an interaction between sampling year and location, since we expected the effect of rewetting to spread outside the ditch. The response variable ('specialist cover') was log-transformed due to non-linearity. To test significant differences between time of restoration, we performed a Tukey HSD test with Bonferroni correction for two sub-datasets separately, i.e. inside and outside the ditch.

## RESULTS

Within 5 years the water table increased in two recently restored sites, stagnated in one degraded, one young and one intermediate site, and decreased in two intermediate and two old sites. In total, we found 90 plant species in 2020 compared to 85 in 2015, among them 44 vascular plants and 41 bryophytes.

*Table 5: Effect of sampling year, location and time since restoration on the cover of plant specialists. * indicates the analyzed interaction effect*

| Explanatory variables | Results of linear model | | |
|---|---|---|---|
| | Df | F-value | p-value |
| Sampling year (2015/2020) | 1 | 1.16 | 0.287 |
| Location (inside/outside ditch) | 1 | 10.60 | 0.002** |
| Time since restoration (young, intermediate, old) | 3 | 20.29 | <0.001*** |
| Sampling*location | 1 | 5.09 | 0.030* |

The linear model showed that the sampling year (2015 and 2020) alone did not have a significant effect on the cover of peatland plant specialists, while there was an interaction between year and location inside and outside the ditch (Table 1). Characteristic plant species increased within the past 5 years inside the ditch, but stagnated or decreased outside (Fig. 1). Furthermore, time since restoration had the strongest effect and specialist cover was generally highest at intermediate and old sites.

The increase in specialists cover since 2015 was strongest in recently restored (young) sites, while at intermediate and old sites the increase was less pronounced (Fig. 1). Outside the ditch changes were also not significant and there was even a decrease in the past 5 years in the oldest sites. Generally, specialist cover was significantly different from the degraded state inside the ditch, but only at intermediate sites outside the ditch.

The ordination (Fig. 2) confirms these findings. Changes in the vegetation composition were most pronounced, indicated by longest arrows from red to grey dots, in most recently restored sites. They became more dissimilar from the degraded ones, while some of the older sites approached the drained state.

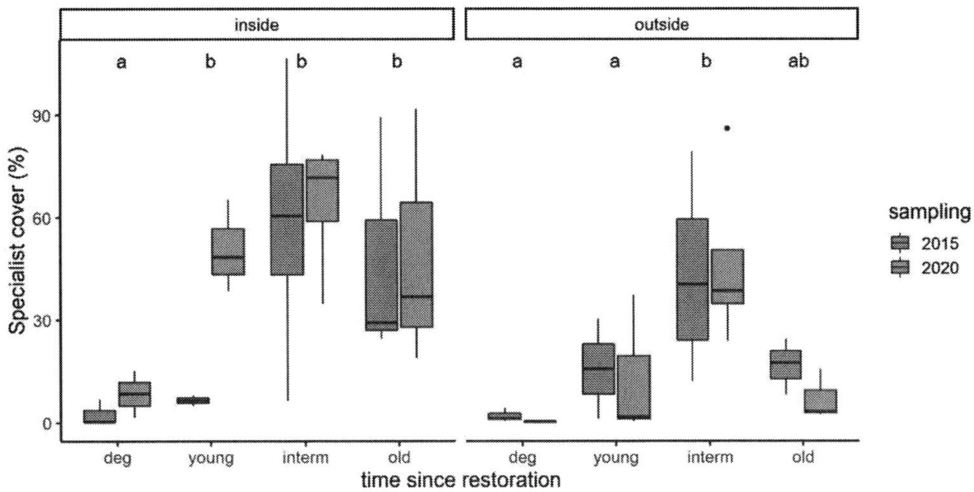


*Figure 7: Changes in cover of plants characteristic for montane peatlands over 5 years depending on their location (inside or outside of restored drainage ditches), and time since restoration (degraded, young, intermediate and old). Different letters above boxes indicate significant differences between age groups (time since restoration) using Tukey HSD test with Bonferroni correction (adjusted p < 0.05).*

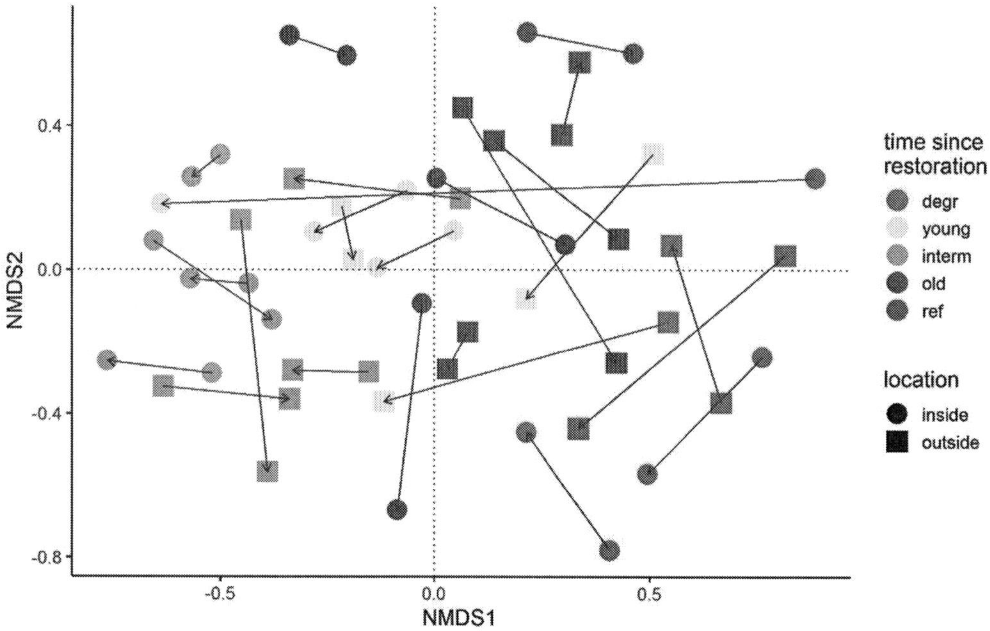


*Figure 8: Nonmetric multidimensional scaling (NMDS) of vegetation relevés indicates a clear difference between degraded (red) and restored (gray) peatlands. Dots represent transects inside the restored drainage ditch and squares outside; grey arrows show the development within five years (sampling 2015 and 2020); blue dots/ squares show the near-natural reference site. Stress level at two dimensions 0.244.*

## DISCUSSION

In our study, rewetting generally led to positive changes in characteristic peatland vegetation, but recovery was heterogeneous. We saw large differences of recovery inside and outside of the restored drainage ditches. Cover of peatland specialists was higher inside the ditch and stayed significantly different from degraded conditions, while it did not improve further away from the ditch. This confirms findings of Hedberg et al. (2012) who observed a much lower increase of water table at larger distances from the ditch highlighting the spatial limitation of the applied restoration measures. It is also in line with our previous findings (Strobl et al. 2019b), where progress of various indicators of peatland restoration success (among them water holding capacity diversity, moss coverage as well as coverage and cover of specialist plants) was mostly observed inside the ditch. Contrary to our expectations improved conditions inside the ditch did not spread to the entire peatland, and spatial limitations of peatland recovery persist.

Concerning the temporal perspective, we observed a strong increase in the cover of specialized plants 5 years after a first sampling in freshly restored sites. This again confirms our earlier study (Strobl et al. 2019b), where we supposed strongest changes shortly after measure implementation based on a space-for-time substitution. It is also in line with Haapalehto et al. (2011), that report a rise of the water table and recovery of peatland-characteristic vegetation in the first 10 years after restoration, but point out that success should not be taken for granted at this early stage.

Indeed, we see that progress did not stagnate as supposed before, but there is a slight trend of further improvement inside the ditch. However, this is not true outside the ditch especially in sites, where restoration measures had been carried out >7 years before sampling (intermediate and old). There, specialist species cover declined and vegetation composition seemed to move back towards degraded conditions. Our data suggests that this is related to a reduced water table in some of the old peatlands, most likely due to leaky dams. Another negative factor are (re)colonizing trees that take up a considerable amount of water as highlighted by Anderson (2010), and we actually observed substantial encroachment by spruce in older and drier sites, similar to Hedberg et al. (2012). This shows, that there can be setbacks after an initial progression towards favorable conditions and that those might become visible only very late in slow-recovering ecosystems like peatlands.

## CONCLUSION

Our findings highlight a considerable effectiveness of rewetting measures in previously afforested and drained montane peatlands. However, recovery did not spread from the restored ditches to the surroundings, and the initial progress did not continue everywhere. Actually, in some older sites vegetation composition moved back to degraded conditions calling for adaptive restoration measures. Additional tree removal and dam reinforcement would stop further degradation; it should be tested, if higher or wider dams support a recovery in larger areas further away from the ditch. Long-term monitoring including the verification of functional dams is essential to ensure long-term success.

## ACKNOWLEDGEMENTS

We thank the 'Bayerische Staatsforsten' for pointing out suitable study sites and allowing their assessment as well as 'Regierung von Oberfranken' for giving us specials permits to access protected areas. We are grateful to Katrin Ketterer for support with moss identification

### REFERENCES

1. Anderson R (2010) Restoring afforested peat bogs: results of current research. *Forestry Commission Report*; 006.
2. Bauer M, Harzer R, Strobl K, Kollmann J (2018) Resilience of riparian vegetation after restoration measures on River Inn. *River Research and Applications;* 34 (5): 451–460.
3. Haapalehto T, Vasander H, Jauhiainen S, Tahvanainen T, Kotiaho J (2011) The effects of peatland restoration on water-table depth, elemental concentrations, and vegetation: 10 years of changes. *Restoration Ecology;* 19 (5): 587–598.
4. Hedberg P, Kotowski W, Saetre P, Mälson K, Rydin H, Sundberg S (2012) Vegetation recovery after multiple-site experimental fen restorations. *Biological Conservation;* 147 (1): 60–67.
5. Londo G (1976) The decimal scale for releves of permanent quadrats. *Vegetatio;* 33 (1): 61–64.
6. McDonald T, Gann G, Jonson J, Dixon K (2016) International standards for the practice of ecological restoration. Including principles and key concepts. Washington, DC: Society for Ecological Restoration.
7. Moreno-Mateos D, Barbier E, Jones P, Jones H, Aronson J, López-López J et al. (2017) Anthropogenic ecosystem disturbance and the recovery debt. *Nature Communications;* 8 (14163): 1–6.
8. Post L von (1924) Das genetische System der organogenen Bildungen Schwedens - Comité international de Pédologie IV. Communication 22. IV. Internationale bodenkundliche Konferenz.
9. Quinger B, Siuda C (2009) Moorrenaturierung kompakt - Teilbeitrag Naturschutz. Allgemeiner Teilbericht B: Vegetationsanalysen zu den Regenerationsflächen in den 28 bearbeiteten Moorgebieten, Allgemeine Gesamtbetrachtung mit Darstellung der methodischen Vorgehensweise. Augsburg: Bayerisches Landesamt für Umwelt (LfU).
10. R Core Team (2015) R: A language and environment for statistical computing. Version 3.2.3. Vienna, Austria: R Foundation for Statistical Computing. Available at https://www.R-project.org/:
11. Strobl K, Moning C, Kollmann J (2019a) Positive trends in plant, dragonfly, and butterfly diversity of rewetted montane peatlands. *Restoration Ecology;* 28 (4): 796-806.
12. Strobl K, Teixeira L, Kollmann J (2019b) Integrated assessment of ecosystem recovery using a multifunctionality approach. *Ecosphere;* 10 (11): 1–17.

ID 72855

# DYNAMICS OF LOCAL GOVERNANCE: THE CASE OF PEATLAND RESTORATION IN CENTRAL KALIMANTAN, INDONESIA

*Rizky Januar, Eli Nur Nirmala Sari, Surahman Putra

World Resources Institute, Indonesia

*rizky.haryanto@wri.org*

Since 2016, peatland restoration policy is implemented in Central Kalimantan province through facilitation and coordination by Peat Restoration Agency (Badan Restorasi Gambut [BRG]), with the goals of reducing the peat subsidence, greenhouse gas emissions, and vulnerability to fire of peat areas. After years of implementation, local peat fires persist, however, and knowledge is still lacking about the challenges and opportunities for supporting the restoration process.

This study examines the dynamics of peatland restoration governance in Central Kalimantan, especially related to the policy implementation. It is expected to provide insights into regional issues and opportunities for restoring local peatlands more effectively. The study uses the deductive approach through use of the Contextual Interaction Theory (CIT) framework. For data collection, the study used mixed (qualitative and quantitative) methods, including a literature review, stakeholder interviews, and questionnaires.

The study denotes that policy implementation has involved cross-sectoral parties at the regional level. Cross-sectoral partnerships have been established on rewetting local dry peatlands, establishing revegetation plots, improving local livelihoods, and facilitating village-level restoration process. These partnerships have led to some progress in the province, where a large number of rewetting units have been constructed. Provision of livelihood packages to communities has made communities largely supportive of restoration.

The analysis yet also reveals several challenges in fully achieving restoration outcome, also in the monitoring and supervision process. Policy measures are further recommended in three fronts: strengthening the roles and capacity of regional actors, avoiding land use overlaps in restored areas, and improving restoration policy process within concession areas. Successful implementation process would actively involve not only the BRG and local stakeholders across sectors, but also relevant ministries at the national level. A coordinating ministry/institution could align and oversee the process.

ID 61372

# RISK GOVERNANCE ON RESTORATION OF PEATLAND ECOSYSTEM

*Ibnu Budiman, Eli NN Sari, Chandra Irawadi Wijaya

WRI Indonesia, Indonesia

*ibnu.budiman@wur.nl*

Since 2016, the Government of Indonesia has conducted peatland restoration programme but fires still occurred on the restoration area in 2019. It implies ineffectiveness of restoration that increases peat vulnerability to fires. One of the reasons for this ineffectiveness is governance issues, which are lack of cooperation and domination of administration in the governance of restoration. This research aims at understanding vulnerability within the governance cycle of peatland restoration and introducing a risk governance framework to increase the effectiveness of the restoration governance. A case study of South Sumatra province is utilised. This research draws on qualitative and quantitative data from interviews with key stakeholders; direct observation; academic literature; experimental modelling; and document review. Findings in this research imply that current governance of peatland restoration is not yet able to stop the cycle of peat vulnerability. The root problem is caused by set up of ambitious target for restoration, absence of ecosystem governance, undetailed restoration planning, not updated peat data, and lacking standard enforcement to restoration activities. These political vulnerabilities caused technological issues, wrong target group, a lack of integration on restoration activities. As a result, several restoration activities were not done in peat area, one out of five infrastructures are dysfunctional, activities overlapped, and not resulting an outcome. From September to October 2019, 6400 hotspots are found on peatland, including on peatland area. Governance issue lays on the unit of restoration activity that is implemented using a conventional administrative approach. Implementation of restoration must consider intercorrelation of biophysics and socio-economic aspects within the peatland ecosystem. This implementation can be done using risk governance framework. Peat data needs to be updated for prioritizing vulnerable peatland to be restored. The result of that detailed planning then must be evaluated and communicated well by and to local stakeholders.

ID 72863

# THE HORTICULTURAL PEAT INDUSTRY AND ACADEMIA: A HISTORY OF A SUSTAINABLE PARTNERSHIP FOR THE ECOLOGICAL RESTORATION OF CANADIAN PEATLANDS

Gwendal Breton, Claire Boismenu, Line Rochefort

Peatland Ecology Research Group (PERG) and Center for Northern Studies (CEN), Université Laval, Québec City, Canada

*line.rochefort@fsaa.ulaval.ca*

## SUMMARY

In Canada, peatlands cover approximately 113.6 million hectares. This represents 13% of the territory, and accounts for 90% of wetland ecosystems found across the country. Peatlands provide many ecosystem services benefiting humans such as carbon sequestration, and are one of the most cost-effective solutions to mitigate global warming effects. In North America, peatlands are exploited to extract peat from which the horticultural industry is the main consumer. However, this industrial activity requires peatlands drainage and vegetation removal which has adverse consequences on hydrology, biodiversity, and associated ecological service losses. Without human intervention, the degraded peatland may witness several decades of bare soils before a typical vegetation spontaneously recovers. In light of this situation, the Peatland Ecology Research Group (PERG) was created in 1992, mainly as a response to a workshop, organised by the Canadian Sphagnum Peat Moss Association (CSPMA), but involving all stakeholders across Canada interested in the management of after-used peatlands. PERG regroups peatland scientists from different Canadian universities and collaborates with provincial and federal agencies as well as the Canadian peat industry. They cooperate on projects aiming towards sustainable and integrated peatland management. For the past 30 years, PERG's research team has developed peatland restoration techniques and significantly contributed to improving knowledge about ecological recovery of these specific wetlands. This case study relates how the sustained cooperative and collaborative history of PERG and the Canadian peat industry over the past 30 years has been instrumental in developing a cost-efficient approach to restore degraded peatlands. The long-term partnership and ecological success are a result of the good corporate environmental vision of the industry since the beginning of the 1990s and the unique Canadian Research Council programmes to funding industry-university research projects.

***Keywords***: long-term collaboration, technique of peatland restoration, restoration success, responsible management.

## INTRODUCTION

Canada is home to a significant proportion of the world's peatlands (27%) and is the second most peatland covered country after Russia (Xu et al., 2017). In their natural state, and because of their unique hydrological function, peatlands provide a specific habitat for many species of flora and fauna. In addition, they provide many ecosystem services useful to human populations, in particular the sequestration of carbon in accumulated peat. By virtue of its structural qualities conducive to water retention, peat is a resource used as a growing medium. In North America, for example, peat is extracted from boreal and temperate peatlands, of which the horticultural industry is the main consumer. This industry has succeeded, in about 150 years, in propelling itself to the world rank of the horticultural peat market (CSPMA, 2014).

Peat extraction obviously has an impact on the environment. This industrial activity, which is carried out using giant vacuum machinery, requires prior drainage and the removal of vegetation within the peatland, generating harmful consequences on hydrology, biogeochemistry, flora, fauna, and therefore on several ecosystem functions of this habitat on a variable time scale. After stopping the extraction operations, the harsh conditions generated by the disappearance of the acrotelm and the lowering of the water table cause modifications of the physicochemical properties of the peat, preventing a return of the plant communities typical of peatlands (Price and Whitehead, 2001; Price et al., 2003). Without human intervention, degraded peatlands can in some cases take several decades for characteristic vegetation – leading to the accumulation of peat – to re-establish spontaneously (Poulin et al., 2005; Graf et al., 2008).

In response to this ecological problem, management methods for the responsible use of North American peatlands have been developed by a group of university researchers (Peatland Ecology Research Group), in association with the Canadian peat industry (Canadian Sphagnum Peat Moss Association and its members). Thus, an ecological restoration method, the "Moss Layer Transfer Technique" (MLTT), has been developed in the 1990s and has proven success in the reintroduction and establishment of bryophytes and vascular plants on ombrotrophic peatlands. This presentation aims to retrospectively describe the achievement of success in the rapid return (less than 15 years) of biodiversity components and ecosystem functions of peatlands restored with this method. In addition, a parallel is drawn to highlight the support for academic research by the Canadian horticultural peat industry and by governments that have made it possible to bring a significant contribution to the field of research in the ecology of peatland restoration.

## DISCUSSION

1) The 1990s: Genesis and consolidation of a collaboration

In the early 1990s, Canada has about 75 companies primarily engaged in peat extraction for horticultural purposes. The year 1992 marks a turning point in the management of peatlands by the horticultural peat industry. In February, a workshop bringing together all the actors revolving around the peat environment is organized with the aim of finding a consensus on the sustainable management of this resource. Unanimously, peatland restoration is chosen from among the post-extraction peatland reclamation options. In that same year, Line Rochefort of Université Laval (Quebec, Canada) created the Peatland Ecology Research Group (PERG). This group is the result of a concerted effort between different actors bringing together university scientists from various disciplines (vegetation, fauna, hydrology, geochemistry), the Canadian peat industry, as well as federal and provincial government agencies. Consequently, various grants will allow Line Rochefort and its collaborators to set up several research projects, in particular on the characterization of peat and the restoration of degraded peatlands.

Post-extraction peatlands located in Quebec (Sainte-Marguerite-Marie peatland) and New Brunswick (Maisonnette and Lamèque peatlands) become the first experimental stations for preliminary tests on peatland restoration. At these sites, several aspects are studied, such as the state of the post-extraction substrate (including peat chemistry and its microtopography), various small-scale Sphagnum reintroduction trials, various ways to rewet or conserve moisture at the sites, plant and animal species present. At the same time, tests are being carried out in the laboratory and in the greenhouse at Université Laval to better understand the biology of Sphagnum mosses, in particular on the survival, regeneration and colonization capacity of Sphagnum diaspores and fragments, in Petri dishes and on peat, depending on various conditions of humidity, fertilization, light, etc.

The results of this research are first reflected in the form of the restoration of 150 ha at the Sainte-Marguerite bog in 1994, using ecological engineering techniques specific to the acid and oligotrophic conditions of the residual peat found in this area. Subsequently, a first Peatland restoration guide for peat managers is published in 1997 (Quinty and Rochefort, 1997). It describes what was at that time called "The Canadian Approach to Peatland Restoration."

From the mid-1990s, several elements made it possible to consolidate a long-term partnership between PERG researchers and their partners of the Canadian peat industry. Scientific conferences and Technology transfer workshops are organized almost every year in order to present the latest developments made within the framework of research projects in peatland restoration and management. A newsletter and a website inform PERG's partners and collaborators about the fieldwork carried out by researchers and their students, and they provide summaries of research publications.

In 1996, Line Rochefort and three other PERG researchers obtain a major Cooperative Research and Development (CRD) grant from the Natural Sciences and Engineering Research Council of Canada (NSERC), in partnership with various Canadian peat-producing companies. The four-year grant focuses on the integrated management of peatlands in eastern Canada. This CRD grant marks the start of long-term funding in the form of various grants from NSERC in partnership with the Canadian peat industry. These grants aim to create mutually beneficial collaborations between Canadian universities and partners from the public or private sectors, leading to breakthroughs that translate into economic, social or environmental benefits for Canada and Canadians. Research funding is shared between industrial partners and NSERC, by matching funds.

2) 1999 and 2000: The Bois-des-Bel restored peatland, an emblematic experimental station

In the fall of 1999 and in the winter of 2000, an area of 8.4 ha of the Bois-des-Bel peatland, in eastern Quebec, is restored using the restoration method for ombrotrophic peatlands developed by the PERG a few years earlier. Part (3.1 ha) of the bog is selected to act as an unrestored control area. In order to assess the success of restoration operations, a database is created: 755 vegetation sampling points, combined with 57 listening points for birdsong, all georeferenced in a geographic information system. Thus, the Bois-des-Bel peatland is given the title of a true open-air experimental site, constituting an essential pillar for the constant improvement of peatland restoration methods.

3) The 2000s and 2010s: The Rise of Peatland Restoration Research in Canada

In 2003, six years after its first publication, the Peatland restoration guide is given a facelift with the publication of a second edition (Quinty and Rochefort, 2003). The content is greatly enhanced with a more detailed approach to the steps of peatland restoration with what is now called the "Moss Layer Transfer Technique" (MLTT) developed in partnership with the peat industry. These steps include:

A. Planning of restoration and various operations, based on site conditions, established objectives, as well as the reference ecosystem serving as a model for restoration;
B. Site preparation (modification of the topographic profile, creation of dikes or basins, scraping of the peat surface);
C. Harvesting plant material (plants or diaspores) at the donor site;
D. Spreading of diaspores and plant fragments on the site to be restored;
E. Spreading protective mulch;
F. Phosphate fertilization;
G. Blocking drainage ditches.

Steps B to G are done using machinery. Other topics are also addressed in this new edition of the guide, including the creation of ponds and the restoration of ecosystem functions through restoration monitoring.

The funding of PERG research by NSERC and by the peat industry partners continues during the years 2000 and 2010. From 2003 to 2018, it is carried out in the form of three five-year terms of the Industrial Research Chair in Peatland Management granted to Line Rochefort. The repeated terms of this Chair demonstrate the real interest of the peat industry in responsible peatland management in Canada. The various projects are supported by several collaborating researchers with complementary expertise (plant ecology, hydrology, biogeochemistry, fauna, and biological invasions). At the same time, an increasing number of post-extraction peatlands are restored each year by peat industry partners in various Canadian provinces: Quebec, New Brunswick, Manitoba, Saskatchewan, and Alberta.

Obtaining the Chair and additional grants make it possible to undertake various research projects with increasingly diverse objectives, such as:

• the expansion of knowledge on the ecological restoration of peatlands dominated by Sphagnum mosses (bogs) and the evaluation of the restoration success, by monitoring the long-term evolution of the restored ombrotrophic peatland of Bois-des-Bel and monitoring the return of plant communities in restored peatlands (through regular inventories of all restored sites in Canada);
• the evaluation of the return of ecosystem functions of restored peatlands, such as hydrology and carbon sequestration (through greenhouse gas exchange measurements);
• the development of techniques for restoring fens, which have characteristics different from bogs (for this purpose, new large-scale experimental sites are created: Bic – Saint-Fabien in Quebec, Elma North, Moss Spur and South Julius in Manitoba, Evansburg in Alberta);
• the development of new restoration approaches for specific environments, such as salted coastal bogs, peatland margins (laggs), peatland pools;
• the reclamation of peatlands that cannot be restored, including the production of berries (e.g., cloudberry) or tree planting;

• the cultivation of Sphagnum mosses (Sphagnum farming) as a renewable resource, which can be used directly for the development of growth substrates or as donor material for the restoration of peatlands.

Collaboration between the peat industry and PERG researchers continues throughout the 2020s, under a grant from NSERC. The research undertaken fills some gaps in specific fields of research. In addition, in order to maintain the co-evolutionary approach favoured by the peatland restoration guide, an update of the latter is carried out in 2019 and 2020 (Quinty et al., 2019, 2020a, b, c). The fine-tuning of peatland restoration methods will help improve the ecological value of restored ecosystems over the next few years.

4) The success of the ecological restoration of peatlands by the MLTT

Since its development in the late 1990s, the Moss Layer Transfer Technique has enabled the Canadian peat industry to restore an ever-increasing number of peatlands (mostly Sphagnum peatlands) in the country. Specifically, 44 peatland sites have been restored nationally, including 31 in eastern Canada (Quebec and New Brunswick), as well as 13 in western Canada (Manitoba, Saskatchewan and Alberta).

Through monitoring of these peatlands, it was possible to demonstrate that this large-scale mechanized technique of restoration has been shown to be successful in the reintroduction and establishment of bryophytes (Sphagnum and Polytrichum) and vascular plants for ombrotrophic peatlands within five years after restoration (González et al., 2013, 2014). PERG has assessed that it facilitates the return of 82% of the biodiversity of vascular plants (Hugron et al., 2020). The technique is effective for reestablishing hydrological attributes (Taylor et al. 2016). It also leads to a return of peat accumulation and to restore the carbon sink function (Strack and Zuback, 2013; Nugent et al, 2018). The work of González and Rochefort (2019) led to the creation of a statistical tool to define the success of the application of MLTT on degraded peatlands. The main advantage of this tool is that it uses simple indicators based on the vegetation layer; it can also be used throughout Canada.

PERG's successes in peatland restoration have led governments in various provinces in Canada to modify their policies on wetlands and peatlands. Some now require restoration measures for disturbances in these environments (New Brunswick, Quebec, Manitoba and Alberta). Several large-scale peatland restoration projects are also being carried out in other countries with the MLTT.

## CONCLUSION

Peat extraction is an important commercial and industrial activity in Canada and must be conducted responsibly. As peatlands provide many useful ecosystem services to human populations, in particular carbon sequestration, their restoration is one of the most cost-effective solutions to mitigate the effects of global warming (Griscom et al., 2017; Nugent et al. 2019).

It is through the long-term, sustained and joint funding of university research by the Canadian government and the peat industry that such results have been achieved in ecological restoration of peatlands in the country. This is a unique opportunity to demonstrate how a partnership between academia and industry can create synergy to help advance knowledge on both practical and fundamental sides.

Continued research into peatland restoration guarantees greater success in restoration efforts from coast to coast in Canada. It helps inform governments to develop better laws, regulations, policies and programs for responsible peatland management across the country. It also provides verifiable evidence that the Canadian peat industry is complying with international conventions as proof of its investment in good corporate citizenship.

## ACKNOWLEDGEMENTS

The authors are grateful to the Natural Sciences and Engineering Research Council of Canada, the Canadian Sphagnum Peat Moss Association and its members, the Québec Peat Moss Producers Association, the New Brunswick Peat Producers Association, the New Brunswick Department of Natural Resources and Energy and the Government of Manitoba for their funding throughout the numerous grants granted to Line Rochefort and PERG researchers since the 1990s. This study was made possible by funding from the Social Sciences and Humanities Research Council granted to Dr. Eric Higgs from University of Victoria (British Columbia, Canada).

## REFERENCES


1. Canadian Sphagnum Peat Moss Association (CSPMA). (2014) 2014 Industrial Social Responsibility Report. Canadian Sphagnum Peat Moss Association, St. Albert, Alberta, Canada. 39 pp.
2. González, E, Rochefort, L. (2014) Drivers of success in 53 cutover bogs restored by a moss layer transfer technique. *Ecological Engineering*; 68: 279–290.
3. González, E, Rochefort, L. (2019) Declaring success in Sphagnum peatland restoration: Identifying outcomes from readily measurable vegetation descriptors. *Mires and Peat*; 24(19), 1-16.
4. González, E, Rochefort, L, Boudreau, S, Hogue-Hugron, S, Poulin, M. (2013) Can species indicators predict restoration outcomes early in the monitoring process? A case study with peatlands. *Ecological Indicators*; 32: 232–238.
5. Graf, MD, Rochefort, L, Poulin, M. (2008) Spontaneous revegetation of cutaway peatlands of North America. *Wetlands*; 28(1): 28–39.
6. Griscom, BW, Adams, J, Ellis, PW, Houghton, RA, Lomax, G, Miteva, DA, ..., Fargione, J. (2017) Natural climate solutions. *Proceedings of the National Academy of Sciences*; 114(44): 11645-11650.
7. Hugron, S, Guêné-Nanchen, M, Roux, N, LeBlanc, M-C, Rochefort, L. (2020) Plant reintroduction in restored peatlands: 80% successfully transferred – Does the remaining 20% matters? *Global Ecology and Conservation*; 22, June 2020, e01000; https://doi.org/10.1016/j.gecco.2020.e01000.
8. Nugent, K, Strachan, IB, Strack, M, Roulet, NT, Rochefort, L. (2018) Multi-year net ecosystem carbon balance of a restored peatland reveals a return to carbon sink. *Global Change Biology*; 24(12): 5751–5768.
9. Nugent, KA, Strachan, IB, Roulet, NT, Strack, M, Frolking, S, Helbig, M. (2019). Prompt active restoration of peatlands substantially reduces climate impact. *Environmental Research Letters*, 14(12), 124030.
10. Poulin, M, Rochefort, L, Quinty, F, Lavoie, C. (2005) Spontaneous revegetation of mined peatlands in eastern Canada. *Canadian Journal of Botany*; 83: 539–557.
11. Price, JS, Whitehead, GS. (2001) Developing hydrological thresholds for Sphagnum recolonization on an abandoned cutover bog. *Wetlands*; 21: 32–40.
12. Price, JS, Heathwaite, AL, Baird, AJ. (2003) Hydrological processes in abandoned and restored peatlands: An overview of management approaches. *Wetlands Ecology and Management*; 11: 65–83.
13. Quinty, F, Rochefort, L. (1997) Peatland restoration guide. Canadian Sphagnum Peat Moss Association. Université Laval, Faculté des sciences de l'agriculture et de l'alimentation, Sainte-Foy, Canada. 21 pp.
14. Quinty, F, Rochefort, L. (2003) Peatland restoration guide, 2nd ed. Canadian Sphagnum Peat Moss Association and New Brunswick Department of Natural Resources and Energy, Québec, Canada. 106 pp.
15. Quinty, F, LeBlanc, M-C, Rochefort, L. (2019) Peatland Restoration Guide – Plant Material Collecting and Donor Site Management. PERG, CSPMA and APTHQ. Québec, Canada. 22 pp.
16. Quinty, F, LeBlanc, M-C, Rochefort, L. (2020a) Peatland restoration guide – Planning restoration projects. PERG, CSPMA and APTHQ. Québec, Québec. 23 pp.
17. Quinty, F, LeBlanc, M-C, Rochefort, L. (2020b) Peatland restoration guide – Site preparation and rewetting. PERG, CSPMA and APTHQ. Québec, Québec. 23 pp.
18. Quinty, F, LeBlanc, M-C, Rochefort, L. (2020c) Peatland restoration guide – Spreading of plant material, mulch and fertilizer. PERG, CSPMA and APTHQ. Québec, Québec. 23 pp.
19. Strack, M, Zuback, Y. (2013) Annual carbon balance of a peatland 10 yr. following restoration. *Biogeosciences*; 10: 2885–2896.
20. Taylor, N, Price, J, Strack, M. (2016) Hydrological controls on productivity of regenerating Sphagnum in a cutover peatland. *Ecohydrology*; 9: 1017–1027.
21. Xu, J, Morris, PJ, Liu, J, Holden, J. (2017) PEATMAP: Refining estimates of global peatland distribution based on a meta-analysis. *Catena*; 160: 134–140; DOI: 10.1016/j.catena.2017.09.010.

ID 72872

# ACCESS ROADS IN PRISTINE AND EXTRACTED PEATLANDS: RESTORATION TECHNIQUES

*Kathy Pouliot[1], Line Rochefort[1], Christine Isabel[1], Pascal Guérin[1], Alexandre Beauchemin[2], Jacques Gagnon[3], Pierre-Olivier Jean[3]

[1] Peatland Ecology Research Group & Center for Northern Studies, Université Laval, Canada
[2] Hydro-Québec, Canada
[3] Premier Tech Horticulture, Canada

*Kathy.Pouliot@sbf.ulaval.ca*

## SUMMARY

Regardless of the resource exploited (peat, oil, etc.), the construction of access roads through peatlands is common in Canada, where 12.5% of emerged lands are peatlands. Mineral roads in peatlands influence the water table level and the physicochemical characteristics of the water and peat. These changes can impact the composition of the plant communities. When these access roads are decommissioned, actions must be taken to restore ecosystem functions. Recent studies are presented about the restoration of peatlands impacted by mineral roads. One of these projects examined if burying the mineral material within the bog is an effective method to restore the peatland conditions. The restoration approach by the Burial Under Peat Technique consists in excavating and burying the mineral material beneath the underlying peat material. The method allowed to reach several restoration goals. An ongoing project is testing this technique in the context of peat extraction for horticultural purposes to allow a better efficiency of the Moss Layer Transfer Technique over wider hydrologically connected areas. Another project tested different peat thickness amendment and fertilization following the partial removal of the mineral road. While the thicker peat treatment (75 cm) presented the higher cover of bog species, asynchronous storage time of peat, and different time gaps between amendments and vegetation introduction did not meet expected results. The last presented approach examines the establishment of fen species directly on the mineral substrate following the partial removal of a road and the efficacy of flow channels to restore water connectivity on both sides of the road. In that case, the mineral surface allowed a gradual return of the targeted plant communities and buried in channels allowed better water circulation, although a dam effect remains. All these projects highlight the importance of long-term post-restoration monitoring to better instruct future peatland management practices.

***Keywords:*** *road decommissioning, burial technique, restoration*

## INTRODUCTION

This presentation is an overview of four projects involving roads in peatlands, from complete decommissioning to mitigation techniques. Here follows a summary of the techniques used.

## RESTORATION TECHNIQUES

### The Burial Under Peat Technique in pristine peatlands

In this research project, the Burial Under Peat Technique was used for the restoration of two peatlands impacted by a mineral road. To avoid habitat loss, to confine nutrients and to recover the functions of the original ecosystem, the road was buried in situ by inverting the layer of mineral material and the underlying layer of peat. The burial of the mineral material aims to restore a layer of at least 40 cm of peat on the surface of the previously disturbed area to allow water circulation and to support peatland plant communities.

The Burial Under Peat Technique was done on site #1 and #2 (Figure 9) in Québec, Canada, using an excavator traveling exclusively on the access road to avoid disturbance to the surrounding peatland. The work was done by repeating each step on small sections of the road, about 5 m each according to the arm of the excavator. First, the materials composing the access road (mineral material, logs, geotextile membrane) were removed and piled behind the machinery on the remaining road. The underlying peat was excavated, creating a pit, and piled up nearby. The road materials were then put into the pit and covered with the previously excavated peat. Subsequently, the surface was reprofiled at the elevation of the surrounding peatland surface and then revegetated with the uniform spreading of a thin layer of diaspores. The diaspores were mechanically harvested on either side of the access road using the excavator bucket. A ratio (area of plant material collected: revegetated area) ranging from 1:5 to 1:10 was used.

Site #1 – Before

Site #1 – 3-years post-restoration

Site #2 – Before

Site #2 – 2-years post-restoration

Figure 9 - Sites #1 and #2 before and a few years post-restoration with the Burial Under Peat Technique

## The Burial Under Peat Technique in an extracted peatland

The recipe to restore *Sphagnum*-dominated peatland in Canada is effective and economically doable at large scales (Rochefort & Lode 2006, Graf et al. 2012, Quinty et al. 2019, Quinty et al. 2020a, b, c). The peat industry, and restoration practitioners, can restore extensive areas using the Moss Layer Transfer Technique, and as a result facilitate the return of the carbon accumulation function around ten years post-restoration (Nugent et al. 2018) and a successful transfer rate of vascular species (Hugron et al. 2020).

Restoration of large areas is limited by the presence of mineral access roads. A testbed of the Burial Under Peat Technique was initiated in 2019 by Premier Tech Horticulture at Paxson, Alberta, Canada (video available at https://youtu.be/18eln47QLqs). Since the area surrounding the road is already disturbed, there is no need to avoid circulation on it. Therefore, instead of repeating all steps of the technique on small sections as for a natural bog road, the burial was instead done in three steps: (1) digging a trench parallel to the road along the entire length of the road segment, (2) burying the road materials (mineral material and fascines), and (3) reprofiling to achieve an elevation similar to the surrounding extracted peatland (Figure 10). The sections of extracted peatland previously separated by the road are now hydrologically connected and can be restored as a whole with the Moss Layer Transfer Technique.

(1)

(2)

(3)

Figure 10 - Steps of the Burial Under Peat Technique in the context of the restoration of an extracted peatland: (1) digging of a trench, (2) burial of the road materials and (3) reprofiling.

**Partial removal of an access road with peat amendment**

The study site corresponds to 200 m of a 400 m long access road made of clay that bisects a poor fen near Fort McMurray, Alberta, Canada (Figure 11). The road's top layer of mineral material was removed to create a trench and subsequently filled up with peat to reach an organic substrate elevation similar to the surrounding peatland. The former road area was divided into eight sections where thickness of peat and fertilization treatments vary.

Clay access road prior restoration

2-years post-restoration

Figure 11 - Partial removal of the road with peat amendment before and 2-years post-restoration

**Partial removal of an access road without peat amendment**

The study site corresponds to another section of the 400 m clay access road near Fort McMurray, Alberta, Canada. This approach consisted of the partial extraction of the mineral substrate forming the road (to reach the mean elevation of the surrounding peatland), of surface preparation (smooth or scratched; Figure 12) followed by the application of the Moss Layer Transfer Technique directly on the residual mineral substrate. Donor site used as supply area for vegetal fragments was composed of brown mosses.

Smooth and scratched mineral surface

Brown mosses 2-years post-restoration

2-years post-restoration

Figure 12 - Partial removal of the road without peat amendment

## ACKNOWLEDGEMENTS

Financial support was provided by Hydro-Québec, Japan Canada Oil Sands Limited, Premier Tech Horticulture and the Canadian Sphagnum Peat Moss Association.

## REFERENCE

Pp. 259-280 in Vitt, D. H. & J. S. Bhatti (eds.), Restoration and Reclamation of Boreal Ecosystems. Cambridge University Press, Cambridge, UK.

Hugron, S., Guêné-Nanchen, M., Roux, N., LeBlanc, M.-C. (2020) Plant reintroduction in restored peatland: 80% successfully treansferred – Does the remaining 20% matter?. *Global Ecology and Conservation* 22. DOI: 10.1016/j.gecco.2020.e01000

Nugent, K.A., Strachan, I.B., Strack, M., Roulet, N.R., Rochefort, L. (2018) Multi-year net ecosystem carbon balance of a restored peatland reveals a return to carbon sink. *Global Change Biology* 24: 5751 –5768. DOI: 10.1111/gcb.14449

Quinty, F., M.C. LeBlanc and L. Rochefort, (2019) Peatland Restoration Guide – Plant Material Collecting and Donor Site Management. PERG, CSPMA and APTHQ. Québec City, Québec.

Quinty, F., M.-C. LeBlanc and L. Rochefort. (2020a) Peatland Restoration Guide – Planning Restoration Projects. PERG, CSPMA and APTHQ. Québec, Québec

Quinty, F., M.-C. LeBlanc and L. Rochefort. (2020b) Peatland Restoration Guide – Site Preparation and Rewetting. PERG, CSPMA and APTHQ. Québec, Québec.

Quinty, F., M.-C. LeBlanc and L. Rochefort. (2020c) Peatland Restoration Guide – Spreading Plant Material, Mulch and Fertilizer. PERG, CSPMA and APTHQ. Québec, Québec

Rochefort, L., Lode, E. (2006) Restoration of degraded boreal peatlands. . Pp. 381 –423 in Boreal peatland ecosystems. R.K. Wieder & D.H. Vitt (eds.). Ecological Studies, vol. 188. Springer-Verlag, Berlin, Germany.

ID 62628

# PALUDICULTURE SPECIES OPTIONS FOR RESTORATION OF DEGRADED TROPICAL PEATLAND IN CENTRAL KALIMANTAN, INDONESIA

Tri Wira Yuwati[1], Dony Rachmanadi[1], Daniel Mendham[2]

[1] Banjarbaru Environment & Forestry R&D Institute, Banjarbaru, South Kalimantan, Indonesia

[2] CSIRO, Canberra, Australia

*yuwatitriwira@gmail.com*

**SUMMARY**

The tropical peatland covers 44 million hectares or approximately 11 % of the total world's peatland. Twenty-one million hectares of it lies in Indonesia. Tropical peatland has important functions ecologically as carbon storage, hidrological control and habitat of flora, fauna and microbes. However, agricultural expansion that required drainage, conversion into other land use such as oil palm, illegal logging and forest fire were among other things the cause for the peatland degradation in Indonesia. Efforts to restore Indonesia's tropical peatland have been accelerated by the establishment of the Peatland Restoration Agency in early 2016. The restoration action policy includes rewetting, revegetation and revitalization of local livelihoods. Paludiculture is one way to restore the degraded tropical peatland in Indonesia. It is not just an action of revegetation but also has potential to contribute to the revitalization of local livelihoods. A survey was carried out in Pulang Pisau district of Central Kalimantan in areas with more than 60% deep peat (>3m). Several species were found that have potential to be developed as paludiculture species, namely *Shorea balangeran, Dyera polyphylla, Cratoxylon glaucum*, Purun, and local fish. All species grew well on deep peat and are economically feasible, however planting tree species should be combined with horticulture and agriculture species due to the long payback period associated with trees.

***Keywords**: paludiculture, tropical peatland, revegetation, revitalization, Central Kalimantan*

## INTRODUCTION

The tropical peatland covers 44 million hectares or approximately 11 % of the total world's peatland (Page, Rieley, and Banks 2011). Twenty-one million hectares of it lies in Indonesia (Wahyunto et al., 2013). Tropical peatland has important functions ecologically as carbon storage, hidrological control and habitat of flora, fauna and microbes. The tropical peatland in Southeast Asia has experienced massive changes and only 6% remains in pristine conditine as of 2015 (Miettinen, Shi, and Liew 2016). The massive changes in tropical peatlands were caused by fire, logging and draination for the conversion into other land uses such as agriculture, oil palm plantations, Acacia plantations and smallholdings(Dohong et al., 2017; Miettinen & Liew, 2010; Silvius &Diemont, 2007; ) To restore Indonesia's tropical peatland, the Indonesian government established the Peatland Restoration Agency or Badan Restorasi Gambut (BRG) in early 2016. The establishment of BRG was motivated by 2015 land fires that had burned 2.6 million hectares of land ((BRG) 2019). The restoration action policy includes rewetting, revegetation and revitalization of local livelihoods. In the rewetting activities, it has established the rewetting infrastructures which comprise 11,800 deep wells, 5,936 canal blockings, and 242 canal backfillings by the end of 2018 ((BRG) 2019). Moreover, in terms of revegetation activities, BRG claimed the construction of 713 revegetation demonstration plots across Riau, Jambi, South Sumatra, South Kalimantan, and Central Kalimantan. Paludiculture is one way to restore the degraded tropical peatland in Indonesia. It is not just an action of revegetation but also has potential to contribute to the revitalization of local livelihoods.

According to Joosten et al., 2016 "paludiculture comprises any biomass use from wet and rewetted peatlands, from using spontaneous vegetation on natural sites to harvesting artificially established crops on rewetted sites".Furthermore, (Uda, Hein, and Adventa 2020) stated that paludiculture can be defined as a sustainable alternative peatland utilization without drainage including growing crops in peatland with no drainage. Although revegetation demonstration plots have been constructed in Indonesia, there is remaining question on the potential species that can be utilized or grown without drainage. The aim of this paper is to provide paludiculture species options for revegetation fo degraded peatland in Central Kalimantan, Indonesia.

## MATERIALS AND METHODS

We did the survery to dig all information regarding paludiculture commodities that were established and potential to be developed in Central Kalimantan. The locations were selected purposively. We did the survey in Pulang Pisau district and Kapuas district of Central Kalimantan. In Pulang Pisau district there were four subditricts namely Kahayan Hilir, Jabiren Raya, Maliku and Pandih Batu sub district. While for Kapuas district only one subdistrict namely Basarang sub district. The respondents were selected by snowball sampling based on the commodities that were cultivated. The data collection was conducted semi-structured and field observation. The data were then analyzed quatitatively and presented descriptively. The information regarding the commodities were including the seed source, land preparation, drainage management, nursery treatments, planting, tending, harvesting, post harvest processing and marketing. Secondary data was also collected through various literatures. Gap analysis and economical analysis were carried out including NPV (Net Present Value/ in rupiahs), IRR (Internal Rate of Return/ in % , BC (Benefit-Cost) ratio and PBP (Pay Back Period) for all the commodities.

## RESULTS

The paludiculture commodities that have been found in Central Kalimantan is presented in the Table1.

Table 1. Paludiculture commodities in Central Kalimantan

| Commodity | Product | Management |
|---|---|---|
| Galam (Melaleuca cajuputi) | Timber (construction) | Un-managed |
| Belangeran (Shorea balangeran) | Timber, seed | Managed |
| Kelakai (Stenochlaena palustris) | Vegetable | Un-managed |
| Local fish in Beje (natural fish ponds) | Food | Managed |
| Jelutung rawa (Dyera polyphilla) | Latex, seed | Managed |
| Gerunggang (Cratoxylon glaucum) | Timber | Managed |
| Nyatoh (Palaquium sp.) | Latex | Un-managed |
| Purun danau ( Lepironia articulata) | Raw purun, Handicraft | Un-managed |
| Purun tikus (Eleocharis dulcis) | Raw purun, Handicraft | Un- managed |
| Pineapple | Food | Managed |
| Spring onion | Vegetable | Managed |

The paludiculture commodities that have been utilized by the local people of Central Kalimantan were mostly peatland species that produce timber, latex, handicrafts and food such as vegetable and fruit. In terms of management activites, there were species that has been planted but also species that can be obtained naturally. For those commodities, we recorded the cultivation or silvicultural technique, harvest, post harvest and environmental risk to peatland. Then, we presented a gap analysis of the paludiculture commodities that is presented in Table 2.

Table 2. Gap analysis of paludiculture commodities in Central Kalimantan

| Focus and efforts to strengthen commodity | Current condition | Expected condition | Gap Analysis |
|---|---|---|---|
| **Cultivation/Silviculture** | | | |
| Belangeran/Jelutung/Nyatoh/Gerunggang | 1. Cultivation technique is available (generative and vegetative)<br>2. Small-scale planting by farmers | 1. The availability of good quality of seedlings and high productivity<br>2. Planting to harvesting is well-planned | 1. The need for identified seed source for good quality seedlings<br>2. Tree improvement efforts of S. balangeran<br>3. Socialization and facilitation of commodities from upstream to downstream |
| Galam | 1. Cultivation technique is available (generative and vegetative)<br>2. Depends on natural regeneration<br>3. There is no yield management | 1. The availability of good quality of seedlings and high productivity<br>2. Galam sustainability through cultivation<br>3. Galam yield management is available | 1. Availability of identified seed source to ensure good quality seedlings<br>2. Galam tree improvement efforts<br>3. Socialization and facilitation of commodities from upstream to downstream |
| Local fish in beje (natural fish pond) | 1. Highly depend on river tidal<br>2. There is no efforts to increase the quality | 1. Dependency on the fish season can be reduced by fish farming | 1. Institutional capacity building to enrich beje fish ponds<br>2. Environmental |

| | | | |
|---|---|---|---|
| | of fish (no fodder application) | 2. The increase of fish quality and quantity | monitoring to support production sustainability |
| Purun | 1. Cultivation technique is available (generative and vegetative)<br>2. Depends on natural regeneration | 1. The availability of high quality and productivity of seedlings<br>2. Land certainty for local people to utilize purun | 1. There is yield management of Purun |
| Pineapple | 1. Cultivation technique is mastered<br>2. Small-scale planting by farmers | 1. The availability of good quality of seedlings<br>2. Planned planting according to market demand | 1. Pineapple improvement efforts |
| Spring onion | 1. Cultivation technique is mastered<br>2. Chemical fertilizer and pesticide application | 1. The availability of certified seed quality<br>2. Organic farming development | 1. Good seed quality<br>2. Facilitation of organic farming<br>3. Looking up for alternative commodity |
| **Harvest and post harvest** | | | |
| Belangeran/ Jelutung /Gerunggang/ | 1.Timber/latex harvested were from natural regeneration, not yet from plantation<br>2. At the age of 5 years, it has produced seeds and can be sold for nursery material | 1. Plantation can be guaranteed for harvest<br>2. Ensuring seed handling and preservation<br>3. Good quality seedling | 1. Facilitating land certainty and harvest certainty<br>2. Facilitating in the production of added value other than timber |
| Galam | 1. Harvesting has been conducted traditionally | 1. More efficient harvesting | 1. Improving infrastructure for business sustainability |
| Local fish/pineapple | 1. There is no post harvest process to generate added value | 1.There is a center for fish processing | 1.Facilitating the post production of fish and pineapple |
| Purun | 1. Harvesting and processing is conducted traditionally<br>2. Harvesting depends on river tidal | 1. Better harvesting technique<br>2. Harvesting does not depend on river tidal | 1. Improving infrastructure and facility to support business sustainability |
| Spring onion | 1. local market supply | 1. A wider market | 1. Facilitating market extend |
| **Environmental Risk** | | | |
| Belangeran/Jelutung/Gerunggang /Galam/Purun/Local fish | 1. Adaptive to peat ecosystem | 1. Positive impact on peat ecosystem | 1. Monitoring and facilitation<br>2. Local development incentive scheme |
| Pineapple | 1. Needs water table adjustion or mounding | 1.To determine the environmental impact | 1. Monitoring and facilitation |
| Spring Onion | 1. Needs water table adjustion or mounding<br>2. Using chemical fertilizer and pesticide | 1. To determine the lowest envirnmental impact<br>2. The development of organic farming | 1. Monitoring and facilitation<br>2. Incentive scheme of bare land<br>3. Establishing organic farming |

The economical analysis of paludiculture commodities in Central Kalimantan is presented in Table 3.

Table 3. Paludiculture business and its economical analysis at Central Kalimantan

| Paludiculture Business | NPV (Rp.) | IRR (%) | Net B/C | PBP | Economy feasibility | Remarks |
|---|---|---|---|---|---|---|
| Belangeran | 10.131.668 | 12 | 1 | 20 yrs | feasible | primary data,2019 |
| Purun | 21.815.362 | 70 | 4,61 | 2 yr 9 mo | feasible | primary data,2019 |
| Jelutung rawa | 29.933.289 | 20 | 7,88 | | feasible | Harun, 2014 |
| Galam | 49.930.081 | | 1,25 | | feasible | GGGI,2017(processed) |
| Pineapple | 90.457.173 | 95,82 | 3,48 | 2 yr 6 mo | feasible | primary data, 2019 |
| Spring onion | 160.387.607 | | 1,3 | 3 yr 3 mo | feasible | primary data, 2019 |

## DISCUSSION

We have found that most species that can survive in the rewetted condition are native species. This is supported by Lampela et al., 2017 that the main focus should be on the native species to reforest degraded ecosystems. The paludiculture species can be distinguished into three categories following Giesen ( 2015). Those are (1) proven commercial crops,(2) quick harvest species and (3) unproven commercial crops. Galam and Jelutung can be grouped as proven commercial crops. Purun and Kelakai can be grouped into quick harvest species and Belangeran, Gerunggang, Nyatoh are put into unproven commercial crops. Although Belangeran is categorized as unproven commercial crops according to Giesen (2015), we have proven that growing Belangeran is economically feasible although it takes 20 years to harvest the timber. Moreover, not only timber, Belangeran can also produce seeds 5 years after initial plant and it can be sold for nursery production. Shorea belangeran has a good growth and survival rate and it has been recommended for restoration (Lampela et al. 2017), is known for its potential in harsh condition (Giesen and Meer 2009) and adapt to acidic soil and resistant to inundation (Giesen, 2013). Another species is Dyera polyphylla. According to (Graham, Turjaman, and Page 2013), Shorea balangeran and Dyera poyphylla are potential for restoration of degraded peatland in Central Kalimantan. It has economical feasibility (Harun, 2014). Moreover, Ulya et al., 2015 stated that Jelutung is financially feasible to be developed in peatswamp area with NPV =Rp. 132,791,740 , BCR = 3.85 and IRR=9,97%. Galam is proven to be another potential paludiculture species (Arifin et al., 2016, Yuwati et.al., 2018). According to Arifin et al., 2016, Galam has multiple use but mainly for house construction. However, based on our survey, Galam has not been cultivated up to present. The supply is still depend on nature. Although it is economically feasible, yield management should also become the focus in the development of Galam. Purun danau and Purun tikus are the next potential paludiculture species (Yuwati, et al., 2018). However, purun is not yet cultivated. Although it is economically feasible but product added value should become the orientation for Purun development. Pineapple and spring onion are not native peatland species. We need to construct mounding to grow them in peatland. Although they are economically feasible and considered as the first top two in NPV with our analysis, they need to be planted intercropped with native perennial species such as Belangeran and Jelutung in order to achieve peatland use sustainability. We have presented some potential paludiculture species in Central Kalimantan. However, some commodities were experiencing constraints such as no product continuity because the raw materials are still collecting from nature or limited cultivation efforts. Another challenge was that the product is still produced in a very simple form resulting in a low price and low consumers motivation to buy. Some commodities owned a long market chain resulting in an unreasonable huge of profit margin. Several technical notes for market breakthrough were (1) changing from "collect from nature" into "cultivation; facilitation, training and incentives should be focused to paludiculture farmers, (2) product diversification to enhance the value of commodity by trainings and market facilitation, (3) the low motivation to buy paludicuture products can be eliminated by promoting as Go Green products and (4) shortening the market chain by establishing a more effective institutional arrangement for paludiculture bussiness. The report of Giesen (2013) Paludiculture: Sustainable Alternatives on Degraded Peatland in Indonesia' provides information on the 534 native peat swamp species that can adapt to acidic soils and are resistant to inundation to support peatland restoration. We need to explore more potential paludiculture species to support peatland restoration.

## CONCLUSION

Several potential paludiculture species in Central Kalimantan and their economical feasibility were determined including Shorea balangeran, Dyera polyphylla, Cratoxylon sp., Palaquium sp., Lepironia articulata, Eleocharis dulcis, Pineapple and Spring Onion. Those species grow well on deep peat and are economically feasible. However planting tree species should be combined with horticulture and agriculture species due to the long payback period associated with trees. Moreover, cultivation efforts should be promoted for those that are still depending on natural regeneration, product diversification shoud be encourage to add product value, shortening the market chain and giving incentives to the paludiculture farmers should be encouraged.


## ACKNOWLEDGEMENTS

The authors gratefully acknowledges The Peatland Restoration Agency for providing financial support for this study. The authors would also wish to thank farmers, government officials and respondents of Central Kalimantan for their contributions in this research. The first author would like to thank ACIAR project FST/2016/144 for providing financial support to participate in the IPC Congress 2021. Tri Wira Yuwati, Dony Rachmanadi conceived and design the research, collected and analysed the data. Tri Wira Yuwati, Dony Rachmanadi and Daniel Mendham wrote and edited the manuscript.

## REFERENCES


(BRG), Badan Restorasi Gambut. 2019. *Three Years of Peatland Restoration in Indonesia Report Badan Restorasi Gambut Republik Indonesia (the Peatland Restoration Agency of the Republic of Indonesia).*

Arifin, Yudi Firmanul, Siti Hamidah, and Yulian Firmana Arifin. 2016. "ECOLOGICAL ANALYSIS OF GELAM (Melaleuca Cajuputi) ON PEATLAND IN SOUTH KALIMANTAN." *Jurnal Silvikultur Tropika* 7(3):S77–79.

Dohong, Alue, Ammar Abdul Aziz, and Paul Dargusch. 2017. "A Review of the Drivers of Tropical Peatland Degradation in South-East Asia." *Land Use Policy* 69(September):349–60.

Giesen, Wim. 2015. "Utilising Non-Timber Forest Products to Conserve Indonesia ' s Peat Swamp Forests and Reduce Carbon Emissions." *Journal of Indonesian Natural History* 3(2):69–72.

Giesen, Wim, and Peter van der Meer. 2009. *Guidelines for the Rehabilitation of Degraded Peat Swamp Forests in Central Kalimantan - Master Plan for the Conservation and Development of the Ex-Mega Rice Project Area in Central Kalimantan.*

Giesen, 2013. Paludiculture: sustainable alternatives on degraded peatland in Indonesia (revised draft). Quick assessment and nationwide screeningof peat and lowland resources abd action planning for the implementation of a national lowland strategy. Euroconsult Mott MacDonald&Deltares. p.71.

Graham, Laura L. B., Maman Turjaman, and Susan E. Page. 2013. "Shorea Balangeran and Dyera Polyphylla (Syn. Dyera Lowii) as Tropical Peat Swamp Forest Restoration Transplant Species: Effects of Mycorrhizae and Level of Disturbance." *Wetlands Ecology and Management* 21(5):307–21.

Joosten, Hans, Greta Gaudig, Franziska Tanneberger, Sabine Wichmann, and Wendelin Wichtmann. 2016. "Paludiculture: Sustainable Productive Use of Wet and Rewetted Peatlands." Pp. 339–57 in *Peatland Restoration and Ecosystem Services: Science, Policy and Practice.*

Lampela, Maija, Jyrki Jauhiainen, Sakari Sarkkola, and Harri Vasander. 2017. "Promising Native Tree Species for Reforestation of Degraded Tropical Peatlands." *Forest Ecology and Management* 394:52–63.

Miettinen, Jukka, and Soo Chin Liew. 2010. "Status of Peatland Degradation and Development in Sumatra and Kalimantan." *Ambio* 39(5):394–401.

Miettinen, Jukka, Chenghua Shi, and Soo Chin Liew. 2016. "Land Cover Distribution in the Peatlands of Peninsular Malaysia, Sumatra and Borneo in 2015 with Changes since 1990." *Global Ecology and Conservation* 6:67–78.

Page, Susan E., John O. Rieley, and Christopher J. Banks. 2011. "Global and Regional Importance of the Tropical Peatland Carbon Pool." *Global Change Biology* 17(2):798–818.

Silvius M, Diemont H (2007) Deforestation and degradation of peatlands. Peatlands Int.2:32 -34

Uda, Saritha Kittie, Lars Hein, and Alma Adventa. 2020. "Towards Better Use of Indonesian Peatlands with Paludiculture and Low-Drainage Food Crops." Springer Netherlands.

Ulya, Nur Arifatul, Efendi Agus Waluyo, and Ari Nurlia. 2015. "Development Prospect of Jelutong as Business Commodity of Forest Management Unit (A Financial Review)." Pp. 471–78 in *Proceedings of International Conference of Indonesia Forestry Researchers III : Forestry research to support sustainable timber production and selfsufficiency in food, energy, and water".*

Wahyunto, Ritung S, Nugroho K, Sulaeman Y, Hikmatullah, Tafakresnanto, C., Suparto & Sukarman (2013) Peta Lahan Gambut Terdegradasi Pulau Kalimantan dan Papua (Degraded Peatland map for Kalimantan and Papua). Indonesia Climate Change Trust Fund (ICCTF)-BAPPENAS, Indonesian Agency for Agricultural Research and Development, Ministry of Agriculture, Jakarta

Yuwati, T.W., Junaidah, Wahyuningtyas R. and Rachmanadi, D. 2018. "Prosiding." edited by E. Tata, Hesti Lestari, Syaufina, L. , Rahmat, M. and Martin. Balai Litbang LHK Palembang.

ID 62703

# MULTI-STAKEHOLDER PARTNERSHIP TO REHABILITATE PEATLANDS IN PAHANG, MALAYSIA

Faizal Parish[1], Serena Lew Siew Yan[1], Aida Hayati Mohd Hassan[1], Muhamad Faizuddin Zainuddin[1]

[1] Global Environment Centre, Malaysia

*fparish@gec.org.my, serena@gec.org.my*

## SUMMARY

Among the challenges of peatland management in Malaysia are over-drainage and associated dry season fires. This paper will share the experiences and results of a multi-stakeholder approach implemented in 1000ha of peatland which was regularly burnt over the past 10 years. The area is within Southeast Pahang Peatland Landscape (SEPPL), the largest peatland landscape in Peninsular Malaysia that is of global importance for biodiversity conservation. The landscape approach was introduced to engage the plantation concession, government agencies and local aboriginal community with a multi-stakeholder partnership. The area has been in high fire risk as there is unsystematic abandoned drainage system left behind by logging company years ago. The drainage has increased fire risk and impacted the local community in terms of water source. A pilot project was started in September 2018 with support from the plantation companies, key relevant government agencies including the District Office, and the involvement of the local Jakun aboriginal community to initiate rehabilitation effort at the degraded peatland area. The rehabilitation through improving hydrological regime and planting suitable indigenous tree species have been executed with agreement by the relevant parties. Free, Prior and Informed Consent (FPIC) procedure was applied to engage the Jakun community at the planning stage. The pilot project has shown a very positive result. This includes advancing economic activities to the local community to address loss of income from degraded peatlands, rewetting the degraded peatland area by installing check dams and encouraging natural regeneration and replanting of the forest. While rehabilitating and conserving the peatland forest, the community has been assisted to establish tree nursery, and offered alternative livelihood option (e.g. bee-keeping, handicraft weaving and mushroom farming) to increase household income.

## INTRODUCTION

The Southeast Pahang Peatland Landscape (SEPPL) is the largest peatland area in Peninsular Malaysia covering 230,000 hectares (ha) of which about 110,000 ha is still covered with peat swamp forests of global significance for biodiversity and climate mitigation (Hamzah, 2012). According to IMP (2011), a total of 58 species mammal were recorded, 54 fish species, 17 Malaysian anurans species, 13 species of snakes and one over third avifauna species can be found in SEPPL. The landscape also has valuable timber species such *as Shorea platycarpa, Anisoptera 378arginate, Calopyhllum* spp. *And Ramin melawis* (Ismail, 2011). As well as other peatland landscape, drainage is still the main threat to degradation of the peatland area. Drained peatlands are susceptible to fire as dry peat is highly inflammable. Peatland drainage and fires are major contributors of greenhouse gas (GHG) emissions thus creating a positive feedback loop between climate change and further peatland degradation (Koh, 2011). Smoke from peat fire has resulted in haze problem which had huge impact on the economy and also public health. As peatland burns with low oxygen levels and hence burns incompletely, it leads to thick smoke haze formation (Parish, 2019). Frequent fires take place in the landscape linked to oil palm plantation development and ex-logging and have degraded portions of the remaining forest and negatively impacted local communities (Lo. J, 2018). Over the years, peat fires have destroyed over 10,000 ha of peat forests causing hundreds of millions on ringgit in losses and impacts.

In relation to these problems, a multi-stakeholder approach is needed involving oil palm companies, government agencies and local communities to modify practices to reduce fire risk and support forest protection and rehabilitation. The start-up project has been conducted on a remote village at Kampung Tanjung Kelapa on the western side of the forest. In recent years, the fires have degraded/destroyed more than 1,000 ha of peat swamp forest as well as plantations of Orang Asli communities in adjacent areas. Analysis based on the satellite images and site visits and interviews with Orang Asli communities indicates that the drainage system in the buffer zone of the Pekan Forest Reserve (FR) is one of the root causes of the regular fires. Oil palm plantations have been identified in the landscape and already developed since 1989 with border to the forest reserve with one kilometre (km) away. In order to develop a landscape programme in the area, Global Environment Centre (GEC) facilitated collaboration between the local indigenous people, the oil palm plantation and a broad range of government agencies (including those responsible for forestry, agriculture, health, local town government and Orang Asli Development). The objective of this programme was to conserve and restore degraded peatland area by rewetting process as well as developing a sustainable peatland management programme while improving the living standard of the local community.

## MATERIALS AND METHODS

### Identification of the landscape

The work started with a desktop study and analyse of satellite images for identification of interest areas prior to commencing of the programme. Peatland management issues then were identified and linked to plantation concerning a drainage canal from the plantation which is linked to large-scale fires in the adjacent Pekan FR. A series of land cover change of adjacent to the plantation reveal massive made from 1995 to 2016 have changed the peatland use with repeated fires (Figure 1). In line with the plantation's commitment to avoid degradation of peatlands, it is important to undertake a landscape approach in its management and operation. The landscape approach then proposed by GEC to overcome the drainage problem at the FR and its buffer zone which is adjacent to the plantation, to prevent future fires as well as to initiate rehabilitation effort at the degraded area within the FR and its adjacent buffer zone.

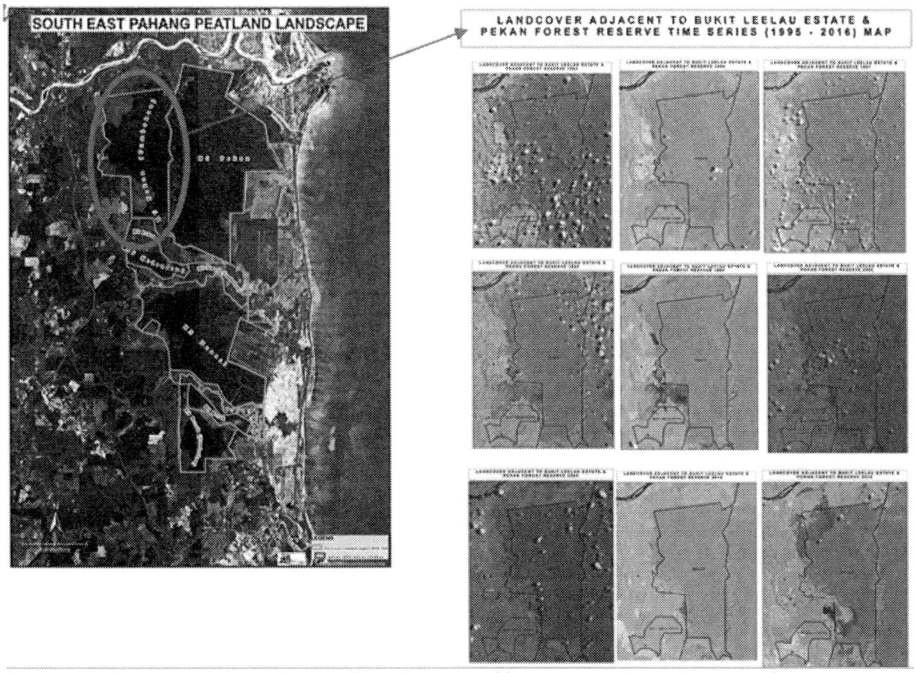


*Figure 13: Southeast Pahang Peatland Landscape and lancover analysis of interested area.*

**Involvement of Bukit Leelau Estate (BLML initiative)**

The Bukit Leelau Mini landscape (BLML) Initiative was started in September 2018, being supported by IOI Plantations and facilitated by GEC, to rehabilitate the degraded peatland by preventing fire, blocking drainage canals and rehabilitating the degraded peatlands. BLML is an area of about 4000 ha within the SEPPL. It comprises oil palm in the IOI Bukit Leelau Estate and the Sri Jelutong Estate together with Orang Asli settlements and peat swamp forests in the Pekan (Extension) Forest Reserve and extensive peatlands on state lands. About 1000 ha of the peatlands have been severely degraded by fire partly linked to drainage canals dug for logging operations 20 years ago and for draining water from the plantations. The Orang Asli from Jakun subgroup, known as Proto Malays, represents a key community in BLML initiative. There are nine sub-villages in the area including Kampung Kernun, Kampung Tanjung Chak, Kampung Keralek, Kampung Meselang, Kampung Tanjung Kelapa, Kampung Sapai, Kampung Melogo, Kampung Tanjung Ipoh and Kampung Betereh. All the sub-villages are rather small, from a minimum of 3 houses to a maximum of 9 houses, owned by a single family to a few families, with a total population of about 200 persons.

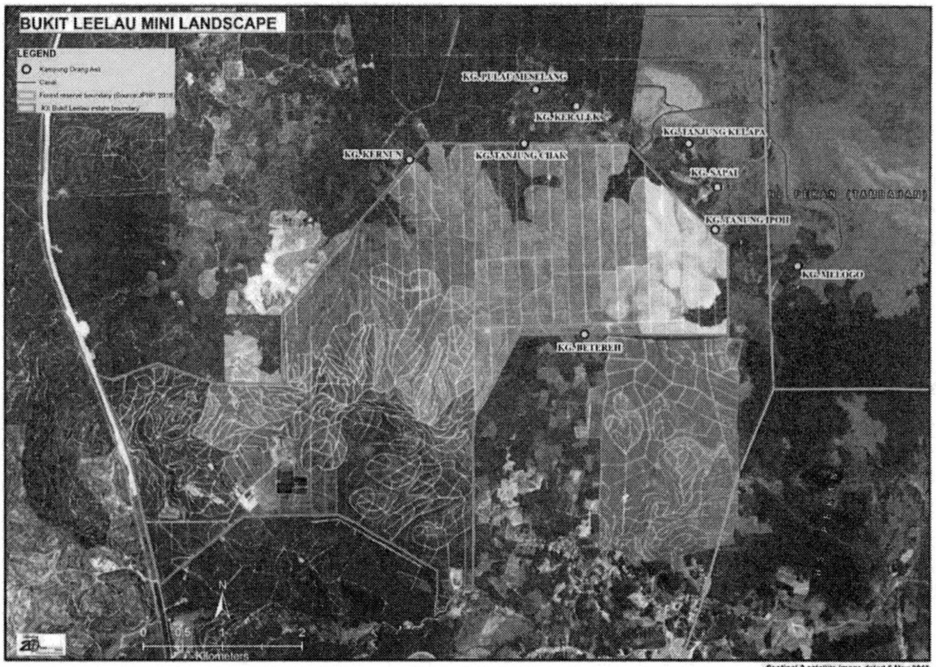


*Figure 14: Map and information on Bukit Leelau Mini Landscape.*

## Multi-stakeholder Approach in BLML

In landscape management processes, every step taken in the landscape is executed in a transparent way to all key stakeholders, especially local community who lives and dependent on the peatland. Frequent fires take place in the landscape linked to oil palm plantation development and logging and have degraded portions of the remaining forest and negatively impacted to local communities. In order to address these problems, a multi-stakeholder approach is needed involving oil palm companies, government agencies (District Office, State Forestry Department, etc.) and local communities to modify practices to reduce fire risk and support forest protection and rehabilitation. Prior project commencing, a total number of relevant stakeholders have been identified (Figure 3).

| | Stakeholder | |
|---|---|---|
| Group | Funders | IOI Plantation Sdn. Bhd. |
| | A<br>Government Agencies | Pekan JAKOA |
| | | Pahang Forestry Department (JPNP) |
| | | BAKAS Unit, Pekan Department of Health |
| | | District Office Pekan |
| | | Pahang Department of Irrigation and Drainage (JPS) |
| | | Pahang Department of Environment (DOE) |
| | | Pekan Fire and Rescue Department (BOMBA) |
| | Private Agencies | Ladang Sri jelutong, Tanah Makmur Berhad |
| | | Bukit Leelau Estate (IOI Plantation Sdn Bhd) |
| | Target Group | Community of Kampung Tanjung Kelapa (KTK) |

**Figure 3: Stakeholder engagement prior to commencing activities of the programme with a) District Office, b) plantation, and c) local community.**

## Rehabilitation work

Restoring hydrological functioning should be the first consideration in the peatland rehabilitation. A rehabilitation plan should focus on rewetting to restore water regime – by installing canal blocks and/or water gates. Repairing hydrological function to raising water table and enable revegetation – natural regeneration has better sustainability for the plants to survive compare to the planted saplings by human. Prior to blocking, it is necessary to carry out a number of analyses including identify suitable locations of the canals to be blocked, affected parties, soil characteristics, vegetation in the surrounding area and socio-cultural characteristics. Free, Prior and Informed Consent (FPIC) process was conducted to make sure community's rights are protected, their voices are heard, consent given and everyone understands the whole effort to be taken in restoring the peatland. A seedling buy-back system has been introduced at nurseries set-up by the local communities living in the BLML – saplings are then purchased from these nurseries for tree planting activities. Community members also are engaged in the planting and maintenance of replanted areas.

Figure 4: FPIC process with effected community surround target areas.(direct impact)

**Introduction to Sustainable Livelihood Options**

It is crucial that assistance is given to the Orang Asli community to improve their living condition before empowering them to the rehabilitation efforts of adjacent forest lands. Rehabilitating peatlands are not solely aimed on restoring its hydrological functions, but with proper planning, various livelihood activities can be adopted for providing alternative livelihood options such as community nursery and integrated farming. The nursery provides a socio-economic opportunity for Orang Asli community, as an alternative livelihood option. Training has been given to local community to enable them to collect wildings as well as set-up and manage their own nurseries (Figure 5 and 6). Integrated farming (e.g. bee farming, aqua-agriculture, etc.) also has been introduced to the local community in this initiative with support of new partners in 2019 and 2020.

Figure 5: Training on collecting wildings and nursery operation were conducted

Figure 6: Wilding collection by Orang Asli Community.

## RESULTS

**Establishment SHGKTK and undertaken activities**

The local community participation is a key element of managing, protecting and rehabilitating the degraded peat swamp forests. A local community committee called Sahabat Hutan Gambut Kampung Tanjung Kelapa (SHGKTK) created with support of GEC to empower the local community in creating awareness and empowering them to manage the peat swamp forests and its buffer zone. The SHGKTK (Figure 7) has jointly and established the wilding nurseries, planting, fire patrolling, and actively participating in livelihood activities. By the end 2019, the cooperation of Orang Asli led by SHGKTK and IOI Bukit Leelau has successfully carried out all main activities under the rehabilitation programme. This includes construction of 10 canal blocks, planting of 5000 *Macaranga* spp. Inside the degraded areas through the multi-stakeholder partnership and fire patrolling by the local community. Alternate livelihood activities also were carried out on top of the community nurseries such as mushroom farming (Figure 8 A-D). The direct financial support by IOI on this BLML initiative was completed in 2019.

Figure 7: Sahabat Hutan Gambut Kampung Tanjung Kelapa (SHGKTK).

Figure 8A: Canal block construction.

Figure 8B: Community Nurseries.

Figure 8C: Planting activities.

Figure 8D: Mushroom farming with empty fruit bunch from mill.

**Participation of Government agencies and new partners**

By mid-2019, the local government agencies have directly involved in the BLML initiative. Additional check dams have been successfully constructed supporting 1500 hectare of rewetting areas in Pekan (Extension) Forest Reserve (Figure 9). Implementation has been carried out by Department of Irrigation and Drainage with supported by State Forestry Department and Department of Environment. The initiative also managed to bring along new partners involving in rehabilitation activities particularly supporting livelihood and welfare of the community in BLML. With participation of Yayasan Bursa Malaysia and Bunge Loders Croklaan in 2019 and 2020, more activities have been undertaken, these include supporting rehabilitation programme by building more canal blocks with livelihood activities.

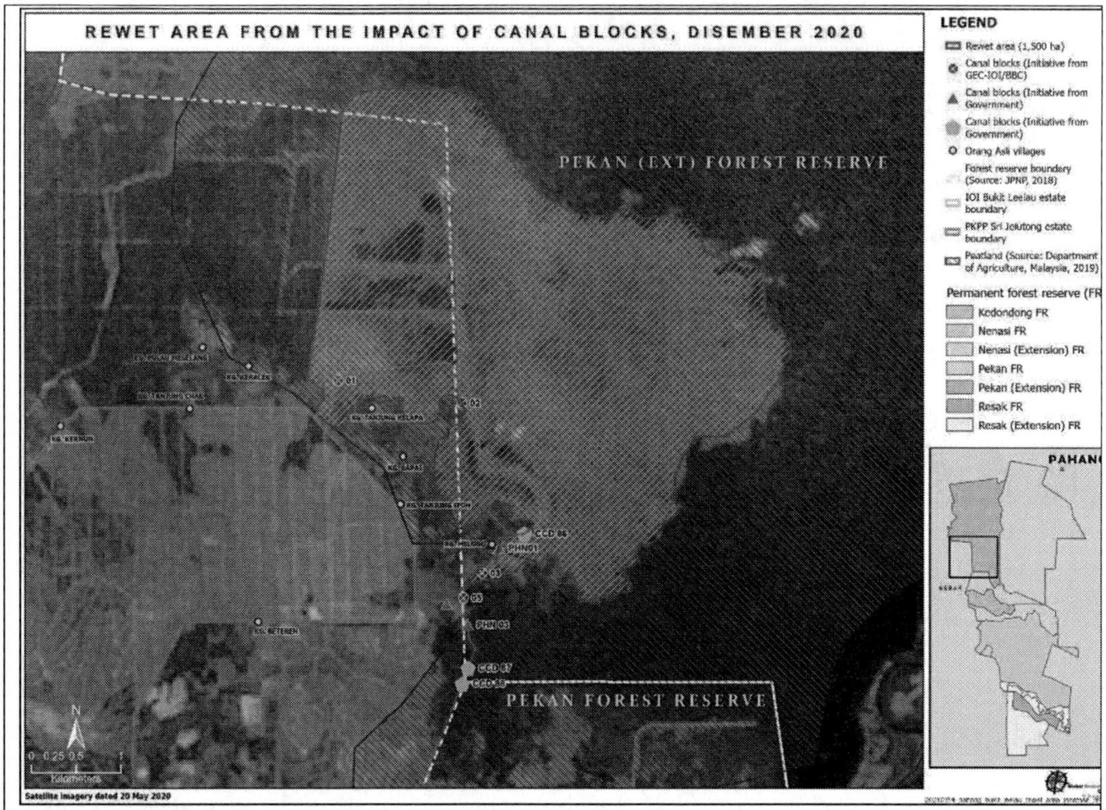

Figure 9: Map of rewetted area of the BLML Initiative.

**Maintaining existing and expansion of the initiative to wider are within the SEPPL**

With the succession of BLML initiative, the rehabilitation programme have been brought to a wider landscape within the SEPPL. With the participation of United Nations Development Program (UNDP) and International Fund for Agricultural Development (IFAD) in 2019, the existing initiative has been maintained and expanded to adjacent areas. Significant funding was gain by IFAD, enabling the initiative to reach-out further collaboration in multi-stakeholder cooperation in developing an integrated management programme for the SEPPL in partnership with state and district governments, plantation sector and local communities. This programme will be developed over the 4 years (2020-2023) with the support of the national project on Sustainable Management of Peatland Ecosystems in Malaysia (SMPEM). Meanwhile, UNDP fund enables further works for maintaining the rehabilitation and blocking structures with supporting the fire prevention in the local OA villages within the BLML and RPS Simpai located in south of the BLML.

## CONCLUSION

Most of the peatlands in ASEAN are under the management of the private sector in particular in the forestry, agriculture and plantation sectors. The oil palm industry has been instrumental in establishing high standards for peatland management and contributing to peatland conservation – for example, through the Roundtable on Sustainable Palm Oil (RSPO). Thus, partnering oil palm industry would be good strategy engagement for peatland rehabilitation. Corporate Social Responsibility (CSR) funds has also been providing significant assistance. Further activity in engaging partners and then channelling funds are crucial in order to support existing implementation, monitoring, maintenance training and empowering communities in rehabilitation activities. Involvement of the government agencies are crucial not only for seeking approval but to become rightful parties that have legal obligation pertaining of undertaking rehabilitation and conservation activities. This includes on law, adoption policies and directive guidelines regarding sustainable peatland management. An Integrated Management Plan (IMP) has been one of the best policy documents could be updated for the landscape. The IMP establishment then will become a guidance for all relevant stakeholders for undertaking rehabilitation and conservation.

## ACKNOWLEDGEMENTS

Global Environment Centre (GEC) as the implementer of the Rehabilitation of Peat Swamp Forest Programme with the Indigenous Community in Southeast Pahang Peatland Landscape, would like to thank our funders i.e. Yayasan Bursa (through its Bursa Bull Charge, 2019-2020), IOI Group (2018-2019), Bunge Loders Croklaan (2019), United Nations Development Program (UNDP, 2020-2021) and International Fund for Agricultural Development (IFAD, 2019-2023) for providing support in peatland fire prevention, forest rehabilitation and community development activities within the Landscape. Special thanks to all key stakeholders from government agencies i.e. Pahang State Forestry Department (JPNP) and its District Forest Offices, Pekan District Office, Department of Orang Asli Development in Pekan (JAKOA Pekan), Pekan Department of Health, Department of Environment, Department of Irrigation and Drainage, Pekan Department of Agriculture, Department of Fishery, Fire and Rescue Department (BOMBA Pekan); private sector i.e. Tanah Makmur Berhad (TMB), Ladang Seri Jelutung, IOI Bukit Leelau Estate; social enterprises e.g. Honey Plus Resources and TONIBUNG; and local communities especially Sahabat Hutan Gambut Kampung Tanjung Kelapa and Kampung Simpai who have been collaborative and supportive towards this effort in preventing peatland fire and rehabilitating the degraded peatland areas within the Landscape.

## REFERENCES

Hamzah, K., A. (2012). Management of Peat Swamp Forests for Conservation and Sustainable Use – An Integrated Approach, Presented at APFP – SEApeat Meeting 9 – 10 July 2012 Pahang.

Ismail, P., Nizam, M.S., Latiff, A., Faridah Hanum, I. & Shamsudin, I. (2011). Phenology of *Gonystylus bancanus* in Pahang, Peninsular Malaysia. Journal of Tropical Forest Science 23(2): 143–151.

Koh, L.P., Miettinen, J., Liew, S.C. & J. Ghazoula (2011) Remotely sensed evidence of tropical peatland conversion to oil palm *PNAS, vol. 108, no. 12: pp 5127–5132*

Parish, F., Mathews, J., Lew, S.Y., Faizuddin, M. and Lo, J. (Eds.). (2019). RSPO Manual on Best Management Practices (BMPs) for Existing Oil Palm Cultivation on Peat. 2nd Edition, RSPO, Kuala Lumpur.

ID 62454

# PRELIMINARY RESULTS OF 10-YEAR EXPERIENCE IN REWETTING PEAT-EXTRACTED BOGS IN RUSSIA

*Kirill Shakhmatov, Vladimir Panov

Tver State Technical University, Russia

*krl81@list.ru*

The central part of Russia features a lot of destroyed peatlands left after a long period of peat excavating that currently are sources of fire and GHG emission.

After fires, especially in 2010 and 2014, a rewetting programme was initiated within the frameworks of "Restoring peatlands of Russia for fire prevention and climate change mitigation" (PeatRus) project in 2011.

By 2020 we have rewetted more than 60 000 ha which is only 20% of the area in need. The most important goal was rewetting drainaged peatlands to achieve the self-restoration of bog's ecosystem.

Because of huge variety and scale of peatlands, as well as different types of peat extraction employed a list of problems to be solved was compiled: identifying most dangerous places, accumulating and analyzing archive data, exploring and monitoring the current state, developing the project and selecting the type of rewetting to name just a few.

Exploring the possibilities to use these places for paludiculture and identifying economic drivers for biomass production became the additional targets.

In the past 10 years of project in Russia we have accumulated unique expertise that allows:

1) to compare main approaches to rewetting peat-extracted bogs disturbed by various peat excavation methods on a large-scale basis (500-1200 ha) in terms of environmental effectiveness, cost, difficulty of implementation and sustainability of constructions;
2) to assess project impact on fire emergence and GHG emission;
3) to develop the technology of paludiculture biomass production and evaluate the cost-effectiveness;
4) to initiate the monitoring of rewetted bogs using ground and remote data.

Our experience and results prove very valuable from both practical and scientific points of view and we are planning to continue research in peatland ecosystems restoration.

Thus the results of this work will be submitted in presentation and further article.

ID 62763

# THE BORD NA MÓNA RAISED BOG RESTORATION PROGRAMME – PROGRESS AND BENEFITS

*Alex Copland, Mark McCorry

Bord na Móna, Ireland

*Alex.Copland@bnm.ie*

Bord na Móna Plc is a publicly owned company, originally established in 1934 to develop some of Ireland's extensive peat resources for the purposes of economic development and to support energy security, In the decades since its establishment the company has employed tens of thousands of people in its fuel, energy, and horticultural growing media businesses. Today, Bord na Móna is undertaking a number of highly significant actions in support of climate policy. These actions involve a radical transformation and decarbonisation of nearly the entire Bord na Móna business. Wide scale industrial peat extraction for energy production is now coming to an end in Ireland. This brings new challenges and opportunities.

Several bogs in the midlands of Ireland were initially drained for industrial peat extraction but were never fully developed. These bogs offer significant potential for raised bog restoration and conservation. These sites now form the basis of the Bord na Móna Raised bog Restoration Programme. Raised bog restoration has now been carried out across 26 sites and 3100 ha have been completed so far. Re-wetting is carried out by blocking drains using peat dams and following best practise methodology. Bord na Móna has targeted an additional 2000 ha for bog restoration as part of this programme.

Raised bog restoration brings significant benefits for biodiversity and for other ecosystem services such as the reduction in carbon emissions. Additional conservation measures for Curlew are being carried out across several of these restored sites by a combination of stakeholders. GHG flux research by academic partners has also demonstrated that Moyarwood Bog has now become a net carbon GHG sink, 8 years after bog restoration was carried out. The paper will discuss the potential for this raised bog restoration programme to support Ireland's biodiversity objectives and its National Climate Action Plan.

ID 62733

# EVALUATION OF GHG EMISSIONS FROM ORGANIC SOILS

*Ieva Līcīte, Ainārs Lupiķis

Latvian State Forest Research Institute "Silava", Latvia

*ieva.licite@silava.lv*

LIFE REstore project aims at development of country specific emission factors for organic soils in Latvia. There are three main greenhouse gas (GHG) inventory improvement targets in LIFE REstore: (a) elaboration of activity data for calculation of GHG emissions; (b) elaboration of $CO_2$, CH4 and N2O emission factors for peat extraction sites; (c) evaluation of potential impact of land use and management changes on GHG emissions.

According to the LIFE Restore area affected by peat extraction reduced from 47.6 kha in 1990 to 39.5 kha in 2016. The most of the land use changes are associated with afforestation.

LIFE REstore covers following land use types: peat extraction, partially extracted peatland without vegetation, partially extracted peatland covered by herbaceous plants, perennial grasslands, croplands, plantations of blackberries and cranberries, pine and birch stands, pristine raised and transitional bog; every type represented by at least 3 sites.

GHG measurements (respiration, photosynthetic $CO_2$ removals) continued for 24 months. Additional parameters, e.g. $CO_2$ removals in tree biomass, carbon input with litter, groundwater level, soil temperature, photosynthetic active radiation and other parameters were continuously monitored.

According to LIFE REstore results net $CO_2$ emissions from soil are twice smaller in comparison to the default emission factors according to Intergovernmental Panel on Climate Change (IPCC) in all managed lands. CH4 emissions, in contrast, are significantly bigger according to the project results; however, they are forming minor part of the net GHG emissions. N2O emissions from soil according to LIFE REstore results are significantly smaller in comparison to IPCC guidelines.

The LIFE OrgBalt project is the next step of evaluation of GHG emissions from organic soils in Baltic states aimed at elaboration of activity data and emission factors for nutrient rich organic soils, thus covering whole range of organic soils and significantly extending the range of evaluated management strategies.

ID 72770

# RETURNING WATER TO CONSERVATION AREAS WILL BENEFIT BOTH FORESTRY AND CONSERVATION

Tiina Ronkainen[1], Samuli Joensuu[1], Jani Antila[1], Juha Jämsen[2], Eerika Tapio[3]

[1] Tapio, Helsinki, Finland

[2] Finnish Forest Center, Pihtipudas, Finland

[3] Metsähallitus, Vantaa, Finland

*tiina.ronkainen@tapio.fi*

## SUMMARY

Forest drainage outside the protected peatland has sometimes dried conservation areas extensively. Sometimes even a single ditch can lead the water flow from the catchment area past the conserved peatland. In connection with the project of ditch network maintenance in the vicinity of the protected peatland, it is possible to return ditch water to the dried protected peatlands. The activity often reduces the costs of the drainage project and has positive effects for example on flood protection and water quality of the water catchment.

Tapio Ltd and the Finnish Forest Centre launched a new cooperation and operating model in which the waters of the forest ditch network maintenance project can be returned to the adjacent dried-up conservation peatland area. The new operating model benefits environment, landowners and also the protection authority and the ditch planners. When planning water management for protected areas, the planner should utilize all new tools based on the application of spatial datasets found on the website of the Finnish Forest Centre. The aim of the action is to improve the conditions of the environment. The operating model for the cooperation of the planner, implementers and protection authorities of the restoration area has been developed in the cooperation project of Tapio, the Finnish Forest Centre and South Ostrobothnia Centre for Economic Development, Transport and the Environment (ELY-Center). The operating model was put into practice in the Hydrology LIFE project (2017-2023).

An important part of the Hydrology LIFE project was to train planners, contractors and authorities to implement the new cooperation and operating model. Also, landowners were educated about the new possibilities that the method offers. This new approach for peatland restoration will benefit not only the environment, habitats and species but widely all stakeholders and different interest groups around peatland restoration.

***Keywords***: *peatland, conservation, rewetting, restoration, forestry, ditch network maintenance*

## INTRODUCTION

In Finland there are many Natura 2000 peatlands, which hydrological state should be restored towards natural state. Natura 2000 sites include a significant number of old forest drainage areas. Natura 2000 sites are often also surrounded by privately owned lands that have been drained for silviculture. In Finland forest drainage was most intensive during 1960-80. Although, as a rule from 1980, forest drainage ditches were not to be dug 40 meters closer to the Natura site, the draining effect of the ditches may have extended to the Natura site, as the drying effect of forest ditches usually reach relatively far. Several working groups promoting the protection of peatlands in Finland have paid special attention to the fact that conditions of peatland habitats in protected areas could be improved by improving the water management of the area (Kotiaho et al. 2016). This could be achieved, among other things, by directing water from the ditch network maintenance sites located in the immediate vicinity of protected areas to the protected peatland, instead of directing waters to the water system. This method works best in aapa mire zone in Finland, where the surface profile of the peatland allows water to be directed from the edges of the peatland towards the center.

During previous project of Tapio, Finnish Forest Centre and South Ostrobothnia ELY-Center an operating model for directing the waters to protected peatlands was made (Autio et al. 2018). Simultaneously a service, which describes those Natura 2000 peatlands which border areas have been found to be dried as a result of adjacent forest drainage, was developed for the Finnish Forest Centre's website. The selection of peatlands is based on inventories and spatial data review. The service includes those dried peatland sites where rewetting is possible on the basis of preliminary estimates based on spatial data analysis.

Current Hydrology LIFE project of Tapio and Finnish Forest Centre concentrated on implementing the operating model to rewet Natura 2000 peatlands with waters form surrounding forestry areas. Metsähallitus Parks and Wildlife Finland acts as the main implementer and coordinator of the Hydrology LIFE project, which aims to implement the restoration of peatlands in Natura 2000 areas during 2017-2023. As an essential part of the project, the Finnish Forest Center and Tapio initated cooperation between the restoration of Natura 2000 areas and the ditch network maintenance areas next to them. The aim of the cooperation is an outcome that benefits both functions, Natura 2000 peatland restoration and forest drainage. During the project, the operating model was tested on pilot sites where water was returned to Natura 2000 peatlands from managed forest areas. The pilot sites were selected on the basis of the previous project of Metsähallitus, where suitable sites were mapped. Part of the pilot sites were bordered with privately owned forestry areas. On these sites local ditch planners were responsible for planning the ditch network maintenance measures and directing waters to Natura 2000 peatland. Rest of the surrounding areas of the pilot sites were owned by Metsähallitus, and the planning was done by specialists Of Metsähallitus. Tapio and Finnish Forest Centre supported planning if necessary.

Operating model

The main aim of the implemented operating model is that at the same time when the ditch network maintenance is being managed, the condition of the neighboring dryish habitats of the Natura 2000 peatland can be improved. The idea of the method is to restore the natural water flow direction, which has been cut off by drainage ditches. As a result, the water flows from the drainage area to water system will be reduced or even retained within the catchment area. When the water flow is reduced, the water protection of forestry operations consequently improves. Most important technique in the planning is the lidar scanned data, from which an exact elevation model of the land area has been constructed. With this elevation model, the former natural flow route in the catchment area can be modeled and used when planning the ditch network maintenance actions nearby the Natura 2000 site. The implementation of the planning is based on the utilization of existing spatial datasets. After suitable sites for returning water are mapped and selected by using the spatial data analysis, their suitability for the planned measures are verified through an on-site inspection. During the field inspection, the actual direction of the water flow and the land elevation differences are verified by measuring elevation differences.

The operating model for returning water from forestry land to the conservation area consists following steps:
- while planning ditch network maintenance the planner notices the possibility of directing water into the protection area. Planner contacts the landowner and inquires landowners' interest to implement the actions.
- ditch planner contacts nature services expert of Metsähallitus. They do a joint field visit to the site. Expert of Metsähallitus writes a memo of the field inspection.
- Metsähallitus issues a permit for returning water to conservation site.
- ditch planner finalizes the plan and makes a drainage notification to supervising regional authority (ELY-Center), a field memo and permit of Metsähallitus are attached to the notification
- authority processes the notification (ELY-Center)
- after the approval of the drainage notification, the project is prepared, and the implementation is put out to tender

Trainings

During the Hydrology LIFE project several trainings were organized for drainage planners and landowners. After the training the drainage planner is able to utilize the available open access spatial data sets from the site (lidar data and the elevation model formed from it, and the flow network data). The aim is to make the planning and implementation of measures as cost-effective as possible and to benefit all parties. Operating model can be implemented both on private or government land. The aim of the training was to inspire drainage planners to adopt the new technology and operating model as widely as possible, especially when ditch network maintenance is limited to a Natura 2000 area. After the training drainage planner is able:
- to identify and take into account those peatlands in protected areas for which returning water is possible and cost-effective;
- to use open access spatial datasets and tools to plan and implement the ditch network maintenance measures
- to assess in field whether it is possible to direct water from the planned ditch network maintenance area to adjacent Natura 2000 area;
- to plan the forest drainage in such a way that no further drying takes place on the protected area;
- to correctly plan the ditches that lead water into the Natura 2000 site in order to improve the condition of habitats;
- to contact the right authorities in Metsähallitus and the ELY-Center when additional information about Natura2000 site near the planning area is needed.

Also, authorities involved in the processing and financing of restoration projects attended the trainings. From the point of view of operational efficiency and overall costs, it is important that all parties involved in the planning, processing and implementation of drainage and restoration projects have a joint knowledge of the operating model and its objectives. The aim of the training was to improve the cooperation and planning know-how of the ELY-Centers, the Finnish Forest Center, Metsähallitus and the ditch network maintenance planner. Private landowners were also invited to the training and a brochure explaining the peatland restoration and forest drainage actions was prepared and distributed for landowners. During the trainings pilot sites were visited, so that the results of the implemented measures were seen in the field. Due Covid-19 trainings were also held online with high success among participators. Online training reach actually almost five times more people than originally planned trainings. Most likely trainings will continue as a part of the Hydrology LIFE project still to spread the word and know-how even further.

## MATERIALS AND METHODS

At the beginning of the project 100 suitable peatland protection sites across Finland were mapped and selected by using spatial analysis. Utilized data is the same data which the drainage planners use. Then 20 sites were selected for more detailed study. The sites were inspected in field to check the surface elevation between forestry area and protected peatland, to assess whether it is possible to direct water to peatland. It was observed at many sites that the forestry area had been depressed due to drainage and the surface of the peatland was significantly higher. Thus, directing the water on these sites to peatland could have been accomplished only by digging a considerably long and deep ditch into the protected peatland. In turn, a shorter ditch poses a risk of waterlogged conditions at the forestry area. These sites were excluded from the selection of pilot sites.

Based on the field inspections 14 sites were identified as a site where water could be directed from the forestry area to the protected peatland. The landowners of the forestry area surrounding these sites were contacted and their willingness to needed measures was inquired. During the project, the operational model was implemented at five pilot sites. Three of the pilot sites were bordered by privately owned forestry area. For these sites local drainage planner planned the directing of the waters from the forestry area to protected peatland. Two pilot sites were surrounded by forests owned by Metsähallitus, for these sites planning was conducted by planner of Metsähallitus. In the case of private own surrounding forest areas, the protection area was expanded at two sites so that the landowner would not suffer from possible waterlogging of the forestry area in the vicinity of protected peatland. At one pilot site on private land, waterlogged conditions emerged. Situation was resolved by digging a longer ditch to the protected peatland.

When designing the actions, the aim of the dry top layer in the forestry area next to the protected peatland was at least 40 cm. Thus, the length of the ditch directing water to protected peatland depends on the elevation between the protected peatland and the forestry area above it. Field visit and especially measuring the surface elevation during the planning is an important part of the planning and successful implementation. Returning of the waters on the pilot sites were carried out between 2018-2020. Pilot sites, conducted actions and observed results are described below.

Vahtisuo

Returning water to peatland was carried out in 2018 from the adjacent ditch network maintenance area. The site was optimal as there was a clear elevation from forestry area toward peatland. The forestry area on the vicinity of the protected peatland, which was mainly poorly growing, was included to the protection area due to the risk of waterlogged conditions. In 2020, the condition of the ditches was reviewed, and it was found that two of the three ditches brought plenty of water to the protected peatland. The water level of one ditch was lower, but the ditch had brought water to the peatland during the spring flood. Although, the ditch had remained a bit short, resulting that the dry top layer did not reach the targeted 40 cm at the starting point of that ditch. For other ditches, the targeted dry layer had been reached. The local Forest Management Association designed the measures for the ditch network maintenance and returning water to protected peatland. (**Error! Reference source not found.**).

*Figure 15. Vahtisuo (photo Jani Antila)*

Pelso strict nature reserve.

On the privately-owned forestry area adjacent to the protected peatland drainage ditches were maintained in 2019, and the ditches towards the protected peatland were dug in 2020. However, the ditch was initially too short due to the low load bearing capacity of the peatland. To gain a sufficient difference in the elevation from the forestry area to the peatland a much longer ditch would be needed (170 m). Still ditch would remain on the poorly growing forestry area outside the protected area. Restoration expert of Metsähallitus negotiates with the landowner about possible corrective measures. The local Forest Management Association designed the actions. (Figure 16)

*Figure 16. Pelso nature conservation area (photo Jani Antila).*

Kinkerisaarenneva
The restoration project planned by Metsähallitus was implemented in autumn 2020. Water was returned to the mire from several different points on the southern edge of the peatland. In addition, water was directed into the mire with a few new ditches from forested land east of the mire. (Figure 17).

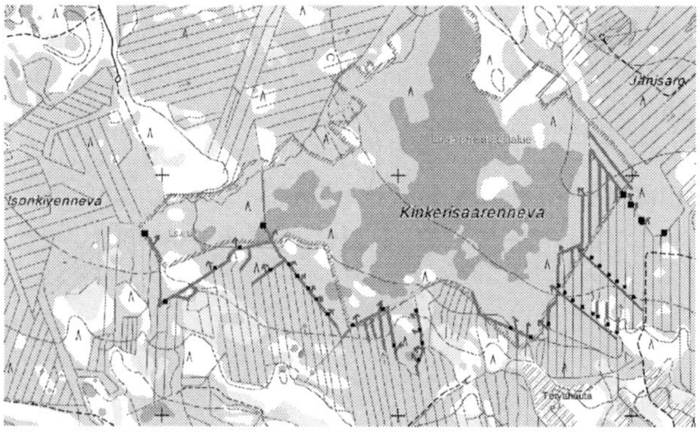


*Figure 17. Kinkerinsaareneva. (map MML & Metsähallitus).*

Suurisuo
Returning water to Suurisuo is planned for the old forest drainage area on the Suurisuo protection area as a part of other restoring activities at Suurisuo. In Suurisuo, the protected area has been extended to private forestry area which will be restored according to plans of Metsähallitus. Old ditches will be blocked, and water will be directed to protected peatland by ditch from the private landowner's forest drainage area. Metsähallitus has planned to conduct restoration project in Suurisuo during the winter 2020-2021.

Pohjoisjärven metsä
Metsähallitus planned restoring actions in 2020. At the site there is sufficient elevation difference between the forestry area and the restoration area, thus short ditch and blocking of few ditches are enough to return the water to the spruce forest under restoration. Implementation is planned.

## DISCUSSION

In Finland several working groups related to peatland protection have identified the need to improve the habitat status of peatlands, especially in the outer parts of the peatlands, which are often affected by the drainage of surrounding forestry area (e.g. Alanen and Aapala, Kotiaho et al. 2015). Returning water from the surrounding catchment area to the dried part of the protected peatland will help to improve the dried habitats. In Finland peatland restoration has been integrated into the nationally funded The Helmi habitats program established by the current government (Helmi 2021). The implementation period of the program is 2021-2030. The program focuses, among other things, on the restoration of Natura peatlands. At the same time the aim of the program is to return water from outside Natura peatlands at 250-400 sites, where, on the basis of a spatial data analysis, measures are found to be possible to conduct.

For successful restoration by returning water to conservation area a detailed planning is essential. Also, it is important that private landowners, through whose lands water is to be directed to peatland, are educated, interested and willing to utilize these new measures. Important part of the planning is accurate mapping and measuring elevations of the sites. In this way, the risks of potential damage to forestry areas due the waterlogged conditions can be minimized. Also, it is important to plan in advance the place for the ditch directing water from forestry area to protected peatland, so that the water can be safely returned to the protected area. Good planning also involves planning the ditches far enough and in the right direction within the protected area. The aim is to have dry top layer with low water level in the forestry area above the protected peatland to avoid damage in three growth due waterlogged conditions. In the planning precision-GPS for measuring elevations (or manual measuring) on site and the elevation model produced with the help of lidar data are utilized. Essential for the implementation of the action is to have an agreement of the landowner for the needed measures.

The implementation of returning water to protected peatland can be linked to the ditch network maintenance actions on the forestry area. In Finland, there has currently been a clear decline in landowners' interest in ditch network maintenance actions. For this reason, alternative solutions to returning water must be considered. One option is nationally managed nature management projects organized by the Finnish Forest Center. In connection with these, different actions can be connected, or the entire project can be built on the implementation of numerous water restoration projects. As a third option, returning water to protected peatland can be linked to the planning and implementation of restoration within a protected area.

Methods to verify the effects of water restoration on hydrology and site vegetation are currently being developed. For example, an ongoing project where methods based remote sensing and drone data are developed to interpret changes in vegetation. To verify hydrological effects of returning water to protected peatland an extensive groundwater monitoring is aimed to be carried out during following years. In this context, it would be important to extend long-term groundwater monitoring also to the surrounding forestry area in order to gain understanding of possible waterlogged conditions resulting from restoration actions. In connection with this, there is also a need for monitoring the adjacent forest more detailed. In order to study the significance of the actions on water protection, monitoring of water quality entering the catchment area and leaving the protected peatland should be initiated.

## CONCLUSION

The aim of implementing the operating model was conducted successfully by the trainings organized during the project. Trainings were aimed to drainage planners, authorities and landowners. During the project water was returned by directing water of the natural catchment area to the protected peatland on five pilot sites. Private ditch planners and specialists of Metsähallitus were responsible for the planning of the pilot sites. On the pilot sites returning of water to the protected peatland was successful, and the surrounding forestry areas did not suffer from waterlogged conditions.

The pilot sites provided good experience on the technique for returning water. The location and length of the ditch which brings water to the protected peatland must be carefully planned, in addition to remote sensing measuring the elevation in field is essential. It was also noticed that water may remain in the drainage ditches located on the forestry area without causing damage as long as the planned dry top layer (ca. 40 cm) is realized.

## ACKNOWLEDGEMENTS

The Hydrology LIFE -project was is funded by The European Union Life funding. Tapio and Finnish Forest Center got funding also from Ministry of Agriculture and Forestry of Finland and Metsähallitus funded part of the Hydrology LIFE project. Cooperation with Finnish Ministry of the Environment was done during the project, and co-operation continues after the Hydrology LIFE -project.
Authors would like to acknowledge the project partners: Metsähallitus Forestry Ltd and Parks & Wildlife Finland, Finnis Forest Center, Natural Resources Institute Finland, Central Finland ELY-Centre, North Savo ELY-Centre, University of Jyväskylä, University of Oulu and University of Turku. Thank you for good co-operation during the project.

## REFERENCES

Alanen A. and Aapala K. (2015). Soidensuojelutyöryhmän ehdotus soidensuojelun täydentämiseksi. Ympäristöministeriön raportteja 26/2015
Autio O., Jämsén J., Rinkineva-Kantola L., and Joensuu S. (2018) Veden palauttaminen kuivuneille suojelusoille kunnostusojituksen yhteydessä. Etelä-Pohjanmaan elinkeino-, liikenne- ja ympäristökeskus. Raportteja 10/2018.
Kotiaho J.S., Kuusela S., Nieminen E., Päivinen J. and Moilanen A. (2016). Framework for assessing and reversing ecosystem degradation – Report of the Finnish restoration prioritization working group on the options and costs of meeting the Aichi biodiversity target of restoring at least 15 percent of degraded ecosystems in Finland. Reports Of The Ministry Of The Environment. http://urn.fi/URN:ISBN:978-952-11-4603-9
Kotiaho J.S., Kuusela S., Nieminen E., and Päivinen J. (2015). Elinympäristöjen tilan edistäminen Suomessa ELITE-työryhmän mietintö elinympäristöjen tilan edistämisen priorisointisuunnitelmaksi ja arvio suunnitelman kokonaiskustannuksista. Suomen ympäristö 8 | 2015
Helmi 2021. Discription of The Helmi Habitat program: https://ym.fi/en/helmi-habitats-programme

ID 62761

# PROGRESS OF THE BORD NA MÓNA CUTAWAY BOG REHABILITATION PROGRAMME IN IRELAND

*Mark McCorry, Alex Copland

Bord na Móna, Ireland

*mark.mccorry@bnm.ie*

Bord na Móna Plc is a publicly owned company, originally established in 1934 to develop some of Ireland's extensive peat resources for the purposes of economic development and to support energy security. In 2021, Bord na Móna recently announced the cessation of industrial peat extraction across its landbank and is now embarking on an ambitious peatland rehabilitation programme.
The Peatlands Climate Action Scheme (PCAS) will support rehabilitation of 33,000 ha of industrial peatlands and is funded by the Irish Government Climate Action Fund and Bord na Móna. It is expected that the Scheme (PCAS) will have benefits accruing from biodiversity provision, water quality and storage attenuation as well as increased carbon storage, reduced carbon emissions and acceleration towards carbon sequestration. The Scheme will also facilitate monitoring of ecosystem services to monitor changes in where the interventions will accelerate the trajectory towards a naturally functioning peatland ecosystem.
Selected rehabilitation improvements will take account of site environmental conditions and are collectively designed to optimise hydrological conditions (ideally and where possible water-levels at the peat surface or <10 cm) for climate action benefits and to accelerate the trajectory areas towards naturally functioning peatland ecosystems, and eventually reduced carbon sources/carbon sinks again. The key to optimising climate action benefits is the restoration of suitable hydrological conditions and more focused intervention means that the extent of suitable hydrological conditions can be increased.
This significant investment in the restoration and rehabilitation of peatlands will quickly yield a range of rich benefits for society and support national policy on climate action and biodiversity. Where once peat was harvested, Bord na Móna will now take meaningful action to reduce carbon emissions from degraded peatlands and create rich and diverse habitats for our native plant and animal species.

ID 62772

# MONITORING MIRE RESTORATION SITES FROM AIR WITH DRONES

*Marko Kohv, Edgar Sepp

Estonian Fund for Nature, Estonia

*marko.kohv@gmail.com*

The hidden values of wetlands are more and more recognized and substantial efforts are nowadays directed to wetland restoration projects. Estonia has lost approximately two thirds of its former mires to agriculture, forestry, oil shale and peat mining and buried them under infrastructure projects. First large scale and clearly defined mire restoration projects started in 2010 and the pace of closing former drainage systems have been increasing ever since.

Unfortunately, accompanying monitoring has been scarce, especially long-term vegetation monitoring, since it is time consuming and therefore expensive via traditional means by permanent monitoring plots. We tested drone-based vegetation monitoring as a possible partner or even substitute for traditional monitoring plots. Multispectral and RGB cameras there used for that task. We also tested different field calibration and post-processing image classification methods in order to achieve high-quality vegetation class maps over mapped areas. Results from five different test sites, each covering 50–70 ha, are presented in the paper.

Drone based vegetation mapping proved to be valuable and cost-effective tool to monitor rapid changes over relatively large restoration sites. However, it has also several shortcomings that must be addressed before heading to field campaigns.

ID 60753

# PROFITABILITY OF BIOMASS PRODUCTION WITH DOWNY BIRCH ON CUTAWAY PEAT BOGS

*Paula Jylhä[1], Anssi Ahtikoski[2], Lasse Aro[3], Jyrki Hytönen[4]

[1,4] Natural Resources Institute Finland (Luke), Kokkola, Finland

[2] Natural Resources Institute Finland (Luke), Oulu, Finland

[3] Natural Resources Institute Finland (Luke), Turku,Finland

*paula.jylha@luke.fi*

## SUMMARY

Annually 2 000–3 500 hectares of mires are released from peat production in Finland. Their afforestation compensates the $CO_2$ emissions of residual peat and reduces erosion and leaching of nutrients into watercourses. The production of downy birch (*Betula pubescens*) for energy biomass without thinnings can be profitable at the recent price level of forest chips (ca. 20 €/MWh) without subvention if rotation exceeds 20 years. Then the leafless whole-tree volume of a naturally established thicket typically exceeds 125 $m^3$ $ha^{-1}$.

The profitability of downy birch production on cutaway peatlands was evaluated based on bare land value. Natural afforestation of the sites was ensured by ash fertilisation immediately after cessation of peat production. A rotation of 15–30 years, an interest rate of 1–5%, and a price of 15–25 €/MWh for forest chips at end-use facility were assumed in the calculations. The stands were clearcut after each rotation applying whole-tree method. The second and third generations after clearcutting were assumed to originate by sprouting, and thereafter reforestation was ensured by mounding. Stand development was predicted using models based on measurements of naturally established, unmanaged downy birch stands located on cutaway peatlands.

Optimal rotation was the shorter the higher price of forest chips and interest rate were used. Wood harvesting was the greatest individual cost item, and it was strongly dependent on tree size. With the lowest price of forest chips, the production of energy biomass was unprofitable in all cases. With the recent price level (20 € $MWh^{-1}$), maximal bare land value was reached only when rotation was ca. 30 years and interest rate 5%. Based on the experiences from peatland forests, thinning response of downy birch is low. Therefore, neglecting thinnings do not affect stand development to great extent, and unmanaged stands can be converted into the production of commercial roundwood at any time.

***Keywords***: *afforestation, bare land value, cutaway peatland, downy birch, profitability*

## INTRODUCTION

In total, 120 000 ha of mires have been harnessed to peat production in Finland (Bioenergia ry 2019), of which 52 000 ha were in production in 2020 (AFRY 2020). The Finnish Government aims at decreasing the use of peat for energy by at least half by 2030 (Finnish Government 2019), but the decline will be much faster than anticipated (Biorenergia ry 2021). Residual peat can be a significant source of atmospheric carbon (Mäkiranta et al. 2007), and erosion and subsequent leaching of nutrients into watercourses may continue for many years after the cessation of peat production (Huotari et al. 2008). Therefore, rapid reuse of former peatbogs is of great importance. On the other hand, the peat used by heat and power plants must be substituted with other fuels. In the present study, the profitability of the production of downy birch on former peat production fields for energy generation was assessed based on bare land value (BLV, € $ha^{-1}$) that measures the net present value of bare land used in perpetual biomass production.

## MATERIALS AND METHODS

Stand development was based on the measurements of 25 naturally regenerated downy birch stands in Finnish cut-away peatlands (Fig. 1). Wood-ash fertilization was assumed to be done immediately after the release of each site. Natural birch seeds drifted on the sites were expected to germinate in the next summer. The mother stands were assumed to be clear-cut at the age of 15–30 years. Coppice regeneration was applied after the second and third rotations. Due to existing root network, these sprout-originated stands were expected to reach two years earlier the same biomass production as the mother stands. From the fourth generation onwards, mounding and natural seeding were assumed for an infinite series of 15–30-year rotations. The cost of ash fertilization was set at 350 € $ha^{-1}$, while the cost of mounding was assumed to be 393 € $ha^{-1}$ (Luke 2019).

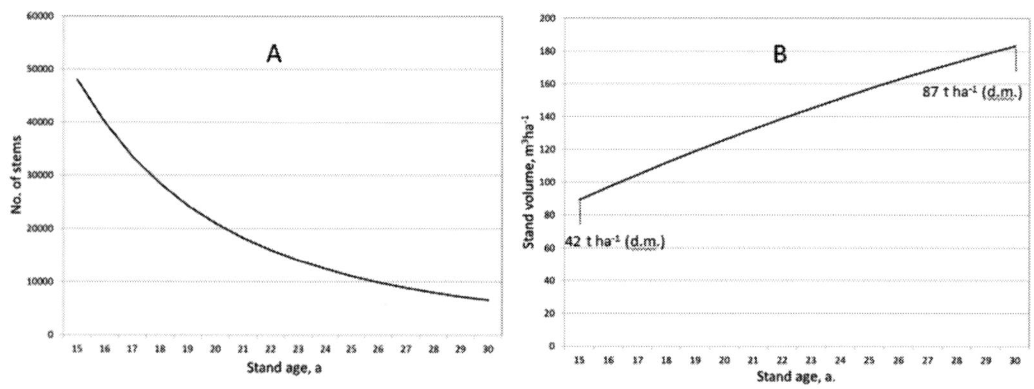


Figure 1. The development of stand density (A) and leafless above-ground biomass (B) of naturally afforested downy birch thickets based on the measurements of Hytönen et al. (2018).

When harvesting, 93% of the leafless above-ground biomass was assumed to be recovered (Jylhä and Bergstrom 2016). In the calculations associated with fuel chip production, the basic density of whole-trees was set at 475 kg $m^{-3}$ (Hakkila 1978). The effective productivities for cutting and forwarding (distance 300 m) were calculated using the models of Jylhä and Bergström (2016). Whole-tree piles were stored covered at roadside for one year, assuming a dry matter loss of 2.7 % (Routa et al. 2018). The cost of covering the piles was set at 2.60 € $m^{-3}$ (Hassinen, Urpo, Finnish Forest Center, Pers. Comm. 18.3.2019). For the fuel chips, a moisture content of 40% (wet basis) on delivery was assumed, resulting in a heating value of 10.6 MJ $kg^{-1}$ (Nurmi 1993, Alakangas et al. 2016).

The productivity of roadside chipping of whole trees with varying size was based on unpublished time study data from the stands described in Jylhä and Bergström (2016). The factors published by Jylhä et al. (2019) and Kärhä et al. (2009) were used when converting the effective productivities of cutting, forwarding and chipping into operative productivities for the cost calculations. The chips were transported to the end-use facility using a 69-ton truck and trailer with a total frame volume of 150 $m^3$ and bearing capacity of 45 tons. Loading and other terminal times were calculated as described by Laitila and Väätäinen (2011). For the chip loads, a solid content of 44% was used (Lindblad et al. 2014). Transportation distance was set at 60 km. The time consumption of trucking was calculated using the model of Nurminen and Heinonen (2017). The hourly operating costs of the machinery were obtained from the studies of Jylhä (2013), Laitila et al. (2015, 2016) and Väätäinen et al. (2017), and updated to the cost level of January 2019 using the forestry machine cost indexes of Statistics Finland (2019). The overhead cost of the wood procurement organization was set at 2.78 € $m^{-3}$ (Strandström 2018). The assumption above resulted in the cost structures illustrated in Figure 2.

The price of forest chips at the end-use facility was assumed to be 15, 20 or 25 € $MWh^{-1}$. The BLVs for each stand with varying rotation length were calculated as the sum of the net present values (NPV, Santhakumar and Chakraborty 2003) associated with the first three generations and the bare land values (F, eg. Chang 2014) from the fourth generation onwards:

BLV = [NPV1] + [NPV2] + [NPV3] + F

In the calculations, five alternative discount rates (1–5%) were applied.

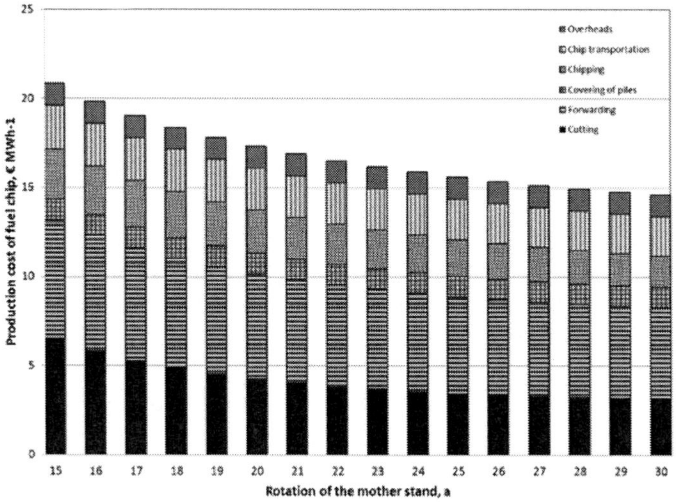


Figure 2. The production costs of fuel chips originating from naturally afforested downy birch thickets managed with varying rotation length. The rotation of the coppice-regenerated stands (2th and 3th generations) was assumed to be two years shorter.

## RESULTS

With the fuel chip price of 25 € MWh$^{-1}$, the production of biomass was profitable in all stand management scenarios and interest rates (Fig. 3). The price of 20 € MWh$^{-1}$ resulted in a positive BLV when rotation exceeded 18–20 years, depending on the rate of interest. With the lowest price (15 € MWh$^{-1}$), production remained unprofitable in all cases. Of the examined alternatives, the maximum BLV with the price of 20 € MWh$^{-1}$ was reached within the rotation span of 15–30 years only with the highest interest rate, at the age of 29 years. With the price of 25 € MWh$^{-1}$, the maximum BLV was reached four years earlier.

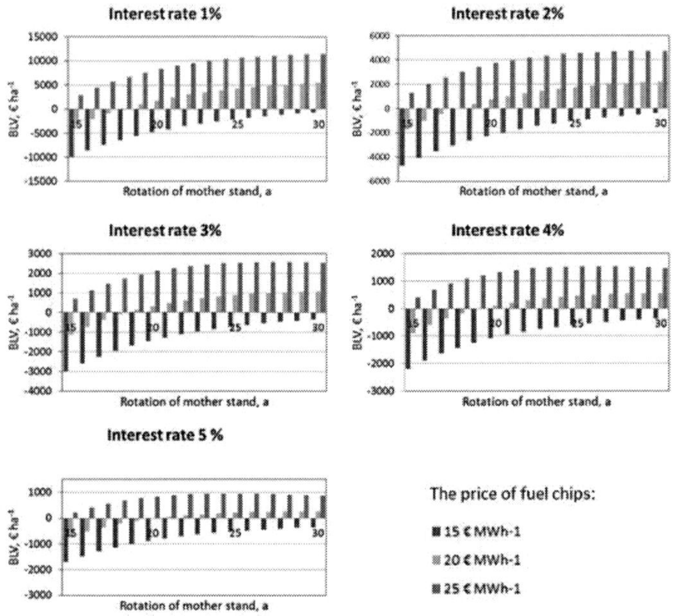


Figure 3. Bare land values (BLV) for various stand management scenarios with varying forest chip prices (15–25 € MWh$^{-1}$) and interest rates (1–5%).

## DISCUSSION

Dense downy birch stands can be successfully established in ash-fertilised peatlands both by broadcast seeding and by natural regeneration (Huotari et al. 2008, Hytönen et al. 2018). Following clear-cut, young birches sprout and grow well (Hytönen 2019). However, birch sprouts are vulnerable to browsing by moose and hares, which can reduce biomass production.

Cutaway peatlands show potential for profitable production of downy birch biomass without subsidies at the recent price level of forest chips in Finland (ca. 20 € MWh$^{-1}$, Statistics Finland 2021). Only minor inputs are required in comparison to other energy crops (e.g. willow, reed canary grass). Profitability was sensitive to harvesting cost, which was highly dependent on tree volume and biomass removal. Therefore, rotation length has significant effect on profitability.

Based on the experiences from peatland forests, thinning response of downy birch is low (Niemistö 2017). Therefore, neglecting thinnings do not affect stand development to great extent, and unmanaged stands can be converted into the production of commercial roundwood at any time.

## CONCLUSION

Downy birch shows potential for profitable production of energy biomass on former peat production areas, but rotation exceeding 20 years is required with the recent price level of fuel chips. The attractiveness of growing downy birch for energy biomass is dependent on the gains provided by alternative forms of land-use. The possibility of converting downy birch thickets into the production of commercial roundwood mitigates the risks associated with the production of energy biomass. When making decisions on the after-use of a former peat-production site, however, one should also consider the biotic and abiotic risks involved in biomass production.

## ACKNOWLEDGEMENTS

The study was conducted in projects co-funded by European Agricultural Fund for Rural Development (EAFRD) and the Centre for Economic Development, Transport and the Environment.

## REFERENCES

1. Alakangas, E., Hurskainen, M., Laatikainen-Luntama, J. & Korhonen, J. 2016. Suomessa käytettävien polttoaineiden ominaisuuksia. [Properties of fuels used in Finland]. VTT Technology 258. 229 p.
2. AFRY 2020. Selvitys turpeen energiakäytön kehityksestä Suomessa. [Report on the development of the peat use in energy generation]. Report for the Ministry of Economic Affairs and Employment 8/2020. Pöyry Management Consulting Oy / AFRY Management Consulting. 69 p.
3. Bioenergia ry, 2019. Turvetuotannosta poistuneet suonpohjat ovat jo hiilinieluja – metsitys tärkein jälkikäyttömuoto. [Sites released from peat production are already carbon sinks – afforestation is their most important form of after-use]. Bioenergia ry, release 8.3.2019.
4. Bioenergia ry, 2019. Turpeen tuotannon ja käytön ilmastopäästöt kolmasosaan jo vuoteen 2025 mennessä [Climate emissions from peat production and use to one third by 2025]. Press release 10.3.2020.
5. Chang, S.J. 2014. Forest valuation under the generalized Faustmann formula. Can. J. For. Res. 44(1):56–63.
6. Finnish Government. 2019. Inclusive and competent Finland – a socially, economically and ecologically sustainable society. Programme of Prime Minister Sanna Marin's Government 2019. https://valtioneuvosto.fi/en/marin/government-programme. [Accessed 24 Nov 2020]
7. Hakkila, P. 1978. Pienpuun korjuu polttoaineeksi. [Harvesting small-sized trees for fuel] Folia Forestalia 342. 38 s. Metsäntutkimuslaitos.
8. Huotari, N., Tillman-Sutela, E., & Kubin, E. 2008. Ash-fertilization improves germination and early establishment of birch (Betula pubescens Ehrh.) seedlings on a cutaway peatland. Forest Ecology and Management 255(7): 2870–2875.
9. Hytönen, J. Aro, L. & Jylhä, P. 2018. Biomass production and carbon sequestration of dense downy birch stands on cutaway peatlands. Scandinavian Journal of Forest Research 33(8): 764–771.
10. Hytönen, J. 2019. Stump diameter and age affect coppicing of downy birch (Betula pubescens Ehrh.) European Journal of Forest Research 138(2): 345-352.
11. Jylhä, P. 2013. Autohakkurin seula-aukon koon vaikutus kokopuun haketuksen tuottavuuteen ja polttoaineen kulutukseen. [The effect of screen mesh size on chipping productivity with truck-mounted chipper]. Working Papers of the Finnish Forest Research Institute 272. 19 p.
12. Jylhä, P. & Bergström, D. 2016. Productivity of harvesting dense birch stands for bioenergy. Biomass and Bioenergy 889(2016):142–151.
13. Jylhä, P., Jounela, P., Koistinen, M. & Korpunen, H. 2019. Koneellinen hakkuu: seurantatutkimus. [Mechanised cutting – follow-up study]. Luonnonvara- ja biotalouden tutkimus 11/2019. 53 s.
14. Jylhä, P., Hytönen, J. & Ahtikoski, A. 2015. Profitability of short-rotation biomass production on downy birch stands on cutaway peatlands in northern Finland. Biomass and Bioenergy 75(2015):272–

281.
15. Routa, J., Kolström, M. and Sikanen, L. 2018. Dry matter losses and their economic significance in forest energy procurement. International Journal of Forest Engineering 29: 53-62.
16. Kärhä, K., Laitila, J., Jylhä, P., Nuutinen, Y. & Keskinen, S. 2009. Kokopuun paalaus - tuotantoketjun tuottavuus ja kustannukset. [Whole-tree bundling – productivity and costs of the production chain]. Metsätehon raportti 211. 68 p.
17. Laitila, J. & Väätäinen, K. 2011. Kokopuun ja rangan autokuljetus ja haketustuottavuus [Productivity of chipping and truck transportation of whole-trees and delimbed stemwood].. Metsätieteen aikakauskirja 2/2011:107–126.
18. Laitila J., Ranta T., Asikainen A., Jäppinen E. & Korpinen O.-J. 2015. The cost competitiveness of conifer stumps in the procurement of forest chips for fuel in Southern and Northern Finland. Silva Fennica vol. 49 no. 2 article id 1280.
19. Laitila, J., Asikainen, A. & Ranta, T. 2016. Cost analysis of transporting forest chips and forest industry by-products with large truck-trailers in Finland. Biomass and Bioenerty 90(2016):252–261.
20. Lindblad, J., Jahkonen, M., Laitila, J., Kilpeläinen, H., Sirkiä, S. & Repola, J. 2014. 20 Metsäbiomassan määrän ja laadun mittaus [Measuring of the amount and quality of forest biomass]. In: Asikainen, A., Ilvesniemi, H. & Muhonen, T. 2014. Bioenerigaa metsistä – Tutkimus- ja kehittämisohjelman keskeisen tulokset. Working Papers of the Finnish Forest Research Institute 289:170–179.
21. Luke. 2019. Statistics database, Structure and production, Silvicultural and forest improvement work. https://statdb.luke.fi/PXWeb/pxweb/en/LUKE/LUKE__04%20Metsa/?rxid=8f416570-a981-43da-a61d-87d24e5035ee.
22. Mäkiranta P, Hytönen J, Aro L, Maljanen M, Pihlatie M, Potila H, Shurpali N, Laine J, Lohila A-L, Martikainen PJ, Minkkinen K. 2007. Soil greenhouse gas emissions from afforested organic soil croplands and cutaway peatlands. Boreal Environ Res. 12:159–175.
23. Niemistö P., Kojola S., Ahtikoski A., Laiho R. (2017). From useless thickets to valuable resource? – Financial performance of downy birch management on drained peatlands. Silva Fennica vol. 51 no. 3 article id 2017. 28 p.
24. Nurmi, J. 1993. Heating values of the above ground biomass of small-sized trees. Acta Forestalia Fennica 236. 30 p.
25. Nurminen, T. & Heinonen, J. 2007. Characteristics and time consumption of timber trucking in Finland. Silva Fennica 41(3):471–487.
26. Statistics Finland. 2019. Metsäalan kone- ja autokustannusindeksit. 25.2.2019.
27. Statistics Finland. 2021. Energy prices made an upturn in the last quarter of 2020. Release 11.3.2021.
28. Routa, J., Kolström, M. and Sikanen, L. 2018. Dry matter losses and their economic significance in forest energy procurement. International Journal of Forest Engineering 29: 53-62.
29. Strandström, M. 2018. Puunkorjuu ja kaukokuljetus vuonna 2017. [Wood harvesting and long-distance transportation in 2017. Metsätehon tuloskalvosarja 8a/2018. 32 p.
30. Santhakumar, V. & Chakraborty, A. 2003. Environmental costs and their impact on the net
31. present value of a hydro-electric project in Kerala, India. Environment and Development Economics, 8(02):311–330.
32. Väätäinen, Kari; Prinz, Robert; Malinen, Jukka; Laitila, Juha & Sikanen, Lauri. 2017. Alternative operation models for using a feed-in terminal as a part of the forest chip supply system for a CHP plant. Global change biology. Bioenergy, GCB Bioenergy 9 11: 1657–1673.

ID 72766

# RAISED BOG RESTORATION THROUGH COMPARTMENTALIZATION: ADUTCH CASE STUDY OF ENGBERTSDIJKSVENEN

*Geert Kooijman[1], Corné Balemans[2], Guus Ogink[3], Nanny Bressers[4]

[1] Staatsbosbeheer, Amersfoort, Netherlands
[2] Staatsbosbeheer, Amersfoort, Netherlands
[3] Province of Overijssel, Zwolle, Netherlands
[4] Province of Overijssel, Zwolle, Netherlands

*g.kooijman@staatsbosbeheer.nl*

## SUMMARY

Engbertsdijksvenen lies in the provincie of Overijssel, the Netherlands, a Natura2000 site of almost 1000ha withmostly bogland. Engbertsdijksvenen is one of the few remaining sites in the Netherlands where hundreds of hectares of degraded raised bog capable of natural regeneration exist (631ha), along with a small segment of active raised bog (0.1ha). Noteworthy is the isolated position of the bog in an otherwise populated area with a dominant agricultural function.
The area is challenged by desiccation, caused by peat cutting and digging of ditches in the past, damaging the impermeable layer. This has been exacerbated by the excavation of the lagg zone, which has left the site elevatedabove its surroundings, where water levels have been kept low for agricultural and residential purposes. As a result, we have a bog that requires very major hydrological and ecological works to be able to regenerate.
In the wider area we take an array of measures, from removing trees and shrubs to creating hydrological protection zones around the N2000 site, to blocking up drains and creating bunded cells (compartmentalization) within the site. This last category (blocking drains and compartmentalization) is part of the *AddMire LIFE* project. From thisproject we want to share our radical and elaborate plan of action to recreate the required hydrological conditionsfor preservation and restoration of the raised bog. We have to take far-reaching measures compared to many European bog sites, due to its isolated location in an excavated area.
To conduct these works in such an inhabited area, means that a proper emphasis on the social and economic environment is also required. We search for the most optimal balance between natural, social and economic values, without compromising the severity of the hydrological measures necessary.

***Keywords**: Restoration, raised bog, hydrology, rewetting, hydrological isolation*

## INTRODUCTION

Engbertsdijksvenen lies in the provincie of Overijssel, the Netherlands, a Natura2000 site of almost 1000ha with mostly bogland. Engbertsdijksvenen is one of the few remaining sites in the Netherlands where hundreds of hectares of degraded raised bog capable of natural regeneration exist (631ha), along with a small segment of active raised bog (0.1ha). Noteworthy is the isolated position of the bog in an otherwise populated area with a dominantagricultural function.
The area is challenged by desiccation, caused by peat cutting and digging of ditches in the past, damaging the impermeable layer, and excavating most of the original bog. This has been exacerbated by the excavation of the lagg zone, which has left the site elevated above its surroundings, where water levels have been kept low for agricultural and residential purposes. As a result, we have a bog that requires very major hydrological and ecological works to be able to regenerate.
In this extended abstract we will shed light on our plans for restoration of this raised bog, and how we intend to restore it to good form, despite the many challenges just identified. Our purpose of this paper is to share our approach, and engage in interaction with other raised bog site managers on their lessons learned for raised bog restoration.

## MATERIALS AND METHODS

The current hydrological conditions form a constraint for achieving the Natura2000 objectives in Engbertsdijksvenen. The N2000 objectives are: 1. preventing further deterioration, 2. improve the quality of bothactive and degraded raised bogs, and 3. increase the surface area of active bogs. Dutch raised bogs covered an areaof 1 million ha before exploitation; 180,000 ha in 1600; 90,000 ha in 1900; in 2000 only 3600 ha were left, only a few dozen hectares of which are active raised bog. As a result of partially successful restoration efforts, 15 ha of active raised bogs have recovered in the Netherlands over the last 50 years. Engbertsdijksvenen is the remainder of a formerly large raised bog area. Between 1850 en 1953 considerable amounts of peat were mined and the laggzone was excavated. A small area of active raised bog was spared (< 1 ha), which makes Engbertsdijksvenen oneof the few Dutch N2000 sites where this habitat can still be found. Key peat moss species are still present there. This active raised bog is surrounded by hundreds of hectares degraded raised bog still capable of natural regeneration, making Engbertsdijksvenen a very promising site for active bog restoration.

To develop and persist, a raised bog requires a permanently wet environment, stable water table and low nutrient conditions. The wet conditions hamper decaying plant material to decompose completely. With time the organic material accumulates and is compressed, creating an impermeable layer (catotelm). However, peat cutting and digging of ditches have damaged the impermeable layer in many locations, causing rainwater to infiltrate to deeper layers, and causing the ecosystem to be no longer hydrologically isolated, similar to a leaky bathtub. This has resulted in fluctuating water levels within Engbertsdijksvenen of 50-100 cm, instead of a maximum of 30 cm required for raised bog persistence. In addition, excavation of the lagg zone has left Engbertsdijksvenen elevated above its surroundings, while groundwater levels around the Natura 2000 area have been kept low to facilitate agricultural practices and to prevent flooding of nearby neighborhoods. This has resulted in the ongoing desiccation of the active and degraded raised bogs.

To counter the desiccation, it is necessary to re-wet the Natura 2000 site and surrounding areas. We will do this through two main type of measures: Converting and creating 27 km of bunds to retain water, using natural materials such as sand, loam and local peat; and Filling 58 km of ditches and trenches with a loamy bottom to restore the catotelm function and prevent water loss by drainage and downward seepage. On top of the loamy bottom, locallywon peat will be applied to diminish horizontal water loss from the system. The resulting raised bog has resemblance of a rice field: compartments are realised that retain the water in the area. In these compartments surface water can be retained more efficiently and the Dutch precipitation surplus can be more optimally used to create permanent wetter conditions and less fluctuating water levels (< 30 cm fluctuation compared to the currentsituation with 50 up to 100 cm fluctuation). We anticipate this will facilitate the growth of bog-forming peat mosses, thus improving the quality of the degraded raised bogs and facilitating their transformation into new activeraised bogs.

The compartments are expected to form a terraced mosaic landscape in which bog forming peat mosses can grow. As an acrotelm is formed, peat mosses will be enabled to cover and pass the bunds in the long term. We have seenthis effect in the Dutch Bargerveen site, and are therefore confident a similar development will take place at Engbertsdijksvenen. Ultimately (over decennia) the terraces would evolve into an undulating raised bog landscape. Hydrological protection zones adjacent to Engbertsdijksvenen are being realised parallel to this, toensure the groundwater loss is not exacerbated in the environment of the bog, thus undoing our work in the bog. Current farming practices in the hydrological protection zone adjacent to Engbertsdijksvenen are not compatiblewith rewetting and will have to be adapted to promote long-term bog recovery. This will take effort as well to contribute to this transition, as making changes to farming practices can be a challenging process, vulnerable tonegative emotions and severely touching upon people's life. We plan to develop together with the local communitynew economic practices that are compatible with bog rewetting, such as development of paludiculture. Therefore, the social-economic aspect of the works is very important as well. This includes the transition to different cropsand different farming approaches, but also the interaction with non-agrarian residents. Concerns have been voicedabout the re-wetting of the lands around the N2000 site, and what that will mean for people living nearby. The measures we take within the N2000 site (the compartmentalization and the filling of ditches and trenches) is notexpected to have a significant impact on the privately owned plots around the site, however, as stated, the water levels of the whole area have to be raised to ensure a thorough bog restoration, and this will of course have a largerimpact. Aside from wetter grounds, residents have voiced concerns about a.o. a possible increase of stinginginsects. Our whole process is aimed at ensuring the degree of nuisance is kept at a minimum, and to address anyconcerns properly, either by monitoring and research to demonstrate the effect is negligible, or through mitigation measures in case negative effects do occur.

Aside from this, we also have to combat nitrogen deposition and the effects of nitrogen deposition, to reduce negative impacts of nitrogen on the raised bog. The Netherlands suffers from high levels of nitrogen deposition, aresult of being a small, densely populated country, with significant amounts of intensive cattle farming, with highamounts of usage of feed concentrates and fertilizers. Also traffic and industry lead to nitrogen deposition. The Natura2000 sites in the Netherlands are further challenged by the fact that many of them are situated on the bordersof the country, making them also vulnerable to foreign nitrogen deposition, which forms 35% of the nitrogen deposition for nitrogen-vulnerable Natura2000 sites (source: RIVM 2019, via website RIVM 2021, see references)[1]. The current nitrogen deposition levels stimulate growth of vascular plants including moor grass, birchand shrubs.

Since these vascular plants in turn cause shadowing and enhance eutrophication and evaporation, peatmoss growth is hampered and an adverse feedback loop occurs. Therefore, we will also (continuously) clear newlygrown trees and shrubs in Engbertsdijksvenen, as long as necessary. In the very long term, raised water levels, recovering peat moss vegetation and lower N deposition are expected to halt further tree growth in Engbertsdijksvenen.

## RESULTS

Currently, we are at such a stage of the works where we have the plan nearly fully formed, the contractor hired, but the actual physical works yet have to start. That means it is too early to share any results yet. As stated, the purpose of this paper and the accompanying presentation is to engage in an interaction with other raised bog site managers about their restoration works. In a few years' time, when we have completed the restoration works, we plan to develop a Best Practice Manual for raised bog restoration, based on the lessons we learned, and the interaction we engaged in with other bog site managers. Of course, we will make full use of existing manuals and papers on this topic. For now, our presentations of Results has to remain short and limited, and we will focuson Discussion for the remainder of this extended abstract. We hope in years to come to be able to share our results with the IPC audience. For anyone interested to follow our current status and our work in progress, pleasevisit our website www.overijssel.nl/addmirelife.

## DISCUSSION

For purposes of discussion we would like to emphasise several topics or issues.
Firstly, the technical choices for the work within the N2000 site, and the interaction between measures within theN2000 site and measures outside the N2000 site. We have made choices about dam construction, excavating the brown moss layer and replacing it by sand with a loam shield, based upon previous breakthroughs of peat dams, and similar choices made in other restored bogs around. We also made choices about compartment-size, based on differences in elevation of the surface, taking into account the maximum required amplitude in water levels.

At the start of the project we formulated four variants for the dams, which we scored based on costs and on criteria such as sustainability/robustness, stability, risks, impermeability, etc. We defined the following fourvariants:

- Dams made of loam and sandy loam, with a top width of 3m.
- Wooden dam walls down to or just in the gyttja layer, made of azobé tropical timber to ensure mold resistance
- Plastic screens down to the gyttja layer
- Soilmix walls made of a mix of cement and bentonite, applied with chain trenchers.

Each of these variants has its own advantages and disadvantages, and differing impacts on the vulnerable raisedbog site. An advantage of the variants 2 and 3 is that the materials can be brought in through the air as construction kits, which reduces the impact on the terrain. Based on all costs (materials, works, transport) the variant 4 (soilmix walls) was by far the most expensive forour site, the variant 1 (loam/sand walls) was the cheapest option. The difference between variants 1 and 2 wassmall in terms of price (10 euro per linear meter).

However, as stated, we also looked at the broader criteria such as robustness and stability.

Each of the variants was scored based on a 4-pt scale (good/sufficient/insufficient/bad). The criteria were: robustness/ natural origin materials/ controllability/ impermeability/ stability/ surface of effects on nature/ risks implementation phase/ risks utilization phase.

Variant 1 scored best overall, with high scores for robustness (long lifespan), natural origins of materials (available in the direct environment), controllability (well accessible for maintenance machines), stability (sufficient height and width), risks in utilization phase (easy to restore with additional sand and loam if necessary). Impermeability and surface size of nature effects score less well, although studies on building on black peat suggest it could have been scored higher. Variant 2, the wooden walls, scored lowest overall, due to the limited lifespan of wood, the difficulties in accessing the dams after construction (because the wood panels covered with peat are not suitable for machinery access), and risks in the utilization phase (leakages are difficultto trace and to repair).

All in all, variant 1 scored best both on price as on qualitative criteria. A challenge this variant presented us was, however the transport of sand and loam: requiring 400,000 cubic meters of sand and loam requires very intensivetransport movements and a massive request on local sand and loam deposits.
Together with the contractor, we were able to address this challenge with a plan to transport the materials through a pipeline to the site (from the nearby local sand extraction site in Kloosterhaar), thus reducing thetransport movements by 75%.
Currently, we are working on a decision matrix for weir selection, based on the exchange we engaged in withother raised bog site managers. We are very curious to hear what choices other bog managers have made for their dam construction, what their considerations were, and what other technical choices they made in their design process and how these played out throughout construction and utilization.

Secondly, the interaction with the social environment and the best approach in strengthening the support base forthe works, without compromising the extend of the works required for nature restoration. As stated, we face a situation in which we take both measures within the N2000 site and outside of the N2000 site. Both actions are required to restore the raised bog. The measures within the site lead to limited nuisance for residents and other stakeholders. However, the measures in the zone around the site might create more nuisance. For the local stakeholders there is no clear distinction, they view the process holistic, which means we have to tread carefully to keep everyone on board, facilitate their opportunities to voice concerns, but at the same time guard that a few concerns become self-reinforcing, thus becoming a catalyst of protest and resistance. We would like to learn from other site managers if they recognise our process, or whether this is a ‘very Dutch situation’, due to our densely populated country and intensive land-use. And for those site managers that do recognise the situation, how they have dealt with this.

We mitigate specific situations by addressing concerns as requests as much as possible. For example, we have left a stretch of forest at the edge of a part of the N2000 site, to maintain privacy for residents next to the bog. Asmany of the hiking paths are on the edges of the bog, the trees give the residents some cover from passing-by hikers. More importantly, the details of the measures and plans is discussed in an Advisory Commission, in which representatives from local and regional stakeholders take seat: formal organizations such as the regional water authority and the municipality, executive organizations such as our own Staatsbosbeheer, but also representatives from the farmers, residents and estates. Together, we seek solutions for the implementation of themeasures, with as much attention for local interests as possible, and in search for synergies and optimalization.

Thirdly, the topic of new business models for farmers, such as paludiculture or green-blue services. Recent papers have identified the design and usage of the buffer zones around the raised bog as the greatest challenge inraised bog restoration (Limpens et al. 2016: 89). Paludiculture can be an important part of these zones, and there have been experiments with a.o. reeds (Phragmites australis) and bulrush (Typha sp.). Even sphagnum could be cultivated here, contributing directly to the recovery of the raised bog site. But how to make this commercially attractive? Are there solutions and business models thinkable in which the cultivations of these crops actually produces a product that is – independent from grants and other financial incentives from the government – truly interesting as a product for the farmer? We greatly welcome experience from other countries, that might be muchmore advanced than we are in this regard.
At our own site, we currently experience that farmers in the buffer zone barely speak about the green-blue services and not at all about paludiculture. The most important factor for this is that the final design is not yet certain and – as a result – neither are the effects of the eventual works. Only when there is absolute certainty thattraditional agriculture will no longer be possible, the discussion about green-blue services and paludiculture is expected to commence. Some local farmers have expressed interest in these alternative forms of land-use, but with the final design and the actual works not yet in place, they are not ready to start the actual thought-process just yet. Addressing the questions above in this IPC2021 setting could provide us with input for the discussion with local land users when the time is right. We greatly welcome any shared experiences.

## CONCLUSION

As stated in the Introduction, we wanted to share our approach, and engage in interaction with other raised bogsite managers on their lessons learned for raised bog restoration. To be able to shape this exchange and interaction we have presented our Natura2000 site, its challenges, our proposed solutions, and the choices and considerations that we have worked on and are currently exploring. We cannot yet share any final conclusions about 'the best approach' for raised bog sites, regardless of the fact that this will always require tailor-made solutions in the first place. We hope to be able to share our insights and recommendations in the future, though,in a Best Practice Manual. In this BPM we also want to include all our lessons learned along the way, and the insights we obtained through the interaction with our raised bog site managers. Today, our main objective is to learn from the IPC2021 audience, and to invite you all to share your experiencesand address the Discussion topics we outlined in this paper.

## ACKNOWLEDGEMENTS

The project AddMire LIFE, in which we conduct the internal measures (compartmentalization, filling ditches) inEngbertsdijksvenen, is funded by the European funding instrument for the environment: LIFE.
The project 'Realisatie PAS maatregel verwijderen bos(opslag) Engbertsdijksvenen', in which tree cutting iscarried out to raise groundwater levels, is funded through the POP3-programme of the European agriculturalfund for rural development (EAFRD).

## REFERENCES

1. Limpens, J. (2016) Sleutels tot herstel van hoogveen (article in Dutch; Keys to raised bog recovery). *Landschap*:2016:2: 82–91
   Accessible via : https://www.b-ware.eu/sites/default/files/publicaties/Limpens_Landschap_2016-2_082-091.pdf
2. Website on Nitrogen from the National Institute for Public Health and the Environment (RIVM): https://www.rivm.nl/stikstof
3. Project website AddMire LIFE, working on the raised bog restoration in Engbertsdijksvenen: www.overijssel.nl/addmirelife

ID 72816

# RESEARCH, RESTORATION AND RELATIONS: THE CANADIAN PEAT MOSS INDUSTRY'S SOCIAL RESPONSIBILITY COMMITMENTS

*Marie-Claire LeBlanc[1], Stéphanie Boudreau[1], Paul Short[2]

[1] Canadian Sphagnum Peat Moss Association (CSPMA) & Peat & Substrate Cluster, Québec Peat Moss Producers Association (APTHQ), Canada
[2] Canadian Sphagnum Peat Moss Association (CSPMA), Canada

*mcleblanc@tourbehorticole.com*

The Canadian and the Québec Peat Moss Industry presented their first Social Responsibility Report in 2014. Its provided benchmarks to quantify the industry's position in relation to governance as well as social, environmental, and economic issues, and to identify the main directions for improvement. In the last years, considerable advances have been made in the three priority areas: support to research to develop Best Management Practices, restoration of post-harvest sites and strengthening of relations with governments, aboriginal groups and various groups. The progress made by the Canadian Peat industry and its members in the last years will be discussed in this presentation, including the progress of research about peatland management and greenhouse gas emissions throughout the peat life cycle and the Best Management Practices tools they led to. The most recent statistics on industry use of peatlands will also be presented, including a follow-up on the implementation of the National Peatland Restoration Initiative aimed at reducing the industry's historical footprint.

ID 72285

# LESSONS FROM 30 YEARS' OF INTENSIVE RESTORATION OF A CUT-OVER PEATLAND - THE UK'S THIRD LARGEST RAISED BOG

*Joan Daniels, Robert Duff, Peter Bowyer

Natural England, United Kingdom

*Joan.daniels@naturalengland.org.uk*

At 950 ha, the Natura 2000 network site, Fenn's, Whixall, Bettisfield, Wem and Cadney Mosses, is Britain's third largest lowland raised bog, comprising active raised bog, a priority habitat type listed in the EU Habitats Directive, and degraded raised bog. The centre of the site is a National Nature Reserve managed by Natural England, England's statutory nature conservation body.
Drained to enable peat cutting, agricultural improvement and afforestation and by transport networks, the centre of the site was rescued in 1990 from near-destruction because of commercial peat cutting. Through continued "first-fix" restoration, this area is now starting to see active peat formation. Under a €7 million EU LIFE Project initiated in 2016 additional intensive management interventions are further rehabilitating the hydrological function of this severely damaged site. Actions include tackling excess evapo-transpiration, inadequate water levels and water and air pollution from unsympathetic land management, including restoration of the important bog-edge lagg zone interface.

Lessons learnt from 30 years of continuous adaptive bog restoration include site management resourcing, the importance in management planning of understanding the hydrological drivers for the peatland, issues arising from the radical reversal of community management activities, the role of socio-economic measures eg management agreements and land acquisition including compulsory purchase on this peatland with multiple private land owners, and use of evolving methods for bog restoration. These have included forest/woodland/pasture to bog reversion, and restoring peat water levels by damming, storm water control, peat bunding, catchment restoration, raising water levels in major drains and diverting canalised lagg streams back to the edge of the bog. Water quality has been tackled by diverting in-flowing pollution and attempting to control the impacts of ammonia deposition.

The varied success of the hydrological restoration will be demonstrated including through the recent analysis of 30 years of hydrological monitoring data.

ID 72866

# AGROFORESTRY-BASED PALUDICULTURE AS A PROMISING ALTERNATIVE TO RESTORE DEGRADED PEATLAND AND IMPROVE THE COMMUNITY LIVELIHOOD IN INDONESIA : A REVIEW

Mashlahatul Umami[1], Eli Nur Nirmala Sari[1]

[1]World Resources Institute Indonesia, Jakarta, Indonesia

*Mashlahatul.Umami@wri.org*

**SUMMARY**

Millions of hectares of Indonesian tropical peatlands have been subjected to unsustainable land management in recent decades. The drainage and land conversion for agriculture and plantation activities have led to the degradation of more than five million hectares of peatlands, resulted in various environmental issues such as massive peat fires, land subsidence, flooding, and the release of gigatons of carbon into the atmosphere. Due to its prominent roles in providing essential ecosystem services at local and global scales, the Indonesian government has initiated restoration efforts to restore the degraded peatlands. Furthermore, as most local communities rely on peatlands as their primary source of living, it is critical to implement a sustainable land management approach that could benefit the ecosystem and society to support the restoration efforts. Agroforestry-based paludiculture is one of the sustainable peatland management approaches introduced in several peatland areas. Adopting a wet agricultural technique that is also combined with multiple land use is seen as promising sustainable peatland management and restoration strategy as it could improve people's livelihood while at the same time gradually improving the degraded peatland condition. However, skepticism arose over the benefits of this land management approach causes some misconceptions in implementing the method. Therefore, this review aims to examine the potential benefits of agroforestry-based paludiculture as one of the restoration approaches that provide benefits not only ecologically but also economically and socially. Several case studies in Indonesia showed that this approach could improve land productivity, provide alternative income sources, support food security, and improve biodiversity. Nevertheless, several challenges might need to be addressed to optimize the benefits of this restoration approach.

***Keywords**: Paludiculture, agroforestry, peatland, restoration*

## INTRODUCTION

Indonesia is the home of the largest tropical peatland areas in Southeast Asia, which accounts for approximately 77% of tropical peatlands in the region. This ecosystem has a significant contribution as one of the global major terrestrial carbon storages that take up more than 11 – 13 % of the global carbon (Page *et al.* 2011). Peatlands also have essential roles in regulating the freshwater system, providing wildlife habitats, and producing natural resources as the source of living (Rieley 2007). Nevertheless, the tropical peatlands have been under threat primarily by anthropogenic factors, including the significant transformation into industrial plantations and agricultural lands in the past two decades (Dohong *et al.* 2017). The development of artificial drainage to support the cultivation activities has degraded its condition, declining the peatlands' ability to regulate water and increase the ecosystem vulnerability to fire (Medrilzam *et al.* 2014). Small-scale unsustainable land management practices such as slash and burn also contribute to declining the peatlands' condition (Dhandapani and Evers 2020). Consequently, more than five million hectares of peatlands are degraded, leading to various environmental issues such as repeated fires, land subsidence, flooding, and the release of gigatons of carbon into the atmosphere (Khasanah and van Noordwijk 2019).

The catastrophic peatland fires in 2015 that account for billion dollars of financial losses and lead to the release of an estimated 1.5 billion tons of $CO_2$ into the atmosphere (World Bank 2016; Setyawati and Suwarsono 2018) became the wake-up alarm for the Indonesian government to set up an initiative in restoring degraded peatlands. Following this unfortunate event, the government made an endeavor to restore 2.6 million hectares of degraded peatlands. The restoration program consists of three main activities, rewetting drained peatland, forest revegetation, and revitalization of the community livelihood (BRG 2016). To enhance the success of the restoration efforts, the government engaged the local communities as the main actor of this project. The purpose of the restoration activities is not solely to restore the peatlands' ecological functions but also to improve the communities' socioeconomic condition. It is mentioned that high level of poverty is one of the drivers of peatland degradation (Wildayana *et al.* 2019). The revitalization of livelihood, therefore, is imperative in the restoration projects as it would potentially ease the socioeconomic pressure on peatlands.

Paludiculture was introduced as a peatland restoration approach that could provide ecological and socioeconomic benefits (Tan *et al.* 2020). This method is considered as a sustainable approach in managing peatland as it requires a wet condition to cultivate the plants; thus, it supports drained peatland rewetting efforts (Wichtmann and Joosten 2007). Furthermore, the species selected for paludiculture should be high economic value local species that can adapt and grow well in the wet and rewetted peatlands and therefore could provide economic benefits while maintaining peatland conditions (Wichtmann *et al.* 2016; Budiman *et al.* 2020). Meanwhile, agroforestry-based paludiculture is the extension of paludiculture method to gain greater benefits of the restoration projects. Agroforestry is a land management approach that combines different land management options in one area to achieve socioeconomic and environmental benefits (Widayati *et al.* 2016a). This system is chosen as it could bind the peatlands' productive and protective functions. Notwithstanding its potential benefits, this method is still undervalued due to insufficient knowledge and evidence. Furthermore, implementing agroforestry-based paludiculture in peatland is not straightforward considering challenges that occurred during the projects, including rewetting activities, plant species selection, and environmental condition that is not suitable for the cultivation. Accordingly, this review paper aims to examine the potential benefits of agroforestry-based paludiculture as one of the restoration approaches that provide socioeconomic benefits while also restore degraded peatland.

## MATERIALS AND METHODS

A non-systematic literature review was conducted. We reviewed seven project reports of paludiculture and agroforestry in some priority areas of peatland restoration projects to examine the variation of agroforestry-based paludiculture implemented in several peatland areas in Indonesia and identify the opportunities and challenges in implementing the system for peatland restoration.

Furthermore, other existing literature, including journal articles, grey literature, government and non-government reports related to paludiculture and agroforestry in Indonesia were reviewed and synthesized to support analysis of potential benefits of agroforestry-based paludiculture for peatland restoration and the enhancement of the community livelihood.

## RESULTS

Four models of agroforestry-based paludiculture were identified to be implemented in several peatland areas in Indonesia, i.e. agrosilviculture, silvosfishery, agrosilvofishery, and agrosilvopasture (Table 1). Agrosilviculture is a form of agroforestry that combines tree planting and crop cultivation, while silvofishery integrates trees with fish farming. Meanwhile, agrosilvofishery incorporates three different land-uses including forestry, agriculture, and fishery, and agrosilvopasture consists of trees, crops, and livestock (Samsudin *et al.* 2020; Shin *et al.* 2020). The selection of agroforestry models was based on several factors, including socio-economic conditions and biophysical characteristics of the peatland areas. It also considered the local knowledge of the local communities, which have been known to implement traditional practices of agroforestry for a long time (Samsudin *et al.* 2020).

A case study in Ogan Komering Ilir Regency, for instance, agrosilvofishery has been adopted since 2002 as a peat-friendly cultivation method that follows the water table fluctuation in the area. This method can maintain peatland productivity despite the dynamics of the water table that often limits farming activities. Since many people in the area highly depend on rice cultivation using *sonor*, a traditional rice planting method that uses fire for land clearing hence harmful for peatland (Mulyanto 2018), and fishing as the source of income, the agrosilvofishery can provide land management practice without burning that is similarly profitable, but more sustainable for peatlands. The agrosilvofishery method allows the community to plant crops in the ridge to provide short-term cash income when the water table recedes on the dry season and do the fish cultivation during the wet season when the water table increase while waiting for tree species to grow (Tim Konsorsium Paludikultur Sumatera 2019). Meanwhile, in Pulang Pisau Regency the agrosilvofishery is also combined with apiculture as another alternative source of income because the area is suitable for bee farming. The existence of gelam (*Melaleuca sp.*) forest in the area could provide nectar that preferred by bee species. The agrosilvofishery in this area also implemented *beje*, the traditional fish trap that using water movement and artificial pond to trap the fish for the fish cultivation (Jagau *et al.* 2018).

Table 6. Model variation of agroforestry-based paludiculture in some peatland restoration priority areas in

Indonesia

| Locations | Types of agroforestry | Area size (ha) | Peat depth (m) | Cultivated species | References |
|---|---|---|---|---|---|
| Kubu Raya Regency, West Kalimantan Province | Agrosilviculture with fish cultivation in some parts of canal | 2 | 2 - 4 | Tree species: Pulai (*Alstonia scholaris*), Jelutong (*Dyera costulata*), Jengkol (*Archidendron pauciflorum*)<br><br>Crop species: Tomato (*Solanum lucopersicum*), Chili (*Capsicum frutescens*), Egg Plant (*Solanum melongena*), Peanut (*Arachis hypogaea*) | (Sanudin *et al.* 2018) |
| | Agrosilviculture | 2 | 3 – 4 | Tree species: Pulai (*Alstonia pneumatohara*), Geronggang (*Cratoxylon arborescens*), Jelutong (*Dyera costulata*), Jengkol (*Archidendron pauciflorum*)<br><br>Plantation species: Pinang (*Areca catechu*) | (Sanudin *et al.* 2018) |
| | Agrosilvofishery | 0.0012 | | Local fish species: Striped Snakehead (*Channa striata*) | (Sanudin *et al.* 2018) |
| Pulang Pisau Regency, Central Kalimantan Province | Agrosilvofishery + apiculture | | 0.5 – 3 | Tree species: Jelutong (*Dyera costulata*), Blangeran (*Shorea blangeran*), Gelam (*Melaleuca cajuputii)*<br><br>Crop species: Taro (*Colocasia esculenta*), Water Mimosa (*Neptunia oleracea*), Lotus (*Nelumbo nucifera*), Water Spinach (*Ipomoea aquatica*), Lily (*Lilium sp.*)<br><br>Other species: Purun (*Eleocharis dulcis*)<br><br>Bee species: *Apis dorsata, Ttrigona sp.* | (Jagau *et al.* 2018) |
| Ogan Komering Ilir Regency, South Sumatera Province | Agrosilviculture | 8 | 1 - 2 | Tree species: Jelutong (*Dyera lowii*), Red Shorea (*Shorea pauciflora*), Gelam (*Melaleuca spp*), Pulai (*Alstonia scholaris*)<br><br>Crop species: Pineapple (*Ananas comosus*), Rice (*Oryza sativa*), Corn (*Zea* | (Sodikin *et al.* 2017; Yazid *et al.* 2018) |

| | | | | | |
|---|---|---|---|---|---|
| | | | | *mays*), Water Spinach (*Ipomoea aquatica*)<br><br>Other species: Purun (*Eleocharis dulcis*), *Aloe vera*, Sagoo (*Metroxylon rumphii*) | |
| | Agrosilvofishery | 10 | 3.5 – 5.5 | Tree species: Blangeran (*Shorea blangeran)*, Jelutong rawa (*Dyera lowii*), Punak (*Tetramerista glabra*), Gaharu (*Aquilaria malaccensis*)<br><br>Plantation species: Pinang (*Areca catechu*), Kopi (*Coffea liberica*)<br><br>Crop species: Galangal (*Alpinia galanga*), Rice (*Oryza sativa*), Corn (*Zea mays*), Pineapple (*Ananas comosus*), Water Spinach (*Ipomoea aquatica*), Spinach (*Basella alba*)<br><br>Fish cultivation: Kissing Gouramis (*Helostoma temminckii*), Sepat (*Trichogaster pectoralis*), Betok (*Anabas testudineus*), Striped Snakehead (*Channa striata*), Walking Catfish (*Clarias batrachus*) | (Tim Konsorsium Paludikultur Sumatera 2019) |
| Tanjung Jabung Barat Regency, Jambi Province | Agrosilvopasture | 10.5 | 0.6 - 1 | Tree species: Jelutong rawa (*Dyera lowii*), Blangeran (*Shorea blangeran*), Medang putih (*Litsea* sp.), Medang mangga (*Litsea sp.*), Laban (*Vitex* sp.), Manggis – manggisan (*Ilex cymosa),* Kelat (*Eugenia sp*), Jambu – jambuan (*Eugenia sp.*)<br><br>Plantation species: Pinang (*Areca catechu*), Kopi liberika (*Coffea liberica*), Mangga (*Mangifera* sp.), Rambutan (*Nephelium lappaceum*), dan Durian (*Durio zibethinus*)<br><br>Pasture species: Goat (*Capra aegagrus hircus*) | (Darwo *et al.* 2017) |

According to the reports, the implementation of agroforestry-based paludiculture in the targeted areas followed three main restoration approaches initiated by Indonesia's Peatland Restoration Agency, including rewetting, revegetation, and revitalization of livelihood. The rewetting efforts were mainly conducted by developing canal blockings in some parts of the areas to increase and maintain the stability of peat water table near the surface (Sanudin *et al.* 2018). Other activities including the measurement of land subsidence, hydrology condition, and carbon stock were also performed to monitor the peat conditions (Darwo *et al.* 2017; Sodikin *et al.* 2017; Jagau *et al.* 2018; Sanudin *et al.* 2018; Tim Konsorsium Paludikultur Sumatera 2019).

Furthermore, the revegetation activities included maintaining the existing peat swamp forest in the area and planting local tree species that can adapt and thrive in waterlogged conditions; thus, the species can sustain in the area for a long time and eventually improve the peat condition. To also support the revitalization of local livelihood, some commercial native tree species producing timber and non-timber forest products were selected to be planted in the area, such as Blangeran (*Shorea blangeran)*, Jelutong Rawa (*Dyera lowii*), Jelutong (*Dyera costulata*), Meranti Merah (*Shorea pauciflora*), Gelam (*Melaleuca spp*), and Pulai (*Alstonia scholaris*). Another profitable plant species, such as sago (*Metroxylon sago*), was also found to be planted in some parts of the area (Darwo *et al.* 2017; Sodikin *et al.* 2017; Jagau *et al.* 2018; Sanudin *et al.* 2018; Tim Konsorsium Paludikultur Sumatera 2019).

Moreover, the revitalization of local livelihood program comprised the cultivation of short-rotation plant species, fish farming, goat breeding and apiculture. These activities were directed to provide an alternative source of quick income for the communities as well as promote the food security program in the area. Additionally, several community capacity building programs including various trainings were conducted to enhance the communities' knowledge about sustainable peatland management, silviculture of paludiculture species and post-harvesting activities (Darwo *et al.* 2017; Sodikin *et al.* 2017; Jagau *et al.* 2018; Sanudin *et al.* 2018; Tim Konsorsium Paludikultur Sumatera 2019).

## DISCUSSION

The notion of agroforestry-based paludiculture is combining two or three different land utilization practices in wet or rewetted peatland areas without draining the peat to attain socio-economic and ecological benefits. This method is projected to improve the peat condition while also financially profitable (Wichtmann and Joosten 2007). However, it is not straightforward to achieve the equity of livelihood and protective aspects of peatlands. Several studies showed that agroforestry-based paludiculture could enhance peatland productivity, provide alternative sources of income, and support food security (Widayati *et al.* 2016a; Prastyaningsih *et al.* 2019; Tan *et al.* 2020). However, the compromises made in implementing this land management approach, particularly related to species selection, might have potential detrimental impacts on the peatland conditions.

As demonstrated by the Ogan Komering Ilir agrosilvofishery project, the agrosilvofishery practice maintains the peatlands' all-year productivity despite the water table fluctuations (Tim Konsorsium Paludikultur Sumatera 2019). The combination between tree species planting, crop cultivation, and fish farming provides the options to manage the land following peatland conditions. Moreover, the agrosilvofishery project in Pulang Pisau illustrated that agrosilvofishery results in a positive financial outcome as indicated by the financial feasibility analysis (Jagau *et al.* 2018). Similarly, the agrosilvopasture in Tanjung Jabung Barat could provide an additional source of income for the short, medium, and longer-term (Darwo *et al.* 2017). Goat farming and apiculture also lead to the diversification source of incomes and reduce the potential financial loss due to the failure of the planting activities that could occur in peatland restoration project (Darwo *et al.* 2017; Jagau *et al.* 2018).

However, the selection of some dryland species such as jengkol (*Archidendron pauciflorum*), pinang (*Areca catechu*), and coffee (*Coffea liberica*) could hinder the restoration activities as those species could not thrive on wet condition. Sanudin et al. (2018) reported that the survival rate of those species on inundation is low. They can only survive up to three days under waterlogged conditions. It suggested that those species could not support peatland restoration in the long run since one essential factor of peat restoration is raising the water table on drained peatland (Ritzema *et al.* 2014). Although those species can be cultivated in drained peatland, this approach is not sustainable (Giesen and Sari 2018). Alternatively, selecting profitable paludiculture species would be a better option to achieve long-term ecological benefits in the peatlands (Tata 2019). About 81 peat swamp local species were identified to have high economic value; hence they could be cultivated on rewetted peatlands and provide economic benefits (Giesen 2015). Due to limited knowledge about economic values, silviculture methods, and post-harvest handling methods, those species remain undervalued compared to the commercial dryland species that have been widely known to be profitable economically for the community (Giesen 2015; Uda *et al.* 2020). Therefore, further research is required to obtain more information of paludiculture species and their benefits to make them more attractive to be planted in the area for the sustainability of peatlands.

Similarly, the selection of dryland crop species to be cultivated in rewetted peatland would not be the best option to support the peat restoration. Species such as tomato (*Solanum lucopersicum*), chili (*Capsicum frutescens*), eggplant (*Solanum melongena*), peanut (*Arachis hypogaea*) could not survive in wet condition. Accordingly, those species were chosen to be cultivated on the ridge or during the dry season when the water table decrease to avoid inundation. However, the dry condition in the ridge is more vulnerable to peat oxidation that contributes to the carbon emission (Uda *et al.* 2020). Instead, the selection of wetland species such as water spinach (*Ipomoea aquatica*), kelakai (*Stenochlaena palustris*), purun (*Eleocharis dulcis*) could be better alternatives to be cultivated in peatland areas. Those species are native to tropical peatland, resistant to inundation, and profitable economically (Uda *et al.* 2020). Nevertheless, the crop cultivation is still considered more sustainable than oil palm plantation and rubber farming system on peatlands (Surahman *et al.* 2018a).

Another concern related to species selection is that the selection of commercial timber-producing tree species for peat restoration might have potential drawbacks for the future environment. While many native peatland timbers producing species such as geronggang (*Cratoxylon arborescens*), pulai (*Alstonia scholaris*), blangeran (*Shorea blangeran*) are selected for restoration projects due to their ability to thrive in peat inundation (Tata and Pradjadinata 2016; Budiman *et al.* 2020), those species might not be the best options to achieve balance between productive and protective benefits of agroforestry-based paludiculture implementation. The timber extraction activities on peatland would likely disturb the ecosystem (Jewitt *et al.* 2014). Therefore, selecting high economic value non-timber forest product species such as jelutong (*Dyera polyphylla*), gemor (*Nothaphoebe coracea*), tengkawang (*Shorea macrophylla*), and candle nut (*Aleurites moluccana*) would be more recommended instead (Giesen 2015). Species such as jelutong has been known to have high economic value to provide latex (Sumarga *et al.* 2016). The community has been tapping jelutong latex from the primary forest since three decades ago. Therefore, jelutong cultivation would be more profitable economically and could support the restoration project (Tata *et al.* 2016).

Notwithstanding those facts, agroforestry-based paludiculture could improve biodiversity and potentially reduce risks of fire on peatlands (Van Noordwijk *et al.* 2019). As noted in some research, multiple cropping activities would increase the plant diversity on the landscape (Widayati *et al.* 2016b; Surahman *et al.* 2018b). Likewise, the adoption of agroforestry-based paludicultre in peatlands could support to revegetate the degraded peatland and enhance the biodiversity in the area (Sitepu *et al.* 2017). Furthermore, the rewetting activities in agroforestry-based paludiculture could maintain the stability of the water table in the area near the canal blocking that could reduce the vulnerability of the peatland to fire (Budiman *et al.* 2020). The peatland management without burning in paludiculture activities also provides a new land management approach that is more sustainable yet similarly profitable than traditional land management practice that involves land burning for the communities (Mulyanto 2018). Therefore, it could reduce the drivers of peat fires in the areas and potentially reduce the $CO_2$ emission (Surahman *et al.* 2018b).

## CONCLUSION

Agroforestry-based paludiculture could serve as a promising alternative to achieve degraded peatland restoration goals by providing a sustainable land management approach to gain financial benefits for the community and improving peat conditions. The studies noted that this method could improve peatland productivity, provide variation income sources, secure food sources, and enhance biodiversity. Furthermore, this method potentially reduces the fire risks on the landscape. However, the scope of improvement of this method is examined particularly related to the technical aspect such as species selection. Therefore, further research is essential in identifying the more suitable species options for agroforestry-based paludiculture as well as analyzing the economic value of those species. It is also equally important to share the research outcome to improve the knowledge of the community as the main actors of restoration efforts.

## ACKNOWLEDGEMENTS

This research is supported by World Resources Institute Indonesia.

## REFERENCES


BRG (2016) Rencana strategis badan restorasi gambut tahun 2016 - 2020. Badan Restorasi Gambut (BRG), Jakarta, Indonesia. Available at http://brg.go.id/wp-content/uploads/2019/04/RENSTRA-OREO-.pdf.

Budiman, I, Bastoni, Sari, ENN, Hadi, EE, Asmaliyah, Siahaan, H, Januar, R, Hapsari, RD (2020) Progress of paludiculture projects in supporting peatland ecosystem restoration in Indonesia. *Global Ecology and Conservation* **23**, e01084.

Darwo, Tata, MHL, Heriansyah, I, Nugroho, A, Bogidarmanti, R, Butarbutar, T, Yuliani, D, Mawazin (2017) Laporan hasil kegiatan pilot project implementasi paludikultur dan agroforestry di lahan gambut. Badan Restorasi Gambut dan Badan Litbang dan Inovasi-KLHK, Bogor, Indonesia. Available at https://kms-troper.brg.go.id/wp-content/uploads/2020/10/29_Darwo_Puslitbang_compressed.pdf.

Dhandapani, S, Evers, S (2020) Oil palm 'slash-and-burn' practice increases post-fire greenhouse gas emissions and nutrient concentrations in burnt regions of an agricultural tropical peatland. *Science of The Total Environment* **742**, 140648.

Dohong, A, Aziz, AA, Dargusch, P (2017) A review of the drivers of tropical peatland degradation in South-East Asia. *Land Use Policy* **69**, 349-360.

Giesen, W (2015) Utilising non-timber forest products to conserve Indonesia's peat swamp forests and reduce carbon emissions. *Journal of Indonesian Natural History* **3**, 17-26.

Giesen, W, Sari, ENN (2018) Tropical peatland restoration report : the Indonesian case. Euroconsult Mott MacDonald Jakarta, Indonesia. Available at https://www.researchgate.net/publication/323676663_Tropical_Peatland_Restoration_Report_the_Indonesian_case.

Jagau, Y, Nion, YA, Jemi, R, Torang, I, Anjalani, R, Anggreini, T, Yuprin;, Damanik, Z (2018) Laporan akhir : Pilot model restorasi gambut terintegrasi. UPT Laboratorium Lahan Gambut CIMTROP Universitas Palangka Raya, Palangkaraya. Available at https://kms-troper.brg.go.id/wp-content/uploads/2020/09/81_Jagau_UPR_compressed.pdf.

Jewitt, SL, Nasir, D, Page, SE, Rieley, JO, Khanal, K (2014) Indonesia's contested domains. Deforestation, rehabilitation and conservation-with-development in Central Kalimantan's tropical peatlands. *The International Forestry Review* **16**, 405-420.

Khasanah, Nm, van Noordwijk, M (2019) Subsidence and carbon dioxide emissions in a smallholder peatland mosaic in Sumatra, Indonesia. *Mitigation and Adaptation Strategies for Global Change* **24**, 147-163.

Medrilzam, Medrilzam, M, Dargusch, P, Herbohn, J, Smith, C (2014) The socio-ecological drivers of forest degradation in part of the tropical peatlands of Central Kalimantan, Indonesia. *Forestry* **87**, 335-345.

Mulyanto (2018) The sonor farming tradition on forest and land fire in Ogan Komering Ilir Regency, South Sumatera. In 'International Conference on Social Science and Character Education. Volume 323 pp. 131-134. (Atlantis Press. Available at https://www.atlantis-press.com/proceedings/icossce-icsmc-18/125909987

Page, SE, Rieley, JO, Banks, CJ (2011) Global and regional importance of the tropical peatland carbon pool. *Global Change Biology* **17**, 798-818.

Prastyaningsih, S, Hardiwinoto, S, Agus, C (2019) 'Development paludiculture on tropical peatland for productive and sustainable ecosystem in Riau, IOP Conference Series: Earth and Environmental Science.' (IOP Publishing:

Rieley, J (2007) 'Tropical peatland-The amazing dual ecosystem: Co-existence and mutual benefit, Carbon-climate-human interaction on tropical peatland. Proceedings of The International Symposium and Workshop on Tropical Peatland.' (Citeseer:

Ritzema, H, Limin, S, Kusin, K, Jauhiainen, J, Wösten, H (2014) Canal blocking strategies for hydrological restoration of degraded tropical peatlands in Central Kalimantan, Indonesia. *CATENA* **114**, 11-20.

Samsudin, YB, Puspitaloka, D, Rahman, SA, Chandran, A, Baral, H (2020) Community-based peat swamp restoration through agroforestry in Indonesia. *Agroforestry for Degraded Landscapes* 349-365.

Sanudin, Hani, A, Handayani, W, Siraudin, M, Sulistyawati, T, Rohandi, A (2018) Laporan akhir : Pilot model restorasi gambut terintegrasi di Kabupaten Kubu Raya, Kalimantan Barat. Balai Penelitian dan Pengembangan Teknologi Agroforestry dan Badan Restorasi Gambut, Ciamis.

Setyawati, W, Suwarsono (2018) 'Carbon emission from peat fire in 2015, IOP Conference Series: Earth and Environmental Science.' (IOP Publishing:

Shin, S, Soe, KT, Lee, H, Kim, TH, Lee, S, Park, MS (2020) A Systematic Map of Agroforestry Research Focusing on Ecosystem Services in the Asia-Pacific Region. *Forests* **11**, 368.

Sitepu, DSM, Tinhout, B, van Amstel, A (2017) Agroforestry-based paludiculture compositions in Indonesian tropical peatlands. Available at https://www.academia.edu/40200829/Agroforestry_based_paludiculture_compositions_in_indonesian_tropical_peatlands

Sodikin, E, Munandar;, Setiawan, A, Prayitno, MB, Suwandi (2017) Laporan akhir pilot project implementasi paludikultur dan agroforestry lahan APL di Desa Perigi, Pangkalan Lampam, KHG Sugihan - Sungai Lumpur,

Ogan Komering Ilir, Sumatera Selatan. Universitas Sriwijaya dan Badan Restorasi Gambut, Sumatera Selatan.
Sumarga, E, Hein, L, Hooijer, A, Vernimmen, R (2016) Hydrological and economic effects of oil palm cultivation in Indonesian peatlands. *Ecology and society* **21**,
Surahman, A, Soni, P, Shivakoti, GP (2018a) Are peatland farming systems sustainable? Case study on assessing existing farming systems in the peatland of Central Kalimantan, Indonesia. *Journal of integrative environmental sciences* **15**, 1-19.
Surahman, A, Soni, P, Shivakoti, GP (2018b) Reducing CO2 emissions and supporting food security in Central Kalimantan, Indonesia, with improved peatland management. *Land Use Policy* **72**, 325-332.
Tan, ZD, Lupascu, M, Wijedasa, LS (2020) Paludiculture as a sustainable land use alternative for tropical peatlands: A review. *Science of The Total Environment* 142111.
Tata, HL (2019) Paludiculture: can it be a trade-off between ecology and economic benefit on peatland restoration? *IOP Conference Series: Earth and Environmental Science* **394**, 012061.
Tata, HL, Pradjadinata, S (2016) Native species for degraded peat swamp forest rehabilitation. *Jurnal Silvikultur Tropika* **7**, S80-S82.
Tata, HL, van Noordwijk, M, Widayati, A (2016) Domestication of Dyera polyphylla (Miq.) Steenis in peatland agroforestry systems in Jambi, Indonesia. *Agroforestry Systems* **90**, 617-630.
Tim Konsorsium Paludikultur Sumatera (2019) Laporan akhir riset paludikultur berbasis agrosilvofishery (Wana-Mina-Tani) untuk mendukung restorasi gambut di region Sumatera. Badan Restorasi Gambut dan Balai Penelitian dan Pengembangan Lingkungan Hidup dan Kehutanan Palembang, Palembang. Available at https://kms-troper.brg.go.id/wp-content/uploads/2020/09/01_Lap-Akhir-Riset-Paludikultur-Region-Sumatera-2019_compressed.pdf.
Uda, SK, Hein, L, Adventa, A (2020) Towards better use of Indonesian peatlands with paludiculture and low-drainage food crops. *Wetlands Ecology and Management* **28**, 509-526.
Van Noordwijk, M, Hairiah, K, Lasco, R, Tata, H (2019) How can agroforestry be part of disaster risk management. *Sustainable development through trees on farms: agroforestry in its fifth decade. World Agroforestry (ICRAF), Bogor (Indonesia)* 215-229.
Wichtmann, W, Joosten, H (2007) Paludiculture: Peat formation and renewable resources from rewetted peatlands. *IMCG Newsletter* **3**,
Wichtmann, W, Schröder, C, Joosten, H (2016) Paludiculture-productive use of wet peatlands.
Widayati, A, Tata, H, Van Noordwijk, M (2016a) Agroforestry in peatlands: combining productive and protective functions as part of restoration (in Lao).
Widayati, A, Tata, HL, van Noordwijk, M (2016b) Agroforestry in peatlands: combining productive and protective functions as part of restoration.
Wildayana, E, Armanto, ME, Zahri, I, Adriani, D, Syakina, B (2019) Socio Economic factors causing rapid peatlands degradation in South Sumatra. *Sriwijaya Journal of Environment* **3**, 87-95.
World Bank, 2016. The cost of fire : An economic analysis of Indonesia's 2015 fire crisis. The World Banck, Jakarta, Indonesia.
Yazid, M, Suwignyo, RA, Sodikin, E, Harun, U, Malahayati, N, Dessy, A (2018) Laporan kajian profitabilitas dan keekonomian komoditi ramah gambut di KHG S. Saleh - S.Sugihan dan KHG S. Sebumbung - S. Batok Kabupaten Ogan Komering Ilir. Badan Restorasi Gambut dan Universitas Sriwijaya.

ID 62804

# MAPPING PEATLAND EXTENT AND PEAT DEPTH IN INDONESIA: APPLYING THE INDONESIAN PEAT PRIZE METHODOLOGY ON BEHALF OF PEATLAND RESTORATION

Florian Siegert[1,2], Anna Berninger[1], Werner Wiedemann[1]

[1] RSS – Remote Sensing Solutions GmbH, Munich, Germany
[2] Department of Biology, Ludwig-Maximilian-University Munich, Germany

*siegert@rssgmbh.de*

## SUMMARY

Sustainable management of Indonesian peatlands and restoration of peatland ecosystems disturbed by fire, logging or drainage is of utmost importance, mainly to reduce the high $CO_2$ emissions which come from these peatlands. Accurate and spatially explicit data on peatland extent, distribution and depth are still missing for many regions in Indonesia. This is because many of the vast Indonesian peatlands are located in remote areas and are very difficult to access on ground for field data collection. We present a sophisticated approach based on historic and recent satellite images, satellite derived digital terrain data, targeted in situ field measurements and spatial 3D modelling to create a wall-to-wall map of most of the Indonesian peatlands. This approach developed by our team was selected as the most accurate, affordable and timely method of mapping the extent and thickness of Indonesian peatlands by the scientific evaluation committee of the "Indonesian Peat Prize Challenge". On behalf of the Peatland Restoration Agency (BRG - Badan Restorasi Gambut) we have mapped an area of more than 15 million ha in search of peatlands. Historical and most recent satellite imagery has been used to map the extent of peatlands and the extensive network of drainage canals. High resolution WorldDEM DTM terrain data and airborne and satellite LiDAR DTM data has been used to map the peat surface topography and to identify carbon rich ombrogenous peat formations. A database of more than 10,000 in situ peat depth corings has been compiled and used to train a model of peat depth in relation to peat terrain elevation. Our methodology allows consistent, large-area mapping of peatlands where sufficient in situ information is missing. Precise and accurate identification of the 3 m peat depth boundary is a requirement for national conservation legislation activities. The 3D peatland map is used by BRG to improve the planning and implementation process of peatland rewetting and restoration. Maps of peat topography and depth are a prerequisite for reliable planning of dam building and hydrological restoration.

***Keywords***: *Peat depth, tropical peat, remote sensing, Indonesia, peat restoration*

## INTRODUCTION

Peatland ecosystems are known as the largest terrestrial near-surface long-term carbon sinks, storing 180–700 gigatons (Gt) C worldwide while covering no more than 3 % of the earth's surface (Agus *et al.* 2011). Indonesia is estimated to contain more than half of all known global peatlands in the tropical zone, ranging between 16–27 million ha (Rieley *et al.* 1992, Page *et al.* 1999) which is calculated to represent a peat carbon pool of 82–92 Gt (Page *et al.*

2011). For millennia, large portions of Indonesia were primarily covered with tropical peatlands and peat swamp forests (Rieley *et al.* 1992, Page *et al.* 1999). Over the last half century, these pristine forests have been degraded through processes such as industrial logging (Barber & Schweithelm 2000), industrial plantation activities and recurrent severe fire episodes (Miettinen *et al.* 2012). Extensive drainage for the establishment of plantations lowers the water level within the peat layer (Carlson *et al.* 2015). A low layer of water exposes the top of the peat layer to oxygen. Subsequently, this leads to decomposition and, thus, carbon dioxide ($CO_2$) emissions (Carlson *et al.* 2015). Furthermore, drained peatlands become extremely vulnerable to massive long-lasting peat fire events. Fires sweeping across the country repeatedly affect the tropical forest ecosystems. This is especially destructive during strong El Niño Southern Oscillation periods (Jaenicke *et al.* 2008). The extreme fire disaster of 1997/1998 was the first to be analyzed by remote sensing. It was estimated that 2.4–6.8 million ha of peatlands burned and up to 9.43 Gt $CO_2$ were released into the atmosphere (Huijnen *et al.* 2016, Lohberger *et al.* 2018). In 2019 alone, 942,000 ha were burned (Suroyo & Diela 2019), which constitutes the most substantial fire-related loss since 2015, when 4.6 million ha burned (Lohberger *et al.* 2018). From the perspective of climate change, the fires in 2015 released 0.89–1.75 Gt $CO_2$ (Huijnen *et al.* 2016, Jayarathne *et al.* 2018, Lohberger *et al.* 2018). Indonesia's current administration has sought to curtail uncontrolled degradation by introducing legislation that has placed a moratorium on new palm oil concession licenses since 2011. Effective protection and restoration activities are heavily dependent on accurate and explicit data of both peatland extent and depth, as well as carbon storage potential. Such data often remain missing or are not consistently available over large areas that can be difficult to access.

To protect peatlands an extensive renaturation project by the Indonesian Peatland Restoration Agency (BRG - Badan Restorasi Gambut) is performed under the management of United Nations Office for Project Services (UNOPS). All together 2.6 million ha of forest and peatlands shall be restored within this project. In the framework of BRG, a total of 106 KHGs (Kesatuan Hidrologi Gambut or Peat Hydrological Unit) comprising an area about 15 million ha were being mapped in 2019–2020 by Remote Sensing Solutions GmbH (RSS). We used an integrative approach with satellite data, field measurements, digital elevation data and sophisticated modelling routines, underpinned with a vast contextual knowledge of the region. The method was selected within the framework of the "Indonesian Peat Prize" (www.indonesianpeatprize.net), developed in direct support of the Indonesian government's One Map Policy, as the best to measure the extent and depth of peat in Indonesia. After extensive analyses proofing their suitability for peatland mapping this methodology was further refined by including the newly available space-borne LiDAR sensors ICESat-2/ATLAS (Berninger & Siegert 2020) and GEDI (Global Ecosystem Dynamics Investigation). Providing consistent, precise and accurate peat extent and depth information allows the identification of critical areas such as the 3 m peat depth boundary recognized in national conservation legislation as well as a more sustainable dam planning strategy in order to renature dried peatlands.

## MATERIALS AND METHODS

The methodological framework is based on observed consistent characteristics between peatland areas across the country and the strong correlation between the convex surface of a peat dome and corresponding peat depths (Jaenicke *et al.* 2008, Vernimmen et al., 2020). Required input data are (1) a high resolution, high quality digital terrain model (DTM), (2) both historical and current satellite imagery of peatland forest extent, and (3) in situ peat depth coring data. Peat domes were visually identified in a multi-staged visual and semi-automized workflow. First, the Airbus WorldDEM DTM was used to identify extremely flat or slightly convex curvature (>1–10 m), which is typical for wetlands and peatlands. Second, historical and current satellite imagery was used to identify the typical vegetation cover, i.e. peat swamp forest, land cover such as plantations, burned peatland, and drainage canals. The WorldDEM DTM is the most accurate terrain model available for the whole country of Indonesia. It is considerably cheaper than airborne LiDAR and provides a spatial resolution of 12 m and a vertical accuracy of <5 m with even lower values in flat terrain. Additional spatial data, such as canal drainage networks, aided in delineation placement for peat domes exposed to extensive land development activities. Furthermore we investigated if the "Indonesian Peat Prize" method can be supplemented by using spaceborne LiDAR data such as GEDI and ICESat-2, which have a similar accuracy than the WorldDEM DTM. ICESat-2 was launched in 2018 and surveys by transmitting and receiving laser pulses with three pairs of beams. The beams have a nominal diameter of 17 m with an along-track sampling interval of 0.7 m and a spacing of 90 m. GEDI, a full-waveform LiDAR instrument, was launched in December 2018 and is carried on the International Space Station. These spaceborne LiDAR instruments can penetrate fine gaps in dense vegetation to collect accurate digital elevation measurements and are - in contrast to WorldDEM DTM - freely available. The elevation measurements of the two satellite LiDAR sensors can be used to model the peat surface using spatial interpolation (Berninger & Siegert 2020). Peat depth has to be measured on ground by peat coring or other ground penetrating methods. A large database of peat depth coring data was provided by BRG. Some of the data was collected following national peat coring protocols. The WorldDEM DTM and LiDAR based terrain data was used to optimize the peat coring sampling design. An ideal minimal sampling design includes both longitudinal and transverse transects, which repeatedly cross the peat dome over the area of highest topographic elevation. Z-score transformed peat depth drilling data and DTM values form the basis of an ordinary least-squares relationship between peat terrain elevation and peat depth, which is then applied across the dome to model peat depth at 25 m spatial resolution. To plan potential dam locations for rewetting purposes, both the DTM and digitized canal polylines were used. Contour lines were generated from the DTM at fixed intervals and then intersected with the drainage network. Dam locations were calculated at 40 cm height intervals, which correspond with the Indonesian regulations for peatland rewetting. This analysis provided important information to BRG in order to allocate appropriate resources for the implementation of rewetting measures.

## RESULTS

Within the investigated area of 15 million ha there were a 9,879,214 ha peatlands (see Figure 18). 4,179,702 ha were located in Kalimantan, consisting of 30 % shallow peat (peat depth 0.5–1 m) and 70 % deep peat (peat depth >1 m). In Sumatra, 5,699,512 ha were mapped as peatland, with 26 % identified as shallow peat and 74 % as deep peat. An intersection of the peatland map with a land cover classification dated from 2017 provided by the Ministry of Environment and Forestry (MoEF) shows, that 3,601,470 ha (36 %) of the peatland have been converted to oil palm plantations and industrial pulp wood forest. Pristine peat swamp forests were found only on 2 % of the area, whereas 9,663,302 ha (98 %) are characterized by a degraded forest vegetation. Besides, an area of 6,856,730 ha peatlands have been drained, which is altogether 67 % of the mapped peatland extent.

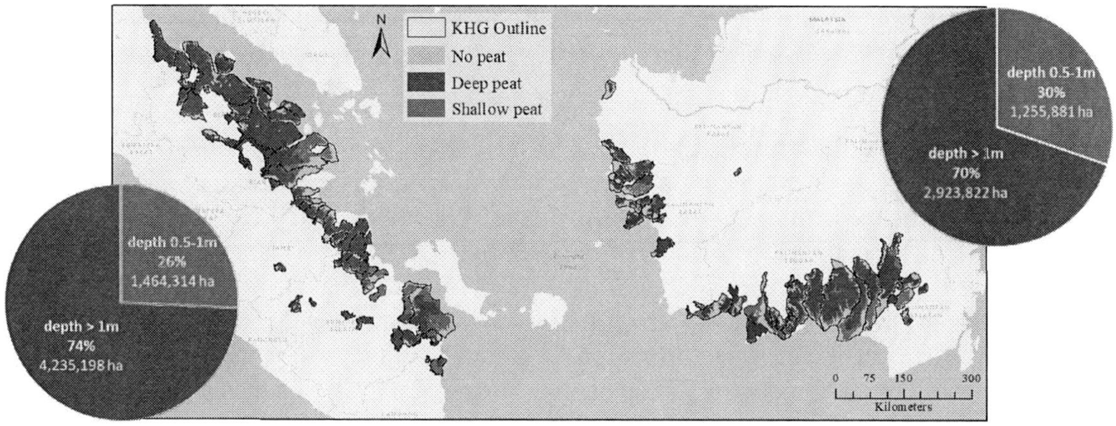


*Figure 18: Peatland extent in the 106 KHG which were investigated in this survey. Dark brown: peat depth >1 m, light brown peat depth 0.5–1 m.*

Peat volume was assessed in KHG where a sufficient number of peat corings was available. For an area of 6,842,036 ha it was possible to not only categorize the peat depth in deep and shallow peat but also calculate a more accurate depth model. The most massive peat domes were up to 14 meters thick. 33 % (2,250,203 ha) have a peat depth of more than 3 m, 37 %. 2,550,036 ha have peat depth shallower than 3 m and 30 % (2,041,796 ha) were mineral soil. Further investigations showed, that an area of 655,474 ha, and thus 29 % of the peat with a depth of 3 m or more, was converted to industrial plantations. 60 % of the deep peat areas was found to be drained and 73 % show a severely disturbed forest vegetation or grasslands and regrowing bushes after severe fire impact.

For modelling the peat volume and to improve the planning of hydrological restoration of disturbed peat domes an accurate digital terrain model (DTM) of the peat surface is necessary. The most accurate DTM is achieved by airborne LiDAR. Since airborne LiDAR surveys are expensive in remote areas, we analyzed the use of more cost-effective WorldDEM DTM and free of charge satellite based LiDAR data (ICESat-2/GEDI). Airborne LiDAR instruments are able to penetrate the dense cover of vegetation and allows to construct a DTM with a vertical accuracy of +/- 10 cm. The radar based DTM generated from TanDEM-X SAR data and the spaceborne LiDAR systems are less accurate.
To investigate the accuracy of both dataset the DTMs were validated with airborne LiDAR DTM's which were available for several KHG (Table 7). In total 13,129 ICESat-2/GEDI footprints were analyzed within the overlapping area of the three datasets (254,055 ha). Within this area the terrain height ranges from 0–13 m. The mean elevation of the airborne LiDAR is 3.35 m. This agrees well with the WorldDEM DTM (3.30 m) and is slightly less than the 3.71 m of the DTM measurements by ICESat-2/GEDI. With an RMSE (coefficient of variation) of ± 0.47 m and an $R^2$ of 0.95, low deviations from the WorldDEM DTM to the airborne LiDAR derived DTM are expected. The strong agreement between the two datasets justifies our approach to use the WorldDEM DTM as a reference dataset for areas without available airborne LiDAR data. Comparing the ICESat-2 DTM to the airborne LiDAR DTM results in an $R^2$ of 0.89 and

*Table 7: Comparison of measured elevation from different tested sensors (Npoints = 13,129).*

| Sensor comparison | Mean elevation [m] | $R^2$ | RMSE [m] |
|---|---|---|---|
| Airborne – WorldDEM DTM | 3.35<br>3.30 | 0.95 | ± 0.47 |
| Airborne – ICESat-2/GEDI | 3.35<br>3.71 | 0.89 | ± 0.85 |

an RMSE of ± 0.85 m and gives thus a good alternative to the WorldDEM DTM. A detailed analysis of ICESat-2 for modelling peat surfaces in Indonesia is given in (Berninger & Siegert 2020).

For 30 KHGs in Kalimantan a DTM was calculated based on ICESat-2/GEDI footprints (Figure 19A). Since for this area no airborne LiDAR DTM was available, the WorldDEM DTM was used for validation. Figure 19B shows the WorldDEM DTM in comparison to the DTM modelled by spatial interpolation of ICESat-2/GEDI footprint data. Sungai Katingan Sebangau (red) covers an area of 828,596 ha, while Sungai Kahayan Sebangau (blue) and Sungai Kahayan Kapuas (yellow) are smaller, covering 454,542 ha and 403,000 ha, respectively. The coefficient of determination for Sungai Katingan Sebangau reaches a value of 0.78 using 1,300 random points. In the smaller Sungai Kahayan Sebangau, the $R^2$ value is 0.84, based on 700 random points. With an $R^2$ of 0.94 for 950 random points, the largely deforested Sungai Kahayan Kapuas KHG showed the strongest correlation. The RMSE is ± 2.67 m for Sungai Katingan Sebangau, ± 1.47 m for Sungai Kahayan Kapuas, and ± 0.68 m for Sungai Kahayan Sebangau. These result in a relative RMSE of 22.5 %, 19.09 %, and 14.3 %, respectively, indicating the lowest errors in areas with low non-forest vegetation.

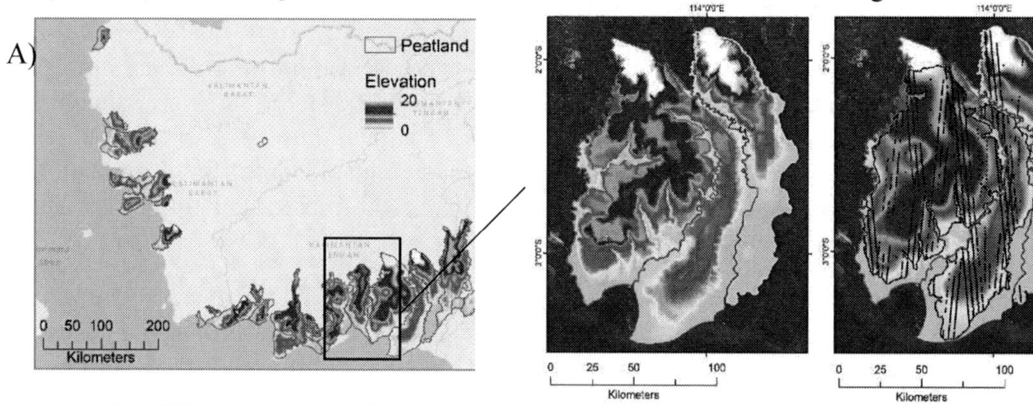


*Figure 19: A) DTM in Kalimantan calculated on the basis of ICESat-2 and GEDI data. Black box highlights the three KHGs displayed in panel B. B) Comparison of the DTM in three KHGs. Left panel: WorldDEM DTM; Right panel: DTM based on ICESat-2/GEDI footprints (shown as black circles superimposed on the DTM).*

## DISCUSSION

Remote sensing by satellites allows a countrywide mapping of peatlands in a fast and cost-efficient way. Since carbon-rich ombrogenous peatlands have a convex-shaped surface topography, it is important to include a DTM in the peatland mapping survey (Jaenicke *et al.* 2008, Ballhorn *et al.* 2011). Since airborne LiDAR surveys and also the WorldDEM DTM are associated with high costs, it may not be a solution for wall-to-wall assessment in large countries like Indonesia. We investigated whether the freely available space-born ICESat-2 and GEDI LiDAR instruments are suitable for identifying dome-shaped peatlands. This was achieved by relating ICESat-2/GEDI measurements to highly accurate large scale airborne LiDAR measurements (vertical accuracy ± 0.18 m, Konecny *et al.* 2016) and WorldDEM DTM (vertical accuracy ± 0.47 m in flat areas with low vegetation cover). Within an overlapping area of all three datasets, we found a good accuracy of the ICESat-2/GEDI derived DTM. In conclusion, it can be stated that peat domes with their smooth topography and convex shape can be identified from space using ICESat-2/GEDI data. The peat surface can be modelled by spatial interpolation of the footprint measurements if a sufficient number of footprints is available. By 2022, ICESat-2 and GEDI will reach almost global coverage, providing flight lines with a distance of less than 2 km at the equator. These more dense measurements will further enhance the interpolated digital terrain model.

This study is the first large-scale mapping of peatland in Indonesia using the award winning multi-scale peat prize approach which uses different satellite instruments and extensive in situ data on peat depth. The area of 15 million ha investigated in this survey on behalf of BRG do not cover all existing peatlands in Indonesia. Important known peatlands not included are located in Central and North Kalimantan, North Sumatra and Papua. The new derived peatland map was compared to the well-known map published by Wetlands International (WI) in 2003. This map was compiled from various data sets on land cover, soil and geology maps. For the overlapping area of the 106 KHG we found 9 % more peatland than previously reported. This increase includes mostly shallow peatland with less than 1 m in depth. Peat depth in a range from 0.5–1 m is given by WI with an extent of 22 % compared to 32 % in this study. Peatland with a depth of 1–2 m is given by WI with an extent of 41 % versus 15 % in this study, peat with a depth of 2–4 m is 19 % versus 17 %. Peat depths > 4 m are found on 16 % of the areas while in contrast to we found 36 %. This significant difference can be attributed to the fact that we could make use of a huge database of peat depth measurements in our analysis. Several KHGs showed peat depths of 12 m and more, while the Wetlands atlas considers only peat deeper than 4 m without providing accurate measurements. In this study BRG collected several thousand peat cores. The stratification of the coring was done on the basis of peatland map and the DTM. Based on the accurate DTM we found that almost all peatlands are of the ombrogenic type and are characterized by a convex surface with steep slopes along the edges of the domes and a smooth or almost flat surface towards the center of the dome. This characteristic shape was derived from high resolution airborne and spaceborne satellite data with an accuracy in the range of 0.1 to 1 m depending on the source of data. The high resolution DTM is not only required to assess the volume of the peat body but also to plan hydrological restoration and rewetting of peatland. For example, more dams have to be built in steep slopes and less in flat slopes. This data helps to reduce costs and facilitates the whole planning process.

## CONCLUSION

Accurate and timely information on peatland extent, distribution and depth are required in order to improve peatland management and to achieve $CO_2$ emission reduction targets announced by the Indonesian government. Several spatial planning and environmental agencies, such as BIG, BRG and KLHK, are in need of accurate peatland maps in order to support spatial planning and efficient restoration of deforested and drained peatlands as well as conservation efforts. Especially peat deeper than 3 m is a key information, since the Indonesian legislation does not allow to develop land to plantations or other land use on these peatlands. Accurate maps of the peat surface topography are required for hydrological restoration and the planning of dam construction sites. The improved "Peat Prize Methodology" presented here is a quick and inexpensive approach to create spatially explicit maps on peat extent and surface topography which can be easily adapted to survey the yet unexplored large peatlands in the Congo basin and the Amazon.

## ACKNOWLEDGEMENTS

We would like to thank BRG for providing aerial LiDAR data and peat coring data.

## REFERENCES


1. Agus, F., Hairiah, K. & Mulyani, A. (2011) Measuring carbon stock in peat soils. Practical guidelines. *Bogor Jawa Barat Indonesia: World Agroforestry Centre (ICRAF).Southeast Asia Regional Program, Indonesian Centre for Agricultural Land Resources Research and Development.*
2. Ballhorn, U., Jubanski, J. & Siegert, F. (2011) ICESat/GLAS data as a measurement tool for peatland topography and peat swamp forest biomass in Kalimantan, Indonesia. *Remote Sensing*, 3, 1957–1982.
3. Barber, C.V. & Schweithelm, J. (2000) *Trial by fire: Forest fires and forestry policy in Indonesia's era of crisis and reform*, World Resources Institute Forest Frontiers Initiative in collaboration with WWF-Indonesia & Telapak Indonesia Foundation, Washington, D.C.
4. Berninger, A. & Siegert, F. (2020) The Potential of ICESat-2 to Identify Carbon-Rich Peatlands in Indonesia. *Remote Sensing*, 12, 4175.
5. Carlson, K.M., Goodman, L.K. & Calen C. M. T. (2015) Modeling relationships between water table depth and peat soil carbon loss in Southeast Asian plantations. *Environmental Research Letters*, 10, 74006.
6. Huijnen, V., Wooster, M.J., Kaiser, J.W., Gaveau, D.L.A., Flemming, J., Parrington, M., Inness, A., Murdiyarso, D., Main, B. & van Weele, M. (2016) Fire carbon emissions over maritime Southeast Asia in 2015 largest since 1997. *Scientific reports*, 6, 26886.
7. Jaenicke, J., Rieley, J.O., Mott, C., Kimman, P. & Siegert, F. (2008) Determination of the amount of carbon stored in Indonesian peatlands. *Geoderma*, 147, 151–158.
8. Jayarathne, T., Stockwell, C.E., Gilbert, A.A., Daugherty, K., Cochrane, M.A., Ryan, K.C., Putra, E.I., Saharjo, B.H., Nurhayati, A.D., Albar, I., Yokelson, R.J. & Stone, E.A. (2018) Chemical characterization of fine particulate matter emitted by peat fires in Central Kalimantan, Indonesia, during the 2015 El Niño. *Atmospheric Chemistry and Physics*, 18, 2585–2600.
9. Konecny, K., Ballhorn, U., Navratil, P., Jubanski, J., Page, S.E., Tansey, K., Hooijer, A., Vernimmen, R. & Siegert, F. (2016) Variable carbon losses from recurrent fires in drained tropical peatlands. *Global Change Biology*, 22, 1469–1480.
10. Lohberger, S., Stängel, M., Atwood, E.C. & Siegert, F. (2018) Spatial evaluation of Indonesia's 2015 fire-affected area and estimated carbon emissions using Sentinel-1. *Global Change Biology*, 24, 644–654.
11. Miettinen, J., Hooijer, A., Shi, C., Tollenaar, D., Vernimmen, R., Liew, S.C., Malins, C. & Page, S.E. (2012) Extent of industrial plantations on Southeast Asian peatlands in 2010 with analysis of historical expansion and future projections. *Global change biology. Bioenergy*, 4, 908–918.
12. Page, S.E., Rieley, J.O. & Banks, C.J. (2011) Global and regional importance of the tropical peatland carbon pool. *Global Change Biology*, 17, 798–818.
13. Page, S.E., Rieley, J.O., Shotyk, W. & Weiss, D. (1999) Interdependence of peat and vegetation in a tropical peat swamp forest. *Philosophical transactions of the Royal Society of London. Series B, Biological sciences*, 354, 1885–1897.
14. Rieley, J.O., Siefermann, R.G. & Page, S.E. (1992) The origin, development, present status and importance of the lowland peat swamp forests of Borneo. *Suo*, 43, 241–244.
15. Suroyo, G. & Diela, T. (2019) *World Bank says Indonesia forest fires cost $5.2 billion in economic losses*, Jakarta. Online at: https://www.reuters.com/article/us-indonesia-environment/world-bank-says-indonesia-forest-fires-cost-5-2-billion-in-economic-losses-idUSKBN1YF0FJ.
16. Vernimmen, R., Hooijer, A., Akmalia, R., Fitranatanegara, N., Mulyadi, D., Yuherdha, A., Andreas, H. & Page, S. (2020) Mapping deep peat carbon stock from a LiDAR based DTM and field measurements, with application to eastern Sumatra. *Carbon balance and management*, 15, 4.

ID 72827

# MEASURING PEAT REWETTING IMPACT USING HYDROLOGICAL MODELING: THREE CASE STUDIES FROM SOUTH SUMATRA AND CENTRAL KALIMANTAN

Dede Sulaeman[1], Ihsan Hafiyyan[1], Hidayah Hamzah[1], Riyandi Nuswantoro[2], Maraya Syifa Widyastuti[2]

[1] World Resources Institute Indonesia, Jakarta, Indonesia
[2] PT DHI Water & Environment, Jakarta, Indonesia

*dede.sulaeman@wri.org*

## SUMMARY

Indonesia is one of the world's largest homes for tropical peatland, with the area reached 14.43 million hectares or more than 30% of the global tropical peat area. Peatlands are fragile ecosystems with essential biological and hydrological functions. However, in recent decades, peatland in Indonesia has been destroyed by human and natural activities, which has created severe problems, including peat fires. Peatland areas were mostly converted into agricultural land where artificial canals were made to supply its water needs and drains its excess water. It caused the decrease of peat groundwater level (GWL) and resulted in a tremendous amount of carbon released, consequently contributing to climate change. Through Peatland and Mangrove Restoration Agency (BRGM), Indonesia's Government committed to restoring degraded peatlands by implementing rewetting infrastructures. However, there are still gaps in identifying the impact of restoration implementation on the peat hydrological properties. Hydrology modeling is an attractive option for solving practical water resource management problems and is widely used to predict peatland hydrological processes. This study aims to measure the effects of rewetting infrastructures implementation using a deterministic and physically-based model coupled with a fully dynamic and one-dimensional modeling system in three Peat Hydrological Units (PHUs) in South Sumatra and Central Kalimantan. Scenario analysis is performed to simulate the water table rise by comparing peat GWL in degraded peatlands with and without rewetting infrastructures implementation. Results showed that the percentage of the rewetted area compared to the PHUs total area, with the threshold of 2 cm GWL rise, ranged from 7.5 – 11.9% in Burnai – Sibumbung PHU, 3.9 – 6.9% in Kahayan – Sebangau PHU, and 8.19 – 13.63% in Kapuas - Barito PHU. This study also indicates that the impact of rewetting activities can be scientifically quantified by using hydrological modeling.

***Keywords***: *hydrological model, peat rewetting, rewetting impact, groundwater level rise*

## INTRODUCTION

One of the world's largest tropical peatland-covered countries, Indonesia, has been struggling to reduce carbon emissions for years. With estimated carbon storage of around 28.1 GtC or approximately 37.4% of global tropical peatland storage (Warren *et al*., 2017), this carbon-densely area could release many greenhouse gasses (GHG) into the atmosphere, which is a major driver in climate change. In 2015 alone, forest and land fires from June to November have resulted in 2.6 billion hectares of land burnt and generating thick smoke and haze (BRG, 2019). In recent decades, by the late 1960s, this fragile ecosystem suffers a high conversion rate due to anthropogenic needs and activities. These natural wetlands are mostly converted into high water-demanding agriculture such as palm oil, pulp, and paper and transportation purposes (Warren *et al*., 2017).

Managing peat groundwater level is one of the primary keys to reducing greenhouse gas emissions from peatlands. Groundwater level decline leads to an increase in oxidation and makes the carbon-rich ecosystem prone to fire. Economic loss in 2015 is estimated at around IDR 221 trillion, which equivalent to 1.9 percent of 2015 GDP due to land and forest fires (World Bank, 2016). Restoring the peatland hydrology is carried out to prevent peat oxidation and mitigate $CO_2$ emissions. Indonesia's President mandated *Badan Restorasi Gambut dan Mangrove*/Peatland and Mangrove Restoration Agency (formerly known as *Badan Restorasi Gambut*/Peatland Restoration Agency) to restore degraded peatlands across Sumatra, Kalimantan, and Papua.

Peat rewetting activities or restoration of hydrological conditions aim to raise the groundwater level and keep the peat moist to prevent fires. Furthermore, these activities also aim to maintain groundwater level fluctuations by reducing water losses from the site and make the peat store enough water during periods of water surplus to prevent drought during periods of water shortage. The success of any restoration project depends on the durable re-installment of appropriate site conditions. There is no universal strategy to restore drained peatlands as conditions differ widely depending on climate, water and peat chemistry, and topography. Hence, there is a need to understand the impact of peat rewetting activities on the hydrological process. Therefore, this study's main objective is to measure the impact of peat rewetting activities through canal blocking and backfilling implementation on the hydrological conditions in three-peat hydrological units (PHUs) in South Sumatra and Central Kalimantan using hydrological modeling.

## MATERIALS AND METHODS

### 1.1 Site Description

This study was conducted in three Peat Hydrological Units (PHUs) in South Sumatra and Central Kalimantan. The first site located in Burnai – Sibumbung PHU (BS site) in Ogan Komering Ilir Regency, South Sumatra with an area of 86679 ha. The other two sites located in Kahayan – Sebangau (KS) and Kapuas – Barito (KB) PHUs in Pulang Pisau and Kapuas Regency, Central Kalimantan with an area of 451507 ha and 558168 ha, respectively (Figure 1).

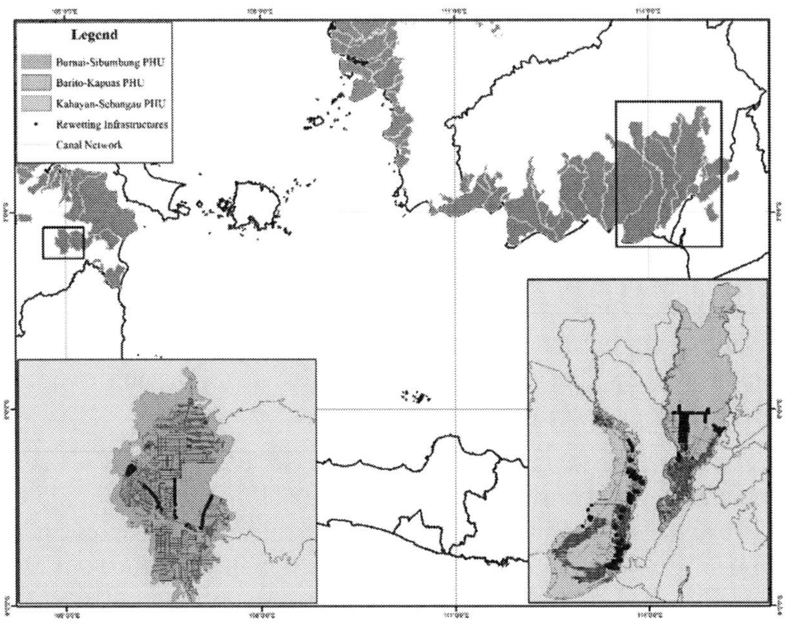


Figure 20. Site locations

### 1.2 Hydrological Model and Data Requirements

MIKE SHE, a deterministic and physically-based modeling system, is used in this study. It is also a distributed model because the model can handle spatial and temporal distributions of parameters. The model simulates all the major processes in the hydrological cycle and includes process models for evapotranspiration, overland flow, unsaturated flow, root zone, groundwater flow, water balance, net recharge to groundwater, and their interactions. The interaction of the processes with channel flow can be handled by coupling the model with MIKE Hydro River, a map-based model, and a highly intuitive graphical user interface. It offers various add-on modules and a large selection of hydraulic structures, including rewetting structures. MIKE Hydro River model contains all the schematization of the canal and river network, as well as the representation of hydraulic structures such as canal blocking and canal backfilling, the structures implemented for peat rewetting purposes. The model contains all the schematization of the canal and river network. These networks were coupled to the MIKE SHE, where it is the main user interface software for the full model for hydrologic processes for surface and sub-surface flows. Peatland is well known for its complex hydrological processes. Therefore, the study needs a lot of data, includes:

*Topography.* Topography is an important parameter in the peat hydrological model, and it is one of the major drivers in groundwater level fluctuation in peatland areas. Usually, peatlands are relatively flat; thus, a good resolution digital elevation model (DEM) is required. In this study, DEM is generated from LiDAR data for KS site and ALOS PALSAR for BS and KB sites with a spatial resolution of 0.5 and 12.5 meters, respectively.

*Meteorological Data.* Rainfall data were obtained from the Meteorological, Climatological, and Geophysical Agency (BMKG), with the period of data from 2016 until 2019. Thiessen polygon method is used to estimate average regional precipitation on each study site. The other four main climatological data needed for this study including average wind speed, average relative humidity, net solar radiation, and average air temperature. The Penman-Monteith method was used to estimate reference evapotranspiration (ETo) and actual evapotranspiration (ET). It depends on the moisture content in the root zone and crop development (FAO, 1998).

*Peat Depth Map and Soil Characteristics.* Peat depth maps produced by Indonesian Center for Agricultural Land Resources Research and Development (BBSDLP) and BRGM, with a scale of 1:50000, were used in this study. BRGM's peat map data has also been validated with some ground measurements. Soil information needed for this study includes soil water content at saturated conditions, field capacity, and wilting point. Additional key parameter such as saturated hydraulic conductivity in the soil was also used in the model.

*Landcover Data.* There are two sources of land cover data in the study area, which are obtained from BRG (2017) and the Ministry of Environment and Forestry, KLHK (2018). In order to simplify various land cover on the study site, several types of land covers were categorized into smaller groups as the raw data consists of numerous categories, and some of them behave similarly from the hydrological aspects.

*Peat Rewetting Structure.* This hydrological model covers two types of rewetting structures, including canal blocking (weir construction) and canal backfilling (only found in KB site) that were implemented by BRGM during 2017-2019. Due to the lack of geometrical structure data, several assumptions need to be made in this study. Each weir that has a spillway is assumed to be modeled ideally, and its width is determined refers to General Director Regulation (PEDIRJEN) No P.4/PPKL/PKG/PKL.0/6/2019.

The other data required for this study includes canal network, canal cross-section data, tidal data (for KS site), and other supporting data (e.g., leaf-area-index/LAI and root depth).

### 1.3 Model Calibration and Simulation

Calibration is an essential process in hydrological modeling to test the model performance. It is the process of estimating model parameter values to enable a hydrologic model to match observations. Manual calibration has been applied to this study by comparing the observed and modeled GWL data. Observed GWL data were obtained from SIPALAGA, a platform developed by BRGM for monitoring real-time data derived from a GWL monitoring sensor. The number of SIPALAGA stations used in this study are 4, 5, and 1 stations for BS, KS, and KB sites, respectively. The parameters used for the calibration process include saturated and unsaturated flow components such as hydraulic conductivities, storage coefficient, specific yield, saturated hydraulic conductivity, conductivity curve parameters, and retention curve parameters. Other parameters were also considered: manning value, surface storage, drain time constants, and evapotranspiration component (LAI, root depth, and crop coefficient).

Model performance was assessed by conducting standard goodness of fit by calculating the coefficient of determination ($R^2$) and Nash–Sutcliffe efficiency (NSE). An $R^2$ value closer to 1 indicates that the regression predictions perfectly fit the data. The NSE is a widely used and potentially reliable statistic for assessing the goodness of fit of hydrologic models. According to Motovilov *et al.* (1999) the model performance at the daily time step is generally judged as satisfactory when NSE > 0.36. A Hydrological model can be used for simulating the scenarios if it meets the minimum satisfaction criteria. There are two scenarios simulated in this study, with and without rewetting structures implementation. A restoration impact assessment was carried out by comparing the GWL data resulted from those two scenarios.

## RESULTS AND DISCUSSIONS

### 1.4 Calibration Result

The measured GWL varies from 0 to -1 m in all study sites. Statistical parameters such as $R^2$ and NSE are presented to quantitatively describe the agreement of model results with the observed data. This study showed that KS site has a higher value of $R^2$ and NSE than BS and KB sites. The highest $R^2$ value resulted in KS, BS, and KB sites were 0.97, 0.82, and 0.71, respectively. The closer the value of $R^2$ to 1 indicates better linear regression between observed and modeled data. The highest all sites NSE value was also observed in KS site with a value of 0.82. Meanwhile, the highest NSE value in BS and KB sites reached 0.48 and 0.38, categorized as satisfactory (>0.36) according to Motovilov *et al.* (1999). The calibration result on each site is described in Table 1 below:

Table 1. The calibration result ($R^2$ and NSE values) for each site

| Site | Number of stations | Lowest value of | | Highest value of | |
|---|---|---|---|---|---|
| | | $R^2$ | NSE | $R^2$ | NSE |
| Burnai – Sibumbung (BS) | 4 | 0.62 | 0.34 | 0.82 | 0.48 |
| Kahayan – Sebangau (KS) | 5 | 0.84 | 0.51 | 0.97 | 0.82 |
| Kapuas – Barito (KB) | 1 | 0.71 | 0.38 | 0.71 | 0.38 |

Asyari et al. (2018) used the same coupled-model to assess peat hydrological processes in Padang Island. Their study showed that the model has a good performance and can be used to predict peat GWL data, with $R^2$ and NSE values by 0.81 and 0.80, respectively. The accuracy of hydrological models is affected by multiple factors. One of the possible causes of the lower model performance in BS and KB sites is due to the topography data used in the model. ALOS data used for BS and KB sites was relatively coarse compared to LiDAR. It may produce some deviation in the Digital Elevation Model (DEM) compared to the site's actual topography. The error associated with the observed data could also be one of these factors (Zhao, *et al.*, 2020)

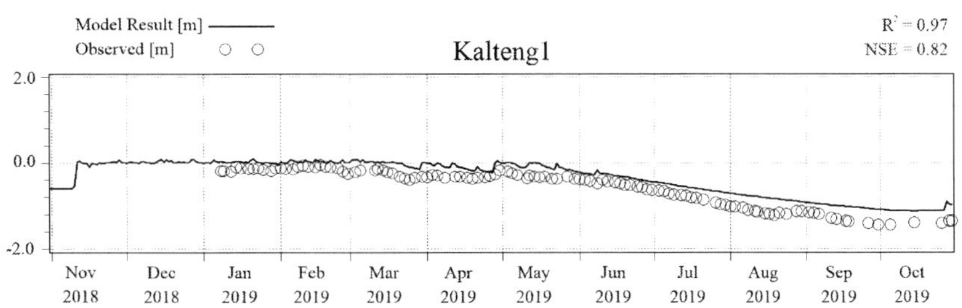


Figure 2. The highest $R^2$ and NSE values in the calibration process (KS site)

## 1.5 Peat Rewetting Impact

Peat Rewetting activities are the first stage in applying peat restoration measures to make the peat rewetted and suitable for peat vegetation to grow in water-logged conditions. Restoring hydrological aspects of peatlands can also reduce greenhouse gas emissions, slow peat subsidence rate, and reduce the risk of fires. The impact of rewetting infrastructures is apparent in the canals where the rewetting infrastructures are located and around the canals affected by the structures. This study showed that the radius of impact in all sites varies from 100 to 300m. These are the distance where the increase in GWL can be observed (e.g., increase by more than 2cm). Another study (Sutikno *et al.*, 2019) showed that the impact of canal blocking could raise peat GWL at a radius of about 170 m from the canal. The rewetting's radius impact might vary depending on the area's hydro-topography situation and land cover in the area. The impacted area (ha) can be seen in Table 2 below:

Table 2. The impacted area (ha) during the wet, transition, and dry seasons

| Season | Impacted area (GWL rise ≥ 2cm) | | | | | |
|---|---|---|---|---|---|---|
| | Burnai – Sibumbung (BS) | | Kahayan – Sebangau (KS) | | Kapuas - Barito (KB) | |
| | Area (ha) | Percentage (%) | Area (ha) | Percentage (%) | Area (ha) | Percentage (%) |
| Wet | 7280 | 11.93 | 12417.75 | 3.91 | 25147.5 | 8.19 |
| Transition | 5155.4 | 8.45 | 15093.33 | 4.75 | 40278.67 | 13.12 |
| Dry | 4576 | 7.5 | 21979 | 6.92 | 41856 | 13.63 |

*Burnai-Sibumbung (BS) Site*. The magnitude of impact varies every month as it also depends on the rainfall intensity. The impact of rewetting structures in BS site is in the range of 7.5 % (4576 ha) to 11.93% (7280 ha) of the total peatland area. During the transition month, the impact was about 8.45% (5155.4 ha). The highest impact is observed in the month where it represents the wet season period (Figure 3). The impacted areas are described by blue-colored patches. The model shows that there is a potential decrease in the GWL downstream of the weirs (yellow-colored canals) as the water flow in the canal is blocked due to the presence of the weirs, causing a lower water level downstream.

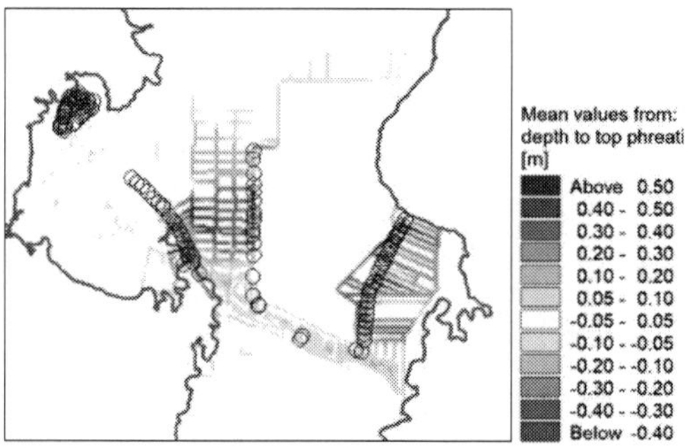


Figure 3. The visualization of impacted areas in BS site

*Kahayan-Sebangau (KS) Site*. The peat rewetting structures in KS site increase the GWL in the area. This study found that the biggest impact of peat rewetting structures in KS site was about 21979 ha or 7 % of the total peatland area in the dry season (Figure 4). The impacted area in the wet and transition seasons reached 3.9% (25147 ha) and 4.75% (40278.67 ha), respectively.

*Kapuas-Barito (KB) site*. The impact of the structures in KB site reached 8 and 13% (25147.5 and 40278.67 ha) in the wet and transition season, respectively. The biggest impact is observed in the dry season, with the impacted areas almost 14% or 41856 ha (Figure 4). The canal rewetting structures act as a storage system to keep and hold water while there is still supply from rainfall in the wet season to prevent a quick drawdown condition of peat GWL in the dry season.

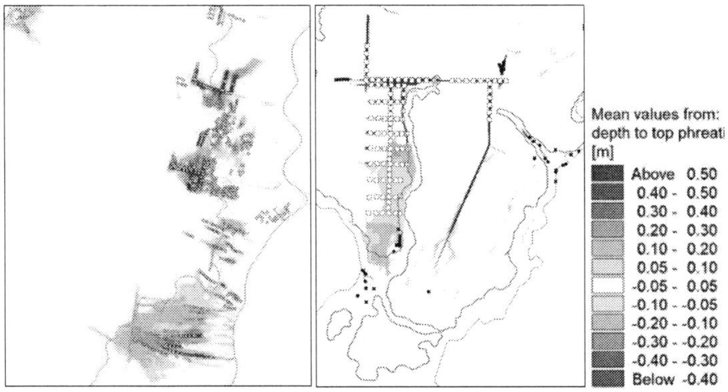

Figure 4. The visualization of impacted areas in KS site (left) and KB site (right)

In the wet season, GWL in peatlands are generally at or very near the surface (Warren *et al.*, 2017), and the ecosystem could be flooded. This is the reason why in KS and KB sites, the rewetting infrastructures have the least impact compared to transition and dry season. For the BS site case, where the biggest impact occurred in the wet season, the canal depth plays an important role. Based on our field observation, canal depths at the BS site are very deep, up to 3 meters below the soil surface. This configuration reasonably returns lower minimum water table depths (about -1.2 meters below soil surface) in the dry season, and the area was not flooded during the wet season.

## CONCLUSIONS

The coupled hydrologic modeling systems used in this study can predict peat GWL and the impact of rewetting infrastructure. Peatland rewetting infrastructures (canal blocking and backfilling) impacted the areas in BS, KS, and KB sites with various impacts. The radius impact of rewetting infrastructure, with a peat GWL increase of more than 2 cm, is in the range of 100 to 300 m from the structure location, depending on the canal depth, slope, and peat characteristic. The biggest impact of rewetting infrastructures occurred in the wet season (BS site) and dry season (KS and KB sites), with the impacted area of 11.93, 6.92, and 13.63 % of the total peatland area. However, it should be underlined that this study only covers the impact of peat rewetting infrastructures implemented by BRGM.

## ACKNOWLEDGEMENTS

This research was part of PRIMS (Peatland Restoration Information and Monitoring System) project activities supported by the Government of Norway through the United Nations Office for Project Services (UNOPS).

## REFERENCES

Asyhari A, Suardiwerianto Y, Balamurugan M, Marpaung SM, Tanjungsari RJ, Hidayat MF, M. I. Harahap F, and Ghimire CP. 2018. Assessing the Impacts of Plantation Forestry on Tropical Peatland Hydrology Using the Coupled MIKE SHE and MIKE Hydro River Modelling System. American Geological Union Conference

Food and Agriculture Organization. 2020. Peatlands mapping and monitoring – Recommendations and technical overview. Rome. DOI: 10.4060/ca8200en.

Motovilov Y G, Gottschalk L, Emgeland K, and Rodhe A. 1999. Validation of a distributed hydrological model against spatial observation Agricultural and Forest Meteorology 98-99: 257 – 277

Peatland Restoration Agency of Republic of Indonesia (*Badan Restorasi Gambut*/BRG). 2019. Three Years of Peatland Restoration in Indonesia Report.

Sutikno S, Nasrul B, Gunawan H, Jayadi R, Rinaldi, Saputra E, Yamamoto K. 2019. The effectiveness of canal blocking for hydrological restoration in tropical peatland. MATEC Web of Conferences: 276

Warren M, Hergoualc'h K, Kauffman J, Murdiyarso D, Kolka R. 2017. An appraisal of Indonesia's immense peat carbon stock using national peatland maps: Uncertainties and potential losses from conversion. *Carbon Balance and Management*; 12: 12. DOI: 10.1186/s13021-017-0080-2.

World Bank.2016. The cost of fire : an economic analysis of Indonesia's 2015 fire crisis. Jakarta: The World Bank. 1–12

Zhao B, Mao J, Dai Q, Han D, Dai H, and Rong G. 2020. Exploration on hydrological model calibration by considering the hydro-meteorological variability. Hydrology Research (2020) 51 (1): 30–46. https://doi.org/10.2166/nh.2019.047

ID 62316

# NATURE AND PREVENTION STRATEGY OF COASTAL PEAT EROSION ANDCOASTAL PEAT LANDSLIDES IN TROPICAL COASTAL PEATLAND, RIAU PROVINCE, INDONESIA

Koichi Yamamoto[1], Hiroki Kagawa[1], Hirotoshi Mori[1], Yoshihisa Akamatsu[1], Motoyuki Suzuki[1], Ariyo Kanno[1],Sigit Sutikno[2], Noerdin Basir[3]

[1]Graduate School of Sciences and Technology for Innovation, Yamaguchi University, Ube, Japan

[2] University of Riau, Pekanbaru, Indonesia

[3] National State Polytechnic of Bengkalis, Bengkalis, Indonesia

*k_yama@yamaguchi-u.ac.jp*

## SUMMARY

Coastal erosion is one of a new but serious problem in the coastal tropical peatland in Riau province. This coastalerosion happens in the Malacca strait side of the peatland. This coastal erosion combines of the peat collapse namely bog burst. We applied temporal UAV observation and chemical analysis for the peat core samples. We estimated that the annual carbon discharge from the coastal peatland per coastal line was around 10tC $m^{-1}$. We evaluated the number of the peaty debris flat appearance, as a result of the bog burst, showed that apparent increaseof peat-tidal flat with the amount of the local precipitation from 2014-2018. The cause of the peat collapse was mainly rainfall.

*Keywords: Bog burst, coastal erosion, Riau, Coastal tropical peatland, Carbon discharge*

## INTRODUCTION

The tropical coast peat islands in Riau province face to the Malacca strait, Republic of Indonesia, peatland cliffsare formed on the coast of the Malacca side (Supardi *et al.* 1993) and coastal erosion is progressing rapidly, reachesup to 32.35 m/year and peat failures were found in Bengkalis Island (Fig.1) (Sigit, *et al.*, 2017). Coastline changesof the Bengkalis Island is shown in Fig. 2. Continuous coastline setback has been observed for around 50 years. This coastal erosion in peatlands has not only the meaning of losing land but also has aspects of organic carbon transport from land. Terrain-to-ocean Particulate organic carbon (POC) and dissolved organic carbon (DOC) fluxes are important in terms of carbon sinks to the ocean. Also, global carbon export from the terrestrial biosphere is controlled by erosion. It is considered to be deposited and buried in the ocean floor for a long time when discharged POC is buried in the seabed (Galy *et al.* 2015). However, carbon discharge due to coastal erosion is not fully considered yet. In the peatland, high concentration of carbon is contained in the soil and when the peat soil is eroded, great amount of POC may discharged. In the upland peatland, POC discharges with erosion of peatsoil by rainfall (Martyra and Kløve 2010).

In the tropical peat coast area, not only coastal erosion but also peat landslides (peat failures) are observed(Sutikno *et al.*, 2017, Kagawa *et al.*, 2017). The phenomenon of peat land slide, so called peat slope failure or peatfailure, that peat accumulated on slopes causes natural slip or landslide as a natural phenomenon, has long been known especially in Scotland and Ireland. One of the feature of the peat failure is bog burst, which has the characteristic that the base occurs even at a very gentle slope (2 to 8 °), such as when the edge of the peat dome collapses or artificially cuts and collapses at a depth of 1.5 m or more is generated. The minimum gradient of the base where collapse occurs is 3-4 ° in the case of peat slide but it is said to occur even in 1-2 ° in case of Bog burst(Dykes and Warburton 2007). These peat failures are mostly reported for the cases in boreal peatland. However, peat failure in tropical peatland has rarely reported. Only the case of the peatland collapse in Tutoh River, SarawakMalaysia (Wilford 1966) was the case other than the Bengkalis Island. In the Bengklais Island's case was reported as bog burst because of its feature of the tension cracks on the peat ground (Kagawa *et al.* 2017).

The aim of this study is to present an importance of tropical peat coastal erosion and tropical coastal bogburst on degradation of the tropical coastal peatland and discuss the prevention method of tropical peat coast degradation.

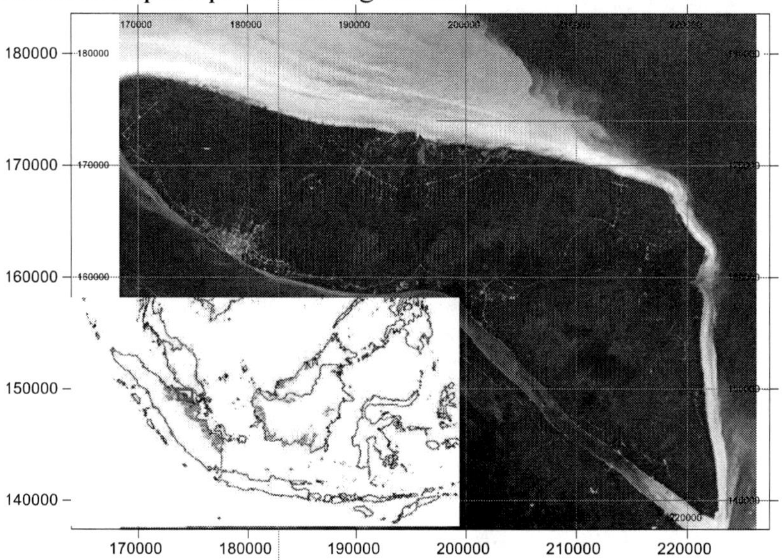


Fig. 1 Bengkalis Island, Riau Province, Indonesia. The coordinates are UTM Zone 48N. Red box shows that thearea of the Fig. 2. Red dashed box shows the area of Fig. 3. Triangle is St. PT as the meteological station

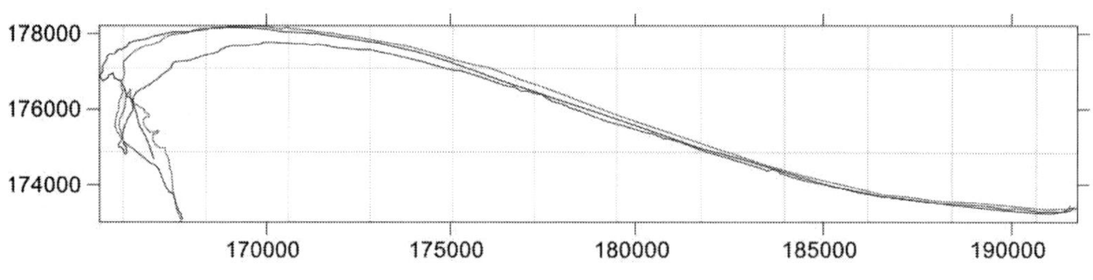


Fig. 2 Coastline changes in Bengkalis Island, Riau Province, Indonesia. The coordinates are UTM Zone 48N.Black: Oct. 5, 1972, red: May 16, 1995, Blue: Feb. 11, 2019.

## MATERIALS AND METHODS

The study area is located on Bengkalis Island, Riau Province, Republic of Indonesia (Fig. 1). The area islocated at latitude 1.6°N and longitude 102°E and has a tropical rainforest climate. The total area of the BengkalisIsland is about 900 $km^2$, and there are four major peat domes in the whole island. A simple meteorological observation station (Midori Engineering SESAME-II) was installed in Perapat tunggal village (St. PT) in western Bengkalis from August 1, 2017 to December 31, 2018 to automatically measure rainfall, wind direction, and windspeed. The wind speed was measured every 10 minutes with an averaging time of 600 seconds.

In order to confirm the occurrence of peatland collapse, the north coast of Bengkalis Island was photographed using an Unmanned Aerial Vehicle (UAV) on March 5, 2016 and March 4, 2017. The area coveredwas about 25 ha (0.25 $km^2$). Used UAVs were Arris M650 and DJI Phantom 4. The images were taken from an altitude of 150 m. In 2016, the shutter speed was fixed at 1/500 and shooting was done in 2 seconds interval withRicoh GR. In 2017, the camera was the one attached to the UAV. In 2017, the camera was attached to the UAV, and the exposure was set to automatic with a 2-second interval shutter.

Satellite images were used to measure the change in the area of the peaty debris fans and coastal erosion. satellite images used were Landsat-8 (resolution: 30 m), Sentinel-2 (resolution: 10 m), and the radar satellite Sentinel-1 (resolution: 30 m) was also used as a supplement. For the estimation of the carbon discharge, World View-1 image on July 23, 2011 and WorldView-3 image on April 2, 2015 were also used to identify bog bursts. Altitudes of the coast area in Bengkalis Island, ALOS World3D (JAXA) was used to estimate volume of the coastal erosion and coastal bog burst.

Peat samples were taken at four points at Bengkalis Island using peat sampler (BH01: 1.6019°N- 102.0218°E, BH03: 1.6025°-102.0218°, L1: 1.5849°N-102.0217°E, E3: 1.5849 °N-102.0090°E) on Aug, 2014,

Sep. 2016 and Aug. 2017. The maximum depths of the peat core samples were at the maximum of 6 meters. Bulk densities and dry densities were measured for the se samples and were dried and carbon contents were measured by J-science JM-10.

Carbon discharge by the coastal peat debris was calculated. At first, vertical carbon mass distribution mc(z) [tC $m^{-2}$] was calculated by Eq. (1) using carbon contents ac [-] and dry densities rd [t $m^{-3}$] of peat samples. Carbon discharge from the coastal erosion area, Mc [tC] was calculated using erosion area Ae [$m^2$] was calculatedby Eq. (2).

$$m_c(z) = \int^{z} \rho_d \alpha_c dz \quad (1)$$

$$M_c = m_c(z_0) A_c \quad (2)$$

Where, z0 is averaged depth of the peat along the coastline [m].

Carbon discharge by the bog burst MB was calculated by Eq. (3). The relationships between affected area AB [$m^2$] and averaged depth of the trough of the bog burst $h_B$ [m].

$$M_B = m_c(z) h_B A_B \quad (3)$$

## RESULTS

Fig. 3 shows the temporal changes of the coastline as well as the temporal changes of the affected area of the bog burst from 2010 to 2018. Peat coast erosion constantly extends with time. The speed of the retreat of the coastline was up to around 30 meter per year. Affected area of the bog bursts are also drawn in the figure. Four colors lines shows affected area of the bog burst in 2011, 2015, 2017 and 2018. After coastal line setback, bog burst occurs behind the new coastal line. The traces of the bog bursts were found in everywhere along the coastline. Peat coast erosion and bog bursts have a chain sequence as drawn in Fig. 3. At first, peat coast cliff appears with peat coast erosion (a). The next, bog burst happens where the instable condition appears because of the existence of the peat cliff. Carbon discharges from the coastal erosion and bog burst was calculated. Relationships between carbon amount $mc(z)$ [t $m^{-2}$] and depth of peat z [m] was

$$m_c(z) = 0.0982z^{0.679} \quad (4)$$

Table 1 shows that the affected area and volume of the peat debris caused by peat coast erosion and coastal bog burst in a part of the northern part of the Bengkalis Island from 2011 to 2018. Initial length of the surveyed coastline was 3457m. Year by year, the coastline shrinks because of the curvature of coastline. Recently, volume of the peat debris from coastal erosion and coastal bog burst were comparable, it reaches 0.41 to 0.59 $Mm^3$ $yr^{-1}$ for around 3 km coastline. Therefore, annual discharged peat debris volume per coastline reaches from 140 $m^3$ -1 -1 3 -1 -1 m yr to196mm yr.

When it was converted to carbon discharge, as shown in Table 2, carbon discharge from coastal bog burst was larger than that of coastal erosion. It was because the carbon concentration of the peat soil tend to increase in the surface of the peat because of the compaction. Because of the coastal erosion and coastal bog burst, around 10 tC $yr^{-1}$ $m^{-1}$ of carbon discharge to sea was estimated.

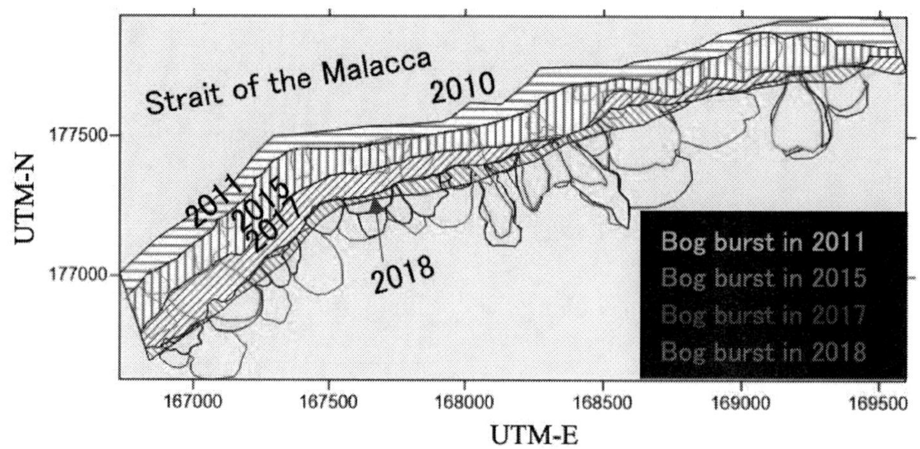


Fig. 3 Traced results of coastline and the are affected area of the bog burst.

Table 1. Affected area and volume of the peat debris caused by peat coast erosion and coastal bog burst in a partof the northern part of the Bengkalis Island, Initial length of the surveyed coastline was 3457m.

| Year | Intervals | Coastline length | Coastal erosion | | | Coastal bog burst | | Total | |
|---|---|---|---|---|---|---|---|---|---|
| | | | area | depth | vol. | area | vol.* | Total vol. | Annual discharge |
| | years | m | ha | m | $Mm^3$ | ha | $Mm^3$ | $Mm^3$ | $Mm^3/yr^{-1}$ |
| 2011-2015 | 3.696 | 3162 | 30.7 | 6.0 | 1.83 | 21.0 | 0.337 | 2.17 | 0.59 |
| 2015-2017 | 1.923 | 3140 | 8.9 | 8.1 | 0.72 | 18.5 | 0.298 | 1.02 | 0.53 |
| 2017-2018 | 1.403 | 3085 | 9.6 | 3.1 | 0.29 | 17.7 | 0.283 | 0.57 | 0.41 |

*Estimated as the depth of the bog burst was 1.60 m.

Table 2. Estimated carbon discharge from the peat debris caused by peat coastal erosion and coastal bog burst ina part of the northern part of the Bengkalis Island.

| Year | Coastal erosion | | Coastal bog burst | | Total | | |
|---|---|---|---|---|---|---|---|
| | Total amount | Annual discharge | Total amount | Annual discharge | Total amount | Annual discharge | Annual discharge per coastline |
| | ktC | ktC $yr^{-1}$ | ktC | ktC $yr^{-1}$ | ktC | ktC $yr^{-1}$ | tC $yr^{-1}m^{-1}$ |
| 011-2015 | 101 | 27 | 28 | 8 | 129 | 35 | 11 |
| 015-2017 | 36 | 19 | 25 | 13 | 61 | 32 | 10 |
| 017-2018 | 20 | 14 | 24 | 17 | 44 | 31 | 10 |

Fig. 4 Coastal peaty debris fan and bog burst of Bengkalis Island, left: UAV imagery on Jan. 10, 2015,center: Landsat8 on Jan. 15, 2015, right: WorldView-3 on Apr.2, 2015. Bar = 250m

## Coastal peaty debris fans generated by the mass movement of coastal peatland

Fig.4 shows the relationship between the extent of the bog burst found in the UAV imagery on Jan. 10, 2015 and the coastal peaty debris fans also found from the Landsat-8 image of 15 January 2015. These figures simultaneously show the trace of the extent of the coastal peaty debris fans and the trace of the collapse area on the UAV Imagery. In the WorldView-3 image on April 2, 2015, a part of the fan has already been lost because about three months have passed since the fan occurred. However, as shown in Fig. 4, when a coastal peaty debrisfans is generated, the trace of bog burst is always visible behind the fan. Therefore, it is clear that the bog bursts cause the peat soil to flow with vegetation and extend over the coast to the sea, forming the fans. Thus, the occurrence of coastal peaty debris fans indicates the occurrence of bog bursts in the hinter coastal peatland.

We compared the time series of the number of coastal peaty debris fans extracted from satellite images with the precipitation at St. PT, which is close to the area where the bog burst occurred

(Fig. 5). Since the intervalsof satellite image acquisition are not constant, the analysis period is unified to 20 days. It is confirmed that 87% of the intervals of all the images fit in 20 days. Fig. 6 shows the increase of the number of coastal peaty debris fansand the total precipitation of the previous 20 days. The number of coastal peaty debris fans increases with 20-day precipitation. In particular, the number of coastal peaty debris fans increases when the 20-day rainfall is higher than around 78 mm. The occurrence of coastal peaty debris fans indicates a bog burst, indicating that heavy rainfallwas a factor in the bog burst, as has been observed in high latitude peatlands.

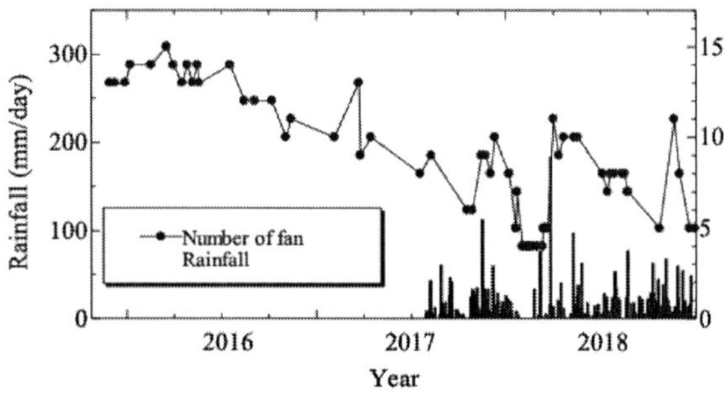


Fig. 5 The numbers of coastal peaty debris fan and dailyrainfall.

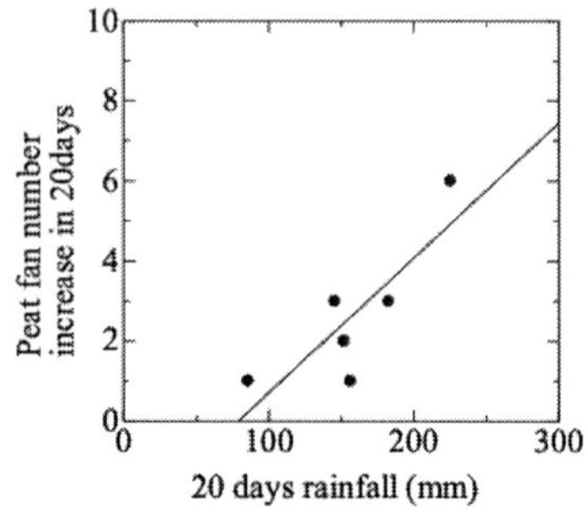


Fig. 6 Relationships between the number of the peat fan increase and 20 days rainfall.

## CONCLUSIONS

Carbon discharge ofthe coastal bog burst and coastal erosion in a tropical peatland, Bengkalis Island was measuredand discussed. The carbon discharge from coastal erosion and coastal bog burst was around 10 tC $yr^{-1}$ $m^{-1}$ in extensively eroded area of the Bengkalis Island. The occurrence of coastal peaty debris fans indicates a bog burst,indicating that heavy rainfall was a factor in the bog burst, as has been observed in high latitude peatlands. To decrease the carbon discharge from the tropical coastal peatlands, it is important to save coastal erosion from the waves and hydrological and geotechnical control in peatland to decrease the risk of the bog burst


## ACKNOWLEDGEMENTS

This study was carried out with the support of MEXT/JSPS KAKENHI Grant number 17H01668.

## REFERENCES


- Alan P. Dykes, Jeff Warburton 2007. Mass movements in peat: A formal classification scheme, Geomorphology 86 (2007) 73 93.
- Galy, V., B. Peucker-Ehrenbrink, and T. Eglinton. 2015. Global carbon export from the terrestrial biospherecontrolled by erosion. Nature 521:204-207.
- Hiroki Kagawa, Koichi Yamamoto, Muhammad Haidar, Ariyo Kanno, Yoshihisa Akamatsu, Motoyuki Suzuki, Sigit Sutikno, Noerdin Basir, Masahiko Sekine 2017. Present Condition of The Coastal Erosion in The Islands in Riau Province, Indonesia, JSCE Proceedings G (Environment) (Proceedings of EnvironmentalEngineering Research), Vol.73, No.7, III_213-III_219.
- Marttila, H., and B. Kløve. 2010. Dynamics of erosion and suspended sediment transport from drained peatland forestry. Journal of Hydrology 388:414-425.
- Supardi and A.D.Subekty, Sandra G. Neuzil 1993. General geology and peat resource of the Siak Kanan andBengkalis Island peat deposits, Sumatra, Indonesia, Geological Society of America Special Paper 286, 45- 61.
- Sutikno, S., A. Sandhyavitri, M. Haidar, and K. Yamamoto. 2017. Shoreline Change Analysis of Peat Soil Beach in Bengkalis Island Based on GIS and RS. International Journal of Engineering and Technology 9:233-238.
- Wilford, G. E. 1966. A peat landslide in Sarawak, Malaysia, and its significance in relation to washouts in coal seams. Journal of Sedimentary Research 36:244-247.

# VII EMERGING TECHNOLOGIES AND TECHNIQUES FOR PEATLANDS AND PEAT RESEARCH

IPC2021

ID 73359

# LANDSCAPE-LEVEL ESTIMATION OF BELOWGROUND CABON STORAGE IN COSTAL TROPICAL PEATLANDS IN WEST KALIMANTAN, INDONESIA

Asep Andi Yusup[1], Tsuyoshi Kato[1], Masashi Hara[1]

[1]PT Wana Subur Lestari/PT Mayangkara Tanaman Industri, West Kalimantan, Indonesia

*asep@wanasl.com*

## SUMMARY

To estimate the peat thickness, the relationship between the elevation of the peat surface and the peat depth has been conventionally used. In particular, the progress and spread of LiDAR technology, although still expensive, has made it possible to easily obtain topographic data, and the relationship between the elevation and the peat depth has become important for estimating belowground carbon stocks at the regional level as well as at specific areas. The study was conducted in a tropical peatland located near the coastal area of West Kalimantan, Indonesia. The target area is 133,700 ha and consists of two industrial forest plantations (115,000 ha) and a protection forest (18,700 ha) managed by the government. The protection forest has been found to form a huge peat dome with a radius of about 24.6 km in the landscape. Within that landscape, we set up 18 transects with distances ranging from 1.2 km to 23.8 km. At the transects, topographic surveying was carried out and at the same time 900 borings were taken to determine the peat depth. The results showed that the relationship between elevation and peat depth was not always consistent depending on the topography of the peatland. Therefore, this study presents the current status and challenges of estimating belowground carbon stocks in tropical peatlands at the landscape level.

***Keywords***: *topographic, peat depth, belowground carbon stock, coastal peatland, landscape-level.*

## INTRODUCTION

Peat is primarily composed of partially decomposed organic matter mainly originated from plant residues under conditions where decomposition factors are not fulfilled, like temperature and oxygen. Peat formation in tropical regions occurs in a condition with oxygen deficiency due to waterlogged or inundated environments for long periods. According to FAO (2020), carbon stock in global peatlands was estimated to be 650 Gigatonnes of carbon (Gt C) which is equal in magnitude to the amount of carbon in the Earth's vegetation, and more than half of the carbon in the atmosphere while peatlands occupy only 3 percent of the Earth's land surface. In Indonesia, peatland area is estimated 14.9 Mha (Haryono et al., 2011) – 20.9 Mha (Wahyunto et al., 2003, Wahyunto et al., 2004, Wahyunto et al., 2006). From these estimations of peatland area, Warren et al. (2017) estimated that 28.1 Gt C (13.6 Gt C – 40.5 Gt C) were stored as belowground carbon in these areas.

To estimate belowground carbon stock in peatlands, the peat volume approach has been applied. This approach focuses on the estimation of peat volume and then uses bulk density and carbon concentration data to convert volume to mass and carbon (Yu et al., 2012). In the peat volume estimation, a peat surface elevation model (along with peat extent) and average peat bottom levels derived from peat depth through field measurements are used (Vernimmen et al., 2020). For the peat surface elevation model, the terrain model technology using airborne and satellite sensors with extensive coverage has grown. It is getting easier to obtain data of ground surface elevation with a newly developed airborne LiDAR technology though the technology is still expensive and requires data validation through a ground truth.

On the other hand, the measurement of peat depth depends on the field survey. To cover a wider area, peat depth mapping has been proposed instead of the survey in the entire peatland. In peat depth mapping, kriging interpolation and an empirical correlation between peat depth and peat surface elevation are commonly used (Jaenicke et al., 2008; Rudiyanto et al., 2015). The empirical correlation depends on the assumption that peat bottom elevation is almost flat in peatlands of tropical Asia (Ruwaimana et al., 2020). However, Dargie et al. (2017) showed that a lacks of linearity between peat depth and surface elevation in a peatland of Congo basin due to the irregular shape of both the top and the bottom of the peatland. As the number of studies about the relation between elevation and peat depth is still limited, there is a possibility that peatlands in tropical Asia also have a similar condition like Congo Basin. The assumption for peat depth estimation in tropical Asia should be evaluated with sufficient data.
Even in a same region, the difference in shape of basal substrate or hydrological process may lead to different process of peatlands formation and different characteristics of peatlands (Rydin & Jeglum, 2013). Uncertainty of peat depth is one of the factors to result in vast range of carbon stock estimation like a case of study by Warren et al. (2017). Further understanding of the relationship between the elevation and the peat depth is required to achieve a more accurate estimation of peat depth and belowground carbon stock. This study presents the relation between peat surface elevation and peat depth at the landscape level with dense survey points to be fundamental information for belowground carbon stock estimation.

## MATERIALS AND METHODS

### Study area

A research was conducted in a tropical peatland located near the coastal area of West Kalimantan, Indonesia (Figure 1). This area consists of two forest concession areas (approximately 115,000ha) managed by PT Wana Subur Lestari (WSL) and PT Mayangkara Tanaman Industri (MTI) and Mendawak protection forest (approximately 18,700 ha) managed by the government. The soil type of WSL is dominated by peat (92%) and alluvial soil at the river's edge (8%). The soil type of MTI is dominated by peat (73%) and mineral soil (27%). Moreover, MTI has non-sedimentary hills with mineral soil located in the Southeast and Northeast of the concession. Meanwhile, Mendawak protection forest is thoroughly covered by peat and has been found to form a vast peat dome with a radius of about 24.6 km in the landscape (Yusup et al., 2016).

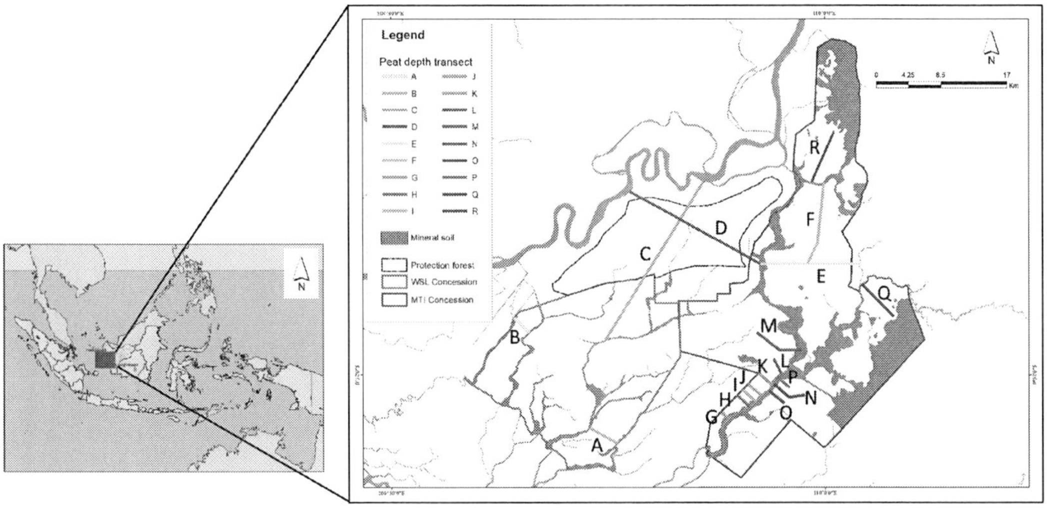


Figure 1. Location of the study area

## Transect Survey

Survey transects were set to cross the peat dome at perpendicular angles to contour. The beginning point of each transect was set on riverbank. We set up 18 survey transects in the area and the length of the transects ranges from 1.2 km to 23.8 km and total length is 114.2 km. In the transects, peat auguring to measure peat depth and levelling to measure ground surface elevation were carried out. Peat auguring was carried out with a peat auger (Eijkelkamp) at 900 points in the transects and the intervals were between 100-500 m. At each location of auguring, the geographical coordinates were recorded with a global positioning system (GPS). Levelling was carried out with auto a spirit level in every 50 m along the transects to capture microtopography of peatland. The elevation of peat bottom was calculated from surface elevation and peat depth.

# RESULTS

## Peat depth and elevation

Among 900 auguring points in the transects, 797 points had peat thicker than 0.5 m, a minimum threshold of peat following criteria by Helmy et al.(2012 ) (Figure 2-a). The maximal peat depth in each transect ranged between 1.0 m (transect A) – 9.5 m (transect C). The surface elevation of transect ranging from 0 m to 14.4 m +msl. The relation between elevation and peat depth is shown in Figure 2-b. The elevation and peat depth seem to have a positive correlation while there are several outliers. Most of these outliers were found in data from Transect Q and R.

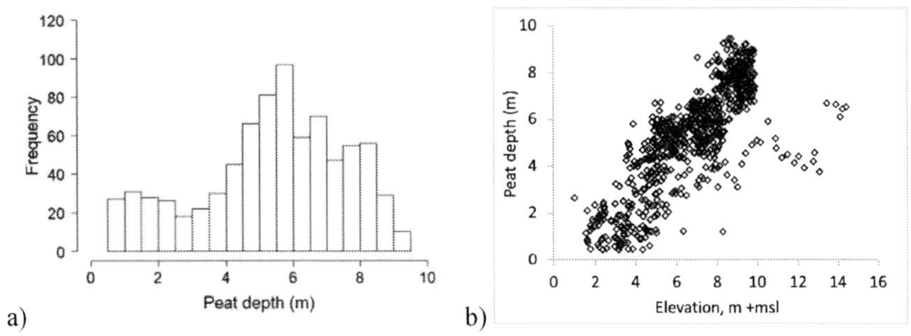


Figure 2. Frequency distribution of peat depth (a) and relation between elevation and peat depth (b)

Some of peat profile along the transect are shown in Figure 3.

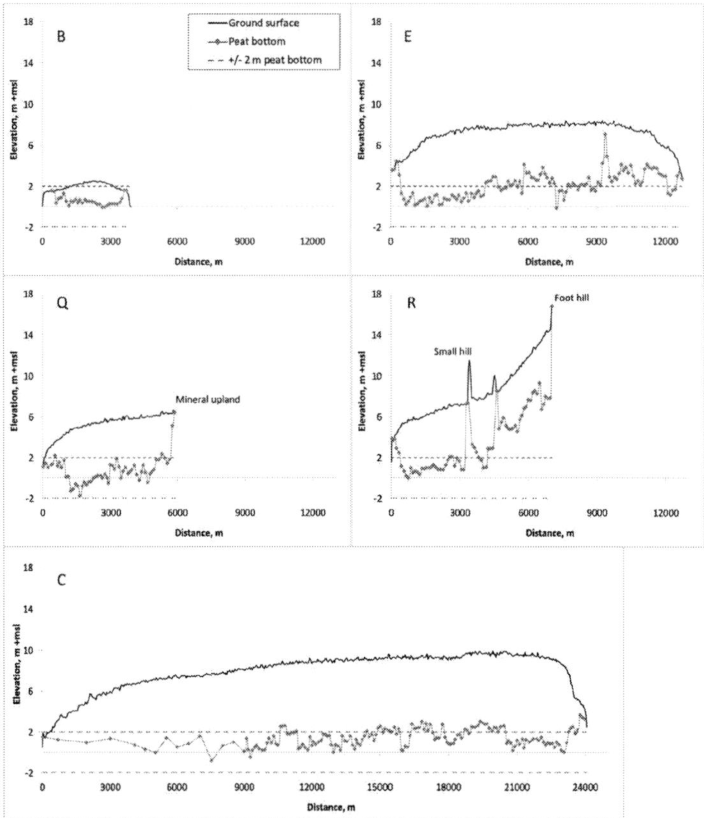


Figure 3. Cross section (500x vertical exaggeration) of peat surface and peat bottom profiles of the transect B, C, E, Q and R

The elevation of peat bottom ranging from -1.9 to 9.3 m +msl. The difference of the peat bottom elevation in each transect reached 9.3 m (transect R) and the average difference among 18 transects were 3.9 m. The numbers of points with an elevation between -2 and 2 m + msl, which have been often considered to the range of peat bottom in Indonesia's coastal peatland (Furukawa, 1994; Rietzema & Wosten, 2002; Hooijer & Vernimmen., 2013) was 563 points (70.6%). The elevation of peat bottom was over 5.0 m +msl in 22 points (2.8%). Though 19 of these points were found in transect R, transect E also had 2 emerging points on the peat bottom.

## DISCUSSION

This study showed undulant peat bottom against the assumption that was used for peat depth estimation in the peatland in Indonesia (Vernimmen et al., 2020). The transects in our study can be divided into two groups, (1) Transition area (Transect Q and R) and (2) peat dome (the other transects). As transition area of basal substrate has a topography continuing to mineral upland, the elevation of peat bottom gets higher near the border between peatland and mineral upland. Though the elevation of peat surface also gets higher following the peat bottom, the peat depth gets thinner in the area (Figure 3). Thus these points became outliers of the relation between elevation and peat depth (Figure 2-b). In the process of peat depth estimation, the transition area should be applied a different method from other areas. To prepare different methods, sampling strategies have a significant impact on data quality. Even before the field survey, we can predict the area with high basal substrate like narrow river valleys or area near hills slope. An intensive survey should be carried out in these areas to obtain sufficient data.

When we focus on the relation of peat surface elevation and peat depth only in peat dome, we still face a variance in the correlation. This variance results from the range of the peat bottom elevation. We couldn't find the correspondence between the topography of peat surface and that of peat bottom. The shape of peat surface on peat dome doesn't depends on the basal substrate as mentioned by Anshari et al. (2010). In transect E, an emergent point close to peat surface was found. This emergent point could be found because of the auguring points arranged with 100 m intervals. In case we had carried out the survey in 500 m interval as Vernimmen et al. (2018), this point couldn't be detected. Peat auguring should also be carried out along the transect for high accuracy regardless of its depth classes. Vernimmen et al. (2018) omitted the survey at the area where peat was thicker than 7 m and assumed flat peat bottom. But peat bottom elevation in transect C changed 2.4 m in 500 m range while the peat depth was over 7 m.

The wide application of a peat surface elevation model must be reconsidered when we see the result of this study. For accurate estimation of belowground carbon, we have to obtain sufficient data from field surveys regarding the peat depth. For the survey of peat surface elevation, a newly developed technology like airborne LiDAR is now applicable. However, the difference of the elevation is larger in peat bottom than peat surface (Figure 3). To improve the accuracy of peat depth estimation, we should make more effort in the measurement of peat bottom elevation even though we have to rely on field surveys for the measurement.

## CONCLUSION

This study showed that the estimation of peat depth from peat surface elevation was not always applicable even in Indonesian peatland. By dividing transition area into mineral upland and peat dome seems to improve the estimation. However, the variance of peat bottom elevation still makes uncertainty in peat depth estimation. As the difference of peat bottom elevation is larger than that of peat surface, we have to obtain sufficient data of peat bottom elevation though we still have to rely on field survey and difficult to cover a wide area. And we have to utilize the result of estimation with the consideration of the risk of overestimation or underestimation of carbon stock through the current method. Finally, we recommend that peat depth mapping and belowground carbon stock estimation in peatlands should be carried out in the entire peatland in landscape level bounded by neighbouring rivers and/or sea instead of only focussing on peat domes.

## ACKNOWLEDGEMENTS

We would like to express sincere gratitude to Sumitomo Forestry, Co., Ltd., Alas Kusuma Group, and The Sustainable Trade Initiative (IDH) for all facilities and making this study possible. The author also thanks the WSL-MTI's topography team for the support in intensive field surveys.

## REFERENCES


1. Anshari GZ, Afifudin M, Nuriman M, Gusmayanti E, Arianie L, Susana RW, Nusantara R, Sugardjito J, and Rafiastanto A. (2010) Drainage and land use impacts on changes in selected peat properties and peat degradation in West Kalimantan Province, Indonesia. *Biogeosciences*, 7, 3403–3419.
2. Dargie GC, Lewis SL, Lawson IT, Mitchard ET, Page SE, Bocko YE and Ifo SA. (2017) Age, extent and carbon storage of the central Congo basin peatland complex. *Nature,* 542 86–90.
3. FAO (2020) *Peatlands mapping and monitoring – Recommendations and technical overview*. Rome.
4. Furukawa H. (1994) *Coastal Wetlands of Indonesia: Environment, Subsistence and Exploitation,* pp.23-57. Kyoto University Press, Japan.
5. Haryono, Sarwani M, Ritung S, et al. (2011) Peatland Map of Indonesia. Center for Research and Development of Agricultural Land Resources, *Agricultural Research and Development Agency, Indonesia Ministry of Agriculture*. Bogor, Indonesia, 2011.
6. Helmy F, Hirose K, Osaki M, Fisher M. (2012) Peatland definition, from uncertainty to certainty. US-Indonesia partnership, *Indonesia Climate Change Center*, Jakarta
7. Hooijer A, Vernimmen R. (2013) Peatland maps for Indonesia. Including accuracy assessment and recommendations for improvement, elevation mapping and evaluation of future flood risk. *Quick Assessment and Nationwide Screening (QANS) of Peat and Lowland Resources and Action Planning for the Implementation of a National Lowland Strategy.* Report on QANS Component 4.
8. Jaenicke J, Rieley JO, Mott C, Kimman P, Siegert F. (2008) Determination of the amount of carbon stored in Indonesian peatlands. *Geoderma,* 147 151–158.
9. Page SE, Rieley JO, Banks CJ. (2011) Global and regional importance of the tropical peatland carbon pool. *Glob Change Biol.*, 17:798–818.
10. Ritzema HP and Wosten H. (2002) *Hydrology of Borneo's Peat swamps.* STRAPEAT-Status report Hydrology.
11. Rudiyanto, Setiawan BI, Arief C, Saptomo SK, Gunawan A, Kuswarman, Sungkono, Indriyanto A. (2015). Estimating Distribution of Carbon Stock in Tropical Peatland Using a Combination of an Empirical Peat Depth Model and GIS. *Procedia Environmental Sciences*, 24, 152–157.
12. Ruwaimana M, Gusti ZA, Lucas CR Silva, and Daniel G Gavin (2020) The oldest extant tropical peatland in the world: a major carbon reservoir for at least 47 000 years. *Environ. Res. Lett.*, 15 114027.
13. Rydin H & Jeglum JK. (2013) *The biology of peatlands*, (2nd (ed) ed.), pp. 199-299. Oxford: Oxford University Press.
14. Vernimmen R, Akmalia R, Fitranatanegara N, Artiyan E, Febrianto T, Yuherdha A, et al. (2018) *Peatland mapping for Kubu Raya, West Kalimantan, using limited LiDAR data and peat thickness field measurements*. Team Deltares report to the Indonesian Peat Prize-final phase.
15. Vernimmen R, Hooijer A, Akmalia R, Fitranatanegara N, Mulyadi D, Yuherdha A, Andreas H and Page S. (2020) Mapping deep peat carbon stock from a LiDAR based DTM and field measurements with application to estern Sumatra. *Carbon Balance Manage,* 15:4.
16. Wahyunto, Heryanto B, Bekti H, Widiastuti F. (2006) Maps of peatland distribu- tion, area and carbon content in Papua, 2000–2001. *Wetlands Interna- tional-Indonesia Programme & Wildlife Habitat Canada (WHC)*, Bogor.
17. Wahyunto, Ritung S, Subagjo H. (2003) Maps of area of peatland distribution and carbon content in Sumatra, 1990–2002. *Wetlands International-Indonesia Programme & Wildlife Habitat Canada (WHC)*, Bogor.
18. Wahyunto, Ritung S, Suparto, Subagjo H. (2004) Maps of area of peatland distribution and carbon content in Kalimantan, 2000–2002. *Wetlands International-Indonesia Programme & Wildlife Habitat Canada (WHC)*, Bogor.
19. Warren M, Hergoualc'h K, Kauffman BJ, Mudiyarso D, Kolka R. (2017) An appraisal of Indonesia's immense peat carbon stock using national peatland maps: uncertainties and potential losses from conversion. *Carbon Balance Manage*, 12:12.
20. Yusup AA, Kato T, Suhandi B, Brady M. (2016) Water management approach in peatlands based on comprehensive field surveys and analysis in West Kalimantan, *International PEAT Congress 15th Proceeding*; 5.1:A-368.
21. Yu ZC, Loisel J, Brosseau DP, Beilman DW, and Hunt SJ. (2010) Global peatland dynamics since the Last Glacial Maximum, *Geophys. Res. Lett.*, 37, L13402.
22. Yu ZC. (2012) Northern peatland carbon stocks and dynamics: a review. *Biogeosciences*, 9, 4071–4085.

ID 62701

# ELMIS - RE-MAPPING OF THE PEATLANDS OF THE EMSLAND REGION AS THE BASE FOR A PEATLAND INFORMATION SYSTEM FOR THE FUTURE TASKS OF NATURE AND CLIMATE PROTECTION

Bernd Hofer

Hofer & Pautz GbR, IPS Commission Peatlands and Environment, Germany

*hofer@hofer-pautz.de*

The basic data of the peatland cadastre in Lower Saxony are mostly from the 60s of the last century and in large parts completely outdated. Therefore, a complete new survey of organic soils for the Emsland region shall serve as a pilot project for the creation of an peatland information system. This digital information system should serve the goals of nature and climate protection with the following Topics:

- current soil map of organic soils
- current biotope types with moisture levels
- current greenhouse gas emissions
- Carbon Storage
- comparison with the data of the old peatland map and analysis of the losses

The collected stratigraphy and vegetation data will be linked in a GIS with the current terrain model of the laserscan flight of Lower Saxony. On the basis of this data evaluation, the potential for ecological development and GHG reduction will be determined for the individual Areas. This forms the basis and at the same time a ranking for future projects of nature and climate protection.

ID 62034

# DESIGN AND CONSTRUCTION OF A LARGE GROUNDWATER LYSIMETER UNDER ACACIA PLANTATION IN TROPICAL PEATLAND

*Yogi Suardiwerianto[1], Sofyan Kurnianto[1], Adibtya Asyhari[1], Muhammad Fikky Hidayat[1], Muhammad Iman Faisal Harahap[1], Rahila Junika Tanjungsari[1], Tubagus Muhamad Risky[1], Sahat Manimbo Marpaung[1], Chandra Shekhar Deshmukh[1], Supiandi Sabiham[2], Fahmuddin Agus[3], Dwi Astiani[4], Chris D. Evans[5], Susan E. Page[6]

[1] Asia Pacific Resources International Limited (APRIL), Indonesia
[2] Departmentnt of Soil Science and Land Resource, Institut Pertanian Bogor, Indonesia
[3] Indonesian Center for Agricultural Land Resources Research and Development, Indonesia
[4] Faculty of Forestry, Tanjungpura University, Indonesia
[5] Centre for Ecology and Hydrology, United Kingdom
[6] Centre for Landscape and Climate Research, University of Leicester, United Kingdom

*yogi_suardiwerianto@aprilasia.com*

One-half of Southeast Asian peatlands are managed for either smallholder agriculture or industrial plantation. This land management system requires maintenance of groundwater table to support optimum vegetation growth. Yet, comprehensive understanding of the link between hydrological processes and vegetation growth dynamics in this ecosystem is still poorly understood.

In this context, we installed polyvinyl chloride piles to the depth of clay layer (~3.75 m) for establishing two groundwater lysimeter plots (30 x 20 m2) under Acacia crassicarpa plantation in tropical peatland of Sumatra, Indonesia. These plots represent the largest undisturbed groundwater lysimeter experiment published to date. The main objective of this study is to investigate the effect of different water table depth on 1) forest plantation growth; 2) transpiration rate; and 3) nutrient dynamics.

We installed artificial water recharge and discharge mechanisms in both plots to maintain two distinct water table depth targets (40 and 80 cm). In order to assess the vegetation growth dynamics, we measured tree height, diameter at breast height, and tree stocking. Transpiration and tree water potential were measured using in-situ xylem sap flow meter and psychrometer, respectively. We conducted baseline measurements of in-situ infiltration rate and saturated hydraulic conductivity. Peat samples were collected to determine peat physical and chemical properties, including macro-micro nutrient content. In addition, rainfall, air temperature, relative humidity, solar radiation, and wind speed data were monitored using an automatic weather station.

The purpose of this paper is to provide an overview of the experimental design and performance of the artificial groundwater table regulating system. Ongoing measurements and further data analysis will establish the link between hydrology and tree growth. Further, modelling work will help to upscale our findings to a landscape scale to guide best practices for supporting responsible peatland management.

Keywords: eco-hydrology, water balance, transpiration, water use efficiency, Acacia plantation

ID 62562

# REGRESSION OF ELEVATION AND PEAT DEPTH VARIABLES AND ITS APPLICATION ON PEAT DEPTH ASSESSMENT FOR THE ADJACENT PEATLANDSCAPE, KALIMANTAN

Chairil Anwar Siregar[1], Asep Andi Yusup[2], Tsuyoshi Kato[2]

[1]Forest Research and Development Center MoEF, Bogor, Indonesia

[2]PT. Mayangkara Tanaman Industri, Jakarta, Indonesia

*siregarca@yahoo.co.id*

**SUMMARY**

Indonesia has not less than 15 million hectares of peat soils outcropping in big islands and some areas are undergoing national development project. In conjunction with an attempt to formulate sustainable peatland management wherein production is as important as conservation merit, this study was designed to examine if regression analysis based on intensive field survey using grid lines on 115 thousand hectares of production forest landscape including 1,500 pairing data of elevation and peat depth, can be employed in the peat depth distribution assessment of Mendawak protection forest (MPF) laid in the adjacent landscape covering areas of 20 thousands hectares.

Based on the 1,500 observations in the peatland of production forest area, simple regression analysis was run and therelationship between two important variables was formulated as Y= 0.92356X–0.6619, $R^2$ = 0.83, wherein X is elevation and Y is peat depth variable. The lowest and highest X value is 0.90 m and 9.98 m above sea level respectively.

In 2018 semi detailed topographic map of MPF was made based on field survey using intensive grid lines, and the lowest elevation is 4.5 m meanwhile the highest elevation is 13.5 m above sea level. The regression equation Y=0.92356X– 0.6619 then was used in the establishment of peat depth map of (MFP) based on topographic map already available, by putting all the elevation data (X) on the equation and then yielding peat depth value (Y). Moreover, ground checking was done based on 31 readings with 1 km interval along 32 km survey line perpendicular to the contour lines. The results of this observation indicates that out of 31 readings, only 2 of them were classified as outliers, meaning that the precision level of the mathematical function formulated is about 94% and good to be used in the MPF.

***Keywords**: Peat depth, topography, mathematical functions, Mendawak protection forest.*

## INTRODUCTION

Peat swamp forest naturally grown in peat-land is one of the valuable natural resources that play very critical role economically and ecologically in Indonesia nowadays. The country, as a matter of fact, has this harsh peat land ecosystem at the extent of about 14.9 million hectares and distributed in along the east coast of Sumatra Island (6.44 Mha, or 43%), the west and south coasts of Kalimantan Island (4.78 Mha, or 32%), and the west and south Coasts ofPapua Island (3.69 Mha, or 25%) (BBSDLP 2013; Osaki and Tsuji 2016). Several type of organic components undergoing different stages of decomposition process in nature so called peat materials, is closely associated with the type of peat swamp forest and as well as its vegetation structure. Moreover, growth of the peat swamp forest is influenced by various features including sites experiencing water logging for long period of time, soil reaction, and low availability of macro nutrient. As a result, tropical peat materials occurring in landscape of peat-lands, are bearing almost similar characteristics of being very rich in dead biomass, and consist of partially or completely decomposed plant debris such as stems, twigs, dead roots and leaves originated from the existing vegetation cover. In addition, climate (high temperature, high humidity, and high rainfall) and topography factors also influence the tropical peat formation in relation to its thickness and peat dome existence (Anshari 2010, Sanchez 2019).

In general, tropical peat swamp forests are grown in lowland and coastal areas, and peat thickness usually somewhat shallow and range from 1-5 m depth; while some are grown in inland areas with altitude up to 20 m above sea level, and peat thickness usually somewhat deep and very deep with value range from 5-15 m depth. The latter peat lands are often accompanied by one or more peat domes. The thickness of peat lands in a given landscape so called peat land hydrological unit has technical and regulation implication in the country today, and this is critical due to the fact that government regulation only permits peat land cultivation in peat land with peat depth less than 3 m, and those with thicker than 3 m has to be classified as conserved peat land areas.

Population growth in Indonesia at rate of 1.6% yearly has caused tremendous pressure on the use of important natural resources including peat lands since the early year nineties. Farmer, private sector and even government started to manage peat lands as a means of developing forestry plantation and agriculture cultivation in line with economic development program. Establishing food estate in peat land, in particular during the Pandemic Covid-19 era, is further directed by the government in order to strengthen national food security.

Carrying chemical, physical, and biological properties in nature and depicted as a closed ecosystem, the peat swamp forest-lands are inherently steady and resilient bodies which are temporarily distorted by natural driving forces like hot dry season and drenched wet season. Nevertheless, the effects of disturbances along with intensive peat swamp forest management on the soil's physical, chemical, and biological properties and long term sustainability inquiries are relatively recent. In addition, forest and land fire including peat land fire has become burning problems and turning out to be a national and global issue lately. Some other main potential threats in relation to peat swamp forest land cultivation are erosion by water, loss of nutrients, subsidence, and irreversible peat dryness.

Strategic policies to hold the ongoing problems of peat land degradation has been evaluated and perceived as top priority. The policy maker has launched several Government Regulations in a way to control the peat land use conservatively. This is true especially when the peat land cultivation in both forestry and agriculture sector are proceeding without putting into account the crucial conservation measure. The spirit of these Government Regulations is designed to strictly conserve the peat land use in wide range of production sector.

In line with an attempt to implement good governance as regard sustainable peat land management in Indonesia, availability of topography map and peat depth map is pre requisite in the establishment of peat land cultivation for both forestry and agriculture sector. This is to say that semi detail or detail topography as well as peat depth map should be constructed prior to properly design hydrological zone as such that water management technology can secure the sustainable cultivation during growing season every year. Currently, constructing the topography and peat depth map is still costly. Examination of relationship between two random variable namely elevation (X) and peat depth (Y) in a given peat landscape based on intensive survey and possibility to apply the relationship in the adjacent peat landscape is very scanty or even none in the country. If this method is statistically proven robust, then the assessment of peat depth and peat land elevation or topography map will become comparatively cheap. This field research, therefore, was designed to evaluate regression analysis between elevation and peat depth based on intensive field survey using grid lines on 115 thousand hectares of production forest landscape including 1,500 pairing data of elevation and peat depth. The regression line then was applied in the adjacent Mendawak protection forest covering area of 20 thousand hectares and then was evaluated employing ground check measurement, to see ifthe regression method is applicable to estimate peat depth based on elevation data in the future.

## MATERIALS AND METHODS

This research was carried out in Mendawak protection forest and industrial forest concession holder area namely PT. Wana Subur Lestari and PT. Mayangkara Tanaman Industri. Administratively this area is located in Kubu Raya District, Sanggau District and Ketapang District, West Kalimantan Province. Geographically this study area is laid in 00° 23'30.76" – 00° 36'35.67" south latitude and 109° 34'54.70" – 109° 49'45.46" east longitude and with altitude ranging from 0 up to 13.5 m above sea level.

The soil type dominated at the study area covering 63.7% area of deep peat, 8.5% area of Mendawai (*shallow peat*), 2.9% area of Kahayan (*riverine plains*), 23.7% area of Honja (*hillocky acid igneous*) and 1.2% area of Pakalunai (*Podsolic*).

In the landscape scale, the study area is situated as shown in Figure 1. Mendawak protection forest is denoted as peat dome in Peat Hydrological Unit of Kapuas River and Durian River; and Peat Hydrological Unit of Kapuas River and Jenuh River. In the northern part, this protection forest is in the adjacent area of huge oil palm plantation concession, meanwhile in the southern part it is in the adjacent area of industrial forest plantation namely PT. Wana Subur Lestari and PT Mayangkara Tanaman Industri. Mendawak protection forest is peatland forest covering an area of approximately 20,000 hectares, and in the meantime PT.

Wana Subur Lestari together with PT. Mayangkara Tanaman Industri covering an area of approximately 115,000 hectares with *Acacia crassicarpa* as a main tree grownfor business purposes.

Topographic survey was executed from October until November 2017 involving 40 well trained technical workers inthe Mendawak protection forest. The topography survey grid line was constructed about 110 km long, and purposiveelevation points and peat depth were recorded.

Figure 1. Map of study area, Mendawak protection forest, West Kalimantan, Indonesia

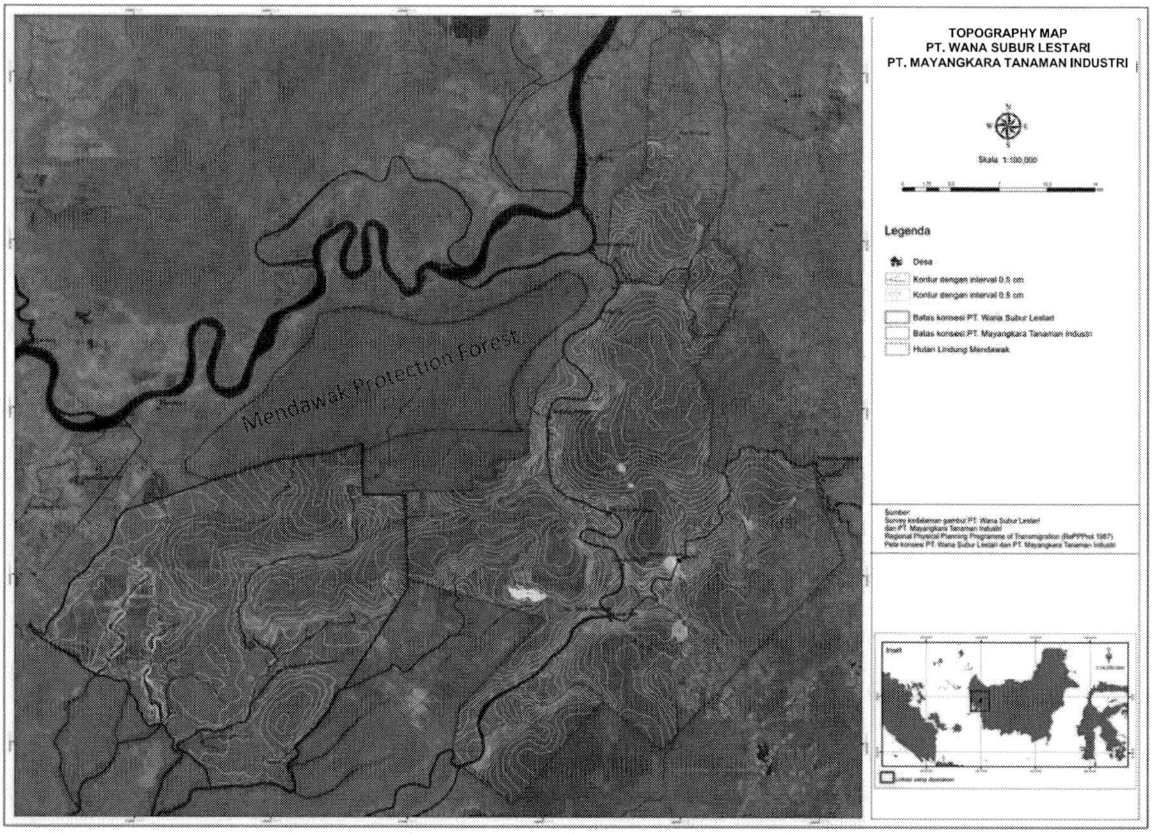


## RESULTS

Based on data collected (points in survey grid line of about 110 km long and elevation data above sea level) topographic map with reasonable precision scale was then constructed and later would be used as a basic working map in the research of hydrological behavior of peat land forest landscape in Mendawak protection forest.

Intensive soil survey covering elevation and peat depth parameter conducted in PT. Wana Subur Lestari and PT. Mayangkara Tanaman Industri was summarized based on 1,500 sampling points and the relationship between peat depth parameter and point elevation parameter was evaluated by employing regression analysis (Kleinbaum *et al.* 2014), and later would be used to estimate the peat depth in Mendawak protection forest. The regression equation isexpressed mathematically as $Y=0.9235X-0.6619$ with $R^2=0.82733$, in which Y is peat depth and X is elevation.

Topography information and contour appearance of the peat land surface is prerequisite to understand the hydrological behavior of a given peat land forest. In this regard, observation on the topography condition is then expressed in the form of topography map and is presented in Figure 2.

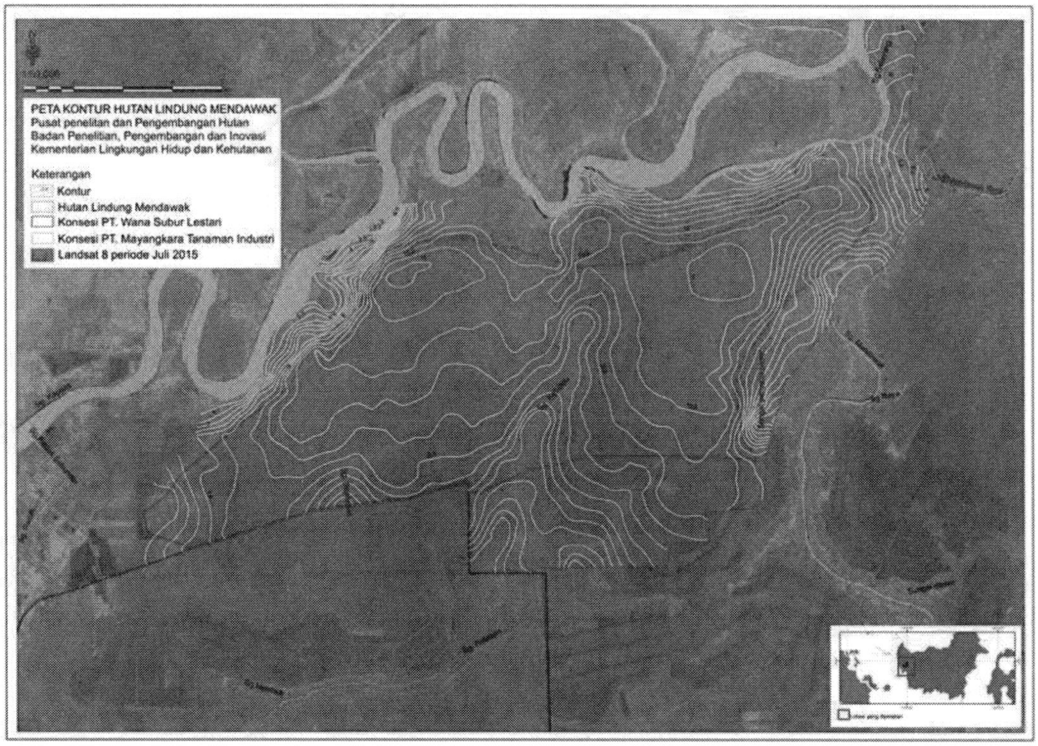


Figure 2. Topography map of Mendawak protection forest

The regression equation Y=0.9235X–0.6619 was then operated to estimate the peat depth in the landscape of Mendawak protection forest. As a result, peat depth distribution over the study area was constructed and shown in Figure 3.

## DISCUSSION

Topography map should enable us to trace direction of water flow from upper stream to lower stream or downstreamin the peat land forest landscape. Further, this map is a basic working map in developing water management means.

Topographically Mendawak protection forest is situated in the elevation ranging from 4.5 m up to 13.5 m above sea level. It is apparent that there are three existing of peat dome in the northern, east and west of the landscape (dark green color). Maximum conservation measure has to be implemented in the peat dome and the surrounding area since these peat domes ecologically play substantial as a gigantic water reservoir for the whole natural landscape. Peat dome will hold very huge amount of water during rainy season and will release some amount of water during dry season in the form of water flowing in the catchment area, from upper stream to downstream. Fail in conservingthis fragile peat mass will end up with disaster as fire risk is elevated while soil productivity may be tremendously dropped. In general, the peat land slope ranges from 3 to 7 %, and then classified as wavy topography, however, somewhat dense contour lines in the northern part of the landscape indicates that this area is steeper as compared to the other areas, and hence can undergo significant soil erosion process. In general, the higher peat land surface in the landscape, the deeper peat land is occurred. Classification of peat depth or peat thickness is then established andit produce 5 classes namely peat depth < 3 m, 3 – 5 m, 5 – 7 m, 7 – 9 m, and > 9 m.

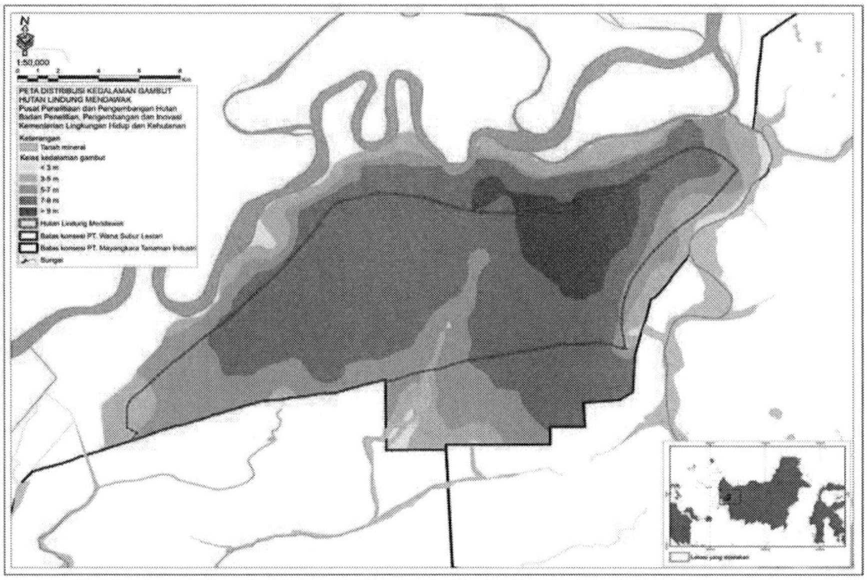


Figure 3. Map of peat land depth distribution in Mendawak protection forest

## CONCLUSION

Mathematically the relationship between peat depth and elevation is expressed as Y=0.9235X–0.6619 with $R^2$=0.82733, in which Y (m) is peat depth and X is elevation (m above sea level). The correlation (r) value 0.91 indicates that there is strong and positive association between the two variables and statistically proven as a robust tool after ground truthing analysis through 31 checking points in which only 2 points on the ground did not fit the equation. However, this occurrence is understandable due to the fact that the two points on the surface are approaching river bank.

## ACKNOWLEDGEMENTS

The authors would like to extend the gratitude to Forest Research and Development Center Bogor and the Forest Concession Holder for all facility provided and make this research possible.

## REFERENCES

Anshari GZ, Afifudin, Nuriman M, Gusmayanti E, Arianie L, Susana R, Nusantara RW, Sugardjito J, Rafiastanto A. (2010) Drainage and Land Use Impacts on Changes in Selected Peat Properties and Peat Degradation in West Kalimantan Province, Indonesia. *Biogeosciences*; 7: 3403–19

BBSDLP. (2013) *Atlas arahan pengelolaan lahan gambut terdegradasi, skala 1 : 250.000*. Badan Penelitian dan Pengembangan Pertanian, Kementerian Pertanian. Jakarta: Bumi Mekar Hijau Indonesia

Kleinbaum DG, Kupper LL, Nizam A, Rosenberg ES. (2014) *Applied Regression Analysis and Other Multivariable Methods*. Boston: Cengage Learning USA

Osaki M, Tsuji N. (2016) *Tropical Peatland Ecosystems*. Tokyo: Springer Japan

Sanchez PA. (2019) *Properties and Management of Soils In Tropics Second Edition*. New York: Cambridge University Press USA

ID 62612

# PEAT AND PEATLAND SERVICES IN GEOLOGICAL SURVEY OF FINLAND

*Tuija Vähäkuopus, Heikki Sutinen

Geological Survey of Finland, Finland

*tuija.vahakuopus@gtk.fi*

Geological Survey of Finland (GTK) is widely recognized in assessment, research and responsible use of Earth resources, including peat and peatlands. Overall ca. 2.3 million hectares of mires and peatlands, almost half of the Finnish geological peatland area, has been investigated since 1970's. The database is a unique world record peat database: it consists totally ~1.8 M peat study points, comprising totally over 18 100 peatlands. The peat database has detailed information on peat thickness and peat quality, mire types, vegetation and bottom soil material among others. Over 18 800 sample points provides information on chemical and physical properties of peat across Finland. In addition to carrying out peat and peatlands resource investigations, studies of environmental effects of peat production, remote sensing methods, carbon stock of Finnish peatlands and GIS based methods of natural state classifications provide solutions for responsible peatland use, carbon stock estimations and utilization of peat in novel applications.

GTK provides research services for peat and peatland resources management and one of the most up-to-date is the Ground Penetrating Radar (GPR)-drone service. Usually the GPR is used in peat production areas to investigate peat resources and the subsoil quality. During peat production, the remaining peat resources can be estimated with updated survey data. The update can be done with modern photogrammetry-based imaging technology installed on a drone, which enables to form an accurate 3D point cloud, an orthophotomosaic and a digital elevation model of the terrain. GPR surveying and updating GPR interpretations with a drone is a very effective combination for energy-peat research among various applications. In addition to being accurate and cost-efficient, the two parts of this method support each other's seasonal nature.

ID 62654

# NDVI AS A PROXY TO ESTIMATE THE CO2 FLUXES IN PEATLANDS: EXAMPLE OF ALKALINE FEN

*Raimo Pajula[1], Anna-Helena Purre[2]

[1] Institute of Ecology, Tallinn University, Tallinn, Estonia

[2] School of Natural Sciences and Health, Tallinn University, Tallinn, Estonia

*raimo.pajula@tlu.ee*

**SUMMARY**

Normalized Difference Vegetation Index (NDVI) is a widely used multispectral vegetation index to estimate vegetation health and its abundance. NDVI is based on the ratio of the red light and near infrared light that is reflected from the surface. Plants absorb red and reflect infrared light, so NDVI reflects density of vegetation. Weaimed at relating $CO_2$ fluxes and NDVI measured by drone to investigate possibilities to upscale $CO_2$ fluxes to larger areas cost-efficiently, and provide more information about relations between $CO_2$ exchange and NDVI in peatlands.

In Estonia, the project “Life Peat Restore” aims at restoring natural water regime and carbon sequestration on large Läänemaa Suursoo mire, where among other measurements, greenhouse gas measurements and vegetation monitoring by drones are conducted. Automated drone SenseFly eBee applied with Parrot Sequoia multispectralsensor was used for NDVI mapping of the study area. Manual transparent chambers and infra-red gas analyser Li-6400 (Li-Cor) were used for $CO_2$ measurements. $CO_2$ measurements and drone monitoring were done simultaneously in May, July, August, September and October in 2019 on the monitoring transect located on near-natural alkaline fen.

NDVI maps reflect pattern of mire plant communities - higher NDVI values reflect higher cover of vegetation, especially sedges, and low values sparser vascular vegetation and higher brown moss cover. Both NDVI and $CO_2$ balance had seasonal pattern during the growing season with highest index values and highest carbon binding in mid-summer. Generally, no significant relation was found between NDVI and measured net ecosystem exchange(NEE) and photosynthesis at ambient light conditions. Whereas during sunny and warm monitoring days the NDVI explained over 30% of the variation in NEE. NDVI was generally positively correlated with ecosystem respiration ($r = 0.44$, $p < 0.01$). NDVI is useful indicator for analysing mires vegetation parameters but relations with $CO_2$ fluxes needs further investigations in different peatland ecosystems and conditions.

***Keywords**: alkaline fen, boreal peatland, NDVI, carbon dioxide, NEE*

## INTRODUCTION

Active mires as well drained peatlands play important role in global carbon budget and greenhouse gas (GHG) balances. Mires restoration is important task for climate changes mitigation. In light of this, GHG measurements continue to be an important activity in the study of natural, degraded and restored mires. Because GHG measurements are labor intensive and costly, there is a need to find indirect methods to estimate GHG balance of mires. One possibility is to use remote sensing methods based on the spectral properties of the vegetation. If smaller spatial resolution is sufficient, satellite monitoring is most suitable for remote monitoring of mires. But if greater spatial resolution is needed then drone monitoring is the most appropriate method. The GHG balance cannot be estimated directly by remote sensing, but can be done through vegetation, provided that vegetation reflects that.

Normalized Difference Vegetation Index (NDVI) is widely used multispectral vegetation index to estimate vegetation abundance and its health. NDVI is based on the ratio of the red light and near infrared light that is reflected from the surface. The standard formula for NDVI is "NDVI = (NIR – Red) / (NIR + Red)". Plants absorbred and reflect infrared light, so NDVI reflects density of vegetation i.e. cover of photosynthetically active parts of plants. In temperate and boreal zone, NDVI of most vegetation types has a clear seasonal pattern with highest values in summer and lower values in spring and autumn (Kross et al. 2013). This pattern reflects the growth of the leaves of grasses, sedges and deciduous plants in spring and summer and the die back in autumn. Carbon sequestration by plants have also similar seasonal pattern (Kross et al. 2014; Mikhaylov et al. 2019; Lees et al. 2021). Therefore, we expect that the NDVI index could reflect carbon sequestration by the plant cover.

Aim of the study is to relate $CO_2$ fluxes measured on field and NDVI measured by drone to investigate possibilitiesto upscale $CO_2$ fluxes to larger areas cost-efficiently, and through it provide more information about relations between $CO_2$ exchange and NDVI in peatlands.

## MATERIALS AND METHODS

The international project "Life Peat Restore" aims at restoring natural water regime and carbon sequestration of peatlands in Estonia, Latvia, Lithuania, Poland and Germany. The project site in Estonia (Suursoo-Leidisoo project site) is eastern part of large Läänemaa Suursoo mire complex (Figure 1, 2). A comprehensive monitoring network has been established on the project area, where among other measurements, GHG measurements and vegetation monitoring by drones and on field are conducted. Monitoring transect containing 4 monitoring points and locatedon near-natural alkaline fen (Figure 2) in eastern part of the project area were selected for the current study. The alkaline fen is near treeless and dominated by *Schoenus ferrugineus*, *Carex davalliana*, *Myrica gale*, *Menyanthestrifoliata*, *Phragmites australis* and *Carex* species. Moss layer is sparse and composed of brown mosses. Shrub and grass layer cover is in the range of 25 % to 45 % and moss layer 10-40%. Water level is in vegetation period
-20 to +10 cm from the mire surface. There is no clear drainage gradient along the monitoring transect but grass layer and moss layer cover and dominant species vary between monitoring points. The site historical backgroundand species composition is described in detail by Truus et al. (2021) in this Congress abstract book.

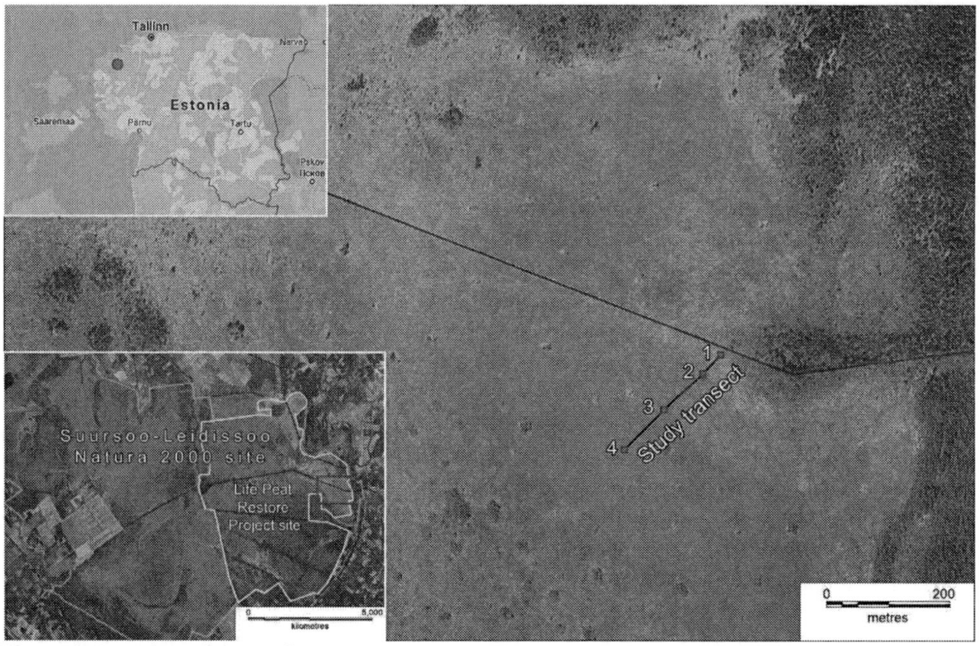


Figure 1. Location of the study area.

Automated survey drone SenseFly eBee with Parrot Sequoia multispectral sensor was used for NDVI mapping of the study area. Flights height was *ca* 65 m above ground and spatial resolution of NDVI output raster was ca 5 cm. Flights were performed around mid-day in same or close day with GHG measurements. In 2018 flights were doneon August 13 and October 16, in 2019 on May 22, July 11, August 13, September 19 and October 30, and in 2020on May 25, September 23 and November 6. Pix4Dmapper software was used for the data processing and NDVI maps creation. For the mire surface and vegetation located inside each 60 × 60 cm GHG measurement collars average NDVI values calculated for the area of ca 50 × 50 cm (0.25 $m^2$).

Manual transparent chambers (60 × 60 × 30 cm) and infra-red gas analyzer Li-6400 (Li-Cor) were used for $CO_2$ flux measurements. $CO_2$ measurements and drone monitoring were done simultaneously in all of the flight days on the monitoring transect located on near-natural alkaline fen. Here only $CO_2$ flux data calculated according to linear change in $CO_2$ concentrations inside the chambers and corrected according to the chamber volume and temperature is presented, and not the $CO_2$ fluxes reconstructed for the whole study period.

Figure 2. Drone photo of the study transect in alkaline fen. Study transect is indicated by red arrow.

## RESULTS

NDVI values of the studied plots ranged 0.18 to 0.75 depending on date and study point. The index values are characterized by seasonal pattern with higher values in summer and lower values in spring and autumn (Figure 3).NDVI maps reflect well pattern of mire plant communities - higher NDVI values indicate higher cover of vegetation, especially sedges, and low values sparser vascular vegetation and higher brown moss cover. There wasslight decrease in the NDVI values along the monitoring gradient moving from the ditch to the more pristine partof the fen. This trend can be explained by differences in cover of the grass layer which was denser near the ditch,while in autumn, NDVI values were higher on the most distant point from the ditch, where brown mosses had significant cover.

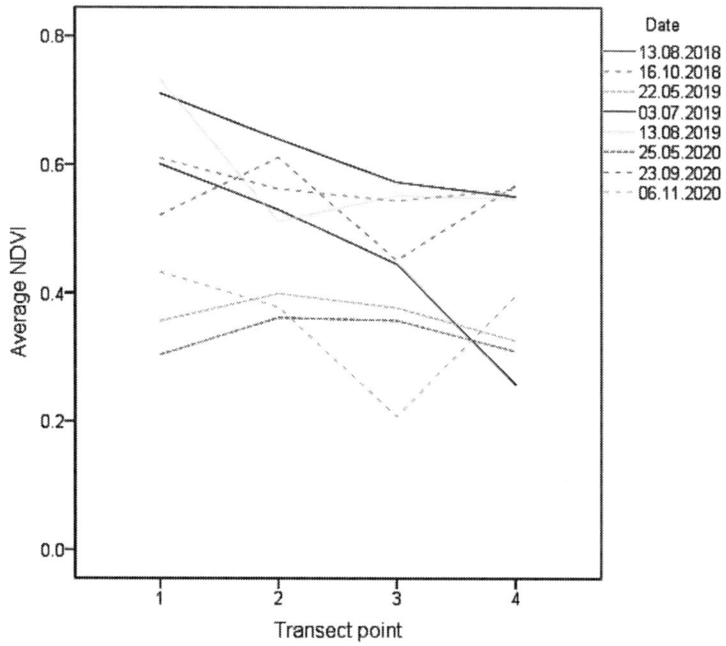


Figure 3. NDVI on study transect points on different measurement days. Solid lines indicate summer measurementdays (June-August), dotted lines indicate spring measurements (May), and dashed lines indicate autumn measurements (September-November).

Generally, plots with higher NDVI had also somewhat higher net ecosystem exchange (NEE) i.e. these plots weresmaller $CO_2$ sinks during the measurements in ambient light conditions (Table 1). Stronger positive correlation was also between NDVI and ecosystem respiration ($R_{eco}$), whereas no correlation was found between NDVI and measured gross photosynthesis ($P_g$). On the three sunny and warm monitoring days (August 13s (2018 ($R^2 = 0.38$)and 2019 ($R^2 = 0.31$)), May 22 (2019; $R^2 = 0.31$)) when photosynthetically active radiation (PAR) was close to or exceeded 1 000 μmol $m^{-2}$ $s^{-1}$, NDVI explained over 30% of variation of the NEE. In the August, 2018 the relationship was positive (higher NDVI led to somewhat higher NEE i.e. smaller CO2 uptake), whereas in both those dates in 2019, the relationship was negative, so higher NDVI led to higher CO2 uptake (Figure 4).

Table 1. Spearman correlations between NDVI, measured $CO_2$ flux variables (NEE and $P_g$measured under ambient light conditions), and environmental variables.

| | NDVI | Transect point | Water level | NEE | $P_g$ | $R_{eco}$ |
|---|---|---|---|---|---|---|
| Transect point | -0,280** | | | | | |
| Water level | -0,331** | -0,096 | | | | |
| NEE | 0,225* | 0,132* | -0,298** | | | |
| $P_g$ | -0,075 | 0,181** | 0,089 | 0,901** | | |
| $R_{eco}$ | 0,424** | -0,085 | -0,546** | -0,226** | -0,585** | |
| $LAI_{vasc}$ | 0,636** | -0,059 | 0,006 | 0,282** | 0,191 | 0,360** |

*- correlation coefficient is statistically significant on level $p < 0.05$; **- correlation coefficient is statisticallysignificant on level $p < 0.01$.

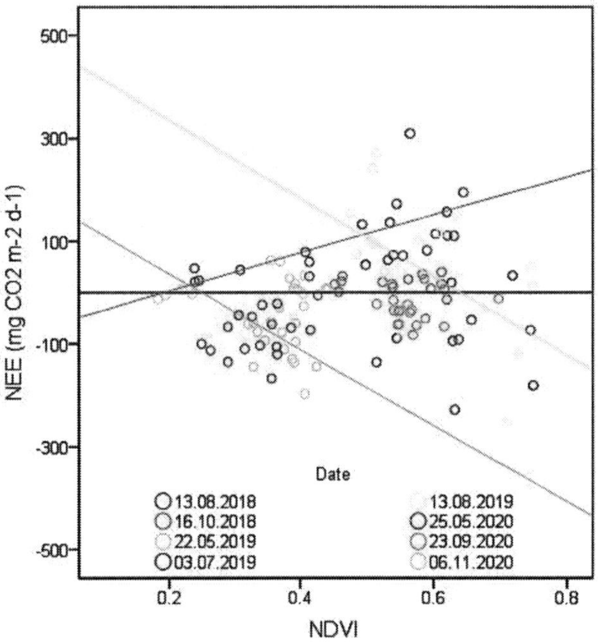


Figure 4. Relation between net ecosystem exchange (NEE) and NDVI. Solid lines indicate the linear regressionon dates when NDVI explained at least 30 % variation in NEE.

## DISCUSSION

Our results support that NDVI has similar seasonal variations as $CO_2$ exchange as reported before (Lund et al. 2012; Kross et al. 2013). NDVI in this study in mildly disturbed fen ecosystem had weaker relationship with NEEthan in restored milled peatlands in our previous study (Purre et al. 2019). Also the general direction of the relationship was reversed, when in restored milled peatlands higher NDVI values resulted in higher growing season$CO_2$ uptake and Pg (whereas no significant relationship was with Reco; Purre et al. 2019), in this study higher NDVI values were related with higher Reco and lower $CO_2$ uptake during the measurements, whereas Pg was not related significantly with NDVI. These differences between the studies are probably caused by different measurement periods. In Purre et al. (2019) NDVI was measured once after the $CO_2$ measurement period and was related with reconstructed growing season $CO_2$ fluxes while here NDVI was measured each time with $CO_2$ flux measurementsand was also related with those. Differences also probably resulted from different peatland ecosystems, as restoredmilled peatlands have more patchy vegetation development with larger areas under bare peat (and therefore high heterotrophic respiration) or open water, and had higher cover of bryophytes, whereas fen ecosystem in this studyhad complete vegetation cover and herb layer dominated over sparser bryophyte layer. In initially bare peat areassuch as restored milled peatlands development of any kind of vegetation is essential for carbon sequestration (Purreet al. 2019), whereas in undisturbed site, the carbon binding through Pg and also release by Reco depend on environmental conditions of the site and plant species and functional types. Site-type (nutrient availability and vegetation) specific differences in relations with $CO_2$ cycling and NDVI have been also reported before by Kross et al. (2013) in different undisturbed peatland ecosystems. Higher vascular cover characterized by higher summerNDVI and Reco values seems to reflect also higher soil respiration which can be caused by plants with aerenhyma.

Our measurements showed that NDVI and NEE related strongly during the more optimal light conditions (i.e. sunnier days), whereas no correlations were found during the clouded conditions. These results support the expectations of Boelman et al. (2003) who proposed that correlations between NDVI and $CO_2$ fluxes during the non-optimal light conditions are weaker than those correlations in optimal light conditions. Differences in NEE response to the differences in NDVI between the sunnier days in 2018 and 2019 could be result of differences in the study year conditions. In early-summer of 2018, heavy drought impacted the development of vegetation, whichcould have resulted in differences of $CO_2$ sequestration later that year. As reported by Lund et al. (2012) drought during the beginning of growing season impacts the $CO_2$ sequestration in greater extent than drought periods laterin the summer. In sedge tundra, Boelman et al. (2003) measured $CO_2$ fluxes and NDVI during the peak of the growing season and at saturating PAR levels, finding that all three $CO_2$ flux components (Reco, Pg and NEE) had higher values (in case of Reco larger $CO_2$ emissions, in case of Pg and NEE larger $CO_2$ binding) on measurement plots with higher NDVI.

## CONCLUSION

Our results show that NDVI can be used for describing temporal development, but also spatial distribution, of photosynthesizing biomass. Still, the relations between the $CO_2$ flux components and NDVI in fen-ecosystem differed from previous results in e.g. restored milled peatlands. Previously NDVI has been generally related with differences with gross photosynthesis, whereas in this study NDVI was more closely connected with ecosystem respiration. This topic should be further developed by relating measured NDVI with reconstructed growing season $CO_2$ fluxes in the future, and testing ways for using remotely measured vegetation indices for modelling and upscaling of $CO_2$ fluxes.

## ACKNOWLEDGEMENTS

The study was conducted under LIFE Climate mitigation programme (2016-2021) project "Reduction of $CO_2$ emissions by restoring degraded peatlands in Northern European Lowland" (Life Peat Restore; LIFE15 CCM/DE/000138)

## REFERENCES

- Boelman N.T, Stieglitz M, Rueth H.M, Sommerkorn M, Griffin K.L, Shaver G.R, Gamon J.A. (2003) Response of NDVI, biomass, and ecosystem gas exchange to long-term warming and fertilization in wet sedge tundra, *Oecologia*; 135: 414–421
- Kross A.S.E, Roulet N.T, Moore T.R, Lafleur P.M, Humphreys E.R, Seaquist J.W, Flanagan L.B, Aurela M. (2014) Phenology and its role in carbon dioxide exchange processes in northern peatlands, *Journal of GeophysicalResearch: Biogeosciences*; 119: 1370–1384
- Kross A.S.E, Seaquist J.W, Roulet N.T, Fernandes R, Sonnentag O. (2013) Estimating carbon dioxide exchange rates at contrasting northern peatlands using MODIS satellite data, *Remote Sensing of Environment*; 137: 234–243
- Lees K.J, Khomik M, Quaife T, Clark J.M, Hill T, Klein D, Ritson J, Artz R.R.E. (2021) Assessing the reliabilityof peatland GPP measurements by remote sensing: From plot to landscape scale, *Science of the Total Environment;*766: 142613
- Lund M, Christensen T.R, Lindroth A, Schubert P. (2012) Effects of drought conditions on the carbon dioxide dynamics in a temperate peatland, *Environmental Research Letters*; 7: 045704
- Mikhaylov O.A, Zagirova S.V, Miglovets M.N. (2019) Seasonal and inter-annual variability of carbon dioxide exchange at a boreal peatland in north-east European Russia, *Mires and Peat*; 24: 34
- Purre A-H, Pajula R, Ilomets M. (2019) Carbon dioxide sink function in restored milled peatlands – The significance of weather and vegetation, *Geoderma*; 346: 30–42
- Truus L, Ilomets M, Pajula R, Sepp K. (2021) Long-term response of vegetation on the water level drop-down ona large calcareous fen (NW Estonia). IPC2021

## ID 61880

# REQUIREMENTS FOR RE-SAMPLING SOIL ORGANIC CARBON STOCKS OF MANAGED PEAT AND OTHER ORGANIC SOILS

*Mareille Wittnebel, Ullrich Dettmann, Arndt Piayda, Bärbel Tiemeyer

Thünen Institute, Germany

*mareille.wittnebel@thuenen.de*

Stocks of soil organic carbon (SOC) as well as further properties of agricultural soils were determined by the first German Agricultural Soil Inventory to improve the national greenhouse gas inventory. Samples were taken at 3104 cropland and grassland sites from a soil pit and eight surrounding soil cores.

Peat and other organic soils made up 5.4 % of all sampling sites and were found to be very diverse in terms of profile development, anthropogenic impact as well as in SOC stocks. Therefore, a new classification scheme was implemented to characterise not only 'typical' fen and bog peat soils, but also shallow peat-derived, covered and deep-ploughed

Stocks of soil organic carbon (SOC) as well as further properties of agricultural soils were determined by the first German Agricultural Soil Inventory to improve the national greenhouse gas inventory. Samples were taken at 3104 cropland and grassland sites from a soil pit and eight surrounding soil cores.

Peat and other organic soils made up 5.4 % of all sampling sites and were found to be very diverse in terms of profile development, anthropogenic impact as well as in SOC stocks. Therefore, a new classification scheme was implemented to characterise not only 'typical' fen and bog peat soils, but also shallow peat-derived, covered and deep-ploughed organic soils. In the upper metre, highest SOC stocks were found in peat soils with a shallow mineral cover and in fen peat soils (655 ± 230 t SOC ha-1 and 638 ± 127 t SOC ha-1, respectively), while, as expected, lowest stocks occurred in peat-derived and deep-ploughed organic soils (333 ± 184 t SOC ha-1 and 331 ± 113 t SOC ha-1, respectively). Overall, total SOC stocks depended strongly on peat depth.

# ID 62462

# LABORATORY EXPERIMENTAL FRAMEWORK TO STUDY PEAT FIRE

Xinyan Huang[1], *Shaorun Lin[1], Guillermo Rein[2]

[1] The Hong Kong Polytechnic University, Hong Kong

[2] Imperial College London, UK

*xy.huang@polyu.edu.hk*

Smoldering fires in peatlands are the largest combustion and fire phenomena on Earth. These mega-scale peat fires can irreversibly destroy ecosystems, produce regional haze episodes, and contribute to 15% of annual global carbon emissions. Many key aspects of peat fire remain poorly understood. On the other hand, wildland fires can influence the climate by changing the atmospheric CO2 and may even regulate the O2 of the atmosphere over millions of years. This work reviews the framework of using small-scale Laboratory experiments to study the mega-scale peat fire. Studying the dynamics of peat fire not only guides us to reduce the natural fire hazards, but also brings scientific tools to geophysics, ecology, and biology to understand the fire threshold of Earth and the evolution of atmosphere and biota on Earth history.

ID 62601

# PEATLANDS OF THE NILE BASIN: DISTRIBUTION, CARBON STOCKS AND CO2 EMISSIONS REDUCTION AND AVOIDANCE POTENTIAL

Samer Elshehawi, Alexandra Barthelmes, *Jan Peters, Felix Beer, Hans Joosten

Greifswald University, Department for Botany and Landscape Ecology, Germany

*jan.peters@succow-stiftung.de*

The total area of peatlands and other organic soils in the total Nile Basin amounts to about 30,445 km2. This area contains a peat carbon stock of 4.2 - 10 GtC (Gt= 1x109 tonnes; C= organic carbon), i.e. 5 to 10 % of the total known tropical peatland carbon stock. The main three regional clusters of the Nile Basin peatlands are: the Nile Equatorial Lakes (NEL), the Sudd wetlands (South Sudan) and the Blue Nile sub-system (Ethiopia).

The NEL region is estimated to contain 12,534 km2 of peatlands and to contribute 58.5 % of the total carbon stock of the Nile Basin. The peatland area estimated within the Sudd wetlands (organic soils) is about ~15,780 km2, which would represent about 50 % of the total peatland area and 37 % of the total carbon stock of the entire Nile Basin. The Blue Nile sub-system (Ethiopia) holds an estimated peatland extent of about 1,110 km2, concentrated in the south-western Ethiopian Highland and around Lake Tana.

Most peatlands are characterized by papyrus (Cyperus papyrus L.), but Raphia palms, other sedges (e.g. Cyperus latifolia) and tall grasses are also common, and partly grow in patches together with papyrus. Peat deposits are mostly found in dendritic shaped valleys, but also in the floodplains of lakes and on river banks, e.g. of the Kagera and Albert rivers. Afro Alpine peatlands occur in various parts of the Nile Basin at high altitudes (>4000 m).

Land use change has recently accelerated especially in the NEL subset and an increasing area of peatlands is being directly and indirectly impacted. We estimate that a minimum $CO_2$ avoidance potential of about 0.2 GtC over the period 2015 - 2050 can be achieved, if no new drainage will be implemented and all drained peatlands are rewetted in 2025.

ID 72103

# TOWARDS ASSESSMENT OF BOG BREATHING WITH SENTINEL-1 DIFFERENTIAL INSAR

Tauri Tampuu[1], Jaan Praks[2], Francesco De Zan[3], Marko Kohv[1], Ain Kull[1]

[1] Institute of Ecology and Earth Sciences, University Of Tartu, Estonia
[2] School of Electrical Engineering, Aalto University, Finland
[3] Remote Sensing Technology Institute, German Aerospace Center (DLR), Germany

*tauri.tampuu@ut.ee*

## SUMMARY

Northern peatlands are significant pools of stored carbon. Though, their ability to be net sequester or emitter of greenhouse gases (GHG) is delicate, depending on water regime. Therefore, understanding of seasonal dynamics of peatland surface and volume, often referred as bog breathing, is the key to improve spatial models of material flows and gas exchange with atmosphere. Differential Synthetic Aperture Radar (SAR) interferometry (DInSAR) is a proven tool to quantify vertical surface movements in sub-mm level. The objective of this study is to examine the applicability of Sentinel-1 short temporal baseline (6 to 12 days) DInSAR to characterize seasonal dynamics of peatland surface. Our study site is located in Umbusi bog in central Estonia and covers an area of the open raised bog where we have in situ peat surface levelling measurements. Also, a stable point on the mineral soil is available as a reference for DInSAR. Our results show a correlation and scale similarity between SAR and the ground truth while the elevation changes are small (in magnitude much below the Sentinel-1 height of ambiguity 2.77 cm). Larger surfaces changes are not reliably detected, probably because of the phase unwrapping errors. We demonstrate how the InSAR coherence reflects the bog surface dynamics and reveals differences for different areas within a bog. We recorded considerable phase changes over a cutaway area which could not be caused by the surface fluctuation but have to be related to the humidity. Our results indicate that the C-band InSAR could be employed in peatlands if the phase ambiguity is solved.

***Keywords**: bog drainage, change detection, peatland, SAR interferometry, surface motion*

## INTRODUCTION

Northern peatlands are significant pools of stored carbon (Leifeld and Menichetti 2018). Though, their ability to be net sequester or emitter of greenhouse gases (GHG) is delicate, depending on water regime (Gorham 1991). Therefore, understanding of seasonal dynamics of peatland surface and volume, often referred as bog breathing, is the key to improve spatial models of material flows and gas exchange with atmosphere (Fritz 2006, Dise 2009). Differential Synthetic Aperture Radar (SAR) interferometry (DInSAR) is a proven method to quantify vertical surface movements in sub-mm level. The previous InSAR studies of Northern peatlands concerning the long term (Alshammari et al., 2018; Fiaschi et al., 2019) or seasonal elevation changes (Alshammari el al., 2020; Tampuu et al., 2020) have lacked the ground truth for comparison and reported considerably smaller motion than what is known of the bog breathing (Fritz 2006). The objective of this study is to examine the applicability of Sentinel-1 short temporal baseline (6 to 12 days) DInSAR to measure seasonal dynamics of peatland surface. To do so, we compare the DInSAR relative deformation values to in situ levelling data and use the shortest temporal baseline available to reduce a chance for mistakes from phase unwrapping.

## MATERIALS AND METHODS

We processed 13 Sentinel-1 A and B ascending orbit (relative orbit number 160) VV-polarization Interferometric Wide swath mode (IW) Single Look Complex (SLC) images from over Umbusi bog in Estonia where we have continuous in situ levelling measurements from the summer till the snowfall in 2016, resulting in twelve 12-day or 6-day interferograms, according to SAR data availability. Coherence estimation window used is 19 range and 5 azimuth, for Modified Goldstein phase filtering window of 15 both in range and azimuth. All calculation carried out in SAR coordinates. No atmospheric correction was applied as the distance is in 1 km only. For comparison to the in situ levelling data, the SAR line of sight (LOS) measurements were projected to the vertical direction ($u_{LOS}$) using the local incidence angle of the SAR sensor (38.43°), assuming no horizontal motion. The in situ ground levelling measurements are from the sites 4 and 6 on the open bog. Measuring devices are attached to T-shaped metal bar penetrating the peat layer and anchored in the underling stable mineral ground. The site 4, lying 50 m from the main drainage ditch separating the natural bog and a cutaway bog, experiences a significant influence of drainage. The site 6, 200 m from the drain, is in an intact condition. At the site 6, one device recorded elevation changes in the hollow and the other on the hummock micro relief. The sites are connected by a transect stretching over the cutaway to a cluster of sheds on the stable mineral soil (Fig. 1) which is used to reference the LOS measurements.

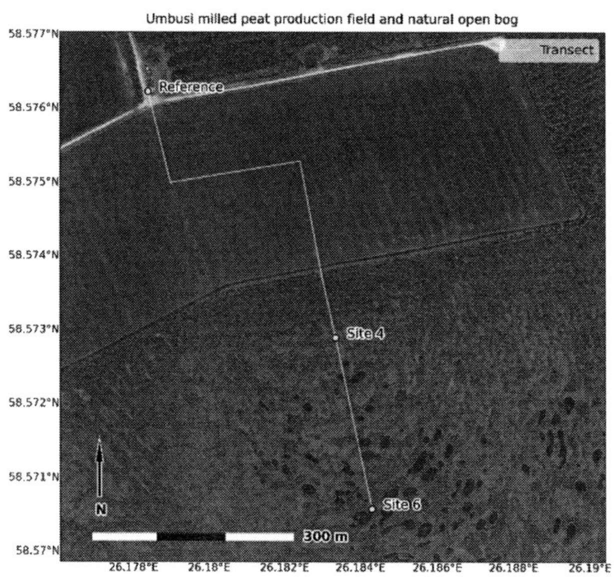


**Figure 1**. Umbusi natural and cutaway bog with a transect from a stable point across milled peat production field to levelling sites 4 and 6 in open bog.

## RESULTS

All the LOS measurements fitted in a single phase cycle which eliminates unwrapping errors, and display considerable differences between the open bog, cutaway bog and the reference site as illustrated in Fig. 2. It is distinctive how during the summer months the InSAR detects a false deformation in the cutaway bog which is characterised by the compacted peat, effective drainage and relative stability (Fig. 2g,f). This spurious deformation is not present in autumn images as illustrated with Fig. 2h when the peat is saturated with water and thus we speculate that it might be related with sub-pixel level spatial inhomogeneity of milled peat extraction field containing drainage ditches and peat with variable soil water content. In all 12 interferograms, the site 4 and the reference site maintained minimal coherence ($\gamma > 0.4$). The point 6 maintained sufficient coherence only in 7 image pairs (illustrated in Fig. 2a–c). The coherence is lost at the site 6 during the summer months when the surface fluctuations are determined by the rainfall and point 6 hollow and 6 hummock fluctuate at different magnitudes. In the autumn when the peat is saturated and the surface fluctuations are caused by changes in water level more uniformly, the magnitude of change at the site 6 hollow and 6 hummock harmonise (Fig. 3). Fig. 2a,b depicts such decorrelation in the natural area whereas Fig. 2.c displays a highly correlated scenes. From the in situ levelling measurements (which are changes of absolute height of the peat layer) we calculated the relative peat surface elevation change (relative surface deformation) between the dates corresponding to an interferometric pair. Shown in Fig.3, the relative surface deformation between 6–12 days lies in most cases in the range of Sentinel-1 LOS height of ambiguity (~2.77 cm), 3.54 cm when projected to $u_{LOS}$ at our site. Nevertheless, it means a natural bog occasionally exhibits elevation changes bigger than the height of ambiguity of Sentinel-1 sensor just in a 12-day period. Our results show the levelling data and SAR measurements display considerable correlation and scale similarity in the autumn when the deformation is small and incorrect phase unwrapping cannot happen. With deformations close to or more than the height of ambiguity, the correlation does not occur. The correlation between the ground levelling and DInSAR $u_{LOS}$ measurements are shown in Fig. 4. Adding or subtracting a phase cycle may improve the values of DInSAR results of the magnitude close to the height of ambiguity as shown. The best agreement was recorded at the site 6 between the elevation changes of the hummock and InSAR $u_{LOS}$.

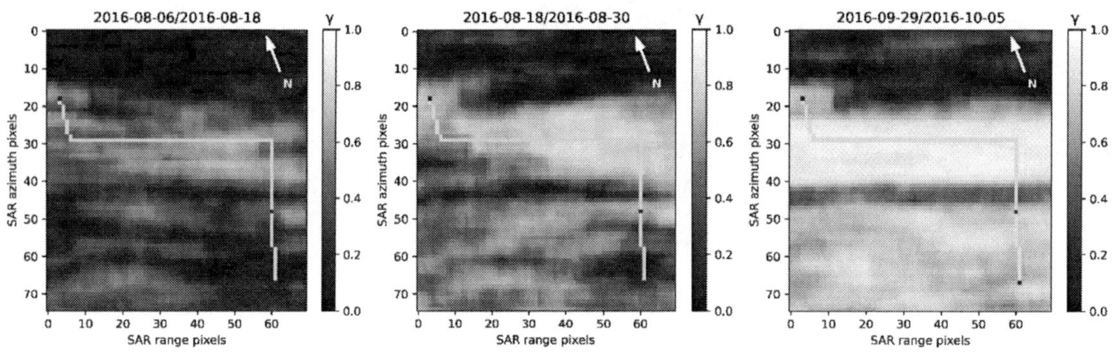


a) b) c)

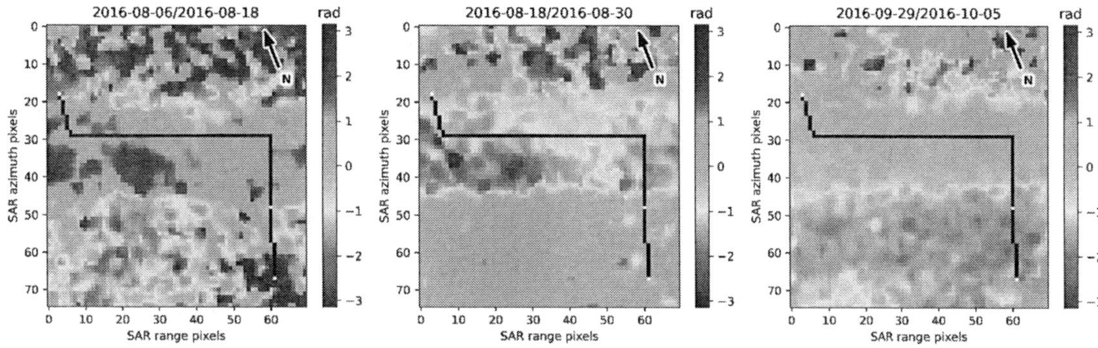


d) e) f)

a)

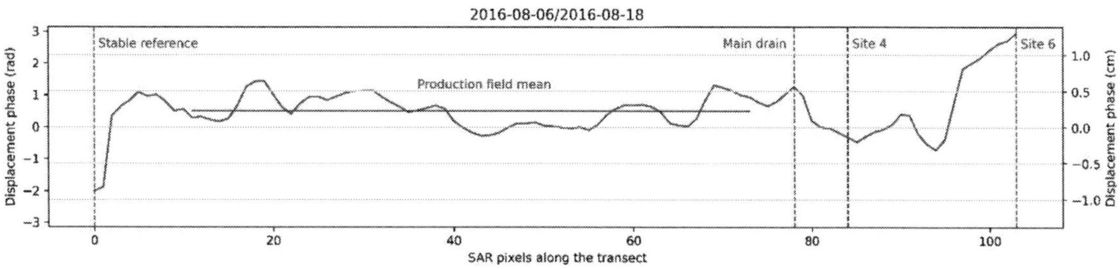


b)

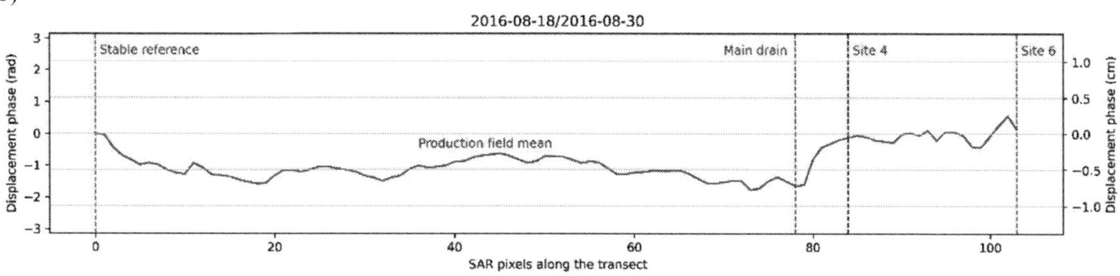


c)

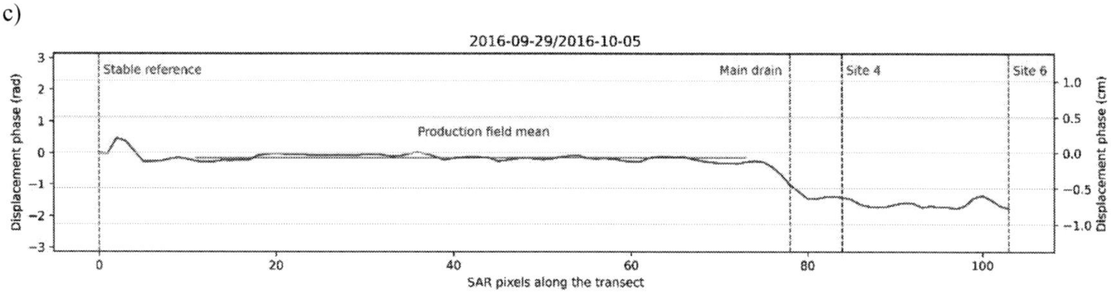


**Figure 2**. InSAR coherence (a–c), phase (d–f) images and LOS measurements along the transect (g–h) in radar coordinates for three interferograms. Transect is the same as shown on Fig. 1.

a)

b)

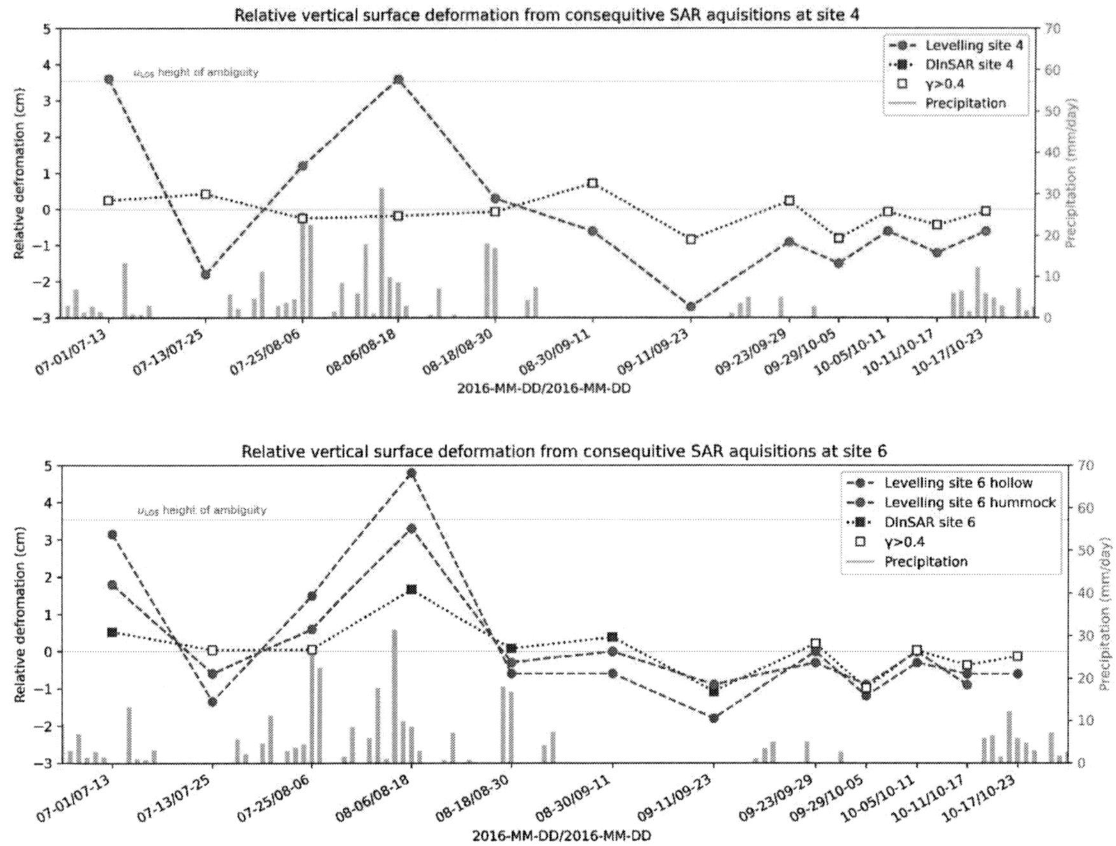


**Figure 3**. Relative deformation between the indicated two dates for the ground levelling and DInSAR line of sight deformation projected to vertical dimension ($u_{LOS}$). The precipitation data correspond to the first of the two dates.

a) b) c)

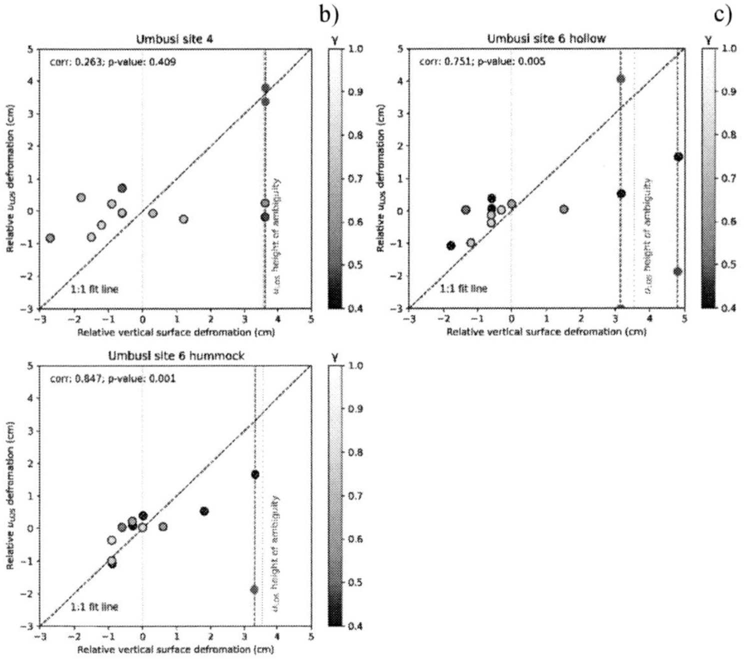


**Figure 4**. Correlation of the ground levelling and DInSAR line of sight deformation projected to vertical dimension ($u_{LOS}$). Dark points mark InSAR coherence less than 0.4. Red points mark an addition/subtraction of a phase cycle is when the in situ value is close to the Sentinel-1 height of ambiguity.

## DISCUSSION

The periodic coherence loss at the site 6 means that in the natural bog where the micro-relief varies, the water level induced subsidence or uplift affects micro-relief elements at a different magnitude causing decorrelation. In the drainage affected areas such as the site 4, the micro-relief is more uniform, peat bulk density higher and the scene retains coherence. These results confirm our previous work showing InSAR coherence conveys the information of the peat moisture (Tampuu et al., 2020). The high coherence of the cutaway bog has to be attributed to the unusually rainy second half of the summer which prevented the peat milling, known to cause decorrelation (Tampuu et al., 2021). We speculate the false LOS change present in the summer scenes over the cutaway is of the electrical origin attributed to changes in peat surface humidity (De Zan et al. 2013) or possibly related to the rain induced water table changes in the drains. In the autumn, when low temperatures and impeded evaporation cause the peat to saturate, no such vertical movement is recorded. The levelling data show a natural bog can exhibit elevation changes larger than the height of ambiguity just in 12 days. Our work shows DInSAR can accurately detect small surface changes but not large ones. The reason could be losing part of the change signal via spatial averaging during coherence estimation and phase filtering or unwrapping errors. Thus, the decorrelation and larger surface changes complicate the use of InSAR in natural bog areas while drainage affected and homogeneous due to higher peat bulk density vertically less changing peatlands are more suitable. Our work doubts an assumption often underlying peatland InSAR studies that the surface fluctuations are of the sufficient magnitude to be detected by C-band. Consequently, we agree with Alshammari et al. (2018) and Fiaschi et al. (2019) who have suggested the further research is needed to assess the accuracy of InSAR time series approaches in peatlands.

## CONCLUSION

Our results show a correlation and scale similarity between InSAR detected elevation change and the ground truth while the change remains smaller than the height of ambiguity (2.77 cm). Bigger changes pose a challenge. However, we have mapped the current limits of Sentinel-1 C-band InSAR and identified problems to tackle while pursuing reliable peatland applications. Natural bog areas with variable micro-relief and larger surface fluctuations are challenging for InSAR due to decorrelation and phase ambiguities. Drainage affected more homogeneous and vertically less changing peatlands could be reliably measured already with current methods. Also, we showed InSAR coherence to reflects the bog surface heterogeneity. We recorded considerable phase changes over a cutaway area not caused by surface fluctuation which we attribute to the changes in the peat surface moisture

## ACKNOWLEDGEMENTS

This study is part of PhD research supported by the European Union from the European Regional Development Fund. Also, this research was supported by the Estonian Environmental Investment Centre grants SLOOM12006 and SLOOM14103, Estonian State Forest Management Centre grant LLTOM17250, Estonian Research Council research grant PRG352, and national scholarship program Kristjan Jaak, which is funded and managed by Archimedes Foundation in collaboration with the Ministry of Education and Research (Estonia).

## REFERENCES


1. Alshammari, L., Large, D. J., Boyd, D. S., Sowter, A., Anderson, R., Andersen, R., Marsh, S. (2018) Long-term peatland condition assessment via surface motion monitoring using the ISBAS DInSAR technique over the Flow Country, Scotland. *Remote Sensing*, *10*(7), 1103.
2. Alshammari, L., Boyd, D.S., Sowter, A., Marshall, C., Andersen, R., Gilbert, P., Marsh, S. and Large, D.J. (2020) Use of surface motion characteristics determined by InSAR to assess peatland condition. *Journal of Geophysical Research: Biogeosciences*, *125*(1): e2018JG004953.
3. De Zan, F., Parizzi, A., Prats-Iraola, P., López-Dekker, P. (2013) A SAR interferometric model for soil moisture. *IEEE Transactions on Geoscience and Remote Sensing*, *52*(1), 418-425.
4. Dise, N. B. (2009) Peatland response to global change. *Science*, *326*(5954), 810-811.
5. Fiaschi, S., Holohan, E. P., Sheehy, M., Floris, M. (2019) PS-InSAR analysis of Sentinel-1 data for detecting ground motion in temperate oceanic climate zones: a case study in the Republic of Ireland. *Remote Sensing*, *11*(3), 348.
6. Fritz, C. (2006) Surface Oscillation in Peatlands: How Variable and Important Is It? Master's Thesis, The University of Waikato, Hamilton, New Zealand.
7. Gorham, E. (1991) Northern peatlands: role in the carbon cycle and probable responses to climatic warming. *Ecological Applications*, *1*(2), 182-195.
8. Leifeld, J., Menichetti, L. (2018) The underappreciated potential of peatlands in global climate change mitigation strategies. *Nature Communications*, 9, 1071.
9. Tampuu, T., Praks, J., Kull, A., Uiboupin, R., Tamm, T., Voormansik, K. (2021) Detecting peat extraction related activity with multi-temporal Sentinel-1 InSAR coherence time series. *International Journal of Applied Earth Observation and Geoinformation*, *98*, 102309.
10. Tampuu, T., Praks, J., Uiboupin, R., Kull, A. (2020) Long term interferometric temporal coherence and DInSAR phase in Northern Peatlands. *Remote Sensing*, *12*(10), 1566.

ID 72803

# UAS IMAGING APPLICATIONS TO MONITOR RESTORED PEATLANDS

*Lauri Ikkala[1], Hannu Marttila[1], Anna-Kaisa Ronkanen[1], Jari Ilmonen[2], Eerika Tapio[2], Sakari Rehell[2], Timo Kumpula[3], Björn Klöve[1]

[1] University of Oulu, Finland
[2] Metsähallitus Parks and Wildlife Finland, Finland
[3] University of Eastern Finland

*lauri.ikkala@oulu.fi*

Peatlands are globally threatened by the increasing exploitation. Majority of peatlands in Finland are severely degraded by land use and drainage activities. Peatland restoration is an effective way to maintain biodiversity, return natural function of peatlands in catchment hydrology and reduce negative impacts of drainage.

Hydrology LIFE project safeguards peatlands, small water bodies and important bird lakes in 103 Natura 2000 areas in Finland during 2017-2023. These environments have undergone major changes in recent decades. The restoration measures recover the degraded habitats towards the original state vital for many valuable species and peatlands ability to store water and nutrients. Restoration activates peat forming processes, and thus reduces long-term greenhouse gas (GHG) emissions in and returns peatlands to act as carbon sinks.

Restored sites are monitored to determine whether the restoration has succeeded and to gather the experiences to further develop restoration methods. The traditional restoration monitoring demands intensive field work with high labor costs and special ecological expertise. Evaluation is mainly based on visual assessment at present. In addition, monitoring typically cannot cover the entire restored site.

There is strong need to develop unbiased indicators and new cost-effective methods producing spatially representative high-quality information on restoration success. We will study new technical possibilities for evaluation of peatland restoration success with unmanned aerial systems (UAS).

The latest image processing techniques and their use in mapping and analyzing peatland areas are to be studied. UAS provides prospects not only to ease the demanding restoration field work but also to transform the discrete nature of conventional single data points into a spatial continuum over the whole restored peatland.

ID 72856

# SPECIES COMPOSITION AND ROOT MORPHOLOGY AT THE TOP OF A PEAT DOME CONSTITUTING TROPICAL PEATLANDS IN WEST KALIMANTAN, INDONESIA

*Natalia Desi Piana Soeka[1], Tsuyoshi Kato[2]

[1]PT. Mayangkara Tanaman Industri/ PT. Wana Subur Lestari, Indonesia
[2]President of PT. Mayangkara Tanaman Industri/ PT. Wana Subur Lestari, Indonesia

*ecisoeka@wanasl.com*

Tropical peatlands have been severely degraded by industrial forest and oil palm plantations, as well as inappropriate peatland management, resulting in the release of carbon into the atmosphere and raising concerns about their impact on global climate change. On the other hand, the biodiversity of tropical peatlands has not been discussed much. Therefore, in this study, the unique vegetation around the tops of a peat dome, which characterizes tropical peatland, is presented.

Two permanent plots of 1 ha in size were established, and DBH and height were measured for all individuals with DBH≥5 cm that appeared in the plots, and tree species and root morphology were recorded. The depth of the peat was almost the same in the two plots, which was 7.9 m. However, plot 1 had an undulation of about one meter, while plot 2 was almost flat. As a result, a total of 72 tree species from 36 families were recorded, including 68 species from 33 families in plot 1 and 51 species from 30 families in plot 2. The dominant species in each were, plot 1 was dominated by *Diospyros maingayi*, *Syzygium longiflorum*, and *Shorea pachyphylla*. Meanwhile, plot 2 was dominated by *Diospyros maingayi*, *Pentace triptera*, and *Syzygium havilandi*i. There was no significant difference in root morphology between an aerial root and mound root where the average were 52.2% and 47.8% respectively.

**Keywords:** tree species, root morphology, peat dome, tropical peatland

ID 62574

# MONITORING CONCEPT FOR PEAT SWAMP FORESTS AND PEATLAND WITHAIRBORNE AND SPACEBORNE SENSORS APPLIED IN THE EX-MEGA RICE PROJECT AREA, KALIMANTAN

Viktor Boehm[1] and Stefan Mühlbauer[2]

[1]Kalteng Consultants, Muenchen, Germany

[2]Aras Software, Gröbenzell, Germany

*viktorboehm@t-online.de*

## SUMMARY

Tropical peat swamp forests are of high significance for climate and environmental studies due to their large carbonstock and rich biodiversity. Therefore, the key importance of peat swamp forests for ecological processes, their resilience to forest degradation, fires, logging and plantations. The need for a comprehensive forest and peatland monitoring is necessary in which LiDAR (Light Detection and Ranging), UAV (unmanned aerial vehicle, e.g. drone) and Satellite information may play an important role.

Changes of forests were detected on basis of multi-temporal LiDAR survey and field measurements on peatland in these areas of the Ex-Mega Rice Project (Ex-MRP) in Central Kalimantan.

LiDAR surveys in 2007 and 2011, the available Satellite images and measurements with drones in 2018 showed many changes in the peatland. Additional yearly peat firers during the dry season in 2009, 2015 and 2019 releasedconsiderable CO2 into the atmosphere and make the local population suffer from smoke and made them ill (ref. 1-5, 7).

A combined use of satellite and airborne high-resolution systems improves the monitoring of peat swamp forests and peatlands especially regarding the interpretation of detected changes with space borne systems. For instance,small-footprint LiDAR has high potential in biomass estimation. Consequently, the biomass estimated with LiDAR can be combined with the change detection from satellite imagery in order to assess the emitted carbon from land cover and land use. Further, UAVs with high-resolution cameras can support the interpretation of facilitating a better distinction between anthropogenic and natural changes. The satellite based change detection may support the focusing of the UAV (drone) flights on areas with high interest like severely changed forests.

***Keyword:*** *Tropical Peatland, Ex-Mega Rice Project, LiDAR and Drone Survey, Sentinel-Satellite-Images, Mawas*

## INTRODUCTION

Tropical lowland ombrogenous peat lands in Southeast Asia are known for their rich biodiversity and huge amounts of stored carbon. In recent years, large natural areas of this endangered ecosystem have been converted into oil palm and acacia plantations. Hence, forest remnants are currently threatened by extensive drainage, logging, hunting and fire. Undisturbed peat swamp forest display specific surface patterns linked to hydrology with respects on biodiversity, vegetation structure and carbon dynamics. The key importance of peat swamp domes to ecological processes, their fragility and impact to global climate and carbon budgets highlights the need for a comprehensive forest inventory of peat swamp resources across Indonesia. Remote sensing data can provide useful information in such environments for hydrological and wild fire modeling, retrieval of biophysical parameters and the management of natural resources. Bi-temporal airborne Light Detection and Ranging (LiDAR) data acquired in August 2007 and August 2011 were used to characterize the peat swamp forest and dome located in Central Kalimantan, Indonesia.

In this study our main objectives were: a) to characterize ground-measured and LiDAR-derived biophysical properties for both forest physiognomy and peat dome slope variations; and b) to present an approach to carbon change assessment based on multi-temporal LiDAR acquisition as the experimental data covers forest regrowth and peat subsidence.

## MATERIAL AND METHODS

LIDAR surveys from 2011 on a BK117 helicopter with a Riegl Laser Scanner and a Hasselblad high resolution optical camera over the Ex-Mega Rice Project (Ex-MRP) in Block C and at CIMTROP Camp were applied (Fig. 1, 2, 3). Peat domes could be analyzed very easy with the data of the Digital Terrain Model (DTM) data. The subsidence of peat domes could be analysed/proofed by comparing their height profile using LiDAR derived terrain elevations from two time stamps, one acquired in 2007 and another one from 2011. The DGPS referencepoint on the airport Palangkaraya (Fig. 14) were used.

Data acquisitions of Sentinel from 20.2.2019 in the EX-MRP and Mawas study area were used for this study of Central Kalimantan (Fig. 4, 7, 10) together with Landsat 8 Images from 3.8.2015 before the strong fires from 2015 (Fig. 8, 9). One additional Sentinel image from 22.10.2020 with many clouds was acquired after the strong fires in autumn 2019 (Fig. 16). This image shows again the impact of the fires in 2019.

In April 2018 drone measurements were performed in the Ex-MRP Block C around the Kalampangan channel between Kahayan and Sebangau river. The acquired images gave good information of local land cover situation along the Kalimantan highway Palangkaraya to Banjarmasin (Fig. 11, 12 and 13).

## RESULTS AND DISCUSSION

The high-resolution Sentinel data from 20.2.2019 shows considerable changes compared to 2011 in the Ex-MRP as well as in the Sebangau National Park coursed by logging, fires and clearing for plantations or for agriculture land use. (Fig. 4).

The forest/non-forest map had an accuracy of 80%. The visual representation of the classification result in Mawas(ref. 5, 8, 9, 10) indicated large forest areas in the north and the west of the study area. Drainage canals and forestsbetween the canals dominated the center and south of the study area. The Kapuas river in the west of the study area was classified as non-forest. In total, 74% of our study area was covered with forest in July 2015. This changed by the fires in 2019 up to now.

Results showed that LiDAR is an interesting instrument to analyze peat profiles, biomass estimation andrelationship between peat dome slope, peat dome depth and tree canopy height (ref. 6). Information on such variables may be useful to assess the dependence of biophysical properties (e.g. tree height, stem diameter and above ground biomass) in distinct peatlands environments. Since peatlands act as a carbon sink, human interventions due to drainage practices for agriculture and selective logging practices of the peat swamp forest mayhave a stronger impact in the carbon release than relative flat areas that still has to be more investigated with LiDAR technology which we did in a survey conducted in August 2007 and 2011. In combination with Drone flights cheaper surveys are possible to get additional information in a time sequence.

The peat subsidence could be measured along the Kalampangan Channel at the boarder to the EX-MRP Block C with 11cm per year between 2007 and 2011.

## CONCLUSION

The optical Sentinel Satellite with 10m resolution give much information about logging, forest fires and land usechanges. Combined with LiDAR surveys and drone flights many new channels, plantation and agricultural activities can be monitored in the Ex-MRP area. To stop the recurring fires is a challenging task for the Kalimantanpeatland area.

## ACKNOWLEDGEMENTS

Kalteng Consultants thanks Dr. Marcel Silvius from Wetlands International (WI) for the contracts of LiDAR measurements in 2007 and data analysis in the frame of The Netherlands – Indonesian CKPP (Central KalimantanPeatland Project) of UNPAR in Palangkaraya.

LiDAR and airborne photographs were acquired by Kalteng Consultants. We would like to thank Prof. Dr. Tatsuo Sweda from the Ehime University, Japan, for the 2011 LiDAR dataset.

Photo data survey 2018 acquired by Drone at Kalampangan Channel in Block C and Sabangau area Central

Kalimantan, Indonesia, sponsored by Hokkaido University, Prof. Dr. Mitsuru Osaki, Sapporo, Japan.

Landsat data were provided from USGS and Sentinel data from Sentinel ESA homepage.

Fig. 1. LiDAR survey 2011 of peat swamp forest near river Sebangau, Kalimantan, Indonesia. (a) Kalampangan channel and (b) CIMTROP transect. The ortho-photo (right) shows the CIMTROP research base camp at the beginning of the LiDAR transect in the Sebangau National Park.

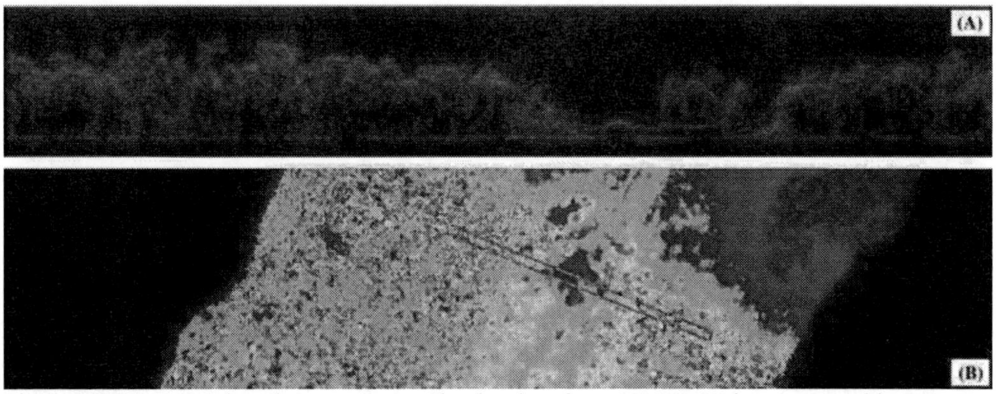

Fig. 2. LiDAR-DSM data shown as Laser Clouds taken from CIMTROP base camp with peat swamp forest, catchment and tree profile (above) (a). The width of the transect is approximately 500 m (below) (b). The tallest trees are approx. 40 m above the ground. The red color indicates tall trees, while blue and violet shows the ground,as shown in Fig. 1 at the beginning of the LiDAR transect.

Fig. 3. LiDAR-DTM data shown the area of Ex-MRP Block C near to the Kalimantan Highway bridge at theKalampangan Channel, 2011

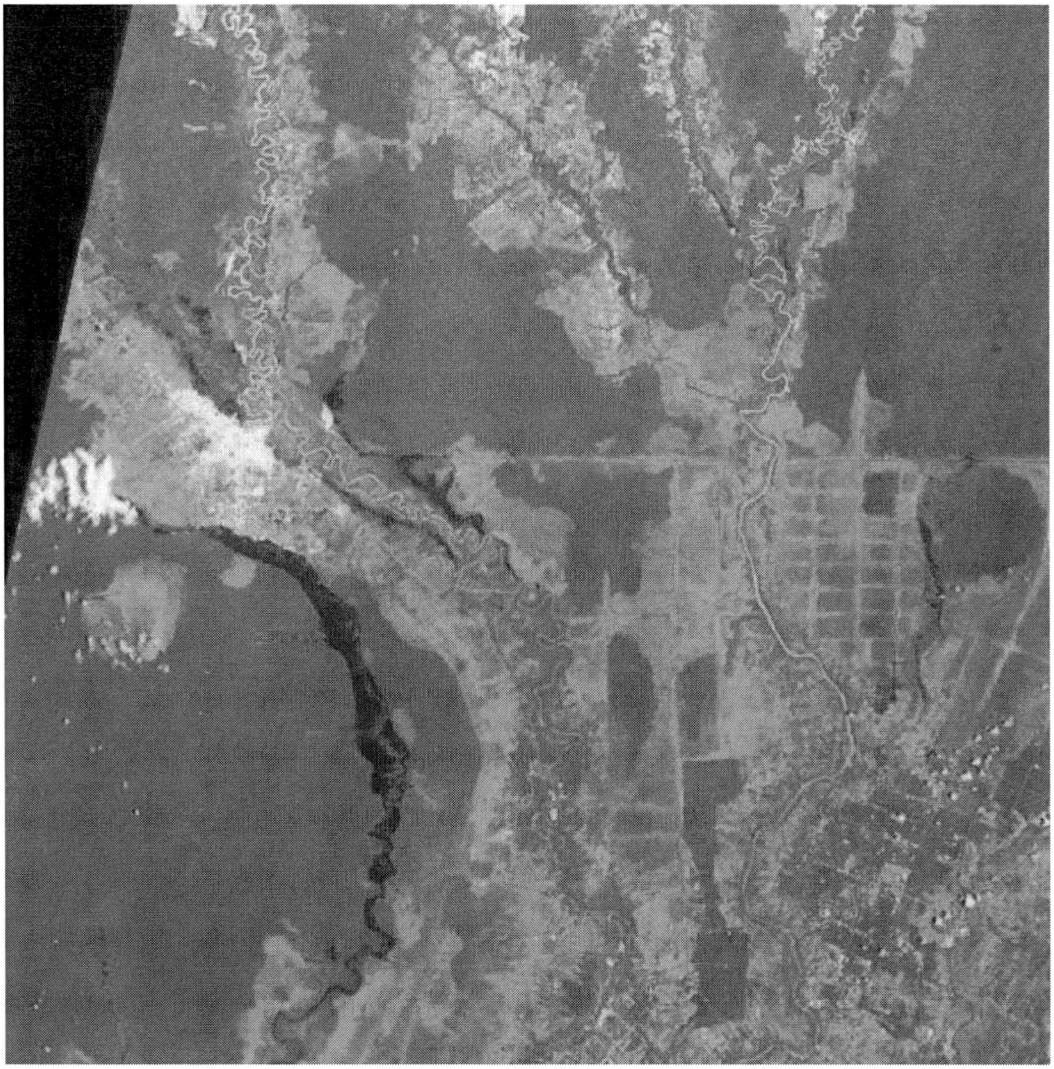

Fig. 4: Sentinel 20190220-Kalteng – Palangkaraya - Sebangau – Kahayan – Kapuas. Mawas and Ex-MRP. A lotof forests were destroyed by logging, fires, gold mining and new oil palm plantations. 10mx10m resolution

Fig. 5: Ex-MRP - Landsat 7 image from 14. October 2015 during strong fires with smoke at Sebangau NationalPark and Ex-MRP

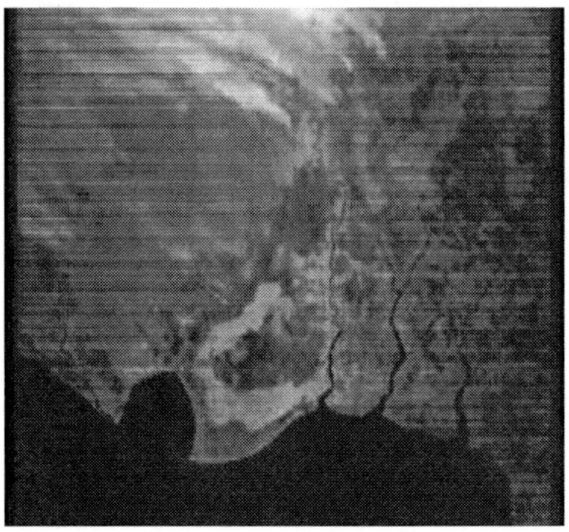

Fig. 6: Ex-MRP Block A+E - Landsat 8 image from 21.9.2016 - part Ex-MRP Block A+E + Mawas area

Alot of forests were destroyed by logging, strong fires during 2015 and new oil palm plantations

Fig. 7: Sentinel 20190220-Kalteng – Kapuas, Ex-MRP Block A+E and Mawas Area. Additional logging wereved in two and a half years later. The fires 2019 came in the dry season, August - October

Fig. 8: Ex-MRP – Block C - LC08-L1TP-118062-20150803-RGB-652 – EX-MRP-Block C between Sebangauand Kahayan River with Kalampangan Channel before the strong fires in 2015

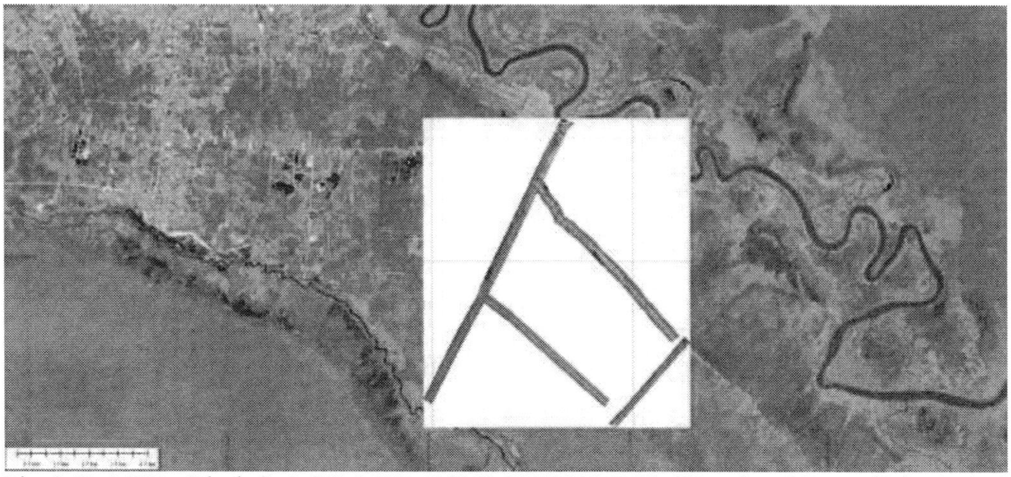

Fig. 9: Ex-MRP – Block C - LC08-L1TP-118062-20150803-RGB-652 – planed Drone-flights in April 2018

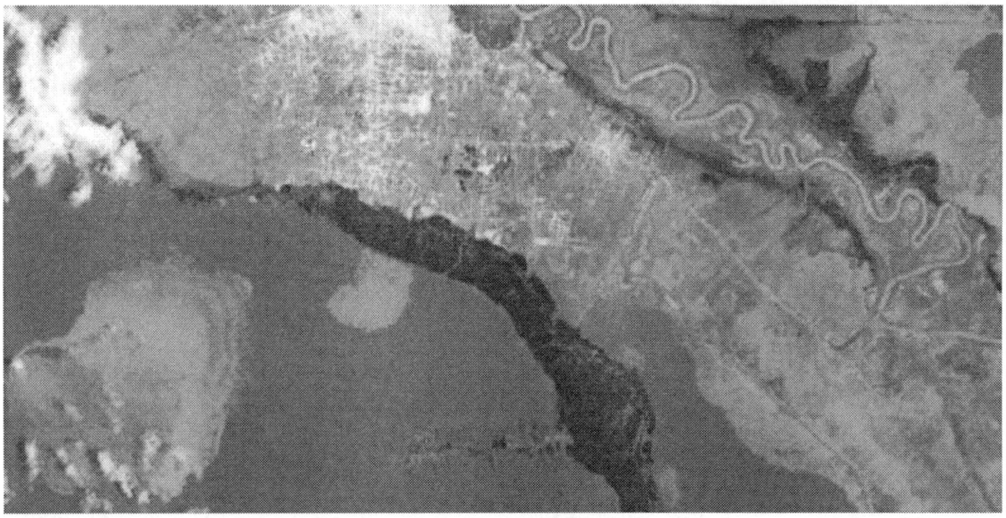

Fig. 10: Sentinel 20190220-Kalteng – Sebangau Area, Ex-MRP Block C and Kahayan areaA lot of fires disturbed forest in the Sebangau National Park and in Block C

Drone-flight preparation in April 2018 near the Kalimantan highway south ofPalangkaraya

Fig. 12: Ex-MRP – Block C Drone-flight in April 2018 along the Kalimantan highway south of Palangkaraya near to the Kalampangan channel

Fig. 13: Ex-MRP – Block C Drone-flight in April 2018 along the Kalimantan highway south of Palangkaraya in the direction of Tumbang Nusa

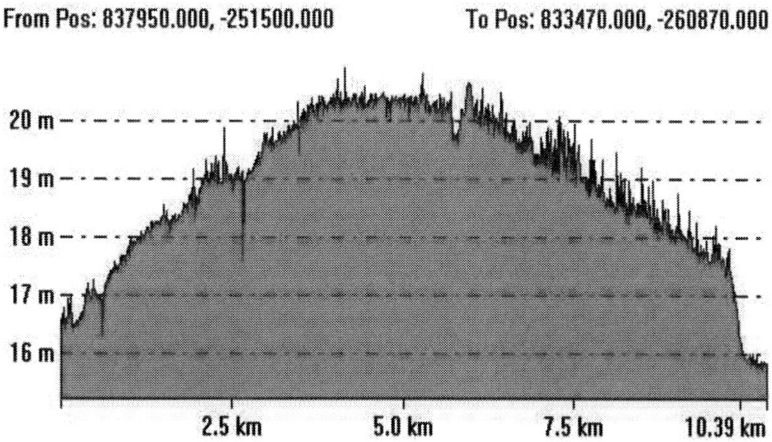


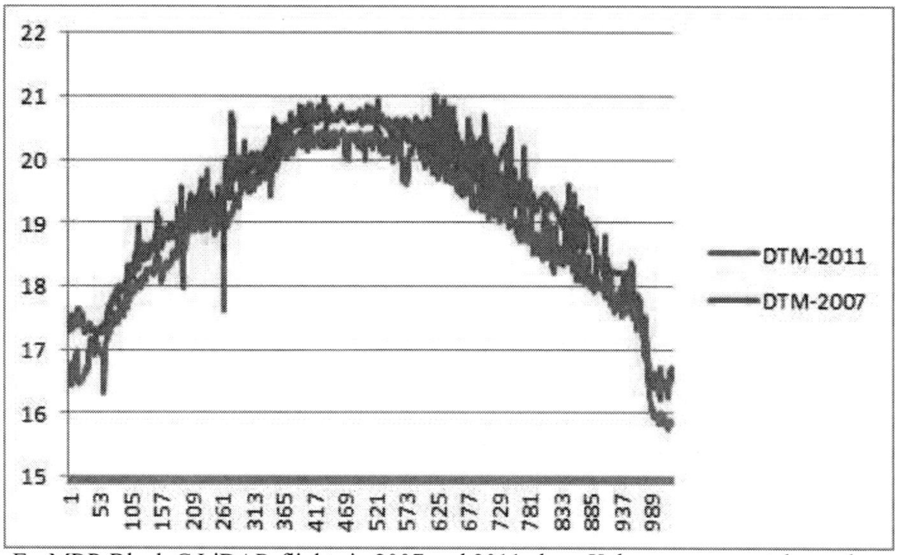


Fig. 14: Ex-MRP-Block C LiDAR-flights in 2007 and 2011 along Kalampangan peat dome channel, to measure
with the DTM-method the subsidence along the 10.4km long channel transect in 4 years with an average of 43cm +-25cm or 11cm per year peat subsidence with 1024 measures. The reference point was the DGPS installed at the airport Palangkaraya

Fig. 15: Kalimantan peatlands under fire. September 2015, courtesy by Björn Vaughn

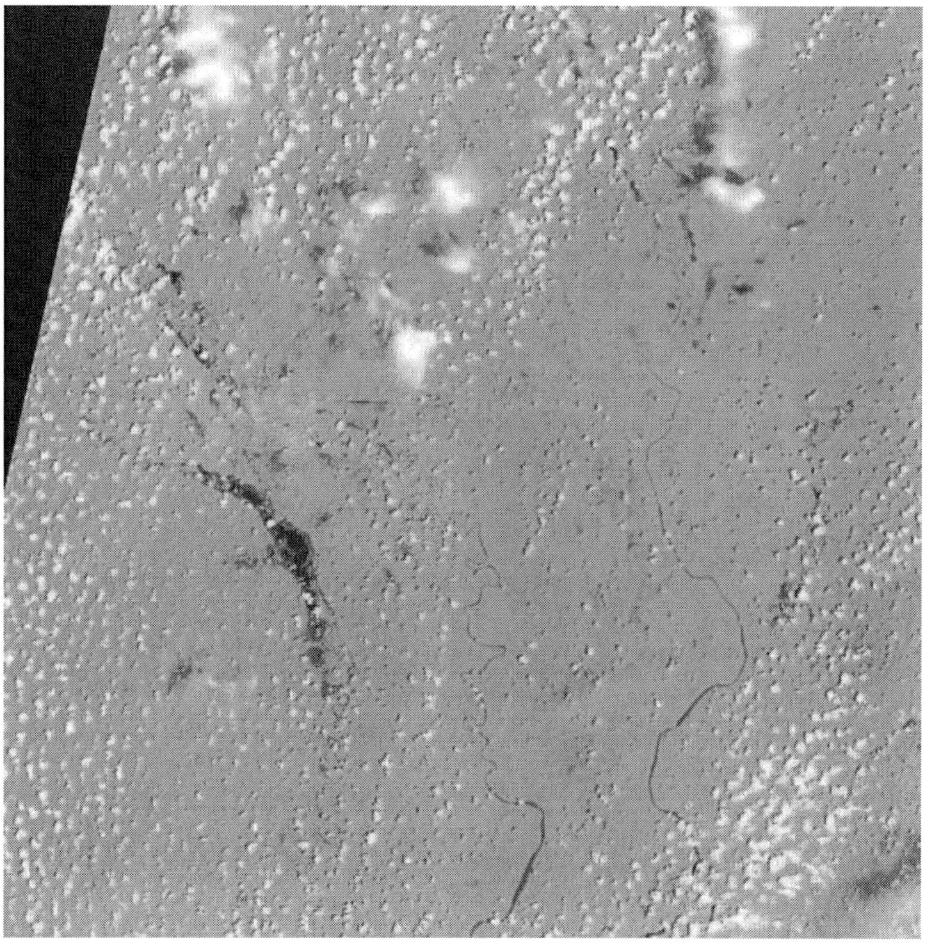

Fig. 16: Sentinel 20201022 with several clouds: Kalteng – Palangkaraya - Sebangau – Kahayan – Kapuas-Mawas and Ex-MRP, taken one year after the strong fires in 2019. Many burnt-scars are visible.

## REFERENCES


- Boehm, H.-D.V., Frank, J., 2008. Peat Dome Measurements in Tropical Peatlands of Central Kalimantan with a high-resolution Airborne Laser Scanner to achieve Digital Elevation Models. In:Proceedings of 13th International Peat Congress, 8-13 June 2008, Tullamore, Ireland, Section 5: Tropical Peatlands.
- Boehm, H.-D.V., Liesenberg, V., Frank, J., Limin, H.S., 2011, Characterizing Peat Swamp Forest Enviroments with Airborne LiDAR, Data in Central Kalimantan, Indonesia, proceedings SilviLaser2011, 16-20 Oct. , Tasmania, Hobart, AU
- Boehm, H.-D.V., Liesenberg, V., Sweda, T., Tsuzuki, H., 2012. Multi-Temporal Airborne LiDAR-Survey in 2007 and 2011 over tropical Peat Swamp Forest Environments in Central Kalimantan, Indonesia, Proceedings of 14$^{th}$ International Peat Congress, 3-8 June 2012, Stockholm Sweden
- Boehm, H.-D.V., Liesenberg, V., Limin, S., 2013. Multi-Temporal Airborne LiDAR-Survey and Field Measurements of Tropical Peat Swamp Forest to Monitor Changes. IEEE Journal of Selected Topics inApplied Earth Observations and Remote Sensing, VOL. 6, No. 3, June 2013, 1524-1530
- Boehm, H.-D.V., Schlund, M., Liesenberg, V., Kuntz, S., Biomass situation of Mawas region in Central Kalimantan between 2007 and 2015 using LIDAR- and TerraSar-X Data. 2016. In: Proceedings of 15th International Peat Congress, 15-19 August 2016, Kuching, Sarawak, Malaysia
- Kronseder, K., Ballhorn, U., Boehm, H.-D.V. and Siegert, F., Above ground biomass estimation acrossforest types at different degradation levels in Central Kalimantan using LiDAR data,. Int. J. Appl. Earth Observ. Geoinf., vol. 18, pp. 37.–48, 2012.
- Page, S., Siegert, F., Rieley, J.O., Boehm, H.-D.V., Jaya, A., Limin, S., 2002. The amount of carbonreleased from peat and forest fires in Indonesia during 1997. Nature, 420(6911), 61-65.
- Schlund, M., Poncet, F. von, Kuntz, S., Boehm, H.-D.V., Hoekman, D.H., Schmullius, C., 2016.TanDEM-X elevation model data for canopy height and aboveground biomass retrieval in a tropical peatswamp forest. International Journal of Remote Sensing, VOL. 37, NO. 21, 5021–5044
- Schlund, M., Boehm, H.-D.V. 2018, Monitoring Concept for Tropical Peatland Swamp Forests with Airborne and Spaceborne Sensors applied in the Mawas Area, Kalimantan, 50. IPS -2018 Sept. 10-13 (Rotterdam, NL)
- Schlund, M., Boehm, H.-D.V. 2021, Assessment of linear relationships between TanDEM-X coherenceand canopy height as well as aboveground biomass in Tropical forests, International Journal of RemoteSensing, SENSING 2021, VOL. 42, NO. 9, 3409–3429

ID 62792

# A PROBABILISTIC APPROACH FOR PEATLAND MAPPING FOR AREAS WITH SCARCE DATA

*Cristina Malpica-Piñeros[1], Laura Villegas-Mejia[2], Alexandra Barthelmes[1], Hans Joosten[1]

[1] University Greifswald, Institute for Botany and Landscape Ecology, Germany
[2] Peatlands team REDD+/NFM Cluster Forestry Department/FAO, Italy

*cris.malpica@greifswaldmoor.de*

Tropical peatlands have high value for biodiversity conservation, climate regulation, flood risk reduction, and human welfare. Knowledge on peatland occurrence and status is urgently important to prevent drainage, deforestation and degradation by adequate land use planning. For some regions, however, this knowledge is limited, while proxy data and maps about soil types, vegetation, flooding period and soil organic carbon are more likely to be available. Using a classification system of direct and proxy secondary information from literature and archives, we developed a cost-efficient method to remotely calculate the probability of peatland occurrence, allowing the identification of confirmed and probable peatland areas at a scale of 250m in Neotropical regions. The semi-automatic probabilistic approach integrates a rating system of spatial resolution, quality and accuracy of the proxy information and reaches an accuracy of 70%. Our results allowed us to identify peatlands from coastal to mountainous ecosystems, adapting the model to different landscapes. The results of this study help to prioritize further field research and support decision making for management and monitoring plans. The approach is a valuable tool to identify peatland areas in regions with little information and the low cost and limited time of implementation facilitate project and fieldwork design, and adaptation to different landscapes and ecosystems.

ID 62794

# PEATLAND FIRE REGIONS AS A MEANS TO ANALYSE GLOBAL PEATLAND FIRES

*Farina de Waard, Hans Joosten, Alexandra Barthelmes

[1] Institute of Botany and Landscape Ecology, University of Greifswald, Germany

*farina.de.waard@greifswaldmoor.de*

Worldwide, peatlands are suffering from human impact and increasingly from climate change. While microbial peat oxidation following drainage and deforestation causes ongoing, huge but 'silent' emissions, peatland fires cause additional strong and more prominent emission peaks. Once ignited, peat fires may burn uncontrollably for weeks or months resulting in rapid ecosystem degradation, excessive $CO_2$- emissions and health risks. Despite their hazardous impact the world distribution of peat fires as a function of climate and vegetation remains poorly understood. Here, we analyse and classify the global occurrence of peatland fires using 'Peatland Fire Regions' (PFRs).

These PFRs base on a global NASA approach to analyse fires in sub-continental regions (GFED regions). As these GFED-regions do not specifically consider peatlands, we adapted them using various fire regime and climate maps. Subsequently we assessed the occurrence of fires from 2009 to 2018 using the Global Peatland Map of Greifswald Mire Centre (2019) and active fire detections from the Moderate Resolution Imaging Spectroradiometer (MODIS) and identified drivers of variability and trends within the various PFRs. Our results indicate that, over the analysed 10 years globally approximately 8 % of the peatlands have been affected by fire, whereas patterns and trends are widely differing. The extent of fire-affected peatland area in the PFRs Boreal North America and Boreal Eurasia both exceeded 80.000 km², which accounts for 3,5 % of their peatland area. In the same time, over 120.000 km² were fire-affected in Equatorial Asia, covering approximately 23 % of the peatland area in this region.

# ID 62667

# ASSESSMENT AND MODELING OF COVARIATES AND FACTORS AFFECTING IRISH PEATLAND PROPERTIES USING MIXED MODELING WITH A FOCUS ON SOIL ORGANIC CARBON

*Kilian Walz[1], David Wilson[2], Kenneth A. Byrne[1], Florence Renou-Wilson[3]

[1] Department of Biological Sciences, University of Limerick, Republic of Ireland
[2] Earthy Matters Environmental Consultants, Republic of Ireland
[3] School of Biology & Environmental Science, University College Dublin, Republic of Ireland

*Kilian.Walz@ul.ie*

In the Republic of Ireland, peatlands constitute the largest soil organic carbon (SOC) stock. Recent research suggests that 75% of SOC is stored in an area covering an estimated 20% of the land surface; predominantly in the form of raised bogs in the centre of the country and blanket bogs along the western seaboard. Despite their importance as an economic resource and ecological refuge, a nationwide assessment of the impacts of land disturbance on peatland properties has been lacking thus far. Current research, funded by the Irish Environmental Protection Agency (EPA), addresses this issue with the goal to fill various gaps related to mapping and modeling the distribution of Irish peatland properties. Data from the first nationwide peatland survey forms the basis for this study, in which the influence of different covariates and factors on SOC in peatlands was examined. As a first step, a data exploratory analysis was conducted to assess the major covariates of SOC properties in peatlands. Then, a mixed modeling approach was applied, in order to identify the relevant covariates and factors that are responsible for the differences observed in SOC properties across the country. In addition, model performance to map peatland carbon properties was evaluated. Results of the study will be presented with a focus on discussing the suitability of the mixed modeling approach to assess the variability in peatland properties and inform climate policy instruments.

ID 72888

# DIGITAL TRANSFORMATION IN PEAT INDUSTRY

Pēteris Gredzens

SIA Intellitech, Latvia

*peteris.gredzens@intellitech.lv*

Digital transformation is an integration of digital technology in all sectors of business. Digitalization creates an opportunity for innovation and increases overall efficiency within the company. It can also be a cultural change within the organization which requires to challenge the status quo and adopt the emerging technologies. For the last years, digitalization has become one of the most important aspects of any business. The peat industry is not an exception. In order to ensure a competitive business environment, the adoption of new technologies is a necessity. Company Intellitech is an IT company that has been working with companies from different industries, helping them to achieve their goal of digital transformation strategy. The main aim is to introduce our experience and show how different digital solutions can help in the peat industry.

ID 72868

# RESTORATION OF WATER TABLE REGIME IN POSTEXTRACTED PEATLANDS: VALIDATION OF THE BOUSSINESQ MODEL ADAPTED TO REWETTING BOGS BY MINI SHALLOW CHANNELS

Sebastian Gutierrez Pacheco[1,2], Sandrine Hogue-Hugron[2], Robert Lagacé[1], Stéphane Godbout[3], Line Rochefort[1,2]

[1] Faculty of Agricultural and Food Sciences, Université Laval, Quebec City, Canada
[2] Center for northern studies (CEN), Université Laval, Quebec City, Canada
[3] Research and Development Institute for The Agri-Environment (IRDA), Quebec City, Canada

*sebastian.gutierrez-pacheco.1@ulaval.ca*

## SUMMARY

*Sphagnum* cultivation is the production of biomass on rewetted bogs. *Sphagnum* moss cultivation offers an optionfor the sustainable restoration of drained peatlands and allows the use of peatlands without degrading the remaining peat horizons. A water management simulation model was used to investigate the suitability of drainage and irrigation systems for *Sphagnum* moss production biomass in post-harvest peatlands widely found in eastern Canada. A modification of Boussinesq's equation is suitable for simulating the water table in the stratified rewetted bogs by mini shallow canals. For this case, a horizontal flow is assumed as the sum of the horizontal flow of eachidentified horizon. For this case, located in Shippagan (NB, Canada), three soil horizons have been identified: 0.7-
1.0 m fibric horizon (von Post H2-H3), 0.4-0.7 m horizon slightly more decomposed (von Post H3); and 0-0.4 mhumic horizon (von Post H5) and the climatological data correspond to the nearby meteorological station and theon-site station.

These soils have low permeability, which limits water transport in the more decomposed and compacted layers. The use of this concept of stratified media represents the different degrees of peat decomposition that vary with depth. Different subsurface drain spacings and combinations of surface and subsurface drainage systems on the peat could be simulated. The results achieved so far suggest that the response time of bog rewetting for Sphagnumcultivation is influenced by the spacing between irrigation canals. Finally, it is suggested to explore the concept of mini shallow irrigation canals to provide a faster response to rewetting.

***Keywords**: Sphagnum cultivation, saturated hydraulic conductivity, stratified soil, Darcy equation, FEM*

## INTRODUCTION

The *Sphagnum* cultivation is the production of biomass on rewetted bogs. A water table near the surface is desiredto stimulate *Sphagnum* growth. For this purpose, the use of channels has reported (Greta Gaudig et al., 2018; Guêné-Nanchen et al., 2017; Pouliot et al., 2015). In *Sphagnum* moss cultivation sites, it is common to find irrigation devices that border the cultivation basins (peripheral channel) or cross the basins (central channel) (Figure 1). These irrigation canals are fed by an irrigation system that takes water from nearby extraction sites or nearby water bodies (e.g., lakes). From a hydraulic point of view, these canals must be filled to a higher level thanthe level expected in the cultivation basins. Thus, a hydraulic gradient is established between the water level of the canal and the water table level of the basin, which favours the movement of water from the canal to the basin.

The irrigation canal network design depends largely on the state of decomposition of the residual catotelm. The spacing of irrigation devices (drains and channels) should consider site conditions, e.g., 5 m is recommended in areas of strongly humified peat (Greta Gaudig et al., 2017) and 10 – 20 m in lightly humified areas (Brown et al.,2017; G Gaudig et al., 2013). These recommendations were made based on empirical criteria, but no technical criteria have been reported in the *Sphagnum* biomass production literature. This paper use the Boussinesq equation (Balliston et al., 2018; Kennedy & Price, 2004) and the Finite element numerical method (FEM) to to examinate the suitability of two irrigation systems for *Sphagnum* cultivation. A modification of Boussinesq's equation is suitable for simulating the water table in the stratified rewetted bogs.

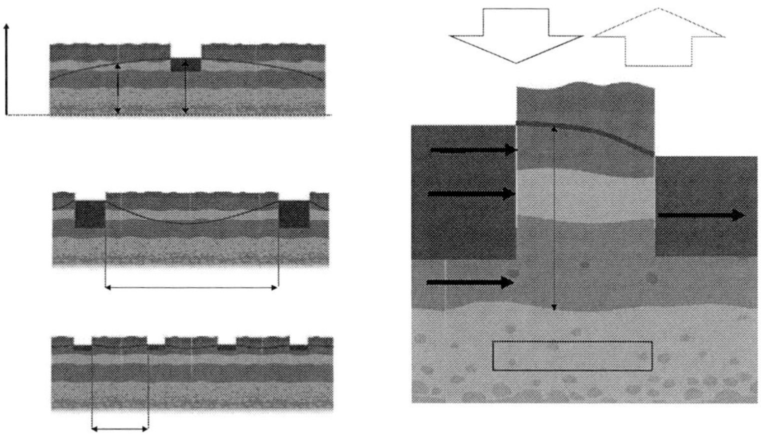

Figure 1. Conceptual model of irrigation system in Sphagnum cultivation context.

## MODEL DESCRIPTION

The modeling approach used in this study consisted of a horizontal flow between the water in the irrigation canaland the water table in the cultivation basins. For versatility and simplicity of the modem, minor processes have been excluded, deep groundwater fluxes are expected to be negligible, and development has focused primarily on stratified rewetted bogs peatlands in eastern Canada. The conceptual model used is summarized below and then explained employing a mathematical model adapted to this type of stratified rewetted bog.

### Conceptual model

After removing the acrotelme and part of the catotelme (Lavoie et al. 2003), peat extraction is carried out down tothe usable substrate (the layer having a von Post of H1-H3 for growing substrates and the layer having a von Postof H4-H7 to make potting soil when mixed with mineral soil; Parent2001). Thus, the remaining horizon, either forrestoration or for *Sphagnum* moss cultivation, is generally quite decomposed and compacted (Clymo et al. 1998).In this horizon, pores are smaller than in the upper horizons, saturated hydraulic conductivity is lower (VanSeters1999), water retention capacity is higher (Schlotzhauer and Price 1999), and pore density may increase after drainage, which reduces interstitial spaces (Price 1997). These are conditions that are not favorable for *Sphagnum*moss establishment, precisely because the flow of water to the capitulum is restricted and it undergoes water stress.

The use of shallow irrigation channels has been reported to maintain water table levels. The main types of irrigationnetwork used in *Sphagnum* cultivation are identified in Figure 1. A simplified conceptualization of the groundwaterflow hydrological has been adopted (Fig. 1). This is used as the basis of a mathematical model constructed in SfePy (Cimrman, 2014, 2013; Cimrman et al., 2019) to represent a one-dimensional *Sphagnum* cultivation basin.The parameters in Fig. 1, as well as others that are introduced in the following sections.

**Mathematical model**

Most of the research associated with groundwater flow modeling uses the Darcy equation, as well as the Richardsmodels and the Boussinesq equation. The Richards equation (Eq. 1) is used to represent the flow in the unsaturatedzone. In the saturated zone (below the water table), the water movement is represented by the Boussinesq equation(Eq. 2), and it is assumed that it is mostly horizontal. Unsaturated zone representation has been excluded for the simplicity of the model and exchanges between the subsurface and the atmosphere (i.e., evaporation and precipitation) were assumed negligent. The validation of the model was done with data collected in periods where precipitation was null, and the vegetation was still in dormancy (evapotranspiration was minimal).

$$\mu \frac{dh}{dt} = \frac{d}{dz}(K(h)(\frac{dh}{dz} + 1)) \qquad (1)$$

$$\mu \frac{dh}{dt} = \frac{d}{dx}(q_x h) \qquad (2)$$

Where $h$ is the water table position, $K(h)$ is the hydraulic conductivity as a function of the water table position and $\mu$ is the effective porosity.

Representing water movement in postextracted peatlands (Ballard et al. 2011; Susilo et al. 2012) and in a *Sphagnum* culture context (Taylor and Price 2015; Brust et al. 2017) has been reported as a scientific challenge. For example, Dimitrov et al. (2010) emphasize the importance of differentiating the porosity present in peat because the horizons typically present (fibric, mesic, and humic) have significant differences that imply significanteffects on hydrologic response. Numerical models rely heavily on measurements of peatland hydraulic conductivity. There is evidence that the hydraulic conductivity of peat soils can vary by several orders of magnitude over just a few meters, vertically or horizontally (Holden and Burt 2003; Taylor and Price 2015).

As a solution to these downsides, the Darcy equation is adapted for groundwater simulation by considering the stratified medium (Dimitrov et al. 2010). The total flow in a stratified medium is the sum of the flows in each of the identified layers. Equation 2 can be expressed as follows for stratified media:

$$q_x = \sum_{i=1}^{m} (\zeta_i - \zeta_{i-1})\, k_i \frac{dh}{dx} \qquad (3)$$

Where *m* is the number of strata or identified layers, *h* represents the water table position, *ζi* is the elevation of *i- th* strata, and *ki* is the saturated hydraulic conductivity of the *i-th* strata.

Other assumptions are considered: No flow in the lower part of the last identified strata. At this depth, the value of the saturated hydraulic conductivity (*k*) is relatively small and can be assumed as an impermeable boundary. Also, the outside of the basin bordering the irrigation channel is of infinite extension. Finally, the *k* values and theboundary conditions (water level in the irrigation channel) are invariant over time.

The equations 2 and 3 to describe the variation of flow depths were discretized in space using finite differences. The resulting ordinary differential equations were then integrated in time using SfePy using a Newton nonlinear solver.

## MATERIALS AND METHODS

### Case study application

*Sphagnum* cultivation sites was located at Shippagan, New Brunswick (47°41'35"N 64°45'47"W), an experimentalsite in production since July 2014. A 20 m x 50 m basin was located on a cutover peatland (Bog 530) slightly decomposed (H4-H5 on the von Post scale, mean peat depth of 2.5 m). The basin had a peripheral channel (PC) and in 2019 the hydraulic network of basin was modified by constructing four 20 cm x 20 cm, 20 m long mini shallow channels (MC), which were connected to the original channels for their water supply. Basin was irrigatedwith water coming from the Martine lake. *Sphagnum* moss was reintroduced over the five basins in 2013 according to an adaptation of Moss Layer Transfer Technique (Graf et al., 2012; Rochefort et al., 2003). Water table was controlled through an automated irrigation installation and each basin was adjusted with different water table regimes. A pumping system sent the water to the irrigation channels arranged in the basins and the target water table level was monitored by ultrasonic sensors installed in the channels. When the water height in the irrigation channel was lower than the target level, the pumping system was activated to feed the channel. The maximum water level in a channel was controlled by the height of a dam, which was a wooden structure that blocked the water flow and increased the water level upstream of the dam. This increase caused a favorable hydraulic gradientfor groundwater flow within the peat for rewetting.

### Field methods

Water table depth (*h*) was recorded every hour by four water level loggers (HOBO U20, Onset Computer Corporation, Bourne, MA, USA, accuracy: ± 0.5 cm) during approximately 10 days. Details of the sampling datesfor each of the sites are given in Table 1. The data loggers were placed inside the observation well located in the middle of basin and, the wells were made of 2-in diameter PVC pipe to record pressure and temperature simultaneously. The wells were installed at a depth of approximately 70 cm using an auger. The wells had nylon stockings on the outer surface to prevent the entry of solids in suspension. All measurements were corrected withthe data logger for Barometric pressure (HOBO U20-001-04, Onset Computer Corporation, Bourne, MA, USA, accuracy: ± 0.5 cm) with the HOBOware Pro software. The daily value of the water table was estimated from hourly measurements as the average between the maximum (*hmax, i*) value and the minimum value (*hmin, i*) recordedduring each day of the growing season (Equation 4).

$$h_i = \frac{h_{max,i} + h_{min,i}}{2} \quad (4)$$

The information of the strata identified in the field are recorded in Table 1. This identification was made with random bore holes in the field. The auger hole method (Lagacé, 2016) was used to obtain the saturated hydraulic conductivity ($k$) value of each strata. For the estimation of the effective porosity ($\mu$), the water table drying curvemethod was used.

Table 1. Parameters for water table simulations based on Boussinesq model for stratified soil using FEM.

| ID basin | $d$ (m) | z (m) | *von Post* | $k$ (m day$^{-1}$) | $\mu$ | $H$ (m) | Sampling days | $h_0$ | $h_f$ |
|---|---|---|---|---|---|---|---|---|---|
| | | 0.7 – 1.0 | H2 – H3 | 1.20 | 0.04 | | | | |
| PC | 20 | 0.4 – 0.7 | H3 | 0.50 | 0.03 | 0.9 | 12 | 0.60 | 0.85 |
| | | 0.0 – 0.4 | H5 | 0.10 | 0.02 | | | | |
| | | 0.7 – 1.0 | H2 – H3 | 1.20 | 0.04 | | | | |
| PC + MC | 10 | 0.4 – 0.7 | H3 | 0.50 | 0.03 | 0.95 | 9 | 0.78 | 0.94 |
| | | 0.0 – 0.4 | H5 | 0.10 | 0.02 | | | | |

**Model validation and performance**

Three statistical measures were used to considered to evaluate the performance of the model: Coefficient of determination ($R^2$), the root-mean-square error (RMSE), and the Index of agreement (IoA). These coefficientswere calculated according to equations 5 to 7:

$$R^2 = 1 - \left[\frac{\Sigma(h_i^2 - \hat{h}_i^2)}{\Sigma h_i^2 - \frac{1}{N}\Sigma \hat{h}_i^2}\right] \quad (5)$$

$$RMSE = \sqrt{\frac{\Sigma(h_i^2 - \hat{h}_i^2)}{N}} \quad (6)$$

$$IoA = 1 - \left[\frac{\Sigma(h - \hat{h})^2}{\Sigma(|\hat{h} - \bar{\hat{h}}| + |h - \bar{\hat{h}}|)^2}\right] \quad (7)$$

Where $hj$ are the observed water table, $hj$ are the estimated water table from each method, $h$ is the mean of observed water table, similartly and $N$ the number of observations.

**RESULTS**

With the 21 days of daily water table measurements, it was possible to compare the simulation results and the comparison ofthe water table depth values can be seen in Figure 2. The statistical measures calculated were RMSE = 32.90 m, R2 = 0.62 and IoA = 0.92.

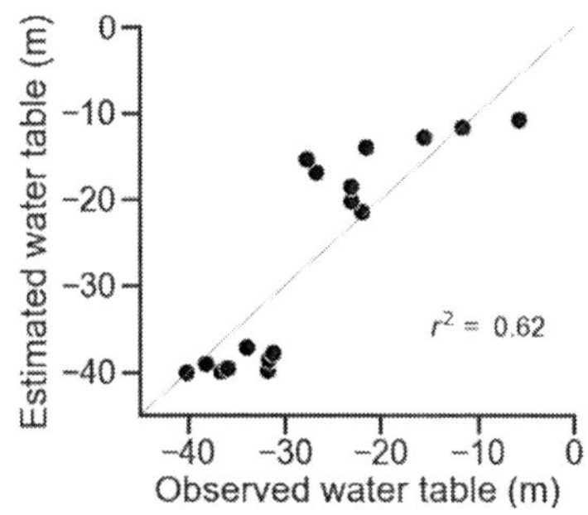


Figure 2. The simulated and observed water table depth.

The results of a simulation of the rewetting after nine days are shown in Figure 2. The mini shallow channel system allowed for faster rewetting and a water table uniformly close to the surface. This is in complete agreement with Gaudig et al. (2017, 2013) and Brown et al. (2017) who suggest a network of irrigation canals spaced 10 m in lightly humified peatlands. However, since the hydraulic conductivity of the last identified strata is relatively low (ten times smaller, Table 1), it is not necessary to dig deep channels. The layers up to 60 cm deep are more permeable, which benefits rewetting. The use of deep irrigation canals is recommended for drainage management (Goulet, 2019).

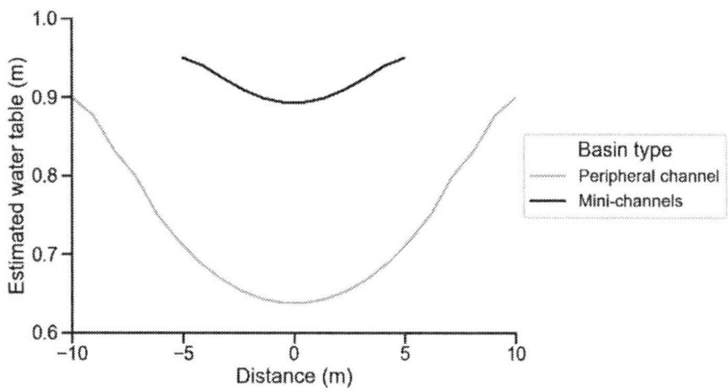


Figure 3. Simulated water table after a time lapse of nine days. The *0-value* on the x-axis indicates the center ofthe basin.

## CONCLUSION

The Boussinesq equation adapted for stratified media provide results comparable to what is observed. Also, this model provides flexibility to represent the irrigation configurations that are used in *Sphagnum* cultivation. The results achieved so far suggest that the response time of bog rewetting for *Sphagnum* cultivation is influenced by the spacing between irrigation canals. Finally, it is suggested to explore the concept of mini shallow irrigation canals to provide a faster response to rewetting.


## ACKNOWLEDGEMENTS

The authors are grateful to SunGro Horticulture and Valorês for site access, specially to Marion Tétégan Simon,Benoit St-Hilaire, and Thomas. Special thanks to Cédric Morin and Guillaume Goulet for field assistance.

## REFERENCES


- Balliston, N. E., McCarter, C. P. R., & Price, J. S. (2018). Microtopographical and hydrophysical controls on subsurface flow and solute transport: A continuous solute release experiment in a subarctic bog. *Hydrological Processes*, *32*(19), 2963–2975. https://doi.org/10.1002/hyp.13236
- Brown, C. M., Strack, M., & Price, J. S. (2017). The effects of water management on the CO2 uptake of Sphagnum moss in a reclaimed peatland. *Mires and Peat*, *20*(5), 1–15. https://doi.org/10.19189/MaP.2016.OMB.258
- Cimrman, R. (2014). Enhancing SfePy with Isogeometric Analysis. *PROC. OF THE 7th EUR. CONF. ONPYTHON IN SCIENCE*, 65–72. http://sfepy.org
- Cimrman, R. (2013). SfePy-Write Your Own FE Application. *PROC. OF THE 6th EUR. CONF. ON PYTHONIN SCIENCE*, 65–70. http://sfepy.org/doc-devel/development.html.
- Cimrman, R., Lukeš, V., & Rohan, E. (2019). Multiscale finite element calculations in Python using SfePy.
  *Advances in Computational Mathematics*, *45*(4), 1897–1921. https://doi.org/10.1007/s10444-019-09666-0
- Gaudig, G, Fengler, F., Krebs, M., Prager, A., Schulz, J., Wichmann, S., & Joosten, H. (2013). Sphagnum farmingin Germany – a review of progress. *Sphagnum Growing*, *13*(08).
- Gaudig, Greta, Krebs, M., & Joosten, H. (2017). Sphagnum farming on cut-over bog in NW Germany: Long-termstudies on sphagnum growth. *Mires and Peat*, *20*. https://doi.org/10.19189/MaP.2016.OMB.238
- Gaudig, Greta, Krebs, M., Prager, A., Wichmann, S., Barney, M., Caporn, S. J. M., Emmel, M., Fritz, C., Graf, M., Grobe, A., & Pacheco, S. G. (2018). Sphagnum farming from species selection to the production of growingmedia : a review. *Mires and Peat*, *20*. https://doi.org/10.19189/MaP.2018.OMB.340
- Goulet, G. (2019). *Système de contrôle automatisé de l'eau en culture de sphaigne*. Université Laval.
- Graf, M. D., Bérubé, V., & Rochefort, L. (2012). Restoration of peatlands after peat extraction. In D. H. Vitt & J.
  S. Bhatti (Eds.), *Restoration and Reclamation of Boreal Ecosystems* (pp. 259–280). Cambridge University Press.https://doi.org/10.1017/cbo9781139059152.015
- Guêné-Nanchen, M., Pouliot, R., Hugron, S., & Rochefort, L. (2017). Effect of repeated mowing to reduce graminoid plant cover on the moss carpet at a sphagnum farm in North America. *Mires and Peat*, *20*. https://doi.org/10.19189/MaP.2016.OMB.250
- Kennedy, G. W., & Price, J. S. (2004). Simulating soil water dynamics in a cutover bog. *Water Resources Research*, *40*(12), 1–13. https://doi.org/10.1029/2004WR003099
- Lagacé, R. (2016). *Chapter 6. Conductuvuté hydraulique*. Notes de Cours Drainage GAE-3001. http://www.grr.ulaval.ca/gae_3001/index.html
- Pouliot, R., Hugron, S., & Rochefort, L. (2015). Sphagnum farming: A long-term study on producing peat mossbiomass sustainably. *Ecological Engineering*, *74*. https://doi.org/10.1016/j.ecoleng.2014.10.007
- Rochefort, L., Quinty, F., Campeau, S., Johnson, K., & Malterer, T. (2003). North American approach to therestoration of wetlands. *Wetlands Ecology and Management*, *11*, 3–20.
-

ID 62259

# BEST MANAGEMENT PRACTICES FOR CULTIVATION OF OIL PALM ON PEATLAND

Faizal Parish, Serena Lew Siew Yan, Muhamad Faizuddin

Global Environment Centre, Malaysia

*fparish@gec.org.my, serena@gec.org.my, faizuddin@gec.org.my*

**SUMMARY**

One of the most extensive land uses on peatlands in Southeast Asia is the cultivation of oil palm which covers more than 3 million hectares (ha) or 12% of the region's peatlands. Oil palm is one of the most productive vegetable oil crops in the world with yields of up to 6 tonnes of oil per ha per year being possible with good techniques. Production of palm oil is very important for the economies of Indonesia and Malaysia which dominate global production and trade. However, the clearance and drainage of peatland for the cultivation of oil palm has a number of significant environmental impacts including high emission of greenhouse gasses (GHG), subsidence of land, loss of biodiversity as well as enhancement of floods and fires in surrounding landscapes. Oil palm production in peatlands is also impacted by significant nutrient limitations as well as pests and diseases such as stem rot fungus (*Ganoderma*). Recognising these significant challenges, both governments and the industry have in recent years put in place measures to stop the further expansion of oil palm plantations on peat. However with a large area of oil palm already cultivated on peat, the industry has documented and promoted a broad range of Best Management Practices (BMPs) to enhance sustainability and reduce impacts – such as through the Roundtable on Sustainable Palm Oil (RSPO) Manual on BMPs for oil palm cultivation on peat published in 2019. The most critical BMPs relate to water management to ensure that the water table in the plantations is maintained at a relatively constant level of 40-50cm below the surface year round. Careful land preparation and ground cover management, integrated pest management and timely application of nutrients is also critical to generate good yields. Fire prevention and attention to a landscape approach is also important.

***Keywords**: Roundtable on Sustainable Palm Oil (RSPO), Best Management Practices (BMPs) Peat Manual, oil palm on peat*

## INTRODUCTION

Oil palm is the world's most planted and fully been utilised as vegetable crop oil. It is grown throughout the Southeast Asia with Malaysia and Indonesia are the world's largest producers. According to Shahbandeh (2020), the global production of palm oil grows to around 73 million metric tons in the marketing year of 2018/2019, up from approximately 65 million metric tons in 2017/2018. With production of 5-10 times (Ling, 2019) more oil than most oilseeds per unit area of lands, oil palm delivering 31% of the world's vegetable oil, followed by soy (24%) and rapeseed (13%) (Traeholt; Ling (2019)). With growing demand of vegetable oil for consumption, it was expected additional 56 million ton of vegetable oil needed for 9 billion world population by 2050 (UN, 2017). Current global consumption for the vegetable oil was 197 million ton (Shahbandeh, 2020). As comparison, it will need an additional of new planting of 94 million ha of soybean or 12 million ha with oil palm (Ling, 2019). Thus dependency of oil palm could not be denies as it becomes most potential crop meeting world future demands.

With land became scarce for plantation expansion, the oil palm cultivation now move to peatlands even though it is less suitable. Currently, it is estimated that there are more than 3.1 million ha of oil palm cultivated on peat representing about 17% of oil palm in the Southeast Asia region and covering about 12% of the region's peatlands (Parish et al., 2019). Peat soils are diverse in physical and chemical properties and not all are productive and easy to manage. A good knowledge, well executed planning and implementation of BMPs are required to reduce some of the impacts caused by oil palm cultivation on peat while enhancing yields. Long term environmental considerations and social aspects need to be taken into account in peat-planting especially minimising subsidence and reducing emissions of GHG. Restrictions on expansion cultivation on peatlands by international and national standards, law and policy imposed good effort promoting oil palm products in world market as it always scrutinises its sustainability globally. For example, current standard requirements by RSPO – a global non-profit initiative that unites stakeholders promoting the growth and use of sustainable oil palm products; there will be no new planting on peat, regardless of depth and all peatlands are managed responsibly by RSPO Principle and Criteria (P&C) 2018.

## BMPs ON OIL PALM CULTIVATION ON PEAT

This paper seeks to address commonly known BMPs in oil palm cultivation on peat in Southeast Asia region. The practice includes water, nutrient, pest & disease, ground cover and Fresh Fruit Bunch (FFB) evacuation. Each plantation may have its own unique practice and standard operation procedures (SOPs) to follow, therefore BMPs included can be used as a guide and not the sole basis for management of plantations on peatlands.

## BMPs ON OIL PALM CULTIVATION ON PEAT – WATER MANAGEMENT

Effective water management is essential to obtain high oil palm yield on peat and also to minimise GHG emissions and peat subsidence as well as vital for prolonging the economic life span of the developed peat. Keeping the peat moist is important for healthy palm growth and high yield. Most palms' feeder roots are concentrated in the top 0-50 cm of the peat; therefore, water level needs to be near this zone, but it should not be waterlogged (Parish et al., 2019). A proper hydrology and water management study should be done in the beginning to design a proper drainage system that can maintain water table at desired level. Failure to do so would have adverse impact such as serious fluctuation of water levels in canals during dry and wet season; detrimental effects to oil palm growth/yield and estate operation. Drain dimension also important in water management. Typical drain dimensions in peat are given in Table 1 below derived from Gurmit (1983), Yin & Chin (1981).

Table 1: Typical Drain Dimension in Oil Palm Cultivation.

| Type of drain | Width (m) | | Depth (m) |
|---|---|---|---|
| | Top | Bottom | |
| Field | 1.0 – 1.2 | 0.4 – 0.6 | 0.9 – 1.0 |
| Collection | 2.0 – 2.5 | 0.6 – 0.9 | 1.5 – 1.8 |
| Main | 3.0 – 6.0 | 1.2 – 1.8 | 1.8 – 2.5 |

Good water management should ensure in-field or field drain water level is maintained at an average of 40-50cm while the collection drain maintain with 50-60cm below the surface (Lim et al. (2012), Eswa (2018), Parish et al. (2019)). Poor maintenance of the drainage system can be a cause of flooding in peat estates although it is often a consequence of subsidence relative to the surrounding landscape. Desilting of drains to required depths is best carried out prior to the rainy season. However, care needs to be taken to avoid cutting drains too deep in peat areas. It is also essential that all weirs and drop-offs are regularly checked and repaired. Water gates and flap gates need to be maintained at minimum every six months to ensure smooth operation (Parish et al., 2019).

Water is the most important element in peatland management, from the formation of peat to maintaining the functionality of the peatlands ecosystem. Peat shrinks when dried and swells when re-wetted, unless it is dried beyond the threshold value where irreversible drying occurs (Andriesse, 1988). Low water tables lead to aeration of peat and oxidation or aerobic decomposition (Wosten et al., 2006). It leads to subsidence and increases the risk of fires. RSPO has adopted the threshold, based on science that each 1 cm of drainage causes a $CO_2$ emission of 0.91 ton $CO_2$/ha/yr (Hooijer et al., 2010). Thus, water management is crucial in peatlands by maintaining desire water table for agriculture purposes, and as high as possible for conservation areas. Listed in Table 2 below two simple devices/tools made to monitor the water level in the field derived from GEC (2020), Parish et al., (2019), Bakewell (2012), and Hudson (1993).

Table 2: Simple Devices to Monitor Water Level in Plantations.

| Piezometer | Description | Water level gauge |
|---|---|---|
| A devise or system by measuring the height to which a column of the liquid rises against gravity. | Definition | Water level gauge is a device to provide a visible indication of water level. |
| 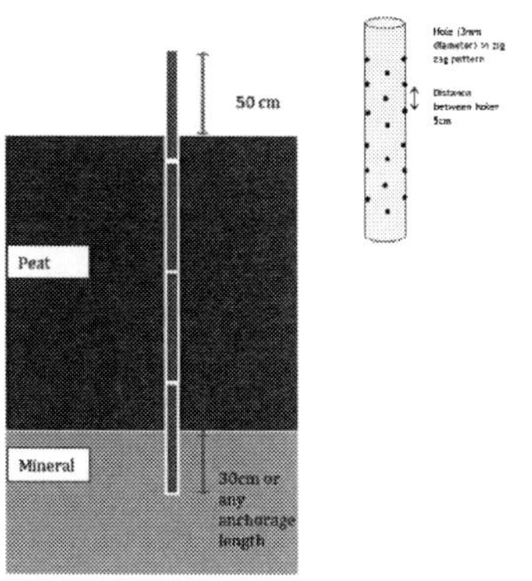  | Design | 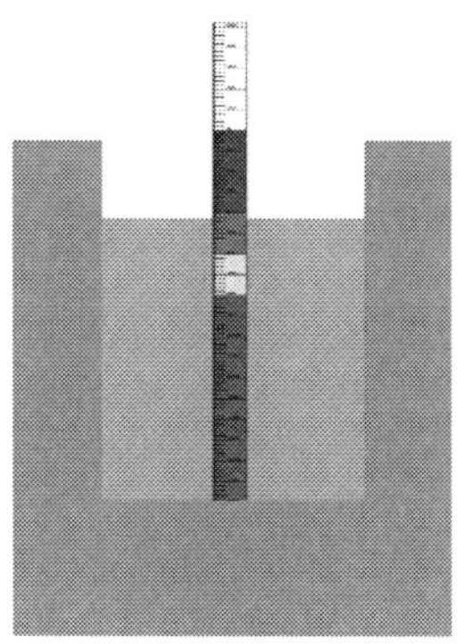 |
| In targeted field area, achor to mineral beneath peat layer | Placement | In collection drain |
| Daily or monthly | Reading | Daily or monthly |

## BMPs ON OIL PALM CULTIVATION ON PEAT – NUTRIENT MANAGEMENT

According to Foster (2003), the fertiliser application and requirements for oil palm depend on many interrelated factors that vary from one environment to another. Oil palm yield response from fertilisers can vary substantially even sharing similar ecological environments. Unlike mineral soils, regardless on the type and depth of peat, retaining the applied nutrients in peat is difficult especially the highly required potassium nutrient due to low bulk density, high infiltration rate and porosity (Parish et al., 2019). Water level in peat should be maintained at 40 to 50cm from the soil surface (Parish et al., 2019). Correct application includes time, dosage and type of fertiliser are crucial in oil plam cultivation on peat. Due to effective root zone for oil palm is nearer to the trunk, application of macro-nutrient fertiliser should be closer to the trunk base ranging from 50cm to 100cm for palm aged 3 years and above. For palms age below 3 years, fertiliser should be applied at a 30 to 50cm radius depending on the growth rate of palms. Contra to macro application, micro-nutrients like Borate, Copper sulphate, Zinc sulphate and chelated Iron fertilisers should be applied closer to palm trunk – within 30cm radius (Parish et al., 2019).

Listed in Table 3 and 4 below suggested that BMPs for management of macro- and micro-nutrient in peat cultivation with suggested dosage, placement and deficiency symptoms on oil palm derived from Parish et al. (2019), Eswa (2018) and Hasnol (2014).

Table 3: Macro-Nutrients Deficiency Symptoms and Recommend Application

| Macro nutrients | Deficiency symptoms | Application |
|---|---|---|
| Nitrogen | Prolong floods: Canopy turn to yellow<br>Imbalence nutrients: single pale yellow to white stripe is seen on the one half of the pinnae | **Fast corrective:** urea of 0.5 to 1 kg per palm (depends to age)<br>**Normal/Maintainance:**<br>1-3 year = 0.5-1 kg of Urea applied in 3 rounds/year<br>>3 year = 1.25 kg of Urea applied in 3 rounds/year |
| Potassium | Confluent orange spotting | **Normal/Maintainance:**<br>1-3 year = Muriate of potash, ranging from 1.5 to 3 kg per palm in 3 rounds/year<br>>3 year = Muriate of potash, ranging from 4 to 6 kg per palm in 3 rounds/year or Bunch ash with 3 kg per palm per year |
| Phosphorous | Stunted growth. Not easy to detect on peat | **Normal/Maintainance:**<br>1-3 year = Rock phosphate, ranging from 0.6 to 1 kg per palm with 1 round/year<br>>3 year = Rock phosphate, not more 1 kg per palm with 1 round/year |
| Magnesium | Exposed old leaf to sunlight will be yellow or orange. Rarely seen in peat. Unless underlying on sulphidic soil | **Corection manuring:**<br>Limestone dust, 2 kg per palm. |

Table 4: Micro-Nutrients Deficiency Symptoms and Recommend Application

| Micro nutrients | Deficiency symptoms | Application |
|---|---|---|
| Boron | Hook leaf on young pinnae of young fronds, round frond tip, blind-leaf, bristle tip and fish bone leaf. | **Fast corrective:** Borate of 200 to 250 g per palm (depends to age)<br>**Normal/Maintainance:**<br>1-3 year = 80-100 g of Borate applied in 2 year interval<br>>3 year = 80-150 g of Borate applied in 2 year interval |
| Copper | Discolouration towards the distal end of the pinnae, necrotic, followed by desiccation developing from the tip of pinnae to downwards. | **Fast corrective:** Copper Sulphate of 200 to 250 g per palm (depends to age)<br>**Normal/Maintainance:**<br>1-3 year = 100g of Copper Sulphate applied per palm/year (depends on agronomist recommendation)<br>>3 year = 100-200 g of Copper Sulphate applied per palm/year (depends on agronomist recommendation) |
| Zinc | Development of pale green to whitish interveinal chlorotic streaks in the pinnae of young opened fronds stretching from pinnae tip to 5 to 8cm of the pinnae base | **Fast corrective:** Zinc Sulphate of 150 to 200 g per palm (depends to age)<br>**Normal/Maintainance:**<br>1-3 year = 100g of Zinc Sulphate applied per palm/year (depends on agronomist recommendation)<br>>3 year = 150-200 g of Zinc Sulphate applied per palm/year (depends on agronomist recommendation) |
| Iron | Chlorosis to young and emerging fronds. At a more advanced stage, the young frond will completely turn yellow with stunted growth of young fronds. Very rare to happen | **Fast corrective**: Foliar application of Ferrous Sulphate ($FeSO_4$) at the concentration of 1% is effective in controlling iron deficiency symptoms. |

| | | | |
|---|---|---|---|
| Leaf eating caterpillars | Holes on the leaves. For severe infestations, only the midribs are left and the fronds appear to be skeletonised | Censuses at an intensity of 1% (1 row in 10, 1 palm in 10) at 2-weekly intervals | **Biological Control:** Establishment of beneficial plants – *Cassia cobanensis*<br>**Chemical Control:** Young palms (1-6 years), spray 0.005% cypermethrin. For tall palms >8 years, trunk injection using acephate (55%) is recommended |
| Rhinoceros beetle | New frond snapping, fan-shaped cut fronds, and dieback of spear and bore holes on the frond bases | Monthly census on every palm (100% census) for newly planted palms | **Biological Control:** Using pheromone traps<br>**Chemical Control:** At low pest levels, carbofuran (3%) or carbosulphan (5%) applied to the spear region and base of new fronds at monthly intervals. At high level 10 beetle per trap use 0.06% Cypermethrin for spraying |
| Rats | Evidence of chew on palm bases (immature). Evidence of chew on fruit bunch (immature) | Fresh rat damage on palms or harvested bunches. Regular censuses on a block-by-block basis | **Biological Control:** Barn owls (*Tyto alba*)<br>**Chemical Control:** Start baiting using anticoagulant baits when census results show more than 5% fresh damage. |

| | | | |
|---|---|---|---|
| Ganoderma | Light-brown dry rot lesions of both the stem and bole fruting body | Three to six monthly censuses of *Ganoderma* infections are recommended | Currently no effective cure for *Ganoderma* infections in an existing stand<br>**Control**: Isolation of *Ganoderma* infected palm using 4m x 4m x 75cm deep isolation trench.<br>**Biological control**: Use arbuscular mycorrhizal fungi (AMF) in nursery stage. |

## BMPs ON OIL PALM CULTIVATION ON PEAT – PEST AND DISEASE MANAGEMENT

Pest and disease for oil palm cultivation differ among regions and palm species. Generally, pests can be classified into insects and vertebrates while the main disease for oil palm cultivation is *Ganoderma* (basal stem rot) diseases Darus & Basri (2000). Close monitoring and early detection especially for young palms are crucial due to their greater susceptibility to pest and disease damage (Lim, 2005). Prevention by early detection, use to measure the extent and severity of any infestation and to determine whether short-term insecticide treatment is required until the pest population returns to normal. Inspections can be less frequent for palms above four years old.

Integrated Pest Management (IPM) emphasises the growth of a healthy crop with the least possible disruption to agro-ecosystems and encourages natural pest control mechanisms (FAO, 2020). IPM means the careful consideration of all available pest control techniques and subsequent integration of appropriate measures that discourage the development of pest populations and keep pesticides and other interventions to levels that are economically justified and reduce or minimise risks to human health and the environment (Ramle et al., 2011). With IPM, the amount of chemicals is reduced, to minimise the impact on beneficial and non-target organisms. Chemical treatments are only carried out by using selective pesticides at low rates and timely applications to ensure minimum impact on the biodiversity and environment (Parish et al., 2019).

IPM procedures includes Biological Control & Cultural Practices, Detection of Pest Damage, Identification of Pests, Enumeration of Pest Population, and Selection of Chemical Control (Wood, 1984). Listed in Table 5 below was identified pest and disease in oil palm cultivation on peat with IPM procedure derived from Parish et al. (2019); Sundram (2015); and Othman et al. (2009).

Table 5: Identified Pest and Disease and IPM Procedure

| Pest/Disease | Symptoms | Suggestion early detection | Treatment |
|---|---|---|---|
| Termites | Presence of fresh mud work or mud galleries on the crown region and palm trunk | Monthly census on every palm (100% census) | **Biological Control:** Using entomopathogenic fungi *Beauveria bassiana* and *M. anisopliae*<br>**Chemical Control:** Fipronil (5.0% a.i.) at 2.5 ml product per 5 liters of water |
| Tirathaba bunch moth | Presence of long tubes of silk and frass (faeces) | Detection in FFB platforms in a block is more than 5%<br><br>Systematic census on 10% of palm population in the block | **Biological Control:** Regulated natural earwigs (*Chelisoches moris*) and Kerengga ants.<br>**Chemical Control:** Spray with *Bacillus thuringiensis* (Bt) at 1 g product/liter of water at 2-weekly intervals |

## BMPs ON OIL PALM CULTIVATION ON PEAT – GROUND COVER MANAGEMENT AND COMPACTION

It is important to increase the water table to reduce GHG emissions or even preventing breeding's of some noxious weed (*Uncaria* spp.). Establishing good ground cover such as natural vegetation such as *Nephrolepis biserrata* in the plantation can help to reduce temperature of the peat by providing shade and also to increase the humidity level (Parish et al., 2019). According to Othman (2012), besides natural vegetation, leguminous cover crops (LCC) are commonly accepted practice in oil palm plantation. Species could be planted include *Pueraria javanica*, *P. phaseolides* and *Mucuna Bracteata*. Main objective of LCC establishment to improve soil fertility by nitrogen fixation and reduce competition of noxious weed to palm growth. In peat, the role becomes broader by conserving soil moisture, minimising peat subsidence hence reducing GHG emissions during land preparation or during immature phase. Listed in Table 6 below are suggestion compositions of LCC guided by MPOB.

Table 6: Suggestion Composition LCC by MPOB

| No | Species | Ratio |
|---|---|---|
| 1 | *Pueraria javanica + Centrosema pubescens + Calopogmium caeraleum* | 4:3:1 kg $ha^{-1}$ |
| 2 | *Mucuna bracteata* | 320 seedlings $ha^{-1}$ |
| 3 | *Mucuna bracteata + Pueraria javanica + Centrosema pubescens* | 320 seedlings + 3:1 kg $ha^{-1}$ |

Apart from establishment the ground cover, weed control is also important in ground cover management. With moist environment in peat, it favours luxuriant growth of weeds. Timely spraying of noxious weeds with selective herbicides to promote the growth of desirable ground cover is advocated to minimise the weed succession problem. The strategy is to keep the palm circles clean and inter-rows devoid of noxious weeds (especially *Imperata cylindrica*, *Mikania micrantha*, *Ischaemum muticum*, etc.). Listed in Table 7 below are examples of the ground cover management in oil palm cultivation on peat with simplified procedure derived from (Parish et al., 2019; Kuntom 2007). Blanket spraying of herbicides should not be permitted in oil palm.

Table 7: Ground Cover Management

| Activity | Frequency per year | Herbicide use in 18 liter knapsack |
|---|---|---|
| Circle weeding with 2.5m radius | 6-9 rounds (depends on field condition) | 100ml Glyphosate isopropyl amine (48%) + 5g Metsulfron methyl<br>Targeted weeds: *Stenochlaena palustris*<br><br>180-240 ml Glyphosate isopropyl amine (41%)<br>Targeted weeds: *Imperata cylindrica*<br><br>15 ml of 26% floroxypyr product<br>Targeted weeds: *Mikania micrantha* |
| Poison woodies | 1-2 rounds (depends on field condition) | Garlon: Diesel (1:19) on a 30 cm band on the basal stems. |

In relation to water management and ground cover management practice peat compaction, are important to oil palm cultivation on peat. Differ from compaction in mineral soil (mainly mechanisation in operation) that reportedly effecting yield reduction, compaction in peat in early land preparation can improve soil bulk density giving positive effects to palm growth, reduce palm leaning, field accessibility and yield production (Parish et al., 2019). Good soil compaction is reported to reduce GHG emissions from peat (Witjaksana, 2011). Additional compaction could be done by excavators about three to four weeks after any construction of additional subsidiary drains (ASEAN Secretariat, 2003).

## BMPs ON OIL PALM CULTIVATION ON PEAT – FFB EVACUATION

Fresh fruit bunch (FFB) evacuation is very important in plantation sector. As peat ground conditions are very soft especially during rainy seasons contain with high water table, crop evacuation is one of the key challenges need to be overcame in peat areas. With labour shortage condition, various scheme have been undertaken by plantation companies. The option includes the process from infield crop collection into crop evacuation to mill, via land or water, with consideration of efficiency, feasibility, and productive method.

In peat areas where there are no suitable sources of road building materials but good natural water sources, especially during dry seasons, water transportation on peat can be considered. The existing drainage system can be modified for water transport by widening the main and collection drains. In this system, boats are used to collect FFB in field collection point then send to main collection point before transport by lorry to designated mill. For example, waterways evacuation known as Pontoon and Container system (P&C) by PT Bhumireksa Nusa Sejati have made labour reduction in operations with minimum manual handling in loading and unloading activities in the estates and at the reception center (Parish et al., 2019).

For consideration in field FFB collection, small dump trucks with large tyres or buffalo assisted field operation is another option, as it involves less capital investment and maintenance. It is important to have interface machine or method between harvester and in field collection to evacuate FFB to platform. This activity also to ensure the FFB can send to mill within 24 hours to process for and produce high quality crude palm oil (CPO). Unloading the FFB have variously method from transfer ramps which must require additional re-handling, into roadside nets or through the use of high tipping dump trucks directly into the transport unit to mill. In addition, using such special vehicles, can save labour by 1:33 ha for machine to land ratio (Syahlan et al., 2017). In contrast, for swampy and a very highwater table condition, the buffalo transportation is an option to choose. A buffalo with two workers should be able to cover 4 ha of land (Zahid, 2018).

## DISCUSSION

Drain peatlands always related to subsidence, increase fire risk and most importantly releasing GHG emissions. For existing oil palm cultivation, it is always important to maintain water table at desire height from 40-60cm from surface to minimise GHG emissions. This is because $CO_2$ emissions always correlated on temperature as well as water level (Hooijer et al., 2011; Carlson et al., 2015; Cooper et al., 2019). Realising the threat of the existing plantation and the big conversion scale of peatlands to oil palm towards environment, more restrictions are coming in place.

For international standard certification like RSPO, members with existing cultivation oil palm on peat, that schedule for replanting must undergone drain-ability assessment. The assessment should be carried out at least five years prior to replanting, then is used to set the timeframe for future replanting, as well as for phasing out of oil palm cultivation at least 40 years, or two cycles, whichever is greater, before reaching the natural gravity drain-ability limit for peat. When oil palm is phased out, it should be replaced with crops suitable for a higher water table (paludiculture) or rehabilitated with natural vegetation RSPO P&C (2018).

Leading countries in oil palm industries mainly Malaysia and Indonesia are now proactively improve policies on peatlands use. Adherence to necessity of sustainable global market requirement, banning oil palm expansion on peat currently taking place for all local and private parties for land development purposes. For example, the adoption of Malaysia cut-off date for oil palm expansion by 2023 (MPI, 2020) and bans all new land clearing and canal building on peatland for Indonesia (PP 57/2016). In addition of implementation for industries, National Scheme for both countries by Malaysian Sustainable Palm Oil (MSPO) and Indonesian Sustainable Palm Oil (ISPO) Standard will be the main key to achieving the sustainable wise use of peatlands for oil palm cultivation.

Continues improvement of BMPs on oil palm cultivation now will become wider. With international and national restrictions to oil palm cultivation on peat, the practice will never limits to existing cultivation, land ownership need to ready for new dimension of field for rehabilitation of peatlands. It will take 35 years' experience to collecting and improving existing knowledge enhancing yields in oil palm cultivation on peat (Parish et al., 2019), thus industries players should be ready to the next phase of collecting new experience rehabilitating the peatlands for plantation concession. Active collaboration with exchange knowledge and experience will be needed in the future forward. For RSPO members, a benchmark have been lifted by introduction of Manual on BMPs for Management and Rehabilitation of Peatlands (Parish et al., 2019b) – it is complement with requirement of the RSPO P&C (2018) and RSPO Drain-ability Assessment (2019) as measure for adoption.

## CONCLUSION

Market will never denie the potential of oil palm potential to fill gaps of food supply. However, the threats of unsustainable use of peatlands resource should never be neglected as well as requirement of sustainable palm product in market. It will take a few more years to see the effect of the implementation of applied restrictions of use of peatlands for oil palm cultivation. The policy makers have made their move, it is back to landowner to implement the restrictions made. In later of future after this paper written, expected more scenario and room improvement gain from main industries players for action taken.


## ACKNOWLEDGEMENTS

We would like to thank all the support and funding gained from this paper through a project funded by the International Fund for Agricultural Development (IFAD) – Measurable Action for Haze Free Sustainable Land Management in Southeast Asia (MAHFSA) through the ASEAN Secretariat and GEC.


## REFERENCES


1. Andriesse, J.P. (1988). Nature and management of tropical peat soils. FAO Soils Bulletin 59. Food and Agriculture Organization of the United Nations, Rome. pp 165.
2. ASEAN Secretariat, (2003). Guidelines for the Implementation of the ASEAN Policy on Zero Burning. The ASEAN Secretariat, Jakarta.
3. Carlson, K. M., Goodman, L. K., & May-tobin, C. C. (2015). Modelling relationships between water table depth and peat soil carbon loss in Southeast Asian plantations. Environmental Research Letters, 10(7), 074006.
4. Cooper, H. V., Vane, C. H., Evers, S., Aplin, P., Girkin, N. T., & Sjögersten, S. (2019). From peat swamp forest to oil palm plantations: The stability of tropical peatland carbon. *Geoderma*, 342.
5. Darus, A., & Basri, M. W. (2000). Intensive IPM for management of oil palm pests. *Oil Palm Bull*, *41*, 1-14.
6. Eswa, M. (2018). Pembangunan dan Pengurusan Sawit Di Tanah Gambut-MPOB, Presented at the *Bengkel Amalan Pengurusan Terbaik Tanaman Sawit di Tanah Gambut di Kampung Raja Musa dan Kampung Seri Tiram*. 27 November 2018, GEC-COSPEC,Selangor.
7. FAO. (2020). -AGP - Integrated Pest Management". Retrieved 11 March 2020.
8. Foster, H.L. (2003) Assessment of oil palm fertiliser requirements. In: Oil Palm: Management For Large And Sustainable Yields (Fairhurst, T. and Hardter, R., eds.). Potash and Phosphate Institute (PPI), Potash and Phosphate Institute Canada (PPIC) and Int. Potash Inst. (IPI), Singapore: 231-257.
9. Gurmit, S. (1983) Micronutrient studies of oil palm on peat. Paper 2. In: Seminar on Fertilisers in Malaysian Agriculture, Serdang, 28 March 1983. The Malaysian Society of Soil Science and University Pertanian Malaysia.
10. Hasnol, O., Farawahida, M. D., Mohd, H., & Samsudin, A. (2014). Re-evaluation of nutrients requirements for oil palm planting on peat soil. *Planter*, *90*(1056), 161-177.
11. Hooijer, A., Page, S. E., Canadell, J. G., Silvius, M., Kwadijk, J., Wösten, H. and Jauhiainen, J. (2010). Current and future $CO_2$ emissions from drained peatlands in Southeast Asia. Biogeosciences, 7, pp 1-10.
12. Hooijer, A., Page, S. E., Jauhiainen, J., Lee, W. A., Idris, A., & Anshari, G. (2011). Land subsidence and carbon loss in plantations on tropical peatland: reducing uncertainty and implications for emission reduction options. Biogeosciences Discussions.
13. Hudson N.W. (1993) Field measurement of soil erosion and runoff - http://www.fao.org/3/t0848e/t0848e-07. Retrieved 10 March 2020.
14. Kuntom, A., Ai, T. Y., Kamaruddin, N., & Beng, Y. C. (2007). Pesticide application in the oil palm plantation. Oil palm bulletin, 54, 52.
15. Ling, A.H. (2019). Global Palm Oil Trade – Prospects and Outlook – Ganling Sdn. Bhd., Presented at Malaysian-China Business Forum, 4 March 2019, Kuala Lumpur.
16. Lim, K.H. (2005). Integrated pest and disease management of oil palm on peat soils. The Planter, 81 (956): pp 671-686.
17. MPI (2020). Briefing on High Level Policies for Malaysia's Palm Oil Industry, presented at the Face

Meeting between TC MSPO and WG Members, 18 February 2020, Holiday Villa, Subang Jaya, Selangor.
18. Parish, F., Mathews, J., Lew, S.Y., Faizuddin, M. and Lo, J. (Eds.). (2019). RSPO Manual on Best Management Practices (BMPs) for Existing Oil Palm Cultivation on Peat. 2nd Edition, RSPO, Kuala Lumpur.
19. Parish, F., Lew, S.Y., Faizuddin, M. and Giesen, W. (Eds.). (2019b). RSPO Manual on Best Management Practices (BMPs) for Management and Rehabilitation of Peatlands. 2nd Edition, RSPO, Kuala Lumpur.
20. RSPO, (2019). RSPO Drainability Assessment Procedure. RSPO, Kuala Lumpur.
21. Ramle, M.; Zulkefli, M. and Mohd basri W. (2011). Susceptibility of termites *Coptotermes curvignathus* (Isoptera: Rhinotermitidae) sampled from oil palm tree against the entomopathogenic fungi. Proc. Fourth IOPRIMPOB International Seminar: Existing and Emerging Pests and Disease of Oil Palm Advances In Research and Management. 14 November 2011. KLCC.
22. Shahbandeh M. (2020). Vegetable oils: Global consumption by oil type 2013/14 to 2019/2020 - https://www.statista.com/statistics/263937/vegetable-oils-global-consumption/ Retrieved 10 March 2020.
23. Sundram, S., Meon, S., Seman, I. A., & Othman, R. (2015). Application of arbuscular mycorrhizal fungi with *Pseudomonas aeruginosa* UPMP3 reduces the development of *Ganoderma* basal stem rot disease in oil palm seedlings. *Mycorrhiza*, *25*(5), 387-397.
24. Syahrizan, Syahlan & Z, Farahida & Khairuddin, Mohd & Bakar, M & Sani, Shafiq & Rakibe, Ismail & Zaini, Rasdi. (2017). Buffalo Assistance for In-Field Collection of Fresh Fruit Bunches in Oil Palm Plantation.
25. Traeholt C. (2019). The Sustainability Pledge: Realising the Potential - Copenhagen Zoo, presented at PIPOC, 21 November 2019, Kuala Lumpur.
26. Othman, H., Darus, F. M., & Mohammed, A. T. (2009). Experiences in peat development for oil palm planting in the MPOB Research Station at Sessang, Sarawak. *Oil Palm Bulletin*, *58*, 1-13.
27. Witjaksana, D. (2011). Recent findings on Greenhouse Gases of Oil Palm Plantation. Presented at the International Conference and Exhibition of Palm Oil (ICEPO 2011), at Jakarta, Indonesia, 11-13 May 2011.
28. Wood, B. J. (1984). Implementation of integrated pest management in plantation crops. In: Integrated Pest Management in Malaysia (B.S. Lee, W.H. Loke and K.L. Heong, ed.). Malaysian Plant Protection Society, Kuala Lumpur. pp 295-309.
29. Wösten, J. H. M., Van Den Berg, J., Van Eijk, P., Gevers, G. J. M., Giesen, W. B. J. T., Hooijer, A., ... & Silvius, M.J. (2006). Interrelationships between hydrology and ecology in fire degraded tropical peat swamp forests. *Water Resources Development*, *22*(1), 157-174.
30. Yin, T. P., & Chin, P. Y. (1981, January). Effect of water management on field performance of oil palms on acid sulphate soils in Peninsular Malaysia. In *symposium on acid sulphate soils* (p. 260).
31. UN (2017). https://www.un.org/development/desa/en/news/population/world-population-prospects-2017.html. Retrieved 10 March 2020.
32. Zahid-Muhamad, M., & Ab Aziz, M. F. (2018). Mechanization in Oil Palm Harvesting. International Journal of Academic Research in Business and Social Sciences, 8(5), 247-256.

PEATWISE

IPC 2021

ID 62695

# A REVIEW OF PEATLAND USE AND SUSTAINABLE MANAGEMENT OPTIONS

*Bjørn Kløve, Kerstin Berglund, David Campbell, Christian Fritz, Poul Erik Lærke, Marja Maljanen Bettina Matzdorf, Merit van den Berg, Nahleen Lemke, Cheng Chen, Hannu Marttila, Lasse Loft, Örjan Berglund, Jussi Ronkainen, Claudia Nielsen, Justice Akanegbu, Maarit Liimatainen, Hanna Silvennoinen

*bjorn.kloive@oulu.fi*

While the use of peatlands is regionally important, peatland drainage and land management lead to environmental impacts such as emission of greenhouse gas emissions (GHG) and changes in water quality. For sound land management policies and decision making, an improved scientific knowledge base of GHG fluxes from different management options as well as transparent and verifiable measuring and accounting methods for emission reductions is needed. The presentation outlines key aspects and results overview of a 3-year international project (PEATWISE- Wise use of drained peatlands in a bio-based economy: development of improved assessment practices and sustainable techniques for mitigation of greenhouse gases.) from work carried out in Norway, Finland, Sweden, Denmark, Germany, The Netherlands and New Zealand. Different conditions found in peatland properties, management and socio-economic settings will be presented covering a wide geographical distribution from the high North, north-central Europe to New Zealand. An outline of experiments to manage soils by water table control and soil amendments will be reviewed and discussed. Rewetting options, related challenges and options for paludiculture will be presented. We also present results from stakeholder analysis and a broader analysis as a basis for management, incentives and funding schemes.

ID 62618

# PEATWISE – GREENHOUSE GAS MEASUREMENTS ON CULTIVATED PEATLAND AT RUUKKI, FINLAND

*Maarit Liimatainen[1,2], Hannu Marttila[2], Justice Akanegbu[2], Erkki Joki-Tokola[1], Timo Lötjönen[1], Liisa Kulmala[3], Henriikka Vekuri[3], Annalea Lohila[3], Hanna Silvennoinen[4], Björn Klöve[2,4]

[1] Natural Resources Institute Finland, Finland
[2] University of Oulu, Finland
[3] Finnish Meteorological Institute, Finland
[4] Norwegian Institute of Bioeconomy Research, Norway

*maarit.liimatainen@oulu.fi*

Agriculture comprises one of the biggest sources of anthropogenic greenhouse gas (GHG) emissions and cultivated peatlands may have especially high emissions of carbon dioxide and nitrous oxide. In addition to high GHG emissions, cultivated peatlands cause high nutrient and organic carbon loading to waterways. In Finland peatlands comprise one third of the total land area and over half of these are drained for forestry and agriculture. Peatlands are actively cultivated especially in Northern Europe and also in Finland about 10 % of total field area are cultivated peatlands. Cultivated peatlands have regionally high importance in agriculture in Finland and therefore there is strong need to get further information on which are the best available cost-effective practices to manage them more climate- and environmental-friendly in the future. We studied the effects of peatland cultivation on both GHG emissions and water run-off quality. The research site is located in Northern Finland at Ruukki (25.00°E, 64.42°N). The unique field research facility was constructed in 2017 and is operated by Finnish Natural Resources Institute (LUKE). The total area of the research field is 19.5 ha. The peat depth varies between 30 and 70 cm and the research field is located in the area of acid soils. The field is divided to 6 different sections, where the water table, soil moisture, leaching of water and its quality are monitored separately continuously. The GHG emissions were measured year-round in co-operation with other research project partners using various techniques including chamber and eddy-covariance measurements. We have combined detailed hydrological analysis and modelling, soil analysis with GHG measurements and have utilized latest measurement technologies. The aim was to study the climatic and environmental effects of peat depth and different moisture conditions as well as various crop rotations and cultivation techniques in production of feed crops on cultivated peatland.

61826

# PEATWISE - EFFECTS OF FOUNDRY SAND ADDITION ON YIELD AND CO2 EMISSION FROM A CULTIVATED PEAT SOIL IN SWEDEN

*Örjan Berglund, Sabine Jordan, Kathrin Hesse, Kerstin Berglund

The Swedish University of Agricultural Sciences, Sweden

*orjan.berglund@slu.se*

Peatlands store a large share of the world's soil organic carbon and are widespread in Northern and Central European countries. Drainage is a precondition for traditional agricultural production on organic soils. Drainage increases peat mineralization and changes the physical and chemical soil properties.

The aim of this experiment was to investigate if the addition of foundry sand to the topsoil will affect the yield and CO2 emission. In the EU-funded PEATWISE project, a field experiment was set up at a former cultivated fen peat. We compared yield and CO2 emission from plots sown with Timothy treated with 0 cm (control), 2.5 cm or 5 cm foundry sand. The sand was mixed in the top 10 cm of the soil. CO2 emissions were measured with automatic dark chambers in frames where vegetation was removed.

The yield (t d.m/ha) 2017 was highest from the plots with 5 cm sand (11.6), lowest from plots with 2.5 cm sand (8.8) and the control yielded 10.3. In 2018 the yield was highest from the control (13.8), lowest from plots with 2.5 cm sand (12.6) and 12.7 from plots with 5 cm sand. In 2019 the yield was lowest from the control (14.1) and highest from plots with 2.5 cm sand (16.3).

The 5 cm plots had the lowest emission (µmol m-2s-1) 2017, emitting an average of 4.53. The 2.5 cm treatment emitted 4.87 and the 0 cm treatment 5.92. 2018 emitted the 5 cm plots the least (6.82) and the control had the highest emission, 7.15. In 2019 the lowest emissions were found from the 5 cm treatment (5.18) and highest from the control plots (7.32). The 2.5 cm treatment emitted on average 6.85. Addition of foundry sand reduced CO2 emission all 3 years.

61553

# PEATWISE - LARGE EFFECTS OF SLIGHTLY DIFFERENT GROUND WATER TABLES ON GHG EMISSION FROM REED CANARY GRASS IN PALUDICULTURE

*Poul Erik Lærke[1], Sandhya Karki[2], Lars Elsgaard[1], Claudia T. Nielsen[1], Tanka P. Kandel[3]

[1]Department of Agroecology, Aarhus University, Denmark
[2]USDA-ARS, Delta Water Management Research Unit, USA
[3]Noble Research Institute, USA

*poule.laerke@agro.au.dk*

Rewetting and abandoning drained peatland to restore the carbon sink function and to reduce greenhouse gas (GHG) emissions have often been recommended. Paludiculture, the combination of peatland rewetting and cultivation of flood-tolerant perennial crops for biorefining, biomaterials or bioenergy, has gained considerable interest as a possible alternative land use option. In 2011, field plots were established with reed canary grass in an agricultural fen peatland in Denmark. From spring 2015, the level of groundwater table (GWT) in four plots was raised to -1 cm (annual mean) below soil surface by pumping water back from the drainage ditch leaving side-by-side plots with slightly lower ground water tables (-3 and -9 cm). Plots were fertilised with 80 kg N $ha^{-1}$ in early spring and 80 kg N $ha^{-1}$ after the first cut in mid-June. The final harvest was done on 1 October in both years. Emissions of $CH_4$ and $N_2O$ were measured with opaque chambers and net ecosystem exchange (NEE) of $CO_2$ was measured with a temperature controlled transparent chamber using four levels of shrouding at biweekly intervals between March 2015 and February 2017.

Harvested biomass yield was on average 13.1 Mg DM $ha^{-1}$ $yr^{-1}$ across years and treatments without significant effect of GWT. NEE of $CO_2$, ranging from -18.3 to -14.1 Mg $CO_2$ $ha^{-1}$ $yr^{-1}$ ($CO_2$ uptake), were similar for all three GWT treatments. In contrast, significant differences in $CH_4$ emissions were measured with 27.8, 14.5 and 1.8 Mg $CO_2$-eq $ha^{-1}$ $yr^{-1}$ at annual mean GWT of -1, -3 and -9 cm, respectively. Emission of $N_2O$ ranged from 1.0 to 2.0 Mg $CO_2$-eq ha-1 yr-1. Thus, the GWT of -9 cm was the most efficient regarding GHG mitigation, however, still being a source with emissions of 10.8 Mg $CO_2$-eq $ha^{-1}$ $yr^{-1}$ including carbon removal with biomass harvest (GWP $N_2O$=265, $CH_4$=28), respectively.

ID 62425

# PEATWISE – EFFECT OF CROPPING MANAGEMENT ON PROTEIN YIELD AND EXTRACTABILITY FROM SELECTED FLOODING-TOLERANT PERENNIAL GRASSES CULTIVATED ON A RIPARIAN FEN

*Claudia Therese Nielsen[1], Lene Stødkilde[2], Uffe Jørgensen[3], Poul Erik Lærke[1]

[1]Aarhus University, Department of Agroecology - Climate and Water, Denmark
[2]Aarhus University, Department of Animal Science - Molecular nutrition and reproduction, Denmark)

*claudia@agro.au.dk*

Paludiculture, defined as agriculture on wet or rewetted peatlands has been proposed as a mitigation strategy to reverse unsustainable environmental impacts such as land subsidence, nutrient release to surface water and greenhouse gas emissions from traditional agriculture on drained peatland. In particular, the production of biomass feedstock from flood-tolerant perennial grasses for green biorefining to protein and other value-added products may be a viable economic and environmental sustainable option for temperate peatlands. However, optimal quality characteristics of the biomass for protein extraction have yet to be defined. In 2018, field plots cultivated with different flood-tolerant perennial grasses were established in an agricultural fen peatland in Denmark. Of these, a total of eight plots cultivated with reed canary grass (RCG) and tall fescue were each subdivided into six sub-plots with different management regarding harvest and fertilisation. Harvest frequencies ranged from one to five times in the period between mid-May to mid-October at intervals of 4-6 weeks. The sub-plots received fertilisation of 100 kg ha-1 of both N and K prior to each harvest. Protein extractability of the grasses was assessed by lab-scale biorefinery techniques using a screw press followed by precipitation of true protein in the resulting juice. This was compared with an analysis of protein fractions as classified by the Cornell Net Carbohydrate and Protein System (CNCPS). Preliminary results of the biorefinery extractable protein yields (fresh weight) ranged from 10 % to 25 % of the fresh mass input, dependent on treatment, with summer harvests having the lowest yield. Evaluation of the easily extractable crude protein (CP) CNCPS fractions B1 and B2 showed yields of between 61.8 – 110.7 g CP kg-1 DM. Precursory processing of data showed that the cumulative yields of extractable crude protein for the growing season seems highly affected by management.

61537

# PEATWISE - INCENTIVE-BASED POLICY INSTRUMENTS GUIDING TOWARDS SUSTAINABLE USE OF PEATLANDS IN EU

*Cheng Chen, Lasse Loft, Bettina Matzdorf

Leibniz Centre for Agricultural Landscape Research (ZALF), Germany

*cheng.chen@zalf.de*

The European Union (EU) is the second largest greenhouse gases (GHG) emitter from drained peatlands. The EU's climate target will not be achieved without reducing GHG emissions from drained peatlands. This will involve significant changes in agricultural production conditions. Despite increasing concerns about the sustainable use of peatlands, there is a lack of assessments of policies steering mitigation measures in peatlands at different governance levels and sectors. In this paper, we aim to understand the institutional setting of such policies in the EU multilevel governance structure, i.e. how are policies adopted by the EU, its member states and at the local level to incentivize climate smart agriculture? Agri-Environment-Climate Measures (AECM) under the EU Common Agricultural Policy (CAP) are the policy in our focus, as they seem well suited to prescribe the new direction for climate mitigation measures in agricultural policy and complementary governmental schemes. For our analysis we build on the concept of Multi-Level Governance (MLG). Our study follows a case study approach by comparing AECMs in three peatland rich countries in the EU: Germany, Netherland and Finland. We reviewed relevant scientific literature and policy documents on sustainable peatland management and conducted 36 semi-structured expert interviews with policy makers, scientists, civil society representatives and farmers. The documents and interviews were analysed through a content analysis, focusing on factors influencing the implementation of incentive-based policy to support sustainable peatland management. We highlight trade-offs and synergies between different governmental and sectoral policies regarding peatland use. We reveal the importance of economic incentives in steering farmer's land use – only if revenues are sufficient, there is a willingness to try new alternatives. This calls for a cross-sector alignment of incentive schemes. At the same time drainage-based agriculture should be phased out while introducing alternative incentives for the reduction of GHGs.